Brenda-

Thanks for all of your contributions
to our staff and students, for [...]
times you sat & listened to me blab away,
and for always taking charge of birthday
celebrations. Best of luck with your future!
Please stay in touch, Nae___

W9-ARA-977

Bren-
I'm really going
to miss having you around.
Who else would go on both spur-of-the
moment trips to Target AND overnight trips to
another state's mall? Both personally + professionally,
I'm so glad you've been through it all with
me & us. No matter what happens, you're
on the right path for you!
Love, KRISTIN

Brenda-
How could you leave us
without helping with staff
training at least one more
time!! Take care and
write often
(E-Mail)
Erin

Brenda-
It's been fun
knowing you. Good
luck always!
Karen Kashayon
have good luck
& fun!
Jessie

Brenda, ? You are
where to start! person +
a very special forgetting
will never being
thanks for
you! Randy

Brenda-
Thanks for all of your
help over the years.
We will miss you -
DAVE & Lin

Dear Brenda, & thanks for
All the best of Great Hall Director!
being A Great Hall Director!
Luv, Val & Brad

Brenda,
It's been great
having you here during
our first year in the halls.
I hope all goes well in your
future! Keep in Touch.
Love,
Colleen & Eric

Brenda —
I can't believe it's been 9 yrs.
since we first met. A lot has
happened during that time. I wish
only the best for you. Please keep in
touch, even if it's only a card (& letter)
at xmas.
Love,
Gwen

The University
in the Pines

The University
in the Pines

Dr. Arthur O. Lee

Published by Bemidji State University
Bemidji, Minnesota, U.S.A.

Copyright© 1994 Bemidji State University
Published by Bemidji State University

"College in the Pines" was originally published by
Dillon Press, Inc., Minneapolis, Minnesota

ISBN 0-943090-04-0

Printed in the United States of America

c

"A permanent institution for training teachers"

CONTENTS

THE MINNESOTA STATE UNIVERSITY SYSTEM

An Overview

T here are seven Universities in the system and all are governed by a nine-member State University Board appointed by the governor. The Board is responsible for the overall educational management of the schools, and to help them in this governance, the Board selects a chancellor (who has a large staff) to make specific policy recommendations to the Board.

Both the Board and the Universities were created by acts of the state legislature and are financed by the tuition and fees paid by the students (one-third) and direct appropriations from the legislature (two-thirds).

The State University System in Minnesota evolved according to a pattern familiar to American higher education: from Normal Schools to State Teachers Colleges (1921) to State Colleges (1957) to Universities (1975). In this pattern of evolvement the schools changed from the training of elementary school teachers only to multifaceted, multiprogram, multi-colleges within a University structure. (For a listing of all the academic areas and programs offered in the System, see Appendix A.)

The most obvious change in the evolving pattern over the past 134 years was size. The first school began at Winona in 1860. The schools changed from tiny training schools to large Universities, with combined enrollments of 65,000. (Two schools became larger than the major universities in neighboring states.) By the 1980s the SUS schools' enrollments exceeded that of the University of Minnesota. (For Bemidji State, the peak enrollment year for on-campus classes was 1971 when there were 4,865 students enrolled. However, the peak enrollment year for all classes on- and off-campus was in 1980 when there were 5,787 enrolled.)

By 1990 the seven Universities employed over 4,000 faculty and staff. Annual budget figures for the combined operation of the seven schools climbed from minuscule numbers to a budget of 650 million dollars for the 1992-94 biennium. (Bemidji State's portion of the budget is about ten percent, i.e., 28 million dollars for the 1993-94 school year. The peak year for Bemidji State faculty numbers was 1970 with 233 members; close behind was 1987 with 225.)

THE CHRONOLOGY LEADING TO THE SEVEN UNIVERSITIES

Winona State was founded in 1860 as the first Normal School in the state, and the first one west of the Mississippi River. Mankato State began in 1868, with 27 students. St. Cloud was next in 1869, created to serve the citizens then in the northern portion of the state's population. Moorhead State began with 10 students enrolled in 1887. Bemidji State started in 1919 and enrolled 38 students for the fall term that year.

Almost 50 years went by before Southwest State (at Marshall) was authorized to open in 1963; classes began in 1967. Lastly, Metropolitan State was established in 1971, with the first students enrolled the next year. Both Metro and Southwest came on line as State Colleges and became State Universities with the others in 1975.

Finally, an "8th campus" of sorts began in 1990 in Akita, Japan. With the new school's building program and operation financed by Japan, the Minnesota SUS Board has served as the consultant and organizer for this two-year school. The mission is in part to provide cross-cultural exchange opportunities for both students and faculties from both nations. The primary administrator of the Akita program is a provost, a Minnesotan selected by the SUS Board.

THE FUTURE IS NOW

The roles of both the schools and the governing boards have changed dramatically in the past half century. (For a more personal and human interpretation of the modern SUS Board's role, see Appendix B and the brief comments made by Board Chairperson Elizabeth Peques at Bemidji State's Commencement Exercises in 1991.) The remainder of this study is concerned with only one of those seven schools, Bemidji State University.

DEDICATION
To All the Many Friends of Bemidji State

ACKNOWLEDGEMENTS to part II, Bemidji State 1939-1994

The author wishes to acknowledge certain people for certain help in the preparation of the most recent manuscript, notably the aid from readers who served as quasi-editors. Keri Mohror, red pencil in hand, went through every page and made corrections in spellings and syntax and on rare occasion she offered an editorial comment regarding appropriate wording. Dr. Mark Christensen read the earliest sections and with perspicacity he wrote little comments in the margins, judiciously phrased such as, "Do you really want to include this?" The needed heavy-hand of an editor came with Dr. Bea Knodel who, with a green felt pen, not only made corrections to words and lines on the pages but she often added thoughtful, useful, challenging, sometimes funny, sometimes acerbic commentaries in the margins on many pages as she responded to the material in the text. Her side remarks made interesting reading, even if her editorializing smarted a little at times. Dr. Knodel's trenchant observations ranged from one-word descriptions ("Neanderthal") to two words ("It's awkward") to three words ("Are you sure?") to making up her own words ("Ibid-iotic") to dire warnings ("Arthur! You can't say that!") to convincing ("Trust me") to grudging acquiescence ("Well, I suppose you really want those caps"). Her green-pen-scratchings led to multiple alterations of the final text and all (well, almost all) of her suggestions were most appreciated.

The final reader was history professor emeritus Dr. Harold T. Hagg (at BSU from 1936 to 1976). Although he can turn a phrase wonderfully well, his role and goal in the perusal was to determine historical accuracy.

For almost all the typing—and retyping, and more retyping to put in/take out ongoing corrections based on the red marks and then the green marks, and then the author changing his mind again on this word or that phrase—I give my sincerest thanks to Peggy Nohner, secretary in Hagg-Sauer Hall. Amid all her efforts on the project (she worked on it off and on for almost a year), Peggy Nohner was always positive, cheerful, always supportive and very helpful.

For all of the above-mentioned kind and helpful people, there's a proper and wonderful Norwegian phrase to sum up the situation: TAKK FOR ALT (Thanks for everything).

BEMIDJI STATE UNIVERSITY'S ROLE AND MISSION

The mission of Bemidji State University is to contribute to the intellectual, social, cultural and economic development of society and, more especially, of northern Minnesota. It fulfills this mission primarily by offering undergraduate programs in the liberal arts, sciences, and professional and applied fields. In addition, the University offers selected graduate programs and provides a wide variety of public services. Firmly committed to academic excellence, Bemidji State University provides a broad liberal education complementing academic specialization so that its students are prepared to function responsibly as members of an interdependent, international community.

THE COMMUNITY
Some Bemidji facts and figures*

Bemidji, with an estimated population of 11,088, is situated on Lakes Bemidji and Irving, sister lakes fed by the Mississippi River. Bemidji was the first Minnesota city built on the Mississippi and now covers an area of 16 square miles at an elevation of 1,356 feet. Bemidji has a manager-council form of government with municipal fire, police, water and street departments. Primarily a retail sales

Mute, Immobile Folk Art
"Bemidji's Most Famous Citizens"

community, contributions to the city's economy also come from forestry, education and the travel industry. The retail sales area is approximately 75 miles in diameter, with a population of about 75,000 people and annual retail sales of nearly $200 million. The principal products and services of Bemidji's 30 manufacturing establishments include lumber, wood products, plywood, hardboard, machining, boats and canoes, steel culverts, computer components, woolens, concrete blocks, garage doors, signs, printing, wood furnaces and fishing tackle. Bemidji's 400-acre Industrial Park is located on the south edge of the city and contains 30 businesses.

*Information provided by the Bemidji Chamber of Commerce.

Education

Bemidji has seven elementary schools, three parochial schools with grades one through eight, one private school with grades kindergarten through 12, a middle school and a high school. Bemidji State University, located on the shores of Lake Bemidji, has an enrollment of more than 4,000 students. The University offers undergraduate and graduate degrees in a wide variety of disciplines. Bemidji Technical Institute offers courses in automotive technology, carpentry, hardware marketing, industrial drafting, practical nursing and office occupations, among others. Oak Hills Bible College is located south of Bemidji between Upper and Lower Marquette Lakes. It is a four-year, college-level school that trains more than 100 people each year for the Christian ministries. The nationally recognized Concordia Language Village is located on Turtle River Lake just north of Bemidji. Here, foreign languages are taught using cultural studies, ethnic atmosphere, food and customs. Programs are offered in Norwegian, Spanish, German, Finnish, Russian, French, Danish, Swedish and Japanese.

Transportation

Bemidji is provided with freight services by the Burlington Northern and the Soo Line railways and daily by several truck lines. Passenger service is provided by Greyhound and Triangle bus lines. Air service is provided by Mesaba-Northwest Airlines, which has three to four daily flights to and from Minneapolis. Taxi and intra-city bus services are also available. Bemidji is located on two major U.S. highways - Highway 71 running north and south, and Highway 2 running east and west.

Recreation

Bemidji has five movie theaters, one drive in and a professional summer theater that presents top Broadway stage fare during a 10-week season. Other area amusements include golf, bowling, bingo, casino gambling, miniature golf, horseback riding, a waterslide, a go-cart track, racquetball, rollerskating and high school and university sports. Winter recreation is provided by a curling arena, two municipal skating rinks, and downhill skiing at Buena Vista Ski Area. The area abounds in trails for snowmobiling and cross-country skiing. Eleven area parks total approximately 150 acres. Public beaches on Lake Bemidji are maintained at Diamond Point, Nymore and Cameron parks.

Services and Groups

Bemidji is home to more than two dozen churches representing leading denominations. The daily newspaper is The Pioneer, with a circulation of more than 8,000, and the area is served by six radio stations. Bemidji has a public library that houses more than 58,000 volumes. In addition, a senior citizen center is located in the downtown area.

Bemidji Climate Facts

Average mean annual temperature	37.2 degrees above zero
Average annual rainfall	23.8 inches
Average annual snowfall	41.1 inches
Average annual humidity	47 percent

Average monthly temperatures

January	2.2	July	66.6	**Coldest month: January**
February	6.9	August	64.7	Mean daily maximum: 12
March	21.8	September	53.9	Mean daily minimum: 11 below zero
April	38.4	October	43.4	**Hottest month: July**
May	50.2	November	25.5	Mean daily maximum: 78
June	61.9	December	11.0	Mean daily minimum: 55

For a 1990 Census Map of Beltrami County (by townships and city wards) see Appendix C.

College in the Pines
The Early Years: 1919-1938

I F STATE COLLEGE alumni everywhere were to be asked whether their alma mater had a unique origin in its founding and early growth, the quick reply would very likely be in the affirmative. It is the contention of the writer that Bemidji State College (BSC) alumni—and all state college alumni—should offer at least a qualified "no" to the question. Although in some circles this position might smack of disloyalty, if not heresy, it is my belief that Bemidji State College simply fits into a pattern of education and institutional growth that was and is nationwide. Indeed, it might be argued with validity that the origin and rise of Bemidji College is essentially the history of every state college, from the initial fight over which community would get the school to the present trend seen in the recent decision to allow Minnesota State Colleges to grant master of arts degrees.

All this is not to suggest that there is nothing unique about the history of Bemidji College, for there is. Most assuredly, for example, there was only one Manfred W. Deputy, the first president, who stamped his long-lasting mark on the institution. As he reads the history of Bemidji College, the reader will, however, widen his view of American educational history if he considers it within the framework of a pattern of institutional growth going on throughout the country.

This section traces the history of Bemidji College but, except for a final summary chapter, it deals primarily with the origins of the school and what the older denizens of Bemidji like to call "the Deputy period" (1919-1937). The early College history is emphasized despite full cognizance that this is the time of the so-called "now" generation that reportedly is interested only in "today" and "relevancy." Alas, but it behooves the writer to remind today's reader that a lot of yesterdays were required to arrive at what we have today. Despite the fact that there are now more than 5,000 students trampling down the grass on this labyrinthine BSC campus, it took considerable background and preparation to get that College grass to trample down. Moreover, to add to the woe of most readers, that bane of history books—footnotes—are sprinkled liberally throughout the chapters. But again, footnotes need to be defended primarily because of the few readers who keep saying, "Now where in heck did he find that?"

In the secular jargon of many college students, history is defined as "one damn thing after another." Even some members of history departments are apt to haul out Voltaire's definition and decide that history is "tricks that the living play on the dead." Hopefully the late historian Carl Becker's idea that history is "knowledge of things said and done" will better serve the purposes of both judging and writing the history of such an institution as a state college. Becker suggests that history is a record of the past, albeit a very incomplete record; it is incomplete because full "knowledge of things said and done" is impossible to acquire. Yet it stands as a desirable goal for historians to tell and record well and accurately—even if not completely--the history of anything. And perhaps George Bernard Shaw's comment should apply to writers of history, too. Shaw once wrote a friend and then apologized for writing so much, concluding, "Had I more time, I would have written a shorter letter."

Several factors prompted the decision to write the history of Bemidji College. Dr. Harold T. Hagg of the BSC history department planted the idea about 1960 and nurtured its growth by indicating that considerable documentation on the subject was readily available. While I was studying as a graduate student at the University of North Dakota during the 1962-1963 school year, my doctoral dissertation committee agreed that the topic had sufficient merit and approved it. Though the topic was approved, such interesting things as passing comprehensive examinations came first. And though sporadic efforts to gather and sift materials occurred after this, not much was accomplished until the administration at Bemidji College gave me a quarter of sabbatical leave at full pay during the spring quarter of 1967. Because my family has the bad habit of eating regularly, without the necessary funds and free time, work on the dissertation would have been long delayed.

Once work got underway in earnest and the chapters began to grow in both size and numbers, it was my committee chairman, Dr. Elwyn B. Robinson of the University of North Dakota, who took my first efforts and red-penciled the many chapter revisions into an organized, readable paper. Because he was always encouraging, always fair—and always demanding better quality--I am most indebted to Dr. Robinson. As for the publication of this history, I thank the BSC administration—and the lucky stars of happy coincidence that this year is the 50th Anniversary of Bemidji State College.

Others whose aid should be acknowledged are: Les Russell of the Bemidji College English department, who made corrections on the final draft; Les Mattison and his cooperative staff at the College library; and Dr. Hagg, a veritable walking encyclopedia on Bemidji's history. And I should also like to thank the many genuinely interested colleagues of mine at Bemidji who said, or refrained from saying, "How's it going?" Finally, after having read hundreds of prefaces, I at last realize why authors pay tribute to the Jobian patience of an understanding and encouraging wife.

Note: Part I, or <u>College in the Pines</u>, was first published separately in 1970 by Dillon Press. The book soon went out of print, hence the need to include it as Part I and thus provide a complete history of Bemidji State over its first 75 years. To aid readers in searching for specific information, an index is included at the end of Part I, (pp. 164-171).

COLLEGE IN THE PINES
CONTENTS

INTRODUCTION
College in the Pines
Part I

LL PERSONS ARE affected by a variety of influences and forces that sweep in and mingle to help shape each individual. The sources of these influences are as many and varied as the complex personalities they affect, but always near the top of the list stands education. Education, realistically conceived, covers the whole life process, for education is inseparable from the total tide of national culture, and the mental set of each person is a product of experiences in which education of some type has figured. Education touches the lives of adults, but in a real sense it is the life of the young as they move toward maturity. And it is the impact of formal education that is beginning to concern more and more historians today who view it as an always pervasive element in American history. A Ford Foundation report put it this way: "The very awakening of Americans to the dependence of prosperity upon education is a great theme, which has recently been opened up but is far from being exhausted."[1]

It should be added, understandably, that to be educational an agency need not be a school. It may be a library, a museum, or a youth movement, for example, since any embodiment of the intent to teach or otherwise influence attitudes is in a sense an educational agency. Yet for the historian, dependent as he is upon documentation, those agencies which have some permanence and produce records are objects of central importance. Colleges and universities are obvious examples of those agencies that leave source materials for historians to read, sift, and synthesize. This, then, is the study of such an agency—Bemidji State College.

For almost 75 years before the middle of this century, the study of the history of American education had a promising future and a disappointing present

---

[1] Education and American History, Report of the Fund for the Advancement of Education (New York: The Ford Foundation, 1965), p. 20.

5

as a subject of investigation and thought by American historians. But this ambivalence began to change, for there began a strong tendency, evident since about 1950, for historians to write both the histories of educational institutions and of American educational thought. All of this is a part of the rather recent historical trend emphasizing intellectual history.

The development of educational institutions as a part of the local history out of which national histories grow has long been thought of as a topic worthy of historical scholarships. The venerable historian Herbert Baxter Adams, director of the then-young seminars in history and political science at John Hopkins University about 1880, believed this to be true. He, like many other professors of his own and succeeding generations, was himself committed to education as a movement that could be thought of in conjunction with such topics as municipal reforms, labor laws, churches, and other largely unexplored subjects which he thought desirable to study. Yet most historians of Adams' period, the 1880s and the 1890s, and even Adams himself, despite their sincere motives, devoted most of their time and intelligence to American political, economic, and constitutional history, regardless of their historical curiosity about, and devotion to, education. It was broad themes, like the roots of democracy and the "germ cell" theory of New England towns, for example, that won their time and interest.[2]

Hence the story of education was neglected by history departments so that, virtually by default, the historical study of American education was carried forward by professors of education and their students. In common usage, the "history of education" meant the history of schooling only, which often took the form of textbooks designed to prepare teachers and school administrators. These works tended to explain schooling more than to clarify history itself, and exemplified the trend of emphasizing schooling as a cause rather than education as a cause. Fitting education into the broad framework of American cultural history tended to be omitted.[3]

In contrast, the more recent works in the history of education involve both professional historians and professors of education, with both seeing education as part of the broad spectrum of the American cultural and intellectual heritage. To cite just one recognized historian as a good example, Columbia University's Richard Hofstadter has published several volumes since 1950 on American education. Columbia University's Education Professor R. Freeman Butts has done the same.

These men serve as a sample of the recent scholarship on American education in general. There are also a growing number of histories of particular

---

[2] Edward N. Saveth, ed., Understanding the American Past: American History and Its Interpretation (Boston: Little, Brown and Company, 1954), pp. 10-11.
[3] For examples of two of the better known works and authors that reflect this interpretation see Edwin Grant Dexter, A History of Education in the United States (New York: Macmillan Company, 1904), and Charles F. Thwing, A History of Higher Education in the United States (New York: D. Appleton and Company, 1906). These examples are cited not to denigrate the works nor the men, as both were capable scholars and their books reflect this scholarship; rather the works are cited as somewhat typical examples of the time. Despite the juxtaposition of historical curiosity and of devotion to education in the minds of many professional historians and educators, few marriages of the two interests took place.

institutions. Examples in this category, to narrow it down to the Midwest, include such universities as North Dakota, Minnesota and Wisconsin. Some college histories in the region recently have been written on Winona, St. Cloud, Gustavus Adolphus, Luther and Augustana.

Isolating one educational institution for study, however, raises some questions of relevancy to the whole theme. Thus it behooves the historian to try to fit his topic first of all into the broader picture and to see the whole pattern of educational experience before narrowing to a discussion of a particular school. One college may, if taken by itself, seem to have little interest or meaning to the whole; but set into the context of the entire movement, its experience becomes a factor in an unmistakably important institutional pattern. Thus writing the history of a particular institution is not necessarily a desirable historical end in itself, nostalgic and sentimental alumni notwithstanding; the initial task is first to make the study relevant to American history as a whole. Then the two can go together to complement each other, for it is axiomatic today in most historical circles to believe that people cannot get good national histories until they first get good local histories. Or as Professor Robert P. Wilkins of Marshall University stated, quoting the late Orin G. Libby of the University of North Dakota, there is always a real need for the "little histories as well as the big histories."[4] The history of Bemidji State College, this first part emphasizing its beginning and formative years, is one of those little histories.

---

[4] Comment made by Professor Wilkins, now returned as a faculty member of the University of North Dakota, in prefacing his remarks before reading his paper, "Porter J. McCumber, Tory Isolationist," at the Northern Great Plains History Conference, University of North Dakota, November 11, 1966.

CHAPTER I

Foundations for Public Education in Minnesota

The Problem of Free Public Schools

T HE FIRST MAJOR issues regarding American public schools involved first of all their desirability, and, secondly, who should pay for them. Essentially, the initial problem became that of awakening, in a new land, a consciousness of need for general education, and then developing a willingness to pay for what finally came to be deemed desirable to provide.

The problem which confronted those interested in establishing state-controlled schools was not exactly the same in any two states, though the battles in most states possessed common elements, and hence had similar characteristics. Paralleling these first major issues arose the problem of where to obtain competent teachers. The academies and colleges in America in the early nineteenth century had not been receptive to incorporating into their curricula a teacher-training program. Even if they had been willing, the colonial colleges and academies did not produce enough graduates to staff the public school faculties. Because no agency existed which seemed both able and willing to undertake the function of educating teachers for the elementary schools, the situation required new agencies. New York and Massachusetts led in the establishment of new types of institutions, of which the normal school was the survivor. The school emerged in the 1840s as the agency that best supplied the teachers for the elementary grades in the United States' public schools.[5]

Throughout their history normal schools were essentially secondary schools, not colleges. The great majority of the normal school students came directly from the ungraded schools of rural districts for one, two, or three years of training at what

---

[5] Charles W. Hunt, "Teachers Colleges," Dictionary of American History, ed. James Truslow Adams (New York: Charles Scribner's Sons, 1940), V, 234. New York in 1834 began state grants for the academies for training teachers. The first normal school opened in Lexington, Massachusetts, in 1839. The name normal school was borrowed from France where the Ecole Normale had a respectable academic heritage. Caggell's French-English Dictionary translates "ecole normale" as simply teachers' training school.

today would be the high school level. The normal schools provided the basic education that is now the responsibility of the high school, as well as the technical training for teaching. The pedagogical methods course and a review of the elementary subject matter to be taught, along with an emphasis on apprenticeship teaching, became the main characteristics of the normal school curriculum until after the first quarter of the twentieth century.[6] The story of the founding and development of the school now called Bemidji State College is essentially, in miniature, the story of state institutions for the training of teachers throughout the United States.[7]

Minnesota's Response to Free Public Schools

As indicated, running parallel with normal schools was the founding and development of the idea and ideal of free, public education for all that has been one of the great contributions of America to the world. The goal of free public education arose from the vision of the early settlers and from their hopes for the future of the region in which they chose to make their homes. In spite of the hardships and limitations imposed by frontier conditions, an interest in and a concern about the education of their children commanded the settlers' early and continuing attention.

Thus, when Minnesota was organized as a territory in 1849, one of the early decisions of the territorial legislature included an act to establish and maintain free common schools. This act became one of the most important of all the early laws as it authorized a tax to raise funds to pay teachers and gave each school district permission to collect money for a school building.[8] No free public high schools existed in the territorial period. If a student wished to go beyond the elementary grades, to "ninth grade," he had to pay tuition at some private preparatory school, academy, or church seminary. Nearly all of Minnesota's private colleges had preparatory departments or grew from them. Colleges begun during the territorial period include Macalester, 1853; Hamline, 1854; and St. Johns, 1856.[9]

During the territorial period, Minnesota, like all territories, had the perennial problem of acquiring trained teachers for its common schools. In 1858, Minnesota became a state. Because, like all mid-western states, it could not depend upon securing enough teachers from existing institutions or from other states, Minnesota decided to train its own teachers. One of the provisions of the constitution directed the state legislature to "establish a general and uniform system of public schools." The first state legislature passed the Act Establishing the Normal School System of the State of Minnesota in July, 1858, signed into law by Governor Henry

[6] Otto Welton Snarr, The State Teachers Colleges in Minnesota's Program of Higher Education, bulletin of the Moorhead State Teachers College, Moorhead, Minnesota, Series 46, No. 2, August, 1950, p. 4.
[7] Ibid. Snarr at this writing was the president of Moorhead Teachers, and he supported this thesis about his school. The same assertion was also made by Archie C. Clark, "The Status, Policies, and Objectives of Minnesota State Teachers Colleges" (unpublished doctoral dissertation, University of Southern California, 1941), p. 22.
[8] Nine years after this common school law went into effect, the state had 72 organized public school districts. A Presbyterian minister, Dr. Edward D. Nell, often called the "father of education" in Minnesota, became the first superintendent of the state public schools in 1851, and he served as an important promoter of education. He was later the first chancellor of the University of Minnesota and helped found Macalester College which he also served as president. Theodore C. Blegen, Building Minnesota (Boston: D.C. Heath and Compnay, 1938), p. 307.
[9] Theodore C. Blegen, Minnesota: A History of The State (University of Minnesota Press, 1963), p. 187. The University of Minnesota was established on paper in 1851 and was conducted as a preparatory school throughout the decade.

Hastings Sibley. The act provided not just one normal school, but three—the first to be established within five years of the passage of the act, the second within ten years, and the third within 15 years. The original act included details of appointment of a Governing Board and its organization, location of the schools, finance and appropriations, and supervision and conduct of the new institutions. Thus, at the very beginning of statehood the legislature provided the basic legal instrument for opening teacher training schools as needed.[10]

The first State Normal School went to Winona and began operating in 1860; it was the first normal school opened west of the Mississippi River. Eight years later, in 1868, the second school opened at Mankato to serve the needs of what was at that time the western part of the settled area, and the following year the school at St. Cloud began to serve what was then the northern settled area.

The legal control of the Normal Schools rested on the provision found in Article VIII of the state constitution; this article gave the legislature complete authority over the system of education for the state. To control the Normal Schools, the legislature in 1858 created the Normal School Board consisting of six members, appointed by the governor and confirmed by the Senate, who served four-year terms, one member to be chosen from each county where a normal school was located and not more than one member from a single county.[11] The Board received the power of management, supervision, and control of the Normal Schools, and of all the property pertaining to them. It appointed the presidents and other employees and determined their salaries; it prescribed courses of study and conditions of admission, prepared and conferred diplomas, reported the number of graduates, and adopted suitable rules and regulations for the schools. A month before each new legislature began, the Board reported to the governor on the conditions, needs, and prospects of each school, with recommendations for its improvement. Except for the supervision over construction of new buildings which was delegated to the State Board of Control, the Normal School Board under this broad grant of authority had entire control over the schools.[12]

The passage of the act creating Minnesota's State Normal School System was also significant in that it indicated the general acceptance on the part of the state's leaders of the need for the professional education of teachers and of normal schools as the most satisfactory institutions to provide that preparation— an idea generally accepted in the older states of the Ohio and Mississippi valleys. There was, however, some active opposition to such schools and even more general indifference on the part of many newcomers in the area, occupied as they were with

---

[10] Minnesota, Session Laws (1858), c. 79. At that time there were eleven state institutions of this type, four in Massachusetts, and one each in New York, Connecticut, Michigan, Rhode Island, New Jersey, Illinois, and Pennsylvania. The movement itself was only nineteen years old.

[11] The Board held its first meeting at the capitol at St. Paul on August 16, 1859. After taking the oath of office before the clerk of the Supreme Court, the four members present chose Lieutenant Governor William Holcomb of Stillwater president, and Dr. John D. Ford of Winona, secretary pro tem. Subsequent legislation increased the Board to eight members and in 1905 the Superintendent of Public Instruction became an officio member and secretary of the Board.

[12] Later legislative acts restricted the Board's powers somewhat by centralizing financial control in a State Department of Administration. Under a 1925 act, the Department of Administration and Finance was given supervision and control over all accounts and expenditures. In 1939 a law placed the clerical and maintenance staffs under classified civil service.

the problems of immediate needs of daily life. To these hostile and indifferent groups, advanced schooling was an unnecessary luxury, and they were content to continue with the primitive school systems then available, including the often inadequately trained instructional staffs. Because of the milieu, most of the people teaching in the elementary schools in the nineteenth century had little formal schooling themselves, teaching often with an eighth grade diploma at best.[13]

Preparation for Teaching Elementary School

Despite a lack of formal schooling, an element of missionary zeal prevailed among many nineteenth century teachers when they chose to forsake worldly gain for the privilege and responsibility of molding young minds. Salaries were pitifully low and working conditions sometimes tortuous, but nonetheless numerous dedicated persons sacrificed personal pleasure to "serve in the vineyard without complaint." It is true that many were attracted to teaching during off-seasons in farming, mining, and other more remunerative endeavors along with better working conditions.[14] While some were well educated themselves, they often lacked the drive to establish continuity in their respective schools and to take more than a passing interest in their students. Others were simply incompetent, but they filled existing vacuums in frontier communities. Some protested that if teaching were a profession, a living wage ought to be paid. More often than not, teachers were subject to the intrinsic values placed on their services by a more materially conscious public. Whether one was imbued with the spirit of Christian service or whether one was seeking a port in the storm, it became evident to leading educators that some formal training and certification programs were necessary for the benefit of the teachers, the teaching profession, and the welfare of the public schools.

Permission to teach elementary school in Minnesota in the nineteenth century—and well into the twentieth—was realistically based on the need for teachers. If the need were great, almost anyone willing was permitted to teach. Separating the qualified from the unqualified, speaking relatively, was based largely on supply and demand. Teachers were often qualified for employment by the simplest forms of pedagogical training. This situation occurred nationally too, of course, when teachers could be certified by examination which could be taken at almost any point in the time sequence of preparation, depending on state and local conditions.[15]

In Minnesota, those who received training for teaching in the elementary schools nearly always did so in one of three ways: attending one of the State Normal

---

[13] Charles A. Harper, A Century of Public Teacher Education (Washington: Hugh Birch-Horace Mann Fund, 1939), p. 16.
[14] In Wisconsin, the average elementary teacher's salary in 1863 was twenty-one dollars a month for men and thirteen dollars for women. Richard D. Gamble, From Academy to University: A History of Wisconsin State University, Platteville (Platteville; Wisconsin State University, 1966), p. 95. Blegen, in Building Minnesota, p. 308, cited comparable wages for his state. He noted also that in 1861, two hundred thirty-five of the four hundred sixty-six school houses were built of logs, "some were scarcely fit for barns or stables." As late as 1876 there were more than eight hundred school districts in Minnesota which had school terms of only three months each year.
[15] Lindley J. Stiles, et al., Teacher Education in the United States (New York: The Ronald Press Company, 1960), pp. 125-126. In Minnesota until the 1920s, the minimum requirement for certification was an eighth grade education, after which one could teach upon successfully completing some examinations.

Schools, enrolling in the teacher-training departments of high schools, or attending summer schools designed for teacher training. These three ways need some brief explanation.

The state made appropriations for the establishment of summer training schools for teachers in the counties under the direction of the county superintendent of schools. Students could attend these summer schools with a view toward teaching after they had completed the eighth grade. While the main purpose of the summer schools was to remedy rural school conditions, they were open to all public school teachers who wished to renew or upgrade their teaching certificates. The first summer schools began before the turn of the century, and each county was to either have a school or have one accessible to it every alternate year. The sessions generally lasted six weeks, and the work undertaken had two phases: the academic or instructional, and the methodic or professional. The instructors at these summer schools were often from the local area. The schools themselves came in for great praise from the area newspapers, the students attending, and the State Superintendent of Public Instruction. He wrote in his 1910 report: "No item of public school expenditure brings greater results than the amount spent yearly for these schools." [16]

In 1895 the state legislature first authorized high school training departments. It offered a subsidy of 750 dollars to each local board of education providing such a department in its high school, but only 32 of the 200 high schools in the state had such a department by 1910. These training departments, usually with just one teacher, enrolled high school students; after completing the one-year program, the student became eligible to teach in any rural elementary school. [17]

The third method of training teachers, normal schools, offered a maximum of two years of work beyond high school. All of the State Normal Schools had the same plan of organization. They were organized into two departments: First, the normal department or place of academic and professional instruction; second, the training department or place of application and practice. The latter was comprised of a campus or model school —an elementary school run in connection with the normal school—in which normal school "college" students observed and did their student teaching. The normal department embraced the following courses of study: an elementary course of three years, designed to fit teachers for work in rural or ungraded schools (students could come in from the eighth grade, take this three-year course and then be eligible to teach in rural or ungraded schools); an advanced course of five years, which gave the preparation for teaching in both the higher and lower grades (students could come from eighth grade, take the five-year course and

[16] Minnesota, Superintendent of Public Instruction, Sixteenth Biennial Report, by C. G. Schultz (St. Paul, 1910), p. 17. Bemidji started the first of its summer schools in 1904 and continued them regularly until the normal school opened in 1919. With sessions held in the local high school, the attendance at Bemidji averaged about fifty students the first five years. A full two-page description of the 1908 session, discussing course offerings, books to be read, faculty, and the like, is given in the Bemidji Daily Pioneer, June 17, 1908.

[17] Because both the normal schools and the high schools with training departments trained teachers for the rural schools, and because the graduates of both competed with each other for jobs, there was not always the best feelings between them. By 1939 there were still thirty-four such training departments in Minnesota, each with one teacher and a total enrollment of four hundred eighty-six. Clark, "The Status Policies, and Objectives of Minnesota State Teachers' Colleges" p. 27. In 1910, there were 4,332 students enrolled in high school teacher training departments. Minnesota, Superintendent of Public Instruction, Sixteenth Biennial Report, p. 245.

then be eligible to teach in any elementary school in the state); a professional course of one or two years, for students who were graduates of high schools (those who went one year could teach in rural schools; those who went two years could teach in any elementary school).[18]

The original statement of the purpose of the Normal Schools, as formulated in the Minnesota law of 1858—"to educate and prepare teachers for teaching in the common school"—was repeated in the revised statutes of 1866, 1873, and 1905. In 1905 the legislature changed the phrasing to read the "training of teachers for the public schools"; at the same time, in the same law the legislature made it clear that "the terms 'common school' and 'public school' are inter-changeable and synonymous . . . including graded and ungraded elementary schools, grammar schools, and high schools."[19] Nearly all subsequent acts of the legislature dealing with the teacher-training institutions reaffirmed the mandate to train teachers for the public schools, and the schools digressed but little from this.[20] Until the second decade of the twentieth century, however, the Normal Schools received little pressure to train secondary teachers. The state university and the private colleges performed this function. From 1858 until 1921 the Minnesota Normal Schools dealt with the problems of training teachers for the elementary schools only.[21]

Some 20 years elapsed from the establishment of the first Normal School to the opening of the fourth State Normal School at Moorhead in 1888. The first three Normal Schools had been located in the southern portion of the state (at Winona, Mankato, and St. Cloud), and in the intervening years the population had spread to the western boundary and moved north into the fertile lands of the Red River Valley. In the year ending July 31, 1892, the four Normal Schools enrolled 1,834 students. The State Superintendent of Public Instruction estimated that there were 483,536 persons of school age in the state, and of these 300,333 were in school more or less during the year ending July 31, 1892. Of those attending, 4,290 were enrolled in the high schools; 100,094 in the special and independent districts (maintaining both elementary and high schools), and the balance, 199,239, in the common districts (maintaining only elementary schools). There were 5,705 common

---

[18] Minnesota, Legislative Manual (1893), pp. 230-231. Two-year graduates received a diploma; those who went one year received a certificate but both were counted as "graduates" of a school. What may seem striking about the early normal schools was the admittance of students completing the eighth grade and the establishment of sub-collegiate curricula. Because there were for many years so few high schools (in 1910, for example, there were twenty-four thousand students enrolled in two hundred high schools with eleven percent of them graduating), normal schools had to adapt to the times if future teachers were to receive any training. The three-year course continued until 1911, and the five-year course was still in existence in the 1920s. Not until 1921 did the Normal Board approve a full four-year degree course; in 1927 the first bachelor's degrees were granted. In 1929 the normal schools, by then renamed teachers colleges, received permission to train teachers for secondary as well as elementary positions.

[19] Minnesota, Session Laws (1905), c. 56. The semantic argument over what constitutes the divisions of public school training still continues today. Though the term common school is now out of date, the issue of whether an "elementary school," for example, constitutes grades kindergarten through grade six, one through eight, kindergarten through nine, and other possibilities, still goes unresolved.

[20] This legislative mandate of 1858 to "prepare teachers" still carries over to the present. For example, even after the Board allowed the schools to offer a B.A. program beginning in 1946, a 1967 memorandum from the Bemidji State College Registrar's Office indicated that eighty-five percent of the four thousand students enrolled were planning on teaching in public schools as a career.

[21] The state high schools did not mushroom in growth until after World War I, and until that time the state university and the private colleges provided an adequate number of high school teachers for the market.

schools, 117 independent, 36 special, and 69 high schools. The average monthly wage in 1892 for male teachers was \$40.79, and for female teachers, \$31.40.[22] Even by the turn of the century, education was beginning to be a big business.

With the opening of the Iron Range, a concentration of population in the northeastern section of the state, and the increasing importance of Duluth as an inland port, the legislature in 1895 authorized the establishment of a fifth Normal School at Duluth to serve the area. Because of several delays, however, the school did not open its doors until 1902. In that year the five State Normal Schools enrolled 2,142 students. In the breakdown of enrollments, Winona had 649 (the total number of graduates since it had opened in 1860 was 1,402); St. Cloud, 357 (it had graduated 1,230 since 1869); Mankato, 649 (it had graduated 1,402 since 1868); Moorhead, four hundred four; and Duluth, 126. These numbers, however, could not fill the demand for teachers throughout the state.[23]

As settlers and their families moved into the north-central area of Minnesota in greater numbers and began clearing the timber and farming the land, a demand for yet a sixth Normal School to serve this section of the state faced the legislators. The precedent of an area state school to serve a given section of the state had been firmly set; historical imperatives seemed to make the issue irrepressible. In the area lived a number of interested people who desired a normal school. Some were altruistic, others were self-centered and shortsighted, and as careless of historical imperatives as their counterparts in other sections of the state who had received a normal school. The stage was set by 1910 for a normal school fight in north-central Minnesota. The big question was: Which town would get the school?

---

[22] Minnesota, Legislative Manual (1893), pp. 230-231. The state population grew rapidly in this period. In 1880, the population was 780,773, an increase of 77 percent in the decade; in 1890, there were 1,310,283 and a 67 percent increase. U. S. Bureau of the census, Sixteenth Census of the United States; 1940. Population, IV, pp. 13, 27.

[23] Minnesota, Legislative Manual (1903), pp. 289-292.

CHAPTER II

The Normal School Fight: 1907-1913

Minnesota After the Turn of the Century

MINNESOTA CELEBRATED THE 50th anniversary of its admission to statehood in 1908, and it was about this time that interested citizens in northern Minnesota began to agitate for another normal school to be located in their area. At this time the state ranked tenth in the union in terms of area, containing 84,287 square miles or about 54 million acres of which 3,500,000 were covered by water. Approximately half of the state consisted of prairie lands interspersed with groves of timber and covered with dark, fertile soil. The rest, embracing the elevated district west and north of Lake Superior, consisted mainly of pine forests along with areas of rich mineral deposits.

The national census of 1910 showed a Minnesota population of 2,075,708, an increase of 324,414 or 18.5 percent in the past ten years. At that time the eight largest cities in the state had the following populations: Minneapolis, 301,408; St. Paul, 214,744; Duluth, 78,466; Winona, 18,583; St. Cloud, 10,600; Virginia, 10,473; Mankato, 10,365; and Stillwater, 10,198. Of the total increase in population during the decade, about one fourth was in rural territory while more than one-half was in places with populations over 25,000.[24]

In 1858, Minnesota's population had been 125,000, and the value of its farm products was estimated at eight million dollars; 50 years later farm products were valued at $275,444,000. In 1858 manufactured products were estimated to be worth 2.5 million dollars, and in 1908, 350 million dollars. Receipts in the state treasury in 1858 were $286,903; in 1908 they were $12,446,280.[25] The total

---

[24] Minnesota, Legislative Manual (1915), p. 211. With the exceptions of Stillwater and Virginia, all of the eight largest cities had a college or normal school located in them (Virginia opened its junior college in 1916). These included all of the cities where normal schools were located, with one exception, Moorhead.

[25] Ibid. The publication went on to editorialize: "It seems probable that Minnesota will hold her place as the greatest wheat-producing state, and will also earn the reputation as the best all-around farming state in the union."

foreign-born population in Minnesota in 1905 was 537,041, about 25 percent of the total population. Scandinavians made up by far the largest ethnic group of these foreign-born: Sweden, 126,283; Norway, 111,611; and Denmark, 16,266. However, there were 119,868 persons who were born in Germany. The next largest group were the Irish with 19,531. There were also 10,225 Indians in the state at the time, most of them located in the northern areas.[26]

Politically the members of the Republican party dominated state politics in the two decades following the turn of the century. This dominance occurred from the federal offices down through the state and local positions. Occasionally a Democrat slipped into office, but this was the exception to the general rule. Democratic governors, however, played an important part in the selection and later the establishment of the normal school in the northern part of the state at Bemidji.

The reports of the State Superintendent of Public Instruction indicate clearly that an elementary school education through the eighth grade prevailed as the top educational achievement for most Minnesota citizens throughout the first decades of the twentieth century. Graduation exercises from the local elementary school, or common school as it was often called, turned out to be the big spring social event in most communities. For example, in 1908, only 3,314 were graduated from high school and only 24,530 were enrolled. At the same time, better than 300,000 students were enrolled in the elementary schools, although the report does not offer any figures on the number of elementary school graduates.[27]

The Calls for Another Normal School

Aside from the university and the private colleges which provided the teachers for the high schools, the most qualified teachers in northern Minnesota schools should have come from the state's normal schools. It was to these sparsely populated rural areas, however, that normal school graduates at this time did not go.[28] To improve school teaching in rural areas became one reason why some public-minded citizens in the northern part of the state started agitating to get a State Normal School to locate there. State Superintendent of Public Instruction C. C. Schultz observed in 1910:

"The chief obstacle in the way of bettering the conditions of the rural schools has been the scarcity of teachers with thorough academic training combined with professional skill. This has made it necessary to employ for the work a large number without teaching experience and without the opportunity of getting even a moderate amount of training for teaching at an expense within their means."[29]

Schultz went on in his 1910 report on normal schools to support the addition of one more. The normal schools, he wrote, were in a "flourishing condition" and had made "marked progress the past few years." Attendance had

---

[26] Ibid.
[27] Minnesota, Superintendent of Public Instruction, Sixteenth Biennial Report, by C. G. Schultz (St.. Paul, 1910), pp. 245-246.
[28] Ibid., p. 17. As late as 1920, Beltrami County Superintendent of Schools J. C. McGhee reported that there were only three graduates of normal schools teaching in the county rural schools.
[29] Ibid.

increased until the full capacity of most of the schools at the time had been reached and in one instance, St. Cloud, had been exceeded. The total enrollment in the five normal schools for the two years ending July 31, 1910, was 7,144, or about 3,500 for each year; the total number of graduates during that period was 1,352. These crowded conditions might be remedied, he indicated, "in one of two ways, namely by establishing a new school—which is needed—or by the enlargement of the present institutions; and my own judgment is that both remedies will soon have to be applied." [30]

Schultz, however, spoke for himself, and not for the State Normal Board which governed the normal schools and made recommendations for changes to the state legislature. The Board did not recommend the addition of any new normal school in either of the first two decades in the twentieth century.

Nearly all of the county superintendents of schools in the north and northwestern parts of the state requested another teacher training school in the area. W. B. Stewart, Beltrami County (of which Bemidji was the county seat), wrote in his 1910 report: "What is needed is a permanent institution for training teachers which will give practice work, with breadth and thoroughness of training, and scholarship for rural work."[31] Presumably Stewart had Bemidji in mind as the site of the permanent institution. In fairness, however, it should be added that when the time came for the legislature to decide on adding a new normal school, the great majority of the citizens in the entire north and northwestern part of the state wanted first an area school to which their young people could go; exactly where it would be was secondary.

Distance was another of the primary factors in the desire to obtain a new normal school in the northern part of the state. The closest normal schools to the Bemidji area were at Duluth and Moorhead, each approximately 150 miles away. In those days when any traveling was an adventure, distance was highly significant.

A sparse population lived in the section of the state that sought another normal school. The three leading contenders became the communities of Bemidji, Cass Lake, and Thief River Falls. Although many community leaders expressed interest in their particular town getting a new normal school, when it came to making the final decision, these largest three towns emerged as the ones likely to be selected.[32] In 1905, Beltrami County, of which Bemidji was the county seat, had 7,017 people living in cities or villages and 12,058 outside of the villages; the city of Bemidji had 3,800 people. Cass County had 2,411 in cities and villages and 7,113

---

[30] Ibid., 52, 248. Schultz, of course, did not suggest in his report where the proposed new normal school should be located. Eventually, however, he was a member of the committee that selected Bemidji as the site in 1913. Because of his office, Schultz was an ex officio member of the State Normal Board. A seemingly incomplete file of his correspondence while in office is on file in the State Archives and Records Service in St. Paul.

[31] Ibid., p. 100. Somewhat strangely, the Cass County Superintendent of Schools was one of the very few who did not desire to have a normal school located closer to home. He wrote: "Our experience is that when our boys and girls who have teaching ability attend the normal schools, that is the last we see of them. The advantage of higher salaries offered elsewhere in city and village schools makes it impossible to keep them in the rural schools." p. 106.

[32] Area newspaper editors soon labeled the issue of which town would get the normal school as the "normal school fight." Because it was drawn out over several years, the names "round one" and "round two" were added. "Round one" was between Bemidji and Cass Lake ; "round two" was between Bemidji and Thief River Falls. Somewhat strangely, even the editors of newspapers located in communities desiring the normal school viewed "the plum," as some called it, going to either Bemidji, Cass Lake, or Thief River Falls.

outside the villages; Cass Lake's population was 1,062. Marshall County, in which Thief River Falls was located before it became the county seat of Pennington County in 1922, had 3,190 in the cities and villages and 14,547 outside the villages; Thief River Falls had a population of 3,502.

A Sketch of the Three Communities

The first settlement had been made in Bemidji in 1888. The town took its name from Lake Bemidji, a shortening of the Indian name, "Bemidjigumag." In 1896 Bemidji became incorporated as a village on May 5, after a referendum passed. In 1900 the population of the town, a thriving lumbering center, was 2,183. In 1905 it became a city and grew to 3,800; in 1910, 5,099, and by 1920, 7,086. Four railway lines provided transportation into the city—the Minneapolis, St. Paul and Sault Ste. Marie; the Great Northern; the Minnesota and International; and the Minneapolis, Red Lake and Manitoba, of which the city was the southern terminus. Though there was some farming in the area, the city was largely a lumbering town from its beginnings until World War I. The town had waterworks, gas and electric lights, four banks, sawmills, a woolen mill, box, brick, tile and turpentine factories, wholesale houses, a creamery, an active civic and commerce association, a Carnegie library, churches of the leading denominations, two newspapers, and good public school buildings. At one time Beltrami County was the largest in the state; after it was reduced in 1922, it still had an area of about 3,000 square miles. Outside of Bemidji, however, not one of the principal villages in the county had a population of more than 800 by 1920. Still it had many organized townships and almost all of them had an elementary school that needed one or more teachers. As one publication put it, the first school in the county began in 1894, and "as settlers came in, little schools sprouted up all over. Every township had its log school."[33]

Cass Lake—15 miles east of Bemidji—was the largest town in Cass County, but the village of Walker held the county seat. The county was named after General Lewis Cass who had visited the region in 1820. Cass County had an area of 2,104 square miles and was divided into 48 townships. The only battle fought between United States soldiers and Chippewa Indians in Minnesota was fought near Walker in 1898. The village of Cass Lake began about 1890 and was situated on the shore of the lake; the Soo Line and Great Northern railroads ran through the community. Like Bemidji, scattered farms existed in the vicinity, but Cass Lake too depended on lumbering as its main industry. The population was 1,062 in 1905, 2,011 in 1910, and 2,109 in 1920. In 1910 the county had three grade schools and 88 rural schools. Cass Lake had two banks, an electric light plant, waterworks, saw and planing mills, a crate factory, five churches, a commercial club, a public

[33] History of Beltrami County (Bemidji: Beltrami County Historical Society, 1957), p. 20. Information on Bemidji, Cass Lake, and Thief River Falls was taken from Joseph A. A. Burnquist ed. Minnesota and Its People (Chicago: S. J. Clark Publishing Company. 1924), II, 373. Burnquist pointedly failed to include the indelicate information that for its first twenty-five years, most of downtown Bemidji was made up of saloons, and that it was most decidedly a rough lumberjack town.

library, and one weekly newspaper, the Cass Lake Times.[34]

Thief River Falls, the third contender for the normal school, began in 1887 and received its name from the fur trading era. An Indian fortification had been built near the mouth of the stream now known as Thief River, but which the Indians called Secret Earth River. The early French in the area called it Stealing River, and this was later translated into Thief River. The first settlers there were attracted by the falls which afforded good water power. Located at the junction of the Minneapolis, St. Paul and Sault Ste. Marie, and the Great Northern railways, the town became the seat of Pennington County. The town owned its electric light plant, a waterworks system, and an auditorium. The community had four banks, a large mill, three grain elevators, a foundry and machine shop, two creameries, a commercial club, churches of seven denominations, a Carnegie library, and two newspapers. The city was the chief trading center for the surrounding farmers living on the flat but fertile land. There were 3,502 people in Thief River Falls in 1905, 3,714 in 1910, and 4,685 in 1920. A small county compared to Beltrami and Cass, Pennington County had an area of only 610 square miles with 22 organized townships. Other than Thief River Falls, no villages in the county had a population more than 400.[35]

Eventually, when the normal school issue came to the legislature, some northern Minnesota legislators began referring to the area seeking the school as the "sixth normal school district" which by 1915 included 13 counties, had a school population of 45,000, and embraced an area of 22,000 square miles or practically a fourth of the state. The legislators estimated there were 225,000 people in the district with the territory valued at 130 million dollars and paying 600,000 dollars in taxes.[36]

The Normal School Fight Begins

John A. Johnson served as governor of Minnesota from 1905 until his untimely death in office in 1909. A popular Democrat bucking the Republican tide, he was elected three times. In his 1904 election, every county in the state voted for the Republican presidential candidate. Johnson, of poor Swedish parents, was born and raised in St. Peter; he made his livelihood there as the publisher of the local newspaper. The first native Minnesotan to be elected governor, he became nationally known for winning as a Democrat in a Republican state. In none of his three addresses to the legislature, however, did he recommend the addition of another State Normal School. His attitude on the subject, as will be shown, prevailed while

---

[34] Ibid., 427. Cass Lake too had its full share of saloons. Both Bemidji and Cass Lake in the period before World War I had all the negative earmarks of frontier communities. There was a great deal of violence; brawls were commonplace, there seemed to be an inordinate number of suicides, and even murder and mysterious disappearances of individuals were not uncommon. Concomitant with this were tar-and-feathering parties and several attempts at vigilante justice and yet, say old-timers in language very up-to-date, a lady then was always safe to walk the streets without fear.

[35] Ibid., 403.

[36] Bemidji Weekly Pioneer, February 25, 1915, p. 9. Excerpts of lengthy speeches by northern legislators praising the "sixth normal school district" are printed in this issue. They maintained that they paid six hundred thousand dollars a year in taxes but didn't get that much back in state benefits; hence, a new normal school would alleviate part of that problem.

he was governor despite the legislature.[37]

The fight to establish a sixth State Normal School began as early as 1907 and continued for six years before successful legislation was passed. Civic-minded citizens in the various communities made a spirited campaign to interest people in the establishment of an additional normal school, and the local newspaper editors took up the task. Editors threw about accolades and pejoratives with reckless abandon in what came down to virtually a no-holds-barred contest among the rival communities for getting the plum of a state institution. To record the long, on-going contest, the newspapers provide the best solid source of information for reference; not only do they shed the most light, they certainly reflect the heat of the battle to obtain Minnesota's sixth State Normal School.[38]

The first mention of the topic in the Bemidji newspapers occurred on January 10, 1907, in an article by Absie P. Ritchie, superintendent of the Bemidji schools, under the headline, "Bemidji Is the Logical Location for State Normal School for the North." Ritchie noted that "the proposition to establish the sixth normal school in this state is being widely discussed," and he went on to argue why the school should be located in Bemidji. He said that the town was the geographical center of the area, that it had excellent railroad facilities, and that it had "a climate for health and vigor that is unsurpassed."[39]

The Cass Lake _Times_ not only picked up the topic but also made an assertion about where the school belonged. The editor, Frank Ives, wrote in the January 12, 1907, issue that "Cass Lake is especially fitted for the location of such an institution. It is the geographical center of this part of the state." The _Pioneer_ editor, A. Kaiser, noted ten days later in a short editorial that State Senator Daniel M. Gunn of Grand Rapids, whose district included Cass Lake, had prepared a bill in the legislature providing for a new normal school at Cass Lake. "The _Pioneer_ moves an amendment, striking out the words Cass Lake and substituting therefore Bemidji, otherwise the bill has our most hearty approval and support." Gunn's reported reason for introducing the normal school bill was to remedy the difficulty of school districts in the northern part of the state of finding enough good teachers. Said Gunn, "It is true that the Duluth Normal is not far away, but St. Louis County [of which Duluth was the county seat] is an empire in itself, and can easily use all the teachers the Duluth school can turn out. Our section is another great empire, and we have trouble finding teachers."[40]

---

[37] In the elections where Bemidji, Cass Lake and Thief River Falls were located, Johnson carried only Marshall County (Thief River Falls) in 1904, all but Cass County in 1906, and all three in 1908.

[38] It seems somewhat ironic that the cause of public higher education is filled with so much bitterness and selfishness among individuals and groups fighting to get a state school located in a given community. Though half a century separated the events, the college-site issue is not out-of-date for there is a parallel between the location of Bemidji Normal in 1913 and the location of the newest state college at Marshall in 1963, as witnessed by the newspapers of both periods.

[39] Bemidji Daily Pioneer, p. 1. In this normal school fight there was enough local puffery to suggest each and every community in northern Minnesota to be a veritable utopia, winters included. In this same article Ritchie knocked the weather on the opposite sides of the state: "We are sheltered from the blizzards of the bleak prairies of Moorhead and the chilly breezes of Duluth by primeval forests." The often hyperbolic claims of the rival communities as to the perfect location, the charges and counter-charges of nefarious favoritism shown by the decision-makers, the hue and cry of "politics," whatever that exactly means, all combine to make a sorry spectacle. Seemingly however, every college in existence today went through a somewhat similar situation. To the victors it was worth the efforts.

[40] Quoted in the Bemidji Daily Pioneer, January 22, 1907. Gunn did indicate that a Cass Lake delegation had requested him to introduce the bill. Gunn had been a member of the lower house when Duluth received its normal school in 1895, and he had helped the Duluth delegation then; it was expected that they would reciprocate for him, and they did.

W. B. Stewart, Beltrami County Superintendent of Schools, tried to stir up enthusiasm for a new school by pointing out the financial advantages for Bemidji. Stewart estimated that the school would average two hundred fifty students a year and that a sum total of "$101,250 would circulate among the businessmen of our city yearly . . . all to be had for the asking.''[41] Along with this article, the Bemidji editor chided the townspeople for their apparent indifference to the topic. Soon afterwards interested citizens held several meetings and eventually chose a committee to go to St. Paul to lobby for a bill to locate a normal school at Bemidji. Representative J. J. Opsahl submitted the bill.[42] After this, almost every issue of the February, 1907, Bemidji papers referred in some way to the proposed normal school. One article told of the local Commercial Club's active support; other articles quoted from outside newspapers supporting Bemidji; one issue published an open letter to the legislature written by Absie P. Ritchie, the person who seemed to be the catalyst in town for promoting the desirability of a normal school for Bemidji.[43]

Some of the area newspapers, however, showed open dismay at the scrapping between Bemidji and Cass Lake over the normal school (Thief River Falls had not yet entered into the fray). Many editors reasoned that it was more important first to get a normal school approved for the north-central part of the state, and then after this, let the Normal School Board select the exact location. From this came what was called the "general bill," introduced into the legislature in February, 1907, and soon afterwards all of the northern Minnesota newspapers and delegations approved the "general bill" idea with the exception of Cass Lake. The people of Cass Lake opposed the general bill because they believed the Normal School Board was prejudiced in favor of Bemidji.[44] The Bemidji papers, of course, became critical of Cass Lake and accused her, among other things, of being very short-sighted, but Cass Lake held its ground and replied in kind.

By March, 1907, the proponents were seemingly reaching into the hat for any kind of support. For example, the Pioneer quoted a lengthy letter from President Webster Merrifield of the University of North Dakota who praised Bemidji as an ideal location for a normal school. And along with editorials that can be described only as vicious in attacking Cass Lake, the Pioneer varied the fare with poetry. The first of six verses suffices to give the content and the quality of the message:

All of you surrounding towns come join together

And help us build the normal this coming summer weather

Why not build it here on the Minnesota ridge?

[41] Ibid.

[42] Opsahl represented the sixty-first district composed then of three counties, Red Lake, Clearwater, and Beltrami. He won his election, according to the Pioneer which strongly supported him, because of his '"firm stand on good roads and drainage," both popular issues at the time.

[43] Ritchie was instrumental in working for the normal school from the inception of the idea until the doors opened in 1919. Born in North Carolina in 1869, one of fifteen children, he moved to Minnesota at age ten. He attended St. Cloud Normal, Hamline University, and graduated from Western University in Chicago. He taught in several Minnesota schools before becoming Bemidji superintendent of schools in 1904, a position he held until 1910. He then became president of the Farmers Mutual Insurance Company. From 1915 to 1923, he held the post of Bemidji postmaster. He died in 1950, survived by his wife and six children. Information supplied by his wife, now Mable Ritchie Goar, age eighty-five, in an interview May 10, 1967.

[44] Cass Lake Times, February 26, 1907, p. 1. "Cass Lake has it on excellent authority . . . that . . . some of the members of the Board are closely related to certain prominent citizens of Bemidji."

For there is no other place as good as 'old Bemidj.'[45]

Despite fulminations and flowery words, by the end of March, 1907, the legislature defeated all the bills regarding another State Normal School. Considering the interest and emotions built up by the newspapers in northern Minnesota, the reactions of the editors seemed mild, and the major protagonists dropped the subject almost entirely, although a few salvos were delivered on the way out. And there the matter rested, like a Lazarus entombed, waiting to be lifted up and restored, the hope still remaining that the forces of right would prevail for each community.[46]

Not until October, 1908, did the Bemidji paper again pick up the topic of normal schools but once started, the topic continued as a regular subject through the early months of 1909 when the Minnesota legislature once more held its biennial session. President W. A. Shoemaker of St. Cloud Normal touched off the issue again when he wrote a letter to the Bemidji editor and asked him to give "a little of your valuable space to spreading the news regarding the congested condition of the school," that is, St. Cloud Normal. In essence he said that no students from the northern part of the state should come to St. Cloud to school because it was so crowded there that it was most unlikely that they could be enrolled (there were 603 enrolled at the time). To this the Bemidji editor sounded the alarm: "The St. Cloud Normal is crowded to the roof and W. E. Shoemaker . . . is sending out warnings that the Normal Board will not care for any more pupils."[47]

There the subject sat until December of that year when a news story told of a recent teachers' meeting (300 attending) in Park Rapids, a town some 45 miles southwest of Bemidji, at which a series of resolutions were adopted, one reading: "Resolved, That we most earnestly advocate the establishment of a sixth normal school to be located at some convenient place in North Central Minnesota, in order to take care of the rapidly growing educational necessities of this section of the state."[48] This helped to refuel the editorial fires.

About this same time, the president of the State Normal School Board, Ell Torrance of Minneapolis, wrote his biennial report regarding the State Normal Schools. Although the Pioneer editor headlined the Torrance report, "A Sixth Normal School Would Furnish Relief," and subheaded its account, "Hon. Ell Torrance, President State Normal Board, Tells of Inadequate Accommodations of Present Schools. State Should Provide Another Normal," at no place in the report

---

[45] Bemidji Daily Pioneer, March 4, 1907, p. 3. Merrifield's long letter appeared in the February 27 issue. President Merrifield had a summer home at Bemidji and apparently liked it: "My family all fell in love with the place last summer and we anticipate the coming summer at Bemidji with far greater pleasure than we did the last. I know of few regions anywhere more desirable whether for a summer residence or for the location of a normal school." The letter was written to a Reverend S. E. P. White of Bemidji, the letter dated February 5, 1907.

[46] A three-man committee from the House visited the area in June, 1907, and looked over the communities. The Pioneer of June 17 noted their presence and said correctly that the normal school issue was by NO means dead.

[47] October 20, 1908, p. 1. It should be noted that the Pioneer changed ownership and editors. In March, 1907, A. G. Rutledge assumed the editorial position. He also wrote a column which he bylined only as "Doc." Rutledge had been active in the normal school issue before becoming editor, and his new position gave him a better advantage to air his views, views that in 1909 became outspoken if not vitriolic. Libel laws of those days had to be much more lax than now. It might also be noted, however, that these early newspapers were much more interesting to read than today's Pioneer; the early editors did not shrink from taking a firm stand on current issues.

[48] Quoted in the Bemidji Daily Pioneer, December 3, 1908, p. 2.

was there mentioned the need for another normal school.[49]

As the 1909 legislature neared, proponents of the new normal school began to gather their forces. The Pioneer headline, "Contest for Proposed Normal Is ON," understated the fracas that followed. The Cass Lake editor caught the spirit: "The battle . . . is yet to be fought and when the carnage is ended and all the dead and wounded are counted, we expect to say to our readers that the school has finally been located on Park Road half a mile north of the business portion of our village, in one of the groves of pine selected by the gods for educational purposes."[50] Other communities, too, warmed up to the heady thought that they might get the new normal school, and citizens formed committees in various communities—Warren, Grand Rapids, Park Rapids, Bagley, Ada, Clearbrook—to consider proper action. What followed, however, repeated the pattern of the 1907 session: Daniel Gunn introduced a bill for Cass Lake, J. J. Opsahl one for Bemidji, and a "general bill" was offered to establish a school somewhere in the northern start of the state. And again, as in 1907, all the northern communities supported the general bill with the exception of Cass Lake.[51]

In the middle of February, 1909, the legislature sent a joint subcommittee of the House and Senate to visit the northern Minnesota towns for the purpose of looking at proposed normal school sites. The committee's visit to Bemidji resulted in one of the rare banner headlines in the Pioneer at that time: "Normal Committee Given Reception," and subheaded down to the centerfold: "Were Tendered Warm and Elaborate Banquet. Hospitality Dealt Out With A Lavish Hand. Visited All Parts of City. Are Surprised at Bemidji's Progressiveness and Pleased With Unlimited Hospitality Which Was Extended." The newspaper devoted the entire front page to the visitors' one-day stay and gave selected quotations of remarks of the committee members. Thus Representative A. Goodspeed of Richfield: "Bemidji and its people are the best on earth."[52]

Rather surprisingly, the Cass Lake paper paid slight attention to the coming of the subcommittee there; yet the editor appeared to be little worried, for he wrote in a short editorial on February 20: "The spoils belong to the finder. So it shall continue to be true, and not even the immense wealth of Bemidji nor her slanderous citizens will be able to remove the custom. Now the fight is practically over. All that remains is to clear away the smoke and the finder will have her spoils."

Even the Bemidji paper and the Bemidji delegation at St. Paul, who regularly filed reports in the newspapers on its progress, acknowledged that Cass

[49] Perhaps both poets and editors are issued poetic licenses. The complete report of Torrance can be found in Minnesota, Superintendent of Public Instruction, Fifteenth Annual Report, by C.G. Schultz (St. Paul, 1907-1908) pp. 61-64. Torrance served on the state Normal Board for eighteen years, the last twelve as president.

[50] Cass Lake Times, January 23, 1909, p. 4.

[51] Bemidji held a mass meeting January 28, 1907, in the Masonic Hall and selected a committee, headed by A. P. Ritchie, to go to St.. Paul to lobby for the Bemidji bill. They held a second meeting February 21 in the reading room of the Crookston Lumber Company and decided then to support the general bill instead, leaving the selection to the Normal School Board.

[52] February 18, 1909, p. 1. The coming of a committee to view the towns had put the Pioneer in a dichotomous position. On the one hand the editor opposed any junket, as he called it, believing it was rigged in favor of Cass Lake; but on the other hand, there was the feeling that once the decision makers came to Bemidji—even in February—and saw the community, they could not help themselves from awarding the school to Bemidji. The editor commented that other members of the legislature came along too,

Lake had the edge in the normal school fight. Apparently Cass Lake had considerable influence in the legislature in the form of Daniel Gunn in the Senate and P. H. McGarry (townsite owner of the village of Walker) in the House. Both men were well liked and respected. Moreover, C. G. Hartley, a wealthy man from Duluth, owned the Cass Lake village townsite and was influential in the Republican party, being considered both as a gubernatorial and a senatorial candidate.

Whatever the reasons, the Cass Lake bill continued to make headway in the legislature. On March 18 the Senate approved the Cass Lake bill by a 32 to 25 vote; about the same time, the House killed the general bill. On April 2, the Cass Lake bill passed the House by a close sixty to fifty-four vote. It appeared that Cass Lake was indeed the winner, and for its citizens it was a time for rejoicing. "Cass Lake Bill Wins 'Against the Field' " ran the banner headline of the April 3 Times and underneath was pictured a large eagle with flags and banners wrapped around its wings and irrelevant Latin quotations coming from its mouth. The triumphant lead article began: "The long fight . . . is ended and Cass Lake by her straightforward manly course has won by a good safe majority."

"The only hope the opposition has," the article continued, "is that Tams Bixby [Bemidji townsite landowner] can induce the governor to veto the act which he will never do."[53]

On April 6, however, Governor John A. Johnson vetoed the Cass Lake bill, and on April 8, 1909, the Pioneer printed the entire veto message:

"I have the honor to return herewith, without my approval, file No. 53, an act to establish a state normal school at the village of Cass Lake, in the county of Cass. In my judgment there is no pressing need for the establishment of an additional normal school at this time. The financial condition of the state is not such to warrant the establishment of new public institutions at this time. It is not my purpose to argue against the wisdom of the legislature in finding this particular site, further than to urge that it never has had the approval of the authorities in charge of normal schools, but on the contrary has met their disapproval for reasons which it is not necessary to assign. In view of the uncertainties of the future development of the region in its relation to education centers; opposed as I am to the policy of establishing new public institutions until there is a decided need for them, I cannot lend my approval to this act. Very Respectfully, John A. Johnson, Governor."

The veto hardly calmed the roiled waters of dispute; on the contrary, it roiled them further, for neither side was yet in a proper state of mind to approach the subject objectively. That tempers were short and invective long between the two towns at this time cannot be denied, and the vitriolic pens of the respective editors

[53] The Pioneer editor did not lose graciously. Though Rutledge sent a very brief congratulatory telegram to Ives, which Ives printed, the pages of the Pioneer avoided any commentary until April 5 when the editor groused that "the bill to establish the sixth state normal school at Cass Lake was passed as a personal favor to P. H. McGarry and Dan Gunn, and not for any real merit which the village of Cass Lake possesses as the best location . . . is admitted on all sides." Before this the St. Pioneer Press,. referred to Gunn as an "oleaginous log-roller" after the Senate passed the Cass Lake bill March 18. Other newspapers too referred to the successful log-rolling act performed by Dunn and McGarry. The Pioneer stated that one of its reporters had personally interviewed all but a few of the sixty men [House members] who voted for the Cass Lake Bill . . . and in every instance the same reply was given: 'McGarry is such a good fellow; we couldn't go back on Pat'."

did little to give credit to either side.[54]

But the emotionalism slowly quieted down, at least publicly, so that even the Times editor in the April 17 issue could view the debacle philosophically and see the whole matter as "a loss for entire Minnesota." After May, 1909, there appeared no mention of normal schools in either paper until January, 1911. Even when Governor Johnson died unexpectedly on September 23, 1909, the Pioneer in devoting two full pages to the man did not mention his veto. The Bemidji paper bowed out of the 1909 struggle by quoting from a Bovey paper in its April 23 edition which called for all the people who were involved to come to their senses about a normal school and "leave the unfortunate matter as dormant as possible." It was appropriately entitled, "Let It Quietly Rest."

The Times soon dropped the topic too; its last mention of the fateful subject that year told of a banquet which in some respects was more of a wake:

"That Cass Lake does not forget its friends was fully demonstrated last evening when the capacious dining hall of the Endion hotel was crowded to capacity . . . to do honor to its representatives [Gunn and McGarry] in the state legislature in the session recently closed. Cass Lakers were advertising to the world that they were just as grateful to their representatives who had fought the fight for them and won it fairly in the normal school matter as if the fruits of their victory had not been snatched from them by the veto of Governor Johnson."[55]

So ended the hopes and dreams of the 1909 legislature to allow some northern Minnesota town to have a State Normal School. One town had come so close to making it, yet lost out by a governor's veto that produced antipathies felt even today. While riding along the shore of Cass Lake in 1963 the late Reverend Harlan Peterson of Cass Lake pointed to a grove of trees and told the author with a touch of bitterness: "There's where Bemidji State College is supposed to be."

The issue of a new normal school lay dormant during the two years following 1909. There appeared to be a consensus among the interested groups not to raise the topic that had wrought up such bitter feelings. Area politicians seeking state offices in 1910 did not mention the topic; in the legislature in 1911, no legislators introduced any bills for any new normal school. Moreover, the area newspapers remained silent on the subject, and it seemed that the political maxim

[54] Understandably, the Times of April 10 reacted in a fit of pique to the veto: "Were it not for the unreasonable, outrageous, and ignominious act of Governor Johnson, the brilliant fight would have been gloriously rewarded. The reasons for vetoing . . . are too weak to be considered." About a week after the veto, tempers had reached a point where Bemidji citizens did not venture to go to Cass Lake. At the same time the members of the Cass Lake Merchants' Association boycotted Bemidji wholesale houses and patronized instead only Duluth merchants. Of course the questionable veracity of editorials like the one appearing in the April 13 Pioneer did not help the situation. "While it is a matter of common knowledge that the Cass Lake people really did have their band out on the street; that flags were flying and that a banquet like unto Balshazzer's feast had been prepared, and was not served, it cannot be said truthfully that Bemidji people gloated over . . . the veto. On the contrary, the Governor's action simply occasioned quiet smiles and nods of approval."

[55] May 13, 1909, p. 1. Though denied by many at the time, there seems little reason today to question Governor Johnson's motives for vetoing the bill. Throughout his public career in the governor's office, both political parties praised the man's integrity although all did not accept his politics. Thus there appears to be no other motives and that Johnson acted according to his best judgment for the state. Grant Utley, age seventy-two, in 1969 the editor of the Cass Lake Times, had purchased the paper from Ives in 1916. He remembered well the normal school fracas and commented: "Wow, that was some fight. There are still a lot of people around here mad about it. I know a fellow who told me he would make a special trip down to St. Paul every year just to spit on the statue of Governor Johnson."

of "action begets reaction" had gone into effect.[56]

Round Two of the Normal School Fight

Not until the summer of 1912 did the newspapers again take up the call for a new normal school. Thief River Falls provided the major competition then for Bemidji, and both publishing the news and reflecting the views of that town was the weekly Thief River Falls News-Press. M. C. Cutter, editor and publisher. The News-Press began drumming up enthusiasm in the summer of 1912 ("Normal School Badly Needed") and continued sporadically to publish similar headlines and supporting stories that fall and early winter. It offered the same arguments of those mentioned in earlier papers of the other communities and need not be repeated. Suffice it to say that the major dissimilarity it offered was that the normal school should be located in Thief River Falls.

After more than a year of silence, the Pioneer mentioned the desire for another normal school in an editorial in its December 12, 1912, edition entitled, "We Refuse to Fight." The article told of a conference of Bemidji men with State Representative Daniel P. O'Neil who was quoted by the Pioneer: "I will favor a general normal school bill, but do not care to have the old trouble stirred up again."[57] Neither did the Pioneer.

But what O'Neil did not care to have came anyway and for northern Minnesota the year 1913 became the year of decision for another new normal school. Into the hopper at the state legislature went bills to locate a new normal school at Bemidji, Thief River Falls, and Cass Lake, and another general bill to locate the school somewhere in northern Minnesota. With a crisis impending, the Pioneer editor showed a reluctance to gird for battle, but felt there was no alternative; he wrote: "Bemidji's attitude is not aggressive but defensive."[58] Delegations from the various interested communities again descended on St. Paul, but after all the oratory and lobbying, the chairman of the House Normal School Committee, W. W. Brown, announced that his committee had decided to recommend the general bill only, and on February 26 the general bill was read for the first time. The crowded conditions of existing state schools and the distance from them were

---

[56] After 1909, reading both the Cass Lake and Bemidji newspapers was comparatively dull. Both dropped their crusading and fiery editorials for a normal school. In the Bemidji paper, part of the reason might be attributed to another change in ownership and editors; by 1911, Ferman A. Wilson had become editor, replacing the outspoken Rutledge. As to Cass Lake, it seemed odd if not unbelievable that it was still the same paper edited by the same man, Frank Ives; he virtually gave up in the normal school fight. Today's Cass Lake editor, Grant Utley, who knew Ives well, stated that Ives was never the leading normal school proponent, that it was the local school superintendent, Peter Larson. "He was the real sparkplug," said Utley, and he sparked Ives. But Larson was relieved of his position (Utley: "The damn fools fired him"), and when he left, Cass Lake's major supporter of a normal school was gone. With Larson gone, Ives was left to write argumentatively about his own favorite topics: saloons, Democrats, and Woodrow Wilson; the topic of normal schools went by the wayside.

[57] Minnesota, Legislative Manual (1913), p. 678, gives this brief sketch: "Daniel P. O'Neil (Rep.) was born in Ontario, Canada, in 1853, moved with his parents to Stillwater in 1872, engaged in lumbering until 1879. Settled on a homestead in Bigstone County, moved to Thief River Falls in 1902. Member of the Board of Education. Common school education. Occupation, farmer. Married." O'Neil won election in 1910 when J.J. Opsahl did not run; he was re-elected in 1912, his district including Thief River Falls and Bemidji. He became embroiled in the normal school fight in 1913 and was accused by both towns of favoring the other.

[58] January 25, 1913, p. 4. O'Neil introduced the Thief River Falls bill, which angered many Bemidji people; A. L. Hanson of Ada introduced the Bemidji bill at the request of O'Neil who said he did not want to appear inconsistent; P. H. McGarry introduced the Cass Lake bill, and the Cass Lake paper made no reference to it even being submitted; Walter Anderson of Badger introduced the general bill. Southwestern Minnesota also contended for the prize as a bill was offered to establish the school at Windom.

the arguments effectively posed by northern Minnesota legislators.[59]

The legislators who had introduced separate normal school bills gave their approval to the general bill in a somewhat rare spirit of compromise. So, too, did the northern Minnesota newspapers. For example, the News-Press agreed that the committee had "acted wisely," concluding that "the natural advantages of Thief River Falls will so outshadow" its opponents that the selection of the site would pose no problem.[60] The Bemidji papers said essentially the same thing except for substituting the word Bemidji for Thief River Falls. The Cass Lake paper said nothing.

But a problem arose long before the issue of site selection occurred. An attempt to scuttle any new normal school by voting down the recommendation of the Normal School Committee nearly succeeded. The first vote to accept the report of the committee was lost, and it appeared that the whole thing was dead. At this rather dramatic moment, Representative O'Neil rushed to the front of the chamber and demanded recognition. Then going out in front of all the seats he protested the action as unfair:

"I am the author of a bill providing for the establishment of a normal school at Thief River Falls, but in the interest of justice and in fair play, I arise to defend this committee bill and to demand that you act as men; that you do not stab this measure in the back. If you do not want to pass a normal school bill, well and good, but you are not men and you are not representatives of the people when you attempt to throttle the bill in this fashion."[61]

The Bemidji paper described O'Neil's statement as "short and dramatic and eloquent an outburst as has rattled the windows at the present session." Anyway, the House promptly proceeded to reconsider its action and voted to accept the committee's report. Then on March 7 the bill passed the House by a 76 to 33 vote. It encountered no great trouble in the Senate either. This was true even though Senate Normal School Committee Chairman Ole Sageng of Fergus Falls was not, according to the Bemidji Sentinel, "wildly enthusiastic over the idea of establishing a new normal."[62] On April 4, the Senate Committee on Normal Schools recommended that the House bill be approved; on April 17, after some discussion but little real opposition, the Senate approved the final passage of the measure, 44 to five, and sent it to Governor Adolph Eberhart for his signature. On April 19, 1913, the governor signed the bill into law.[63]

[59] Unfortunately the Minnesota State Archives do not have any records of the normal committee hearings of either the House or the Senate that go back that far. Neither did the members' papers available in the Minnesota State Historical Society lend much light on the attitudes of the committee members, though one might presume that they believed another normal was needed but that politics should not govern its location. The Archives, however, do have the original copy of the general bill.

[60] February 27, 1913, p. 1.

[61] O'Neil's short outburst was recorded in the February 28, 1913, Bemidji Sentinel, a weekly newspaper under the guidance of former Pioneer editor Ferman A. Wilson who had become both its editor and publisher. Wilson had a reporter at every legislative session and supplied long columns on legislative happenings.

[62] March 14, 1913, p. 1. Sageng believed that students could be sent to high schools with normal training departments and that would relieve the normal schools. Training departments of high schools, however, were by law limited to twenty students, though out of necessity they often accepted more. In appealing for another school, northern legislators used the big argument of the crowded conditions of the existing normals, along with the distance from them.

[63] Minnesota, Session Laws (1913), c. 362. The only Senate opposition noted in the newspapers was the unsuccessful attempt to limit the power to select the men to choose the site to the governor. Minneapolis Journal, April 19, 1913, p. 22.

The Bemidji newspapers reacted to the news of a new normal school for the northern part of the state with little emotion. It would appear that such good news should conjure up some thumping editorials, but the Bemidji papers ran none (the lead editorial in the Daily Pioneer the day the bill became law was entitled "Death to Stray Cats"). The Thief River Falls paper printed a most interesting reaction; it ran a headline reading, "Normal School for TRF" but hurriedly acknowledged in the first paragraph that "we use the above headline advisedly because of the fact that we are certain no committee can determine otherwise than on Thief River Falls."[64]

So the next step lay with the committee, and all sides waited to see who would be appointed to choose the site. Newspapers quoted the governor's frequent statement that he would insist that no prejudiced person would be appointed to the commission. Northern Minnesota editors, while they waited and speculated about the commission, chose up sides. Understandably those closest to Thief River Falls supported that community whereas Bemidji's area supported that town, with one exception, the Cass Lake Times editor who at first said nothing. Newspapers began to view the issue as one between the "prairie counties"—the flat, fertile, generally treeless counties surrounding Thief River Falls—and the "wooded counties" around Bemidji.[65] It appears rather strange that most editors saw either Thief River Falls or Bemidji as receiving the normal school when theoretically any of the area communities were eligible if they provided the state a suitable site for the school. But as Editor Wilson wrote in the Sentinel on April 25, 1913: "Either this city will be named as the proper place for the new normal school . . . or it will go to Thief River Falls. That is the way it looks at the present time. Cass Lake and other towns . . . may become active aspirants, but as a matter of calm, cool conclusion, it looks like a fight between Bemidji and Thief River Falls."

On May 8, 1913, appeared the names of the persons chosen for the commission (it was often referred to as the committee) to select the site of Minnesota's sixth normal school: James A. Ferguson, Duluth; S. B. Wilson, Mankato; Representative W. W. Brown, St. James; Senator Ole Sageng, Fergus Falls, State Superintendent of Public Instruction, C. G. Schultz. The Bemidji and Thief River Falls papers gave their full approval to the men selected, the latter labeling the decision of this fine commission to be "a foregone conclusion." It went on to add that as to Bemidji's claim about offering a better site, "there is nothing in the proposition where the cold hard facts are concerned."[66]

But one cold, hard fact still unclear was an exact location for the school at Thief River Falls, should it be selected. With the commission announcing plans to

---

[64] April 24, 1913, p. 1. If there was one trait that the News-Press exhibited consistently in this normal school business, it was confidence. The Minneapolis papers made only oblique reference to the establishment of a new state school. Though it did not mention the normal school bill, the Journal stated that the legislature "has scattered the people's money with a liberal hand. It is the fruit of the 'pork barrel'." April 26, 1913, p. 4.
[65] The counties around Thief River Falls were Marshall, Polk, Red Lake, Norman, Mahnomen, and Roseau; those around Bemidji were Clearwater, Hubbard, Cass, Koochiching, Lake of the Woods, and Itasca.
[66] Thief River Falls News-Press, May 15, 1913, p. 1.

visit the sites in early June, the Thief River Falls paper put out a call for help: anyone having land to offer, immediately communicate with the local committee. Although the article stated that the committee did have some tentative offers, it "should have a complete list of desirable sites on file so that no time may be lost in viewing the same."[67] An editorial in the same edition urged the townspeople to "clean up the city streets" because the Normal School Commission was coming. Apparently the call for new sites got results; two weeks later the paper announced the town had "not less than six 20 acre sites" to offer, all within easy walking distance of town, all donated, while Bemidji had only one site to offer, owned by the Townsite Company, which "will cost not a small sum to acquire. It is at least two miles from a railway in a dense jackpine thicket with a constant menace of fire about it "[68]

The one site offered by Bemidji lay about one mile north of town in a densely wooded area that bordered Lake Bemidji. The Bemidji Townsite and Improvement Company, then headed by A. A. White of St. Paul, owned the land. A committee of three, J. J. Opsahl, F. S. Arnold, and A. P. Ritchie, went to St. Paul and completed arrangements with White to secure the property should Bemidji be chosen for the normal school.

As the communities awaited the coming of the commission, and the newspapers continued to banter back and forth, Bemidji received an unexpected boost and considerable state publicity resulting from a meeting of the Northern Minnesota Editorial Association held in Bemidji in early June. The Association voted to endorse Bemidji as the site for the normal school. This unusual if not remarkable resolution found the Bemidji editors as confounded as anyone, but they hastily recovered and exploited it for propaganda reasons.[69] They also quoted, selectively, from the papers of the editors who were at Bemidji for the Association meeting and who wrote about the town when they got back home. This included one from St. Cloud whose columns praising Bemidji were so long that the Pioneer ran it in installments.

Just before the commission began its tour of the towns, a statement made by the editor of the Menahga Journal touched off an editorial row. He said essentially that the location of the normal school was already set for Thief River Falls in order to pay off the political debts of the lieutenant governor and the speaker of the House, who along with the governor had appointed the five-man commission to select the site. The Thief River Falls paper used up four full columns to denounce the charge of any "fix," calling the accusation, among many things, "the last gasp of the cut-over jack pine territory" to smear Thief River Falls. Even the Cass Lake Times came to life over the allegation; in its first editorial comment

[67] Ibid., May 29, 1913, p. 1.
[68] Ibid., June 12, 1913, p. 1. Much of this description was true. There were only two small houses on the twenty-acre tract at the time; it was mostly covered with trees and underbrush. The site, however, went to the city at a cost of one dollar.
[69] A copy of the resolution is printed in the Bemidji Daily Pioneer of June 16, 1913, p. 1; a sample of the editorial results can be seen in the Bemidji Sentinel, June 20, 1913, p. 4: "This Association, made up of nearly two hundred members representing more than thirty counties, wields a mighty influence. Some of these men came with their minds clouded by the 'lumberjack village' libel . . . and yet when the resolution . . . was read, a spontaneous applause burst forth and the resolution was adopted without one dissenting vote."

on normal schools that year, Editor Ives called the whole thing "a vision" that "none of the rest of the newspaper boys can fathom." He added: "That Thief River Falls is not a logical point for the location of a great educational institution is well known. Its water facilities are not good and what is worse, never will be."[70] The Bemidji papers dismissed the whole idea, but the Minneapolis Journal hinted that there might be something to the charge; it concluded, however, by quoting Lieutenant Governor J. A. A. Burnquist saying in exasperation: "I never inquired and do not know now what town is favored by any member of the commission."[71]

Into northern Minnesota and into this unenviable situation came the commission early in July to view the sites and make the decision that would ecstatically please the few and disappoint if not embitter the many. All the towns that the commission visited played the role of the gracious host, each trying to outdo the others in impressing the visitors. The commission made its first stop at Thief River Falls, and after the departure the next day, the News-Press for the first time qualified its confidence in getting the school; yet the paper went on to suggest how favorably impressed the commission members were with the community and the sites available.

The commission arrived at Bemidji on July 8, the next stop after Thief River Falls. A delegation of Bemidji business and professional men met the commission at the train depot and escorted them to the Markham Hotel. From that place the members were escorted to the city dock, where the big city boat took them for a ride around the lake. In the afternoon, five automobiles took the party for a drive around Lake Bemidji. That evening they held a banquet for the commission at the Markham Hotel. After the meal, County Superintendent of Schools W. B. Stewart, City Superintendent of Schools W. P. Dyer and attorney E. E. McDonald presented plans, arguments, and statistics. The speakers used charts to illustrate the points made, and according to the Bemidji Sentinel, "each chart contained a vast amount of information scarcely less astonishing to the many businessmen present than to the visiting commissioners."[72] Dyer and Stewart brought out points about the amount of money spent to maintain the area school system, the rapid gain in volume of railroad freight and in number of passengers, the postal receipts, the size of the lumber industry and general indications of the future prosperity of the city. Attorney McDonald spoke of the city as one of homes and "stabbed the oft-repeated libel that this city is a wide-open lumberjack town." McDonald declared, "There is not a more moral or law-abiding city of its size in the state."[73]

Apparently this assertion of righteousness was not fully accepted by one commissioner; State Superintendent of Schools C. G. Schultz broke in on McDonald

[70] July 3, 1913, p. 4. After 1909, the local news that Editor Ives wrote most heatedly about was keeping the Cass Lake saloons from being closed by federal agents ("those scum," he called them) led by a colorful though hated figure referred to in his papers only as one "Pussyfoot" Johnson, the appellation in reference to his alleged sneakiness in achieving his goals. The issue was over an old law forbidding liquor to be sold in Indian territory. Interpretation of this law was never clear nor consistent, and the saloons in both Cass Lake and Bemidji were opened and closed with regularity. In this fight, Ives eventually won. It seems unnecessary to add that the liquor issue received much more space in the local papers than the topic of normal schools.
[71] July 2, 1913, p. 19.
[72] July 11, 1913, p. 1.
[73] Ibid.

to ask: "How many saloons?" Replied McDonald, "We have 29 and the number is being decreased," although he did not say either how or by how many. "It has been reported," Schultz continued with a stern voice, "that you have sporting houses here. Is that true?" McDonald: "That is not true. There is not a place of that kind within the city limits of Bemidji." McDonald then added the curious statement: "Bemidji has nine churches and the city is well policed both day and night.''[74]

When the commission left the next day, July 9, for Cass Lake, Commission Member W. W. Brown summed up well its difficult if not impossible position:

"Thief River Falls proved to us beyond any question of doubt that the school should be located there. Bemidji has shown us that to locate the school at any other point would be little less than criminal, and we expect that Cass Lake and Park Rapids will each offer proof positive that each of those towns should have the institution."[75]

After the sojourn in Cass Lake, the Cass Lake Times reported their big day with the commission. "After luncheon the visitors were taken for a trip around Pike Bay [a large bay that is part of Cass Lake] and through the forest preserve. In the afternoon . . . a trip to Star Island . . . and six o'clock dinner at Star Island Inn. At eight o'clock . . . the arguments were delivered.... It was nearly midnight when the session ended." And the editor added, seemingly with a sigh of relief, "The report of the location will be filed on or before October 1, and the infamous normal school fight will be ended."[76]

At this point all that the towns could do was to sit back and wait expectantly for the decision which Schultz, chairman of the commission, said would be announced July 15.[77] And then came the day. The Pioneer on July 15, 1913, shouted the news with an "EXTRA!" that read: "Bemidji Wins the Sixth Normal School by Unanimous Vote." That late-evening edition of the Pioneer captured well the atmosphere of the celebration and general hoopla that followed the announcement:

"A. P. Ritchie was present when the message was received and immediately went out on the streets shouting out the good news to the people.... As the news reached Bemidji ... the town almost went wild. The fire whistle was blown and both whistles of the lumber company mills were set off and continued to blow for almost an hour. Automobiles paraded the streets tooting their horns, and shouts of joy from boys and men were heard everywhere. The fire bell was clanging and together with the firecrackers and other explosives Bemidji celebrated one of the greatest events of its history. A procession of automobiles loaded with enthusiasts was quickly formed and crowded the streets of the city, taking entire possession of every

---

[74] Ibid. An interview with Herbert Warfield, seventy-two, and a life-long resident of Bemidji, found Warfield highly amused by McDonald's statements: "McDonald couldn't count very well." Warfield added that he remembered "very well" that when World War I broke out, "there were fifty-four saloons and seven licensed sporting houses, mostly double deckers."
[75] Bemidji Daily Pioneer, July 9, 1967, p. 1.
[76] July 10, 1913, p. 1. In the issue the week before, Editor Ives had grumped that "the location here will end a disagreeable fight that has been brewing between other applicants since our rights were so unceremoniously taken from us."
[77] In the interim between the visit of the commission and the announcement of the location, the Bemidji papers heaped praises on the Bemidji Townsite Company for donating the land which was valued at thirty thousand dollars. Recent storms had cut nearly all telephone lines making it impossible to receive word directly from St. Paul. When the message came, it came in a telegram to A. P. Ritchie. Prior to this, rumors circulated wildly regarding which town won.

THE BEMIDJI DAILY PIONEER

BEMIDJI, MINNESOTA, TUESDAY EVENING, JULY 15, 1913.

NUMBER 68   TEN CENTS

ADDRESS GETTYSBURG

BREWERY CUTS MELON

DENIES ATTACK ON CHARACTER

OFFERS $5 FOR A NAME

EXTRA
Bemidji Wins the Normal School by Unimous Vote

St. Paul, July 15. (3:45)—Bemidji selected for new Six Normal school at meeting at capitol. Won from Thief River Falls by five votes. American Press Association.

Thief River Falls, Minn. July 15. Thief River Falls confirms the report that Bemidji was chosen for the next Normal school. The city sends congratulations.

St. Paul, July 15. (3:30 P. M.— "Bemidji Wins the Normal School." was the message sent over the wire to this city, at three-thirty. Practically all the telephones were down and it was impossible to get word direct from the capitol building. The message was sent by relay and came direct from the governor's office.

PRANK CAUSES DISASTER

Meddling With Whistle Causes Bad Crash—Result, Bodies Are Cut To Pieces

TWELVE KILLED, 200 INJURED

BUILDS NEW FIRE WALLS

Troppman Building To Be Remodeled With Full Basement Under Structure

DOUBLES SALESROOM CAPACITY

NEW RIVER

Every Man To His Own Trade

By "HOP"

SCOOP THE CUB REPORTER

available thoroughfare. The Reynolds and Winter's car, loaded with Professor Dyer, Ritchie, F. S. Arnold, and others who were active in securing the school, led the big parade. To say that all acted like a lot of 'crazy hoodlums' is putting it mildly. Boys formed in line with tin pans and sticks and all in all the town presented one of the wildest scenes ever known in its history."

The weekly Bemidji <u>Sentinel</u>, July 18, with three days' perspective, described the scene this way:

"Within fifteen minutes after a bulletin had been received Tuesday afternoon—a week to a day after the commission's . .visit here flashing the news that Bemidji had won--the city had gone crazy with joy. As soon as it was known . . . the city's great fire siren was turned loose and almost simultaneously the fire bell began clanging out a joyous message to the startled populace. An impromptu automobile parade formed quickly and a mile of machines heavily loaded with men, women, and children began circling the business streets, the occupants of each crashing tin pans, blowing horns, pounding drums, dangling cow bells, tooting whistles, firing revolvers, and making any other noise possible, and from out of the pandemonium continuously came the shout, 'We win.' Bells in all parts of the city joined in and locomotives in the Minnesota and International shops shrieked back a reply. When the Soo train bound for Thief River Falls arrived at 4:35 p.m., the pavement leading to the station was packed with automobiles, and the platform was filled with a thousand delirious citizens dancing about like maniacs. A circle was formed on the platform and in an Indian pow-wow led by W. P. Dyer . . . one hundred shouting men joined in. For two hours the noise would make a boiler factory appear as silent as a tomb. It was 11 p.m. before the band stopped playing and the last tune was 'Cheer, Cheer, the Gang's All Here,' and it was too.... Farmers and others in the country who heard the weirdly shrieking fire whistles and din of other noises bellowing out from the one city were struck with terror, believing the city to be at the mercy of an Indian uprising . . . or that an earthquake had broken loose, or more logically that the place was in flames." [78]

According to next day's <u>Pioneer</u>, the celebration lasted "until nine o'clock this morning." It also added that the noise the day before had broken up a district prayer meeting: "When the whistles sounded the glad tidings the district prayer meeting . . . was suddenly brought to a close. Those attending found it more advantageous to give vent to their feelings and rejoice in the open air than within the walls of Mrs. Muncy's home." The paper added that "the band was seated under an electric light which was lowered to within six feet from the ground and played as never before"; the music "was snappy and popular and received with great applause."

If there was one hero to be singled out by the crowd, it was Absie P.

---

[78] Interviews with several people who lived in Bemidji and remembered that particular day resulted in their general confirmation of the newspaper accounts, along with some added color that the papers missed. For example Herbert Warfield said he still had a vivid memory of the Soo train pulling into town and bound for Thief River Falls." Some of the boys painted big letters in red paint all along the train reading: 'Hello Thief River Falls— Congratulations On Your New Normal.' As a result of this act, the Soo company sent a bill for four hundred dollars to the city for cleaning expenses, but of course they never paid it."

Ritchie. The Pioneer described one spur-of-the-moment tribute:

"Calls for speeches were heard from the masses, and a group of husky young fellows, led by Wilbur Lycan, immediately took hold of A. P. Ritchie, carrying him on their shoulders to the Kreatz automobile which stood in the center of the crowd. He was so hoarse as a result of his over-indulgence in the celebration that he could be heard but a short distance."[79]

At the same time that the front page stories told of the jubilant celebration, the inside pages had editorials acknowledging the wisdom of the commissioners, praising the local men who had helped the most, and soothing the despair of those towns which had lost.[80]

Surprisingly, the Thief River Falls paper printed mild reactions to the normal school location and at first showed little resentment. After the announcement, the News-Press ran a long one-column news story giving all the particulars, but it was devoid of opinion. It did add, however, that the vote of the commissioners had been "four to one, Ole Sageng of Fergus Falls voting for Thief River Falls." On the editorial page, the editor asserted once more that Thief River Falls had the best site and deserved the school. "However," he concluded, "we believe we should be good losers and therefore extend congratulations to our friends and neighbors of the pine country—Bemidji, but at the same time can't help but recall that our old friend Bobby Burns . . . [wrote] 'The best laid schemes o' mice and men gang oft a-glay, an lea'e us naught but grief and pain, for promised joy.' "[81] The Cass Lake Times also ran a straight news story on the normal school decision in its July 17 paper but made no editorial comment.

A week after the announcement, however, the bad feeling over the normal school decision heated up again but was shortlived, at least in the newspapers. In the Thief River Falls NewsPress, the editor wrote that there were rumors going around the town which called the normal school decision "the most damnable outrage ever perpetrated on the people of this city." The rumor included the allegation that Representative O'Neil, who lived in Thief River Falls, had "sold out" to Bemidji. All the rumors, concluded the editor, were "totally unwarranted by the facts," and the editorial finished with a stout defense of the integrity of O'Neil. But on July 31, an editorial entitled "Was It a Political Job?" asserted that nefarious "politics" had been behind the decision favoring Bemidji. Suspicious, the editor wrote: "From appearances it is evident that outside influence dominated the action of some of the members of this commission . . . and we believe . . . that the people . . . are entitled to a complete and detailed report."

Exactly what were these "outside influences" was not made clear either in

---

[79] July 16, 1913, p. 1. In an interview, Mrs. Ritchie, eighty-five, spoke proudly and at length about her husband's active role and continued interest in the school. She added that he had "made over forty trips to St. Paul" to help get the school. Wilbur Lycan, one of those "husky youths" who carried Ritchie on their shoulders, is recently deceased at age 74. He had called the day of the site selection one of the most exciting in the town's history. Lycan served one four-year term as resident director of the college from 1939 to 1943.

[80] The names of those singled out by the papers were Ritchie, H. C. Baer, J.J. Opsahl, A. P. White, F. S. Arnold, F. S. Lycan, E. E. McDonald, W. P. Dyer, W. B. Stewart, A. A. Warfield, R. E. and N. E. Given, C. E. Battles, G. T. Baker, David Gill and Miss E. L. Calihan.

[81] July 17, 1913, p. 2.

the newspapers or in interviewing people who were around at the time, or in the available papers of the men closely involved. This is unfortunate, for a bit of a pall hung over the normal school decision for several years, and even the allegations never became clear, let alone the validity of them. Whatever the situation, the area newspapers leaped in again with charges and counter-charges that collectively helped to muddle more the troubled waters and to predict an uncertain future for the school.[82]

By the fall of 1913, however, newspapers abandoned the subject of normal schools once more. The Thief River Falls paper went back to quoting, and without malice, from the Bemidji papers about a variety of subjects. It also began worrying about some socialists who were skulking about town, allegedly attempting to take over the city government; the Cass Lake paper went back to flaying the federal Indian agents. The issue, though not completely dormant, became submerged, and did not rise again until the next legislature when it came time to get some funds to get the school started.

In the meantime, rising land values became the first palpable gain from the location of the state institution in the community. Lots in the vicinity of the normal school site jumped from 25 to 40 percent by the end of July, 1913, and what was described as a "run" was made on the local office of the Townsite Company. This company owned almost all of the land surrounding the proposed normal site, and practically all of the land was still forest. One of the first acts by the company was to temporarily suspend all land sales while it reappraised the land values: "T. C. Bailey, who represents the Townsite Company, immediately received word by telephone, instructing him to take all lots in that vicinity off the market for the time being."[83] Apparently this action produced some local grumbling which the Pioneer editor tried to assuage in a commentary labeled "Our Townsite Friends." He praised the company for its "magnificent donation" and concluded that Bemidji "was but a child of fifteen and has not yet reached that stage where it has a right to assert its absolute independence. It needs the Townsite people and the Townsite people need Bemidji."[84] Now whether or not Bemidji citizens accepted such pleas, at least the newspapers avoided the topic when the lots went up for sale again at greatly increased prices.

---

[82] The available documentary evidence offers little to answer the question of possible skullduggery. Interviews with elderly people in both Bemidji and Thief River Falls proved just as fruitless in getting any answers. Because of this, the writer is tempted to conclude that there really was nothing behind the allegations other than rationalizations to soothe injured pride. After the normal school decision, there grew an intense rivalry among the communities of Bemidji, Cass Lake, and Thief River Falls. Today, however, this parochial rivalry is essentially seen only in the sophomoric intensity of competition between their respective public school athletic teams. Thus it is only the adolescents, of all ages, who continue the 1913 battle, and one might surmise that few if any of the public school students today have any notion of its background.

[83] Bemidji Daily Pioneer, July 19, 1913, p. 1.

[84] Dr. Harold T. Hagg, a member of the Bemidji College faculty since 1936, and author of a book on Minnesota history and several published articles on Bemidji history, called the Townsite Company a "closed book" for historians. He tried unsuccessfully several times to peruse the books of the company that were held by Miss E. L. Calihan. In interviewing her in 1940 he said she simply refused to let him see the books, nor would she answer any questions about this important and somewhat shadowy business. The County Register of Deeds informed the writer that only with the recent dissolution of the Townsite Company could a landowner in the college area get a clear title without going through the Company. Two major streets close to the college are named after members of the Townsite Company, Calihan and Bixby avenues, the latter after Tams Bixby, the person the Cass Lake editor claimed had persuaded Governor Johnson to veto the Cass Lake bill giving that town the normal school. Descendants of Bixby, now in Oklahoma, still maintain a summer home on the east side of Lake Bemidji.

The Normal School Commission—the one that chose the site —paid Bemidji one last visit before disbanding. With it came the State Normal School Board members, and these two boards were joined by the Beltrami County Board of Commissioners who "together . . . visited the site for the normal school and approved" it, seemingly one last time, on August 13, 1913. The Bemidji <u>Pioneer</u> reported the action of the boards and described the site location in a rather vague manner:

"The site chosen begins at Fourteenth Street from Doud Avenue [now Birchmont Drive] to the lake front and follows the lake shore to the Kelsey residence . . . to within two hundred feet of Grand Forks Bay. The tract comprises from twenty to twenty-five acres. The deeds and necessary papers were properly executed and the transfer to the state will be duly effected as soon as the attorney general approves the title."[85]

Approval of the deed by the state attorney general, however, seriously threatened delay if not the loss of the normal school to Bemidji. When the deeds for the site were presented, the attorney general late in September indicated objection to the title on the grounds that the portion donated by the city could not be transferred without the vote of the people, and moreover that all the deeds had reverting clauses in case the site should ever cease to be used for normal school purposes. Because of this possibly dangerous situation, A. P. Ritchie and Frank S. Arnold went down to St. Paul again and spent a whole day in the attorney general's office, and they ironed out the difficulties at literally the eleventh hour. The deeds were signed the evening of September 30, which fact was of vital importance because the legislature specified that the site should be chosen and the title approved before October 1, 1913.[86]

Thus did the normal school fight end. After six long years of an intermittent struggle, Bemidji in 1913 won as the site for Minnesota's sixth State Normal School. Only the appropriation of the state legislature for the first buildings would be needed for the school to open its doors. It would be six more years, however, before the school on paper became the school of brick, and the long metamorphosis would involve not a few problems.

---

[85] August 13, 1913, p. 1. One of the state Normal School board members, John Wise, owned the Mankato Daily Review. When Wise returned to Mankato, he wrote about his recent trip to Bemidji which the Pioneer quoted in two lengthy installments. Wise concluded: "While we have not viewed the other sites offered . . . it is our opinion as well as all those in Wednesday's party [the combined boards] that the commission acted wisely and conscientiously in making the selection they did."

[86] The Northern Student, Bulletin of the State Teachers College, Bemidji, Minnesota, Vol. XI, No. 2, January, 1938, p. 8. An unconfirmed report has it that some Cass Lake men were in St. Paul at the time for the express purpose of getting the Bemidji delegates inebriated so they would be unable to sign the deeds in time.

WARRANTY DEED
BY CORPORATION

White & Street

Townsite Company

-to-

City of Bemidji.

Office of Register of Deeds
County of BELTRAMI

I hereby certify that the within Instrument was filed in this office for record on the 15 *day of* Sept *A. D. 191*3*., at* 2 *o'clock* P *.M., and was duly recorded in Book* 27 *of Deeds, on page* 304

CR Moon
Register of Deeds

By *E Murphy* Deputy

Taxes paid and transfer entered this 15 *day of* Sept 191 3

J. L. George
County Auditor
By

2134000

I hereby certify that the _____ for the year 1912, on _____ assessed lands are paid.

Earl Gail

CHAPTER III
Opening the School Doors: 1913-1920

O NE SET OF POLITICIANS gave life to Bemidji Normal School, a second set nursed it, got it started, soon named it "teachers college," and sent it on its way, until, something like Topsy, it just grew. Once the site was selected, it was this second group of men who simply got the thing going, though it was not simple, who deserve much credit; at the start the infant came close to dying in the maelstrom of biennial legislative exigencies. Thankfully for Bemidji, some politician godfathers saved its life.

Because the school was brand new—existing only on paper— the central difficulty was getting the initial appropriations to get it started. In the face of economy-minded legislatures, along with the unsettling times around World War I, getting started provided real difficulties. Those men who struggled for the school in the first formative years set a precedent for determination and stamina that may well be unsurpassed in the history of the College. They emerge as the major protagonists if not the heroes of the early years of Bemidji Normal School. The politicians acted as spokesmen for the civic-minded people of Bemidji and the surrounding community, and they represented their constituency well. For it is politicians, when one really gets to the heart of the matter, whose actions move the legislative machinery which in turn moves—or stalls or kills—a state run institution; it is the legislators who must first make the world go 'round for the State Colleges. This is a lesson that Minnesota State College faculties are reminded of every two years.

Receiving the First Appropriation

In the 1915 legislature, the group of northern Minnesota legislators made up, in general, a new team from the one of 1913, although a few of the old names were back. But in the interim, a couple of them had switched sides. P. H. McGarry,

38

from Walker, who had plumped so long and hard before for Cass Lake, became exceedingly active in supporting Bemidji's new normal school once the site had been selected. Conversely, Daniel P. O'Neil, who had once supported Bemidji but who most recently had worked hard for the location of the school at Thief River Falls, fought vociferously against any legislative appropriation for the new school.

The political makeup of the state legislature in 1915 was difficult to ascertain. Caught up partly in the wave of progressivism that was sweeping the country, the legislature in 1913 had declared itself to be nonpartisan; hence the legislative manual for 1915 gave no political affiliation for the legislators. However, comparing the same names with lists of previous legislatures when there was party designation, one can see that the Republicans had a clear majority in both houses. And with the exception of the governor, all of the major state officers were Republicans.[87]

Many northern Minnesota legislators aided Bemidji's normal school in 1915. Most of the more active ones in the House were listed as collectively sponsoring the bill (House File No. 84) appropriating $150,000 dollars in the next biennium "for the erection of a normal school building at Bemidji, Minnesota." The sponsors were L. G. Pendergast, Bemidji, Beltrami County; H. J. Miner, International Falls, Koochiching County; Farley A. Dare, Walker, Cass County; E. R. Hinds, Hubbard County; and G. S. Wilkins, Wadena County. Leonard H. Nord of International Falls introduced the same bill in the Senate, and he along with McGarry supported it actively in that wing of the capitol.[88]

Editors expected the year 1915 to be a year of retrenchment in state spending. As the January 29, 1915, Bemidji Sentinel correspondent said of the legislature: "At present everybody is talking and preaching economy, and the general tendency seems to be in that direction." Without belaboring the point, suffice it to say that for several reasons the year 1915 was not a year for legislative largess.[89]

Into this fiscally conservative arena came Absie P. Ritchie, by then Bemidji postmaster, and Beltrami County Superintendent of Schools W. B. Stewart to join Representative Pendergast and State Superintendent of Education C. G. Schultz to testify in behalf of the Bemidji Normal School appropriation before the House appropriations committee. Farley A. Dare, a member of the House who was also the publisher of the Walker Pilot, recorded the interesting action taken by the committee on the Bemidji request:

"It is quite probable that Bemidji will secure a small appropriation for a

---

[87] Winfield S. Hammond, Democrat, was the governor in 1915. A native of Massachusetts and a graduate of Dartmouth College, he had come to Minnesota in 1884 as principal of the high school at Mankato. Admitted to the bar in 1891, he made his home at St. James and practiced law. From 1898 to 1906 he was a member of the State Normal Board; in 1906 he began the first of four consecutive years as United States Representative from the Second District. Aided by a split in the Republican party, he was elected governor in 1914, but in that election only one of the three counties which had sought the new normal school—Beltrami, Cass, and Marshall—gave a majority of their votes to Hammond. Minnesota, Legislative Manual (1915). p. 609.

[88] As indicated in the previous chapter, the State Archives do not contain any records of the normal school committee hearings dating back that far; hence one has to rely largely on area newspaper accounts for news as the Minneapolis-St. Paul papers gave short shrift to regional bills in the legislature.

[89] Minnesota was very much an agricultural state at the time, and the wholesale price index for farm produce had not changed from 1913 to 1915; it was still at 71.5, based on 1926 equals one hundred. U. S. Department of Commerce, Historical Statistics of the United States: Colonial Times to 1957. Washington, D. C.: Government Printing Office, 1960), p. 116.

normal school. The original bill calls for $150,000 but its author, presumably Pendergast, dropped a remark . . . to the effect that he would be glad to get $25,000 a year for two years, and the appropriations committee passed on that amount before the author had a chance to change his mind."[90]

As for the chances of the bill in the Senate, the Sentinel observed that not only was money hard to get but also there was a member in the Senate out to "get" Bemidji, an old nemesis, Ole Sageng. Sageng had been on the 1913 committee to choose the site and had himself voted for Thief River Falls. "It is understood," remarked the editor, "that ever since the commission that located the normal . . . disregarded his advice . . . the man has been antagonistic . . ." to Bemidji.[91] Money, however, proved the greater problem, and in view of the loud cry for economy by legislators, the northern Minnesota contingent felt well satisfied with a $50,000 appropriation for Bemidji after talking with the House appropriations chairman and the Senate finance committee chairman. So Bemidji partisans sought this reduced amount, but even this figure was not easy to attain.[92]

Meanwhile, one public act occurred to indicate that a normal school existed in some form at Bemidji. On April 8, 1915, Governor Hammond appointed A. P. White, president of the Bemidji Northern National Bank, as a member of the State Normal Board. The local Sentinel interpreted the appointment to be "a recognition by the executive of the fact that the sixth state normal school, yet to be built, has been definitely located at Bemidji." Just that statement suggested that there had been some lingering doubts before.[93]

When the 1915 legislature began its last week of the session, the Bemidji appropriation request had become absorbed in the House omnibus bill for general state appropriations. But judging by the general tenor of the legislature and the specific description of the House, this money bill was anything but safe: "The only words that express the condition existing in the House are chaos and turmoil. These, however, are really inadequate to give an idea of the real situation," wrote the correspondent of the Bemidji Sentinel.[94] Despite the turmoil, the House approved the omnibus bill by a 78 to 15 vote. Before the vote, however, a motion had been made to have the Bemidji appropriation of $50,000 stricken from the bill, but this amended motion lost by the same 78 to 15 vote.[95]

Over in the Senate a similar clash over the Bemidji appropriation occurred

[90] Quoted in the Sentinel, March 19, 1915, p. 1.

[91] March 19, 1915, p. 1.

[92] After the Senate Finance Committee at first turned down any request for Bemidji Normal, editor Ferman A. Wilson of the Sentinel on April 19 wrote an open letter "To the Legislature" and said in effect: you decided to locate the school here, we gave you the land, so the legislature was "in honor bound to fulfill its part of the obligation. Bemidji has kept faith with the state," and the legislature must in turn keep the faith.

[93] Added insight into this appointment appeared in a bulletin printed in 1938. In the brief historical sketch of the college, it was stated that Hammond had spoken at an Educational Association meeting in Bemidji on February 12, 1915, and "on this occasion the governor was requested to appoint a Bemidji member on the College Board which procedure it was assumed might aid the cause of an appropriation. Governor Hammond agreed to do so." The Northern Student, Bulletin of the State Teachers College, Bemidji, Minnesota, Vol. XI, No. 2, January, 1938, p. 9. White met with the Board for the first time on May 11, 1915.

[94] April 16, 1915, p. 1. In contrast with today, both Bemidji newspapers had a special correspondent employed during the legislative sessions to report at length on legislative happenings.

[95] L. O. Teigen of Jackson made the motion to amend, and he received strong support from Oscar Stenvick, whose district included Thief River Falls, even though Stenvick's home was Bagley, a town twenty-five miles west of Bemidji. The debate on the motion was described as "heated."

between Senators Nord and McGarry on one side and O'Neil on the other. By then the figure had been cut in half to twenty-five thousand dollars, the last minute cutting done by a conference committee of both houses, but O'Neil objected to any amount.[96] However, he could not muster up enough support to kill the appropriation. The measure became law: "For aid to commence erection and construction of a normal school building at Bemidji as authorized by law, available for the year ending July 31, 1917—twenty-five thousand dollars."[97]

The reactions of the two Bemidji papers to this first small legislative appropriation present a curious contrast. The Pioneer deemed it a "brilliant victory" for the city and northern Minnesota. In view of the stringent attitude toward spending by the state in general, "it is a source of great satisfaction that our northern legislators were able to muster sufficient assistance to secure any amount whatever."[98] The Sentinel, however, ran the headline: "Bemidji Fares Poorly at Hands of Legislature," and went on to say that any hope of an adequate appropriation had "faded away" for at least two years more.[99]

Nevertheless, when the area legislators arrived home at the close of the session, the local papers praised them for their efforts. They, in turn, praised each other; they especially commended the work of Senator McGarry of Walker, with Senator Nord maintaining that had McGarry opposed the appropriation or even been neutral about it, the money would never have been approved.[100]

The topic of normal schools appeared one more time in the 1915 newspapers before taking a year-long recess. It occurred when a party of about 40 members of the legislature, their wives, and state officials visited Bemidji June 17 on one of their stops in their long itinerary. The group included two men who would become the next two governors: J. A. A. Burnquist, then lieutenant governor, and J. A. O. Preus, state auditor. City officials attempted to give them the royal treatment, complete with banquets and tours; the Pioneer seemed almost obsequious in playing up their presence in town. For their part the group of visitors conducted a mock session of the Senate in the local armory building for the public in which, reported the Pioneer, "Lieutenant Governor Burnquist presided in true legislative style."[101] Two days after they left town, June 19, 1915 the Pioneer quoted from the Minneapolis Tribune a story filed by one of its reporters traveling with the party:

---

[96] The cut was not unexpected, "it being generally understood that the $50,000 bill could not pass the Senate," Pioneer, April 20, 1915, p. 1. Said the Duluth News-Tribune: "Stenvick . . . made an impassioned plea for the amendment and Senator O'Neil . . . also appeared to work for the amendment against Bemidji. This action . . . was owing to his resentment over the failure of his city . . . to obtain the designation for the sixth normal." Quoted in the Pioneer, April 22, 1915.
[97] Minnesota, Session Laws (1915) c. 375.
[98] April 22, 1915, p. 1. An editorial in the same paper revealed much foresight, though it probably appeared as wishful thinking at the time: "It means that the day is not far distant when the attractive site . . . will be adorned with appropriate buildings and this section of the state will be blessed with this needed educational institution."
[99] April 23, 1915, p. 1.
[100] Pioneer, April 24, 1915, p. 1. Pendergast said he was well satisfied with the small amount because it would give enough money to properly erect a basement and foundation. But most important, he said, "From now on the normal school will be in the hands of the State Normal Board and further appropriations will be secured through its recommendations." In effect, he felt the hardest part was over.
[101] What seemed to impress the visitors the most in their two-day stay was a large grove of virgin timber along Lake Bemidji called the Ruggles Forest, which they hoped would be saved from the woodsman's ax. The only bill passed in the mock session was "unanimously passed" and "appropriated $250,000 for the purchase of the Ruggles timber." Would that they were so free with money for the local normal school buildings.

"The autos . . . transported the visitors to the new normal school grounds and the Bemidji citizens, when they had the legislators on the beautiful grounds . . . took occasion to intimate that at the next session a substantial appropriation for this institution will be desired."[102]

Approaching the Time To Build

The state authority that oversaw the normal schools was the State Normal Board. It took charge of Bemidji Normal once that first appropriation was made in April, 1915. But the Board delayed any action on Bemidji for a year. Not until June 10, 1916, did the Board arrange for architectural plans of the first building at Bemidji. Resident Director A. P. White, who had attended a recent Board meeting, told the local paper that the Board had decided to send "landscape gardeners" (architects) to Bemidji to look over the site, and that the Board had also agreed to construct a main building, a dormitory, and a central heating plant for the present, and would ask the 1917 legislature for $250,000 to complete these plans.[103]

State Architect C. H. Johnston and Landscape Engineer A. R. Nichols were the "gardeners" who arrived in Bemidji on June 17, 1916, to inspect the grounds for the normal. That evening they outlined their plans before the city council, reported the <u>Pioneer,</u> and said they would have sketch plans ready for approval by the Board when it met in Bemidji in August. When the Board assembled on August 22, 1916, in Bemidji's Carnegie library building, now the Community Arts Center, Johnston was there with his drawings and plans which he presented to the Board. The Board approved them. Though not mentioned in the official minutes, the August 23 <u>Pioneer</u> stated that Board President Ell Torrance had also appointed three Board members—White of Bemidji, J. L. Washburn, Duluth, and C. G. Schultz, State Superintendent of Public Instruction—"to confer with the state architects who represent the Board of Control as to the arrangement of the main building." There the matter rested for another year. From the available evidence, it appears that the Board decided not to proceed with any plans for a building at Bemidji until after the 1917 legislature convened and presumably acted favorably on its requests for the next biennium.

The Normal Board's 1917 requests totaled $1,413,000 for all six normal schools, $579,3 44 of which was for new buildings (the total appropriations made to the normal schools in 1917 had been $787,310). As to Bemidji, the request read: "Central building, including heating plant, auditorium and gymnasium, two hundred sixty five thousand dollars. Girls' dormitory, eighty-five thousand dollars."[104]

---

[102] Quoted June 19. 1915, p. 1.

[103] Pioneer, June 10, 1916, p. 1. The official Board minutes, however, do not mention this meeting. The Board had met with the State Board of Control because the building finances of the university and normal schools had been placed under the supervision of the State Board of Control by the 1911 legislature in the attempt to secure administrative efficiency. These unofficial decisions regarding Bemidji Normal were formally included in the minutes of their November 14, 1916, meeting.

[104] Minutes of the Normal School Board, November 14, 1916. Though the board recommended a lump sum appropriation from the legislature, the legislature itself made allocations to the individual normal schools; hence each normal school waged a battle for money and competed with the other normals to get it. This competition continued despite several resolutions passed by the Board to discourage it. Today, however, the money is allotted to the Board which in turn distributes it to the schools.

Again it would depend on what the politicians decided in St. Paul. The 40th session of the state legislature extended from January 2 to April 19, 1917. Incumbent Republican Governor J. A. A. Burnquist, who had succeeded to the position upon the death of Winfield Hammond late in 1915, had been elected in 1916. Minnesota went Republican in 1916, including the state going for Charles Evans Hughes for president.

Efficient government was the keynote of Governor Burnquist's opening message, one of the shortest ever given. He recommended holding the budget to the minimum. The Normal Board's budget requests had been lumped together with other requests of the state-expense budget which totaled over $27,000,000. Burnquist lopped 7.5 million dollars off this budget before sending it to the legislature, and one of the items he struck out was the $350,000 request for buildings at Bemidji. He suggested that the legislature defer until 1919 "the building of large educational structures because of high costs of material and scarcity of labor."[105] Moreover, the governor pointed out that the Normal Board had asked for $625,000 more than had been allotted to it in the last session, and that the current requests were out of line. After this the Bemidji Sentinel concluded, "The attitude the governor has taken . . . is that of asking the legislature to spend as little as possible." The Pioneer echoed, not without reason: "All there is to show for the proposition now is the site."[106]

For many reasons Bemidji partisans in 1917 lacked optimism for any appropriation. With the conservative attitude of the governor, the elimination of Bemidji's request from the first appropriation bill, and the current worry about the war which overshadowed all other topics the Bemidji newspapers and the northern Minnesota legislators resignedly expressed little hope of getting any money out of the 1917 legislature. The local newspapers almost dropped the subject until the perennially wild last week of the session. An educational omnibus bill had come out of the House Appropriations Committee without any money stipulated for Bemidji Normal. When it reached the floor, L. G. Pendergast of Bemidji proposed an amendment to included $150,000 for Bemidji Normal. This 75 year-old Civil War veteran, who had gotten up out of his sick bed that day, then made an impassioned plea on the floor of the House. In his talk he reviewed the long fight for the location and then the very small appropriation that had been made in 1915. He concluded by saying:

"It has been almost my sole ambition during the past ten years to build up this additional institution in Northern Minnesota, and when the time comes when my good friends will sound taps for me, I want to go knowing that this institution is built so that people may say of me when I have passed beyond, he gave all the energy and influence which God Almighty entrusted to him to build up this institution of learning for future generations. I would consider it a greater honor to me to have this said than all the monuments of granite, or marble or bronze which

---

[105] Quoted in the Bemidji Sentinel, February 2 1917, p. 1.
[106] Ibid., February 1, 1917, p. 1.

the United States has ever erected to the memory of her military heroes. This is all the honor I want, it is enough for any man."[107]

The House adopted Pendergast's amendment by an 80 to 11 roll call vote; the entire omnibus bill was then approved without an opposing vote. The bill next went to the Senate, was recommended for passage by the finance committee, and passed without opposition. But trouble came when it went to the governor, and this apparent $150,000 victory, much ballyhooed in the Bemidji press, was very shortlived. Burnquist exercised his right to alter or veto separate items included in appropriation bills, and he slashed the figure in half.[108] Yet the $75,000 dollars was a big victory, and Bemidji's civic-minded citizens poured out to welcome home their hero-of-the-day, Pendergast, upon his return to Bemidji. According to the Pioneer:

"A spontaneous outpouring of Bemidji's citizenship was at the depot to welcome him and his good wife.... And while it might seem an amusing human interest feature, the grizzled veteran of the Civil War had . . . lost forty pounds of weight. His kind face was wreathed in smiles as he emerged from the car to be greeted by band music and the outstretched hands of a throng of friends. Instantly he was surrounded by the crowd, everyone eager to grasp his hand, and cheers rent the air. He was escorted to the car of A. P. White, the band played, the civilian auxiliary fell into line, scores of autos followed in turn and the procession passed through the business district to the city hall. In response to a query about giving up hope for any appropriation for the normal school he replied, 'Well, it did look that way, but I felt just like Paul Jones did—just commenced to fight'."[109]

With the 1917 legislature over, and the final action of the governor, there remained $100,000 to start building the Bemidji Normal School, $25,000 from the 1915 session and $75,000 available after August 1, 1917. The time to build had arrived. In a relatively short time the bureaucratic machinery moved, for at the August 14, 1917, Board meeting, State Architect C. H. Johnston presented the sketches of the proposed building to the Board, and they were approved.[110] The Board approved the final plans on February 18, 1918, and bids were solicited and announced to be opened on March 12, 1918. When that day came, the number of bids totaled 45, 13 for the general construction, 20 for mechanical equipment, and 12 for electrical equipment. However, bids were not let for a few days until State Architect Johnston went over them and gave his approval. Finally on March 19 the Board of Control awarded the contracts for the building of the first structure of Bemidji's normal school: F. M. Klarquist and Sons, Minneapolis, general construction, $72,075; M. J. O'Neil, St. Paul, heating and plumbing, $19,376;

---

[107] Quoted in the Sentinel, April 20, 1917, p. 1. Pendergast died that fall, November 21, 1917, in Nevada where he had gone for the winter, said the newspaper, "to regain the health he had lost in the desperate fight he waged against great odds to secure the normal school appropriation." Reportedly he had lost forty pounds during the session. His body was returned to Bemidji June 19, 1918, and in the news story about it, again the same point was made as to how he lost his health.

[108] Minnesota Session Laws (1917), c. 437.

[109] Quoted in the Bemidji Weekly Pioneer, April 26, 1917, p. 2.

[110] In retrospect, the most interesting decision of the State Normal Board at that meeting was the unanimous approval of the resolution, "That the teaching of the German language in the normal schools of this state in all departments be discontinued forthwith."

Today's News Today From the American Battle Front In France---By the United Press

BEMIDJI DAILY PIONEER

VOLUME XVI. NO. 183　　BEMIDJI, MINN., MONDAY EVENING, AUGUST 12, 1918　　FORTY-FIVE CENTS PER MONTH

CORNERSTONE OF NEW NORMAL IS LAID

ENEMY STARTS RESISTENCE TO ALLIES; BEGIN TO TIGHTEN UP

EXTRA!

JUDGE C. W. STANTON

Who Performed the Ceremonies of Laying the Cornerstone of Minnesota's Sixth Normal School at Bemidji

STANTON PERFORMS RITES; BURNQUIST IS ORATOR OF THE DAY; CEREMONY SIMPLE

CONTENTS OF CASKET

Governor Burnquist

LITTLE GIANT SHOWS ARE COMING UNDER AUSPICES OF BAND

OFFICERS ARE ELECTED FOR POTATO PRODUCTS CO.: DIRECTORS CHOSEN

TOWNLEY CANDIDATES MUST BE FILED AS INDEPENDENTS

NEW DAUGHTER MAKES DEBUT AT STANTON HOME

1000 CAMP DODGE MEN MADE AMERICAN CITIZENS

OLD ENGLISH TOWN IS FULL OF YANKEES

EIGHT HUN AIRPLANES BAGGED BY BRITISH

THREE MORE VESSELS ARE SUNK OFF COAST

SWEDISH STEAMER IS SUNK BY SEA RAIDER

PERSHING'S CASUALTY LIST

BRITISH CONTINUE TO ADVANCE; CAPTURE CITIES

Minnesota Electric Light and Power Company, Bemidji, electrical work, $1,758.

Laying the Cornerstone

On April 3, 1918, work began on clearing the trees on the site and excavating for the foundation, with teams of horses used in the excavation. The first carload of brick arrived by rail the next day for the 145 by 55 foot, three-story building to have 26,100 square feet of floor space. By April 25, the excavation for the basement had been completed and workmen began to pour cement for the foundation. When the building of the foundation began, the city Commercial Club began to plan for the cornerstone-laying ceremony. On May 2 the Pioneer reported that the superintendent of construction of the building had spoken to a noon luncheon of the Commercial Club the day before, and afterwards "it was voted to have a big celebration at the laying of the cornerstone."[111]

Cornerstone laying (August, 1918)
"From a photograph of Chief Bemidji to copies of 11 newspapers"

---

[111] The Commerce Club named a committee to head the arrangements: H. E. Reynolds, chairman; A. P. Ritchie, A. P. White, W. Z. Robinson, and W. C. Bolcum. The Sentinel on May 3 added that it would be "a celebration to which all of the members of the last legislature and many other prominent men will be invited . . . when the cornerstone of the new building is formerly [sic] laid."

The Commercial Club president announced on June 26 that the day for the ceremonies had been set for August 10, 1918, at 2 p.m. The club sent out invitations and began to make final preparations. Two days before the ceremony, however, the Pioneer announced with an air of sophistication that there would be no parade and no demonstrations on the part of the city in general; instead, it continued, the "ceremonies will be simple and impressive, the address of the governor being the feature of the day." And the brief article concluded, "The entire populace of Bemidji is urged to attend the ceremony."[112]

The ceremony took place on an improvised platform erected at the main entrance of the building. The newspapers gave no estimate of attendance, but stated only that there "was a large assemblage of Bemidji people and visitors." The visitors were not identified. District Judge C. W. Stanton of Bemidji presided; after some opening band numbers and the invocation, he gave a brief address, incident to which he set the cornerstone in its allotted niche. Stanton then introduced Governor Burnquist, who delivered the major address.[113]

The prediction by the newspaper of a sedate ceremony was apparently correct; this one-day ceremony was not a celebration in the sense of a big outburst of show or emotion. For whatever reasons--perhaps mainly the overwhelming tenor of the current war then going on—the public show for the actual building of the long-fought-for normal school appeared anti-climactic. The newspapers agreed afterwards that simplicity marked the ceremony, and interviews with persons who were there confirm this general opinion.[114]

Choosing the First President

Though the workmen obviously made progress on the construction of the building after the cornerstone-laying ceremonies, the local papers did not report it. The State Normal Board, however, observed the strides being made so that at its November 12, 1918, meeting, President Ell Torrance appointed Board Members A. P. White, Bemidji; S. H. Somesen, Winona; and H. T. Welter, Moorhead, to constitute a committee "to consider persons for the position of president of the

---

[112] August 8, 1918, p. 1. Nearly all the news about the building progress of the new normal was sandwiched in comparatively small spaces among war news stories. And rarely during this first building period were there any editorials about the school, these too dealt nearly always with some phase of the war or war efforts at home. The chauvinism, the shrill headlines, the articles equating nonconformity with treason were epitomized in the 1918 Bemidji newspapers. For just one example, the June state primary election found several candidates who were members of the controversial Nonpartisan League, among them Charles A. Lindbergh, Sr., and the day after the election and subsequent defeat of League candidates, the Pioneer doubledeck banner headline read: "Minnesota Responds to Loyalty Call; Slaughters Advocates of Sedition." Civil liberties had adjourned in Bemidji.
[113] War news was put aside for one day in the local newspapers, the day of the cornerstone laying. A full account of the ceremony appears in the Pioneer of August 12, 1918, and the Sentinel of August 16, 1918. Lengthy excerpts, seemingly the entire talk of Stanton, appear in the Pioneer. Neither paper quotes one word of Burnquist's speech, despite the Pioneer statement that "Governor Burnquist made a most masterly address which was listened to intently and commanded applause at frequent intervals."
[114] Fred Troppman, a still-active Bemidji businessman at age ninety-five, recalled that the day of the cornerstone laying "was all very nice, but I don't remember it being anything so extra special." Regarding the cornerstone, it would appear that it took a large container to accommodate all the memorabilia that went into it. As the Sentinel article of August 16, 1918, read: "Records of practically all the proceedings connected with the development . . . were placed within the casket that is now covered by the cornerstone." The items ran from a photograph of Chief Bemidji to copies of eleven different newspapers to another photograph and biographical sketch of the late Representative Pendergast, plus literally dozens of other items.

Bemidji school and make a report at the next quarterly meeting." At this November meeting the Board made a decision that for the time being affected Bemidji negatively. A motion carried that "no appropriations for any buildings for the normal schools be requested from the next session of the legislature by this Board, or otherwise." In this decision, the Board showed caution and to no avail members White and Schultz voted against it. Thus it appeared that there would be no chance for a dormitory for Bemidji at least until after 1921. To help change the Board's decision, the Bemidji Commercial Club named a committee of three —County Attorney Graham Torrance (son of Normal Board President Ell Torrance), Postmaster A. P. Ritchie, and Superintendent of Schools W. C. Bolcum—to meet with the Board. Although the Board's minutes do not mention the meeting, the Bemidji delegation—subsequently changed to Ritchie, F. S. Lycan, and Judge C. W. Stanton—went to St. Paul in February, 1919, to plead its case. One might presume that its influence was significant, judging by the resolution passed by the Board on February 11, 1919:

"Whereas, since the last meeting of the Board, it has been made to appear that a liberal building policy is to be adopted with reference to state institutions, therefore Resolved by this Board that requests for appropriations for dormitories and equipment at normal schools be made of the present legislature, instead of postponing the same for two years."

So the Board recommended $100,000 each for dormitories at Bemidji, Winona, and Mankato, and instructed the secretary to "present these resolutions to the proper committees in the legislature."

At the same time the three-man committee chosen in November to recommend a president for Bemidji Normal had been active. By mid-January, White informed the Pioneer after recently returning from Minneapolis where he had attended a meeting of his committee, that "there were about fifteen or twenty applicants for the position, some of them educators of good reputation and standing."[115] Moreover, White reported, the choice had been narrowed down to three persons, but he named no names. The Pioneer did, however, and concluded in its speculation that it would most likely be John Munroe, superintendent of schools at Faribault, even though "he is known as a progressive in education, even to the point of radicalism." The suspense was lifted, and the Pioneer's prediction proved wrong, when the State Normal Board selected Bemidji's first president at their February 11, 1919, meeting. The manner in which the official minutes reported the selection, however, conjure up all kinds of questions that were not answered. Let the minutes themselves present the enigma:

"Mr. White, Chairman of the Committee to consider persons for the position of President of the Bemidji School reported that the Committee had not agreed upon a man to recommend for the position and the Committee would require

---

[115] January 14, 1919)p 1. Though hardly intended, the phrasing of White is such to suggest the questionable reputations of the remaining candidates.

more time. An extended discussion followed. No decision was reached at this time.

"The Board reassembled at three o'clock and unanimously elected Mr. M. W. Deputy, formerly of Mankato but now of Kansas City, Missouri, as president of the Normal School at Bemidji at a salary of $4,000. Mr. Deputy was communicated with by long distance telephone. Further assurance was given him of increase of salary so as to place him in two years upon the same basis as the other presidents, if the school progressed satisfactorily."

Deputy accepted two days later and arranged to begin his duties al Bemidji on May 1, 1919. Bemidji Normal School had its first president, although it may never be known just what went on at the Board meeting the day he was chosen.[116]

The Pioneer ran a picture of Deputy in its February 24, 1919, issue along with an article on his background. Manfred Wolfe Deputy was born in 1867 on a farm near Vernon, Indiana, and attended rural schools. His first teaching experience was in rural schools, and he later became a high school principal, a city superintendent of schools, and a county superintendent of schools, all in Indiana. His professional preparation included a two-year course at Southern Indiana Normal, Mitchell, and four years as a student at Indiana University. He received a B.A. degree in philosophy and psychology in 1904, and an M.A. in education in 1905. Beyond this he did graduate work at Teachers' College, Columbia University. In 1909 he went to Eastern State Normal in Charleston, Illinois, where he taught pedagogy and served as director of the elementary school connected with the normal. From 1911 to 1916 he served as a teacher of pedagogy and director of the elementary school at Mankato Normal. From 1916 to 1919, he served as director of teachers' training and extension work in the public schools of Kansas City, Missouri, and organized a standard two-year normal course there. Deputy was married and had one daughter.[117]

Funds for a Dormitory

By the end of February, 1919, the Bemidji Normal School had a president selected and one building half completed. It next wanted funds for a dormitory. Again the immediate future of the new school lay in the bills before the state legislature and in the hands of the politicians who would guide them along their difficult route.

Fortunately for the newly founded school, two new representatives from the sixty-second district, the district in which the new normal was located, proved to be stalwarts in supporting the school. Representative Arthur E. Rako of Bemidji

---

[116] A bulletin printed by Bemidji College in 1938 gave some additional information on what went on at that February, 1919, Board meeting: "From the forty or more active candidates the committee did not arrive at a conclusion and asked for an extension of time. It was the Board opinion that the selection should no be longer deferred. During the discussion director J. L Washburn suggested the name of M. W. Deputy. Because Mr. Deputy was well-known to other members of the Board and to the presidents of the other colleges, his appointment was unanimously favored." The Northern Student, Bulletin of the State Teachers College, Bemidji, Minnesota, Vol. XI, No. 2, January, 1938, p. 10. That the Board would select a president in this almost casual, spur-of-the-moment manner seems difficult to accept.

[117] Several years after Deputy had been in Bemidji, the May 27, 1927, Pioneer quoted him as saying: "I had expected to spend the rest of my days in Kansas City, but I had been raised and brought up on a farm, and had the true spirit of the Northwest within me. I had been at Mankato and knew the sturdiness of the people. I had faith in this northern Minnesota country. I was sure that the Bemidji school was being established because you needed it."

and Franklin J. McPartlin of International Falls both landed seats on the all-important Appropriations Committee; Rako had the further advantage of sitting as a member of the Committee on the University and State Schools, a position which provided him an additional lever for getting appropriations. Then, too, Senators Nord and McGarry were back to espouse the cause of Bemidji Normal in the upper house. Nord was in an advantageous position in that he was a member of the Finance Committee.

Besides having good representation in the legislature, several other factors aided Bemidji's quest for funds in the 1919 session. The general attitude of the state administration had brightened since the previous year and understandably so in view of the fact that the anxiety connected with the war had given way to optimism and a desire for revitalization of the state and its agencies. A second factor which provided impetus to a greater expansion of state educational facilities in general, and of normal schools in particular, was the appointment on January 20, 1919, of James M. McConnell as State Superintendent of Education. McConnell, who replaced C. G. Schultz, served in this position until his death in 1933. As a former teacher of history at Mankato Normal, he was already aware of the numerous problems facing teacher-training schools. His sincere devotion to forwarding the cause of teacher education in Minnesota proved to be a boon for all the struggling schools.[118] Still another favorable circumstance was the fact that able Judge Ell Torrance presided over the State Normal School Board. Judge Torrance of Minneapolis was the father of County Attorney Graham Torrance of Bemidji—the county seat of Beltrami County—and the local citizens had great faith in Judge Torrance's ability. They felt that they had a staunch supporter in an influential position, one who would not necessarily show favoritism but who on the other hand would not permit the well-established schools or any other pressure group to force the newest normal school into a disadvantageous position.[119]

When the legislature began, Bemidji partisans had a slight scare thrown into them when it was discovered that the appropriations for Bemidji Normal had not been included in the budget submitted by Governor Burnquist. But the omission proved to be an error, and a correction was forthcoming immediately, averting a costly setback. Once the Board's resolution calling for a $100,000 dormitory appropriation reached the legislature, Representative Rako and his compatriots assumed the task of guiding it, along with a $40,000 maintenance and equipment appropriation, through the tortuous course of budget snipping. Both Rako and

[118] There were several changes in title of the person who served in the capacity as the head of the state public schools; regardless of the title, the person served as ex officio member and secretary of the State Normal Board. Almost all the authors who have written on Minnesota public education during McConnell's long tenure have paid warm tribute to the man. An example of this can be seen in a small book by Dudley S. Brainerd, History of St. Cloud State Teachers College (St. Cloud: St. Cloud State Teachers College, 1953), p. 47. McConnell's work is also noted in J. McKeen Cattell, ed., Leaders in Education (New York: The Science Press, 1932), p. 592.

[119] Editorial originally published in the Minneapolis Tribune, reprinted on the editorial page of the Pioneer, March 18, 1919. Torrance served as a Board member for eighteen years, the last twelve as president; he retired from the Board in 1920. Torrance had also been the national commander of the Grand Army of the Republic; his papers are on file at the State Historical Society and are filled with correspondence regarding the G.A.R. He was listed in Who's Who In America, 1920-1921, Vol. XI (Chicago: A. N. Marquis Company, 1920), p. 2848. At the University of Minnesota, Duluth, "Torrance Hall" is a dormitory named after him.

Senator Nord kept a close watch on developments while Bemidji newspapers and other backers supported their legislators with editorials and letters.[120]

On March 18 the Appropriations Committee of the House reported favorably on the dormitory request; within a week a joint committee of the House and Senate met and placed in their recommendations all the Bemidji requests. The legislature approved these recommendations, as usual, in the closing days of the session. The financial struggle had been waged successfully again, and it was a jubilant Bemidji when the good news arrived. The distribution of the funds for Bemidji Normal included the following:[121]

Maintenance, including summer sessions and library	$ 27,400
Repairs, betterments and equipment	$ 1,250
Equipment for the new building available for the year ending July 31, 1919	$ 10,300
Maintenance available for year ending July 31, 1919	$ 3,000
Women's Dormitory	$ 100,000
Total	$ 141,950

One problem that luckily ended up being a diversion occurred in the 1919 legislative session. A rumor of a proposal spread among the legislators that the newest school at Bemidji be permanently limited to being an academy for the training of rural teachers. The proposal, whose origins were vaguely traced to "state education circles" or "the Education Department," came under immediate attack by Bemidji area legislators and the regional newspapers.[122] Fortunately, perhaps, the proposal was never drafted into bill form, and the local papers paid tribute to the legislators for not allowing the plan to gain any real backing.

Selecting the Teaching Staff

All in all, the 1919 session proved to be a very successful one for Bemidji Normal. With sufficient funds secured, a president hired, and a building nearing completion, plans could be readied to open the doors to the first students. The Normal Board had already made plans back in March for its opening when State Superintendent McConnell announced that there would be a six-week teachers' training school held in Bemidji starting June 23, 1919, with President Deputy in charge of arrangements.

Deputy arrived for a one-week stay in Bemidji in April, and Resident Director White showed him around. After spending some time at the site where the construction was progressing on the main building, Deputy addressed a Commercial Club meeting and announced that a regular year's session would open that fall if equipment could be secured. That same week Deputy traveled around the area,

---

[120] Bemidji Sentinel, February 28, March 7, 1919.
[121] Minnesota, Session Laws (1919), c. 466.
[122] A sample response can be seen in a Sentinel editorial on February 7: "Students in this section of the state will grow to depend on the local Normal for a full course in education. To many it will fill the place of a university, and the expense of going to the Twin Cities will be eliminated." Later years bore that statement out, although it must have sounded far-reaching in its day.

visiting schools and giving short talks to students and teachers. Before returning to Kansas City to conclude his business there, he announced via the newspapers that there could be no dormitory that first year of school and appealed to Bemidji residents to "open their homes that proper accommodations may be provided for the one-hundred-and fifty students expected to enroll" in September.[123]

Deputy attended his first meeting of the State Normal Board on May 13, 1919. At the meeting the Board approved the general plans submitted by the architect for the Bemidji dormitory. They also approved the summer school plans and accepted the position that the faculty for the summer session be selected by the Department of Education with the approval of Deputy and Resident Director White; the Board then designated the summer school as the first regular session of the Bemidji Normal School. Apparently two members of the Bemidji staff had already been selected, because the Board in its last-minute business approved formally the hiring of Miss Mabell Bonsall, mathematics; and Miss Emma Grant, methods and training work. (These two were the highest paid on the staff that summer of 1919, getting $311 and $383 dollars respectively for teaching in the one six-week session.)

On June 10, 1919, two weeks before the school would open, Deputy announced that the selection of the faculty had nearly been completed; that the building was nearly finished and that much of the equipment for it had arrived;[124] that sidewalks had been laid in front of the building; that he "was much encouraged by the number of requests for information" and felt that there would be about 100 students in the first summer session. City officials, for their part, announced that they would provide sidewalks from town to the school, and that they would pave the street in front of the school before paving any other major town street.[125]

With Deputy again present, the Normal School Board met on June 17, 1919, and gave official approval to the Bemidji faculty and their salaries for both the summer school and the first full school year beginning in September. For the latter, the faculty included the aforementioned Misses Grant of Springfield, Illinois (who had taught the previous year in the Kansas City Normal), $2300; and Bonsall, Terre Haute, Indiana (who also became acting Dean of Women), $1,900; Mr. Marion J. Atwood, Madison, Wisconsin, history and geography, $2,00 for ten and one-half months (though Atwood was hired for the full school year, he resigned at the end of the summer session); Miss Eunice Asbury, Bloomington, Indiana, $1,700 for nine months; Maude Kavanaugh, Rural Department, $1,600 for nine months; Miss Helen Reinheimer, secretary (to Deputy) and accountant, $1,250 for

[123] Quoted in the Bemidji Weekly Pioneer, April 30, 1919, p. 1. The Bemidji Womens Community and Civic Club conducted a canvass of the town of rooms available for students and prepared a directory of them for Deputy to send to students who made inquiry. By May 14 they reported having sixty rooming places, and at forty of them students could also take their board.
[124] There were no electrical fixtures installed that first summer, however.
[125] Neither the street nor the sidewalks were completed for many years, however. As late as 1932, Deputy wrote to the city council: "We respectfully call attention to the fact that ... the City Council would provide for the paving and laying of sidewalks to the proposed college. Undoubtedly some of the council members and the mayor will recall the former enthusiasm which the city had about this matter and will think it proper to carry out the work." Letter from Deputy to City Council and Mayor, June 29, 1932. Random correspondence of Deputy on file in the Special Collections Room; A. C. Clark Library, Bemidji State College.

full year. Only half of the faculty members that first year held a degree of any kind. What also might be noted were the several persons—Grant, Bonsall, Asbury—whom Deputy essentially brought along with him when he came.

In addition to the above persons who were to teach in both the regular year and the summer vacation, the Board also approved for the 1919 summer term: Miss Ellen Nystrom, writing and handwork, $225; Harry Olin, agriculture, $100; James W. Smith, physics, $100; Ernest Durbahn, manual training, $100. The last three persons were listed as part-time only.[126]

The School Doors Open

Bemidji accepted the first students to its long-awaited normal school on June 23, 1919, at 8 a.m. Said the Pioneer that evening, the school opened "under the most auspicious circumstances and the outlook is indeed flattering." By noon the first day the enrollment had reached 60, and Deputy was reported as "much

First Faculty Members, June, 1919
"It's a great thing to be a teacher; it's a greater thing to be a teacher of teachers."

encouraged" by the numbers. By the end of the third day and supposedly the last day to register, ''there were 123 enrolled and more coming," said the Pioneer, which then announced that Deputy had extended the registration period to the entire week. The final total reached 130 students (only six were men) from 17 Minnesota counties. (At the opening of the College there was no library and not a single book

---

[126] Minutes of the Normal School Board, June 17, 1919; information on background of faculty provided by the June 20, 1919, Pioneer. Olin, Smith and Durbahn were on the Bemidji high school faculty during the regular school year. Smith later became Bemidji Superintendent of Schools and served in that capacity until his retirement in 1966.

with which to begin one.) [127]

When the summer session ended on August 1, 1919, the <u>Pioneer</u> that evening wrote glowingly of the school's success and the "splendid work" of President Deputy in getting everything organized and operating after being on the job such a short time. In view of such an excellent start, the article predicted, the first regular session to start the next month would see over 100 students enrolled.

Meanwhile, Deputy and Resident Director A. P. White continued to worry publicly about the recently financed but unbuilt dormitory. Though the state promised that the architectural plans would be ready in June, and the newspapers predicted its completion by the start of the winter term, it was not until August 11, 1919, that bids were called for. The sum of $100,000 had been allotted for the dormitory, the amount to include both construction and equipment. When the Board opened the bids August 20, the lowest bid for the general construction alone was $102,000. The plans went back to the drawing boards. The original building

The "main building" (1927)
"The school opened under the most auspicious circumstances."

---

[127] Between the registration period and the end of the first session, the local Bemidji papers offered no news about the normal school. Miss Maria Krogseng, now age seventy and a retired school teacher living in Saum, Minnesota, was one of the students enrolled that first session. In an interview she indicated that because of the distance from the school to downtown eating places, noon lunches were prepared by the domestic science class and sold for seventeen cents a meal. However, students regularly walked up town for noon meals anyway, said Miss Krogseng, because "we were used to walking great distances in those days." What she remembered most fondly about the first session was "that nice Mr. Deputy" talking to the students at regular meetings ("we called them convocations"). Miss Krogseng is remembered in the records for having written the winning lyrics to the school song "Hail to Thee Bemidji College" which she wrote during the regular school year of 1921-1922, and first sung to the tune of "The Battle Hymn of the Republic." Later the melody was changed, and later yet the school song was changed.

was to be L-shaped, but the wing was eliminated to cut costs. When the Board submitted the readjusted plans, the contracts were awarded September 10, 1919, and construction started soon afterwards. Klarquist and Sons, the builders of the first building, again received the bid of $66,470 for the general construction of the two-story brick structure which would contain 14,816 square feet of floor space and a root cellar.[128]

In preparation for the students' arrival for the regular session to begin September 2, 1919, the Women's Community and Civic Club announced that it had found 130 rooming accommodations available in town. Miss Bonsall, acting dean of women, received the list of rooms and assigned students to their quarters. President Deputy publicly emphasized that even though students would be housed in various parts of the city, they would still be required to observe dormitory rules and violators would be reported. As one editor later observed, "The school was run on rather strict Methodist lines in the first years."[129]

The first regular year's session began with registration on September 2, 1919. "Every one of the thirty-eight students enrolled for that quarter registered between eight and ten o'clock. No one dropped out during the term," said a later College bulletin regarding the first enrollment.[130] Fourteen of the students who enrolled in the summer session stayed on for the fall term. On Saturday afternoon, September 6, the Women's Community and Civic Club sponsored a get-acquainted reception at the Normal to which the general public was invited. The local papers estimated that between 200 and 225 people attended, a large turnout in comparison to the number enrolled. There was a program which included several musical selections, and which concluded with an address by President Deputy. The Pioneer deemed the entire event "decidedly successful."

The courses offered during the first year—and in subsequent years—were: (1) a two-year curriculum for high school graduates leading to the advanced diploma allowing holders to be eligible to teach in any elementary school in the state; (2) a one-year course open to high school graduates which awarded them a certificate permitting the holder to teach only in rural schools; (3) a five-year course in which eighth grade graduates were eligible to enroll to pursue what was then called "undergraduate" studies, or high school courses. Essentially students in this five-year program took four years of high school in three years and then two years of normal school work; at the end of the fifth year, they received the standard two-

---

[128] The building was used as a dormitory until 1966, when it became faculty offices. The basement of the building was used as a dining area until after World War II, when it became a student union. When a separate student union building began operation in January, 1968, the basement was used for classrooms. Recently the basement was renovated and now houses the Counseling Center.

[129] A Brief History of Beltrami County (Bemidji: Beltrami County Historical Society, 1963), p. 56. Deputy was a very strict Methodist himself, according to statements made by his contemporaries. For example, Deputy allowed no one, including male faculty members, to smoke on campus.

[130] The Northern Student, Bulletin of the State Teachers College, Bemidji, Minnesota, Vol. XI, No. 2, January, 1938, p. 11. That "no one dropped out" was not confirmed by Kenneth Kenfield, age sixty-eight, one of the students enrolled that first fall term, who indicated in an interview that he dropped out after one month and transferred ("There was nothing but girls here," he said). The Sentinel of September 5, 1919 said more hopefully than honestly that there were forty students enrolled and "new students are arriving daily."

year diploma.[131]

In connection with the Normal, Bemidji ran an elementary school—or Observation School as the first brochure called it— that consisted of kindergarten through grade four, inclusive. Deputy saw this Observation School as the heart of a normal school. The classrooms were on the basement floor of the building, and the enrollment totaled 81. Miss Emma Grant was in charge of the school; Miss Letheld Hahn taught kindergarten and grades one and two; Miss Lucy Dunigan taught grades three and four in the school. The purpose of the school was, said Deputy, to illustrate the best methods of teaching for the Normal School students enrolled. The "college" students also did their observation and student teaching in this on campus elementary school. (Deputy's extraordinary interest and concern for this campus elementary school caused one faculty member in the late 1930s to grouse that "the tail was wagging the dog.")

Once the first session with its 38 students began, the local papers offered little news about the school, very likely because there was not too much news to report. There were no men's athletic organizations at the time; indeed, there were only ten men enrolled. The only extra-curricular activity provided was a Dramatic Club. The school purchased a Webster's dictionary for its first library acquisition in the fall of 1919. To this lone volume the school added a second-hand set of the Encyclopedia Britannica which the school bought for ten dollars.[132]

The Normal School Board at its October 14, 1919, meeting, routinely approved the employment of the aforementioned Misses Hahn and Dunigan, and also the hiring of Miss Mary Deputy, President Deputy's daughter, to teach physical education and English at a salary of $1,200 for nine months.[133] (The physical education instruction was limited, and no credit was given for it until the next year, 1920-21.)

The existing records of the College registrar do not list the names of the students for each quarter; instead they are lumped together as "Students Enrolled, 1919-1920," with their names and hometown addresses. The list for the first year totaled 58 names of those enrolled for some portion if not all of the school year. That ten of the names were male was a bit out of the ordinary; the Pioneer found it remarkable and wrote on December 8 that "several young men enrolled and according to percentage of attendance, the young men are greater in number than

---

[131] The State Department of Education then offered a variety of teaching certificates, most of them temporary, to accommodate the need for teachers; realism dictated that the standards could not be high for certification, an eighth grade diploma being the minimum. All the so called undergraduate work was discontinued in 1927, except that in summer sessions teachers in service below high school graduation still had the privilege of enrolling to improve their certificates, to meet the requirements for certification renewal, or to work toward graduation.

[132] The Northern Student, Bulletin of the State Teachers College, Bemidji Minnesota, Vol. XI, No. 2, January, 1938, p. 11. The library holdings, or lack of them, remained a constant problem throughout Deputy's nineteen year tenure. It had to be an understatement when he wrote in his report in October, 1920: "Because of the lack of funds, only the beginning of a general reference library has been made." Minnesota, Report of the State Board of Education, Twenty-first Biennial Report of the Department of Education, 1919-1920, p. 63.

[133] Miss Deputy's background and training had been in landscape gardening, despite what she taught at Bemidji. (As one instructor put it who had taught under Deputy: "In those days we were all Renaissance men.") Miss Deputy had both a B.A. and M.A. degree from Indiana University. She married F. Vernon Lamson, Bemidji, one of the students enrolled in the first regular school year. She later became a professional landscape architect in New York City. She had no children, and at this writing is living in Chicago.

in any other normal in the state."

At its January 15, 1920, meeting, the Board gave Deputy an early vote of confidence for the work that he had done by re-electing him as president for the ensuing year of school. Meanwhile work continued on the dormitory through the winter, and the superintendent of construction indicated that it would be completed by June, 1920, in time for summer school. Because of this progress, Deputy announced he would accept applications for rooms and boarding at the dormitory for the 1920 summer session. Still, the completed dormitory would only hold about 50 students, so again from Deputy's office the call went out to Bemidji citizens to provide rooms for the summer students. Deputy estimated that the number might be as high as 300.[134]

The Bemidji Normal School conducted its first commencement exercises on June 3, 1920. State Commissioner of Education James McConnell delivered the

Sanford Hall (1920)
"The domicile for girls at college should be a dormitory."

main address, and Resident Director A. P. White gave out diplomas to four graduates.[135] It is fitting that the names of these first graduates should be recorded: Mrs. Cora Bernhard, Bemidji; Georgia L. Brown, Brainerd; Josephine H. Parker, Bemidji; and Margaret Romens, Happyland.[136]

Summer school sessions for the first 12 years brought in more students

---

[134] The biggest news regarding higher education that winter and spring dealt with the widespread rumor that Hamline University was leaving St. Paul and would move to Bemidji, or at least to some town in the northern part of the state. The local editors fulminated at great length on the pristine virtues of the country versus the inherent sinfulness of the city. By the end of May, however, Hamline officials announced they were staying in St. Paul and the local editors went back to reporting the possibilities of the local normal.

[135] Those who graduated were able to do so after only one year at Bemidji because of the transfer of credits from other schools.

[136] Prior to graduation, Miss Deputy's physical education classes put on an outdoor pageant during the last week of school for the general public, and the pageant became traditional for the next few years. The show was mainly dancing and an exhibition of body exercises, "including the aesthetic dancing of the high school girls. In spite of the strong wind which made it difficult to give some of the exercises, the results were excellent," concluded the Pioneer, May 27, 1920, p. 1.

than were enrolled in the regular years' sessions. President Deputy prepared for the 1920 session by enlarging his faculty to 12 members. In addition to those on the regular year's staff—Grant, Bonsall, Asbury, Kavanaugh, Hahn, and Dunigan—(but not Mary Deputy) he added G. H. Sanberg, superintendent of schools at Crookston, history and civics; Bemidji High School Principal J. W. Smith, physics; Bemidji Superintendent of Schools R. O. Bagby, history and grammar; A. E. Shirling, Polytechnic Institute, Kansas City, geography and hygiene; Florence Musch, sewing; Mrs. Grace Thacker, Northwestern University, home economics. Deputy also employed Mrs. Thacker for the next regular year, and besides her teaching, she was appointed dean of women, or as the Normal Board minutes called it, "Preceptress."[137]

The bulletin prepared by Deputy describing the summer offerings in 1920 varied little from the first one. The most significant addition for 1920 was the statement that women could stay on campus, at least some of them, living and eating in the newly completed dormitory named Maria Sanford Hall. This one factor aided significantly the initial growth of the school. Without the building of this residence hall, it would have been exceedingly difficult for the school to attract a student body of measurable size. It must be remembered that the student body in its first years was made up overwhelmingly of girls, that the town did not have the facilities to house a large influx of youthful schoolgirls, and that the prevailing moral and ethical standards of the time dictated that the traditional domicile for girls at college should be a dormitory.[138]

Thus with an almost new main building and a brand new dormitory, the school welcomed students for its second summer session of 1920. "The enrollment exceeded all expectations," said the Sentinel, and whether this was true, 292 students—only eight of them men—enrolled for the session. This figure nearly tripled the previous summer session and augured well for the future. Deputy revealed extra pleasure in pointing out that the summer enrollment was larger than that at Duluth Normal School.

Judge Ell Torrance, Normal Board president, filed a report to the State Department of Education on the normal schools covering the biennial period ending June 30, 1920. Among the many items mentioned in his lengthy review, he noted that the highest total enrollment for all the normals in the 1913 to 1920 period was 4,208 for the year 1916, and the lowest was 3,233 for 1919. At the end of the 1920 school year, St. Cloud Normal had the largest enrollment with 1,057, and Moorhead next with 900; Bemidji, of course, had the lowest with 58. The enrollment

---

[137] Minutes of the Normal School Board, April 13, 1920. The home-towns of the summer school faculty are given in the Bemidji Sentinel, June 4, 1920, p. 1. Of note to high school history teachers, the Board at the April 13 meeting appointed Fremont P. Wirth to instruct in history at Bemidji beginning in the fall of 1920. Wirth later went to George Peabody College and while there wrote several very successful high school history textbooks.
[138] The school named the dormitory after Maria Sanford, a Minnesota teacher; although eighty-three years old, she had come to Bemidji Normal to speak in both 1919 and 1920. Ten days after her second visit to Bemidji, she passed away after delivering an address ("An Apostrophe to the Flag") to the Daughters of the American Revolution in Washington, D. C. "As a memorial to this woman whose matchless spirit, speaking power, and character had made a profound impression on all members of Bemidji College, the dormitory was named Maria Sanford Hall." The Northern Student, Bulletin of the State Teachers College, Bemidji, Minnesota, Vol. XI, No. 2, January, 1938, p. 14. It was not recorded if the faculty was consulted on naming the building, for no minutes were kept of any faculty meetings during Deputy's nineteen years as president.

of the remaining State Normal Schools in 1920 were Winona with 732; Mankato, 755, and Duluth, 330. Receipts and appropriations for Bemidji Normal in its first school year totaled $30,328.65.[139]

President Deputy's first published report appeared in the same publication; he covered the period ending September 30, 1920, the time when his school was just starting its second regular year. He began by writing that the establishment of the Bemidji Normal "came at one of the most critical periods through which the schools of the state and nation have passed," namely World War I. He blamed the decreased attendance in all normal schools on the current economic conditions caused by the readjustments following the war; these conditions "without a doubt have curtailed the initial enrollment of this school," he emphasized. Deputy presented the figures of attendance for the first regular year and the two summer schools, and then wrote what he called the two large aims to be kept in mind in developing the school: (1) school standards conducive to sound scholarship; (2) well-trained teachers. Further on in his report he added the additional aim of service, "especially to the rural schools." Expanding on this topic, he added, "Probably more than three-fourths of all students who have enrolled have been rural teachers, and due attention has been given their interests." As to major problems, he cited lack of housing for both faculty and students, and a shortage of classroom space, especially for the elementary school, the latter being "located on the basement floor . . . in rooms designed for science and industrial departments." He concluded by stating essentially that the problems of the fledgling Bemidji Normal could be ameliorated by a generous appropriation from the next legislature.[140]

Before the reports were published, the second regular year of school had begun on September 7, 1920. The courses of study were practically the same as the year before and were the same offered by the other Minnesota Normal Schools. Among the changes, the school had added a fifth grade to the elementary school, and now had a faculty of ten. The biggest change was the enrollment; it went up from 38 to 97 for its second regular school year.

Thus one can say that by the fall of 1920, Bemidji Normal School had gotten started. From a school on paper in 1913, it had become a school of brick by 1919 along with a faculty and a student body. It had one regular year and two summer sessions of operation by 1920; it had a faculty of ten, two new buildings, and had graduated four students. But its permanence was by no means assured. For the next decade the faculty and the Normal Board were forced to meet numerous problems ranging from apathetic legislatures to opposition from liberal arts colleges. It had been hard to get it started; it would be just as hard to keep it going.

---

[139] Minnesota, First Report of the State Board of Education, Twenty-first Biennial Report of the Department of Education, 1919-1920, pp. 52-55.
[140] Ibid., p. 63.

CHAPTER IV

From Normal School to Teachers College 1920-1929

T IME, PERSPECTIVE and closer study reveal the importance of Bemidji Normal School's getting two buildings— the main building and the dormitory—almost from the start in 1919 and 1920, because essentially those were the only two buildings used during Deputy's entire 19-year administration. The only additions in his tenure were a wing added to the main building for an elementary school and a heating plant, both structures begun in 1925. That was all. Not until December 15, 1937, did work begin on another building on campus. Despite crowded conditions in the 1920s that required the use of tents in the summers and hall corridors in the winters, the legislature gave money for building purposes only once in this long period.

Legislative and State Board Actions

Plausible reasons can be offered for the failure of the legislators to bestow funds for more building in the 1920s. Minnesota experienced a 15 percent rise in population between 1910 and 1920, and this rise, plus the fact that the value of more education was slowly being realized by the citizenry in general, tended to bring about an increase in normal school enrollments. But unfortunately the over-all wealth of the state did not grow as fast as the demand for new educational facilities. These two incompatible factors meant trouble for expansion-minded normal schools as the 1921 legislative session ended.[141]

In outward appearance, the Bemidji Normal's representation in the

---

[141] The increase from 1912 to 1922 in the estimated wealth of Minnesota was at the modest rate of fifty-seven percent while that of the whole country was seventy-two percent. In 1920 the purchasing power of the dollar was forty as compared with one hundred in 1913. William W. Folwell, A History of Minnesota (St. Paul: Minnesota Historical Society, 1926) III, 322. U. S. Department of Commerce, Historical Statistics of the United States: Colonial Times to 1957 (Washington, D. C.: Government Printing Office, 1960), p. 12. The changing Minnesota population figures as listed: 1910, 2,075,708; 1920, 2,387,125; 1930, 2,563,953; 1940, 2,792,300; 1950, 2,982,483; 1960, 3,413, 864.

legislature, that is, the representatives and the senator from the sixty-second district, seemed to be as strong as ever. Along with Senator Leonard H. Nord, the voters returned Representatives Arthur E. Rako and Franklin L. McPartlin. Senator P. H. McGarry, from the fifty-second district at Walker, another former supporter of the College, also won reelection. Again, as in 1919, these men obtained their same, rather influential committee memberships.[142]

But one startling difference set the 1921 legislature off from its predecessor. No longer were the legislators prepared to support an expanding building program on a statewide basis. Times were not that good economically. Certainly the residents of Bemidji favored a building appropriation for their Normal School, just as citizens of other localities favored state-sponsored projects in their hometowns, but economic and political realities combined to prevent any specific area from imposing its wishes on the legislature, since cooperation within the respective houses and between them was necessary before allocations for state buildings could be made. But a preponderance of the constituents did not favor building projects which were downstate or upstate, as the case might be. In short, Minnesota was caught in the recession that followed World War I.[143]

An abetting factor that curtailed the legislature's desire to build was the decline in the ability to pay taxes. With the legislature under predominately agrarian influence, and with the wholesale price index of farm products falling from 150 in 1920 to 88.4 in 1921 (on the basis of 1926 equals 100), it seemed obvious that the farming areas would be vociferous in their opposition to expanded state spending. Shrinking tax revenues accompanied by an abhorrence of deficit financing presented little alternative for the state building program for 1921-1922; it had to be reduced.[144]

To make matters even more unfavorable, the wholesale price index of building materials had not fallen as much as the wholesale price of farm products. The disparity in the decline brought about a relative rise in building costs and affected both private and government contracting. In turn, the lack of building served to depress the economy even more. Indeed, editorials advised that the cost of building materials be reduced to stimulate the lagging economy. These realized little effect, however, and Governor J. A. O. Preus, along with the legislators, had little grounds for optimism as the session began.[145]

The Normal School Board had sensed the temper of the times the previous fall. In a meeting at Moorhead on October 12, 1920, the Board returned to the presidents their previously submitted budgets with the notation that the schools must retrench, cutting out all but absolutely necessary expenditures. The budgets then would be significantly reduced by the time they were to be presented to the legislature in hopes that the legislators would recognize the austere nature of the

[142] Minnesota, Legislative Manual (1921), pp. 179, 181, 183.
[143] Bemidji Weekly Pioneer, January 13, 1921, p. January 20, 1921, p. 1.
[144] Historical Statistics of the United States. p. 116; U. S. Bureau of the Census Statistics Abstract of the United States, 1965, p. 13.
[145] Editorial in the Bemidji Weekly Pioneer, February 3, 1921, p. 4.

requests and approve them as submitted. The Board granted to Bemidji Normal, however, permission to submit its requests without retrenchment since, in the Board's judgment, Bemidji had not received a sufficient appropriation after actual operations had begun in 1919. To cut Bemidji's budget after only two years of operation would have had the effect of nearly stifling the school's program before it got started, and the Board acted accordingly and, to Bemidji partisans, wisely. Bemidji's recommended appropriation for maintenance was set at $72,700 and $77,300 for the two fiscal years 1922-23. Moreover, the Board approved a $75,000 request for an addition to the dormitory at Bemidji.

Minnesota State College Board (seated) and State College Presidents (1935)
"That is a matter exclusively for the Board to determine."

At the next Board meeting held less than two weeks later, October 23, 1920, President Ell Torrance resigned from the Board. Reluctantly, the Board moved on without him, realizing that asking him to continue despite his age (76) would be asking too much from the august gentleman who had served on the Board for 18 consecutive years, the last 12 as president. Into the position of president moved Edwin J. Jones of Morris, who, though an able man, did not have the veneration and experience that Judge Torrance had been able to acquire in his long tenure. Bemidji Normal thus suffered a loss, for the judge had always expressed a friendly attitude towards the little normal school in northern Minnesota.

Still it seemed doubtful that Torrance or anyone else could have insured that Bemidji's financial requests would be approved by the 1921 legislature. The realities of the situation dictated otherwise, and gradually the Bemidji supporters at home, in the legislature, and on the Board saw the futility of struggling for any large appropriations. Instead the Board led a drive to update the state statutes which had an important bearing on the normal schools.[146]

The normal school presidents brought three proposals to the Board meeting on January 25, 1921. In a suggestion that aroused considerable controversy, the presidents recommended that the Board abolish the students' pledge to teach in Minnesota in order to get free tuition at the normal schools. This oath, which apparently many regarded as a rather odious device, had provided a form of insurance against students obtaining a free education when that education would not be used in Minnesota's classrooms. The oath read:

"I declare that I will faithfully attend the State Normal School for the purpose of fitting myself to teach, and that I will, upon ceasing to be a student of the school, teach in the public schools of Minnesota for two years unless excused or time extended by the president of the school; in lieu of the fulfillment of this pledge by so teaching and as compensation for the privileges of the school, I will pay cash tuition at the rate of ten dollars per term. I will report annually to the school until fulfillment of this pledge."[147]

The presidents opposed this requirement; they had asked the Board on several occasions to recommend eliminating it. The Board had hesitated to act because of frequent criticism from sources unfriendly to the normal schools alleging that many graduates did not or would not teach in Minnesota without the oath. The presidents, however, had found enforcement difficult. If a graduate married or for any other reason failed to secure a teaching position in the state, an obligation to pay existed. To collect the back tuition was not easy, and the attorney general's office had not been especially interested in bringing a considerable number of suits for the collection of small sums.[148]

From all this came the Board's decision to approve a milder version of the oath: "I declare it to be my intention to teach in the public schools of the State of Minnesota for not less than two years after leaving the State Normal School."[149] Students who would not sign the pledge, and apparently they were rare, could continue taking courses as in the past at the rate of ten dollars per term. While the new oath was not a complete success in the eyes of the normal school presidents, at least a modification had been achieved.

The second suggestion of the presidents concerned the authorization of the Board to seek legislation which would expand the normal school curriculum to four years and allow the conferring of the degree of Bachelor of Education, or Bachelor

[146] Ibid., April 7, 1921, p. 6.
[147] Adopted and printed in the Minutes of the Normal School Board, June 2, 1913.
[148] Dudley S. Brainard, History of St. Cloud State Teachers College (St. Cloud, Minnesota: St. Cloud State Teachers College, 1953), p. 48. This small publication traces quite carefully the shifting policies of the Board throughout the Board's long history.
[149] Minutes of the Normal School Board, January 25, 1921.

of Science in Education, on four-year graduates. Four-year graduates who followed a prescribed curriculum would then be allowed to teach in any elementary or secondary school in the state. This proposed move from a two-year normal school to a four-year teachers college, whether or not it was a mistake, was part of a trend in higher education then going on throughout the country.[150]

That the private colleges in Minnesota would be opposed to this proposition was understandable. When such an expansion of the normal schools had been proposed just before World War I, opposition had come from the liberal arts colleges and the university, since they provided the high school teachers for the state. While it may have been instinctive for private liberal arts colleges to protect their programs and graduates, they seemingly failed to realize that the number of high school students was growing, and that the number of towns which could support a high school was growing, and that other sources of high school teachers would be needed.[151]

The major argument that the liberal arts colleges and the university used was similar to that used in the middle of the nineteenth century when normal schools were beginning to be established, that is, that the existing schools would adequately provide enough school teachers. Moreover, though not openly stated, it was implicit in the argument of the liberal arts colleges that any preparation outside of their own kind was *ipso facto* inferior.

Opposition, however, did not come from all the educators connected with the liberal arts colleges or the university, for a great number recognized the future need for more secondary teachers and favored the proposal even though it meant a possible reduction of their own prestige as well as a loss of students who would be drawn off to the new teachers colleges. In any event, the Board approved the proposal to make the normal schools four-year colleges and named a committee to prepare legislation to give effect to their recommendation.[152]

The third proposal of the presidents asked to change the names of the "normal schools" to "teachers colleges." On the surface this seemed a rather mild proposal and an inevitable consequence of the four-year curriculum, and its adoption would be in keeping with some of the other states in the nation.[153] Yet semantics entered in as the term "normal school" had, in some circles, connotations of derogation at worst and at best was certainly inferior to the term "teachers college."

---

[150] Lindley J. Stiles et al., Teacher Education In the United States (New York: The Ronald Press Company, 1960), pp. 97, 98. Normal schools were at the peak of their numerical strength around 1900, with two hundred ten institutions in 1890 and two hundred fifty-eight in 1910. Twenty years later, one hundred ninety-six normal schools were still in operation, and the number declined rapidly thereafter as four-year teachers colleges developed. By 1910 there were eleven teachers colleges, and by 1930 there were one hundred forty. Then began the trend towards state teachers colleges becoming simply state colleges which offered B.A. as well as B.S. degrees.

[151] Ellwood P. Cubberly, Public Education in the United States (Boston: Houghton Mifflin Company, 1947), p. 627, gives the growing number of pupils per thousand in public high schools nationally; for Minnesota, see John E. Dobbin, Ruth E. Eckert, T. J. Berning, eds., "Trends and Problems in Minnesota's Public Schools." Higher Education In Minnesota, Minnesota Commission on Higher Education, 1947-1949 (Minneapolis: University of Minnesota, 1950), p. 36 and Table 6.

[152] Minutes of the Normal School Board, January 25, 1921.

[153] Iowa, for example, had changed the name of its one state teacher-training institution at Cedar Falls to teachers college in 1909; see footnote 10 for a brief discussion of this trend.

This alleged inferior status was a rather standard interpretation of why the liberal arts colleges had regularly attempted to keep the term "normal school" in vogue for those schools other than themselves.[154] The Board adopted this third proposal, too, on January 25, 1921, the resolution reading:

"Resolved, that this Board approve the recommendations of the Presidents of the State Normal Schools that the State Normal Schools and the State Normal School Board be designated hereafter as State Teachers College and State Teachers College Board respectively; and that said Board be authorized to award appropriate degrees for the completion of the four-year courses in said schools..."

All of the Board's recommendations went to the legislature with the vigorous support of James McConnell, Commissioner of the State Department of Education. All subsequently became law, the legislators offering no serious objections to the Board's proposals.[155]

Unfortunately, this could not be said of the budget struggle, the ramifications of which were to be felt by all the state schools. At the March 4, 1921, meeting of the State Normal Board—the final one using the old title—the problem of limiting the collective budget to $1.6 million faced the Board members. A committee of the Board had met with the finance committee of the Senate and the Appropriations Committee of the House. On March 4 the chairmen of the two legislative committees met with the Board and told them in effect that the Board could not expect to get more money than had been appropriated in the last biennium for maintenance, that there would be no money for the purchase of land or for additions to buildings, and, most likely, no money for faculty salary increases.

The figure of $1.6 million was far below the Board's original request of $2 million early in the session. It must also be remembered that the request had been a scaled down version of an even higher budget. Faced with the further cut, the Board had to forego its land procurement plans entirely, and reexamine its building plans. The faint hopes of a dormitory extension for Bemidji shrank to minuscule proportions.[156]

A further blow fell when Senator Leonard H. Nord, Bemidji's representative and a member of the Finance Committee, died on March 5, 1921, at a time when his voice was sorely needed. While the Normal Board had viewed Bemidji's budget as an exception, there was no evidence which indicated that the legislature would do the same.[157]

The outcome of the budget struggle, as expected, cut deeply into all departments, with the normal schools getting about two-thirds of the amount requested. The collective budget voted the normals came to $1,422,955, well below the projected figure presented to the Board in March. The legislature killed the

[154] Chris A. DeYoung, Introduction to American Public Education (New York: McGraw-Hill Book Company 1950), p. 366.
[155] Minnesota, Session Laws (1921), c. 260. It appeared that the legislators were far more concerned with the present than the future. Though the decision to allow the normal schools to become four-year, degree-granting teachers colleges would eventually cost the state much more money, this argument was not voiced effectively in 1921.
[156] Minutes of the Normal School Board, March 4, 1921; editorial in the Bemidji Weekly Pioneer, April 21, 1921, p. 6.
[157] Bemidji Weekly Pioneer, March 5, 1921, p. 1.

proposed addition to the Bemidji dormitory, and $12,000 per year was slashed from the recommended maintenance appropriation. The final figure for Bemidji read:[158]

Maintenance, including summer sessions and library
    available for the year ending June 30, 1922 ....$ 60,650
Maintenance, including summer sessions and library,
    available for the year ending June 30, 1923 ....$ 65,650
Repairs, betterments, and equipment available for
    year ending June 30, 1922 ....$ 9,000
Repairs, betterments, and equipment available for
    year ending June 30, 1923 ....$ 6,000
Maintenance available immediately...$ <u>11,000</u>
Total ....$ 152,300

    With resignation, Bemidji and the other normal schools, by then teachers colleges, curtailed their plans and hoped that the allotted sums would reach far enough to sustain their minimum programs. Moreover, there was some reason for taking heart, for the proposals regarding extra-financial matters were enacted into law. Most notably the legislature laid the basis for conferring four-year degrees. (Because it took so long to draw up an acceptable curriculum and then implement it, it was not until 1928 that Bemidji awarded a bachelor's degree.) The fact that the legislature authorized the State Normal Schools to become teachers colleges and award degrees was as propitious an action as could have been desired. Indeed, for the infant Bemidji school, the advance in three years from a pine-covered site on the shores of Lake Bemidji to a teachers college with authorization eventually to grant degrees was nothing short of tremendous. Hence, though the over-all results of the 1921 legislature were not as financially advantageous as hoped for, the term was not a failure. The school had not been cut off without funds nor lessened in its scope of activity, and the laws other than those concerning money were progressive.[159]

    The need for more money in 1921 can be seen in the actions of the State Board on March 4, 1921. Though there was no tuition charge per se for those who signed the pledge to teach in Minnesota, the Board at that meeting allowed the schools to charge a fee of three dollars for activities, e.g., concerts, ball games, and the like, and another five dollars for book rentals; the two charges together were collectively called "term fees."

    When the Board reconvened on April 26, 1921, it met for the first time as the State Teachers College Board. At this meeting, it passed several items directly related to Bemidji: It set the president's salary at $5,400 for the next school year; it formally approved summer session faculty members; it ruled that the one-year

---

[158] Minnesota, Session Laws (1921), c. 473. The 1919 allotment for Bemidji Normal had been $142,950 for the biennium.
[159] An argument can be supported that some of the older Minnesota normal schools had already moved towards the ends set forth in the new laws, and that the laws were a recognition of circumstances existing. For example, most of the schools by 1921—Bemidji excluded—had a three-year program that led to a special certificate allowing holders to teach in junior high schools in such fields as physical education, music, and drawing.

(beyond high school) elementary diploma would no longer be continued after June of 1922 (this seemed to be more of a semantic change, for while the diploma was discontinued, the one-year curriculum continued as a course of study for the preparation of rural teachers leading to a certificate rather than a diploma). The Board expressed—again—its marked disapproval of independent action on the part of the presidents in connection with the budget and the presentation of the same to the legislative committees. It authorized the colleges to charge a tuition fee of not more than $25 per person per term for those enrolled in the three-year program who did not sign the pledge to teach in Minnesota. Lastly, the Board adopted a new type of two-year diploma that the presidents had recommended.

The year 1922 proved to be a very difficult one for the Board and for all of the new Colleges. Vexatious financial problems compounded by costly fires early in the year at Mankato and late in the year at Winona required the Board to meet in extra sessions to ameliorate the situation. Prior to the second fire, at its August 8 meeting, the Board passed a motion to include in the proposed legislative budget for Bemidji $113,000 for a wing to the main building for an elementary school, $90,000 for a dormitory wing, and $50,000 for a heating plant. But the second fire forced a drastic alteration in the legislative requests. By the time the 1923 session of the legislature met, little hope remained for any major appropriations for Bemidji.[160] Yet the Board did ask for a dormitory extension for Bemidji Teachers College.

The legislative strength of Bemidji had diminished for the 1923 session due to the loss of several friendly legislators. In the sixty-second district, David Hurlbut of International Falls replaced F. J. McPartlin as representative from Koochiching County, and W. T. Noonan of Baudette replaced A. Rako as representative from Beltrami County.[161] McPartlin, a staunch backer of the College while a house member, chose to run for the vacated seat of the late Senator Leonard Nord and lost the election. In the primary election, McPartlin placed second in a field of three candidates. The other two contenders were Harry A. Bridgeman and Absie P. Ritchie, both of Bemidji, and though the Bemidji papers boomed Ritchie for the position, he placed third behind McPartlin. In the general election, Bridgeman won handily. The new senator retained his predecessor's seat on the Finance Committee, but being a first-year man, he could not speak with the authority of former Senator Nord.[162]

As mentioned, David Hurlbut, city attorney of International Falls, filled the vacated seat of McPartlin. He failed to obtain a committee membership on the Appropriations Committee which McPartlin had held, a setback for the College. Lastly, Alfred L. Thwing, a newcomer to politics, replaced P. H. McGarry of

[160] Editorial in the Bemidji Sentinel, December 29, 1922, p. 4.
[161] Minnesota, Legislative Manual (1923), pp. 147, 681. Rako, who had fought successfully for the dormitory appropriation in 1919, did not seek reelection in 1922. Noonan, his replacement, had been the columnist writing the legislative news for the Bemidji newspapers during the 1919 and the 1921 sessions; his style of writing was excessively breezy though colorful.
[162] Bemidji Sentinel, June 30, 1922, p. 1.

Walker, and thereby the College lost another former supporter who had four previous terms in the Senate and two in the House. All in all the legislative representation from the Bemidji area lost a wealth of experience along with important committee assignments. The closing hours of the session proved how costly those losses would be.

Problems of growing magnitude faced the 1923 legislature as only spotty gains could be noted in the state economy. Certainly the building picture was no brighter than in 1921. The cost of materials increased 11.3 points on the wholesale price index between 1921 and 1923, while the wholesale price of farm products increased only three points during the same period, to 91.6 (1926 equals 100). Concerned citizens again led a drive to hold down spending by the state.[163] And on the local level, in Bemidji, a rather typical example of a town struggling against higher taxes on all levels, meetings were held and committees formed, all pointed at reducing the tax bill.[164]

As if a less experienced group of legislators and an unfavorable economic situation were not enough of a handicap, the destructive fires on the campuses of Mankato and Winona Colleges added more gloom to the hopes of a dormitory appropriation for Bemidji. The first fire in February, 1922, damaged the main building and library at Mankato severely, the loss amounting to well over $100,000. Even after renovations were made, the public examiner's reports showed a net loss in the value of the buildings at Mankato between June 30, 1921, and June 30, 1923, to be $70,900. Insurance did not cover the costs of the fire; consequently, the state bore the full impact of the loss.[165] The second catastrophe occurred at Winona on December 3, 1922, with the loss estimated at $500,000. This figure was borne out by the public examiners reports which showed that the decline in the value of the Winona buildings after June 30, 1923, was $254,635. The remainder of the loss consisted of equipment, books, and personal effects. The destruction, not being covered by commercial insurance, was paid out of a state insurance fund, which meant out of the general revenue.[166]

The College Board met within a week of the Winona fire and voted to include a request for appropriations of $525,000 for Mankato and $750,000 for Winona in their budget to replace damaged or destroyed buildings. This resulted in the drastic cutting or complete elimination of other proposed building projects. Yet the Board had little choice, for the school at Winona, the oldest in the state (1860), had to be rebuilt, and the main building at Mankato had to be repaired. So into the hopper of the legislature went a bill which authorized the issuing of certificates of indebtedness in the sum of $1.3 million for rebuilding purposes at Mankato and

---

[163] Historical Statistics of the United States, p. 116; editorials in Bemidji Weekly Pioneer, March 22, 1923, p. 9; April 12, 1923, p. 9.
[164] News items in the Bemidji Sentinel, January 19, 1923, p. 1; February 2, 1923, p. 1.
[165] Minnesota, Twentieth Biennial Report of the Public Examiner, 1921, p. 151; Minnesota, Twenty-First Biennial Report of the Public Examiner, 1923, p. 134.
[166] Ibid., p. 129; Irwin S. Selle, ed., The Winona State Teachers College (Winona, Minnesota: By the author, 1935), p. 52. For a more recent history of Winona, see Jean Talbot, First State Normal School: Winona State College, Quarterly Bulletin of Winona State College, Series 55, No. 4, August, 1959.

Winona. The legislature reduced the amount to $900,000, and it was this figure that appeared in the 1923 Session Laws. Bemidji's projected dormitory addition, amazingly enough, was not killed until the fading hours of the session. Amid the confusion, excitement, and last-minute compromising that usually characterized the last days of the session, the Bemidji bill floundered in the house and died.[167] What was appropriated was $72,000 per year for maintenance, including summer sessions and library, and $15,000 for the two years for repairs, betterments, and equipment. In reviewing the 1923 session, Bemidji College could see only an improved chance for building appropriations in 1925, a wispy hope that would depend on no more calamitous fires, a good economy, and convincing and experienced representatives in the legislature.

The recommendations of the State Teachers College Board, of course, also had an influence on the legislative field. Though the legislature did not approve all the Board's recommendations, unless a College's proposal was endorsed by the Board nothing came of it. Bemidji had marked success in getting its requests put into Board recommendations; the rub lay in getting them transformed into laws.

Other facets of legislative reality also played an important role in determining legislation. For example, pressure groups representing liberal arts colleges and the university exerted efforts from session to session in an attempt to mold legislation. The conclusion that appears most plausible regarding these groups was that their desire to see the youth of the state educated transcended the desire to protect any special school.[168]

While all of the above factors had tangential bearing, it was the poor financial straits of the state that caused the most difficult problems which Bemidji and the other State Colleges experienced in the first years after 1920. In this period the state seemed torn between what appeared to be a prosperous industrial group and a decidedly depressed agricultural community. But compared to the national industrial outlook, Minnesota lagged in manufacturing, too. In 1919, Minnesota produced 2.03 percent of all manufactured goods in the nation; in 1923, this figure went down to 1.65 percent. Essentially neither industry nor agriculture was economically healthy, and the spending of the state legislature reflected it. These facts and conditions collectively accounted for the demands to hold down state spending. President Deputy and his supporters would have to wait until 1925 before seeing any further building appropriations.[169]

As indicated, the State Teachers College Board sympathized with the needs of Bemidji. In the budget requests of the Board, adopted October 14, 1924,

---

[167] Senator Harry Bridgeman, despite being new, waged a commendable battle and the senate approved the appropriation. Recognition of Senator Bridgeman's many years of service in behalf of Bemidji College occurred in 1964 with the naming of a new six hundred thirty thousand dollar industry and arts building after him. Bridgeman was senator from 1922-1950.

[168] Though liberal arts colleges received no state money directly, many graduates of them—some on the boards of directors of the colleges--were members of the legislature, and some tried hard to protect their alma maters. Their role is discussed in Archie C. Clark, "The Status, Policies, and Objectives of Minnesota State Teachers Colleges" (unpublished Doctor's dissertation, University of California, Los Angeles, 1941), p. 80.

[169] Minnesota, Economic Analysis of the State of Minnesota, Report to the Minnesota Resources Commission by the J. G. White Engineering Corporation, 194S, vol. II, p. 171. The index of real income of farmers by 1921, on the basis of one hundred for 1910-1914, was down to seventy-five, and never passed the high point of ninety-three in June, 1928.

three of the seven items that Deputy had called his "greatest needs" were sent to the legislature; $120,000 for an extension to the main building for an elementary school, $100,000 for a dormitory extension, and $65,000 for a heating and power plant building.

Economically, the times were a little better when the forty-fourth legislature began in 1925. The index for all farm products had gone up to 109 compared to 91.6 in the previous session; the prices on all commodities rose to 103.5 compared to 100.6 in 1923. Nationally, the country had moved into the period of what historians call the "seven fat years" before those seven lean years of the Depression. But again in the jargon fitted to those times, agriculture was one of the "sick industries" of the 1920s, and Minnesota was then primarily an agricultural state.[170] To illustrate, in 1919 the farm crops of Minnesota were worth $506 million and in 1929 only $310 million; in that same period the amount of land on which crops were grown increased by nearly 16 percent. It seemed understandable that Republican Governor Theodore Christianson called for careful fiscal responsibility in his message to the 1925 legislature. Christianson, along with an all-Republican slate of state officials, began the first of three consecutive terms in 1925. As to representation from the Bemidji area, only Bridgeman in the Senate and Hurlbut in the House were experienced representatives. The Pioneer interpreted the governor's message this way: "Governor Christianson will become Minnesota's economy executive if he has his way." All in all, Bemidji State Teachers College expected no largesse from the 1925 legislature.[171]

Thus, in summary, when the session ended, the Pioneer wrote with honesty and surprise, "Considering the state of the legislature . . . the institution fared well under the circumstances." [172] Bemidji College was the institution that fared well, receiving $105,000 for construction of the elementary school wing to the main building, and $65,000 for the heating and power plant building.[173] The Pioneer went on to speak hopefully of even larger building appropriations for the local college in the following legislatures, not realizing, as was indeed impossible then, that 1925 would be the only year between 1919 and 1937 when the state would allocate any money for buildings for Bemidji Teachers College. After 1925, it was back to receiving only maintenance funds, and in the 1930s, even these funds proved difficult to obtain.

Enrollments, Students, and Student Life

Unable to build any more buildings until after 1925, school officials had

---

[170] Theodore C. Blegen, Building Minnesota (Boston: D. C Heath, 1938), p. 389. Farm lands in Minnesota increased from 18.4 million acres in 1900 to 30.9 million by 1930. By 1936, Minnesota ranked first among states in production of butter, rye, barley, and flaxseed; second in corn, and third in oats.
[171] Bemidji Daily Pioneer, January 7, 1925, p. 1. Price index statistics taken from Historical Statistics of the United States, p. 116. Information on governor taken from Minnesota Legislative Manual (1925), pp. 691, 735.
[172] April 27, 1925, p. 1.
[173] Minnesota, Session Laws (1925), c. 424. Bemidji's appropriations and receipts for maintenance and equipment totaled by June 30, 1925, $84,784.26. Minnesota, Financial Statement of the State Board of Education and Public School Statistics, 1925-1926, Bulletin No. 4, p. 190.

to learn to get along with the facilities available and make its development around them. Though very new and not very big, Bemidji attempted to continue its function of serving the citizens of northern Minnesota. That function, as Deputy always saw it, was to provide facilities for young people to learn to become school teachers. The students who attended came predominantly from the region close to Bemidji; most came from the rural communities and farms.[174] Ninety-seven students enrolled at Bemidji in September, 1920, and this was the same number when the school closed its regular year June 3, 1921. In the fall, the Board and all the College presidents had a meeting at Bemidji and several members of both groups gave short talks to the Bemidji student body at one of the regular assembly programs which were mandatory for students to attend. The newspaper account of the talks inadvertently suggested the general tenor of the school, the paper indicating that before the men spoke "the regular program of hymns and responsive readings was given."[175]

The student body was composed of three groups or classes which at that time were called the junior class (first year beyond high school), the senior class (second year beyond high school), and the five-year class (those who had not graduated from high school). In the 1920-1921 school year, at its highest enrollment point, there were 68 students in the five-year course, 46 juniors, and 23 seniors.[176] In these last two groups, a large student turnover occurred each year throughout the decade. Naturally the seniors left, and a considerable number of juniors did too because one could get a certificate to teach in rural schools with one year of training beyond high school and many took advantage of the opportunity.

Faculty members organized extra curricular activities during the 1920-1921 school year. Misses Eunice Asbury and Edith Morse formed two literary clubs, the Bi Nor Sku and the Athenian, with the student body divided into two groups. Membership was mandatory. Miss Morse also organized the Tanki Ki Ci Camp Fire Club the same year, with membership optional. When Mrs. Dorothy Torrance MacMillan, granddaughter of Judge Torrance, became the music instructor in the spring of 1921, she organized the first girls' glee club.[177]

One of the school traditions adopted in 1920 was the school colors of green and white. Reportedly, an assembly hour had been set aside for the selection of colors, and after the initial balloting resulted in a deadlock, a student named Cyrillus Freeman arose from her seat and said, "As we sat here discussing the question, I happened to glance out the window. The sight that met my eyes was fresh green pines silhouetted against pure white snow. What could be more appropriate than green and white." On the first round of balloting, Miss Freeman's choice of

---

[174] More information on the background of the Bemidji students is given in Chapter V. A detailed analysis of the background of all the teachers college students can be found in A. C. Clark's doctoral dissertation, "The Status, Policies, and Objectives of Minnesota State Teachers Colleges," Chaps. vii, viii, i.

[175] Bemidji Daily Pioneer, September 17, 1920, p. 1.

[176] Not all of the one hundred thirty-seven students were enrolled at the same time; as indicated, the most enrolled for any one quarter that year was ninety-seven.

[177] The Northern Student, Bulletin of the State Teachers College, Bemidji, Minnesota, vol. XI, No. 2, January, 1938, p. 12. The information in this Bulletin was approved by Deputy; it was published to honor Deputy upon his retirement. A men's glee club began in 1924. Not until Carl Thompson came in 1937 was there an a cappella choir.

colors had received one vote, but after her remarks, according to the report, her idea "was immediately accepted unanimously." [178]

In the fall registration of 1921, 157 students enrolled; 164 enrolled in the winter term, and 158 in the spring quarter. All in all a total of 211 different students enrolled for some portion of the school year and the number included only sixteen men. All of the state teachers colleges faced a relative dearth of males on campus. For example, Winona never had a student body with more than ten percent men until 1924, and it had been in operation since 1860.[179]

President Deputy required Bemidji students to attend twice-a week assembly programs and to go to classes on Saturdays. There were, however, no Monday classes in the 1920s. Deputy believed strongly that Sunday should be a day of rest, a rest which should include no student having to study for Monday classes.

Senior Class (1921)
"From normal school to teachers college in two years."

For the sports-minded, the most interesting extracurricular activity begun in the 1921-1922 school year was the organization of the first basketball team by Fremont Wirth, who aside from Deputy was the only male member of a faculty of

---

[178] Ibid., p. 14. For the record, the assembly program was held in the month of February, but in view of the climate, the same scene described by Miss Preeman could have been viewed three months on either side of the date given. In some of the publications, Miss Freeman's first name was listed as Phyllis rather than Cyrillus
[179] Erwin S. Sells, ed., The Winona State Teachers College, p. 52

fifteen. On the eve of the school's first game, December 16, 1921, the Pioneer wrote that Coach Wirth "had developed a formidable squad and indications are that the school will stand on its own against any school in this section of the state." Bemidji won the game, fifty-one to eleven, over Kelliher High School because, according

"Seventeen cents . . . for basketball season expenses."

to the Pioneer the next day, "They had the advantage of weight and previous basketball experience." (Coach Wirth refereed the second game at Kelliher that evening between two local teams, and the score of that game, six to two, was more typical of the period.) Bemidji played 18 games that first season, mostly against area high schools. However, they traveled as far as St. Cloud for a game against the Teachers College, and also to the Iron Range where they played Hibbing and Virginia Junior Colleges. Home games were played in the armory, a distance of about a mile from the school, and the slate included as one opponent the "Bemidji Naval Militia."[180] (The Fifth Minnesota Naval Militia was the first civilian American unit to be called into active duty at the beginning of World War I.)

Beginning with the fall session of 1922, Bemidji printed the first of its annual or biennial catalogs or bulletins, as they were sometimes called. This first 43 page catalog gave the essential information found in most college catalogs today: faculty names, costs, course descriptions, student organizations, and the like. It also included the names of every student registered, hometown included, beginning with the first 1919 summer school. The catalog separated the faculty into the Academic and College Department, and the Elementary School Department,

---

[180] After Wirth left Bemidji in 1924, his first college teaching job, he received his Ph.D. degree in history the next year from the University of Chicago, and then began to teach history at George Peabody College, a position he held until his retirement in 1955. While there he wrote several highly successful textbooks used in junior and senior high school American history classes. He died in 1960, at age seventy. Mississippi Valley Historical Review, XLVII (December, 1960), p. 561. E. W. Beck succeeded Mr. Wirth as coach until 1926.

the former having twelve members and the latter six. The publication stipulated the grading system used, noting that percent equivalents were in general use in the state, and so along with letter grades, for transcript purposes the school would employ the following percent values: 93 percent for A; 87 for B; 82 for C; 77 for D. Along with the explanation came the vague warning: "It is expected that a student shall have at least as many grades above D as D's before being recommended for a certificate or before receiving a diploma from the College."[181]

The oldest record-book that the Bemidji State College Registrar's Office has is a little black book labeled only "Journal." The carefully scrolled handwriting inside it began with the fall registration of 1922 and indicated that on September 16, 1922, 187 students paid a student activity fee of three dollars each. The rest of the 201 students that fall—all but 12 were women—came straggling in later, the last entry showing three registrations on October 13. Apparently all the students signed

Skiing down the hill behind Deputy Hall
"The girl who gives all her time to work is not an ideal student."

the pledge to teach in Minnesota, as no indication was given of any student paying any more than the activity fee (fees from 202 students were collected but one student's check bounced). By the end of the quarter, November 29, the student activity fund had amassed $642.52, all safely deposited at the local Farmers State Bank. The first activity expenditure in the fall of 1922 had been $8.40 for an all-

---

[181] First Annual Catalog, State Teachers College, Bemidji, Minnesota, 1922, p. 13. The practice of listing the names of the most recently enrolled students in the college catalogs continued through the 1939-1941 publication, and then it was dropped. Enrollment was lowest during the years of World War II; in one summer session, only thirteen students were enrolled. Though it is difficult to document, contemporaries of Deputy who worked with him maintained in interviews that the quality of academic work done in classes was at a high level.

school party on September 20, and then five days later, an all-school picnic costing $19.90.

The College Lyceum Program, open to the public, began in 1922 with Miss Mabell Bonsall of the faculty as chairman. The program offerings that year included three lectures and two musical groups, for all of which the sum of $1,475 was paid out of student activity money.[182]

The enrollment continued to grow steadily those first years of the 1920s, and the school seemed to be progressing well towards meeting the definition of a college. In the fall of 1923, the enrollment figure came up to 223, with a then record male population of 25 on campus. The student-faculty ratio was a highly desirable 14 to one. Despite the men students enrolled, the college catalogs couched their terminology as though aimed only at the females. For example, in the 1923 catalog under the section called Student Welfare, it said: "The girl who gives all of her time to work and none to play is not an ideal student." It should be noted quickly, however, that Deputy's definition of play was most austere; only reluctantly did he allow dancing on campus even if properly chaperoned, but he himself would not participate.[183]

In the social calendar listings for the school year 1923-1924, the College promoted and featured the lecture-music series in connection with the Lyceum programs. The varied fare included a lecture by Arctic explorer Vilhjalmur Stefansson. Throughout the decade, the published College social calendar always included mention of a dinner at the home of President and Mrs. Deputy for fall and winter quarter graduates, and a reception at their home for the entire student body and faculty held near the end of the spring term.

Student organizations for 1923 included the Musical Art Club, which was actually a community organization outside of the College to which students could belong; a girls' glee club; two literary societies—the aforementioned Athenian and the second one by then called the Laurean; Camp Fire Girls, connected with the physical education classes; the first student government association; and various athletic groups for both sexes, although the only interschool competition was in boys' basketball. One last organization connected with the College was the Parent Teachers Association, in connection with the College elementary school which by then, 1923-1924, had 205 children in grades kindergarten through eight inclusive.

The registrar's book showed that 223 enrolled for the fall term in 1924, and that 24 dropped out before the term ended. In the winter quarter, 244 started and 31 dropped; and lastly, in the spring term, 31 more students were added to make a total of 244 at the end of the school year. Rather curiously, the registrar's book indicated that 25 "Mid-Spring" students enrolled—rural teachers who had finished their

[182] "Journal," (unpublished record of student enrollments at Bemidji State Teachers College from 1922-1939, on file at the Registrar's Office, Bemidji State College), p. 7. Along with enrollment figures, this book also recorded disbursements paid out of student activity fees. No item was too small to dismiss as miscellaneous. For example it duly recorded that $1.49 was paid to Mary Deputy, as chairman of an indoor track meet; and that seventeen cents went to Fremont Wirth for "basketball season expenses."

[183] According to a faculty member who taught under Deputy, Deputy put up with dancing on campus to keep the students from frequenting "those awful gas houses," as Deputy reportedly called the filling stations near the college, and also he did not like to have students associating with "those rowdies downtown."

school year and took double sessions of classes on Saturdays—but this number was not included in the official enrollment for the spring quarter. Of the 244 students in the 1924-1925 year, 30 were boys. From this number a men's glee club was organized, and according to the catalog, "any young man having reasonable ability and interest is eligible to the club, which meets twice a week for the study of part songs." In athletics, the school became a member of the Minnesota Junior and Teachers College Conference (The Little Ten Conference); to basketball the school added men's track in the spring of 1925 as an intervarsity sport.[184]

BSTC Band (1920s)
"Any young man having reasonable ability is eligible."

According to the College catalog for the 1924-1925 school year, the school adopted the 3.0 honor point system (A, three points, B, two points, etc.) and a stiffer grade point average for graduation. All students had to have at least as many honor points as credits—an average of C—before they could graduate. Another rule required that a minimum of one year of resident work be required of every candidate for graduation with a two-year diploma. Board officials would not allow newly enrolled students to get their diplomas without spending at least one year on campus. Though not all were offered, the catalog listed 77 different courses and course descriptions; of these, education had the most courses with 16.

Throughout the decade the College had the perennial problem of finding student housing. The only dormitory, Sanford Hall, housed about 50 girls, although

---

[184] The Northern Student, Bulletin of the State Teachers College, Bemidji, Minnesota, Vol. XI, No. 2, January, 1938, p. 12; Catalog, State Teachers College, Bemidji, Minnesota, 192S-1927, p. 17. Basketball games were played in Bemidji high school beginning in 1922. The Little Ten went defunct and in 1931 all six teachers colleges joined The Northern Teachers College Athletic Conference.

double that number could eat there in the basement cafeteria. Living rates at the dormitory were uniform; board and room were furnished for six dollars a week. Those living elsewhere--at costs of rent varying from one and a half dollars to six dollars a week— could take their meals at Sanford Hall for four and a half dollars a week. Each year Deputy was required to ask Bemidji residents to furnish lodging for College students, and somehow the students were accommodated.

Scene from the Play "Ice Bound" (1932)
"The student should make every effort to eliminate . . . foreign accents."

That the crowded conditions that Deputy complained about were real was indicated in the State College Board authorization of March 26, 1925. The Board allowed Bemidji "to rent for the spring term additional rooms in a private dwelling located one-half block from the college building, at a rental of twelve dollars per month, to be used to provide additional recitation rooms necessary because of lack of capacity in the main building."

Total enrollment reached a new high in the fall term of 1926. The figure totaled 254, and a Saturday extension class added twelve more. The College charged eight dollars a term from each student, which entitled the student to "the use of all textbooks and of the library; admission to lectures, concerts, entertainments, and other functions of the College; and tickets to contests in which the college teams compete," according to the college catalog that year. Excluding these "term fees," as they were called, tuition was free to students who signed the declaration to teach in Minnesota two years; the rest were to pay $20 tuition a term in 1926. There is no indication, however, noted in the registrar's book of anyone paying anything but the term fees in the entire decade.

The College had organized several new student clubs by the 1926-1927 year. These included a Sketch Club, which met one hour a week; the Kindergarten-Primary Club, for students who planned to teach in those grades; the Century Club, an organization for the furthering of outdoor activities; the Little Theater Club, a group interested in drama; the Women's Athletic Association; and the Nautilus Club, a somewhat deceptive title as the purpose of the organization was to "enable the members to be discriminating in their reading, and to develop an appreciation of literature."[185]

In the fall of 1926, R. E. Mendenhall organized the College's first football team. Considering that there were only 26 boys enrolled, this was no small accomplishment. The school played four games that fall, one each against high schools at Deer River and Thief River Falls, and two with Cass Lake High School (Bemidji won one, lost two, and tied one). After their first game and first loss to Cass Lake, 33 to 0, the local newspaper felt that "the Peds," as the town papers nicknamed the athletic teams, had done very well considering the male personnel available: "Barely enough have turned out to form one team, and Coach Mendenhall was forced to go through scrimmage work with the local high school eleven, so as to have the practice."[186] The second meeting against Cass Lake, October 27, 1926, found the Peds winning their first game 13 to 0, and it was the first football game played on the College field by the lake near Diamond Point Park.

The 1927 fall quarter enrollment dropped to 207, 36 of them men, from the 1926 high of 254. The enrollment declined, as usual, during the year so that by the end of the school year, only 194 were on the registrar's list. In the breakdown of classes, the registrar's figures indicated that there were 99 in the freshman or, as it was then called, the first-year class; 139 in the second-year class; five in the third-year class (i.e., college juniors enrolled in the new four-year curriculum); and one member of the fourth-year class. There were also seven in what was called the fifth-year course, a course designed for non-high school graduates leading to a two-year diploma. Although newly enrolled students had to be high school graduates by the fall of 1927, those who previously had been enrolled were permitted to complete the five-year programs under which they had started.[187]

As the above figures suggest, the march to become a viable four-year college was very slow. Despite the ballyhoo made over the adoption of the four-year curriculum for the teachers colleges, there was at first little attraction for students to obtain a bachelors degree. There seemed, however, to be little embarrassment suffered by school officials in the late 1920s in pretending it was a four-year college when it was hardly that. The attitude and remarks attributed to Deputy regarding this reflect more of a philosophical resignation on his part rather than any embarrassment. In effect he said to keep on going as before, do as well as possible with the popular two-year program, and gradually the four-year program

---

[185] Ibid., p. 13.
[186] Bemidji Weekly Pioneer, October 14, 1926, p. 9. Athletics very much interested Deputy, who often went out to watch practice. It is he who gave the current nickname of "Beavers" to the college athletic teams. Reportedly, at a practice in 1932 he called one of the football squads into a huddle and christened them Beavers as this animal symbolizes hard work and endurance.
[187] The last section in this chapter gives a more complete discussion of the changing curriculums in the 1920s in the state colleges. Phasing out the five-year program brought an end to ex-eighth graders on campus who were barely teenagers in years.

would appeal to more students. (Even in the late 1920s, Deputy would remind his staff that the College "was still in its swaddling clothes.")

Only a few changes occurred on campus in the 1927-1928 year in student organizations. The Athenian and Laurean literary societies merged into the Nautilus Club with Miss Ruth Brune as advisor, and a "B" average was made a requirement for membership. The school added a publications committee, and whether there was a cause and effect relationship, the College published the first formal issue of the Northern Student. This first issue had in its contents the announcements for the 1928 summer session, the calendar for the 1928-1929 school year, and four articles on current educational topics written by members of the faculty. The second issue was devoted entirely to news about and articles by the elementary school pupils enrolled in the Observation School. In the years following these first publications, the College used the name Northern Student on all of its printed materials whether they were newspapers, bulletins, or articles written by faculty members.[188]

Bemidji Teachers College held its first Homecoming on October 6, 1927. The event was held at the same time as an area teachers convention in Bemidji so a considerable number of alumni were present. Rather strangely, President Deputy was not in town that weekend. The Northern Student portrayed vividly a description of a portion of the day:

"At twelve o'clock the day of the game, the college students including the members of the football squad assembled in front of the high school building, some afoot, others in decorated cars, and led by a pep band, paraded through the downtown district. Then came the big game. The whistle blew at three o'clock and the game was on. In a short time one thousand fans present saw the seasoned St. Cloud team carry the ball over our goal line...."[189]

At an alumni association meeting the morning of the game, it was voted to telegraph the score of the Homecoming game that afternoon to President Deputy who was visiting in the East. In view of the 26 to 6 loss, one wonders if it was carried out. However, in this their second season, the football team won five and lost three games, with scores ranging from a 44 to 0 win over Park Rapids High School to a 69 to 0 loss to Hibbing Junior College.

The Northern Student is an invaluable source of information on Bemidji College, especially after it began publication regularly in 1929. Though much of the information in it might be labeled historical trivia, nevertheless a great deal of what went on at the College regarding enrollments, students, and student life was recorded in these publications.

What happened to students after graduation from Bemidji was noted in the June, 1928, Northern Student. From 1919 to 1928, the number of graduates totaled

---

[188] President Deputy gave the name to these publications. According to a historical sketch of the college written in 1938 and appearing in one of these Northern Students, Deputy had remembered his college newspaper, the Indiana Student, and he substituted Northern for Indiana for the new title. Vol. XI, No. 2, January, 1938, p. 14. Former faculty member Ruth Brune Mangelsdorf, who was the editor of this particular bulletin, indicated in an interview how hard she and Deputy had worked together on it both for inclusion of important facts and the accuracy of them. However, other documentation does not always confirm the information given in this aforementioned bulletin which was published to honor Deputy upon his retirement.
[189] Ibid Vol. I, No. 4, June, 1928, p. 26.

385, and 293 of them were teaching at the time; 92 were not teaching. Of the 92 not teaching, 54 were "married and homemakers"; ten were attending school; four were doing office work; three worked in hospitals; three clerked in stores; 11 were working at home; two were unable to teach because of ill health; and of five there was no record.

Commissioner of Education James McConnell offered more statistics on all Minnesota Teachers College students which he presented to the Board and which were included in the Board Minutes of August 17, 1928. His figures dealt with enrollment and graduation statistics over a period of three years, 1925-1928. With the exception of summer school enrollments, Bemidji was bested in numbers by her sister colleges in this period. Still new, still remote—in a sparsely populated area without good roads to provide easy access—it could not catch up very fast with the rest. Limited essentially to just two buildings that were already overcrowded with the small enrollment it did have, the enrollment peaked in 1926 and then started downward. All the State College enrollments show this downward trend, and the College Board interpreted it largely as the workings of supply and demand in the elementary teacher market. Moreover, the reason that more were not enrolled in the four-year program seemed clear: Teachers with only two years of training could obtain teaching certificates and secure jobs at salaries almost as high as those paid to four-year graduates. Because neither economic nor social rewards were that much greater, there was little external motivation to go to college an extra two years.[190] Indeed, it appeared that many students would not have entered the teaching field at all if more than two years of training had been required. And certainly the two-year enrollment drained away many students who might possibly have entered the four-year curriculum. All in all, Bemidji and the others felt declining enrollments in the late 1920s that did not pick up significantly again—and somewhat ironically—until the earliest years of the Depression.[191]

In 1928, Bemidji's enrollment dropped below the 200 mark for the first time since 1921; 194 students, 29 of them men, signed up for school that fall. By the next spring the number dipped to 184. The continued relative disinterest in working for a degree might be seen in that only 14 members of what would be called juniors and seniors made up the 194. But interestingly enough, of these 14, ten were men. Slowly, very slowly, more males began to move into teaching positions in elementary schools, and many had hopes of moving into the position of principals.

In the 1928-1929 school year, the clubs and organizations on campus remained the same. In women's athletics, the College added basketball and track to soccer, volleyball, and baseball —all intramural—and in the summer, Red Cross awards were presented in swimming for the first time. In connection with the

[190] The Bulletin, Bulletin of the State Teachers College, Moorhead, Minnesota, Series 46, No. 2, August, 1950, p. 19. The report indicated that even as late as 1948, the average salary obtained by Moorhead two-year graduates was $225.44 per month for nine months, while that obtained by the few elementary degree graduates was $276.94. In that same year, only 10.9 percent of all Minnesota teachers college students were enrolled in the four-year programs in the various colleges.
[191] Minnesota State Teachers Colleges In Transition, Bulletin of the State Teachers College, Moorhead, Minnesota, Series 42, No. 2, August, 1946, pp. 27, 28.

College, the elementary school, or the training school as it was often called then, added a ninth grade in 1928 with a total of 245 students in grades kindergarten through nine inclusive.[192]

As the College began its tenth year of operation in the fall of 1929, the enrollment figure crawled over the 200 mark again but just barely as 208 enrolled; by spring quarter the figure went down to 181. Thus it was around the figure of 200 that the enrollment seemed to settle during the regular school year in the 1920s at Bemidji State Teachers College.

Faculty and Staff

During his entire presidency of 19 years, Deputy did not have his faculty separated into either departments or divisions. Nor were any faculty members given any rank or classification under him. Regardless of the degree held, all faculty members were called "instructors," a title that apparently grated a very few who held advanced degrees. Others on the faculty supported this non-ranking. As Training School Director Telulah Robinson said when the subject of ranking came up for discussion, "Ranking is undemocratic."

The faculty had no organization of any kind to promote and work for benefits for itself; such an attempt by the faculty would have then smacked of unionization and would have been regarded by Deputy as a direct slap in the face to him.[193]

Judging from interviews with those who worked under him, President Deputy was paternalistic to both faculty and students alike. A strong Methodist, there was always the touch of the lay preacher in what he did and said, and he apparently felt honor-bound to guide the morals of those with whom he came in contact. For example, he would chastise on the spot any male faculty member who came on campus smoking. And the thought of any female smoking, faculty member or student, was abhorrent to the man.[194] Indeed, there was no smoking in any College buildings until after World War II. (Harold Hagg, who joined the Bemidji faculty in 1936, and who shared an office with A. C. Clark, recalled that even in the middle of the winter, Clark would leave his desk and go for a walk around the block so that he could smoke his pipe.)

Deputy knew personally every student and regularly helped them to work out their class schedules. He also knew of their personal and financial problems, often digging into his own pocket to help some student out. His large home two

---

[192] The Northern Student, Bulletin of the State Teachers College, Bemidji Minnesota, Vol. XI No. 2, January, 1938, p. 18. These same grades were continued until 1962 when the junior high grades were phased out. In 1950, the elementary school moved into a new building and was renamed the Laboratory School.

[193] The smallness in numbers of the faculty under Deputy (seldom more than thirty) meant very few formal faculty meetings, and no minutes of the meetings were kept. Regarding the meetings, one male faculty member under Deputy put it this way in an interview: "A couple of times a year, Deputy would call his flock together, deliver some pleasant homilies, and then dismiss the group."

[194] Reportedly, it was to Deputy's traumatic dismay when he learned of his daughter Mary smoking in the attic of their home. "He never fully recovered from the shock," said a former faculty member in discussing this. Another reported incident involved Deputy chastening a male faculty member for allowing the stem of his pipe to stick out from his vest pocket, thus permitting students to witness the hateful thing.

blocks from the campus (now 1121 Bemidji Avenue) was regularly opened to students. Mrs. Deputy, described in all interviews as "a very pleasant woman," seems best remembered for maintaining an outstanding flower garden. As one lady said, "All flower gardens in Bemidji were always compared to hers."

All faculty members were expected to be present at every school function, and if someone missed, Deputy would corner the absentee as soon as possible to inquire if the person had been ill or out of town. Apparently these were the only excuses he would allow. The subject of salaries was supposed to be taboo among the faculty, and no one was to know what anyone else received during the year

Sanford Hall Basement (1920)
"With candles on the table and linen tablecloths."

(though faculty salaries were published in the State College Board Minutes, they were not made available to faculty members). However, like now, they had a vague understanding of what everyone made. A raise in salary of $100 a year was regarded as almost excessive, and who got the raises, of course, Deputy alone decided.

The dean of women, Miss Margaret Kelly, worked very closely with Deputy to make young ladies out of the students. Though the community still had the aura of rough lumberjack days, Deputy was insistent that his staff indoctrinate the students in proper etiquette. Miss Kelly was also in charge of Sanford Hall, and at evening meals—with candles and linen table cloths—the girls, and the boys who ate their meals there, were instructed, sometimes reluctantly and painfully, in the proper social graces.[195]

In the fall of 1920, Deputy had a staff of seven women and one man, Fremont Wirth, who taught history. Physically on campus, there was one main building and one half-completed dormitory. The grounds surrounding the construction site were described as a mess. In the spring of 1921 the school spent $3,000 on improving the campus grounds. The underbrush between the buildings and the lake was cleared, a thousand yards of black dirt was leveled and seeded for lawns, and the College constructed several drives and walks along the lake shore.

When the fall term of the 1921 year began, Deputy had a faculty of 15, again with only one male counterpart, Fremont Wirth. Including Deputy, 11 held at least a bachelor's degree; only four had a master's degree, and none had a doctorate. Salaries averaged about $1,800 for nine months for the teaching faculty while Deputy received a 12-month salary of $5,400. Considering the times and what money would buy, Deputy's salary seemed substantial.[196] Faculty and students, however, had very limited library facilities to use in 1921. Authentic library records

Sanford Hall Lounge (1926)
"As a memorial to this woman . . . of matchless spirit."

began with the books accessioned that year, during which the number of volumes was estimated at 900.[197]

---

[195] Information derived from interviews with Professors Emerita Mabel Parker and Ruth Brune Mangelsdorf who both joined the Bemidji faculty in 1924. They indicated that though there was some negative reaction to the efforts of Miss Kelly to improve the students socially and culturally, all realized after graduation what good she had done for them, and alumnae eagerly sought her out at alumni gatherings for belated thank yous. Both spoke very highly of Deputy as a person, with Mrs. Mangelsdorf referring to him as "the most humble, the most unpretentious man," who yet "towered above his faculty" and was "a wonderful person."

[196] In 1920, Deputy received five thousand dollars. For sake of comparison, Thomas Kane became president of the University of North Dakota that year and received six thousand dollars. Louis G. Geiger, University of the Northern Plains: A History of the University of North Dakota, 1883-1958 (Grand Forks: The University of North Dakota Press, 1958), p. 290.

[197] The Northern Student, Bulletin of the State Teachers College, Bemidji, Minnesota, Vol. XI, No. 2, January, 1938, p. 11. The Bemidji library still has the first book accessioned on September 10, 1921: Handbook of Nature Study by Anna B. Comstock.

Deputy showed constant concern for a neat-looking campus, and a campus that would have plenty of trees, trees that are now mature. Each spring he presided over an annual "tree planting day," and apparently felt strongly enough about this to include it regularly in the calendar of events published each year in the College catalog. By the end of the 1922 school year, he could happily write in his report that driveways and walks had been laid on campus, and that athletic grounds, including tennis courts, a running track, a hockey field, and recreation grounds had been partially completed. Regarding the two buildings, he wrote, "The ground had been regraded, lawns started, and trees, shrubs, and vines planted."[198] The following

Tennis Courts by the Lake (1922)
"The underbrush was cleared and courts constructed."

year, with a $7,000 legislative allotment for repairs, betterment, and equipment, the recreation grounds were completed, including the leveling and surfacing of a football field. There was still plenty of work to be done, however, for in 1923 "the campus east of the building the area between the lake and the main building was a wilderness," according to a later description of the campus.[199]

Two more male members joined the staff in 1923 along with Deputy and Wirth: Roy Schofield, geography, and Elton W. Beck, education. Though neither held doctorates, both came in at $2,800 which was above the average salary of about

---

[198] Minnesota, Tenth Second Biennial Report, Department of Education, 1921-1922, pp. 137-138. Beginning with 1920, each graduating class had dedicated a tree or a vine on the campus; this practice continued until 1940.
[199] The Northern Student, Bulletin of the State Teachers College, Bemidji, Minnesota, Vol. XI, No. 2, January, 1938, p. 9.

$2,000. Deputy's salary jumped to $5,500 that year as he presided over a faculty that numbered 20, with six of these teaching in the elementary school.[200]

Deputy summed up the progress of his school in its first few years in his summary report to the State Department of Education which appeared in the fall of 1924. He began by giving the enrollment figures, noting that the interesting feature of the enrollments for each year to date had been the substantial increase in the number of high school graduates who were starting college (between 1921 and 1924, the number of high school graduates rose from 109 to 232). He attributed this desirable trend to three causes: first, the development of more extensive high school facilities in northern Minnesota; second, the greater emphasis placed on high school graduation as an entrance requirement; and third, the tendency of public schools to employ teachers with broader academic and professional training. Because of the greater supply of better qualified teachers and the corresponding decrease in the number of five-year students (those who had not graduated from high school), wrote Deputy, the College Board at its April 8, 1924, meeting had passed a resolution providing that only students with at least one year of high school work be admitted in the regular year, beginning September, 1924. Deputy was pleased to see the standards being raised. "Probably it will be only a short time until the five-year course should be discontinued," he concluded on that topic. (It was discontinued in 1927.)[201]

Deputy went on in his 1924 report to list what he called the "greatest needs of the college;" whether they were in order of preference he did not indicate. Provision for more classrooms and a larger library space were the first needs mentioned; after this he listed dormitory expansion, an auditorium, a gymnasium, a training school, and lastly, a separate heating and power plant building. He lamented that during the regular school year there had been 500 students—the College students and the elementary school pupils—in the one main building, and under the present conditions, it was impossible to control the ventilation and heating. He complained that the library would seat only 40 students; that there were no extra classrooms or study rooms available for either faculty or students during periods of no classes; that a large tent had to be used for three summers in a row to accommodate the numbers; that the College was compelled to depend on "uncertain arrangements made temporarily" with the renting of the armory or high school for all indoor events to which the public was invited. Alas, said Deputy essentially, will not the legislature recognize our needs and help us out? Other than the enrollment growth, the only positive remarks on the biennium just ended that Deputy made were words to the effect that at least the campus looked good, and that it had been developed to provide for "athletics and outdoor activities through tennis courts,

---

[200] With the exception of St. Cloud, all of the state college presidents received the same salary. In the history of St. Cloud College (see footnote 8), Dudley Brainard wrote briefly about the disparity, stating only that "the Board recognized his outstanding leadership by re-electing him at a salary of $6,200, which was $700 more than was paid to presidents of other teachers colleges," p. 60. Their president, J. C. Brown, left St. Cloud in 1927 to become president of DeKalb, Illinois, State Teachers College.
[201] Minnesota, Twenty-Third Biennial Report, Department of Education, 1923-1924, pp. 158-160. Though the errors may be clerical or mechanical, it might be noted that Deputy's enrollment statistics do not always agree with the Registrar's figures.

running track, soccer and football field, baseball diamond, and swimming docks."[202]

When the school began in the fall of 1924, the faculty of 25 had been upgraded so that 17 had at least a bachelor's degree and 11 held master's degrees. Fremont Wirth took a leave of absence for that school year, the leave turning out to be permanent, and Archie C. Clark, who received a beginning salary of $2,700, replaced him. Clark remained on the faculty in a variety of roles, including the presidency, until his retirement in 1964.[203]

As indicated in the section on legislative action, the legislature came through only that one time in 1925 with money for new buildings. That summer and fall, continued interest grew as to when these two structures—a wing to the main building for the elementary school, and a separate heating plant—would be started. Delays for many reasons found the final bids for both buildings put off until December 10, 1925, when contracts were let. The company of A. G. Wahl and Sons of St. Cloud received the contracts for the general construction of both buildings for $96,149. C. H. Johnston, who had designed the school's first two buildings, was again the architect. When completed, the wing to the main building contained 20,376 square feet of floor space, and almost doubled the available floor space that there had been before. Construction on both buildings began in earnest in the spring of 1926 and was completed the following summer in time for summer school. At the same time the College enlarged the library in the main building to give seating capacity for 85 readers, doubling its former capacity. (The term "main building" was used until 1959, when the Board officially named it "Manfred W. Deputy Hall.")

The 1926-1927 regular school year found several important faculty changes. The College hired its first staff member with a Ph. D. degree, Raymond E. Mendenhall, who taught history and physical education.[204] Of the remaining 25 faculty members, 11 held a master's degree and five had a bachelor's degree. Nine members, however, nearly all instructors in the elementary school, had no degree. Deputy received a salary of $5,500; the next highest paid was Miss Telulah Robinson, director of the campus elementary school, who received $3,000. Only one other staff member received at least $3,000 that year, Roy Schofield in geography. As was very common throughout the decade, the pay raises from the previous year averaged less than $100 per person, and several received no raise at all.

Not until 1929 did Bemidji and the rest of the State Colleges belong to any national accrediting agency. Until then both the Board and the presidents—as

---

[202] Ibid. After 1924, the State Department of Education did not publish the reports of the state teacher college presidents; at the same time the name of the publication was changed to Financial Statement of the State Board of Education and Public School Statistics, and the information pertaining to state colleges was limited to amounts of money appropriated and enrollment figures. Although the presidents filed quarterly reports to the Board, neither the Board office nor the State Archives have copies of these reports; however, there is an incomplete set of Deputy's reports in the Deputy papers on file in the Bemidji State College library.
[203] "I believe I held almost every job at this school except that of dean of women," Clark once remarked. For most of his tenure, Clark was chairman of the division of social studies. Clark passed away in 1966; the school named its new 1.4 million dollar library after him in formal ceremonies at commencement exercises, June 4, 1967.
[204] Mendenhall left after two years, and no one else with a doctorate was hired that decade. In 1928 Miss Elsie K. Annis joined the faculty in women's physical education and remained at Bemidji until her retirement in 1963.

separate groups and together— had often discussed the advisability of applying. After consideration, based largely on the assumption that they could meet the requirements, a motion carried at the meeting of the presidents on March 19, 1928, to approve the plan of inspection by the American Association of Teachers Colleges and recommend to the College Board that Minnesota Teachers Colleges apply for membership.[205]

The presidents appointed Deputy to bring the recommendation to the attention of the Board, and this done, the Board members discussed it off and on throughout the year. Finally, on February 6, 1929, the Board approved it with the stipulation that "if any one or more of these six colleges fail of such accreditation, all applications be withdrawn." Subsequently, the Board made application and all the State Colleges were accepted as Class A Colleges.[206]

In summary, regarding the faculty of Bemidji College in the 1920s, the staff did not experience a big turnover each year. For example, between the staff of 1926 and 1929, there were only three replacements. Deputy's paternalism did not drive faculty members away. By the end of the decade, salaries for nine-month teaching duties averaged about $2,500 for a faculty that numbered around 25 for the regular school year. One thing grew faster than the faculty in the decade, however; that was the number of faculty committees. For the 1929-1930 school year, the College catalog listed the following faculty committees: athletics, lectures and entertainment, loan fund, extracurricular activities, social affairs, scholarship and graduation, entrance requirements, student activity budget, and publications. As president, Deputy became an ex officio member on all of them. It appeared that Parkinson's Law had taken effect at Bemidji State Teachers College.

Summer Schools

In terms of enrollment, summer schools brought the most students to Bemidji in the decade of the 1920s. The total enrollments were as follows: 1920, 292; 1921, 428; 1922, 476; 1923, 531; 1924, 537; 1925, 469; 1926, 336; 1927, 340; 1928, 298, and 1929, 334.

The College held one six-week summer session each year, the session beginning about the middle of June and continuing to the end of July. Though a boon to the school, it also brought problems. Judging from the descriptions in the local newspapers and the reports of President Deputy, housing both on and off campus provided the major problem. The newspapers seemed cooperative in aiding Deputy to find rooms each summer, but, generally, once that was done and the attendance figures duly reported, the local papers forgot about the summer session

---

[205] Minutes of Presidents Meetings, Minnesota State Teachers Colleges, March 19, 1928 (in the files of the President's Office, Bemidji State College). The Teachers College presidents met irregularly several times a year, but official minutes were not kept until July 27, 1927. Prior to this, if a president missed a meeting, one of the other presidents would write him a letter telling him what had happened. At this first meeting at which minutes were taken, they authorized six one-man committees; Deputy headed the committee labeled Relationship to Public Schools of Minnesota. At their meetings they worked on such things as a uniform calendar for the school year, athletic eligibility, standards, and the like.

[206] In view of the fact that Bemidji had graduated not a half-dozen persons with a degree by that day, it seems strange that the school would be given a Class A rank. Conversely, this does not say much about the accreditation standards of the agency or of the period.

news. But Deputy could not forget it; he had to find some way to accommodate the large numbers on campus, and the means he used, if not the final answer, was to erect a large tent between the main building and the lake. Out of necessity, the College used the tent for several summers in a row. Normally the College used the tent for assembly programs of the entire student body. It was, however, sometimes used for larger classes and as a practice area for choir rehearsals.[207]

One significant characteristic of summer schools was the importance paid to visiting lecturers. In the brochures sent out announcing summer school dates and courses available, Deputy regularly inserted a paragraph emphasizing the assembly programs.[208] He seemed capable of corralling any man of note who came into the area to speak at his summer school assemblies. When Governor J. A. O. Preus came to Bemidji primarily to address the annual convention of the Minnesota Fire Department Association held in town, Deputy got him over to talk at a morning assembly program. Sometimes the lecturers would stay a week or longer and give talks every day. For example, William L. Bryan of Indiana University came for a week in the summer of 1922 and lectured twice a day—in the tent. The College invited the general public to all the lecture programs.[209]

As Deputy pointed out in his official reports to the Board, Bemidji College aimed its summer school programs at meeting the needs of the rural teachers. He believed that most of the students in the summers were interested in meeting certain certificate requirements in order to qualify for positions in rural and semi-graded schools, and the College would help to serve their needs. To substantiate this point, he listed several statistical tables in his reports, including the following:

	1920	1921	1922
Enrollment (Summers)	292	428	484
Credit toward First Grade Certificate	71	126	173
Credit toward Second Grade Certificate	119	191	115
Credit toward college diploma	59	93	107
Intending to teach in rural school the following year	171	251	302

In many respects, students at summer school got the full treatment just as they would were they in the regular school year. Along with the assembly programs—held each day with attendance mandatory—the College also held summer graduation exercises. Nineteen students received diplomas at graduation

[207] The tent was first put up in the spring of 1922—and used for graduation exercises that year—"to take care of the exceptionally large enrollment which was anticipated" for summer school. Bemidji Sentinel, June 2, 1922, p. 1.
[208] Under the section called Special Features in the 1921 summer school brochure, it states that "provision will be made for special programs of interest to all, including a series of lectures" to be given in the tent.
[209] The only news item played up in the local newspapers regarding the 1922 summer session suggested the cooperativeness of the townspeople in promoting good relationships with the college. About four hundred twenty-five students were taken by the citizenry on an "auto ride around Lake Bemidji and a trip through the big sawmill of the Crookston Lumber Company," located across the lake from the college. There must have been some logistics problem, for Deputy said there were still some seventy-five students who did not get to go because there were not enough cars, and he asked if someone would please take them, too. Whether this last group got to make the epic journey was not recorded. Bemidji Daily Pioneer, July 15, 1922, p. 1.

exercises on July 24, 1923, marking the completion of their work and the end of summer school. Essentially full graduation exercises were held, as there was a principal speaker, Judge C. W. Stanton of Bemidji, and the College's Resident Director A. P. White was there to hand out the diplomas. There was a full program; Deputy made brief comments, the glee club sang several numbers, and what sounded the most interesting of all, "Mrs. Edith B. Ness, secretary to President Deputy, gave a whistling solo."[210]

The peak enrollment figure during President Deputy's tenure occurred during the summer school of 1924 when 537 students enrolled. That summer also marked the fifth anniversary of the opening of the school, and the occasion was not overlooked. The State College Board members and all of the teachers college presidents came to Bemidji as special guests. The school held two programs—in the tent—one in the morning and the other in the afternoon of June 24. At the morning assembly program for the students, Presidents Charles Cooper of Mankato and B. W. Bohannon of Duluth spoke. In the afternoon program for the public, along with musical selections between talks, Commissioner of Education James McConnell, former Board President Judge Ell Torrance, and St. Cloud President J. C. Brown all spoke. After the program, the guests went on a boat ride around Lake Bemidji and then traveled by automobile to Itasca State Park for evening dinner, a distance of some 40 miles from Bemidji.

In relation to the fifth anniversary program that summer, the Bemidji Daily Pioneer made one of its rare editorial comments about the local College that decade, but what it said should be said of any College in any community at any time: "The College means much to the city . . . not alone from a financial point of view as a source of steady revenue to the businessmen of the city, but its effect on the atmosphere of the community is a helpful and inspiring one." The editorial went on to note how the entire area benefited from the many worthwhile College-sponsored functions available. All in all, concluded the editor, the College made the city the "educational center for all this part of the state."[211]

Having reached the high point of enrollment of 537 in the summer of 1924, the following summer began the first year of an almost steady decline in students for the next ten years. In part, all of the teachers colleges experienced this decline. After fees were returned to four students, the registrar's book indicated the final figure for the 1925 summer school to be 469, which was still a sizable number for that time. The ten-page, five by seven inch brochure describing the features of the session revealed little changes from the past, with one significant exception. The College held morning classes of sixty-eight primary children in connection with summer school for the College students to observe and do practice teaching. Again listed first in the special features of the session were "the fine course of lectures and entertainments." At the end of the session, the school held another commencement

---

[210] Bemidji Weekly Pioneer, July 26, 1923, p. 8. Commencement programs appeared to be more interesting in those days. However, the use of the tent for graduation facilities left much to be desired, according to interviews with participants who fought off mosquitoes during ceremonies.
[211] June 24, 1924 p. 2.

ceremony, with Miss Mabel Bonsall of the faculty giving the address for the 14 students who received their diplomas.

Summer enrollment for 1926 went down again to 336, down 100 from the year before and almost 200 from 1924. President Deputy found some grace by noting the growing number of advanced students, that is, students in the third or fourth year of the four-year curriculum, enrolled and working towards a degree; there were 32. At summer graduation, Edith Bader, grade supervisor of the Ann Arbor, Michigan, public schools and a summer instructor at Bemidji, gave the commencement address.

Summer school mathematics classes did a very interesting study in 1926. What Bemidji College meant to the town financially was the subject of a project directed by Miss Mabel Rice, training teacher in the junior high portion of the campus school. The figures reported were based on 600 questionnaires sent to various people associated with the College, and also available financial records were used. The results make interesting reading and tell a great deal about the financial impact the College had on the community. The total expenditures for each school year were listed as: June 15, 1919, to August 1, 1920, $53,272.58; August 1, 1920, to August 1, 1921, $84,666.82; August 1, 1921, to August 1, 1922, $116,771.33; August 1, 1922, to August 1, 1923, $138,905.15; August 1, 1923, to August 1, 1924, $130,344.59; August 1, 1924, to August 1, 1925, $161,424.78; August 1, 1925, to September 1, 1926, $166,106.40; the grand total: $851,396.65.[212]

During the 1926 summer term, based on the questionnaire returns, students and faculty spent $25,181.60 in the community; during the regular school year just completed, the same groups spent $102,591.70. The report estimated that the total amount spent by students and faculty in Bemidji from 1919 to 1926 was $780,366.50.

In the breakdown of figures cited, the College since 1919 had spent $36,927.54 for maintenance; $2,734.93 for postage and telephone; $2,573.99 for hauling, or as the report phrased it, "drayage"; $2,900 for printing; $20,445.89 for fuel, water and electricity; and $4,175 for other supplies.

The report also cited the results of questionnaires completed by 30 workmen then currently building the heating plant and the wing to the main building. As reported, they each spent an average of $102.83 per month for the eight months they would be working at the College, or a total of $24,679.30. The building contractor had spent an added $3,453 in Bemidji for supplies.

In conclusion, the report stated that the eight summer sessions had brought expenditures in Bemidji totaling $202,487.84; seven regular years of operation brought about expenditures of $577,878.66 for a total of $780,366.50. When the Pioneer ran a synopsis of the report, it headlined the article: "State College Has Brought [sic] Huge Revenue"; though the adjective might have been hyperbolic,

---

[212]Exactly how these figures were arrived at was not made clear in the report; presumably they were based partially on the annual appropriation from the state. The full report, along with samples of the different types of questionnaires used, appeared in the Northern Student, Bulletin of the State Teachers College, Bemidji, Minnesota, Vol. 1, No. 1, March, 1928, pp. 13, 16; a synopsis of the report appeared in the Bemidji Weekly Pioneer, July 22, 1920, p.3.

nevertheless the revenue brought into the community by the College was impressive. A potpourri of items in the report dealt with money spent in Bemidji. Summer session students in 1926 each spent an average of $9.51 a week in town. Three hundred fifty-four students from Bemidji had attended the College, and if there were no college in town, 35 percent or 129 would never have gone to college while 225 indicated they would have gone to school elsewhere. This would have taken $77,031 out of the city. Thirteen summer school students in 1926 owned cars purchased in Bemidji; nine faculty members bought automobiles in town; eight faculty members owned homes; and the total amount paid the faculty in the 1925-1926 school year was $65,527 of which they spent $44,991.36 in Bemidji.

To summarize this report, despite the large number of overlapping figures that make the whole pattern a bit jumbled, and admitting that the validity of the statistics is questionable, one has to agree essentially with the local paper: "Thus it is demonstrated that Bemidji State Teachers College is among the most important industries in Bemidji, if an educational institution is rightly classed as an industry." It observed that the report had aroused considerable comment among the businessmen in town "who previously had but a vague idea as to the commercial value of the college. The survey indicates that too often we overlook the value of existing institutions in our anxiety to secure new ones."[213]

Very likely aided by a State Board ruling, the summer enrollment in 1927 increased slightly to 340, or four more than the previous summer; of these, 32 were enrolled in the four-year degree program. The Board had ruled in February, 1926, that as of July, 1927, in order to renew a first grade certificate that had been issued upon examination (i. e., to those who did not have a two-year diploma) the holder must have attended a State Teachers College for a six-week term and completed full work. Also, those having teaching certificates but who had not taught in the past five years would have their certificates renewed for two more years only if they each attended at least one summer session in a State Teachers College. These and similar rulings in the continual but slow upgrading of teacher certification helped eventually to sustain enrollment in the teachers colleges.[214]

There was little positive effect, however, in sustaining Bemidji's summer enrollment for 1928. It fell to 298, the lowest figure since the second summer session of 1920. The numbers rose to 334 in 1929 before ebbing downward in the Depression and war years. Many persons speculated as to the reasons for the declining enrollments. Some saw it as a direct result in the gradual decline of population growth in the state. Some viewed it as reaching the point where the majority of elementary school teachers had obtained life-long teaching certificates

---

[213] Ibid. Though the figures were formidable for that time, they are dwarfed by today's budgets. That is, in 1968-1969 fiscal year, Bemidji State College spent $4,836,000; of that amount, $3,760,000 went for faculty salaries. The annual payroll increased twenty-three percent for 1969-1970 to 4.6 million dollars and the total budget to six million dollars.
[214] Teacher certification in Minnesota throughout the 1920s and 1930s was in a continual state of flux. What seemed to dictate eligibility to teach was the reality of supply and demand. The upgrading of teacher preparation culminated at long last in 1961 with the ruling requiring all beginning teachers in both elementary and secondary schools to have a bachelor's degree. At this writing there is a move to require all public school teachers to have had a year beyond the bachelor's degree in order to remain certified. It is not expected to happen soon.

and did not need to return to school. As long as the requirements for legally qualified candidates remained somewhat meager, there was no need to go back to college. Others saw the decline related to the movement of people away from the rural areas and into the larger cities. Yet others believed that the numbers were smaller because young adults saw little financial reward in the profession of teaching; it would take more than internal motivation to lure them to college. Lastly, it was postulated that the agricultural areas around Bemidji were already depressed financially before 1930, and the young people of the area simply could not afford to go on to college.[215]

Senior Class (1926)
"The president's secretary gave a whistling solo."

---

[215] Chapter IV of Clark's dissertation, "Population Trends, School Enrollments, and Teacher Demand," discusses the times.

For whatever reasons, the summer schools at Bemidji which had started out so well at the start of the decade trailed off by the end of it. Still the regular faculty nearly always found employment in the summer session, even at the low point of enrollment. When the enrollment was at its peak in the middle of the decade, Deputy would have to bring in almost a dozen extra faculty members for the summers; even at the low point he usually added three or four to the summer staff, and by the end of the decade salaries for summer school teaching were averaging $400. All in all, summers in the 1920s were pretty good times at Bemidji College.

Graduation and the Alumni Association

Graduation time at any school can be a festive occasion, and Deputy attempted to make it that at Bemidji. The school had only one spring commencement as a Normal School, the June exercises in 1920. In June, 1921, it held its first commencement as a teachers college. Throughout the decade one is struck by the generally high quality of the persons brought in to speak at both baccalaureate and graduation exercises. Clearly, Deputy sought out talented people, cooperating closely with Bemidji High School in paying speakers' fees. Often the College and high school shared the costs, the speakers talking to both groups of graduates at separate exercises.

The State Colleges adopted a new diploma and Bemidji used it at the June 3, 1921, graduation. Dr. George D. Strayer of Columbia University delivered the graduation address for 23 graduates, which included three men. (There were only five males enrolled in the College.)

A tradition of an outdoor pageant accompanied graduation exercises for the first few years. The pageants were held during the last week of the school year for the general public and often grew out of work in physical education classes. By 1925, however, the pageants had given way to either plays or operas, performed by the seniors at the College in the high school auditorium.

Considering the small number of graduates, the turnout of people for the College commencement exercises was considerable. For example, in 1922, with 21 graduates, the _Pioneer_ estimated the crowd at the morning program to be over 500. That was the year the tent was first used. Dr. Lucius Bugbee, pastor of the Hennepin Avenue Methodist Church in Minneapolis, gave the commencement address in the morning at the College, and in the evening he addressed the 53 graduates of Bemidji High School.

It was in connection with the 1922 graduation that the Bemidji State Teachers College Alumnae Association was formed at a luncheon held June 2 at Sanford Hall. The minutes of this first meeting, recorded by Secretary Anne Brundin, a 1922 graduate from East Grand Forks, stated that the gathering occurred "at the invitation of the College extended by President Deputy." After the luncheon, Deputy acted as chairman and introduced the proposition of forming an association.

Dr. Bugbee, commencement speaker that day, then spoke "on the great opportunities of such an association in connection with this new college." Several others, both faculty and alumnae, were called on to speak, "and all seemed of the opinion that as one-half of all the graduates were present then, it was advisable to take steps of organization at that time."[216]

Miss Telulah Robinson of the faculty outlined a plan of organization for an alumnae association that called for a president and a secretary-treasurer as officers and the appointment of a committee to write a constitution. A motion then carried that an alumnae association be formed, and Miss Laila Jerdes, also a 1922 graduate from Bemidji, was elected president with Miss Brundin as secretary-treasurer. Faculty members were declared to be honorary members of the association. A committee was appointed to write a constitution and the group adjourned after deciding to meet that fall in connection with the Northern Minnesota Education Association meeting to be held in Bemidji.[217]

Autumn Dance Pageant along the Lake (1924)
"In spite of the strong wind . . . the results were excellent."

In its fourth regular year of operation, Bemidji College graduated 60 students (only one man)—on June 7, 1923. This was more than the total number of the past three years and altogether made 111 graduates. The high school and College again cooperated on a speaker: Dr. Edward A. Steiner of Grinnell College spoke at the baccalaureate service for the College in the morning of June 2, and that night he spoke for high school commencement (the College's share in the expense

---

[216] Getting one-half of all the graduates there at one time was not so difficult considering there were only fifty-one graduates in all, which included the twenty-one of the class of 1922 who had graduated that morning and who were all invited to the luncheon. Minutes of the Meetings of the Alumnae Association of Bemidji State Teachers College, 1922-1937 (on file in the Special Collections Room, A.C. Clark Library, Bemidji State College), pp. 2-3.

[217] Ibid The group did meet that October with eleven alumnae present; at that meeting they set the annual dues at 25 cents.

for Steiner was $165). Dr. Lotus D. Coffman, president of the University of Minnesota, delivered the commencement address for the College graduates; he accepted no fees for his services.[218]

The Alumnae Association again met in connection with graduation at a Sanford Hall luncheon. At this meeting, the secretary-treasurer reported that 27 persons had paid their dues, and after disbursements for the year of three and a half dollars, there was a balance in the treasury of $5.95. The group elected new officers for the coming year, and they adjourned until the same time the next year.[219] In reading through the minutes for the entire decade, there seemed to be a pattern followed at each alumnae meeting: There was a luncheon, the president of the association welcomed the returnees, a faculty member introduced the members of the current graduating class who had been invited to attend, the secretary-treasurer told how much was spent and what was left in the treasury, Deputy made a few remarks, the alumnae debated about having a fall meeting at teachers' convention time, officers were elected, "Old Lang Syne" was sung, and the meeting adjourned until the next time when the whole performance was repeated. With minor exceptions, little was accomplished for the College at these meetings, although one may concede that the meetings offered group sociability and a chance to renew acquaintances.

Tent Erected behind Deputy Hall (1920s)
"Swat mosquitoes and pick off bugs."

[218] Annual Catalog, State Teachers College, Bemidji, Minnesota, 1923, p. 60 Bemidji Weekly Pioneer, June 7, 1923, p. 1. As a note of interest, when Coffman left his position as head of the Model School at Eastern State Normal School, Charleston, Illinois, in 1909, to go to the College of Education at the University of Minnesota, it was Deputy who succeeded him at the Charleston job. As president of the university, Coffman did not accept fees when he gave speeches in the state.
[219] Minutes of the Meetings of the Alumnae Association of Bemidji State Teachers College, 1922-1937, p. 9. Erin McPherson, an alumnus, also paid his dues in the year 1923. How Mr. McPherson fit into the Alumnae Association before it became the Alumni Association in 1927 was not recorded. According to one graduate, the "invitation" of Deputy's for the graduating class to attend the alumnae meeting during graduation was akin to a ukase.

When graduation came in 1924, the large tent—set up mainly for summer school purposes—was again the scene of the exercises, first to hear the baccalaureate address on June 1 by Dr. Thomas F. Kane, president of the University of North Dakota, and then the commencement talk on June 5 by Dr. Paysen Smith, Commissioner of Education for the state of Massachusetts. A. P. White, resident director, awarded diplomas to 25 students. By the end of that summer session, 47 diplomas had been awarded for the 1923-1924 school year.[220]

In 1925 Dr. Henry C. Swearingen of St. Paul gave the baccalaureate address, and Francis B. Blair, State Superintendent of Public Instruction in the state of Illinois, and a long-time friend of Deputy, gave the commencement address. Seventy-two received their diplomas that spring, a new high.[221]

In 1926 the College used the Methodist Church as the site for both its baccalaureate and commencement exercises. Dr. Roy Smith, pastor of Simpson Methodist Church, Minneapolis, delivered the baccalaureate talk; Dr. J. S. Young of the political science department of the University of Minnesota gave on succeeding days the commencement addresses to both the high school and the Teachers College graduates. Forty-two College students received their diplomas that June.[222]

In 1927 the College and high school again shared both the baccalaureate and commencement speakers, Dr. T. W. Stout, pastor of the Methodist Church in Bemidji, and Commissioner of Education James M. McConnell. The Pioneer gave a lengthy synopsis of McConnell's talk which discussed the big changes in Minnesota public schools. McConnell stated that in 1910, there were only about 14,000 enrolled in Minnesota high schools with 11 percent of them graduating; in 1926, he said, there were 84,000 enrolled and 17 percent graduated. He estimated that 15,000 would graduate from Minnesota high schools that year, 1927, or 1,000 more than the total high school enrollment in Minnesota in 1910. He saw this as having a distinct bearing on the State Teachers Colleges in the training of teachers for high schools as well as elementary schools.[223]

At the end of the 1928 school year, the College graduated 81 students. The first person to receive a bachelor's degree from Bemidji State Teachers College did so in the spring quarter commencement exercises: Leonard H. Vogland, Milaca, Minnesota. President A. F. Hughes of Hamline University and Dr. M. E. Haggerty, Dean of the College of Education, University of Minnesota, gave the baccalaureate and commencement addresses.

---

[220] This was White's last graduation as Bemidji College resident director, a position he had held since before the school opened. Taking his place on the Board on September 29, 1925, was his successor, R. H. Schumaker, of the First National Bank, Bemidji. Schumaker completed one four-year term.

[221] Pioneer, June 4, 1925, p. 1. As to those commencement exercises in the tent, a faculty member who went through several shook her head at the thought of them. She told in an interview how the faculty would march up the aisle in the loose sand and the straw spread around, sit in their academic garbs and often swelter in the heat, and at the same time swat mosquitoes and pick off bugs. Moreover, she added, as they sat there trying to look serious, there was one male faculty wag who would rustle the straw behind the women and then loudly whisper "Mouse!"

[222] The graduation brochure indicated that the seniors put on a production of the play "A Mid-Summer Night's Dream" in the high school auditorium. According to the Pioneer, the performance was excellent and it played before a full house. Today it is unlikely that the seniors would ever select such a play, and if they did, it is more unlikely yet that it would be performed before a full house.

[223] June 3, 1927, p. 1.

At the 1928 spring alumni meeting, with about 70 present, the Alumni Association passed a significant resolution. It voted to offer an Alumni Scholarship "for the best all-round first-year student. The award to be . . . in the form of free tuition for the second year of the two-year course." It also voted that the "best all-round second-year student working for the two-year diploma be presented a specially engraved pin." To finance these awards, which were subsequently carried out—the recipients to be selected by a special committee of the faculty— a motion carried that the constitution be changed to read, "The membership fees shall be 50¢ per year."[224]

The final year of the decade of the 1920s found Bemidji College awarding diplomas to 79 graduates. Though hardly a high figure, nevertheless the number of graduates had risen considerably since that first 1920 graduation when four received diplomas. In the decade, the graduation figure averaged 54; the highest number for any one year was 82 in 1927. And along with the stability shown by increased numbers of graduates was the organization of a body of College alumni. From these two things Bemidji partisans could hold cautious optimism for the College's future.

Curriculum Changes

When students enrolled at Bemidji Normal and later at Bemidji State Teachers College, the school required 96 hours of credit (24 term units) for graduation.[225] Such a diploma allowed the holder to teach in any type of elementary school in Minnesota. After two years of successful teaching, the diploma holder received a life certificate to teach from the State Department of Education. Two years of schooling beyond high school permitted a person to teach elementary school the rest of his life. Those high school graduates who completed one year (12 term units) beyond high school received a first-grade certificate from the state to teach in rural schools or ungraded elementary schools. After the first two years of teaching, this certificate had to be renewed. The bases for renewal changed regularly, depending upon the need for teachers. Non-high school graduates who came to Bemidji took a five-year curriculum and were required to earn 240 quarter hours (60 term units) in order to graduate and receive a diploma, the same diploma that was awarded high school graduates who took the two-year course. Essentially, those students in the five-year curriculum took their high school work in three years and then did two years of college work. These were the options open to the students until 1922.[226]

---

[224] Minutes of the Meetings of the Alumnae Association of Bemidji State Teachers College, p. 32. The wording of the secretary appears to be in error regarding a scholarship for "tuition" as tuition was free to those who signed the pledge to teach in Minnesota; hence it would seem that she meant a scholarship for the payment of "term fees," that is, activity and book rental fees. Fern Ramsey won the first award in 1929.

[225] A term unit consisted of the work in one subject for twelve weeks amounting to sixty class hours of forty-five minutes each, or forty-eight class hours of fifty-five minutes each.

[226] In reference to the need of the area and the opening of the school in 1919, Deputy wrote: "It was thought that not a few young people in northern Minnesota were without high school facilities, and that among them were many who would ultimately become teachers." Consequently, a five-year curriculum was provided for such students. Minnesota, Twenty-Second Biannual Report, Department of Education, 1921-1922, p. 137. Whatever the changes in the curriculum, the presidents on every occasion referred to education of teachers as the only function of the teachers colleges.

In 1922, Bemidji added what the other State Teachers Colleges already had in operation. It was called the three-year course, that is, three years of college beyond high school, and graduates from this course received a special diploma permitting its holders to teach physical education, drawing, and music in the junior high schools. Thirty-six term units were required for the special diploma. This program had little appeal in Bemidji. In 1926 there were two enrolled and it was discontinued after that year.[227]

The courses of the two-year curriculum give the best indication of the preparation of elementary teachers in the 1920s. In the first year there were no electives; the school required students to take grammar, composition, reading, geography, United States history and civics, music, psychology, sociology, introduction to teaching, arithmetic, and drawing. With the exception of United States history and civics, which was a two-unit course, all were for one unit. In the second year students took special methods of teaching, hygiene and sanitation, literature, psychology, observation of teaching, penmanship and spelling, teaching, and electives. Teaching in the campus elementary school counted three units; observation and penmanship and spelling counted one-half unit each, and all the rest were for one unit, with four units of electives allowed.[228]

The course of study for the five-year curriculum was similar to the courses required in high schools today. Only in the last year of the program were students allowed two units of electives; all the rest were prescribed.

College Campus School Band (1930s)
"Was the tail wagging the dog?"

[227] Six general electives beyond those included in the two-year curriculum and the following six specified subjects were required for the three-year special diploma: history of education, psychology, advanced composition or literature, supervision or administration, educational sociology, teaching of special subjects. It is difficult to see much special training in this curriculum.
[228] First Annual Catalog, State Teachers College, Bemidji, Minnesota, 1922, p. 20.

After approval (in April, 1921) by the legislature to allow the normal schools to become teachers colleges offering a four-year curriculum, the Board governing the Colleges met on June 2, 1921, to act on the authorization. It passed a resolution: "Resolved, that it is the intention of the Board to establish and develop the four-year curriculum as soon as possible. That the presidents be directed to prepare a curriculum, based on a four-year course, and report the same for the consideration of the Board."

The presidents went to work on a four-year curriculum. But not until March 26, 1925, did they submit what they called a "tentative program" for elementary teachers. The Board adopted the program provisionally and instructed the presidents to work on a permanent four-year program.[229]

Meanwhile, little by little, the Board raised the entrance requirements. It began by requiring students to have at least one year of high school, then two, then three, and finally by the fall of 1927, only high school graduates were allowed to enroll during the regular school year. As more high school work was required, the Board phased out slowly the old five-year curriculum so that by the fall of 1927, the College catalog read, "Sub-collegiate work will be discontinued beginning with September, 1927. Non-high school graduates are no longer admitted to the college except teachers in the summer session," when programs were arranged to allow those to finish who had already started in the five-year curriculum.[230]

For those who enrolled in the four-year program when it started in the fall of 1926, 192 hours of credit representing four years of work beyond high school were required (the two-year diploma required 96 quarter hours) and this figure is the same today. Students who had taken their two-year diploma could come back and start in the third year of the four-year curriculum. In addition to meeting general education requirements, such students were required to organize their work to include two majors, one of which had to be in the field of education, and two minors, one of which had to be in a field other than either of the majors. A major consisted of 24 quarter hours, exclusive of required subjects in the first two years, and a minor consisted of 12 quarter hours, also to be taken in the third and fourth year. Majors were offered in the following groups rather than in single subjects: (1) education and teaching, (2) science and mathematics, (3) social science and geography, (4) language and literature, (5) arts and expression. Courses were numbered in the 100's, 200's, 300's, and 400's, corresponding respectively to freshmen, sophomore, junior and senior courses. Students were required to take 48 quarter hours each in

[229] The newly adopted four-year program for elementary majors is described in the Minutes of the State Teachers College Board, May 5, 1925. The problems of the presidents and the on-going discussions on curriculum changes can be followed in part in the Minutes of the Meetings of the Presidents, Minnesota State Teachers Colleges, July 27, 1927, to March 29, 1943 (on file in the President's Office, Bemidji State College). These questions were also taken up by Dudley S. Brainard, History of St. Cloud State Teachers College (St. Cloud, Minnesota- St. Cloud State Teachers College, 1953), pp. 61-62.
[230] Annual Catalog, State Teachers College, Bemidji, Minnesota, 1927-1928 p. 10. Classes for the five-year students and the two-year students were supposed to be separate, but according to a faculty member who taught at the time, this was not always the case and it proved difficult to teach people in the same class with a wide variety of backgrounds. In the summer session of 1928, there were sixty-six students still in the five-year program; they kept coming well into the 1940s. The catalog suggests the influence of other cultures on the speech patterns when it stated that using good English would be a mandatory requirement for graduation. "The student should make every effort to eliminate personal speech defects, foreign accents, and obscure enunciation." p. 14.

groups 100 and 200, and 96 quarter hours in groups 300 and 400.[231]

With the temporary four-year program launched for elementary majors, the questions connected with adopting a permanent four-year course of study presented not a few problems for the presidents and the Board. They discussed them at length at different Board meetings and at separate meetings of the presidents. Some of the questions that had to be worked out included: Should the new curriculum consist of two years added to the existing two-year curriculum or should a new unified course of study unrelated to the existing curriculum be adopted? Should the first two years of this new course include a general education curriculum, or as it was called then, a "junior college" curriculum which two of the Colleges already had? How about certification of four-year graduates to teach in comparison with graduates with similar training in the liberal arts colleges? Should the new program include preparation for secondary school teachers as well as elementary?[232]

Not until March 19, 1928, at a meeting of the College presidents, did the presidents give their approval to the "Preliminary Report Concerning the Degree Curriculum" which had been worked out after many meetings and which they presented to the State College Board the next day. This lengthy report recommended a four-year course for both elementary and junior high school teachers to be built on a "unity basis" rather than consist of a patchwork of the existing two year program with an additional two years of work tacked on. (The presidents still wanted, however, to allow two-year graduates to return to college and complete their degrees in two more years.) They recommended that the permanent four-year curriculum prepare teachers for both elementary and junior high schools; the program would include training for: (1) teachers or principals in elementary schools of either the six or eight-year type, (2) teachers or principals in junior high schools organized as such, (3) teachers in high school teacher-training departments, (4) supervisors of elementary schools, and (5) teachers of physical education, general industrial training, music, and fine arts in the junior high schools. When these recommendations came to the Board, it took them under advisement for further study, and the knotty problem went back to the talking stage again for almost another year.[233]

Significantly, it may be noted, the presidents did not recommend that their Colleges prepare teachers for senior high schools. It would appear that they still acquiesced to the negative attitudes maintained by the university and the liberal arts colleges. To recommend junior high training but not senior high presented obvious problems. For example, are the two clearly separate? Thus at the September 25, 1928, Board meeting, Commissioner McConnell recommended extending the work of the four-year course to include the training of senior high school teachers

---

[231] Minutes of the State Teachers College Board, May 5, 1925. Understandably the three-year program in all the colleges was dropped when the four-year program began in the fall of 1926.
[232] Despite the great amount of time and effort that went into the starting of the four-year curriculum, large numbers did not enroll in it at first. Bemidji had only two students enrolled in the program in the 1926-1927 regular year.
[233] Minutes of the State Teachers College Board, March 20, 1928.

as well as elementary and junior high teachers. On this proposal, the Board again procrastinated, the secretary's minutes reading, "The manner was discussed at length, with the conclusion that the question should be presented for formal action at the next meeting."

The next meeting occurred on December 4, 1928, but still the Board did not come entirely to grips with it. What it did was to pass a resolution which would add McConnell's recommendation to the earlier presidents' report received by the Board in March, 1928, but not yet formally adopted or approved. Finally, three Board meetings later, on May 10, 1929, the Board formally approved the new four-year curriculum as recommended by the presidents along with McConnell's addition. This curriculum, then referred to as "permanent," covered eight pages in the minutes of the meeting. In brief, it provided for 34 credits of required work for the first year, 30 the second year, 20 in the third, and 12 in the fourth year of subjects which were called "constants"; the constants would be roughly akin to general education courses in colleges today. For both elementary and secondary teachers-to-be, general fields to major in were specified as education, English, social science, science, mathematics and foreign language; special fields of majors were specified as music, fine arts, industrial arts, and physical education. One minor and one major were required. There was a definite provision as to the courses and number of hours constituting a major and minor in each of the general or special fields. These ranged from 20 hours in mathematics to 42 hours in music. Ninety-six credits of constants, plus the credits required in a major and a minor, plus credits for elective courses had to total 192 credits for graduation. Those who fulfilled these requirements would be awarded a Bachelor of Education degree.[234]

Perhaps the most important effect of this action by the Board can be seen in the gradual enrollment growths in the junior and senior years throughout the College System in the years following. The increase became attributed mainly to the number enrolled for the preparation of teachers for secondary schools, especially men. To illustrate, in 1929-1930, 67 students were graduated from the State Teachers Colleges with degrees; in the 1939-1940 school year, 448 were graduated with degrees. In the secondary field, there were no graduates, of course, in 1929-1930, but ten years later there were 331 graduates from the State Colleges. There was a steady decrease in the number who finished Five-Year courses for the diploma, and on the other hand a constant increase in the number who finished four-year courses. By 1939-1940, the total number of four-year graduates was about three-fifths of the number who finished the two-year course. Though the goal of a college degree for every public school teacher was still in the future, an important trend in that direction began with the Board action of May, 1929, and the State Teacher Colleges played a significant role in sustaining the drive to upgrade public school staffs.

---

[234] Catalog, State Teachers College, Bemidji, Minnesota, 1929-1930, pp. 242. The title of the degree was changed to Bachelor of Science in 1939.

Summary

By 1929, by the end of the first ten years of Bemidji State Teachers College and the first decade of the presidency of Manfred W. Deputy, some important goals had been secured and milestones reached. Though still the smallest Teachers College, the school had taken its place with its sister institutions and became comparable to them in most criteria. In a sense, the College became taken for granted, a position not necessarily undesirable; it had achieved the position comparable to the other State Colleges in the minds of the public and the purse of the legislature. It had developed from a normal school of secondary grade to an institution of College grade; as the high school grades were slowly deleted, expansion into the third and fourth years of college work were allowed, even though few students at first went beyond two years. This curriculum development culminated in the decision to organize a completely new four-year course instead of merely adding two more years to the existing two-year program. A decisive measure was the adoption of the program for the preparation of secondary teachers as well as elementary, a decision that significantly aided its operation in the difficult decade that followed.

At the end of the first ten years, Bemidji Teachers College became accepted as a member of the American Association of Teachers Colleges. While only 50 percent of the first 1919-1920 faculty held degrees of any kind, 80 percent of the 1929-1930 staff of 30 members had this qualification. From that first Webster dictionary in 1919, and the first book accessioned in 1921, the library by 1929 counted 5,000 volumes. The size of the student body had settled down to about 200 students in the regular school year while the one six-week summer session approached an average of 400 in that beginning ten-year period of operation.

Under the capable leadership of President Deputy, a personal leadership that found him involved closely with both students and staff, the school had gotten started, and it kept going; its future appeared promising.[235] The Depression years following, however, constrained this promise, and the 1930s, too, became a period of trying to keep going.

---

[235] Apparently Deputy's stature didn't reach down through the entire school. Once when Miss Robinson was introducing Deputy to the Primary Training Department, she asked, "Do you know who this is?" A first grader instantly replied: "Yes, it's the college janitor."

CHAPTER V

The Lean Years: 1929-1937

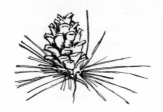

I
N MANY WAYS FOR Bemidji State Teachers College, the Depression years were as difficult as those beginning years. As it was for many individuals in the Depression, so was it for the institution: a difficult period of trying to retain what it had, to simply hang on, as it were, making the best of what was available and hoping for better days ahead.

The Shrinking Finances

The dismal economic decline following the stock market crash of 1929 rendered more serious the Depression in Minnesota which had already been in existence in the rural areas since 1922. For example, farm product prices sank to new lows. Beginning with 1930, the price index for farm products was at 88 (based on 1926 equals 100), and in the succeeding years it went to 64, 48, 51, 45, 78, before it even reached 80 again in 1936. Moreover, as the country sank into the Depression, a dry period unprecedented in the history of Minnesota came in the years 1933, 1934, and 1935. Land values decreased and bank failures increased, particularly in the smaller rural communities.[236]

Consequently, and quite obviously, for the State Teachers Colleges the generally steady progress that characterized much of the previous decade came to a temporary halt. A temporary halt came also for the graduates seeking employment. In the 1920s all graduates, both of the two-year and the four-year programs, readily obtained positions in city and village school systems as well as in schools in rural areas. But in the early years of the Depression especially, the comment made by

---

[236] U. S. Department of Commerce, Historical Statistics of the United States: Colonial Times to the Present (Washington, D. C.: Government Printing Office, 1960), p. 116.

President Deputy in a letter to a faculty member on leave was quite typical: "Not many graduates are yet placed. There are absolutely but few vacancies."[237]

By 1932 the consequences of the Depression were visible on every hand, and the State Teachers College Board reacted to the times with the resolution:

"Resolved, that this Board recognize the widespread economic depression throughout the state and nation, the necessity or limiting except in cases of emergency . . . all increases in salaries or expenditures for other activities until such time as present economic conditions shall have passed."[238]

In March, 1933, the legislature cut salaries of all state employees receiving more than $1,200 a year by 20 percent, and at the same time required that the College Board establish a tuition charge for all students. The Board fixed the tuition charge at ten dollars a term with an additional five dollars for non-resident students. Since tuition was charged, the legislature canceled the pledge to teach for two years in Minnesota. When tuition charges began in 1933, reportedly the wry comment of the students was, "We get a raise and the faculty gets a cut."

The position taken by the legislature to allow Bemidji State Teachers College to hang on, but little more, can be seen in the total legislative appropriations for Bemidji in the years 1930 to 1937; there was little variation in the annual appropriations (about $100,000) in this seven-year period, regardless of the changing enrollments. In fairness, however, and in comparison with Minnesota's neighbors—North Dakota for example—the maintenance of the same level of appropriations in these troubled times was a remarkable achievement by the legislature.

Table 1 shows the money allotted to the State Colleges for building purposes in the 1930 to 1937 period; as indicated previously, Bemidji fared very poorly in receiving building appropriations.

Enrollments

The Depression did not adversely affect college enrollments in the first years of the decade. The regular school years ending in 1929 and 1930 showed the normal 200 students enrolled at Bemidji. During the following two years, with the country sinking to the bottom of the Depression, the enrollment in the State Colleges often increased, as can be seen in Table 2.

TABLE 1

STATE APPROPRIATIONS FOR BUILDINGS AND LAND

	1930	1931	1932	1933	1934	*	1937
Bemidji	$220,000						

---

[237] Letter from Deputy to Miss Talulah Robinson, April 20, 1932. In the Manfred W. Deputy papers in the Special Collections Room, A. C. Clark Library, Bemidji State College. All letters hereafter cited are in this collection. Miss Robinson served as Director of Training (akin to Division Chairman today) and next to Deputy was the highest paid person on the staff.
[238] Minutes of the State Teachers College Board, April 25, 1932. Representing Bemidji College on the board as resident director from 1931 to 1939 was Dr. D. H. Garlock, a Bemidji physician.

	1930	1931	1932	1933	1934	*	1937
Duluth	$ 21,400						
Mankato	$ 5,605	$ 21,270					$240,000
Moorhead	$740,000			$29,400			
St. Cloud	$225,000		$10,000	$ 780	$ 2,211		
Winona							

*1935 & 1936 No amount allotted.
Source: Table from President's Office Files, Bemidji State College.

TABLE 2
ENROLLMENTS OF THE SIX STATE COLLEGES
(Based on the maximum enrollment of the three quarters)

	1930	1931	1932	1933	1934	1935	1936	1937
Bemidji	210	293	335	287	233	234	213	193
Duluth	445	521	607	446	456	454	449	448
Mankato	522	607	679	577	538	546	575	566
Moorhead	541	662	688	527	468	429	497	514
St. Cloud	883	1001	1101	855	703	728	727	724
Winona	443	506	485	448	388	391	401	392

Source: Table from President's Office Files, Bemidji State College.

It appeared that during the first few years of the Depression, if college age persons could not find an available job, they went to college. It seems evident that numerous young people came to college during these years who would have obtained work in other vocations had conditions permitted. However, these somewhat strange enrollment increases did not continue, as the above table indicates. Difficulty in obtaining a teaching position combined with the fact that many parents could no longer afford the costs of college produced a slump in enrollment after 1932.

The Depression period also showed a steady increase in the proportion of students who sought and received a four-year degree. The fall term of 1930 found only 18 of 210 Bemidji College students working for a degree; the fall term of 1937 found 42 out of 193 students seeking a degree.

A larger proportion of men enrolled also characterized the decade of the 1930s at Bemidji College. Again using the same years, 1930 and 1937, the fall enrollment of 1930 had fifty-three men out of 210, the highest ratio of men to date; in the fall of 1937, 83 out of 193 were men, or 43 percent of the student body. At no time in the short history of the school did the percentage of men get so large on the Bemidji campus as in the late 1930s, and this increase was directly connected with the growth of the four-year curriculum in the preparation of men for secondary school teaching positions.

Summer school enrollments did not change much in the period of the

Depression; in comparing the figures with those summer sessions in the previous decade, however, the average was 275 or nearly 100 less than in the 1920s. Indeed, for the first time the regular year's enrollment exceeded the summer session enrollment in 1932 and thereafter kept pace with or exceeded the summer enrollments throughout the 1930s. The attendance figures for the summers were as follows: 1930, 269; 1931, 301; 1932, 318; 1933, 262; 1934, 200; 1935, 253; 1936, 241; 1937, 255, first session and 49, second session.[239]

As in earlier years, the percentage of men enrolled in the summer schools during the Depression years was less than during the regular school years. During this period male enrollment varied from 11 percent in 1930 to 30 percent in 1937.[240]

Never had the student body contained so many persons who faced financial difficulties as in the 1930s. Student loan funds had first begun with a $100 donation from the Bemidji Women's Study Club given on September 13, 1921. In the Depression years, these funds were used to a much greater extent, but the amount of money available to loan was never enough to meet the demand. Even with regular contributions, including donations from the student activity budget, the figure never got up to $1,000 in the 1920s. At the start of the fall quarter in 1930, there was $121.52 in the bank. No loan exceeded $100 to any individual, and as repayment came trickling back, the money was loaned out just as fast as it came in. Though thousands of dollars were loaned out in small amounts in a revolving account, the balance on hand never got above the high of $748.56 on March 25, 1935. From the beginning of the loan fund in 1921 until 1935, $11,715 was loaned out to students, and $10,200.84 had been repaid.[241] Both the amounts of the gifts and the donors to the loan fund are shown in Table 4. Bemidji College had no generous benefactor who came along either before or after the Depression to plunk down some large endowment for student financial aid. The only thing remotely similar to significant outside help was aid to the College from the National Youth Administration which came through with approximately $3,000 per year from 1933 to 1938.[242] The available correspondence of Deputy and interviews with faculty members who were with him revealed Deputy's deep distress at the financial plight of students who could neither come to college nor stay in college because of lack of finances. It was during these years, said one person, that Deputy regularly dug into his own pocket to help students out and that he neither wanted nor expected repayment. (The cost of attending Bemidji State Teachers College in 1935 was estimated at 70¢ a day, according to the Northern Student, or $225 a year.)

---

[239] In Deputy's last year as president, 1937, the college started a second session of summer school, a practice continued to date. Although the second sessions always produced smaller enrollments than the first sessions, the results were nevertheless important as it enabled students to press more rapidly towards graduation and gave summer employment to more faculty. Deputy bowed to faculty wishes for a second summer school. This is noted to point out that the usual paternalistic Deputy was not always that rigid nor was the faculty only servile.

[240] Information on summer enrollment figures taken from the Registrar's Journal, unpublished record of student enrollments at Bemidji State Teachers College from 1922-1939, on file at the Registrar's office, Bemidji State College.

[241] Information on Student Loan Fund and repayments taken from General Accounting Record, on file in Special Collections Room, Library, Bemidji State College. Even in the affluent 1960s the percentage of repayment of National Defense Education Act loans nowadays is not that good, according to the Financial Aids Director.

[242] Report to the Interim Committee on Administration (mimeographed). Bemidji State Teachers College, 1933-1943, Bemidji Minnesota, January, 1944 p. 58. The N. Y. A. appropriations to Bemidji as cited in this report, were: 1933-1934, $1,964; 1934-1935, $4,590; 1935-1936, $3,780; 1936-1937, $4,803; 1937-1938, $2,835.

TABLE 4
BEMIDJI STATE TEACHERS COLLEGE STUDENT LOAN FUND

Gifts to Fund—

Women's Study Club of Bemidji	9/13/21	100.00	
	2/l0/21	100.00	
	5/1/22	75.00	
	6/27/22	40.00	
	2/9/23	125.00	
	6/20/24	91.00	
	3/17/26	50.00	581 .00
D. A. R of Bemidji	6/6/24	18.25	
	6/30/24	16.50	
	11/11/24	6.00	
	2/11/25	34.10	
	5/1/26	36.75	
	3/25/27	25.00	
	3/25/27	25.00	
	3/9/28	10.00	
	1/27/30	10.00	
	2/2/31	10.00	
	2/21/33	20.00	211.60
Student Activity Fund	10/22/23	300.00	
	6/20/24	300.00	
	9/9/24	243.09	843.09
American Association of University Women—Bemidji Chapter	3/21/31	10.00	
	6/10/32	10.00	20.00
Miscellaneous or Single Gifts			
Senior class of '24		15.00	
Proceeds of faculty party	6/14/24	5.00	
Musical Arts Club, Bemidji	4/2/26	5.93	
Roy Luttrell—in appreciation of loan	10/7/27	5.00	
President Deputy	7/ 1/37	9.21	
President Deputy	1/11/34	1.50	
Mary Bangs	4/1/37	1.00	42.64
Interest collected to 8/l/37			654.35
Total			2,352.68
Notes written off			-236.00
Balance - of Principal			2,116.68

Source: Table from President's Office Files, Bemidji State College.

Numerically, the Bemidji faculty remained rather stable both in numbers and in turnover during the Depression years. Such was the case in the rest of the State Colleges, too, as Table 5 shows. Table 6 reveals the number of students per teacher in this same period.

In academic qualifications, the Bemidji faculty showed improvement in the 1930s. In 1930, 80 percent of a faculty of 30 held degrees; 14 of these had master's degrees but there were no doctorates. When Deputy began his last year in the fall of 1937, on his staff were five with doctorates and 24 with master's degrees. The group without any degree on the faculty had disappeared, while those holding only bachelor's degrees fell to five, and two of them were school nurses who taught part-time classes in hygiene. In 1929, Bemidji's library counted 5,000 volumes; in 1937, there were 15,000 volumes and 125 periodicals, all of which, said the catalog that year, were "carefully selected."

Student Background and Student Life

Bemidji and the other teachers colleges in Minnesota provided higher education for the men and women from the small towns and farms. Questionnaires filled out by students in the teachers colleges of the state in 1935 indicated that 35.7 percent came from farms and 27.1 percent of the remaining students came from communities with a population of less than 2,500.[243] A later study of "What Happens to High School Graduates?" showed that in 1938, high school graduates who were children of farmers made up 39 percent of the new freshmen in the teachers colleges, 18 percent of the freshmen in the liberal arts colleges, and 13 percent of the freshmen in the junior colleges. According to this same study, 25 percent of the 1933 high school graduates from schools outside Minneapolis, St. Paul, and Duluth who continued their schooling went to teachers colleges; 24 percent to liberal arts colleges; and only 17 percent went to the university.[244]

TABLE 5
NUMBER OF TEACHERS ON STAFFS

	1930	1931	1932	1933	1934	1935	1936	1937	1938
Bemidji	25	25	27	29	29	29	30	30	31
Duluth	33	31	32	36	39	43	43	41	43
Mankato	45	46	44	47	48	53	521/2	53	51
Moorhead	39	39	43	44	44	45	46	46	46
St. Cloud	59	60	61	63	61	59	57	60	61
Winona	36	391/2	401/2	401/2	401/4	41	39	421/2	43

---

[243] Archie C. Clark, The Status, Policies, and Objectives of Minnesota Teachers Colleges; (unpublished doctoral dissertation, University of Southern California, 1941), p. 298.
[244] Paul Heaton, Minnesota State Teachers Colleges in Transition, Bulletin of the State Teachers College, Moorhead, Minnesota, Series 42, Number 2, August, 1946, p. 7. Of the remaining forty-four percent, some went into nurses training, music schools, trade schools, and the like.

TABLE 6
STUDENTS PER TEACHER

	1930	1931	1932	1933	1934	1935	1936	1937	1938
Bemidji	8.40	11.27	13.15	9.90	8.03	8.07	7.10	6.12	9.81
Duluth	13.48	16.81	18.97	12.39	11.69	10.66	10.44	10.93	12.42
Mankato	12.14	13.80	16.17	12.82	11.69	10.50	11.42	11.09	14.26
Moorhead	13.87	16.97	16.00	11.95	10.64	9.53	10.80	11.17	13.70
St. Cloud	14.97	16.68	18.05	13.57	11.52	12.36	12.75	12.07	14.15
Winona	12.31	12.89	11.98	11.06	9.64	9.54	10.09	9.22	11.00

Source: Information for both tables taken from the files of the President's Office, Bemidji State College.

Both the cultural backgrounds and the general nature of the student body at Bemidji during the Depression years can further be seen by reading the student newspapers of the period. Students began to publish a weekly called the <u>Northern Student</u> on November 20, 1929. In the first years after this date, the paper was usually six pages in length, and generally mimeographed on eight and one-half by 14-inch paper. In reading the contents, one is struck by the "one-big-happy-family" atmosphere that seemed to have permeated the student body and which was reflected in the school paper. With the apparent paternalism that was a part of President Deputy and the smallness of the student body, no doubt this somewhat casual type of family togetherness was reasonably easy to achieve.[245]

The small number on the faculty allowed for a closeness of its members also. The entire faculty associated a great deal with each other, both on and off campus, and usually once a month they met in each others' homes for pot-luck dinners. (Perhaps it stands without saying that there was no smoking nor drinking of alcoholic beverages at these gatherings.) Faculty sleigh rides were regular winter social events, and Sunday afternoon teas with students at the Sanford Hall lounge were also part of the regular social calendar. The alumni fondly remember the frequent all-school picnics at Diamond Point beach near the College and the watermelon eating contests during the summer.

Several times each year the faculty met for formal dinners at the Markham Hotel, with formal wear being *de rigueur*. Before one such dinner two male faculty members thought they would not wear their formal clothes that evening and called up President Deputy to inform him of their decision. The reply from Deputy: "It

[245] Some of the general tenor of the school might be seen in a letter from Deputy to H. T. Hunter, president of Western Carolina Teachers College, on December 4, 1931: "We opened this Teachers College twelve years ago and were much interested in establishing the proper social standards in laying the foundations of the College. Our school functions are limited to college students and faculty members except on special occasions.... At the time we opened the College we concluded that unless we provided for reasonable opportunity at the College under our own supervision . . . we might have considerable trouble with the out of school conditions, particularly with the downtown unchaperoned type of dances."

would please me very much if you would wear them." They wore their tuxedoes.

Four faculty members (A. C. Clark, E. W. Beck, Cal McClintock, and Alfred Elliott) and their wives were members of an informal group called "The Sunday Evening Club"; they would have dinner at one home every Sunday night and after the meal go downtown to see a movie. As one person said, "In those days you went to the movies; you didn't go to a particular movie." (Clark, Elliott, and Carl Thompson showed the temerity to build homes together "way out in the woods," as one observer said, on Lake Bemidji—an area that was then indeed regarded as forest, but is now only the 2300 block on relatively posh Birchmont Drive.)

Deputy himself did not associate a great deal with Bemidji townspeople

BSTC "Icicles" in Winter Carnival Parade (1937)
"The average temperature for February was below zero."

except through his role in the Methodist church. His contemporaries maintain there were few in town with whom he desired association, outside of fellow faculty members. One of these few was District Judge Graham Torrance, the son of Judge Ell Torrance, the influential Board member when Deputy was made president in 1919. (An alumnus told with some glee how Deputy got his first taste of alcohol. It occurred when the Deputys had dinner at the Torrances and Mrs. Torrance served rum sauce on the dessert. Not knowing what the sauce contained, he thought it was so good that he asked for a second helping. This story was spread all over campus by a college girl who served as the waitress for Mrs. Torrance that night and witnessed what was then thought to be a highly amusing event.)

If there was one faculty member and wife who did associate a great deal with downtown people and clubs, and hence made better public relations for the College, it was Mr. and Mrs. A. C. Clark. Clark was very active in the American Legion Post and in the Chamber of Commerce; he later became president of the Chamber. (Hence the Clarks were "accepted," so the story goes, in the "better society" of Bemidji.)

Almost out of habit, faculty members attended all school functions at the College in the 1930s and the 1940s. (This practice leveled off in the 1950s, a factor that distressed a goodly number of the older faculty who had remembered the days of close student-faculty relations. By 1969, however, it was as odd to find a faculty member at a winter prom, for example, as it was odd for a 1939 faculty member not to be there.)

One thing Deputy did not like was bobbed hair, and he would not hire any prospective teacher who had such a hair-do. One woman faculty member, however (best unnamed), bobbed her hair after she was hired and compounded her sin by pulling down the shade while talking with a male student in her office. When this was reported to Deputy, she was called into his office and only tears, promises and pleading saved her from being fired immediately. (These were the days before modern tenure laws, of course; nowadays to have tenure and still get fired requires, says one male faculty member, that person "to commit incest, arson and murder all in front of the State College Board. Even then you might win your case by calling it academic freedom.")

Several distinctive features about the school stood out in the pages of the student newspaper. First of all were President Deputy's twice-a-week assembly programs, each lasting nearly one hour, which all the students were required to attend. Anyone reading about these many assembly gatherings can easily conjure up the image of an English headmaster calling his charges before him regularly to bestow upon them the mantle of civilization which would uplift them, whether or not they wanted to be uplifted, to cultural civility. This appeared to be the case with Deputy, who called his brood together twice weekly to be edified or entertained, chastised or cultivated. In most of the sessions, Deputy or one of the other faculty members headed the programs. All the faculty sat on a small platform in the front of the room. There were slides shown of someone's trip to China, a talk on character education, a symposium on proper dress, a debate on political or educational problems; often Deputy would simply read to the assembled group, sometimes from the Bible, sometimes from Charles Dickens, William James, or Rudyard Kipling, and when he felt in a lighter mood, he would read from the writings of Mark Twain. Later in the decade students and student organizations took a larger role in putting on assemblies, and they offered songs, acts, skits, readings, and the like. And of course Deputy brought in many out-of-town visitors to speak at the assembly gatherings. When the lecturer or entertainer was judged to be of sufficient quality or reputation, the performance would be moved from the smaller assembly room in the main building of the College to the high school auditorium, a distance of three blocks from the College, and the public would be invited.[246]

One other feature apparent in student life at Bemidji College in the 1930s, as revealed in the student newspapers, was do-it-yourself entertainment. The various clubs and organizations seemed most active in putting on some type of weeknight entertainment for the rest of the student body. One might surmise that this was their substitute for today's television viewing.

The student newspapers also, of course, contained the usual news stories of who was elected to such and such position, who won or lost the athletic contests and why; editorials then were still asking the professors to stop lecturing when the bell rang ending the class period; emotion-charged editorials perennially exhorted students to show more school spirit; there were the usual quips about who was running around with whom, about some *faux pas* made in class, about alumni news, and new books, and how great it was to be going to a small college. All of these things were reported with an air of folksy clumsiness and an absence of journalistic style. Though the reader could easily look back on these old student newspapers with a feeling of quaintness and a smile of condescension, the social historian would likely judge them to be an illuminating find of primary source material on the lives of a small group of rural young people tucked away in the woods of northern Minnesota during a grave national period of stress and strain. Though the country might have been in grave financial peril, however, the strain and worry were not to be seen in the pages of the student newspaper. Showing the optimism of youth, they knew things like depressions would pass. After all, they had a faculty whom they admired and trusted, and a president who was highly revered, one who watched over and took a personal interest in each student. The Depression would be weathered.[247]

Mrs. Deputy had suggested in 1929 that it would be fine if the College had an outdoor fireplace near the lakeshore. The idea was turned into reality when students, alumni, training school children, and faculty began collecting stones from which the fireplace and seats were constructed in the spring of 1932 by M. O. Morse. The fireplace was dedicated by President Deputy June 6, 1932, "to the spirit of recreation, friendship, and good will." (From lack of use and repair, by 1960 the fireplace was crumbling and the immediate area grown up with tall weeds; thinking that 50th anniversary alumni might be searching this place out at homecoming time, College officials had the fireplace repaired in the summer of 1969.)

The record is clear that during the Depression there was little significantly

---

[246] Information from student newspapers and interviews with former faculty members who taught under Deputy. Students had assigned seats at assembly programs and the president's secretary took roll. Assembly programs concluded with all saying the Lord's Prayer (Methodist version) in unison; they also sang songs from the Methodist hymn book.

[247] According to John Schuiling, a former student at Bemidji in the late thirties, Deputy's failure to stamp out smoking was revealed each spring when the snow melted and cigarette butts were found on the ground outside the back door of the main building. The revealing evidence led to a stern lecture at the next assembly program. Deputy's paternalism extended to the janitorial staff too; in a letter from him to Mr. and Mrs. Will Clark, April 21, 1932, he wrote that he would rehire Clark "only on condition that your domestic affairs have become reconciled so that you will be maintaining your home and living agreeably...." Clark was later rehired.

new. The school added no buildings until 1938, and the numbers of faculty, students, and appropriations to run the school remained relatively the same. And though the College newspaper records the weekly comings and goings of the school personnel, this source too had a repetitive sameness. A better picture of the College in this Depression period is revealed in the correspondence that came in and out of the president's office; these letters shed a great deal of light on both the school, the times, and on Deputy as the president of a small teachers college struggling to keep going during the worst of the Depression years. Hard times indeed.

Dedication of College Fireplace (June, 1932)
"All fixed up for returning alumni."

The Problems of President Deputy

In Deputy's report to the State College Board on September 12, 1931, he wrote with some alarm about the 33 percent increase in enrollment (to 273) over the previous fall; the number was considerably higher than the facilities could accommodate. "Because of the increase we are pressed for room, particularly in library accommodations and in the assembly room which seats only two hundred seventeen students." (The chairs were rearranged to get all the students in the assembly room.) He added that " One of his surprises in our enrollment is the number of students in the rural department...." This statement indicated part of the trend going on throughout the state, that is, the growing number of two-year graduates going out to teach in rural schools. Prior to the Depression, graduates with the two-year diploma could and often did secure positions in towns and villages whereas the one-year graduates went to the rural schools. By the end of the decade nearly all of the two-year graduates were entering the rural field. Because of this trend, the two-year curriculum at Bemidji was revised in 1931 and became designed to prepare students for both the graded and ungraded elementary schools.[248]

Deputy's letters in the early 1930s often mentioned automobile transportation and improved road conditions. Deputy believed that better roads had contributed to the enrollment growth; he wrote that this growth "would not have been possible a few years ago without much inconvenience and additional expenses to students because of long distances, poor roads, and limited means of conveyance."[249]

Deputy wrote many letters to the commissioner of education, James McConnell. In several cases, when some question of interpretation came up that needed clarification, he would write to McConnell or to the state attorney general. For instance, on December 4, 1931, he wrote McConnell wondering if faculty members could buy books at a discount for Christmas presents, the purchases to be made from the College book and supply department. To this McConnell scribbled on the bottom of the same letter and sent it back saying, "Dangerous practice, I think...."

In the quarterly report to the Board sent at the end of the fall quarter, 1931, Deputy stated that with the large increase of College students, plus some 290 students in the campus school, the main building had about reached its capacity. "The increased enrollment causes over-sized classes, with much over-crowding in library, toilets, locker and work rooms." He added, "It has become necessary to arrange some regular classes for the noon hour, on Saturdays, and in the evening, made possible only through the good spirit of faculty and students." Thus at the end of the report, Deputy again, perennially again, called for Board appreciation of Bemidji's building needs, especially for some type of physical education facility that might serve also as an auditorium.[250]

President Deputy had long wanted some type of structure to replace the tent used in summers and which would be used for an auditorium and physical education plant during much of the regular year. On his own, he sought out the costs

---

[248] Quarterly Report of Deputy to the State College Board, September 12 1931. He discussed the change in the two-year curriculum in his December 11, 1931, Quarterly Report. All the presidents filed these reports to the Board Office, but today neither the Board Office files nor the State Archive have these reports. An incomplete set of these Quarterly Reports that Deputy filed are located in the Special Collections Room, Library, Bemidji State College.

[249] Letter from Deputy to H. Z. Mitchell, September 28, 1931. The college also owned one car at that time, a Chevrolet. One of his letters about autos included a bill to someone for seventeen and a half dollars for damage to Deputy's car. There seemed little doubt in his mind as to who was at fault: "Because of the fact that I was on the right of way and that you gave no warning that you were backing out, necessarily makes you responsible for the damage." Letter from Deputy to John C. Johnson, October 20, 1931. One final sample of his correspondence dealing with cars was about a near accident he was in along with the president of the Charleston, Illinois State Teachers College: "How thankful I am that there was no injury to you . . . in the near accident that we had on the way to Moorhead. I hope that your nervous system was not unduly disturbed. I do not like night driving." Letter from Deputy to L. C. Lord, November 11, 1931.

[250] Quarterly Report of Deputy to the State College Board, December 11, 1931. The two hundred ninety pupils in the campus school were under Miss Ruth Jessup, principal, a fair but stern disciplinarian. Once a city workman was flushing a large hydrant and was permitting the heavy stream of water to tear up the college lawn. A third grade boy, upon hearing Mr. Deputy chastise the man, sidled up to the president and whispered, "Why don't you send him to see Miss Jessup?"

of some structure to fulfill the needs, for in March, 1931, he received a reply from the Dickinson Construction Company of Bemidji that a building 40 by 80 by 12 feet would cost approximately $8,500 and if it were done in the summer, a considerable reduction of $500 to $800 could be made "by use of regular College force of men to do excavation, rough work, and some carpenter work."[251] Though the idea must have intrigued him, Deputy was not able to do anything about it.

Deputy led a busy life, judging from all the correspondence passing over his desk, along with his frequent trips out of town. It seemed understandable when he wrote to a teacher on leave of absence, "I was very glad indeed to receive your letter several weeks ago, but have neglected to answer it because of so much demand upon my hours."[252] Some of his trips he had to forego. For example, he wrote that he could not make a national meeting of educators in Washington, D. C., in 1932 "because of the economic depression."[253]

The question of whether the Minnesota State Teachers Colleges should seek entrance to the North Central Association of Colleges and Secondary Schools vexed the presidents and the Board from the time they began talking about it officially in 1929. Finally, on June 13, 1931, the Board decided that the Colleges could qualify and that in becoming members they would not establish themselves as liberal arts colleges. The Board then authorized the presidents to make application for accreditation. The first assessment of Bemidji College made by the North Central officials was not especially favorable as might be expected. Among the two pages of criticism sent to Deputy were these: the North Central Association required colleges to have at least eight departments, and Bemidji had none. The Bemidji library was too small both physically and in number of books, especially so in that part of it which was used by the campus school elementary pupils; the course offerings were too limited in academic areas, notably science; the percentage of junior and senior students was too small. As to faculty standards, "I feel fairly safe, however, in saying that it is distinctly too low."[254]

Apparently the other Teachers Colleges did not fare much better in the evaluation because the Board withdrew the applications and decided to defer the matter indefinitely. The attitude of Deputy to the North Central Association's Preliminary evaluations can be seen in this letter to Commissioner of Education McConnell: "It is evident that the judgment concerning our eligibility is based entirely on the Liberal Arts standards which do not fit our methods or purposes. Until such point of view can be changed, I see no reason why we ought to push our

---

[251] Letter from C. M. Dickinson to Deputy, March 14, 1931.

[252] Letter from Deputy to Alice Frederickson, January 6, 1932. Miss Frederickson was studying at Columbia University and wrote to Deputy on November 8, 1931: "Whoever invented the saying that a degree from Columbia was easily acquired evidently thought merely in terms of thesis. Those people who are interested in advanced degrees would find it profitable to return to school soon or all possible research problems will have been solved."

[253] Deputy to Charles W. Hunt, January 25, 1932.

[254] Letter from George A. Works of the North Central Association of Colleges and Secondary Schools to Deputy, January 27, 1932. There was one statement made in the letter that might he construed as a compliment to Bemidji but which did not say much about her sister colleges: "In one respect you show a decidedly better condition than obtains in the other Minnesota Teachers Colleges," but he did not explain what this respect was.

case."[255] McConnell, who had seen the reports on the Minnesota Teachers Colleges before the presidents, wrote, "Frankly, I am a good deal out of temper with this whole North Central situation, and I am ready to tell them to go hence."[256]

Exactly where the power lay in running the Teachers Colleges could be seen in a sharply worded letter from a Board member to Deputy. Deputy had requested that the Board allow the American Legion Auxiliary the use of Bemidji's dormitory for occupancy by the area gold star mothers and the district and state officers at a convention in Bemidji, August, 1933. Wrote Stephen Somsen, resident director from Winona, to Deputy, "I think you know my attitude with reference to allowing these people the use of state property." His attitude on this was negative; apparently even female legionnaires presented a threat, as he went on to explain in no uncertain terms:

"I sincerely hope that the Minneapolis people will take time in renovating the bedding so that it will not be returned in time for the Legion meeting. In any event, you have no authority to give any permission to the Legion or to anyone else to make use of any of the school buildings. That is a matter exclusively for the Board to determine, and it is my suggestion that if any application is made to you for the use of the dormitory, you respond with the statement that it is a matter wholly within the jurisdiction of the Board, and that application must be presented to it." [257]

Deputy also received a minor rebuke via the mails from the state offices. State Auditor Stafford King wrote to Deputy in 1932 and told him to please fill out the state forms correctly. A little later when Deputy wrote for some missing reports, the reply to him came from the deputy state auditor and seemed most intemperate for a public official: "I distinctly remember sending copies each two years to the libraries of all state institutions. Inasmuch as complaint has been made to the present State Auditor that requests for the State Auditor's report have been made as many as ten times in the past five years and no reply or report has ever been received, I take this as a direct slap at me personally...."[258] Deputy did not back down in his answer. He did acknowledge that he was certain "there has been no intention upon your part or that of the State Auditor not to send the above reports," but the fact still remained that he did not have them and still wanted them sent to him.[259]

In Deputy's quarterly report to the Board on April 21, 1932, he submitted the names and the proposed salaries for the faculty for the next regular school year. In every case he proposed the same figure as the year before. (The salaries for the 1932 regular year had averaged less than $3,000 per member; E. W. Beck was the highest paid member of the teaching staff with $3,400.) The Board had cut summer school salaries that year 14 percent (the average pay had dropped to about $300 per

[255] Letter from Deputy to McConnell, February 3, 1932.

[256] Letter from McConnell to Deputy, January 26, 1932. Full accreditation by the North Central Association of Colleges and Secondary Schools was not granted to the Minnesota teachers colleges until 1943.

[257] Letter from S. H. Somsen to Deputy, February 22, 1932. At the April 25, 1932, Board meeting, the request for the Legion to use the dormitory at Bemidji was approved without a dissenting vote recorded.

[258] Letter from M. J. Desmond to Deputy, May 7, 1932. It seems inconceivable that Deputy, described by his contemporaries as so gentlemanly, would ever complain in the manner suggested by Desmond.

[259] Letter from Deputy to Desmond, May 16, 1932.

person), but at its April 25, 1932, Board meeting, it accepted Deputy's proposed salaries. This was the same meeting in which the members had passed the resolution recognizing "the widespread economic depression throughout the state and nation...." As it turned out, even those recommended salaries were too high, as Governor Floyd B. Olson wrote letters on May 21, 1932, to all of the elected and appointed heads of state government and to the University of Minnesota asking to have all permanent employees "join me in giving up one-half month's salary—we might call it having our vacations without pay."[260] The Board agreed, and on June 19, 1932, passed a resolution that put the cut into effect that month for all those whose salaries were paid in twelve monthly installments of at least $100 per month. During the months of September and October, all permanent employees of the state receiving a salary of $1,200 a year or more for nine months, received another deduction of one-twenty-fourth of their salaries for these months. The Board also considered seriously the proposition to limit the enrollments at the Colleges, but aside from recommending that the presidents admit only the very able students, it took no formal action to do so.[261]

This dilemma of increasing enrollments and limited funds can be viewed in a letter from Deputy written to a former faculty member after the fall session opened in 1932: "To our surprise we have a very great increase in enrollment and now have 345 students and need extra teachers now, but there are no funds to pay them."[262] There was no shortage of teachers applying for positions at Bemidji, however, and to these often imploring letters Deputy replied courteously and said in effect to all: alas, we have very few vacancies and no funds to hire more but we'll keep you in mind if something should open up.

On September 15, 1932, Deputy wrote to the commissioner of administration seeking to enlist his aid in supporting Bemidji's budget proposals for the next biennium. Significantly, the Bemidji College needs met the Board's definition of spending for buildings "only in cases of emergency" and, along with maintenance appropriations of about $110,000 per year, the Board's budget requests included $100,000 for a building at Bemidji. This was the only school that the Board allowed a building request that year. In his letter to the commissioner, Deputy wrote that "from its opening the College has had the constant problem of meeting required standards each year at minimum cost and also of making new developments and providing additional work required through natural growth." He went on to trace briefly the enrollment growth, noting pointedly that of the 345 students at the time, all were high school graduates or the equivalent. Notwithstanding this increase of more than 60 percent from 1929 to 1932, Deputy continued, which compelled the overcrowding of classes and the inability of offering some further necessary work, Bemidji was not recommending an increase in maintenance except to provide for

---

[260] Letter from Governor Floyd B. Olson to Deputy, May 21 1932.
[261] Minutes of the State Teachers College Board, June 10, 1932. The secretary noted that "it was the consensus of opinion that while at present it appears impractical to fix more highly selective standards for admissions, the Colleges should consistently advise against enrollment of persons whose . . . limitations are such as to indicate lack of ability to become successful teachers."
[262] Letter from Deputy to James M. McArthur, September 27, 1932.

two additional teachers. The Board had recognized Bemidji's needs for building extensions too, he concluded, and "because of our lack of facilities we are under the greatest handicap with an *emergency situation*. There is congestion in every department...." Thus, because of all this, he pleaded, please do not reduce our budget.[263]

Deputy's communication to the commissioner came soon after an architect had been sent to Bemidji to survey the situation and make recommendations. The report of the survey came out November 4, 1932, and confirmed Deputy's position and plight: "The main building is extremely crowded as it was designed originally to accommodate about 200 students" and there were 345 college students there. The elementary school wing of the building was built to house 250 students and there were 315 of them. The three-page, typed report discussed classrooms ("eight

Library (Deputy Hall) in 1920s
"One dictionary and a used set of encyclopedias."

classrooms built to accommodate 30 students have 12 classes composed of 40 to 42 students"); the science department ("the rooms are so small that it is impossible to give the students individual laboratory work of any nature"); manual training ("only one room and used by both the College and the elementary school students"); art and music ("one small room is devoted in each case to these departments"); library ("this room is very small for a student body of 661"—since both College and elementary school students used the same room); assembly room ("the room used

---

[263] Letter from Deputy to the Commissioner of Administration and Finance September 15, 1932. The underlining was done by Deputy. In Deputy's nineteen years as president, the 1932-1933 regular year was his "best" year in terns of high enrollment and his "worst" in trying to accommodate that enrollment. After 1933, the regular year's enrollment steadily went down.

. . . is also very small, seating under crowded conditions only 190 students"); physical education ("we would term this a 'play room' rather than 'gymnasium' which should be devoted to physical education"); administration ("four small rooms provided for this purpose are scattered throughout the building"); faculty room ("a small room is devoted to 28 women faculty members"); nurse's office ("the nurse has her office in the rear of another small office with a screen division"). The report concluded:

"In closing, permit us to say that under the present arrangement it is utterly impossible for proper instruction to be given to an enrollment that has experienced such tremendous increase. We strongly advise that a sufficient appropriation be made in order to cover the cost of the work set up in this report."[264]

Despite all such reports, letters and testimonials, the legislature allocated nothing for any building additions. Not that some legislators did not try, for the Bemidji area representatives certainly worked to get building money for the College out of the 1933 legislature, and Deputy wrote several letters to Harry Bridgeman in the Senate and Gustav Erickson in the House, offering encouragement and advice. For example, because the Board had already taken steps to recommend a building for Bemidji and felt no further resolution was needed by them, Deputy wrote Bridgeman, "The situation is now open for you and Mr. Erickson to proceed in such manner as seems best to get our building need before the legislative committees as an emergency need. Dr. Garlock, Resident Director and I will give all the help we can." Bridgeman replied that after talking it over with Erickson, they had concluded that it would be best to "let this matter come up in the usual manner and not attempt to make an emergency of this appropriation. From my observations so far it would appear that the legislature is in a rather hysterical mood. . . "[265]

His observation of the 1933 legislature seemed accurate. As it turned out, Bemidji State Teachers College was lucky to emerge at the end of the session as still an educational institution and not an insane asylum. State Senator Charles Orr, St. Paul, chairman of the Rules Committee, submitted a proposal to abolish the work of any or all of the State Teachers Colleges so that the buildings might be used for insane asylums, reform schools, or prisons. He asked that all of the six schools be investigated, placed under the State Board of Control, and if the schools did not appear to be vitally needed—he felt that at least three could go—the buildings should be turned over for better state use. At the very minimum, Orr and his supporters maintained, all the State Colleges should be turned back into two-year Normal Schools. Orr reasoned that teacher supply exceeded teacher demand, and that this demand could be easily supplied by the university and the liberal arts

---

[264] Preliminary Report of Requirements, Bemidji State Teachers College, Bemidji, Minnesota, for the Commissioner of Administration and Finance, State of Minnesota, prepared by Nairne W. Fisher, Architect, St. Cloud, Minnesota, November 4, 1932, on file in the President's Office, Bemidji State College. The "play room"—gymnasium—described was twenty-eight by fifty-eight feet with a twelve foot high ceiling between beams. To accommodate students for assembly programs that year, the student body was split into three groups and met separately. For full assemblies the high school auditorium three blocks away was used when available. A faculty member recalled that year "every nook and cranny of the building" was used, including faculty offices under stairwells and in closets.
[265] Letter from Bridgeman to Deputy, January 10, 1933.

colleges. Of course, all of Orr's suggestions were purportedly made in the interest of economy.[266]

Deputy wrote to Bridgeman that he had read about Orr's resolution in the daily paper, and gave a partial rebuttal: "Senator Orr probably does not understand that the School of Education at the University does but little in the training of elementary teachers, and the private schools do nothing in that field of work."[267] He next wrote to Representative Erickson, "I hope and have confidence to believe that the legislature cannot be stampeded into such reactionary enactments as has been suggested by Senators Orr and Schweitzer."[268]

But Orr continued his attack and brought five of the presidents of the Minnesota liberal arts colleges to St. Paul to testify before the Finance Committee, at which time the presidents indicated that under the circumstances, their Colleges could not compete with the State Teachers Colleges and might have to close their doors. The arguments of the presidents, as indicated in the newspapers, might be summarized: privately endowed colleges and the university are amply equipped to prepare teachers for high schools, a function that the Teachers Colleges had usurped; private colleges cannot compete with Teachers Colleges with their low tuition rates; Teachers Colleges should limit their training to teachers in the elementary grades; it would save the taxpayers much money if Teachers Colleges were turned back into Normal Schools; ideals in education "must be safe-guarded —there is too much tendency to develop colleges, we even have some 'Barber Colleges'."[269]

TABLE 7
APPROPRIATION PER STUDENT
(Based on maximum enrollment)

	1929	1930	1931	1932	1933	1934	1935	1936	1937
Bemidji	472	469	359	296	366	404	456	503	631
Duluth	349	274	234	199	281	278	330	312	355
Mankato	311	306	256	228	266	225	289	264	295
Moorhead	293	277	227	223	238	270	323	280	302
St. Cloud	240	248	228	207	218	260	292	286	316
Winona	343	372	304	316	276	320	371	347	417

Source: Information from President's Office Files, Bemidji State College.

[266] Orr's proposal was met by anguished cries in the Bemidji newspapers. The Sentinel called it unthinkable and the Pioneer "a grave error." Before this Deputy had been working on his own economy program and had written his fellow presidents, January 19, 1933," Should we not seriously consider doing away with the awarding of sweaters, blankets, trophies, etc.?"
[267] Letter from Deputy to Bridgeman, January 24, 1933.
[268] Letter from Deputy to Erickson, February 6, 1933. Both representatives assured Deputy that they believed the legislature would not act precipitously on Orr's proposed resolutions.
[269] Minneapolis Journal, January 26, 1933, p. 8. Hearings on the Orr proposals were held between January 25 and March 8 of that year. The records of the Senate Finance committee to which the proposals were referred make no reference to committee action. The chairman, A. J. Rockne, however, spoke disparagingly of putting tax money in competition with privately endowed institutions, while Orr, incidentally a member of the board of trustees of one of the church-related colleges, was quoted in the Journal as saying: "We should cut out three of our six teachers colleges; we should make a start and eliminate one anyway."

The presidents of the Teachers Colleges went in turn to the legislature to testify against the Orr proposals. Deputy came armed with support ranging from student-body-signed petitions to comparative figures of total enrollment costs in neighboring states and supporting brochures published by alumni. Bemidji had especial cause to feel endangered judging by the high costs per student, as Table 7 indicates. The smallest of the Teachers Colleges, Bemidji did not have, consistently, enrollments high enough to match the high fixed costs of operating a school at optimum efficiency. For example, Deputy received the same salary to run a school of 350 as the St. Cloud president who had a school of 1,000 in 1932.

Deputy even sent Bridgeman the deed that ceded the land for the College and noted that the deed states that "the land was granted for 'Normal School' purposes. We hope that the issue will not come to the point where we will have to use this argument."[270] They did not have to use it. By the end of March, 1933, Deputy felt that the Teachers Colleges were saved and safe. He wrote to a faculty member on the staff at George Peabody College, "There has been quite a fight on in this state, as well as other states, but now it seems that the teachers colleges will not be disturbed in their present status as four-year training institutions. I am sure the fight is practically over...."[271] Deputy was correct, and at the end of April he wrote again, "Our legislature is just closed and I am informed that we are still intact as a four-year degree granting college, but that our budget along with all others has been slashed."[272]

About all that was accomplished by the opponents of the Teachers Colleges in the 1933 session was to reduce the budget and to require that all the Colleges had to charge tuition. This latter decision reversed a practice that had stood since the founding of the schools of allowing free tuition for all who intended to teach.[273]

Perhaps the most important loss suffered in 1933 by the Teachers Colleges occurred with the death of Commissioner of Education James McConnell in April. McConnell had served as commissioner since 1919 and had been a most able friend of the Teachers Colleges. Those who followed him found the State Teachers College Board unfortunately getting deeply involved in partisan politics, and

---

[270] Letter from Deputy to Bridgeman, February 6, 1933. As if legislative problems were not enough, Deputy on the same day received an anonymous letter from a student reminding him that college dances are supposed to be for college students . . . not for outsiders from the high school across the tracks, or from behind the gashouse, and would he, President Deputy, please keep these outsiders out.

[271] Letter from Deputy to R. L. Goulding. March 18, 1933. Amid this legislative struggle, problems in and out of school continued for Deputy. For example, in early March, 1933, Deputy became most alarmed over some alleged misbehavior of two Bemidji women graduates teaching in Cass Lake. The superintendent of schools there wrote Deputy that the Cass Lake townspeople were very disgusted with Bemidji College because of these two women who went so far as to spend weekends with traveling men... With Deputy's firm approval, both were fired.

[272] Letter from Deputy to Dr. Thomas H. Briggs, April 20, 1933. The records of the House committee to which the proposals had been referred indicate a hearing on March 1, when three teachers college presidents spoke against the bill. One week later the record indicates the passage of a recommendation for indefinite postponement of the bill. On file in the State Archives. These records are not verbatim accounts of the hearings. Some hearings apparently were not reported, and those that were are in summary form, their completeness depending on the diligence of the committee clerk.

[273] Minnesota, Session Laws (1933), c. 294. Former faculty member Fremont Wirth of George Peabody College wrote to Deputy May 19, 1933, "I hope your state legislature treated your institution better than the state legislature treated the Tennessee institutions. They were obliged to take a very drastic cut in appropriations, so severe, in fact, that I do not see how they can operate efficiently." Further attempts to curtail if not eliminate the Minnesota Teachers Colleges were made in 1943, but all legislation regarding these closings failed.

political situations became a factor in Board decisions, something not present when McConnell was commissioner.[274]

More bad news in 1933 for Bemidji came in a report of the American Association of Teachers Colleges which said in effect that Bemidji's library was terrible, and if it were not soon improved, Bemidji College would lose its accreditation. Moreover, the report read, the Association Committee "somewhat reluctantly approved the educational qualifications of your faculty this year. Next year it hardly seems likely that the Committee will do this under the standards as they were interpreted at the last meeting." To meet these situations, the College newspaper led a drive for getting more book donations to the library and for students to return those books which they had "borrowed." Also, Deputy was able to hire two new faculty members with Ph. D. degrees for the next year. The upshot of all this found Bemidji College keeping its accreditation.[275]

It did not seem strange that Deputy would write in his quarterly report to the Board on June 5, 1933, that the past school year had seen "difficult conditions." Nevertheless, he concluded, "there has been a good spirit and a conscientious effort shown by both faculty and students in the face of these discouraging conditions and we pledge ourselves to carry on with renewed hope for the coming of better times when our conditions can be alleviated."

But times were hard for the College, and its frozen assets of $811.46 in the local bank did not help matters. Deputy wrote to the United States comptroller of the currency on August 28, 1933, regarding the closing of the Northern National Bank of Bemidji in March and which had not yet been reopened: "We urge that you authorize the local bank to pay the above amount which is due the State Teachers College immediately." He went on to rebuke mildly the government for its action: "It [the bank] has always been a leading institution of the community, and undoubtedly would have continued to do business in a most satisfactory way had the closing act been rescinded." Though the cause and effect relationship of the letter would be highly questionable, the local bank soon reopened.

When the fall session opened in 1933, the enrollment dropped about 25 percent (346 to 284) from the previous year. In his report to the Board, Deputy wrote that "this was to be expected because of the financial handicap which many students are under to pay tuition and the cost of living while attending college; also because of the disappearance of the one-year course under the provision of the recent Board regulation May 10, 1933 the announcement of which, no doubt, has caused a number of one-year students not to apply." He added that the large enrollment the previous year had brought in many students who were unable to do

---

[274] The Grand Rapids, Minnesota, Superintendent of Schools, C. C. Baker, wrote to Deputy on February 10, 1933 and quoted from a letter he had received from the Mayo Clinic: "Mr. J. M. McConnell was operated upon here this morning.... During the exploration it was found that his liver was full of cancer. Of course the prognosis is poor." The State Board Minutes of May 1, 1933, record a lengthy tribute to McConnell, following his death.
[275] Letter from Charles W. Hunt, secretary-treasurer of the American Association of Teachers Colleges, to Deputy, May 24, 1933. This possibility of the College losing its accreditation proved a constant threat to Deputy throughout his tenure. His correspondence reflected the fears preceding the time for reaccreditation and the sighs of relief that followed the announcement that the College was accredited for the immediate future.

college work and had been advised not to continue. Hence, he wrote, the quality of the students had improved that fall although the total number of students was less. His closing line in his report offered the enigmatic statement, "The outlook for the year is auspicious."[276]

When the fall quarter ended in 1933, Deputy wrote to the Board regarding the difficult times for students financially: "More than in any previous year, the students are under the handicap of limited means which makes it necessary for them to curtail their expenses, and in some cases live below their actual needs for wholesome food and clothing." He added that the College had tried to do everything possible to aid worthy students within the limited means available, but that many more students had applied for government work-relief jobs than could be selected.[277]

Deputy saw the way to raise more state taxes in 1933 in the same way that the 1967 legislature did: pass a sales tax. "This, as you know, is in operation in two or three states," he wrote to Senator Bridgeman, and "I see no reason why it is not equitable and fair." Certainly, he continued with a statement echoed today, there should be no additional tax on real estate or personal property, "both of which are now staggering under too heavy a load." Neither did he believe that there should be an additional tax on gasoline, as he said he found on a recent trip that there "was considerable reaction against high taxes on gasoline, resulting in the curtailment of the use of motor vehicles because of it."[278]

The legislature of 1933 had required that the State Colleges add an extra five dollars per term for non-residents, and Deputy wrote to the commissioner of education, E. M. Philips (who succeeded McConnell and served only one year to 1934), seeking a clear explanation of a non-resident student. As indicated, Deputy often wrote for clarification of duties. The reply to Deputy was long and complicated, and ended by giving Deputy a loophole by stating that "about all that can be done is to apply the general principles in each case."[279] This explanation did not satisfy Deputy, and so Deputy asked the other presidents for their opinions and also for the opinions of the Board. Their replies, however, did not completely clarify Deputy's questions, and the problem continued to come up regularly at registration times.

The State Teachers College Board appeared sympathetic to all Deputy's problems whether they were rather minor, like definitions of a non-resident student, or major, like adding more buildings. In the latter case, the Board continued to try to alleviate Deputy's crowded conditions by passing a resolution

[276] Quarterly Report of Deputy to the State Teachers College Board, September 8, 1933. Deputy's interpretation regarding the many students who allegedly could not do college work is not born out in the Statistical Report of the College for the 1932-1933 school year, on file in the President's Office, Bemidji State College. The overall grade point average was 1.28 on a three point basis. In percentages of 4,870 grades given, 7.7 were A's, 27.3 were B's, 53.2 were C's, 8.8 were D's, and only 2.8 were E's.
[277] Quarterly Report of Deputy to the State Teachers College Board, December 7, 1933. The enrollment for the second quarter was two hundred eighty-four, with ninety-two men and one hundred ninety-two women enrolled. Deputy also made reference to a common topic of conversation in Bemidji in the winter, the weather. In view of the fuel costs, he hoped that the approaching winter would not be as cold as the previous one. The average temperatures for January and February in 1933 were thirteen and four degrees, respectively. Information from the Department of Conservation Office, Bemidji.
[278] Letter from Deputy to Bridgeman, December 18, 1933.
[279] Letter from P. C. Tooning, deputy commissioner of education, to Deputy, September 11, 1933. Three years later Deputy still wanted to know what a non-resident was, and in letters to the other presidents on September 10, 1936, he told what he got for his efforts when he asked the attorney general: "I wrote to the Attorney General and was mildly chastised because I wrote on my own initiative instead of presenting the matter through the College Board." College presidents too had to follow the pecking order and observe proper procedure.

at its January 25, 1934 meeting requesting funds for a building at Bemidji, the money to be taken from an emergency fund passed by the legislature for such contingencies. The resolution read that if the state would allow this money for Bemidji, "none of the other five Teachers Colleges in the state of Minnesota will present any requests for new buildings to be paid for out of such fund." This was a fine gesture, but to no avail; it turned out to be only a gesture, and Deputy continued to get along with the three buildings he had.

In Deputy's quarterly report to the Board dated March 12, 1934, he reported very satisfactory results from the government plans of work-relief for students. Thirty-three students during the winter term were assigned work, he wrote, which included repair of chairs, furniture, and library books; office, library, and laboratory work; redecoration of basement rooms in main building; campus and dormitory work. Though he did not give the amount of their wages, he did write that "eleven additional students at fifteen dollars a month or equivalent had been allotted for spring term," so presumably the 33 received the same approximate figure. In choosing those students to work in the program, Deputy emphasized that "care is used in assigning this work to those most in need and with eligibility to do work as prospective teachers."

In this same March 12, 1934, report to the Board, Deputy said that he was happy to report that Bemidji College retained its accreditation in the American Association of Teachers Colleges despite the library deficiency. The standard required 15,000 volumes and 150 magazines while Bemidji's attainment at the time of the survey was 10,500 volumes and 110 magazines. (Deputy's reporting of this to the Board gives the impression that he was as perplexed as anyone as why Bemidji was still accredited.) Near the end of the report, Deputy wrote about his recent attendance at a meeting in Cleveland, Ohio, of the American Association and Department of Superintendents [sic] and reminded the Board of the current national trend for curriculum revision which included "provision for more liberal culture than now obtains." Deputy implied that the Board's supposedly permanent four-year curriculum adopted in 1929 should be updated with the trend of the time.

In Deputy's last quarterly report for the school year, dated June 1, 1934, he included a special section headlined "Handicaps." His first sentence was the terse announcement that Bemidji College "has again been compelled to raise the tent on the campus in order to take care of our late spring and summer conditions." And once more he asked, again underlining it, for more buildings. "We anticipate," he concluded, "that the Board will find it possible to assist us in vividly putting our situation before the forthcoming legislature with such effect that our conditions will be improved." Again the Board agreed to try. At its July 21, 1934 meeting, it approved in its legislative requests a sum for another building at Bemidji. The legislature, of course, rejected this in its 1935 session.

Deputy summed up the work of the 1934 summer school in his September 7 report to the Board. The school enrolled 37 men and 163 women; but of this small number, he noted with satisfaction, 82 were in their third or fourth years, that is, working for a degree. The trend toward declining summer enrollments he understandably placed in part on "the general economic conditions with doubtful outlook for those employed; in part to the elimination of all under high school graduate courses," as he phrased it, "and in part to the gradual readjustments in the curriculum and in state certificate requirements causing the summer session to be quite similar in numbers, purpose, and content of work to the regular year." In short, Deputy seemed to say that the times were bad, it was harder to get certified and harder yet to find a job, and that the College could offer little out of the ordinary.[280]

The difficult times and the pinch of money can be seen throughout the quarterly reports that Deputy filed with the State Board in the 1930s. On December 5, 1934, he wrote, "Many students find it difficult to continue school because of lack of means. Federal and state relief funds in the amount of $600 a month are of material aid to 58 students who otherwise could not attend. Doubtless many others, including those who could not be admitted on work-relief, are unable to be in school." (Though the Deputy home was always a center for students to visit regularly, it was in the 1930s that Mrs. Deputy found out which students were the worst off and thus regularly had them come to her home for a square meal. Reportedly, many students had as a usual diet only oatmeal and beans.)

That the pinch of money was real to the College might further be seen in Deputy's letter to the attorney general, January 11, 1935, asking him to collect from two sets of parents for failure of their children to pay college debts of $49 and $19. Four days later the reply came back from the attorney general's office that the parents had been notified, and that "unless settlement is made in the near future, we shall commence suit to recover same." Despite Deputy's sympathy, students paid their bills or else. Another stern measure of Deputy's was the expulsion of any student who was not back to school the first day after any vacation ended.

Much correspondence passed between Deputy and legislators in the 1935 legislature, which lasted from January through April. Deputy first worried about an Associated Press story citing the State College maintenance budgets, and Bridgeman sent back a telegram to Deputy saying that indeed an error had been made but was corrected. Then Deputy wrote Bridgeman again, "We are all anxiously waiting with our thumbs crossed for favorable consideration concerning our much looked for building."[281] The bill for the building came out of committee favorably but was stricken on the floor of the Senate. After the session ended, Deputy wrote to the Department of Administration and Finance, "The legislature has closed and we know our budgets for the coming two years. We are distressed to have lost out on our building."[282] But to another person, he wrote characteristically, "While all of us

[280] It might be noted that between the regular school years of 1928-1929 to 1933-1934, Winona showed a one hundred twelve student loss, Mankato a gain of sixty-four, St. Cloud a loss of twenty-seven, Moorhead a gain of ninety-seven, Duluth a gain of fifty-three, and Bemidji a gain of fifteen. Of the graduates of Bemidji in 1934, fifty-four percent of the degree students and fifty-seven percent of the two-year graduates held teaching jobs as of October, 1934. Northern Student, October 23, 1934, p. 1.
[281] Letter from Deputy to Bridgeman, March 27, 1935. Interestingly, the college student newspaper kept closer watch on the progress of the bill than the town newspapers.
[282] Letter, April 27, 1935. The Journal of the Minnesota Senate showed that the amendment striking out the Bemidji building appropriation was supported by all the senators having teachers colleges in their districts, with two exceptions. There was obviously a lack of unity of interest on the part of those whose constituency was in an immediate college area.

were very greatly disappointed, we shall carry on and shall try to make the school even better, with the hope of getting results later."[283]

The only money outside of maintenance allowed Bemidji College by the 1935 legislature was $4,000 to construct a tunnel to take care of underground water and steam mains, and gas and electric lines. Even the spending of this relatively small amount involved much red tape and correspondence before work began. Still in this limited project, Deputy saw hope for future structures, as he wrote to the architect and suggested having one of the tunnel walls from the power house run to a certain spot because "it might be very desirable to be used as a foundation for the possible building we have under consideration on the north side of the power house."[284]

Delay followed delay in the building of the tunnel. Contracts were not let until the third bid and it was not completed until 1936. Some of the delay was caused by the question of who should be hired and the wage scale to be paid. Some indication of the wages paid in the middle of the 1930s can be seen in the commissioner of finance and administration's letter to the architect informing him of the local rates paid around Bemidji. On a per hour basis, he gave the following figures: common labor, 35 to 40¢; carpenters, 65 to 85¢; cement workers, 90¢; bricklayers and plasterers, $1.00; expert electricians, $1.00; journeymen plumbers, $1.00.[285]

The addition of lights to illuminate the athletic field provided one of the few significant physical changes on the Bemidji campus in the early 1930s. There were 40 lights mounted on eight 60-foot poles. Deputy again took the lead in sponsoring this, and in the initial drive to raise funds, he was aided by local organizations, citizens of the community, and faculty members. The total cost of the construction, completed in 1935, was $2,175. By the time Deputy retired two years later, only $300 remained to be paid.[286]

Curriculum Changes

The Colleges adopted a new four-year curriculum in 1935, replacing the one that had been in effect since 1929. The presidents had continued to work on curriculum revision after 1929, as directed by the Board, and the Board adopted the new program on January 25, 1935, to go into effect June 1 of that year. This program did not bring the matter to an end, of course, as discussion continued, and changes in the curriculum were made from time to time.

While it is the immediate and often flamboyant events that grab the headlines, such things as curriculum revision are more important in the long run. Such was the case with the adoption of the 1935 curriculum, a program which,

[283] Letter from Deputy to Daisy Brown, April 27, 1935. Deputy could probably find but thin solace for his efforts in articles like the one appearing in the February 4, 1935, issue of the Minnesota Journal of Education under the title of "Makers of Better Schools." In a short tribute to Deputy, the article concluded: "The State College at Bemidji is one of the recognized four-year institutions of the Northwest—and it is the lengthened shadow of this man." Indeed it was.
[284] Letter from Deputy to Nairne W. Fisher, May 22, 1935.
[285] Letter from J. Earle Lawler to Nairne W. Fisher, May 27, 1935; copy sent to Deputy, on file in the Deputy papers, Special Collections Room, A.C. Clark Library, Bemidji State College.
[286] Northern Student, Bulletin of the State Teachers College, Bemidji, Minnesota, January, 1933, Vol. XI, No. 2, p. 10.

though partially altered, has remained basically the same up to the present.[287] Essentially, the 1935 four-year curriculum was general education in the first two years and broad majors and minors in the last two years; it thus counteracted the old program of scattering courses throughout the whole four years of work which belonged in the first two. Moreover, the plan of requiring education courses every year of the four-year course was omitted.[288] The 1935 curriculum required 100 hours of constants (general education requirements) while the former had required 96 hours. In addition to constants required in both the elementary and secondary fields, the elementary field required 40 hours of work from five fields; the secondary field was set up in terms of majors and minors. Every secondary student was required to complete either one major other than education and two minors, or to complete two majors other than education. Majors consisted from 32 hours in mathematics or education to 48 hours in each of the special fields of industrial arts, physical education, music, or fine arts. A minor was to be not less than 20 quarter hours in one of the designated fields, including constants. This left about 52 hours of elective work for elementary majors and 24 hours for those in the secondary fields, all combining to make a total of 192 quarter hours of credit for graduation.[289] Soon after adopting the new four-year curriculum, there followed an attempt to revise the two-year curriculum also, but for a variety of reasons, often political — two Board members who were not educators sat on the committee to make the revisions—the two-year curriculum revision was delayed until after Deputy left office in December, 1937.

Deputy's Letters

President Deputy received a large number of questionnaires to be filled out and returned. He dutifully answered nearly all of them, and often added a personal letter. One such letter attached to a reply gave some insight into the pragmatic character of the man regarding what he called "the coming and going of educational slogans." He wrote to a doctoral candidate that he had watched for 40 years the periodic enthusiasm about how to succeed in teaching centering around such words as correlation, motivation, problem solving, unit organization, and others, and allowed there might be some value in each. However, he admonished, "All pedagogical valuation does not exist in any one. Each is as old as good teaching, but when any one is singled out as an educational 'Eureka' it becomes wooden and often defeats its own value in becoming an end instead of a means." He ended his letter with some advice: "If you are interested in working out a college thesis, I hope you can find a more profitable topic."[290]

[287] In 1939 the Board authorized the change from Bachelor of Education degree to Bachelor of Science. After 1935, the next extensive curriculum change came in 1945, and thus the next year, 1946, the Board authorized granting the Bachelor of Arts or non-teaching degree.
[288] After the Board approved the program, the college newspaper quoted Deputy as saying, "An outstanding feature of the new four-year program is the provision for a more general cultural education in the first two years ... with professional training concentrated in the last two years." Northern Student, February 27, 1935, p. 1.
[289] The description of the new four-year course takes up six pages in the Minutes of the State Teachers College Board, January 25, 1935.
[290] Letter from Deputy to Marjorie Potter, January 30, 1936. Perhaps Deputy's philosophy about teachers colleges is summed up in the phrases he quoted so often: "It's a great thing to be a teacher; it's a greater thing to be a teacher of teachers."

Deputy also wrote personal letters of appreciation to all who donated to the student loan fund, regardless of the amount donated. Some of these replies give added information about the College. For example: "We have had more requests for loans than usual this year," wrote Deputy in 1936, "so many in fact that we have recently borrowed $200 to help along temporarily. This very greatly appreciated gift of $50 will help out in a significant way."[291]

At the end of the regular school year, 1936, Deputy wrote a short and perfunctory quarterly report to the Board, and in it stated that things had not changed much during the year nor from the year previous, except that because of the "long, severe winter, the fuel bill of the College for the year has been nearly one thousand dollars more than usual, which fact handicaps our budget possibilities for the coming year." When unanticipated expenses came along, Deputy had to be extra cautious.[292]

Though the quarterly report omitted it, Deputy might have added that the College received a $3,300 federal grant in biology to add mounted specimens and skeletons of fish, birds, small animals, and reptiles to its collections. Certainly Deputy appeared most pleased with the grant: "This project is a great boon to this College, and I shall personally be interested in seeing it properly carried out."[293] (The guiding hand behind the growth of the science department was Dr. Alfred Elliott. Former students described him as "an outstanding teacher"; also cited was Elliott's interesting habit of locking the door at the start of a class period and not permitting tardy students to enter the classroom.)

When school opened in the fall of 1936, the first issue of the College newspaper had a headline reading, "Four-Year Students Win Lead in Fall Enrollment." For the first time in the history of the school, the number of four-year students (116) exceeded those in the two-year course (98); of the total, 82 were men. This change was significant, for the school had slowly evolved from its normal school beginnings to a closer approximation of a college. And also important, at least for those involved, the newspaper said that all of the last year's graduating class in the two-year course had teaching positions. As to the four-year graduates: "Twenty-one of the 28 four-year graduates have schools, and the others are employed in various fields." Only two four-year graduates were teaching in rural schools, while 46 out of the 64 two-year graduates were placed in rural communities. The news article concluded by giving the names and addresses of each of the 1936 graduates.[294] To suggest that all was well with the State Colleges

---

[291] Letter from Deputy to Mrs. De-Witt Garlock and the Bemidji Women's Study Club, March 18, 1936. See Table 4 for record of the income to the loan fund throughout nearly all of the Deputy period. Mrs. Garlock also regularly had students come to her home for meals. Mr. Garlock was the resident director of the college from 1931-1939.
[292] Quarterly Report, May 28, 1936. It had been a cold winter; the average temperatures for December, January and February were 12, minus 2.5, and minus 6.2, respectively. Alas, Bemidji still holds the dubious honor of being the icebox of the nation. It's no wonder that some wags call it Burrrr-midji.
[293] Letter from Deputy to G. W. Friedrich, chairman of the Minnesota Department of Conservation, August 14, 1936. The project was delayed because of the reluctance of the conservation authorities to issue collecting permits for game birds, fish, and other animals. A similar project, though much smaller, had been carried out the previous year under the heading of "historical project." About fifty specimens were collected and mounted at a cost of three hundred dollars, of which the college contributed seventy-five dollars. Northern Student, October 31, 1936, p. 1.
[294] Northern Student, October 7, 1936, p. 1.

by 1936, of course, would be misleading. For example, that summer the College presidents passed a resolution urging the National Youth Administration to provide additional funds to the Colleges "because of increased requests for aid due to extreme drought conditions, forest fires, poor crop conditions, and other economic causes preventing students from enrolling or continuing in college." [295]

In Deputy's fall quarterly report to the Board, 1936, he dwelt mainly on his school's proposed budget for the next biennium. It would appear that he could have copied the same letters that he had written to the Board in the early 1920s, as the requests and the phrasing of the requests changed but little: "We strongly urge the approval of the building requests as proposed." Possibly anticipating the worst again, he concluded, "If it is necessary to consider curtailment of the building request, the elimination of the dormitory expansion could better be deferred than either of the other building items." These other building items were a gymnasium-auditorium, a classroom building, and appropriate laboratories.[296]

On this same topic of budgets, Deputy wrote a long letter to the State Department of Administration and Finance on September 22, 1936. He told them that Bemidji's proposed budget had "been prepared carefully . . . and has been unanimously approved by the College Board . . . September 14." The situation seemed identical to what had occurred on many occasions before: The budget was carefully prepared, the State Board approved it, but the legislature did not.[297]

Deputy went on in his letter to the State Department of Administration and Finance to justify his building requests. In its physical plant and equipment, he wrote, the College "was scarcely half-completed," and the inadequacy of buildings and operating space "was a most serious handicap" to do the best work. Because of lack of space, he informed them, it had become necessary to cut off each end of the hallways on all three floors for office and storage space, and the hallways on the lower and upper floors were further partitioned off to provide temporary room for laboratories and library stacks. Moreover, he continued, the school never did have a gymnasium nor an auditorium, thus compelling the rental at high cost of the city armory building a mile away for physical education purposes. Unfortunately, he said, but true, it was almost impossible to have an assembly of the entire school at any time "except by use of a Chatauqua tent in summer or the rental of the high school auditorium in the winter." He concluded, "Notwithstanding the most favorable location of the new College in the extensive Northern area of the state,

---

[295] Minutes of the Presidents Meetings, Minnesota State Teachers Colleges, August 26, 1936.
[296] September 10 1936. The laboratory facilities were sadly lacking. In a letter to a newly hired science teacher, Alfred M. Elliott dated December 3, 1934, Deputy wrote: "You probably know that the college is just a few years old and is just getting underway. Only last year did we begin to place science work on a college basis." At the end of the letter, in a line that was akin to Calvin Coolidge's remark on unemployment, Deputy added: "As a teachers college our main work is the preparation of teachers." Elliott is credited with building the science department at Bemidji. He stayed until 1947 when he went to the University of Michigan as chairman of the Zoology Department. His son, Dr. William Elliott, joined the B.S.C. English department in 1967.
[297] Apparently Deputy's budgets were too carefully prepared, according to some faculty members who worked many years with him. In an interview with two of them, who did not wish to be quoted, they pointed out with some reluctance and some embarrassment that Deputy was too honest. By this left-handed compliment it was meant that Deputy never padded his budget but always asked for exactly what was needed. Subsequently the legislature assumed otherwise and cut his budget, leaving him to operate his school on a shoestring. A retired businessman in town, who said he knew Deputy well and liked him as a person but not as an administrator, put it this way in an interview: "He was no fighter; he was an educator." Exactly what this terminology implies makes interesting speculation.

the handicap of building facilities naturally curtails enrollment and hinders the best development of the institution."[298]

When Deputy filed his quarterly report to the State Board at the end of the fall quarter, 1936, he surprisingly saw the decline in enrollment (216 to 211) in a positive way. He reasoned that the decline was "due to the fact that all graduates of the past year and others unplaced in previous years have secured teaching positions or in a few cases other work positions, whereas in previous years a considerable number of the unplaced graduates returned for further work." Though some might question this rationale, Deputy went on to add, "We consider this condition wholesome, indicating a close correlation between graduation and service rendered to the state."[299]

Deputy's Last Year as President

Though unaware of the fact, in January, 1937, Deputy began his last calendar year as president. The decision for mandatory retirement came with a five-to-four decision of the State Board on May 4, 1937, "that the retirement age of 68 be set for all staff members and employees, administrative and otherwise, of the State Teachers Colleges," to become effective January 1, 1938. Deputy was 70 years of age. "News of retirement came rather as a surprise," the student newspaper quoted him as saying.[300] "Oh, but that was a dark day around the halls of the main building; it came as a real blow," said a former faculty member remembering the day the Board's decision was announced.

In view of the many things that motivated the State Teachers College Board that decade, the decision to make retirement mandatory was not surprising. Political factors entered into the decisions of the Board after 1933. After the death of Commissioner of Education James McConnell that year, and then the one-year term of E. M. Phillips, John Gunderson Rockwell became the commissioner and held the post the rest of the decade. Rockwell was an ardent supporter of the Farmer-Labor Party which held the governor's chair from 1931 to 1939 when Republican Harold Stassen became governor. The Board went into executive session more frequently in this period than had been the custom for many years.[301] Sometimes the Board's Farmer-Labor members caucused in private and agreed upon decisions without consultation with the other members of the Board or the College presidents. And more and more the Board began to interfere in the internal administration and in the curriculum of the Colleges to a degree considered

---

[298] Letter from Deputy to State Department of Administration and Finance, September 22, 1936. As indicated, such imploring letters, as well as any other approaches, were not successful for Deputy in getting money for building purposes at Bemidji after 1925. After considering the statements made in the interviews with people who knew him well and worked with him, there seems to be a consensus that as a person he was a virtuous and wonderful man, and in getting the College started he was equally wonderful and capable; but when it came to expansion and growth of the school, he did not measure up to what was needed. As one former faculty member remarked with a sigh of resignation: "He was so good, and did so well with what he had. But had he stayed on, this school would not have grown."
[299] Quarterly Report, December 2, 1936.
[300] Northern Student, May 14, 1937, p. 1.
[301] The presidents of the colleges normally met with the Board at its regular meetings. When Rockwell became commissioner, however, it was not uncommon that the presidents be sent out of the room, like miscreant schoolboys, when the Board wished to discuss something in private. Though perhaps letters regarding this rather irregular Board behavior may have been removed, there is nothing in the Deputy files to suggest that he looked upon the Board with any disfavor.

improper by many educators. For instance, the Board ruled that emphasis should be given such subjects as cooperatives and the labor movement, and later encouraged the faculties to unionize. And on May 4, 1937, the Board requested outlines of all courses offered in the social studies fields in the Colleges; on June 8, 1937, the Board appointed two members to work with the presidents in reviewing the curriculum of the two-year graduates, an educational problem for which lay Board members had questionable qualifications. Moreover, that same year the Board appointed a committee on educational appointments to recommend candidates for election to the faculty, to the business office, and even to the janitorial staffs.[302]

The Board decision to terminate employment at age 68, however, had been discussed off and on in Board meetings for two years before the decision was finally made in 1937. Presumably, the Board's decision was prompted by the desire to get younger staff members and improve the unemployment situation, but also it appears that it wished to find replacements with the correct point of view. The more radical of the Board members fought for retirement at age 65, but they lost out.[303]

Possibly the biggest solace that Deputy found that spring of 1937 was in the legislative act allowing $220,000 for the construction of buildings on the Bemidji campus.[304] The College newspaper greeted the final passage of the bill with the headline of "Hope of Decade Realized." There was more than hope that went into this. In the fall of 1936 all faculty members went out to collect contributions from townspeople to be used in lobbying for the new building. The legislature voted the money to "build a physical education building and wings for the main building and the dormitory," read the newspaper, although it did not turn out that way as all of the money was used up just on the physical education building. Even before construction started, it was realized that the amount granted was insufficient; the Board therefore formulated a request to the Public Works Administration for aid to complete all the buildings.[305] The request was not approved. The next course was to apply to the Works Progress Administration for aid, which was granted for the physical education building only. Hopes ran high that the Works Progress Administration would come through with more funds to finish the architect's plans for the entire gymnasium complex which included two gymnasiums, a swimming pool, an auditorium, and several classrooms. After simply a morass of red tape, work finally started on December 15, 1937, with plans to construct the main portion of the gymnasium building only. Yet the College newspaper wrote optimistically:

---

[302] Five years later, 1938, the Board established two more committees, a personnel committee to study and review the credentials of all candidates for appointment, and a business committee to do the same for the office staffs. In June, 1938, the Board passed a resolution authorizing the faculties to organize a union if they so desired. The Farmer-Labor Party dominance on the Board came to an end with the appointments of resident directors by Governor Harold Stassen, beginning in May, 1939. Soon afterwards, the special committees dissolved, and the Board went back to its former policies. Dudley S. Brainard in his history of St. Cloud was highly critical of the Farmer-Labor dominated Board, but Jean Talbot in her history of Winona College avoids mentioning the issue.
[303] Though difficult to document, contemporaries of Deputy asserted in interviews that no one on the Board was out to "get" Deputy; rather, if the mandatory retirement was aimed at anyone, it was at the Duluth president, E. H. Bohannon, who had some difficulties in his last years getting reappointed by the Board.
[304] Minnesota, session laws (1937), c. 385.
[305] Northern Student, April 30, 1937, p. 1. Four of the five pages of the May 4, 1937, Board Minutes are taken up by the results of a discussion with a P. W. A. official at the meeting who then spoke optimistically of easily getting federal monies for college projects.

"Before this unit is completed, plans will be arranged to complete the remainder when it becomes known what further grants will be possible...."[306] No more grants came, and all the allotted funds—$220,000 from the state and $140,000 from the federal government—were used to construct only "Plan A" of the physical education unit. This included a main gymnasium (to serve also as an auditorium), locker and shower rooms, and classrooms as one might expect, but out of necessity the gymnasium came to include also a recreation room, a lunch and social room, a bookstore, student union, three industrial arts rooms, one classroom, a laundry room, offices, workrooms, and closets. Before workmen finally completed the building in 1939—which required another $25,000 from the legislature—it was the largest W. P. A. project going on in the state, and it became a *cause celebre* for state politicians to successfully exploit. Such things as accusations and counter accusations on alleged mishandling of funds, false charges of having to knock out a newly constructed brick wall in order to remove a large cement mixer, along with reporters listening in at open transoms on secret sessions of the State College Board, and the like, were used effectively and to a degree aided the election victory of Republican Harold Stassen as governor in 1938. Deputy, who saw only the groundbreaking for the building 16 days before he retired, was not present to witness the alleged scandals that followed.

When Deputy began his last term as president in the fall quarter of 1937, he regretted to see student enrollment down to 193, the lowest fall enrollment since 1921. Deputy also much regretted not being able to see the new gymnasium building rise. He could, however, take comfort in the fact that he had laid the plans and helped untangle the red tape to get construction going, and he was present with pick and shovel for opening ceremonies on December 15, 1937, the day work began on excavation.[307]

The State College Board began seeking Deputy's replacement soon after it announced the mandatory retirement age, May 4, 1937, and formed a committee to suggest candidates. On August 2, 1937, the committee presented the names of seven candidates to the Board; the Board by a six-to-one vote chose Charles R. Sattgast. The Board member who voted against Sattgast wanted Sattgast as president of Duluth Teachers. At the time, Sattgast was at Columbia University completing his work for a Ph. D. degree, and for the seven years prior to his going to Columbia, he had been president of Sioux Falls College, Sioux Falls, South Dakota. His duties at Bemidji were to begin January 1, 1938, but because of a delay in completing his doctoral thesis, he received permission from the Board to begin February 1, 1938.[308]

During that last quarter of Deputy's presidency, recognition and tribute

---

[306] Northern Student, December 10, 1937, p. 1.
[307] Northern Student, January 14, 1938, p. 1. Another ceremony, this time with W. P. A. officials in attendance, occurred January 15, 1938, but Deputy was not present for it. The new building lay between the main building and Sanford Hall and adjoined the latter. When completed in 1940 it was thought then to be a marvelous structure, and people drove from miles around just to see it.
[308] Dr. E. W. Beck of the Bemidji faculty served as acting president for the month of January, 1938, and he is sometimes counted as the school's second president. Dr. Beck left Bemidji after World War II; he currently lives in Demorest, Georgia, and is retired.

were shown to him in many ways. The school published a special bulletin of the Northern Student, to honor him; the Northern Minnesota Educational Association set up a "Special Deputy Scholarship Fund"; the School Master's Club in the state gave him a gift in honor of his services; several banquets and teas, both on and off campus, were given. At a banquet December 18 at Sanford Hall, he received a book containing 260 letters from alumni, students, and friends. Deputy himself spoke more often than usual that fall at the student assembly programs, and he also gave

WPA Officials at Groundbreaking Ceremonies for Memorial Hall (Jan. 1, 1938)
"Was a new wall knocked out to remove a cement mixer?"

the address at fall graduation exercises. Community and school newspaper editorials about the man reflected the warm regard held for Deputy because of what he had done for Bemidji, the College, and the entire area. A phrase so oft-repeated as to become a cliché was the statement that Deputy "was the best-loved school man in Minnesota." The State College Presidents held a dinner for him and Duluth President E. H. Bohannon "as an expression of the long-time cordial relations among the individual members of the group."[309] The State College Board added a resolution to its December 14, 1937, minutes in behalf of both Presidents Deputy and Bohannon: "Realizing as we do that the services of these men are largely

---

[309] Minutes of the Presidents' Meetings, December 14, 1937. E. H. Bohannon retired at the same time as Deputy; his replacement was named at the same Board meeting that chose Sattgast to replace Deputy.

responsible for the gradual development and efficiency of the institutions named, we take this occasion to thank them for the wisdom, faithfulness, and efficiency with which they have governed and guided their respective institutions."

On December 31, 1937, Deputy affixed his signature on a state document for the last time as president of Bemidji State Teachers College; seven days later he and his wife left on a 9,000 mile tour of southern and eastern United States. They returned the next May, and after spending the summer in Bemidji, he and his wife moved to Florida where he accepted a teaching position at Southern College, Lakeland, Florida. He taught classes in the related fields of education until 1942, and after the death of his wife that year, he enrolled again as a graduate student at Indiana University. (Deputy made very few trips back to Bemidji after his retirement; one of these was on the occasion of the 25th anniversary of the College in 1944.)

Sporadic illnesses, including an operation at the Mayo Clinic, interfered with his doctoral studies. Just prior to his death on March 13, 1947, however, he completed the last of his requirements and received his Ph. D. degree at the age of 80, an achievement referred to by university officials as "notable and unique." He was buried in New York, reportedly wearing his doctoral academic robe and hood.

In the fall of 1967, as a result of minor student agitation, the words "State Normal School" over the entrance to the main building on campus were plastered over, and in large steel letters the words "Deputy Hall" were substituted. Considering the man, Deputy, his personality, and all the honorable things for which he stood, one can surmise that he would have much preferred the original name on the building.

CHAPTER VI

Bemidji College Since 1938: A Summary

C HARLES R. SATTGAST, one of the younger college presidents at age 39 when he began as Bemidji State College president on February 1, 1938, served as president until his death on March 24, 1964. He interrupted his tenure of office when he went into the military service from 1943 to 1946; Dr. Archie C. Clark served as president during his absence.

Sattgast was born at Mount Vernon, Illinois, January 26, 1899, and received his bachelor's degree from Southern Illinois University, his master's degree from Stanford University and his Ph. D. from Teachers College, Columbia University. He did public school and college work all of his life except for one year, 1919-1920, when he was a dairy extension agent for the University of Illinois. He taught in the rural schools of Illinois, was superintendent of schools at Richfield, Kansas, a member of the faculty at Colorado State College, Greeley, Colorado, from 1926 to 1930, and served as president of Sioux Fall College, South Dakota, from 1930 to 1937.[310]

Sattgast had some characteristics similar to those of his predecessor, Manfred W. Deputy. He too held strongly to strict Methodist mores; he also showed paternalism towards students and faculty; and he was totally dedicated to serving and improving the College. Sattgast, a big man physically, was also a dynamic personality; he nearly always spoke with force and gusto. In his years as president, Sattgast led the school in some of the worst times during World War II, and some of the best of times in the early 1960s. His initial year, 1938, found the College with an enrollment of less than 200 and a faculty of 25; by his death in 1964, the enrollment had reached 2,500, the faculty 125, and the school was then the fastest-

---

[310] Northern Student, April 9, 1964, p. 1.

growing college in Minnesota in terms of percentage increase in students. The physical plant increased from one classroom building, one dormitory, a small heating plant, and a half-completed gymnasium on a 20 acre campus in 1938 to 12 modern buildings on a 74 acre campus by 1964.[311]

Homecoming Royalty (1938)
"What could be more appropriate than green and white?"

Sattgast's first significant change in the structure of the College took place in 1938 with the decision to divide the faculty into five separate divisions with a chairman for each. These included: Dr. Philip Sauer, Languages and Literature; Carl O. Thompson, Fine and Applied Arts; A. C. Clark, Social Science; Dr. Alfred Elliott, Science; and Dr. E. W. Beck, Education and Psychology.[312] (This divisional structure is still in use in 1969-70, although there are now seven divisions, most of which have sub-divisions or departments. The seven are: Fine, Performing, and Communicating Arts; Physical Education, Health and Recreation; Behavioral Sciences; Business and Industry; Science, Mathematics ; Humanities; Education.)

As might be expected, the tone of the College changed under Sattgast. It seems understandable and reasonable that a new president would want some things done differently, and so it was with President Sattgast. And of course the times were different too, and this should make one qualify any judgments when comparisons between Presidents Sattgast and Deputy (and later Bangsberg and Decker) are

---

[311] Ibid. A thorough history of the Sattgast era (1938-1964) should and will be written someday, perhaps for the College's centennial celebration. This writer did not attempt it for two reasons: (1) it's a long story and the book is already too long, (2) it is too recent to get proper historical perspective. In the latter case, people outside of history cynically view this interpretation as copping out just when everything is starting to get interesting. However, it is virtually impossible to write a proper history of something that is regarded as current events. There are, to illustrate, too many emotions surrounding the Sattgast period, and too many source materials available that would either hurt or embarrass people living today—and perhaps be of no historical significance.
[312] Sauer and Thompson are still on the BSC faculty; both remained as chairmen of their divisions until July 1, 1969; Dr. Clark is deceased; Dr. Elliott retired July 1, 1970, from the Zoology Department, University of Michigan; and Dr. Beck is retired and living in Demorest, Georgia.

President Sattgast Presented Beaver Award to C.W. Richards (1938)
"I christen thee 'Beavers'."

Dr. Alfred M. Elliott (1938)
"Tardy students don't get in."

considered.[313] One might cite as a small but telling sample of change the different type of student assembly programs run by Sattgast. Under him, assemblies gave way to weekly programs called convocations led mainly by outside speakers and/ or entertainment, and student attendance was no longer mandatory. As another example, the campus elementary school was of lesser significance to Sattgast, a situation not necessarily negative as the personnel in the campus school were suddenly given more freedom to innovate without interference from the president. Moreover, the faculty started an organization to promote its own welfare, and it slowly became a moving force in affecting College decisions. In this latter case, size helped as much as anything for, very simply, the place got too big for one person to be in on every important decision. To illustrate, Dr. Sattgast had felt it his responsibility to do the hiring of all new faculty, and this he tried to do until well into the 1950s when it finally got to be too much and he eventually turned most of it over to deans and division chairmen.

Further indications of changes in faculty involvement can be seen in the way committee appointments were made and are made. Under Deputy and Sattgast (and Acting President Clark), the president simply said to a faculty member, in effect: you are on this committee and somebody else is to be on that committee, and that is that; don't argue, don't fight it; the president has made his decision. It may not have been democratic —but it was efficient, and was then very much accepted by the faculty. Nowadays, [written in 1969] according to one observer, the administration is so democratic that between the time your name is first submitted and the time you begin on a committee, half the year has gone by.[314]

Sattgast held at least one faculty meeting a month (now there are three a year) which he, of course, usually dominated and used as a platform to espouse his views and feelings and he had strong feelings on a myriad of topics. Some topics were regularly on his agenda: the need for promoting the image of "the friendly college"; the need for complete faculty unity and harmony, a faculty that all worked together and did not break up into small groups or cliques (when he first came, he looked with apprehension on the old "Sunday Evening Club"); the need for a neat and clean-looking campus free of debris. Though he might chide the members for not always exhibiting the proper spirit, he invariably ended by praising the faculty with vigor for their loyalty and dedication. And though his remarks seemed unctuous to some, he was sincere in making them.[315]

When Sattgast began in 1938, the faculty of 25 met in a small classroom,

---

[313] On one occasion when this writer was having a cup of coffee with President Sattgast in the old student union in the basement of Sanford Hall, Sattgast made this comment on the role of a college president: "Perhaps ninety percent of what a president does can be done by almost anyone, it's that remaining ten percent that counts in making a successful president."
[314] Perhaps a striking example of Sattgast's paternalism can be noted in this situation. The faculty was to have a Christmas dinner at the local Elks Club in 1961. A few days before the gathering, a memo regarding the party came from the President's office (which many faculty saved as a historical memento) which contained the stern admonition: "There will be no drinking." And there wasn't.
[315] In his last years he was especially vehement about students smoking in the buildings. Especially if he found cigarette butts lying in the halls, he would begin faculty meetings with a virtual harangue about helping to stamp out smoking in the buildings. (Still he had come a long way in changing, for in 1939 students were not to smoke unless they were at least one block away from the campus.) In fairness it should be noted that Sattgast's opposition to smoking was primarily practical rather than moral; essentially he feared fires.

Homecoming (1938)
"With scores ranging from a 44-0 win to a 69-0 loss."

Homecoming (1938)
"Football starts in '26 . . . with 26 men enrolled."

and as the numbers grew, so did the size of the meeting place so that by his last year, 1964, they met in the Laboratory School auditorium, the largest room available on campus where there were chairs with backs. (Now [1969] the only room large enough to hold the whole faculty of some 300 members is the gymnasium, and with no backs to the seating, most are glad there are only three meetings a year.)

In the first three years after Sattgast's appointment, the enrollment climbed about 100 students each year so that by the fall of 1940, 501 students were enrolled.

This figure made an all-time high enrollment for the regular year and augured well for the future. Then came World War II and an almost steady decline in the student numbers. (In a <u>Northern Student</u> poll taken in the fall of 1939, 84 percent of the students believed the United States would not get into the war that had begun in Europe.) In the fall of 1942, there was a 23 percent drop, and only 98 out of the 283 students were men. Then it got worse, for in the following two years, the enrollment fell precipitously to 141 and 146 students, the lowest enrollment since 1920, the school's second year. In the second summer session of 1942, only 13 students registered.

The College placed a service flag in the entry of the gymnasium in 1942; the stars on the six-foot-by-nine-foot flag represented the number of former Bemidji College students and faculty in service since 1940. There was a blue star for every serviceman (360 by October, 1944), and the blue star was replaced by a gold one for those killed in action. By the end of the war, 20 former members of the Bemidji student body had been killed in the war.[316]

Dr. Sattgast left Bemidji for voluntary military service in the fall of 1943 and began training at Fort Custer, Michigan. He served as a major in military government in England, France, Germany, Austria, and Italy. He returned as president to start the fall session in 1946.

Flight Training Class (1941)
"The male population kept dropping . . . to 18 men."

[316] Bemidji Daily Pioneer, January 4, 1960, p. 1. (This particular issue was called a "souvenir edition" devoted to College news and history, and published in connection with the dedication of the new physical education building.) A War Activities Committee of the Student Council was formed in 1943 which assisted in Red Cross service. As a result, that year 8,143 bandages were made by students at the College in rooms designated as Red Cross rooms.

Faculty Members In Armed Forces

Top left: Lt. (JG) R. Daggy, U.S.N. Top right: Major R.B. Frost, U.S.A.F. Bottom Left: Lt. E. Smith, A.N.C. Bottom center: Ensign O. Sand, U.S.N.R. Bottom right: S2/c H.T. Hagg, U.S.N.R.

1944 Faculty: Pictures taken from the 25th anniversary brochure.

The small male population at Bemidji State kept dropping during World War II so that by the fall of 1944, only 18 men remained on campus. Despite this fact, Bemidji became the only State College to continue football without interruption throughout the war years. Indeed, the 1944 team had an undefeated season,

The Faculty

Top, left to right: Miss Elsie K. Annis, Miss Waunita B. Bell, Miss Ruth E. Brune, Mr. Harry E. Bucklen, Miss Bertha A. Christianson, Dr. Alfred M. Elliott, Miss Alice C. Fredickson, Mr. H.J. Erickson, Mr. John S. Glas.

1944 Faculty: Pictures taken from the 25th anniversary brochure.

The Faculty

Top, left to right: Miss Mabel E.Parker, Miss Dorothy A. Pulley, Miss Telulah A. Robinson, Dr. Phillip R. Sauer, Miss Esther D. Schroeder, Miss Harriet L. Seeling, Mrs. Gladys B. Stapleton, Mr. Carl O. Thompson, Mr. James H. Witham.

1944 Faculty: Pictures taken from the 25th anniversary brochure.

The Faculty

Top, left to right: Miss Margaret E. Kelly, Mr. C.H. McClintock, Miss Mary McClintock, Miss Clara M. Malvey, Miss Mary Lee Marksberry, Miss Janet Matthews, Miss Alice Melby, Mr. Gordon M. Mork, Miss Alice G. Nesvold.

1944 Faculty: Pictures taken from the 25th anniversary brochure.

although reportedly H.J. ("Jolly") Erickson, the coach, had to round up some townspeople to fill in occasionally on the day of the games. (They played four games, home-and-away contests with Eau Claire and Concordia, Moorhead.)

Of some aid to College enrollment in the war years were summer and winter off-campus extension classes. For example, in the 1943-44 school year,

Coaches "Jolly" Erickson and
Jack Frost (1938)
*"Round up some townspeople to
fill in occasionally."*

there were 111 people enrolled in the regular year's extension classes, a figure that nearly matched the number enrolled on campus (135). Missionary ardor came out in these classes as many extension sites were reached under adverse conditions. For instance, former teacher (1928-1946) Esther Schroeder (retired in 1969 from Western Michigan College, Kalamazoo) recalled in an interview how she and Dr. E. W. Beck taught Saturday extension classes at Baudette (115 miles from Bemidji) at no extra pay during a winter quarter in the war years. They left in the morning when it was still dark and returned late at night. There was a stretch nearly 50 miles long where there were no homes or buildings along the road, but they took some comfort in the fact that there were at intervals some telephone boxes on poles along the highway that could be used to call for help in case of emergency. Only after the quarter had ended did they learn that all the phones had been removed for the war. It might be added that today those who teach an extension class during the winter quarter at Baudette take along what some call their "survival kit," i.e., winter sleeping bag, heavy boots, mittens and the like. (Regular year off-campus extension classes still continue at the College with 1,275 enrolled in 2,100 hours the 1968-69 school year; summer extension classes were discontinued in 1960.)

When the war ended, the veterans began to pour back into school in the fall of 1946. That year the fall enrollment went up 300 percent to 575, or 391 more than the previous year, and men outnumbered the women three to one. Also in 1946, the State Teachers College Board authorized the granting of the Bachelor of Arts degree and approved a new curriculum appropriate to the B.A. degree. Very few, however, pursued the B.A. degree at Bemidji during the first decade it was available. One important event for the College in the war years was the accreditation of Bemidji College by the North Central Accrediting Association.

In 1947 the Board authorized the Associate in Education degree to replace the old two-year general education program that attracted students mainly interested in secretarial work. (This A.A. degree is still offered, but it now attracts very few students.) [317] In 1949, students interested in elementary school teaching could still finish a program in two years and become certified, but gradually throughout the next decade the State Department of Education raised standards for certification (first to seven quarters, then eight quarters, then three years) so that by the fall of 1961, all beginning teachers in elementary schools were required to have a bachelor's degree.

"It will fill the place of a university."

In 1950 the College was authorized to give a four-year B.S. degree in business education, and a two-year secretarial science and a two-year business management course. Also in 1950 the American humanities major was added, and in 1951 a library science minor became available. In February, 1952, the drama workshop was created to offer practical experience in directing, makeup, costuming and acting. This workshop is still offered during the summer sessions, using the professional Paul Bunyan Summer Playhouse as their laboratory.

Honors to graduates were begun in 1955, including the *cum laude, magna cum laude*, and *summa cum laude* awards. The speech and drama major was added in 1958. Additions in 1959 included the full quarter of student teaching, and minors in recreation, physics and Russian. That year the College added a new division of philosophy and psychology.

The College Board authorized Bemidji to offer the Master of Science in Education degree in 1953, and the first graduate classes began that summer. Enrollment in the program began slowly with nearly all of the graduate students in summer schools. By the 1968-69 school year, however, there were 60 full-time and 185 graduate students enrolled on campus during the regular school year. Bemidji

---

[317] Ibid., p. 8. Also in 1947, Dr. Ruth Brune of the English department organized the first journalism conference for high school students with forty delegates attending. This became an annual event and last fall, 1969, under Jim McMahon, seven hundred fifty delegates from fifty-one area schools came on campus for the conference.

awarded its first M.S. degree in 1955. The number of graduate degrees awarded increased each year so that in 1969, the College awarded 55 master's degrees.[318]

Until well after World War II had ended, President Sattgast had the use of only one more building than his predecessor, the physical education building (Memorial Hall). Out of necessity, parts of the building came to be used for a variety of purposes other than physical education. These ranged from a lunch bar and student union in the basement to an assembly hall to a post office to the holding of classes in the lobby. The first new structures to appear on campus after World War II were two, long, wooden government-barracks units to be used for "temporary housing." Though no longer used for housing by 1969-70, these two eyesores still grace the campus, are still in use as storage sheds and are known unaffectionately as "the shacks." The first major building project on campus after the war came with the erection of a $240,000 library building adjacent to the main building (Deputy Hall), and first used in 1947. The heating plant building was again enlarged in 1949. Next came a $600,000 new Laboratory School building (campus elementary school) in 1950. Sanford Hall, the only residence hall in use since 1920, finally received some relief from its many years of cramped quarters when Birch Hall, providing living quarters for 200 students, was completed in 1952 at a cost of $700,000. Birch Hall eventually included a food service building, a large reception lounge, and a recreation area. The erection of Birch Hall completed what could be labeled the first phase of the building program that followed the war. An interesting feature regarding these buildings was the fact that all were connected by underground tunnels for student use. Especially in the rugged Bemidji winters, students made use of these warm underground thoroughfares, and this use gave rise to apocryphal stories of some students who never once went outside between January and April.

Beginning again in the late 1950s, and continuing to the present, buildings began to spring up on campus like the proverbial mushrooms. (Students graduating as recently as five years ago come back on campus and state that they can't recognize the place anymore.) Starting with another food service building in 1958, the school added two more dormitories in 1959 and 1960, and expanded the heating plant facilities once again. Also in 1959, workmen completed the first unit of a new physical education complex at a cost of one million dollars, and Governor Orville Freeman gave the dedication address on January 4, 1960. This large building contains a gymnasium a swimming pool, classrooms and faculty offices. The College completed the second unit of the complex in 1967; it houses a large indoor practice area for athletic teams (it is also used for commencement exercises), and in the winter it serves as an indoor hockey arena with seating for some 3,000 spectators.[319]

[318] Information from Dr. William Sellon, Graduate Office, Bemidji State College.
[319] Bemidji Daily Pioneer, January 4, 1960, pp. I, 10, 12. Bemidji College had a hockey team in 1949 and played pick-up games in the outdoor (natural ice) city arena, until literally the roof fell in on the place. Attempts were then made to shovel off snow from Lake Bemidji, using a caterpillar bulldozer but this time the "cat" fell in the lake. That ended Bemidji hockey and it wasn't revived again until 1959. Since the indoor arena opened, hockey has perhaps become the major spectator sport the past three years. Winning teams (two recent N.A.I.A. championships) have packed the arena with vocal fans, though some bemused philosophers see all this hockey as confirming the views of Thomas Hobbes in action.

A legislative money bill in 1959 provided for a new science laboratory and classroom building; it was completed in April, 1962, at a cost of $1,080,000. By action of the State College Board, the building was named the Charles R. Sattgast Hall of Science. The 1961 legislature provided $630,000 for an industry and arts building, but after some delay over a referendum changing the state constitution regarding indebtedness, the new building was not completed until 1964 and named Harry A. Bridgeman Hall.

Aerial View of Campus
"A victory for the 'wooded' counties."

Construction of new dormitories, or wings to existing dormitories, reached the point at which one has been underway every year since 1960. All dormitories have been named after trees and have such names as Birch, Pine, Maple, Oak, Linden, and Tamarack. The major buildings most recently completed are the A. C. Clark Library, a $1,400,000 structure completed in 1966; a one million dollar student union, first occupied in January, 1968; another $1,350,000 food complex building (Walnut Hall) first used in the summer of 1969; and a two million dollar high rise (13 story) dormitory used in the fall of 1969— despite the fact that the elevators weren't working. Currently [1969] under construction are a two million dollar classroom building and a three million dollar fine arts building. However, virtually all the buildings recently completed have one thing in common: They are too small to accommodate the mushrooming number of students the past ten years.

Classroom space is in especially short supply. Registrar Ed Aalbert's report of classroom usage indicates that general classrooms have been used an average of 37 hours a week between 8 a.m. and 5 p.m. for the winter term, 1970. This compares with the following statement from *University Space Planning* book, 1968: "There are a few institutions . . . who have set a standard as high as 36 hours per week usage of their classrooms. This is considered maximum and not attainable by most colleges and universities during the daytime schedule."

The end of the building boom is not in sight. College officials have made requests totaling $15 million to the Minnesota State Legislative Commission. Projecting an enrollment of 8,919 students by 1975, Bemidji College is asking from the 1971 legislature: $5.7 million for an administrative and business classroom building; a $3.3 million science building; the second phase of the fine arts complex costing $1.1 million; the conversion of Sattgast Hall at $151,000; a football, track and stadium on a new site north of the city at $2,130; and a central receiving building with garage at $775,000.

In contrast with the almost total lack of building under President Deputy in the 1920s and 1930s, this recent dramatic building program is the antithesis of the Deputy period. It has caused much wonderment, head-shaking, and speculation on when, or if, it will ever end. Understandably, it has brought with it not a few problems, notably with townspeople living in the area of the College who are finding their homes being taken by the College for necessary building expansion (and their driveways blocked by student cars). While interested townspeople in the Deputy period worried about the College because it was too small, they now worry because the College is getting too big, and town-and-gown relationships have been strained at times because of it. Now almost half the population of the community is made up of College students, and each year the numbers keep increasing. A telling point is the fact that there have been more students graduating from Bemidji College in the past ten years than there were in the first 40.[320]

The costs for students are escalating also. In 1937 students paid ten dollars tuition charges per quarter (three quarters in the school year), and a five dollar activity fee which entitled the student to the use of free textbooks as well as free admission to all College-sponsored activities. By 1947 students paid $20 tuition per quarter, and the activity fee went up to eight dollars, but students had to buy or rent their own books. In 1957 the College Board upped tuition rates to $35 per quarter and the student activity fee to ten dollars. In 1967, the tuition figure was set at five dollars per credit, or approximately $80 per quarter for an average class load of 16 quarter hours or credits; the student activity fee went to $15, the extra five dollars going for student union fees. In 1969 tuition went up once more to $6.75 per credit ($15 for non-residents of Minnesota), and the student activity fee to $25.

---

[320] The amount of money spent in town is welcomed, of course. The budget for Bemidji College in 1969-70 is six million dollars just for maintenance and operation (not buildings), this represents a one million two hundred thousand dollar increase from the previous year, or nearly twenty-five percent. Just this one-year increase is the equivalent of bringing in a new industry to the community. Chamber of Commerce President Dr. James Ghostley estimates that students and College employees spend approximately eight million dollars a year in Bemidji.

According to the College catalogs' estimated costs for a student during the school year (tuition, fees, books, board and room for three quarters), it would take $250 to go to school at Bemidji College in 1937; $400 in 1947; $700 in 1957; and $1,150 in 1967. The Field Services Office estimates that the 1969-70 basic costs are $1,368, and then note that this figure does not include any extra spending; hence, it was estimated that in the 1969-70 school year, a student "would get by comfortably at somewhere between $1,700 and $1,800."

Rising costs of attending college have not deterred enrollments, as indicated. The size of the student body has continuously increased since World War II, with the exception of two years during the Korean conflict in the early 1950s. Beginning again in 1953 and a 471 enrollment, the number of students rose on the average of about 100 each year until 1958 when it jumped 25 percent, from 847 to 1,231 in one year. Between 1958 and 1962, enrollment rose nearly 200 a year; since 1962, with 2,222 students, the enrollment figures have gone up nearly 400 each year so that in the fall of 1969, 5,011 full or part-time students were enrolled. The projected figure for 1975, as stated, is 8,919.[321]

The student numbers keep high even though the attrition rate is high. To illustrate, in the fall of 1968 there were 1,021 new freshmen enrolled; the fall of 1969 only 589 of these students returned. What happened to the other 432? The Registrar's Office reports that 101 transferred to other in-state colleges; 29 transferred to out-of-state colleges; 140 were on academic suspension or probation; nine were listed as simply "miscellaneous"; and of the 153 remaining, their whereabouts is "unknown."

BEMIDJI STATE COLLEGE
Bemidji, Minnesota
ENROLLMENTS

YEAR	Fall	Winter	Spring	Ist SS	2nd SS	Reg.Year Extension	Summer Extension
1919	–	–	–	130			
1919-20	38	41	38	292			
1920-21	97	94	97	428			
1921-22	157	164	158	476			
1922-23	201	186	185	531			
1923-24	223	238	224	537			
1924-25	223	244	242	469			
1925-26	245	241	222	336			30

[321] Information from E. J. Aalberts, Registrar, Bemidji State College. If this 8,919 estimate is like the one made ten years ago, there will have to be some quick adjustments made. To quote the Pioneer (January 4, 1960, p. 8), "By 1969 the estimated enrollment for BSC will be 2,612." However, the estimates made in 1968 by the State College Board of the number of students in the whole system in the fall of 1969 was 99.29 percent correct; they guessed 34,466 and there were 34,221. Computers are wonderful, explained the chancellor.

Year							*I	*II
1926-27	254	248	219	340				18
1927-28	207	193	194	298				16
1928-29	194	193	184	334				32
1929-30	208	204	181	269				38
1930-31	208	210	193	301				23
1931-32	293	288	259	318				22
1932-33	346	355	335	262				
1933-34	284	287	254	200				
1934-35	233	273	217	253				12
1935-36	228	234	216	241				11
1936-37	211	213	190	255				28
1937-38	193	189	182	255	49			21
1938-39	301	304	286	281	84			24
1939-40	410	421	400	272	112			36
1940-41	501	452	423	253	63			
1941-42	397	369	341	167	13	15		12
1942-43	283	259	194	106	25	3		65
1943-44	141	135	133	65	128	111		33
1944-45	146	134	123	61	30	89		44
1945-46	184	241	279	127	44	70		22
1946-47	575	580	555	116	45	10		37
1947-48	598	591	563	140	67	23		207
1948-49	573	579	544	139	97	10		195
1949-50	604	611	572	140	97			195
1950-51	575	530	451	85	68			153
1951-52	462	463	420	308	216	22		124
1952-53	471	445	423	279	204	27		94
1953-54	513	473	476	398	308	33		186
1954-55	601	549	601	426	371	30		198
1955-56	706	651	692	402	336	160		301
1956-57	847	834	793	416	301	403		439
1957-58	847	865	1,134	943	573	759	415	196
1958-59	1,231	1,163	1,240	913	664	600	302	216
1959-60	1,558	1,575	1,506	917	698	835	257	187
1960-61	1,724	1,669	1,721	824	602	714	0	0
1961-62	1,917	1,798	1,800	824	628	696	0	30
1962-63	2,222	2,061	2,001	1,068	789	756	69	52
1963-64	2,554	2,337	2,312	1,197	945	843	63	62
1964-65	2,920	2,592	2,730	1,216	989	733	58	205
1965-66	3,390	3,134	3,089	1,424	987	589	236	76
1966-67	3,866	3,701	3,658	1,525	1,331	1,061	248	331

| 1967-68 | 4,554 | 4,178 | 4,473 | 1,913 | 1,639 | 1,372 | 342 | 262 |
| 1968-69 | 5,082 | 4,578 | 4,471 | 2,192 | 2,128 | 1,525 | 464 | 569 |

(for enrollments since 1968, see Appendix D)

*The above figures for total enrollment include extension and institute enrollment. There have been no summer extension classes since the summer of 1960. The figures on the report are for workshops and institutes held at the College during the summers. These are also included in the total enrollment figures.

• • •

Faculty growth has been commensurate with student growth so that in the current 1969-70 school year there are 255 on the instructional staff alone, and 297 on the entire faculty.[322] Of the 255, 39 hold the rank of professor, 47 are associate professors, 75 are assistant professors, and 94 hold the rank of instructor; there are also 36 others, mainly graduate students, having no designated rank. Eighty of the 255 (31.3 percent of the faculty) hold an earned doctorate. The mean average salary for the academic year 1969-70 according to professorial ranks are the following: professor, $16,404; associate professor, $13,152; assistant professor, $10,786; instructor, $8,758. Just nine years before this, in the 1960-61 school year, with a student enrollment of 1,724, Bemidji had only 85 on the instructional staff and 90 on the full faculty. Twenty-six of the 85 or 30 percent of the staff held earned doctorates. The mean salary for the faculty of 1960-61, according to rank, was the following: professor, $8,950; associate professor, $8,113; assistant professor, $7,335; and instructor, $6,461. Financially, things have improved considerably for the faculty in these last few years. The 1967 and 1969 legislatures proved to be most beneficent for State College faculty members, at least for those members who held the rank of professor or associate professor. For the years 1967-68 and 1968-69, it raised the salaries of professors 30 percent from their 1966-67 figures; for associate professors, salaries went up almost 20 percent. Gone, it seemed, was the penury that marked the legislatures while Deputy was president; since World War II, money from the legislatures both for buildings and salaries has been forthcoming, and though the appetites for money are insatiable, the state of Minnesota has not been stingy in the recent past in building up the State College System. The System now has 34,000 students on six campuses; at present [written 1970] there are 1,200 faculty members in the System which has a biennial budget of over one hundred million dollars. By 1973, the system is expected to enroll 44,000 students.[323]

Two Bemidji resident directors on the State College Board who served with President Sattgast are still living [statement written in 1969]. In interviews, each commented on what he regarded as the most important events at the College while each was resident director. Wilbur S. Lycan, owner of the Markham Hotel in

---

[322] Faculty members not on the instructional staff include such persons as financial aids directors, field services directors, and the like.

[323] For the sake of salary comparison, in 1957 the maximum salary for faculty members in the Minnesota State Colleges was the following: Group I (professor) $7,008; Group II (associate professor) $6,308; Group III (assistant professor) $5,440; Group IV (instructor) $4,740; Group V (assistant instructor) $3,672. The annual increase for the respective five groups that year was $144, $144, $120, $120, $96.

Bemidji, resident director from 1939 to 1943, stated, prior to his death in December, 1969: "In my estimation the most important event that happened was that the Bemidji State Teachers College became fully accredited as a degree-granting college in 1943 by the North Central Association of Colleges and Secondary Schools. By this action we gained full academic respectability." Lycan also noted that in 1939 the legislature granted an original appropriation of $160,000 for a library building, and although the library was not built until some years later due to the war, "this was an important appropriation" because any appropriation was hard to get in those days.

Clarence R. Smith, an attorney in Bemidji, served as resident director from 1944 to 1948. He stated, "Possibly the most important development at Bemidji State Teachers College during my term as resident director was the authorization and approval for the granting of Bachelor of Arts degrees. Previously the only degree awarded was the Bachelor of Science degree." He added that "another very important development or possibly difficult task during this time was the maintaining of the College. At one time during those war years we had almost as many faculty members as students. Many attempts were made to close Bemidji State Teachers College and convert the buildings and premises to other state use. With the present enrollment and expansion at the College, it is now easily seen that all efforts on the part of College officials and the citizens of Bemidji in keeping the College at Bemidji were and are well justified."

Herbert E. Olson, also a Bemidji attorney, was resident director from 1955 to 1967 (Dexter Duggan, deceased, was resident director from 1948 to 1955). Olson emphasized three important developments. "First is enrollment," he said. In 1955, the number of full-time students was 601; in 1960 there were 1,724; in 1967 there were 4,554. Olson attributed much of physical growth and change on campus to the state's allowing the sale of revenue bonds to finance the building of new dormitories. This meant, he indicated, that the state did not have to dip into its own treasury but allowed building to continue, the bonds to be paid off by the students from the normal costs of living and eating in the dormitories. The third important development cited by Olson was the acquisition of more land. The College acquired a 50-acre open tract of land adjoining the campus which was owned by the city and generally called "the city forest." This increased the size of the campus to 74 acres. It was also during Olson's term as resident director that the College name was changed from Bemidji State Teachers College to the present name of Bemidji State College, the change of name coming by action of the 1957 legislature.

At present there are no resident directors on the State College Board. The 1963 legislature eliminated the provision for appointing members from the counties in which colleges are located; the only limitation currently in force is that no more than one member may be from the same county at the time of appointment. There are today eight Board members serving four-year terms, but by action of the 1963 legislature, the terms will be progressively changed to six years. The ninth member of the Board is the state commissioner of education who also serves as secretary to the Board. All Board members serve without compensation, although expenses of attending meetings are reimbursed. Regular meetings are held quarterly, although it is commonly found necessary to hold meetings more frequently. The Board maintains a central administrative office in St. Paul under the direction of the State Colleges' Chancellor who is appointed by the Board. The purpose of this office is to coordinate the activities of the State Colleges, to provide certain accounting and budgeting services, to provide the Board with reports and statistical information, to serve a liaison function with other elements of state government, and to carry out the policies and directions of the State College Board.[324]

Beaver mascot and friend
"Showing the optimism of youth."

Since World War II, graduates of Bemidji College have found little difficulty in securing employment. In 1943, Dr. A. C. Clark, acting president of the College, was quoted as saying that there were so many teaching positions open that "students interviewed superintendents instead of superintendents interviewing the students." Clark added that year, "I can safely say there are ten positions or more for every individual we can possibly place." Although it is hardly that situation today, almost all the 1968-69 graduates of Bemidji on the Bachelor of Science teaching curriculum found employment in teaching. There were 591 graduates— 257 in elementary education and 334 in secondary education. The mean average

---

[324] Minnesota, Legislative Manual (1967-68), pp. 191.

salary for these beginning teachers was $6,485, which does not include extra-curricular activities pay. This represented an increase of $426 over the salaries of beginning teachers for the preceding year; and 12 years before this, 1957, the average mean salary paid for Bemidji graduates was $3,864. Beginning teachers from Bemidji in 1969 found employment in 67 of the 87 counties in the state. A total of 218 elementary and 201 high school teachers, or 86 percent who accepted teaching positions, secured employment in Minnesota. In addition to placement in Minnesota, beginning teachers found positions in 18 states, and four accepted positions in Canada.[325]

The number of students seeking a B.A. degree at Bemidji has grown from a minuscule figure of less than one percent of the students in 1950 to about 25 percent of the student body by 1969. The number of B.A. graduates in 1966-67 increased from 75 to 198 in 1969; of the latter figure, ten percent went on to graduate school. Excepting those in graduate school or in military service, the mean average salary for B.A. graduates in 1969 was $8,413 or nearly two thousand dollars better than their B.S. degree counterparts in teaching. In any event, both B.S. and B.A. graduates of Bemidji have found it relatively easy to secure employment in the affluent times since World War II, that is until 1969.[326]

After the death of Sattgast on March 24, 1964, the State College Board chose Dr. Harry F. Bangsberg to succeed him. Bangsberg began his duties September 1, 1964, although official inaugural ceremonies were not held until April 21, 1965.

Bangsberg was born in Minneapolis, April 7, 1928, the son of Roy and Marie Bangsberg. He grew up in LaCrosse, Wisconsin, where he attended public schools. He left high school during the latter part of World War II and served as an infantryman in the Army in the Pacific Theater. After being discharged from service, he attended Wisconsin State University and then transferred to Luther College at Decorah, Iowa, where he received a B.A. degree (*cum laude*) in June, 1950. The next year he attended the State University of Iowa at Iowa City where he received his M.A. His master's thesis was, "The State University of Iowa During World War I," part of the history of the university series.

During his post war and college years he worked as a newspaper reporter, and after completing his M.A., he returned to La Crosse to work on the *LaCrosse Tribune*. After a year he returned to the State University of Iowa for doctoral study.

He taught history at Western Illinois University and Wisconsin State University at Eau Claire while continuing his doctoral studies which were completed in 1957. The title of his dissertation was, "The Evolution of the Colombo Plan for Cooperative Economic Development in South and South-East Asia: 1950- 1956."

In 1959, Dr. Bangsberg resigned as associate professor of history at Eau Claire to become assistant director of the Wisconsin State University System at Madison. He left Madison in 1963 to become the first executive director of the

[325] Bemidji State College Placement Bureau, Annual Report, 1968-69, pp. 1 , 4. (Mimeographed.)
[326] Ibid., p. 3. Employment problems did show up for some of the 1969 graduates with B.S. degrees and the immediate future for B.S. graduates is not totally optimistic.

Higher Educational Coordinating Council of Metropolitan St. Louis. He left there to become president of Bemidji State College September 1, 1964.

At Bemidji State College he led in encouraging student participation in making decisions affecting the College. He believed that faculty and students should get involved in the world around them and through his work with the Boy Scouts, his church, as a Rotarian and as a member of many North Central Association accrediting teams, he led the way. He worked to develop a cultural arts program at Bemidji State College which would attract people of northern Minnesota to the campus so they could share in the good things that the world of music, arts and letters offers.[327]

Under his guidance, the curriculum was strengthened in the direction of liberal arts and he worked to develop programs in the Asian studies, in social science, and in literature. He initiated the work that led to the 1967 legislative decision to allow Bemidji State to offer a Master of Arts degree.

Dr. Bangsberg knew the meaning of cooperation and was quick to develop programs involving Bemidji State College with the University of Minnesota, the Red Lake Indian Reservation and other reservations, the Bemidji Public Schools, other branches of state, county and local government, and the many federal projects aimed to improve the educational, cultural and economic resources of this area. He worked successfully to bring federal funds to Bemidji State and brought to the campus such programs as Upward Bound, Community Action Programs, and institutes from the National Science Foundation. And in spite of Dr. Bangsberg's professional and community achievements, he was a family man. Weekend afternoons in the winter would find him on the ski slope or at the pool with his five children and his wife, Trudy. In the summer, he enjoyed his garden, sailing, and fishing for walleye.

Many at Bemidji compared Bangsberg's college presidency to the national presidency of John F. Kennedy. Bangsberg, a young college president at age 36, was full of ideas and zest, and he brought to the campus a freshness and vitality that were infectious in the College and community. Probably more than specific reforms and innovations, he added to the atmosphere a spirit of enthusiasm and a general feeling that the whole school was moving ahead in a useful, positive direction.

Bangsberg believed firmly that the College faculty should be involved in projects off campus as well as on, and in that light he accepted an assignment to Viet Nam which ended in tragedy. Bangsberg became a member of a team of nine United States educators sponsored by the United States Department of State through the Agency for International Development. The group went to Viet Nam to advise the government of Viet Nam in the development of a system of public higher education. Bangsberg left Bemidji on January 1, 1967; he never returned. He and six others in his group were killed in a plane crash in Viet Nam on March 23, 1967.

---

[327] The fine arts complex now being built will be named after Bangsberg. Mrs. Bangsberg and their children now live in Madison, Wisconsin, at this writing, 1969.

John S. Glas
(Interim President, 1967-1968)
"First clear it with John."

After Bangsberg's untimely death, John S. Glas served as acting president for the next year and a half, until September 1, 1968. Formerly he had held the title of assistant to the president under both Bangsberg and Sattgast (he is in 1969 vice president for administrative affairs). Glas has been on the Bemidji faculty since 1939, usually in the role of business manager, but in all his roles or capacities, he has been an influential figure in the operation and guidance of the school's direction.

The period that Glas served as president was a holding period and perhaps a watershed period in the history of the College. At the time the new president, Robert Decker, took over, September 1, 1968, the College was operating under an acting president, an acting academic dean, an acting associate dean, and an acting chancellor of the State College System. Many Bemidji College partisans waited with some impatience for the State Board to act on permanent appointments. Then finally on March 13, 1968, the Board appointed Dr. G. Theodore Mitau, chairman of the political science department at Macalaster College, to be the new chancellor of the State College System. Mitau, 47, assumed his duties July 15 at a salary of $30,000 a year. Mitau foresaw a trend in the State Colleges from major emphases on teacher training and traditional liberal arts to more specializing in the training of para-professional personnel for business, industry, engineering, and health sciences. These graduates will be the "practitioners and supervisors" much in demand by Minnesota employers, he said.[328]

Mitau's appointment was followed shortly by the Board's appointment on April 15, 1968, of Dr. Robert D. Decker as the seventh president of Bemidji State College.

Dr. Decker's early life, schooling, and professional training were all in the state of Texas. He was born in Hays County Texas, November 12, 1922, the son of a county judge and rancher. He graduated as valedictorian of his class from Kyle High School, Kyle, Texas, in 1940. Prior to entering the service during World War II, Dr. Decker attended South-West State College at San Marcos. He enlisted as a private in World War II and was released as a first lieutenant, seeing service in the Pacific theater, including the Philippines and Japan. Dr. Decker continued his

---

[328] Minneapolis Tribune, March 14, 1968, p. 1: September 10, 1969, p. 5. The ubiquitous Mitau and the role he played as chancellor thus far might be noted in the remarks of President Decker when he introduced Mitau before Mitau spoke to the combined Bemidji service clubs at a noon luncheon July 28, 1969: "Sixteen months ago a whirlwind hit the Minnesota State College System, and when it had settled down there were no longer six individual colleges but a true State College System working toward a common goal." Bemidji Pioneer, July 29, 1969, p. 1.

education after the war and received his B.S. degree in 1948 from Texas A. & M. He returned to San Marcos where he was agriculture teacher for the Hays County Veterans' Vocational School for one year, and from 1949 to 1955 he was vocational agricultural teacher at San Marcos High School.

He received his Master of Education degree in agricultural education from Texas A. & M. in 1954 and from 1955 until 1957 he worked as a research assistant for Texas A. & M. at its Agricultural Experiment Station. From 1957 until 1959 he was assistant professor of agricultural economics and economics at Sul Ross State College, Alpine, Texas. In 1958 he received his Doctor of Philosophy degree in agricultural economics from Texas A. & M. He remained at Sul Ross State until 1961 where he was associate professor of economics, plus serving as registrar. In September of 1961 he moved to Odessa College, Odessa, Texas, where he was dean of admissions and registrar.

President Bangsberg (in beret) welcomes Norwegian National Symphony to Bemidji (1966)
"A freshness and vitality that were infectious."

Dr. Decker moved to Minnesota in February, 1966, to be assistant to the State College chancellor, and when the chancellor left in July, 1967, Dr. Decker served as acting chancellor until the appointment of Mitau in March of 1968. At that point Decker soon became both president-elect of Bemidji State College and assistant chancellor of the Minnesota State College System. He became president of Bemidji College September 1, 1968. Dr. Decker and his wife Jacqueline have two sons and one daughter.

President Decker addresses graduation audience (June, 1969)
"The times . . . they are a' changin'."

Dr. Decker leads Bemidji State College into its second 50 years. What direction the College moves, what new programs the school begins, what different services the institution provides the area and the state are largely up to the president. Curious and interested partisans of the school await his decisions. To aid him in his decisions he has chosen an essentially new team to lead a somewhat new college structural organization. There are now three vice presidents: (1) administrative affairs vice president, the aforementioned John Glas whose canny knowledge of the laws and the whole system, along with his hand on the purse strings, give credence to the oft-said faculty line, "First clear it with John"; (2) Academic Affairs Vice President Richard Beitzel, whose open-door policy for everyone has already favorably impressed all with a reputation of openness and fairness, and whose occasional gruff manner belies a quick wit and mind. (3) Student Affairs Vice President Cletus Kemper, new to the position in the fall of 1969, and whose

Classtime on the Lakeshore
"Likely the best campus location in Minnesota."

significance in the position is yet to be fully appreciated.

In the new administrative structure, there lies beneath the vice presidents seven division chairmen, all appointed to their positions by the president on July 1, 1969, and all responsible to the academic affairs vice president. The divisions and their chairmen are: Fine, Performing, and Communicating Arts, Ronald Gearman; Physical Education, Health, and Recreation, Victor Weber; Behavioral Sciences, Lewis Downing; Science and Mathematics, Evan Hazard; Humanities, Myron Swanson; Education, John Yourd; Business and Industry, John Warford. And under the division chairmen are the department chairmen, all responsible to their division head; and under all—and yet curiously "above all"—are the faculty members who with no titles make the world of BSC go 'round for President Decker and all his administrative lieutenants.

And last of all, and most important of all, are the students for whose benefit alone the entire institution exists, whether it be in 1919 or 1969 or 2019. It is well to be reminded of this fact, often. Students, and they alone, were the criteria for establishing the "sixth State Normal School"; they, and they alone, are the criteria of existence for BSC in the next 50 years.

Since the days of President Deputy, many changes have taken place at

Bemidji College. The physical plant improvements are visible, but other changes undoubtedly have greater significance. The students have changed; the curriculum has changed and the teaching is changing. Change has been imperative; without it the school would have deteriorated. However much some faculty and alumni might nostalgically long for the Bemidji College of 1929 or 1939 or 1959, or however much they would like the quiet serenity of a small, homogenous student body, the fact is that such longing is fiction; for a college today cannot be that simple (and probably never was). The problems only shift to new areas, and the participants seem to have but little control over the shift. There is no escape to an ivory tower fantasy, nor should there be. The college must live in the real world— although one would hasten to add that the real world in Bemidji affords far more isolation and insulation than is normal for most colleges and universities. This may be an advantage if the College makes use of the environment. The future will bring new problems, unforeseen challenges, and complex involvements that might frighten people if the crystal ball were illuminated. Fortunately, they see only in a mirror darkly and move forward with a quiet confidence that the school has the resources to enhance the traditions that it has inherited.

But whatever the future, whatever the past, perhaps the closing lines of Bangsberg's inaugural address best offer the challenge for tomorrow's Bemidji State College: "Let us work together as faculty, students, administration and friends and supporters of this College, and we can accomplish so much. Let us do as Edwin Markham urged in his poem:

> I am done with the years that were, I am quits,
> I am done with the dead and the old;
> They are mines worked out, I delved in their pits,
> And I have saved their rains of old—
> Now I turn to the future for wine and bread—
> I have bidden the past adieu—
> I laugh and lift hands to the years ahead,
> Come on! I'm ready for you."

End of Part I

PRESIDENTS

Manfred W. Deputy (1919-1937)
*"The College . . . the lengthened
shadow of this man."*

Charles R. Sattgast (1938-1964)
*"The best of times . . . the worst
of times."*

Harry F. Bangsberg (1964-1967)
"An assignment . . . in tragedy."

Robert D. Decker (1968-1980)
"Lively times . . . for level heads."

PRESIDENTS

Rebecca Stafford (1980-1981)
"Bright spots . . . amid turbulence."

Lowell R. Gillett (1982-1990)
*"The right man . . . at the right
time."*

Leslie C. Duly (1990-1993)
*"The unchangeable optimist . . . he
loved this place."*

M. James Bensen (1994-   )
"A new man . . . and a new merger."

College in the Pines

Introduction

PREFACE TO PART II

T he history of Bemidji State has been written in two different parts and at two different times by the same author. Likewise, both parts were written and published for special events within the history of the school, namely the 50th Anniversary and the 75th Anniversary of the school's founding in 1919.[1]

The first book published, <u>College in the Pines</u>, in effect Part I, was published in 1970 and dealt essentially with the earliest years of the school's opening and operation. Of the six chapters in the book, five were concerned with the location of the school in Bemidji and its start and operation under the leadership of its first president, Manfred Wolfe Deputy. Chapter Six was entitled, "Bemidji State College Since 1938: A Summary," and the chapter summed up a broad overview of the school's history from the years 1939 to 1969.

Now comes Part II, and this large section attempts to tell a more complete history of Bemidji State since World War II. However, given the time period to be covered, 1939-1994, this "new history" by necessity also becomes a general survey of that lengthy period. Also there is some repetition from the "Chapter Six Summary," but an effort has been made to expand on some topics. There have been no changes, no editing in the Part I portion, despite the later observations of the author that such-and-such could and probably should have been done differently. Whatever, all the facts,

---

1)The opportunity to write Part II of the history of Bemidji State came as a pleasant surprise. I certainly did not have this in mind when Part I was published. At the time I expected that "that was it," and answered negatively to those persons who then questioned the possibility of doing a second history or some kind of an "update" 25 years later. Back then it seemed so far away; now it seems, of course, that the time in between has gone by too fast - and too much has happened to be adequately recorded.

interpretations, and general observations remain as first published.[2]

This general history, both "old" and "new," Parts I and II, has been written primarily for students, former students and friends of Bemidji State University. But Part II will read differently from Part I in that it will, by comparison, be more personal. Moreover, the style and layout will be more journalistic and the overall tone less formal, making the whole history simply better reading. (Well, such is the intention, anyway.) Basically because "I was here" on the faculty of Bemidji State since 1959, I found it difficult to remain the "outside narrator," that distant voice chronicling the institutional developments and ringing-the-changes-of-history *vis a vis* all the historical documentation, those musky, dusky primary sources that supposedly guide the way to the final writing of "the truth"—all to be presented in scholarly, academic verbiage, the turgid likes of which can make any possible student of history switch his major to math.

When writing Part I, it was far easier to be on the sidelines—that third-person-outside-historian—because at the time the research and writing began, circa 1963, I was still rather new to the community and had yet little "feel," let alone perspective, for the institution. Nor had the school changed that much by 1959; the great burst of change would come in the next ten years. By 1969 it had changed markedly and remarkably! Wow, how it changed!

THE PRESSURES AND SIGNS OF CHANGES

Of course the school of the Post-War Years—or any time afterwards—never did or could operate in a vacuum. Like individuals who are subjected to the legion of external pressures of societal changes, so too did Bemidji State adopt and adapt to the changing times. Sometimes the outside motivation came from popular culture, and it was all for fun, like the once-popular Sadie Hawkins Day dances in the Fifties, a' la Al Capp and L'il Abner. Nothing like that for the students of the Nineties; indeed, most of them never heard of Capp. Nor would Fifties students understand any Nineties mandatory requirement that they complete a sexual harassment/assault training program—or else not be allowed to register for subsequent quarters. Forties students appreciated the technology of electric adding machines, while a word like "computer" appeared in science fiction. Any Nineties student illiterate in computer use remains that—illiterate. Those new electric typewriters in the Fifties were state-of-the-art technology; in the Nineties they're museum pieces. AIDS to Seventies students could mean financial, an insurance

2)Whether critics and/or correctors following the printing of College in the Pines chose to be generous in not pointing out presumed necessary corrections, the overt responses arriving in the mails singled out few needed changes. The most useful letter came from a 1929 graduate, Irvin Keeler (then of Naperville, IL; letter dated 11-8-77 and in author's files). He noted that there were four students who received their bachelor's degrees in the 1920s, not just one (see p. 131), namely: Keeler, Leonard Vogland, William Elliot, and Casper Dahle. Keeler added that Elton Beck in retirement (p. 191) went to Demorest, not Damascus, Georgia, and served as assistant to the president of Piedmont College, which is not a Negro college. And "It wasn't volunteer work. If you had known Beck, you would appreciate the underline." Finally, wrote Keeler, in the picture section (after p. 112) the automobile shown in the picture in front of the Main Building "is our 1925 Dodge. I worked in the office that summer and this must have been one day when my Dad let me use it. No parking problems then."
Lastly, for corrections, 20, not 21, died in WWII (p. 194).
(Amid the generally favorable mail, there was one very short and very angry note from a former faculty member who wrote, "How dare you use my name without my permission!" And now I dare not use her name again, even if she can't write another nasty note from the Great Beyond.)

company, or the American International Development Services; a decade later it became a dreaded medical term. Obviously the times—1939-1994—"they-are-a-changin'"—and not always for the better.

The Rigors of Registration
"In the late 1940s . . . 3x5 cards . . . coming up in the 1990s, register via telephone."

THE STUDENTS
"I'm the first person in my family to go beyond high school."
That simple statement essentially explains both the reason for Bemidji State University and what it has meant for the people of northern Minnesota. This basic declaration could have been written by at least three-fourths of the over 30,000 students who have graduated. Moreover, there would likely to be double that amount of could-be-writers who once attended but did not officially graduate.[3] The line would—and did—appear when the school first opened its doors in 1919;

---

3)It is easy to get the actual total of BSU graduates (30,283 by 1992) but it is near impossible to determine the numbers who once were enrolled but never graduated. An official in the Records Office said, we can give only "a SWAG estimate," which acronym stands for "Scientific-Wild-Ass-Guess," and the SWAG guess came out that 80,000 persons at one time took at least one class between the years 1919-1994.

it would—and did—appear once more 75 years later.[4]   And it will likely still be used come Centennial time as well because the line continues to solidify one major reason for the existence of Bemidji State.

REVERSE SNOBBERY
Bemidji State is not and never has been a snob school. The only thing there is to be snobbish about is being unsnobbish. Thus there is in effect reverse snobbery, and this is a good thing. Instead of feeling any remorse or embarrassment about lacking Ivy League fame or luster, students and faculty alike have felt instead a source of pride that on the quasi-frontier in northern Minnesota was located a pretty good school which over 75 years kept getting better and better. Bemidji State has met the needs of those thousands of unsnobbish students who chose to come here. This is in the best American tradition because our history is replete with figures who had humble backgrounds but who made the best of opportunities available to them and rose to become not only acceptable members of society but real assets to that society. Here in the northland, Bemidji State has offered extraordinary opportunities; of this all Minnesotans can and should be proud.[5]

THERE'S HONOR IN "SCRUBS"
The public's perception of Bemidji State students always seems to have included those who view students negatively, alas. I recall sitting in a local barber-chair and listening to some of the town gentry in the room refer to the College students as "a bunch of scrubs." The remark hurt at the time because I knew differently, but most curious was their ongoing, rambling "definition" of these "scrubs." Despite their labelings, sarcastically delivered as put-downs, the labelings were accurate! - and they were positive! - if the word "Scrubs" is changed to "Scramblers." According to the critics' blanket assertions, these College kids were nobodies; their parents were nobodies and "didn't have no education"; they came from the wrong side of the tracks; they came from Podunks and Nowheresvilles; a bunch of uncouth Jackpine Savages—or Winchester Farmers—or Remington Ranchers, right out of the brush—with the bark still on some of them; their family names meant nothing to this glorious state's history and honor; and many of their names were funny-sounding and often hard to pronounce; naive neophytes, they're the first ones in their families to ever give college a try. And on and on. . . .

4)The words were quoted again in a 1992 thank-you letter sent to the vice president of development, Dr. David Tiffany, from a graduate who had contributed to the BSU Scholarship Fund. This time the words of the former student were followed by the line, "I probably would have stayed home and worked, but the scholarship made the difference." (In 1992, BSU provided $328,000 in scholarships to 500 students.) It is unlikely that any BSU faculty member at any time in the history of the school did not hear students regularly say that they were the first in their family ever to go to college.
5)The impact of college snobbery came up abruptly to this author while attending a graduate school at the University of Wisconsin one summer in the 1950s. Across from my dorm room lived a young man who attended Princeton University during the school year. For "variety," he came to Madison via his Jaguar convertible to what he called "flyover-country" and enrolled for one credit of phy ed, which allowed him sufficient time to party steadily for eight beer-soaked weeks. Although pleasant enough in personality, he'd come up with one indelible response after he once asked what I did in the summers when I was an undergrad, and I told him that I worked as a laborer on a section-gang on a railroad. His quick reply was part shock but all honest upper class scorn, "Work is for horses." Bemidji State reverse snobbery would take proper issue with that line. We're work-oriented pragmatists, one and all, and proud of it.

These judgmental barbershop buffoons were so "right"—but so "wrong" in what they were inferring from the students and their backgrounds. Unfortunately, but true, the immediate area surrounding Bemidji has held for too long the dubious, ongoing distinction of being one of the poorest sections of the state. As well as

Crowd Scene at a Homecoming Game
"Students see any new school year with a vibrant and positive view . . . Time to live!"

being forever economically depressed, the regional mental health center in Bemidji long ago (1966) labeled the area as "a twilight zone of poverty in which 31% of all households lack a hot water system; 30% lack indoor plumbing, and less than half of the households have a furnace. The average education of the head of the household is 9.1 years of schooling for the male and 10.2 for the female. Persons with low incomes show a very high depression level and show a social introversion." (Thankfully there have been significant improvements since that '66 report.)

So this is the region that Bemidji State serves; from this area have come two-thirds of our "scramblers."[6]

SO HOW DO THE STUDENTS DO, ONCE THEY GET HERE?

If the great majority of students who attended Bemidji State never did have

6)A major reason the scrubs-and-scramblers at Bemidji State dismay me not is that I was once a scrub myself in an Iowa college, one who scrambled to survive, one who literally scrubbed the floor of a local restaurant in town every Saturday night for four years, starting at 1:00 a.m. and ending at 6:00 a.m. And my three roommates for four years were scrubs: one a big Swede, a bear of a man who was twice all-conference in football and who was afraid of only one thing: girls. Today he's the top CPA in an accounting firm. Another roomie was a gangling apparition who scrambled for subsistence but not for grades. (Like a good roommate should, he helped pull us all through, bless him.) Today he's a judge on the Minnesota State Appellate Court. The last fellow-scrub was a test of endurance for himself, us, and all officialdom; it took him five and a half years of scrambling before graduating magna-cum-thanks, but he did make it, finally! He would become a head coach and eventually an athletic director; he died of a heart attack at age 59, in 1990. (Actually I wrote and had published a book about my college and roommates in the 1950s; it had the unpronounceable title of Brother Hottenbotten; no wonder it only had two printings.)

the fanciest of backgrounds, then how did they do once they got here? For this answer, as former 1920s New York Governor Al Smith said so often, "Let's look at the record." A most important measurement is the graduation rate, and the record shows that the graduation rate is over 40% for Bemidji students who have enrolled as freshmen, which is considerably higher than the national average of one in three graduates.

Every faculty member from the past 75 years could come up with the names of certain graduates he or she personally had and knew and hold these graduates up as successful, or even outstanding, Bemidji State alumni: "Look at so-and-so, a major executive with _____, and take _____, what a fantastic career in public education that person had after college . . . and then there's _____." Of course any college faculty member anywhere can come up with such a list, and thus the rhetorical if cynical question: Did these people do well in life because they went to Bemidji State? Or would they have succeeded anyway? This is a difficult question to answer but I honestly believe that in most cases Bemidji State made the difference in their lives. At a crucial time period for them, these students came to this institution and both directly and indirectly were molded positively by their experiences here. The record proves it.[7]

LEFT-HANDED COMPLIMENT: "SCRAMBLING TECH"

There appears never to have been such a thing as the stereotyped rah-rah kind of college spirit at Bemidji State. And because it has not met that definition, some surprised new students and fledgling faculty have complained about "the lack of school spirit." Not to worry. To deplore this absence of overt controlled hysteria is both blind and unimaginative but, granted, the student body, since about 1965, has lacked cohesiveness. Most come to Bemidji State on their own because they want a college degree (I'd like to say "education," but can't), and it has always been the kind of place where it is possible somehow, with enough hustle and scramble and stick-to-it-iveness, to get that elusive sheepskin—and learn much at the same time.

When new students arrive on campus, they may appear to have little in common with their cohorts except the shared notion that it is hustling and scrambling that will get them through—eventually. This scrambling breeds a kind of comradeship, but they are not a homogeneous group, and because they are not all alike, they come to think it is normal and healthy to be individualistic—but always practical. They discover, for example, that there are many different kinds

7)Former students have over and over said as much. I really believe that we have done better with our raw material than many if not most colleges. (A colleague once told me back in 1964, "And believe me, some of it is pretty raw.") Since my arrival here in 1959, I have been part of the crew responsible for preparing secondary school social studies teachers and over that time period I can confidently assert that it has been "the scrubs" who have become the best high school teachers! The reports from the superintendents and classroom supervisors came back over the years with all essentially declaring the same thing, Bemidji student teachers are commonsensical. They're not starry-eyed idealists living in La-la Land. Because of their own backgrounds, they can easily identify with the school kids they must deal with every day. So practical-minded. So understanding and patient, with good senses of humor - who don't take themselves too seriously. But still solid. And decent. So fully aware of the fact that for most of the families from which public school kids come from, life is pretty basic; it's bread and butter and how to raise the rent money—and keep that TV set on day and night. Good mentors, good teachers. Give us more!

of intelligence and many places to learn outside of the classroom. College life, college living, college extracurricular activities, teach many valuable things even if those "things" are often difficult to define. One byproduct of individualism, of course, is that they never develop a total-group-spirit, that so-called "college spirit." For example, at athletic contests they have seldom all yelled very effectively in unison and have been the despair of all Beaver cheerleaders for decades! (Without the ongoing pep bands for inspiration, cheerleaders would have been in a pickle.) Bemidji students have never performed well to orchestrated enthusiasm. They do yell mightily when there is something to yell about, but not when the cheerleaders direct them. It's an independence that is not all bad. (And when considered carefully, is there anything more phony than organized enthusiasm?)[8]

BEMIDJI STATE: WHAT PURPOSE AT START? (Easy to Answer)

Bemidji State emerged out of the normal school tradition, that is, the tradition of teacher-training institutions, which in turn grew out of the European tradition of educators/philosophers like Pestolozzi. Originally, normal schools

Lecturing on Literature from Ruth Stenerson
"The epitome of a fine teacher: kind, caring, patient -- and demanding."

---

8)The "shock of the silent crowd" hits most freshmen, especially those from small towns who recently left their high schools where "school spirit" had verged on the manic.

were not part of the American system of higher education to which universities and liberal arts colleges belonged.[9] (Normal school graduates received a one-year or two-year teaching certificate allowing them to teach in elementary schools.) However, that began to change in Minnesota in the 1920s when all the State Normal Schools became designated teachers colleges and were authorized to give four years of schooling leading to a bachelor's degree in either elementary or secondary education. For all students attending Bemidji State at either stage—normal school or teachers college—there was the expectation that they would become—or at least could become—school teachers. (No liberal arts or business administration non-teaching B.A. degrees then.)

As expected, the faculties hired reflected the temper of teacher-training, with both classes and instructors weighted heavily in the direction of professional education. In 1946, for example, Dr. Harold T. Hagg could almost alone handle all the history course offerings necessary.[10] That year, out of a total staff of 48 faculty, 16 members were in professional education. But already the forces of change were moving the school into different directions.

BEMIDJI STATE: WHAT PURPOSE BY 1960?—2000? (Not Easy to Answer)

Certainly by World War II Bemidji State began hiring more faculty members who were products of the liberal arts tradition, and a slow transformation began taking place. The result might be noted in an article called "The Short and Happy Life of the State Teachers College," the title suggesting that changes had come to the former normal schools, whether wanted or not, and World War II had brought those changes. The G.I.s came back from "The Good War" and enrolled in college in record numbers, and many of the men—and women—had no intention of becoming school teachers. Even those who did wanted more depth in subject matter fields and demanded appropriate and more diverse curriculum offerings. Bemidji State met these demands by creating its first non-teaching B.A. major, and although this might appear on the surface as a trivial change if not ho-hum and boring, the school would never be the same again. Bemidji State's representative on the State Colleges' governing board then (1944-48) was local attorney Clarence Smith who later said, "Possibly the most important development at Bemidji State Teachers College during my term as resident director was the authorization and approval for the granting of bachelor of arts degrees. Previously the only degree awarded was the bachelor of science degree."

9)The term "normal" was borrowed from the French, who called a teacher-training school an Ecole Normale, technically meaning model or ideal school. In the early years of the 19th century, the preparation of teachers was so bad that leading political figures such as John Quincy Adams, Daniel Webster, and Horace Mann decided to do something about it. Mann, a lawyer, abolitionist, congressman, and later president of Antioch College, got a modest appropriation for a public institution at Lexington, Massachusetts, and called it a normal school after the French usage. It opened in 1839 with three women students. The movement spread rapidly to other states as the effectiveness of the school became known. One started in Winona in 1860, the first normal school west of the Mississippi River.
10)Perhaps the shifting size of the history department faculty reflects the shifting significance of history in the curriculum since World War II. From Hagg virtually alone in 1946, the number inched up slowly (Dr. Bernie Friedman came in 1955) by 1960. Then came quantum leaps! A history faculty of 16 in 1970! Then came ongoing decline and almost demise; the department has limped along with four members since 1992, and thus must be added an editorial boo-hoo.

'Signing' for the hearing impaired in Alan Brew's Anthro Class
"All this illustrates again that neither high school nor college is what it used to be."

Not that Bemidji State students rushed immediately into non-teaching programs; that came later. For example, even by 1965, when there were 3,000-plus students, there were only 57 B.A. graduates. The big swing into non-teaching areas, most notably business administration, began in the 1970s and has continued with little let-up since then. Essentially the school that began only to educate and train teachers eventually became a college for non-teachers. In the 1992 graduating class, only 23% received degrees in public school teaching.

BUT HOW ABOUT STANDARDS? WHOM DO WE LET IN? (KEEP OUT?)

Alumni of the 1940s may have thought their school to be just fine, but it wouldn't do for their children, from whom more was expected—and to whom more should be offered. And should not student standards and requirements and grade points be raised?—say all the ones who have graduated. Certainly! And should not admission requirements be raised to keep out the . . . uh . . . "undesirables"? Of course. Well, maybe; then again, maybe not.[11]

Discussion of these issues has continued with little abatement since The War, and certainly no consensus has ever been reached. Overall since '45, the issue of "access"—that is the chance for admittance—has been answered by the basic decision to allow essentially anyone with a high school diploma to be admitted to Bemidji State. In effect the reasoning has been, "Give the kid a chance." Almost all the College presidents have argued for the right-to-try-college, with one (Harry Bangsberg) saying that given his (Bangsberg's) terrible high school record, any stipulation on enrollment admissions would have kept him from starting college. Only in the last few years (since 1990) has this policy been altered; and requirements for admission have gone up to the point that over 400 students were denied admission to BSU in the fall of '93. Among the unhappy responders to the latter policy change are those legislators who get phone calls from unhappy parents wondering why their genius-offspring can't get into "the local teachers college."

KEEPING GOOD STUDENTS OUT: SOARING COSTS; THE ECONOMY

So why are capable students who are highly motivated and want to go to college NOT going to college? More and more the simple answer has become that they can't afford it. This has been most apparent the past ten years when the mushrooming of costs—over a 100% jump—to attend college have far exceeded growth in costs in other areas—and in wages. More than the policy barriers keeping young people from attending Bemidji State—A.C.T. scores, S.A.T. scores, class rank, *et al*—it's simply the shortage of the big bucks needed that disallows hundreds of potentially fine students from coming to Bemidji. 'Tis sad, especially considering that it was the Bemidji States that were historically established for those students from families whose income meant they "couldn't afford to go to college."

Despite a system of government and private financial aid based on need, going back to the first monumental federal aid precedent set in 1958 with the National Defense Education Act, lower income families in Minnesota have borne a heavier burden than did the more affluent families. It was not supposed to be that way. Consider the costs of going to Bemidji State over ten-year blocks:

In 1947, with tuition at $20 a quarter, the overall cost for one school year was determined to be $400. Ten years later—tuition at $35—the year's cost was set at $700. By 1967, tuition was based on credits taken at $5 a credit; the final figure for the year went to $1,150. The total jumped to $1,900 in 1977; tuition at

---

11)Over the past 30 years, I have heard faculty profs, who themselves graduated from Bemidji State, say—and say proudly— that if they were to enroll today, they would never make it academically. A curious compliment. Most faculty go grudgingly along with accepting a kind of academic social Darwinism, i.e., letting any student enroll, after which it's strictly survival-of-the-fittest; the strong live, the weak die (flunk). However, there is one very vocal supporter of raising enrollment standards; a former department chair, she says to "show me in the Constitution where it says that every citizen is guaranteed the right to go to college." (For the majority of teachers, however, it's the waggish line of a grad school dean who said it right, "Many are called; few are chosen." In Bemidji, there's an awful pun-ish line to punish people with, "Many are cold; few are frozen.")

$9.25 a credit. What then followed were horrendous leaps in the next decade so that by 1987 the estimated expenses a year totaled $3,600. By this point financial "gradualism" over the decades abruptly became year-after-year escalation so that in 1990, $4,600 was the year-end cost figure, and it was $5,400 just two years later when cost per credit reached $42.35 for residents (and $83.80 for non-residents)!

Minnesota's public colleges and univeristies have become less affordable since the early 1980s because of steep tuition increases. Between 1981 and 1992, tution of the University of Minnesota went up 153 percent, the community colleges 151 percent, and the state universities 204 percent! That even exceeded medical costs in that time period which went up 133 percent--while per capita income in that period rose just 87 percent. (Source: Minneapolis Star Tribune, February 26, 1994, 1B.) By Diamond anniversary time, students can expect to pay some $6,000 for a year at Bemidji State.[12]

Concurrent with the rising costs of the past ten years has been the rising time needed to graduate. The once normal expectation of four-years-and-you're-done has given way to a new near "normal" notion that it takes five school years to get a degree. Moreover, with the combination of many problems, there is little surprise in noting that by 1992 the average graduate has left with a loan-indebtedness of over $7,000.[13]

Both Artist and Art Professor Marley Kaul
"The art department FINALLY got some decent facilities."

12)There's actually some "good news" in these college costs because money/loans/debts are all and always relative. To wit, Bemidji State expenses have been a bargain compared to the costs of going to almost any of Minnesota's private colleges! To take the extreme example, attending Carleton College for one year at this writing (1994) costs over $20,000 and its neighbor in Northfield, St. Olaf College, costs $15,000. Comparatively, Bemidji State is back to being "inexpensive."
13)Unfortunately that substantial debt figure has been surpassed by some (too many) BSU graduates who looked at college loan bills well over $10,000 their day of graduation. To compound the problem, there's yet another factor—labeled by students "a real bummer"—to this negative story, namely the difficulty in finding well-paying employment after graduation. Since the heady wine of jobs-jobs-jobs in the 1960s, the employment picture has not been totally good for any grads, and for those majors who were in areas where there was the least hiring, it was downright bleak (read horrible).

ARE THE STUDENTS GETTING BETTER AND BETTER?
HOW 'BOUT FACULTY?

Julius Caesar likely turned to his Preceptor of Education and asked, "Are the students not getting better over the years? And is the faculty not showing ongoing improvement?" And likely the Preceptor responded with a murky line like, "Well, it depends on how you define the word 'better.' It's a 'weasel-word,' y'know. And as to the teachers, well, that's a little more measurable, but not much." The better-and-better-student statement has kept getting mouthed about Bemidji State students each decade since The War and thus it has become an accepted if not necessarily a valid cliche—but it remains impossible to answer, let alone prove. What remains somewhat answerable and measurable is faculty improvement over the last 40 years, assuming that advanced degree attainment is an acceptable measure of improvement. With that standard in mind, the statistics show that only 30% of the 1950 faculty held the terminal (normally a doctorate) degree, while in 1990, 70% of the faculty had achieved that distinction. The latter figure is the highest in the entire Minnesota State University System.[14]

WHAT CAN BE MEASURED EASILY AND ACCURATELY?

The easiest and most obvious way to determine changes at Bemidji State since World War II is to count the buildings on the campus and to look at the changing campus itself. In 1944 there were three buildings on a 20-acre campus; in 1964 there were 14 buildings on an 84-acre campus; in 1994 there were 23 buildings (including the Physical Education Complex which is essentially three separate buildings) on 89 acres of land. A veritable building boom starting in the 1960s marked the transformation of a tiny teachers college on the shores of Lake Bemidji into a major University. What cannot be empirically measured but nevertheless can be agreed upon by everyone is the beauty of the location of Bemidji State. It is the loveliest location of any college in the state of Minnesota, period.[15]

MORE THAN A COLLEGE—THE CULTURAL
"MECCA" OF THE NORTHLAND

Question: "But . . . but what is there to do in Bemidji in the arts? What is there to hear, to see way up there amid all this . . . er . . . woodland?"[16]

---

14)There are as many hairy doctorate stories as there are hairs on a dog. Horrid tales follow about "ABDs,"—All-But-Dissertation, almost always stories which fall in the category of Tragedies, namely persons who came as close as you can to completing a doctorate—but not quite. Something happened; something went wrong, and that something is something one does not ask about. It's too touchy a subject, too emotional, too upsetting to even bring up in the presence of the ABD person.
15)Parochialism aside, the campus sells itself to prospective students. Admissions counselors indicate that once an inquiring student comes to the community and tours the campus, their selling job has ended; the location is a major factor in student selection of a college to attend. It is the rarest of students—and they're from metropolitan areas—who find the Bemidji campus undesirable. One such person whom I got to know well (we're still exchanging Christmas letters after 25 years) was from Detroit and she simply could not stand the quiet and all those trees! Indeed, without the night sounds and police cars and/or fire sirens going off every hour on the hour, she could not get to sleep!
16)This was the rather carefully phrased question once asked me by my oldest brother, then of Minneapolis and cognizant of the virtues of concerts and theaters and galleries surrounding the area (question asked when we first moved to Bemidji in 1959)—and oh-so-slightly suggesting that amid the jackpines and mangy moose, there was little aesthetically available outside of the sun shining off the ice on Lake Bemidji in July. He was wrong then and even "wronger" now (1994). Still the perception of outstate Minnesota (officially we're declared "Greater Minnesota" as a barren cultural wasteland unfairly continues.

Answer: There is so much to do and see and hear in Bemidji that the question becomes rather, "Which cultural attraction will I have to miss because there's something else going on at the same time?" The primary reason there are so many cultural and artistic events in the community is Bemidji State University. That simple. It has become a widely known fact that persons choose to move to Bemidji—whether for employment or as a retirement spot—because of the multiple and ongoing cultural offerings provided by the University. It can be cold outside, but inside there is a plethora of cultural activities all year 'round! (Much more on this subject in a later section called "The Eye (and Ear) Catchers.")

SO WHAT RANK SHOULD BE GIVEN BEMIDJI STATE TEACHERS COLLEGE? BEMIDJI STATE COLLEGE? BEMIDJI STATE UNIVERSITY?

The three designations deserve in order the answers Good, Better, Best. Obviously this becomes another "qualification statement" but one that will be answered—and supported at length—in the text following this Introduction.

The changing times have been good for the school. Bemidji State, although on the surface geographically "isolated," has benefited mightily from the Information Revolution. Technology and transportation improvements have nullified what had been provincialism. Fax machines move information as quickly to and from Bemidji as to Burnsville—or London. The new Beltrami County Airport on the edge of town constantly finds faculty and administration in the morning flying off to meetings in Minneapolis and flying home that same evening. Vax computers and E Mail enable profs to communicate not only nationally but internationally. The information age has been good to and for once remote Bemidji State.

Although the school may specifically focus on the region—and get most of its students from the region—the graduates go all over the country and the world. By design—indeed, by decrees of the presidents, starting with Bangsberg in the mid-'60s—international students have been recruited to this campus by the hundreds so that the student union has at times resembled a little United Nations. If there were not at least 20 countries represented in the student body during any school year the past 25 years, there has been something amiss in recruiting. The many foreign students have been good for Bemidji State and vice-versa.[17] In a legion of ways—and measured by a variety of criteria—it's a different school and yes, a constantly

---

17)"Foreigners" in large numbers came to Bemidji State somewhat suddenly in the middle 1960s. In looking back, their arrival seems almost quaint, but then it was just provincialism. There was then a form of xenophobia on campus, but with a twist; these "foreigners" were all from New Jersey! But they were certainly "different"; they talked funny, and they were so loud! That made them really different, so much so that there was student agitation both open and covert (it included homemade, sometimes obscene signs on the walls) to keep them out! Eventually adjustments were made, grudging acceptance was allowed, and these "foreigners" became tolerated, at least in part. Their arrival from Jersey had been prompted by a precipitous jump in college costs there; they viewed Minnesota rates as virtually free education. Although most returned to the east coast, a few stayed in the region, including a young man who gave his own (really!) famous name to the establishment he owns in Erskine, "Joe DiMaggio's Bar." As to the truly international students at Bemidji State (always 200 or more the past 10 years), they have added a desirable flair, and with their clothes and cultures, they have provided a multi cultural mix. It would be an overstatement to indicate that all of them have been welcomed with open arms and easily or totally assimilated, but it can be stated that there has not been a single incident of overt nativism. Their most positive public contribution is their well-received, looked-forward-to Feast of Nations banquet and program, which they have put on each spring since 1970, a credit to them and to their American advisor on campus since 1969, Lorna Sullivan.

improving school, since 1945. How good? Well, a retiring board member of the entire State University System privately told a retired BSU president in 1993 that "Bemidji State is the flagship of the System."

WHAT'S THIS? BEMIDJI STATE UNIVERSITY
NOW THE BEST IN EVERYTHING?

NOoooo, not really; no pretense to that category. Just ask the students. If there's any doubt, the students will tell you as much, as there's a combination of healthy skepticism and independent spirit in this unrarified atmosphere. Staff and students together can admit to the institution's being far from ideal and a shade short of perfection. The best students say openly that some programs are weak, some majors "thin," some courses cheesy, some instructors bad, and they don't feel obliged to gloss over their criticisms while at the same time having faith in and giving support to their alma mater. Good combination.

End of Quarter Exams Once Taken in Memorial Hall
"Faculty tests (too hard; too easy; too canned) . . . unfathomable grading standards."

Anytime pedantic profs get too caught up in their own self-importance, they get reminded quickly of the most elementary fact about the history of Bemidji State: It is here for the students, not for the faculty nor administration. Students have forever remained an amazing and varied lot: They're young (lots of high school kids taking college classes on campus) and they're old—and getting older (average age by 1990 almost 29)[18]; many are very smart (these merit scholars are a challenge to any Ph.D.) and some moderately dumb (in an intelligent way, of course). But all of the above have remained respectful and anxious to please.

These wonderful "scramblers" have over the many years remained independent and practical and have learned not to take academia too seriously in a world in which they have had to scramble to survive. They do not lie to themselves or become smug, as some elite college groups do. Almost all of the students in Bemidji's short history have had to take extra jobs in order to make it through college. One sees them employed everywhere: Working in the union, taking tickets, clerking in stores, tending bar, fighting fires, serving as night watchmen; they're anywhere and everywhere they can pick up a needed buck that can keep them enrolled. Many work too hard; they often get C's and D's when they could earn A's and B's if they did not have to scramble so hard. For this the faculty makes concessions they perhaps should not make, but they do anyway. A one-page statistical report from the Chancellor's Office labeled "Percentage of Students Employed" in 1989 finds Bemidji with the highest percentage of any State University at 73.3%; that's on-campus jobs only and NOT off-campus employment.

THE "NON-ACADEMIC SIDE" OF LEARNING: WHO'S RIGHT?

Whether '94 or '44—or forever—supporters of academics as the soul of learning vs. extracurriculars as the REAL learning have been at odds. Too many students have perennially neglected their coursework because of too much time and commitment for out-of-class activities; moreover, there are other students so narrowly class-oriented that they miss the fun, the excitement, the bonding that comes from involvement in tangential activities outside the lecture halls.

Yet only the extremists in both camps object totally to the other. Most have agreed that if a college works well, academic rigor goes along well with outside vigor. Both are necessary for a complete college education. And there have always been and still remain so many ways and places and opportunities for the expression of interests and talents that few, if any, students have failed to participate in extracurricular effort of some kind. Indeed, it's been clear over the years that extracurriculars have been the major factor in keeping large numbers of students in school.

Each new activity opens up vistas and encourages development. The "outside stuff" has meant a full and often exhausting life for students, especially when at the same time their teachers have "piled it on"; this regular combination has too often brought a student to the inevitable stern accounting and self examination

---

18)Teachers of vintage age are constantly asked, "Who have been your best students?" That question is also constantly ducked, but to those of us who have taught in the Elderhostel Program, the answer is simple, the senior citizens, who should be renamed "seasoned-citizens"; they're the best students on campus! To be eligible for Elderhostel, one must be at least 60 years old, and the average age of those attending the Bemidji State program (not incidentally the biggest in the state) is closer to 75. They go because they want to learn. As one elderly woman (she was 88) told me after one session, "We long ago made the discovery that the real action in life is inside the head." They are absolutely delightful students who are fun to be around and to have around; they're bright and eager, with a lifetime of experiences to draw from. The Elderhostel program, which began in 1978, has been one of the most successful collegiate programs nationally since World War II.

of his or her priorities. If the pace has become too fast, student common sense usually asserts itself; deceleration takes place, and books get more attention; the sound, serious business of getting a college degree is not lost sight of amid the whirlwind of often frantic activities. Now and then these active young folks have taken time off to sleep, sometimes in classes.[19] Only alumni can look back and declare college to be their "happy years." The scrambling undergrads at the time aren't always that sure.

Sanford Hall Lounge
"Set up for the 50 women who lived upstairs . . . board and room $135 a quarter."

SYNOPSIS TIME FOR PART II
This lengthy narrative which follows has been an overall attempt to record the story of the struggling years of the school since World War II; of both the subtle and the obvious ways in which it adjusted to the changing times; of the place it filled in the ever-widening community of northern Minnesota; of the difficulties which beset it because of financial difficulties; of the internal and external adjustments made to meet the needs of the times; of the little changes hardly noticed from day to day, even year to year; of the big changes which transformed its burgeoning student body and its growing constituency to meet head-on the newest challenges, always there; of the expansion of its curriculum and the growth of faculty; of its intellectual interests and aesthetic endeavors; of its pop-culture absorption and

19)For paying parents, their children's over-extension in non-class interests has led to some unhappy situations. One frustrated father summed it up in a memorable line, "My kid is majoring in Extracurriculars and minoring in Sin. If those were marketable skills, he'd be a millionaire."

athletic endeavors; of the enlargement of aim and extension of mission; of opportunities and palpable achievements and clear successes which have collectively won for Bemidji State a growing and continuing loyalty of alumni and friends.

In short, this history is an attempt to tell the story of ever-changing Bemidji State in such a way that understanding of its ongoing place and mission may grow. It is not an account of an unbroken succession of triumphs. No school operating for three-quarters of a century is so fortunate as to warrant such a narration. It is rather an attempt to tell the history in a readable style which simply and directly unfolds the tale made by the principal actors in the production.

More difficult to single out from the 75-year-old production are the roles played by the alumni and friends of the school. These have not yet been fully appraised nor fully appreciated. But they are out there everywhere. In public service, public office, law, medicine, ministry, business, mass communication, teaching—especially teaching—Bemidji alumni and friends are active in large numbers, almost 35,000 of them.

A FINAL WORD

Bemidji State has passed from infancy, toddling stage, childhood and youth—from Normal School, Teachers College, State College, and University— and now has moved into full adulthood, ready to serve, ready to challenge and ready to be challenged. Those who know the school best understand it best and admire it most. This history, whatever its imperfections, seeks to contribute to that knowledge, understanding and admiration.

Commencement Marshal Gerald Schnabel (caught in a touch of levity)
"The only thing there is to be snobbish about is being unsnobbish."

"Public education, along with home and church, forms the very foundation of American democracy. Freedom and representative government can survive only in the hands of enlightened people."

Luther Youngdahl
Governor of Minnesota 1947-51

The 1940s

THE WAR YEARS in Beltrami County, Bemidji, and at Bemidji State.

World War II was a total war in which nations centralized political power, mobilized resources, organized society, and directed cultural life toward the end of achieving victory in a long struggle. Obviously the requirements of total war affected colleges and universities in the United States as the nations were drawn into the global conflict. The wartime experience of Bemidji State, like that of higher education in general, mirrored that of American society. Both society and academic institutions suffered initial short-term dislocations; both enjoyed eventual long-term benefits; and both were sustained by appeals to greater community effort towards a grand cause.

Officially, World War II began on September 3, 1939. Yet long before the United States entered the war following the Japanese attack on Pearl Harbor on December 7, 1941, the town's two newspapers, The Pioneer and The Sentinel, gave frequent and vivid accounts of the war in Europe and Asia to the area readers. Regular full-page, banner headlines brought the conflict into Beltrami County homes. Often they were ugly: "Nazis Advance Over Own Corpses"; often they were scary: "U-Boats Seen Off Newfoundland"; but never in headlines, stories or editorials was there any pretense of neutrality. Bemidji's newspapers were totally anti-Germany and anti-Japan. Of extra concern for the many Scandinavians in Beltrami County was the German invasion of Norway on April 9, 1940, and seen in Pioneer headlines such as "Struggle For Norway Intensified."[1]

---

1)Because of close Norwegian ancestral ties, local hearts were stirred by the invasion and subsequent fall and occupation of Norway. Both newspapers (The Sentinel was a weekly; The Pioneer a daily) tried to follow closely the ongoing tragic events there, knowing the special interests of their readers. Norway was "close" to Minnesota. For example, the Norwegian Crown Prince Olav and Princess Martha had visited several Minnesota communities in the spring of 1939. Norwegian-Americans were heartened by President Franklin Roosevelt's praise of early Norwegian resistance and his famous line, "Look to Norway!" The owners of both papers during the war years were Henry Zehing Mitchell, who went by the nickname of "Heinie," and Walter Marcum; hereafter the newspapers will be cited as simply Pioneer and Sentinel. Marcum and Mitchell had owned the weekly Bemidji Sentinel before buying the daily Pioneer in 1924. It is the first time in newspaper history when a weekly bought out a daily. The Sentinel continued as a weekly.

191

The German invasion of the low-countries that spring of 1940, along with their subsequent rollover of France, would be news as disturbing to Beltrami citizens as to the rest of the nation. However, in an apparent effort to cushion any emotional upheaval and demand for immediate war involvement among Minnesotans, a variety of exhibitions were staged by anti-war leaders, one of which was a 30-plane sweep, flying over Bemidji and other towns in northern Minnesota. The planes dropped peace leaflets, with directions to sign them and return them to the Minneapolis Tribune as part of a petition to be sent to Congress to stay out of the war.

Meanwhile, the National Guard members in Bemidji, Battery H (anti-aircraft unit), increased both the number of men and their training. Civilian activities, meanwhile, included scrap-aluminum drives in town long before Pearl Harbor Day. The fall of France in late June had made it clear to most thinking citizens that the U.S. was indeed threatened by Axis military greed and power, and the Bemidji editorials promoted the need for vigilance and for increased military preparedness.[2] Despite intense opposition, Congress passed America's first peace-time draft bill on September 16, 1940, and the Pioneer explained its details.[3] The next month Beltrami County established its draft board, but before it was a month old and before any men had been picked to go, 18 area young men had already enlisted, enough to fulfill the county quota for several months. Patriotism had started early.

The Bemidji airport was of extra importance since Beltrami County was so near Canada, that country going to war officially June 10, 1940. The possibility for sabotage seemed feasible, as did illegal border crossings by the enemy. Because the National Guard units were to be federalized, local civilian defense units were called for in the form of a temporary (it ended in March, 1942) Homeguard made up of men not eligible to be drafted. In Bemidji, the men of the Homeguard became Company K and were fitted with winter clothes and ordered to guard Bemidji's airport and watch for aircraft; moreover, given the shortage of available men, they were also to guard the airport and border crossing at International Falls. All airplanes sighted throughout the war would be reported to a central state control agency. In February of 1941, an army major general addressed the state legislature and urged that a practice bombing range be established north of Red Lake in that 3,000-square-mile open area between Red Lake and Baudette. The Bemidji airport would be the advance base for communications, fuel, and briefings for airplane crews in training, according to the proposed plan. Little or nothing came of this

---

2)The Bemidji National Guard Unit, Battery H, would be called into the U.S. armed forces in January, 1941. Editor Mitchell was all for more preparedness, "As can be seen in Norway, Holland and Poland, courage is not enough. Present hysteria indicates that German theory was to let others sleep in their ignorance and build as fast as they could." (Editorial, May 20, 1940, p. 4.)
3)Commonly called "the draft," it was officially the Selective Service Training and Service Act. Initially all U.S. males ages 21 to 35 had to register; these numbers would soon be moved from 18 to 44. Anyone within that age bracket was eligible to be drafted into military service. The first board members for Beltrami County were C. Linnum of Kelliher, G. Carlson of Grygla, and from Bemidji were Dr. E.W. Johnson, A. Brattland, and A. Molander. They had the unenviable job of deciding which young men would be sent to war and who could stay home. The key terminology for physically fit men was 1-A; those not fit were determined to be 4-F. In between were designations of deferment set by draft boards for persons "needed at home" for reasons either accepted or not accepted by boards. Sometimes men were needed on the farms and hence deferred. With parental consent, a young man age 17 could join the Navy.

proposal. Obviously, however, given the growing concerns and fears of approaching war, it is understandable that the large number of ideas floated around at the time made semi-sense, even if years later these same ideas would be viewed as amusing only. For the most part, common sense prevailed in Bemidji throughout World War II, something that cannot be said of the community in World War I.[4]

THE OL' HOMETOWN . . . ON THE EDGE OF CHANGE
          During the summer of '41, life went on pretty much as usual in this town that had always been concerned with tourists and fishing, much of it then centering on the long city dock extending east into Lake Bemidji. The popular dock, almost an extension of Third Street, was right near the statues of Paul and Babe, of course. The Bemidji Boat Club on Lake Bemidji helped promote the tourist trade, making boat rides available daily all summer long from the dock. The dock was also a kind of "parking lot" for people who lived along the lake and who came by boat to town to do their shopping.
          The most prominent homes in the city in 1941 stretched from Fifth Street north along Lake Boulevard. There stood the big old houses built early in the century. Several families who owned these Lake Boulevard homes also had summer cottages directly across the lake in the section called Lavinia; there the lakeshore was sandy and clean and good for bathing beaches.
          In all the homes then, it was radio that brought most of the distant news and entertainment, including special events in professional athletics: Heavyweight champion Joe Lewis fought seven bouts in 1941; the U.S. Open Golf Tournament was won by Patty Berg. Joe DiMaggio, the Yankee Clipper, set the record of hitting in 56 consecutive games, and for Boston's Red Sox, Ted Williams set another record as the last player to hit for a season batting average of .406. The other Boston team that year changed its name from the Bees to the Braves. That year saw the tragic death of the Iron Horse of Baseball, Lou Gehrig, at age 38. His still-existing record was to play every Yankee game for 14 years: 2,130 consecutive games.[5]
          Summertime, with its summer sports, drifted into fall so that soon the local high school and teachers college football teams moved into action, the latter having a most successful 6-2 season, with special credit given to BSTC quarterback and captain Clarence "Bun" Fortier.[6] But already the war in Europe had affected BSTC negatively, its enrollment dropping that fall to 397 from the previous year's all-time high of 501. The student newspapers mirrored the uncertainty of the times while

4)For some information and insight into this scary subject, see "Hometown Hysteria: Bemidji at the Start of World War I," by Art Lee; Minnesota History, Summer, 1984, pp. 65-72. For example, in the first war the State Colleges were forbidden to teach the German language. In contrast, in World War II, at Bemidji State, Dr. Philip R. Sauer continued his German classes; indeed, at Christmas-time the German Club went caroling downtown, singing some songs in German.
5)Local movie fans in 1941 took parochial delight in film star Jane Russell. Born in Bemidji in 1921, she spent her youthful years in Grand Forks, North Dakota, and made trips for summer activities in Bemidji. Under contract with movie mogul Howard Hughes, she brought some national recognition to Bemidji. Her later starring in the controversial film, The Outlaw, brought fame/infamy to her name. See Pioneer, August 21, 1941, p. 10.
6)BSTC football coaches were R.B. "Jack" Frost and head coach H.J. "Jolly" Erickson, the latter staying and coaching throughout the difficult war years when almost all the eligible men went into military service. Bemidji State was the only State College to continue a football program throughout the war, albeit with shortened schedules. Fortier would go on to become Bemidji High School's most successful coach in the won/lost column. His overall career record as basketball coach was 424-92 in the 1950s and 1960s, a time period when the high school routinely won its way to the state tournaments.

at the same time trying to bolster spirits and show optimism. It was not easy, given the momentous war going on, especially in the news regarding that huge Eastern Front and the cataclysmic struggle for Russia.[7]

The town newspapers by November of '41 gave almost daily commentary on the impasse between Japan and the U.S. over Asia in general and China specifically. Lengthy headlines and sub-heads summed up the situation in the November 18 Pioneer, "Japs Prepare for any Eventuality; Relations With U.S. and Russia Sharply Strained."

In the fall issues came grisly, hand-drawn cartoons portraying Germany's military monstrousness in all of Europe. Other Pioneer drawings gave artists' views of the Nazis' blatant submarine attacks damaging two American ships, along with their sinking of the U.S.S. Reuben James. Already America was in a shooting war with Germany on the high seas. For those in the know, it was only a matter of time until war would come with Germany or Japan or both, unless, of course, President Roosevelt could meet face to face with their representatives and get things straightened out. Thus readers could only hope when the Nazi ally Japan sent special envoys to Washington in late November to respond to the American position on Asia. The uncertainty of the big-powers meeting was stated in the Pioneer December 6 full-page headline, "Nature of Jap Reply Not Disclosed." War could come; then again it might not.

In this mood, Americans were shocked but not surprised by the Pearl Harbor attack and the response of the U.S. Congress the next day. Read the December 8 Pioneer in extra black headlines, "U.S. Declares War on Japan; Congress Enters War with Only One Dissenting Vote."[8]

The biggest war on earth had begun for America. However, at home this war was "different" than World War I. The tone of the home front support for World War II might be summed up in the banal phrase, "It's a tough and dirty job, so let's go at it sensibly and get it over with as soon as possible." The nation had learned something from history.

The hysteria and emotionalism that had engulfed Americans in the first world war did not get repeated in the second war, with the obvious black-mark exception, of course, of the treatment of Japanese-Americans. The prevailing commonsense attitude had already been revealed in Bemidji. Three days after Pearl Harbor, Pioneer Editor Henry Mitchell would write with apparent equanimity:

"President Roosevelt, Governor [Harold] Stassen, and Mayor [Earl] Bucklen have urged that business 'proceed as usual'. . .and that we go on about our work as

7)Following the German attack on Poland on the first day of September, 1939, a special BSTC all-school assembly met to speculate on what this would mean for the U.S. All faculty members speaking at the assembly predicted that the U.S. would not get into conflict, which, though incorrect as it turned out, did at least partially ameliorate some student fears for a brief time. The war's outbreak in '39 had found many collegians opposed to U.S. entry. The Student Opinion Surveys of America, conducted by an association of college newspapers, and regularly reported in the Northern Student, revealed a waning but stubborn persistence of neutralist sentiment throughout 1941.
8)The one dissenting vote came from Congresswoman Jeanette Rankin of Montana. The first woman ever to be elected to Congress, she had also cast a "No" vote in 1917 against entering into World War I. She showed immense courage in her actions, arguing that someone has to stand up publicly and say that there has to be a better solution to human conflict than war. The public did not agree; after each vote she was not reelected to office. Her anti-war consistency continued so that she led anti-Vietnam War marches in Washington when she was in her 80s. She died in 1973 at the age of 93.

quietly and efficiently as possible. Let's keep cool and do the job that is expected of us."

OFF THEY GO INTO THE ARMY, NAVY, AND MARINES

The day after Pearl Harbor hundreds of thousands of American young men went to recruiting offices to join the military services. At the same time new selective service regulations called for inductions of literally millions of others into military service. Beltrami County alone had a quota of 147 men just for the month of April, 1942. Those inducted who had no special skills were classified as enlisted men, and they received the lowest pay, $21 a month for the first four months and then a raise to $30 per month. American women were given the opportunity to enlist when Congress in March of '42 approved the Women's Auxiliary Corps, and they too received the initial pay of $21 a month.

Beltrami County had been the site of some half-dozen Civilian Conservation Corps camps established as job work in the Depression years. Young men ages 17 to 24 had volunteered to work in these CCC camps—receiving $30 a month—which were run by U.S. Army personnel. But these camps were deemed unnecessary because of the need for manpower in the military. With only a tinge of regret, the CCC camps were soon phased out one by one, never to be resurrected again.

BSTC from Above
"Public education . . . forms the very foundation of American democracy."

THE HOME FRONT

Mobilizing for the Bemidji home front began immediately after the Pearl Harbor attack, with the formation of a Salvage for Victory Committee. Salvage drives had started by January 1 as people began their ongoing four-year donations of items like silk hose, rubber items, tin cans, and metal products of any kind. Scrap metal was badly needed, so area junk yards were the first to supply government requests. Basements and garages were next to be cleaned out.

Within a few weeks of the war's start, the Chief Theater in town advertised that any adult accompanied by another with a paid ticket would be admitted free if that person presented a set of 1941 license plates for the war effort. (All men in uniform were also admitted free.) But driving to any theater anytime during the war could be a moral problem in that it could be considered a waste of fuel and tires. If one chose to "motor" to the movie, then the national speed limit of 35 miles an hour was to be observed.

Tire rationing began 20 days after Pearl Harbor, the War Production Board announcing its strict control of rubber. Before long there were no new tires to buy, let alone girdles, garden hoses, water bottles, tennis or golf balls, erasers, and bathing caps. Manufacture of each of the items mentioned was reduced 75 percent below prewar production.[9]

"Bureaucracy Begets Bureaucracy," or so reads Parkinson's Law. This statement seemed most apparent in the war years when agency after agency was created, the head agency over the other agencies centered in the U.S. Capitol. The "alphabet soup" of multiple agencies in the Depression years gave way to a near-equal plethora of wartime committees and commissions that soon became familiar to all citizens. The Office of Transportation, created because of gasoline rationing, was one of them.

Gasoline was needed badly for the military. An infantry division required six times as much gasoline as food, and an armored division needed eight times as much. Their needs meant the rationing of gas for civilian use, carried out in the form of ration cards with individual stamps in books required to be surrendered by auto owners whenever purchasing gas at gas stations. Any car owner could get an "'A' Card," allowing the purchase of three gallons per week, and this figure was later reduced to two. Those who could demonstrate need for more gas moved up to a "'B' Card," and so on upward for persons like medical doctors who had unlimited amounts. Moreover, car owners were limited to owning five tires; amounts above that had to be turned in. Any driver caught exceeding the 35 mile an hour speed limit forfeited his gas ration card. Obviously there was little auto traveling, and those who did travel were queried by that familiar guilt sign everywhere, "Is This Trip Really Necessary?" Small wonder that many car owners found it more practicable to put their cars up on blocks and leave them there until the war's end.

9)Editors everywhere urged citizens to do their patriotic duties by NOT over-buying any product for storage. This was called "hoarding," but appeals to patriotism often fell on deaf ears, at least in our house. My father used one room in our home for nothing but hoarding! The Bemidji editor said the only proper way to spend extra money was to buy war bonds. For a useful look-at-length into the war years in Bemidji, there is a master's paper by Don Hammer called "The Home Front in Bemidji, Minnesota During World War II." The unpublished paper is on file in the BSU history department storeroom. At the time the paper was written, 1980, Hammer was a junior high social studies teacher in Bemidji; at this writing, 1994, he has been retired three years but still lives in Bemidji.

Nothing seemed too small to be saved for the war effort. A barrel was placed by the front door of the Pioneer office for the collection of toothpaste and shaving cream tubes. A plea was also made for aluminum foil found on some candy, cigarette and gum packages. Each strip was to be peeled off, rolled into a ball, and when large enough, placed in the collection terminal.[10]

THE START OF THE AMERICAN "CLEAN PLATE CLUB"

The wartime agency closest to every Beltrami County citizen was the OPA, the Office of Price Administration, as that agency governed the rationing system for various foods and certain other products, such as shoes. Within 90 days after Pearl Harbor, rationing began on meat, cheese and butter, and regularly afterwards another product would make the ration list. Within a year after the start of the war, 21,038 food-ration books went out to county citizens, while 8,087 were issued in the city of Bemidji. Every person, regardless of age, was allowed one ration book by the local WPA officer. The arrival of a new baby usually sent the new father heading immediately for the WPA office to get a new set of books. Deemed necessary for the war effort, ration stamps were equally deemed a headache for merchant and buyer alike.[11]

MORE BAD NEWS THAN GOOD FOR BSTC

School supporters have to search hard to find much "good news" for Bemidji State during World War II. Some can be found in employment opportunities, a wonderful change from the Depression times when finding a job, any job, was a major achievement. The steady depletion of men from the public school system teaching ranks found women in large numbers taking positions that included assignments considered strictly "men's jobs" before the war, such as principals, administrators, and coaches. BSTC Placement Director A.C. (Archie Clair) Clark announced in June of 1943 that there were ten teaching positions open for every graduate. At this point candidates interviewed superintendents about the job, rather than vice versa.[12]

The obvious "bad news" for the school was the continued decline in the numbers of students attending, a slide that by spring quarter of '45 found only 123

10)Sentinel, July 31, 1942, p. 1. The area downtown around Paul and Babe became the site for collected materials. The city's devotion to the cause of scrap collection can be noted in that on October 13, 1942, every store and business, as well as all the schools, closed in order for citizens to spend the day collecting scrap metal. By day's end, the College students delivered 50 tons but the high school students came up with over 100 tons. No surprise that the huge scrap-iron pile stood so high that it dwarfed Paul Bunyan. The day ended with a band concert downtown by the BSTC band under director Milton Dieterick.

11)Housewives had the eternal hassle of planning and preparing meals, all determined, of course, by rationed foods and the stamps necessary for their purchase. And even if they had the stamps, it was just as likely that the store did not have the product anyway. Americans never did get used to the grocery store signs reading, "No Milk or Butter Today. Please Do Not Ask for Coffee. Limit of One Pound of Hamburger." (Only a few years ago, about 1990, I had an older woman student in class who was a housewife in World War II. I had brought some old food-ration stamp books to show class members and her first response when she saw them was to blurt out, "Oh, those damn things!")

12)On a personal note, my only sister, now deceased, graduated from college in 1943 and accepted a job as a classroom English teacher in a rural Iowa town. By the end of the war, every male member of the faculty had gone into military service except the superintendent, and he went insane. The entire K-12 system was run by women. My sister's duties expanded to include being assistant principal and head basketball coach. (She was offered the football job but turned it down.) Moreover, all the teachers were "frozen"; that is they could not quit and take another job somewhere else. The government had and used the authority to declare certain positions so important to the war effort that the personnel could be "frozen."

enrolled. Only 24 senior students graduated that year, and of that number only three were men. The sinking enrollments again jeopardized the school's very existence, with some fiscally-responsible downstate legislators openly proposing closing Bemidji State and turning it instead into a state insane asylum.[13] Once again local legislators came forward to prevent the school's demise, with considerable credit for its continued life going to Bemidji's representatives, Leonard Dickinson and Harry Bridgeman.

The shortage of men at BSTC was noted in a variety of ways, and one Northern Student editor came down hard on the few men remaining:

"College girls are appalled at the absence of reasonably presentable males, for after draft boards and defense industries have weeded out the more likely looking prospects, what is left besides a large and unlovely group of adolescents? Sorry-looking individuals with mental deficiencies, adenoids, flat feet, spinal curvature, faulty vision, or less than 10 opposing molars."[14]

The war dominated the home front. It affected the lives of every citizen, whether in Beltrami County or Washington, D.C. BSTC officials made decision after decision based on wartime conditions. Curriculum offerings changed to meet the obvious needs of the men on campus and to better prepare them for what they could expect anytime, getting drafted. New courses became available on military geography, sending and reading international radio code, organization of the armed forces, blueprint reading, and of course, first aid. The best-selling book in the country during the war was the Red Cross First Aid textbook.

Another change allowed students to graduate after ten quarters of attendance, rather than the previously mandated twelve. In this the College followed national trends toward accelerated programs and more utilitarian courses. Considered a form of service to the country, wartime adaptations fostered institutional pride and raised expectations of a brighter future. Summer school programs were augmented to allow for earlier graduation as well as to provide opportunities and incentives for former teachers to become recertified and meet the desperate needs of public schools for teachers.[15]

Both the impact of the war and its effect on BSTC might be seen in the president himself going off into the military. President Charles Richard Sattgast

---

13)There are a few wags in town who believe that goal was inadvertently achieved anyway. It was already noted in College in the Pines that Bemidji State's only undefeated football squad was the '44 team which, with a squad membership of 14 men, won the four games they played that truncated season, home-and-away games with Eau Claire, Wisconsin, and Concordia College, Moorhead, Minnesota.

14)Northern Student, January 28, 1942, p. 2, under the caption of "War Cry." The women on campus did considerable volunteer work to help in the war effort, including the wrapping of thousands of surgical dressings. There was also a knitting organization, "The Knit-Wit Club." Following the Pearl Harbor attack, for young men of military age there began an overwhelming desire, yea passion, to be a part of America's fighting forces. It became not the thing one might do but something one absolutely had to do. Conversely, not to be a part of this crusade could leave rejected men with deep, invisible scars of failure. Case in point: Life-long Bemidjian Chester Swedmark (long of Swedmark's Hardware) fit the classic case of must-do the military. By 1943 almost all of his friends had either enlisted or put themselves up for an early draft call, and Swedmark was part of the latter. However, he had failed his physical exam (poor eyesight) and was declared 4-F and unfit. He would say that after that letdown, he would not venture downtown in the daylight because he felt so ashamed, so like a slacker. If he had to go on the streets of Bemidji, he took the back alleys so no one would see him. Despite being married, and with a child on the way, Swedmark continued to see the local draft board members, pleading with them to take him. He even threatened to sit on the city hall steps day and night until they agreed to draft him! Finally, with later physical requirements loosened, he retook his physical and passed. His only return to Bemidji before being shipped overseas was to see briefly his wife and new baby in the hospital. (In the ongoing humor of things that only the Army would and could do, said Swedmark, it made him a forward observer.)

War-Time Registration
"The shortage of men was noted..."

enlisted as a captain in the U.S. Army in September of 1943. He was replaced by
Archie C. Clark, with the understanding—and it was the law—that Sattgast would
return as president at war's end, whenever that would be. Sattgast would later write
several letters back to the school which were published in the Northern Student, and
these notes were a combination of information, chattiness, and motivation.[16]

Meanwhile, the campus numbers continued their steady decline. In the fall
of 1944 there were only 18 men on campus, and thus there was little surprise that
the graduating class the next spring would, as mentioned, have just three men in a
class of 24.

Because the College community defined itself as family, those on campus
maintained contact with the servicemen. The student newspaper reported inductions
and casualties; ran advertisements for war bonds and stamps; and proudly related
the whereabouts, special assignments and decorations earned by the Beavers in the
military. For the entire Bemidji community, the first thing done each morning was

15)Again on a personal note, my father was a supervising principal of a small high school in Wisconsin during the war years.
The need to find a "qualified science teacher" found him hiring a retired teacher in his 80s. The music teacher was primarily
the village rural route mail carrier. The athletics coach had himself just graduated from high school the year before; he was
exempted from the draft because of farm work. A motley faculty ranging from teenagers to octogenarians. And only a few years
previous, in the Depression, there had been way too many available teachers. He told of making a mistake by informing the area
(Stevens Point) teacher's college placement bureau that there was an opening at his school. As a result of this "error," he
practically had to go into hiding to escape the applicants, some of whom came to the door of our home at all hours of day or night
seeking the job, and willing to work for just board and room. The war totally reversed this process.
16)Sattgast was hardly alone among school officers in the military. Indeed, while in England he wrote of an informal meeting
of his with the ex-presidents of Gustavus Adolphus College and St. Cloud State who both happened to be stationed at the same
base where he was located.

to scan the Pioneer to look for news on area servicemen—and who might have been wounded or, worst of the worst, who might have been killed. The first Bemidji man to die in the war was 20-year-old Bennie Bylcum, whose ship was sunk in February, 1942. By war's end, 20 former Bemidji State men had died in the conflict. Their names are listed in the footnote.[17]

The war dominated lives in the Bemidji community. Any hint of grumbling over the absence of prewar commodities and reduced lifestyles was met with the familiar line, "Don't you know there's a war on?" Thus there was obvious disappointment but no opposition to the decision to cancel the annual 4th of July celebration in 1944; it just did not seem right to be so festive at home when there was so much suffering going on throughout the world.

On June 6, 1944, the same day as the Allied invasion of Normandy, Bemidji State ran a full page ad in the Pioneer inviting all area people to attend the 25th anniversary commencement exercises. President Emeritus Manfred Deputy was returning for the occasion to be both honored and also to serve as speaker for the ceremonies. A sidenote to the ad was the notation that some 350 students and staff of BSTC had entered the armed forces in some capacity since 1940. That same day the Bemidji Sentinel ran a cover story on the approaching graduation and included the entire list of the 1944 graduating class. The list took up two brief paragraphs.

Bemidji participated wholeheartedly in the several practice "blackout" drills during the war, when all lights in town were turned off in planned preparation for any would-be bombing raid, along with the "brownouts" implemented in 1945 when restrictions limited outdoor advertising and ornamental display use. Theater marquees could have nothing bigger than 60-watt bulbs; wasteful outdoor home-lighting at Christmas time approached un-Americanism. There was an added threat: Open flaunting of excess electrical use could result in the penalty of having one's electric power cut off.

Not only city people but also every Beltrami County farmer had been made aware of energy needs and conservation. Hence any farmer with a woodlot was told that he could make a contribution by burning only wood for heating. Heating values of different woods were measured by the amount of heat given compared to burning coal. White oak, black cherry and green ash had one cord equaling one ton of coal. Wood types producing less heat but equal to 1,800 pounds of coal were white ash, red oak, elm, and hard maple. One cord of popple was equivalent to only 1,200 pounds of coal. Whatever the wood, it was still patriotic to burn it rather than coal or fuel oil.

17)Giving their lives were Edgar Arnold, Bagley; Walter Brotherton, Williams; Howard Cords, Bemidji; Will Erickson, Red Lake; Robert Frazer, Minneapolis; Malcolm Getchell, St. Paul; Archie Graves, Bemidji; Kenneth Gregg, Bemidji; Amel Hocking, Hibbing; Bruce Johnson, Boy River; Willard Johnson, Sebeka; Donald Jones, Upper Darby, Pennsylvania; Jim Lizer, Litchfield; Jack McCormick, Bemidji; Robert McPartlin, St. Paul; Harry Rose, Jr., Bemidji; Robert Tesch, Bemidji; Robert Worth, Bemidji; James Koefod, Bemidji; and John Schock, Nashwauk. For each former student body member who died in the war, a gold star was added to the flag that hung in the gymnasium. The Northern Student of October 24, 1945, p. 2, lists their names, rank, place and cause of death, if known; above their names it reads: "THEY GAVE THE LAST FULL MEASURE OF DEVOTION."

By spring of 1945, with the success of the military fronts suggesting an end in sight, ongoing shortages had made home front pantries more empty year by year. Meat supplies became lean if not totally absent, so much so that horse meat was being offered for sale, though only the brave ventured to try it. The name Steakhouse for any restaurant was more of a dream than a reality. By July of '45 the chance to buy a steak dinner was one in 400 for any Minnesotan stopping to eat at a roadside haunt.[18]

A direct war-related industry in Bemidji was a Munsingwear plant that produced underwear, jungle hammocks, wing covers for C-47 transport airplanes, and bras, girdles, underpants, and shirts for the Women's Auxiliary Corp (WACs). Over 100 persons were employed; total production values exceeded $16 million by spring of '45.[19]

The whole county took extra pride in learning that a transport ship being built by the Kaiser Shipyards of Richmond, Virginia, would be named U.S.S. Beltrami, and county citizens were asked to donate books to be placed on the ship for the crew's leisure reading. Pictures of the ship placed in the Pioneer office window on Beltrami Avenue drew many onlookers, and inside the newspaper office were more pictures, including those of the crew members.[20]

Creeping inflation throughout the war, with average costs on everything going up one-third, proved distressing to thrifty citizens. Government efforts to control rising prices were a combination of rationing, emotional appeals, and war bond sales. Only two special war loan drives were planned for 1945, as compared with three the year before. The figure of $14 million was set for the spring of '45, with one-half of that aimed at individuals of modest means who would buy the least expensive bond, the E-series which cost $18.75.[21]

THE WAR SEMI-ENDS

Early in the war anyone making an extra nickel who used the money to buy anything but war bonds was portrayed as unpatriotic if not a thief. The same held true for the upholding of rationing and controlled pricing, but near the end of the war enough people winked at the regulations to make enforcement difficult. Buying through the "black market" became a common practice, with somebody always knowing somebody else who could come through with a half a pound of butter or an extra gallon of gas or a box of shotgun shells, all sold illegally at extra high prices.

Enthusiasm for the war effort on the home front tended to be transient in Bemidji and throughout the country. It peaked by the end of 1943 and then declined

18)Sentinel, July 13, 1945, p. 1.
19)Sentinel (October 5, 1945, p. 1). The article tells of wartime employee picnics held on Lake Bemidji in the summers, sponsored by the company. That one-time factory building in town is, at this writing, Bethel Lutheran Church.
20)Pioneer, August 2 and August 11, 1944, pp. 1-2.
21)Pioneer, May 12, 1945, p. 4. There were seven major bond drives during the war, and in each drive the figure was exceeded, usually phrased as "going over the top." The E-series allowed even young children to buy bonds, often little by little as bond books were distributed to students in which stamps with values as low as ten cents would be glued in the books, eventually reaching the $18.75 value. At this point the stamp book was brought to the post office and the recipient received a bond in exchange. After ten years, the bond could be cashed in for $25.

gradually due to improved fortunes of war as well as inattention from the federal government.

Nonetheless, by sacrificing as they did for the greater cause, Bemidji students and all citizens forged a sense of national community. Their wartime sacrifices were not painful because, as historians have noted, Americans have regularly derived great satisfaction from contributing to the common good.

Patriotism was still there in '45, but its rigidity had slipped a cog or two. No longer did it seem un-American to acquire a few of the former "good things in life," even when paying outrageous prices. After all, went the rationalizing, the war would soon be over. By late April of 1945, the Allied armies were pressing the Germans so hard everywhere that their defeat seemed imminent, and the expected German surrender came on May 8, 1945, on what was called "V-E Day," Victory in Europe. The five-year-long war in Europe, the most costly, murderous conflict in history, ended when the German High Command surrendered to the Allied armies.

As the anticipated surrender approached in Bemidji, merchants informed Mayor Earl Bucklen of their intention to close their businesses that day, but to have no celebration. A quiet tribute only. Municipal liquor stores were scheduled to close also, and churches began preparing for special services. V-E Day meant the war was only half over for Americans; there was still Japan to conquer.

Hundreds of Bemidji residents went to their churches on V-E Day to offer thanks for the conclusion of half of the great conflict. The town schools remained in session that day but all held special programs of commemoration.

Immediately following V-E Day came a noticeable return to prewar times when Governor Ed Thye announced that the midnight curfew for all entertainment spots in the state would be lifted. Following close behind this announcement came another allowing horse racing in the state to start up again, although horses could not be shipped in from out of state because of controlled transportation requirements. By the end of the month the OPA announced an increase in gas allowances, with "'A' Card" holders allowed to buy six gallons per week! As the war's end came closer, the prewar civilian days were gradually returning.

On August 14, 1945, came the greatest news of the decade, with one headline saying it all in two words, **"It's Over!"** World War II ended with V-J Day, Victory over Japan. In Bemidji the emotional but well behaved celebration was the exact opposite of the almost somber V-E Day, beginning with an impromptu large crowd of people racing downtown to mill around, shouting prolonged cries of joy and waving flags. A snake dance of teenage bobbysoxers wound its way through and around the throng of happy people, many throwing confetti in the air, while more paper came sailing out from upstairs apartments above the stores.[22] This was pure celebration, the spontaneous, unbridled variety loved by everyone. Seldom in a person's life could this experience be matched: Celebrating the end of mankind's

---

22)For a complete description of events on V-J Day in Bemidji, see The Pioneer, August 15, 1945, p. 1.

greatest war. The "Good War" was over! It was no overstatement then to believe that civilization had been saved.

A SIMPLE SYNOPSIS ON POSTWAR AMERICA

Any American history telling about the end of the second world war reads very much the same; it goes something like this:

Americans went wild on August 15, 1945. It was V-J Day, Victory over Japan, and it marked the triumphant end of World War II, the most expensive and savage war in history. On that glorious day Americans looked forward to the blessings of peace and prosperity. Most Americans looked not backward, but forward with positive hopes. A new age was dawning.

Packing to Aid America's Newest Ally
"The 'Good War' was over . . . civilization had been saved."

The vastly powerful federal government, which touched the lives of all Americans in a variety of ways, evolved during the presidency of Franklin Delano Roosevelt through the two most important events of the 20th century, the Great Depression and World War II. For women and persons of color, the war years brought expansions of opportunity, along with rising hopes and frustrations, that would have a great effect on postwar society. Most dramatically, the U.S. assumed a new, all-important position in international relations; America had become a super power, the new world leader in everything.

Before the war Europeans believed they occupied the center of progress, civilization, and power. No more. The war altered Europe's position. The

American Age had arrived.

However, pressing problems and hard decisions did not end with the war. Postwar reconstruction and the development of a Cold War between the U.S. and the Soviet Union kept international affairs in a state of near perpetual crisis. Thoughtful citizens knew as much before the World War II guns were silenced.

Before the Cold War could dominate both the news and the budgets, however, Americans enjoyed a brief period of heady optimism, marked most openly by the jubilant return of the men and women from military service. They came home—the lucky ones—by the millions (200,000 a month!) and world peace was here to stay, along with national prosperity, or so it seemed at the time. Even if cynics and major magazines like Fortune were, in the fall of '45, predicting a return to the depression and a coming war with the Russians, the great majority of citizens set those negative notions aside. The reasoning seemed simple enough: If we could lick Hitler and Tojo, and fat-jowled Mussolini always seen in the newsreels mugging on some Italian balcony, we could lick any depression, too, along with those Ruskies.

Meanwhile the boys were coming back from the wars, back from hundreds of places Americans had never heard of before the shooting started—Iwo Jima, Remagen, Okinawa, Buchenwald—to their hometowns. But then the ex-servicemen started doing something that no other generation before them had done in such large numbers; they were going off to college under the new GI Bill of Rights.

Even before the end of the war, in June, 1944, Congress passed what was officially labeled the Servicemen's Readjustment Act, but known popularly as the GI Bill. It was the most generous act ever devised for American ex-military personnel. It entitled veterans to unemployment insurance for a year (popularly referred to as the "52-20 Club," i.e., 20 tax-free dollars a week for one year); guaranteed loans for building homes or establishing businesses; and payment for virtually all the costs of veterans' education in colleges or vocational schools, proportionate to the length of their service. A new age of education had dawned, and colleges like Bemidji State had to adapt quickly to postwar America.

BACK TO BEMIDJI . . .

All kinds of good things happened to Bemidji civilians following V-J Day, despite the fact that rationing and controls continued, at least in name. By the end of the month a new cry was heard in town, "Fill 'er up!" Gasoline could be purchased in any quantity with no qualifications except the money to pay for it, and there was plenty of that around, thanks to wartime prosperity. Butter, cheese and milk were soon available without stamps. Seats on airplanes and trains now became available on first-come, first-served basis; no more priorities in public transportation. Even the clocks came back to normal, the public turning back one hour from CWT, Central War Time.

Even if by fall of '45 there were still shortages of civilian products—caused by workers' strikes everywhere—there was still optimism for the future.

The great horn of plenty would soon be flowing again. That fall three Bemidji gasoline service stations reopened, now that the basics of that business, fuel, tires and manpower, were becoming available.

A building boom began immediately at war's end for Bemidji. A car dealer bought four lots on West Second Street that became a new and impressive Chevrolet dealership. (This would later become a Chevy-Buick business, and later yet, at this writing, would be converted into a complex of rooms for social gatherings run and owned by the VFW, the Veterans of Foreign Wars organization. The Chevy-Buick business moved out on Highway 2 West in 1989, there to join almost all the other car dealers in Bemidji.)

Construction continued throughout the downtown. A gas station on the corner of Beltrami and Fifth Street was bulldozed away and in its place came a new two-story building, first called the Glass Block Drugstore; in the early 1980s the drugstore closed and was purchased and used by the owners of KBUN radio station, which started in 1946. Up the street from the Glass Block, a new Doctors' Medical Clinic building (now the home of the Beltrami County Social Services) was built. Leonard Dickinson added a large addition to his building, just across the street from Paul and Babe; a new farm implement building and dealership was built on the corner of Fifth and Minnesota Avenue; a new sheet metal and roofing company opened at 2300 Bemidji Avenue that fall of '45. A new era had begun in Bemidji signaled by this building boom.[23]

Despite some shortages, despite spiraling inflation, people were still happy and confident. Not only was the war over, the home front war was over also, and best of all, the men were coming home! The bright future was here.

BACK TO THE "GOOD OL' DAYS"; THE MEN RETURN TO CAMPUS

The brighter future for Bemidji State began that fall of '45 when enrollments increased 20 percent, and kept going up every quarter for the next two years. The obvious change came with "men, Men, MEN!"—or so ran the Northern Student headline for the September 26 issue, with the subhead, "Over 50 Enrolled!" On the sports page of the same issue came more good news, "Happy Days are Here Again!," after which came the happy story that 26 (count 'em) men had turned out for the first football practice. The GI Bill fueled the postwar surge of students which kept increasing with no letup, no down-turn in numbers until another war, the Korean Conflict, began in 1950. (See Appendix D for all Bemidji State enrollment figures since 1919.)

Housing the veterans became the immediate problem. Bemidji State first accommodated the GI upsurge by negotiating for and then receiving two long barracks buildings from the closed CCC Camp at Bena, east of Cass Lake. The

23)Often anecdotal citations are better than some scholarly footnote reference. Such is the case with Bemidji postwar prosperity. Among the venerable businesses in town is Naylor Electric, which at World War II time was run by the Naylor Brothers. Charlie Naylor told me that Naylor Electric did as much business in each month after the war as they had done in an entire year before the conflict. Similarly, Ron Patterson of Patterson's Clothing indicated that before the war, his father felt he had a very good sales day if he sold one suit. Postwar Bemidji gave a new definition to a good sales day.

structures had been recently used to house German prisoners of war. (There were 12 such POW camps in the state during the war, housing 1,275 German POWs.) The white-framed, wooden structures were moved the 30-mile distance and, despite some difficulty in maneuvering, were placed side by side behind the gymnasium (the latter building to be renamed Memorial Hall).

A 'Dorm Room' -- of sorts -- in 'The Shacks'
"The structures had been recently used to house German prisoners of war."

One of these "dormitories" was to house 32 single men; the other was set up for five separate apartments for married veterans and their families. The buildings were immediately deemed "temporary housing only," but necessity made the word *temporary* last for another 25 years. (They were still in use by 1971, but not as dorms; by then they had become classrooms and departmental offices for the music department, something the members were less than enthusiastic about.) Off campus there were 15 privately owned apartments just for veterans and families; they were located near the Beltrami County Fairgrounds, west on Highway 2.

IT WAS SO SMALL, BUT IT SEEMED SO BIG
    The number of students enrolled, and the importance of that number at

Bemidji State is relative, but numbers do tell much about the changing times. That is worth noting when reading the Northern Student front page of the October 25, 1945 issue:

"BSTC, the youngest state teachers college but no longer the smallest, with 55 men enrolled, now boasts the largest male enrollment of any teachers college in the state. Dr. Clark agreed with the general opinion that this abundance (?) [sic] of males was due in part at least to the fact that BSTC has the only teachers college football team in the state this year."

And some kind of team it was, defeating both North Dakota State and South Dakota State Colleges. Of special interest was the win over South Dakota State at Brookings. Read the Northern Student version, "Sparked by halfback Jack Luoma, BSTC scored a 6-0 victory. . . ." Years later Luoma would add amusing insight into this win. He first emphasized that South Dakota State had a V-12 program, a military-training program on campus which allowed an extra large number of men to be enrolled. This large number was reflected in a very large football squad who, prior to the game, lumbered all the way around the field, parading both their new uniforms and multi-bench strength. "Then we came ambling out on the field, all 17 of us, looking like a bunch of scrubs," added Luoma. David and Goliath, with many of the latter. Then Luoma laughed and suggested they won the game because Bemidji State had a "ringer" playing for them in the form of superb athlete W.J. (Buster) Spaulding. Buster was still in the Navy and playing service football, but he happened to be home on furlough and went to see the game as a spectator. While the teams were warming up, Buster went down from the stands just to say hello to his former coach Jolly Erickson, but when the coach saw him, he told him to hurry up and put on a Beaver uniform! Buster also got a "new name" for the game, one he forgot when the public address announcer introduced the starting team. "Buster," whispered Erickson, "that's you. Get out there!" And Buster played the entire game, both offense and defense. "That was a fun one," concluded Luoma.[24]

THE RETURN OF "THE BOYS"

While 55 men came on campus in September of '45, and 90 had arrived by winter quarter, almost none of the former faculty members were by then out of the military, and most of them were not even close to American soil, let alone Bemidji. President Sattgast was in Austria, Harold Hagg in the Philippines, Ole Sand in the Aleutians, Eleanor Smith in England. Elton Beck was on the American mainland, stationed on the West Coast; same with Reuben (Jack) Frost, stationed in Florida.

24)Anecdote relayed by Luoma to this writer at a social gathering December 20, 1992. With the exception of one year's teaching in Wyoming, Luoma taught high school math in Bemidji until his retirement in 1989. He also succeeded Bun Fortier as basketball coach and in his first year (1972) he coached Bemidji to the Minnesota State Basketball Championship. Luoma and his wife, the musical Marie (Cahill), spend their summers in Bemidji at their home on Turtle Lake and their winters in California. Buster Spaulding—always "Buster" (not two people in Bemidji know his real name, Willis Joseph)—stayed on in Bemidji and is the present-day owner of a large, successful Cadillac-Oldsmobile-Honda dealership located on Highway 2 West. He did not start "large," he told me. His used car lot entrepreneurship began on a shoestring after the war with one car—which he also used as his "office." But one led to two, and so on. Though remembered at Bemidji State as a three-sport athletic star, he was also a fine piano player. In how many dealer showrooms today can you find a grand piano? Perhaps only at Spaulding Motors.

Several of these far away faculty wrote letters home to Bemidji State which the Northern Student printed that school year.

Already this normalcy was noted in the tone of the school papers, with stories and articles reflecting not the world news but local concerns and local events and the small-school folksiness of the past. Apparently there was reader interest in the kind of news stories associated with small town newspapers: Who got engaged, who was married, who on the faculty had new babies (Coach Jolly Erickson and wife had Boy #4), who became a grandparent (the Student listed "grandpappy status" for the much-revered C.V. Hobson, he of many hats, all worn well: Geography teacher, conservationist, counselor, personnel director, perhaps "moral environmental conscience" of BSTC), which former student was stationed where, who was mustered out and would be returning to BSTC soon. It was all so wonderful at the time; the "family" would soon be reunited, and for the staff of the Northern Student, "the good ol' days are now." With the extended family reuniting, the Student could indulge in some not-great journalism but well-read journalism, a "gossip column," in which one phase of newspaper mandates was emphasized, Names Make News! Hence the teasing writer, using the imperial "we," wondered in print: "Wasn't that Bill S. that we saw with Suzi B. Saturday night at Shorecrest?[25] Now what would Alice G. say, knowing that Suzi was apparently stepping out on John A.? Of course we'll never know, but we surely wonder . . ." and on to the next name-dropping of alleged romantic Beaver Tales to be told in print to a readership that never missed a word of good gossip.

And the sports-minded student body in '45-'46 reveled in the winning 15-2 basketball season, even if Coach Erickson made it clear afterwards that he could hardly wait for regular basketball coach Jack Frost to get out of the Army and return to relieve him of the job so he could concentrate on football.

With the limited number of graduates in these postwar years, there was a limited problem in getting every grad's picture in the Northern Student, along with the briefest of biography on each, even if the Student came out only eight times a year.

Although, as has been mentioned, the B.A. non-teaching degree was first offered in '46, the importance of this change seemed less than super newsworthy to Student editors, even if, as they wrote, "the emergency regulation was passed by the State College Board in August of 1946." However, editors did recognize celebrity status by emphasizing in the April 10, 1946, issue the recent marriage of former BSTC student and Bemidji native Mary Welsh to famous author Ernest Hemingway, then age 47. The article noted that this was the second wedding for

---

25)The term "Shorecrest" conjures up immediate memories to those readers who lived in Bemidji during the war and postwar years. Shorecrest really meant Shorecrest Ballroom, a dance hall/pavilion located on Lake Bemidji about four miles north of the College on Birchmont Drive. The popular dance hall overlooked Lake Bemidji (private homes now stand on the site) and was especially appealing to Bemidji State students who spent considerable time there. The place did on occasion attract "live bands" of national renown (the Tommy Dorsey Orchestra, the Chick Webb band, for example) but mainly it was area "big bands" who played Shorecrest. And on weeknights there was always the jukebox. For many Beavers, it was "the College hang out." Its demise in the Minnesota North Country was on account of weather; too much snow caved in the roof and it was never rebuilt. By the late 1950s, it was just a place students heard about—and missed the fun there.

Welsh and the fourth for Hemingway. (As it turned out, it was the last wedding for both; they remained together until Hemingway's death by suicide in 1961. Mrs. Hemingway made a number of semi-secret trips back to Bemidji to visit a few select friends, but her clandestine appearances were not noted publicly until after she had left, at which time the local newspaper would mention her having been in town.)

THE RETURN TO NORMALCY; THE FACULTY IS BACK, TOO
The fall of '46 found the once-absent wartime faculty back on campus, ready to take up from where they left off. President Sattgast returned that summer. And along with the old came 17 new faculty members, bringing the total faculty to 50, another record for BSTC. These numbers reflected the bulging enrollment, 570 students. "Biggest Enrollment Ever at BSTC This Quarter," read the headline of the first issue of the '46 school year.

Instructor Ron Gearman Points to the Piano
"In 1947 he and his class collectively wrote GO, BEMIDJI BEAVERS fight song."

Faculty members come and go, but there are a few who stay many years and become an important part of the institution. Such was the case for special arrivals to BSTC in '46: Edwin Nordheim (BSTC class of '41) in biology; John Warford (BSTC, '43), industrial arts; Norman Christensen, English; Ronald Gearman, music; Ida Mae Talley, art supervisor in the Laboratory School. All of these people would take leaves and/or sabbaticals in the next few years, primarily to complete their doctorates, but all returned to campus at some point.
Also arriving that fall was Judson P. Martin as registrar, and Martin too

would fill several important positions over the next 20 years, notably #2 man (academic dean) to the president. With Sattgast's return, A.C. Clark went back to his former title of vice president but returned as chairman of the social studies division.[26]

Other long-staying stalwarts on the faculty who arrived in the postwar years were (in '45) Harold Peters, biology; Ruth Lane, chemistry; Myrtie Hunt, physical education; ('47) William Britton, chemistry; Stanley Hall, physical education; Marion Sletwick, library; ('48) Maurice Callahan, music; Wesley Winter, physics.

These newcomers would soon become acquainted with the already-stalwarts on campus: Elsie Annis, physical education (who came to BSTC in 1928); Ruth Brune, English (in '24); Harry Bucklen, education ('39); Bertha Christianson ('41); H.J. Erickson, physical education ('38); Alice Fredrickson, education ('26); Harold Hagg, history ('36); Hazel Hogenson, education ('43); C.V. Hobson, geography ('31); Margaret Kelly, English ('21); Calvin McClintock, industrial education ('27); Francis McKee, education ('32); Gordon Mork, education ('40); Mabel Parker, sociology ('24); Philip R. Sauer, English ('37); Harriet Seeling, art ('25); and Carl O. Thompson, music ('37).

More solid administrative figures to greet the postwar newcomers included powerful Business Manager John Glas (came in 1939), and certain support staff personnel like Hazel Shimmin, office manager; Otis Mandrell, building custodian; and top secretaries Marie Peterson (to the president) and Nora Mae Smith (to the registrar). It was a well-known fact then and always that if one wants to know how a school is run (and who runs it), consult the campus secretaries and the janitors. They know everything!

THE "LAY OF THE LAND"

In the years right after the war, BSTC operated on a 20-acre campus, with all activities going on essentially in three buildings: The Main Building (in 1959 to be named Deputy Hall), the Physical Education Building (in 1959 to be named

---

26)Sattgast as a G.I. in World War II, like a million or more other men, had experiences that he would never talk about later; things no one would ever know, something no one would ever have known, except for a strange gift to the BSU library from Mabel Sattgast, his wife. Many years after Sattgast's death, Mrs. Sattgast was cleaning out a closet in preparation for her moving from Bemidji to California (about 1980), and in the closet she found a worn, leather satchel she had not seen before. She looked briefly at the satchel's contents and decided to give them to Bemidji State's archives collection. Acquisitions Librarian Mary Kay Smith, in preparing to catalog the items, called me and a student worker named Randy McGuire to be witnesses to the contents. When Ms. Smith dumped everything on a table, there seemed little unique there except for a tiny notebook, which turned out to be a very incomplete wartime diary that Sattgast kept. Let the words of Sattgast reveal some wartime experiences:
20 April, 1945.
"Entered Nurnberg today while the fighting was still going on within the city. We made temporary headquarters in an apartment house at the edge of town while the town was being cleaned up. Tanks were being used for patrol purposes."
21 April, 1945.
"I killed two men today. It was all very quick. One a Hitler youth about 16, the other an SS lieutenant about 30."
22 April, 1945.
"Got an order from S.H.A.E.F. to pack and ship the records. Good to be out of the hellish cellars."
23 April, 1945.
"Shot my third man. Can I always be first? He was in the book stacks of Germanic Museum."
In giving the luncheon address to alumni attending the 1990 homecoming, I quoted the above lines from Sattgast's diary, and the audience was palpably shocked. No one knew anything about this, said everyone afterwards, including faculty members who were around Sattgast 30 or more years. The most telling response that day came from a fellow World War II G.I. who afterwards said simply to me, "Unfortunately, that's what war is all about."

Memorial Hall), and Maria Sanford Hall, the women's dormitory. The three-story Main Building, appropriately named for what it held, had most of the science department on the lower level; the upper levels included all the administrative offices and classrooms, faculty offices, the library, and a little theatre seating 100 people but used also for large classes, conferences, and small recitals as well as play productions. The south portion of the building, added in 1927, housed the Laboratory School, which included grades kindergarten through nine. The "dividing line" between the Lab School section and the College was marked by the composition of the floors: The Lab School had a cork-based flooring while the College had wood flooring.

In the late 1940s at BSTC, the eating area for students was in the basement of Sanford Hall. Although initially set up for the 50 women who lived upstairs in their dorm rooms, the opportunity to receive three square meals a day was expanded to allow any non-dormitory student to eat there, including the vets in the barracks buildings. The costs for board-and-room together was $135 a quarter; board alone cost $105 per quarter.

'Jukebox Saturday Night'
"There was also a jukebox and a space for dancing for those so inclined."

Students could also buy snacks and lunches at the student union, called the Beaver Union (eventually "The Beavers' Den" in the 1950s), located in the physical education building (now Memorial Hall). Tables were provided for sitting there and enjoying a cup of coffee, but also for ubiquitous card games. There was also a jukebox and a space for dancing for those so inclined. Naturally it became the daylight social gathering spot for both students and faculty to mingle, even if there was a kind of no-no-table where only faculty were to sit.

With more students than dormitory rooms available, most students sought accommodations in private homes in town. Room rents ranged in price from $15 to $35 a month, depending on a number of factors. Some off-campus rooms included cooking facilities, allowing students to work on their culinary skills. A number of women students earned their monthly "rent money" by assisting with the housework in private homes, and these students became known as "board-and-room-girls." (This once-common method of working your way through college went well until the federal government initiated loans and grant programs in the late 1950s, after which time the board-and-room girl became a historical artifact. No more swabbing toilets, washing ceilings, and scrubbing floors when the Pell Grants were offered or free-and-easy low interest loans became easily available. An era ended.)

WHAT'S THERE TO DO OUTSIDE OF CLASSES?

ANSWER: Plenty. Maybe too much to do.

Extra-curricular activities were encouraged, the student handbook stating that "the College endeavors to provide a well-rounded program for all students." That "all students" actually participated is not likely, but the following official activities were listed (alphabetically) in the '48-'49 Catalog:

A Cappella Choir. Founded and directed by Carl Thompson (more, much more on him later);

Alpha Phi Sigma. The Nautilus Chapter of Alpha Phi Sigma was the local scholastic society affiliated with the National State Teachers College Scholarship Fraternity;

Association for Childhood Education. Local club affiliated with the National Association for Childhood Education;

"B" Club. The Lettermen's Club; membership open to all men who had won letters, sweaters or other athletic awards;

Band. Open to any student who played a musical instrument sufficiently well to qualify. The band rehearsed three times a week, played for College games and gave concerts in Bemidji and other cities of northern Minnesota;

Beaver Sportsman's Club. Opened to all interested in individual sports, with emphases on hunting, fishing, fencing, archery, skiing, and camping. Met twice a month;

Class Activities. The organization (officers elected every fall) of freshman, sophomore, junior, and senior classes to promote "wholesome class spirit, friendship and social qualities." Classes assumed responsibilities for special programs to be presented to the entire student body;

In full Uniform on the Steps of Memorial Hall (1948)
"A community with a college or university is the most fortunate of towns or cities."

Footlight Guild. Organization to promote amateur dramatic art;

Franspandeu. A club composed of the members of the modern language classes—French, Spanish, and German; met once a month;

Industrial Education Club. Students registered in Industrial Ed courses were eligible for membership; met one evening a month;

International Relations Club. Affiliated with the Carnegie Endowment for International Peace; held biweekly meetings to discuss events of current interest;

League of Women Voters. Affiliated with the local, state and national organization; met once a month; membership open to any woman student;

Northern Student. Official newspaper of the College and a member of the Associated Collegiate Press and Columbia Scholastic Press Association. Responsible for eight issues a year;

Orchesis. A club for students interested in dancing;

Orchestra. Open to any student; orchestra furnished music for College operas and annual oratorio productions;

Pi Mu Epsilon. Organized in the spring of 1948, this local society selected its members from male seniors with high scholarship who showed promise in the field of education;

Rural Life Club. Affiliated with the national Rural Youth of the USA.

Club met monthly to discuss rural problems and topics;

Sans Serif. Club for anyone interested in journalism; members assisted in the publication of the Northern Student;

Science Club. For any student interested in pure or applied science; met twice each month;

Sketch Club. For students interested in drawing, painting or crafts; met once a month; did publicity work for College activities and also made and annual creative Christmas project;

Student Council. Elected students who worked in cooperation with faculty committees "in promoting and controlling such student activities as athletics, social functions, pep meetings and convocations, campus religious activities and the student handbook";

Veterans' Organization. All vets in school were automatically members; formed to help veterans with school problems as well as keep all informed on changing rules and regulations of the national Veterans Administration;

Women's Athletic Association. Open to all women; club sponsored inter-class and inter-group sports and activities;

Social and Co-Recreation. Planned different types of parties and formal and informal campus dances. Promoted seasonal sports such as hiking, swimming, canoeing, boating, skiing and ice skating;

Intramurals. Phy ed representatives promoted sports for all students, with activities and games, which included basketball, bowling, boxing, badminton, softball, horseshoes, ice hockey, curling, tennis and table tennis.

THE "LOWLINESS" OF HOCKEY

Of special notice in the Activity section above is the listing of hockey as an intramural program only. (How times change. By the mid-1960s, Bemidji State hockey exploded in growth and interest and went on to become the most popular athletic sport on campus. Obviously not so in the late '40s.) Even the tiny program of intramural hockey had been dropped during the war, but a revival of sorts came in the fall of '46. The November 11 Northern Student showed a headline reading, "BSTC Hockey Team Given Official Sanction," but the article did not make clear what this sanction was or meant. An explanation of sorts came the next year in a fall Northern Student column. "Last season was the first time the College entered competition hockey. There was no coach, no equipment, very little financial help from the College and the players had to fend for themselves," according to one unhappy player who was quoted. A related picture showed 10 players in uniform. Student Ed Johnson, a freshman from International Falls, served as the coach. Better days were coming—but not for a while; the "golden days" were a dozen years away. Meanwhile, postwar BSTC hockey limped along; the small squads played limited schedules, with home games held in the downtown ice arena (Northland Apartments building now on that spot)—until literally the roof fell in (nobody

Workers Retrieve Sunken Bulldozer (1949)
"The 'cat in the lake' signaled the essential end of hockey for the next ten years."

injured) because of heavy snow build-up, and the arena was never rebuilt. So back to Lake Bemidji for the hockey team until the January day in 1949 when a bulldozer was plowing away the snow in preparation for a game—and the bulldozer fell through the ice. End of season. A squad member summarized their plight succinctly and well, "First the roof fell in, then the bottom falls out." The "cat in the lake" signaled the essential end of hockey for the next ten years.

FIRST POSTWAR BUILDING APPROVED FOR BSTC
        Receiving a state appropriation to construct a new building on the Bemidji State campus has remained forever a problem, the issue arising almost every year. In the '40s it was even worse because the State Colleges did not act in unison in going before the legislature. Although on the surface there was "harmony" among the State Colleges' administrations, it became dog-eat-dog in the legislature when it came to funding. Schools fought each other for precious money in a perennial struggle to grow—and sometimes just to survive. Having the "right" legislators from your region didn't hurt either—but it did hurt when these solons had little clout under that capitol dome in St. Paul. Then another school got the largesse.
        Amid this mess, something financially positive did happen downstate so that in January of 1947, President Sattgast could announce that an initial sum of $170,000 had been approved for a new library, to be attached to the Laboratory School—thus really an addition to the south end of the Main Building. By May of that year excavation began, and the funding was raised to $232,000. This would be the first of many new buildings to come to the College in the pines (the only one in the '40s), and each and every one would be a struggle to achieve.

CHANGING JOBS, ALAS

Exploding numbers of college students throughout the nation after the war meant opportunities for professors to find employment at other institutions. Thus did several Bemidji State faculty members choose to leave, presumably for the proverbial greener pastures.

It came as quite a surprise when Ruth Jessup, principal of the Laboratory School since 1922, left Bemidji State in the summer of 1947 to become principal of the elementary school at Schofield Barracks, Hawaii.

Reuben H. "Jack" Frost, who had first come to the campus in 1935, returned from the war in '46, leaving the Army with the rank of lieutenant colonel. The popular teacher and coach apparently had a number of schools who wanted him, according to the Northern Student writers who speculated with sadness about his likely resignation. It turned out that Frost also left in the summer of '47 to accept the position of athletic director at South Dakota State University, Brookings.

The year 1947 was not a good one for BSTC, bringing the loss of several fine teachers. Another long-time BSTC professor, Dr. Alfred Elliott, left to become a zoology teacher at the University of Michigan at Ann Arbor. The remaining faculty, however, did take pride in the quality of both Elliott and the prestigious school to which he was going. (Elliott remained at Michigan until his retirement in 1970. His son William, however, joined the Bemidji faculty in 1967 as a professor of English.)

Dr. Gordon Mork, called "a crackerjack schoolman," left the education department in 1949 for the University of Minnesota, another important prof on the make.

In addition to the faculty loss in '47, there was an economic loss for students, announced in the campus newspaper that fall, "Students Will Buy Books Next Term," decreed Business Manager John Glas. The days of furnished "free books" going along with activity fee payments had ended, and students would then have to add the "book bite" to their budgeting.

TOO MANY MEN?!

So different was the composition of the student body by 1948, compared to war years, that the first fall edition of the newspaper could run the headline, "BSTC Overrun by Males!" The eye-catching title was as much a spoof as it was news, a tongue-in-cheek story followed about "too many men?" written by someone taking the nom de plume of "Virginia Beaver." Actually the writer was pleased with both the men and the state of the campus—and the state of the state. They were all looking good.

Another student writer in that same paper was not pleased with the results of a straw vote election for U.S. president that year (1948); the article was headlined, "Who Stuffed the Ballot Box?" and this was followed by the vote tally.

The "winner" on campus was Dixiecrat Party candidate J. Strom Thurmond who received 30 votes. Next came Democrat Harry S. Truman with ten, followed by Republican candidate Thomas E. Dewey with six. Gaining only two votes was

1949 Winter Graduates in Formation'
"So different was the composition of the student body . . . 'BSTC Overrun by Males!'"

Socialist Norman Thomas while there was one vote each for Progressive candidate Henry Wallace and one write-in for Communist Earl Browder. The real winner in the real election was, of course, Truman, an item not mentioned in this November 24 issue.

What was mentioned was something closer to the students' most sensitive nerve, the pocketbook-nerve. These future teachers could appreciate the headline, "Teachers' Salaries Increase." Public school contracts for Minnesota grads ranged from $2,400 to $3,300 for the '48-'49 school year, with the median salary at $2,886. This latter figure was compared with the '44-'45 year when the median was $1,775. Still, noted the writer, the "big money" lies in becoming a school administrator as salaries for the '48-'49 school year found principals averaging $3,200, while superintendents did even better at $4,900.

MOMENTOUS DECADE COMES TO AN END WITH "NORMALITY"
The final school year of the '40s found Earl Gregoire of Bemidji elected student body president, replacing the retiring Louie Marchand, also of Bemidji. Of some interest, always, the new editor of the Northern Student was Bruce Atwater

of Williams, Minnesota.[27]

By this time the school was back to the routine considered normal before the war. There were by then enough "fresh" freshmen right out of high school who acquiesced completely to proper subservience, including the requirement of wearing those little green-and-white beanie caps. (What some of the freshmen World War II vets told upper classmen to do with their beanie requirement cannot be repeated in a family newspaper.)

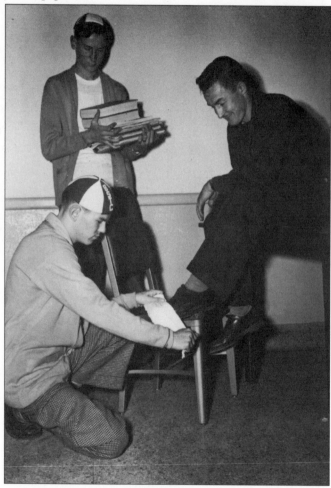

Beanied and Lowly, the Freshmen do their Duties
"There were by then enough 'fresh' freshmen . . . who acquiesced completely."

27)The three men mentioned would all have successful careers and eventually all become an important part of Bemidji. Gregoire went on to medical school and returned to Bemidji to become a noted "baby doctor." His lovely home stands near the University on the corner of 16th and Bixby Avenue. His love of the North Country was reflected in his passion for fishing, including regular excursions into the Canadian wilderness. His career ended abruptly and sadly with a fatal heart attack in 1986 at the age of 64. Marchand went on from Bemidji State to schooling at Syracuse and the University of Denver, returning to his alma mater in 1955 as speech teacher and director of dramatic arts. His play-directing—and his own playwriting—for the next 36 years made him a legend in his own time; he retired in 1992. Atwater spent almost all of his public school teaching career in Warroad, there on the Canadian border, teaching high school English and also directing speech and theater students. When he retired in 1980, he moved back to Bemidji and soon began another "career" in city politics. At this writing (1994), Atwater still sits on the city council representing the 5th Ward of Nymore.

Certain social activities before the war at BSTC were restored to their same elevation afterwards. Over 300 couples attended the formal, senior prom—and the faculty was also fully represented at the dance. Paul Bunyan Week came and was again enjoyed, with the proper spirited election of a Paul and Carrie to preside over the Woodchoppers Ball, highlighted by the nationally famous Big Band that made the song "Woodchoppers Ball" famous, Woody Herman, playing for the dancers on the basketball floor in Memorial Hall. That week all got into the spirit of Paul Bunyan Week, some of it enforced by the student Kangaroo Court who "sentenced" malefactors who were not wearing proper attire, namely a plaid lumberjack shirt and jeans, each day.

Letters to the editor appeared on banal but ongoing topics, *ad infinitum*: school spirit, and/or the lack thereof; convocations/brought-in speakers and their quality, and/or the lack thereof; faculty tests (too hard; too easy; too canned) and strange, unfathomable grading standards of some profs; cheating (an honor code needed?); theft (missing pocket books); boorish behavior of certain men; blind referees who robbed us . . . but wait'll next year; and more on those topics so important to undergraduates at all times, including the perennial problem of registering.[28]

Meanwhile, the administration went ahead and held a dedication of the library on February 2, 1949, and in the same month promoted publicly the attempt of the State Colleges to seek approval to offer a much-needed master's degree program, and at the same time drop the word "Teachers" from Bemidji State Teachers College. (Both requests were approved by the legislature in the next decade, the M.S. in 1953 and the name change to Bemidji State College in 1957.)

What the legislature did do for Bemidji State in 1949 was also big news; they approved funding for a new separate Laboratory School to the tune of a half a million dollars! Bids were awarded in February, and construction began in the spring, with completion the following summer, 1950. Thus the new decade began on this auspicious note—and more good things would come to BSTC in the 1950s, like an unimaginable 1,000 students!

---

28)Registration procedures in the postwar years seemed simple enough, and only later would they be viewed as something lying historically between quaint and ancient. To register in the late 1940s, students filled out a separate 3x5 blank card for each class they wanted to take. They also filled out a card listing all their classes and turned in all the filled-in cards to the Registrar's Office. Registration workers then sorted by hand all the 3x5 cards by means of dropping the class cards into "pigeonhole" mailboxes, with the instructor's name above each box. The teacher then had a card for each student enrolled and used the same card for turning in each student's grade at the end of the marking period. The schedule-cards for each student were also counted by hand, with the statistics on the cards reported to President Sattgast and appropriate chairpersons. Later the cards were used to compare them with the tuition receipts to determine which fees were not paid. Information from Arleigh Chandler, a long-time BSU employee (since 1949); memo dated March 31, 1992, copy in author's file. Added Chandler about veteran's payments, "We had some delay, mainly because we still had the World War II vets in school and their G.I. pay was consistently late—some things never change." Her final line about postwar registration at Bemidji State, "We were not very automated, but I think it was more fun." Arleigh Chandler started working at Bemidji State when she was 17 years old. She retired in January, 1994, after working there 45 years! That record should stand forever.

The 1950s

"Those 1950s! Wow! Now that was really a weird decade!" To this can be added, "But weren't they all!" for each time period in American history has its uniqueness that can flippantly be described as "weird." That "wow" description of the '50s does indicate a common emotional response to a ten-year period, and yet the "wow" hardly gives any insight or information about that particular time-span. Moreover, today's "wow" is tomorrow's cliché and the next day's nostalgia, and nostalgia is insidious. Waiting for a time when our defenses are low and our need for respite high, it worms into consciousness with half-remembered notions of simpler times and supposedly sweeter people. The older you get, the more sneakily does nostalgia overtake you. Now, come to think of it, the 1950s really was a "wonderful" decade.

When looked back on, certain touchstones pop to mind, all of them made indelible in the mind by that then newest and most attractive medium, television. TV was all so new and so wonderful then; it started out in the barrooms and people moved in off the streets to see the flickering gray images cavorting on tiny screens. And when the neighbor down the street got his own set, well, then everyone else had to have one too, and they soon did. And the watching began with such fascination that, verily, people turned on their first sets early just to view the test pattern! And which of the programs are remembered? Why, there's Howdy Doody screaming an appropriate, "Hey kids, what time is it?" Elvis Presley and Marilyn Monroe and Marlon Brando excited and scandalized us. Superman, Davy Crockett, Paladin, and Sergeant Bilko were our folk heroes. Uncle Miltie, Jackie Gleason - "Norton! Norrrton!" - Sid Caesar, Lucy and Desi were court jesters to "Queen for a Day." As to popular music, there was something new, something pounding a primeval beat throughout the land for the affluent young; it was the record industry-contrived

220

marvel of sound, rock 'n roll, and the brand new faces and voices promoting and exploiting it. And above them all was Elvis Presley, Elvis the Pelvis. Elvis Presley was an evil dude; he was Grease in the flesh. He looked like his idea of a good time was to lead the Blackstone Rangers into a Saturday night rumble. The way he waggled his crotch drove mothers of teenagers to apoplexy - "Harry, tell me! What is this world coming to?" - and Ed Sullivan into not allowing the cameras to view him from the waist down the first time Elvis appeared on national TV. Only the studio audience caught sin-in-motion in his pelvic gyration; the multi-millions watching TV saw only a sneering young man who was waiting to sing dirty-ol' rock 'n roll. The combination of raunch and rock seemed to be unbeatable for this ex-Tennessee truck driver. Heck, anyone who could so thoroughly offend everybody from high school age on up must have something going for him.

And then there was that war in Korea, Truman firing MacArthur, fall-out scares, evacuation routes, the Rosenbergs, Army-McCarthy hearings - "Point of Order!" - the Checkers speech, quiz shows and payola scandals, Hungary in '56, Sputnik in '57, Cuba in '58, and among all the political stars of all those years was Mr. Nice Man himself for whom everything is summed up in his campaign slogan, "I Like Ike"; and millions did, including his twice-defeated opponent Adlai Stevenson, who said he liked Ike too, but not Ike's running partner.

For readers who were not old enough to know what was going on in the '50s, or maybe not even born yet, all those aforementioned items ticked off are just so much schlock out of the past. Even to those who lived in the '50s, the decade seemed sort of bewildering as to significance and meaning. But to the then young, to college kids, it was usually all fun and often funny, too. It was strange, confusing and sometimes goofy.

Among America's permanently bewildered are its college students who are smart enough to know they're bewildered, although seldom admitting as much, and dumb enough to enjoy it all—well, anyway most of it—meanwhile living in limbo, neither adult nor kid, living in a special world often far removed both physically and mentally from "the real world," expecting always that good and not bad will happen to them, believing that if they can just somehow hang on and get a degree, well, then they'll "have it made," and this bewilderment, this cloud of doubt above them, will somehow miraculously disappear with the reception of a sheepskin. The worries, the uncertainties, the vagaries of life will end come graduation day, according to the dream formula.

The college kids' quasi-answer phrase to any problem in a bizarre if not stupid world is the line, "This too shall pass." They loftily assume that in the totality of life not much is important; therefore, whatever the issue, eventually, "it, too, shall pass." Meanwhile, students must live, though they know not just why, only live, just live, live for the day, and maybe for the week because a full week means a weekend and a party; live until the next exam is over, don't think beyond the next test; infinity means the end of the semester; the brave new world is out there *someplace, and one joins it when the diplomas are handed out on that glorious June day. So hang in there, and stay brave; learn enough just to pass, learn enough just to get the grade point up; learn enough to avoid the draft; just hang on; "want-to" is more important than I.Q. Just keep jumping the hurdles one by one, and if you stumble or fall, then get up and try again. The country will keep until graduation, at which point you can join it, but not before, 'cause there is safety in being at college. Just graduate, graduate any way you can; graduate summa cum laude or magna cum thanks, but graduate. The degree means success; at least it's supposed to mean that; it means money (which is success), and success, when normally translated into American English means money; and money means security, security in an insecure world. A world in which the Russians threaten the globe by putting a round hunk of metal into orbit. But why is Sputnik threatening? Well, it just is, that's all, 'cause Khruschev said, "We will bury you," and Sputnik is the start of the funeral. And so is the Russian victory in the Olympic Games. But what do a bunch of husky, Rusky superjocks have to do with monolithic Communism taking over the world? Well, they just do, that's all. It's unAmerican to think otherwise, to question, to criticize. Whose side are we on, anyway? Will Ike hold off the burial? Will SAC deter ICBMs? Will NATO have a showdown with the Warsaw Pact nations? Will Godless Eastern Communism win out over Godly Western Christianity? These are the big questions of the '50s. Or are they? Depends. Will Steve Allen's TV show knock out Ed Sullivan's "Toast of the Town"? Will Hamm's outsell Grain Belt? Will Iowa win the Rose Bowl? Will Iowa pigs stop smelling up the countryside? These are/aren't the big questions. How about all those Reds and Pinks in the State Department? And in Hollywood? And on the college campuses? Will someone ever step on Elvis's Blue Suede Shoes? Would someone please just stamp out Elvis? Who will follow Eisenhower to the throne? Will Julius LaRosa regain his humility enough to get back with Arthur Godfrey? Who knows? Who cares? Does it make any difference? Who cares who controls the "hot spots" of the world—Lebanon? or Venezuela? or Matsu and Quemoy? or even Little Rock, Arkansas? Certainly not the "leaders of the future," with the emphasis on "future"; not these college kids of the '50s who find the University of Pittsburgh significant in the news because of its number-one ranked football team rather than for its chem prof named Jonas Salk. Who cares? Who should care? Let the students care about student-cares. They'll join the nation later, say, like after graduation.**

*(for samples of historical trivia on the '50s, see Appendix E)

◆ ◆ ◆

COLD? SURE, BUT IT'S SO PRETTY. . . .

Bemidji State at the start of 1950 was similar to the school of 1940. First of all—in January—it was still cold. Very cold. Down-to-the-bone-marrow cold. Square-car-tires-cold. Minus-20/30/40/50-below-zero cold. Frozen-fuel-lines cold. Sky-high-fuel-bills cold. Freeze-your-buns cold. Death-by-wind-chill cold. Survival-kit-in-the-trunk cold. It's cold!

Not one student or faculty member could ever leave Bemidji and not have at least one cold weather story tattooed in his or her mind.[1] But beautiful cold, too. Breathtakingly beautiful views of nature. A veritable winter wonderland everywhere. Gorgeous snow-laden pine trees. Even the lowly jackpine looks great when drooping with white stuff. And clean air. Amazingly fresh, clean, unpolluted fresh air to breathe.

Downstate Minnesota may get snow, sometimes in huge amounts; then again maybe not. Whatever, the snow seldom stays long "down south." Twin Cities winters find "snirt"—a combination of snow and dirt—everywhere. Ugly. Dirty. Yucky. Not so in Bemidji. One can depend on snow; snow on snow; clean, pure snow arriving all winter long. Aesthetically lovely.

Complaints and complainers? Sure. But only "foreigners" (read anyone who came from south of Brainerd) get "disturbed" by Bemidji weather; who cannot understand why most students are not bothered by the frightful cold, who do not even wear caps or gloves or even winter coats; who matter-of-factly go ahead with plans whether it's a hot 25 above or cool 25 below zero. Minor problem.

An extraordinary testimonial of student response to winter and cold and storms comes from a story President Sattgast enjoyed telling. In his many years as president, from 1938 to 1964, he called off classes for the day only once because of a severe snowstorm. (Sattgast walked to school that morning on snow shoes.) He was concerned about student safety and did not want to endanger anyone. But what did many students do when the word got out that there would be no classes? Defying no-travel warnings, they got in their cars and hit the snowstormed highways and headed through the snowdrifts for their homes! Sattgast never canceled classes again.

Only foreigners in Bemidji find crazy the voices of the local radio commentators who talk flippantly about "the slight drop in temperatures," and who routinely and unemotionally mention "the wind chill factor today is 75 below zero." Outlanders find little funny in common lapel pins worn by the locals, some which read, "-41 Keeps Out the Riffraff," "Have You Noticed There's No Mosquitoes?" or "Winter is Our Best Kept Secret in Brrrrmidji."

Only the snide, wimpish, waspish strangers-in-the-land can label Bemidji State in January as Tundra Tech, The Ol' Miss of the Muskeg. TRUE Beavers have always taken pride in their special North Country, whether January in 1920 or 1990.

Not that school officials have ignored weather concerns. Just the opposite. Indeed, perhaps Bemidji State is the only university in the nation in which essentially all buildings on campus are connected by either underground tunnels or

1)Dr. Harold Fleming came to Bemidji from Tennessee in 1950 to head the division of education. He would soon see things he could not believe, like a large house being moved across the ice on Lake Bemidji. He found it hard to convince his southern friends of the degree of cold in Bemidji winters until one day he took a photograph of his thermometer when it hit 50 below zero and sent the picture as proof. The coldest "dip" this writer personally observed on a thermometer was -46°; on that same day he routinely pulled his kindergartner son on his sled to the Laboratory School. Just a normal January day. Ho-hum.

overhead walkways. (Today, only at Bemidji State can a student attend one full winter quarter and never once have to go outside between January 1 and April 1. It can be done.)

THE UNITY FOUND IN A SMALL SCHOOL

In 1950 Bemidji State was still small enough—almost all classes held in the one Main Building—so that the one-big-family atmosphere continued. Basically everybody knew everybody—or as much as they wanted to know. This togetherness would be seen and maintained in a variety of ways, notably the weekly all-student-faculty convocation. One hour each week—Wednesdays at 9:00 a.m. in the

'The Fireplace': Built in '32, Unused by '62; Almost Unknown by '92
"Certain social activities before the war . . . gave way to a different school."

gymnasium—had been set aside for this assembly and assembling; no classes were allowed that hour. Attendance, however, was voluntary. Depending on the program-appeal of the week (and Carl Thompson of the music department coordinated and planned all of these programs for 27 years! A herculean task!) there could be a full house—filling up both sides of the bleachers—or there might be less than a dozen folks taking up a tiny space in the south bleacher section. Whichever, there was a wide variety of programming:

Lectures, slide shows, movies, musical programs ranging from soloists to

75-piece bands; one-act plays; inspirational orations from speech students; club and/or class skits; parodies; pep rallies; introduction of sports team members; homecoming rallies; political speeches; debates—and more—and always there for introductions was school President Charles Richard Sattgast, who also could and did use the setting and opportunity to bestow some needed/unneeded advice to both the undergraduates and the faculty in attendance.

These convocations allowed for a full measure of student and faculty unification; it fit perfectly for the small college that Bemidji State once was.[2]

"THE FAMILY" THAT WORKS TOGETHER . . . CAN GET TOO CLOSE

Having almost all (except phy ed) classes in one building had both good and bad points. Certainly there was the convenience factor; no one had to go very far to find anyone else. The president could and would roam the halls upstairs and downstairs, bestowing presidential presence to everyone—and checking carefully for clean floors and NO cigarette smoking. When machines in a classroom broke down, well, just call that nice Wesley Winter, new in the physics department. Either he or Eddie Nordheim would come around eventually, and they could fix anything. After all, in the '50s, there was no such title on campus as an audio-visual director; profs figured out their own A-V technology—or called Wes or Ed.

No one bothered the science people downstairs until they "bothered" the rest of the people upstairs by occasional offensive odors emitting from their laboratories. Sometimes they stunk up the whole building, resulting in windows upstairs being thrown open on the coldest of winter days, just for fresh air. No one in the decade of the '50s could accuse other departments of aloofness; they were all together, basement smells included. Curiously, the chemistry department was on the top floor and the rest of science in the basement. Between the two areas, their scientific formulas and mixes became well known to all non-science majors as well. (Sattgast was once to accuse the chemists of allowing nitric acid to seep through the floor above his office and land on Sattgast's head—but that's a later story. See "As I Remember Charles Sattgast," by Richard Beitzel, in later section.)

WHAT DEANS MUST DO

The wooden floors in the Main Building carried sounds well, too well. Profs were told to close their classroom doors, not for privacy so much as for keeping out the competing noise from other profs. On occasion, when door-closing

---

2)Convocations had started with President Deputy back in 1920, but then they were held twice a week and student attendance was mandatory (his secretary took roll). Sattgast changed the format soon after he arrived in 1938, and it stayed his way until his successor, Harry Bangsberg, abolished the weekly convocations in 1966, arguing that the limited monies available should be spent not on dozens of unknown persons but only on a special few, well-known figures of national reputation. The first person Bangsberg brought in was military historian S.L.A. Marshall; his "name" filled the high school auditorium, the largest "nice" auditorium in town, where all these "major figures" appeared. Alas, this format did not always succeed because too soon some alleged "big names" attracted only sparse attendance, embarrassingly so, expensively so. However, this irregular "convocation" plan—moved back to campus—continued until the present, with one small turnaround—or 'what goes around comes around.' Starting in the fall of 1992, one College—Arts and Letters (formerly the division of humanities and fine arts)—alone set aside 11:00 a.m. on Tuesdays for convocations. 'Tis too soon to assess its success at this writing (1994) but the initial responses have been less than overwhelming. Since 1966, with both bigness of numbers and no planned all-student-assemblies, the only time the student body comes even close to "getting together" is at home hockey games, alas.

was forgotten, stentorium lecture voices from down the hall could overwhelm sotto-voiced presenters in other rooms. Hence the academic dean had more to do than to plan Great Curriculum, he had also the task of leaving his office to moderate and/or referee competing faculty lecturers who were annoying each other. He also shut a lot of classroom doors.

Although later changed to "academic dean," the title used in the 1950s at Bemidji State was "dean of instruction." Except for the president, that dean was considered the most important administrator on campus. With degrees from the University of Wisconsin, Dr. Judson P. Martin came to Bemidji in 1946 as registrar but was later appointed dean of instruction, his title for most of the 1950s. A short, small man physically, he dressed rather nattily and became famous for his "trademark," the clip-on bow tie, an item of fashion at the time. Physical appearances of the faculty were then a concern of the dean, reflecting the common view of school officials everywhere that if men were not wearing coats and ties and women were not wearing dresses or skirts in their classrooms, they simply were not dressed properly. Martin's views of propriety of appearance included the eschewing of beards. (Mustaches were all right; they had to be!—because A.C. Clark had one and nobody messed with A.C. Clark.) By decade's end, only one man wore a small goatee, the new speech teacher Jim Ertresvaag, and Martin persuaded him to shave it off. But the next year he grew it back again—and kept it on. (In the '60s, beards became as common on men as the pantsuits on women.)

THE POWER OF THE PRESIDENT

If the dean of instruction appeared paternalistic, that was the way it was done in the 1950s—and before. The administration had full autonomy. The president, and his top designee, could be, and often were expected to be, benevolent dictators.

In loco parentis (in place of the parents) was more than a fancy phrase. With the real parents home, the next-in-line "parent" was the president of the college. He had full authority to discipline and/or expel any student without any hearing; he determined the rigid regulations for women (men were excluded) in dormitory hours; he determined which off-campus rooms were acceptable and which were not. There were no national social fraternities or sororities on campus because Sattgast said there would be no fraternities or sororities on campus.

Sattgast could and did rule over his faculty with power nearly equal to that with which he ruled the students. When authorized by the legislature, he alone decided who got raises and who did not deserve them; he ultimately determined who got promoted in academic rank; who got sabbaticals and who got leaves with no pay. Sattgast did all the firing and did all the hiring, regardless of the esoteric needs of a department he may/may not have understood. (In fairness, Sattgast did seek opinions from the committees he appointed.)

Sattgast asked job-seeking candidates bluntly in interviews if they were churchgoing folk; he also asked them if they smoked and drank in moderation. He asked them the standard if non-academic question of whether they liked hunting and fishing as hobbies.[3] When he told faculty members that they were expected to be in attendance at certain social functions of the College, they were there. When he told each member to purchase an activity ticket, they did, or they did not stay around long. If he wanted to change a faculty grade given to some student, he could—and did. He took seriously the line in the school catalog under the section called Objectives, "To foster growth of moral and spiritual values and to develop a mature sense of social and civic responsibilities."

To help him achieve these proper objectives, and more, the president selected proper people with proper titles: dean of men and dean of women. They also had proper authorized power to expel or suspend students on their own. At the decade's start, these positions were held by C.V. Hobson and Margaret Kelly. The aforementioned Hobson also was the director of student personnel, the umbrella office for student help. Miss Kelly had come to Bemidji State as an instructor in English in 1921; as the housemother for Sanford Hall women, she immediately gained notoriety, at first the grudging kind, but later pure admiration. Kelly was always addressed as "Miss Kelly," although at a distance she became "Ma Kelly." The latter title is not pejorative; she was truly a substitute mother to the women. Contemporaries describe her favorably, if not with devotion, as "genteel, motherly, ladylike"—and a no nonsense person of probity and high standards demanding in others the integrity that was already in herself.

WHEN DEANS WERE "LAWYERS"

The format, the policy and the personalities changed for students. Newly hired (in 1952, at the request of Dean Martin) Raymond Carlson came on the scene, starting as a one-man psychology "department." He received the titles, and duties, of both coordinator of student services and dean of students, men and women. Student services, such as they were, were fragmented and scattered; Carlson was to try to integrate these services under his direction. The youthful-looking, crew-cut Carlson radiated kindness and help-for-students, markings of the man that never changed over the next 40 years (although he finally let his hair grow longer).

Among the first real changes sought by Carlson were the role, nature, need and even the definition of counseling. As stated and defined in the school catalog under Counseling, "Each student is assigned to a faculty member who acts as his counselor, conferring with him on scholastic achievement, work load, personality

---

3)Faculty members hired by Sattgast loved to get together later and swap stories about what happened when he interviewed them. One told of being interviewed by Sattgast simultaneously with another candidate, and when the question of hunting and fishing came up, the one candidate said no, he didn't care for either one. Sattgast was taken aback by the answer, finding it unbelievable, and pursued it by demanding that he just had to have some hobbies. The man said no, he didn't have any, and then his wife beside him whispered in his ear, after which he said, "I guess I do have a hobby; it's reading." "Is that it?" asked the president. "Yes, that was it," replied the man. He was not hired.

There is likely a tone of implied criticism of Sattgast in the above section, which is really not intended as it is not fair to him. He truly acted always in what he believed was best for his school. Only later—with the changing attitudes—would he be viewed as some kind of martinet. He always tried to be fair and was certainly "small-d" democratic. For example, he vetoed any attempt to allow a faculty-only parking lot because he maintained it was simply not democratic. As to church attendance, he bragged to St. Olaf President Clement Granskou that his Bemidji State faculty had a higher proportion of Sunday church attenders than Granskou had at St. Olaf.

development and other problems concerned with his happiness and success." To Carlson this seemed inappropriate for teaching faculty; they simply were not counselors in the true sense but primarily academic advisors.   When Carlson pushed for added personal counseling, the faculty then defined it as some form of "crying towel," or "silly hand-holding," obviously not needed.   Harrrrumph. (Carlson eventually won; a counseling center was established by 1960 and expanded thereafter.)

The '50s found Dean Carlson a busy man both day and night, especially those nights when the phone calls came from the police. The expected procedure was for the police to call the dean whenever some College student had been

Dr. Ray Carlson
"The '50s found Dean Carlson a busy man both day and night, especially nights."

apprehended for some alleged crime. Thus Carlson would regularly be awakened by late night calls and summoned immediately to the police station to do his duties as dean of students, even though he lived 15 miles north on Lake Beltrami. As a result, a great deal of predawn, pre-court plea bargaining got done in the 1950s, with "Attorney Carlson" in the middle of it.

His law work went even further. When the degree of the crime went beyond the informal plea bargaining/commonsense solutions outside of court, then Carlson and the judge got together before the trial, the latter seeking Carlson's opinions on what his ruling and/or sentencing should be. It was all very pragmatic; it was all very paternalistic; it was all very illegal. But they did it anyway. Such were the times.

Only gradually could Carlson convince the administration to accept these strange theories called "student rights" or the even weirder one of "due process." Finally, said Carlson, by 1956 we got semi-due-process in the form of Student Review Boards, soon called J-Boards, for Judicial Boards. The spark that pushed Carlson to act in the name of common sense occurred when a woman student was about to be expelled because she had been exactly 22 seconds late in getting inside the dormitory door! The forthcoming J-Board hearing saved this particular malefactor from expulsion. "That nice Mr. Carlson" had won again.[4] (More on Carlson and the shifting patterns of personnel/student rights rulings in the section on the 1960s.)

RESPONSIVE, RESPONSIBLE CLUBS
    The temper of the times, the Return to Religion associated with the '50s, can be seen in part on the Bemidji campus by the addition that decade of several church-sponsored organizations. All would be authorized by the school and listed under Clubs and Organizations in the '58-'59 catalog (pp. 24-30):
    Canterbury Club, for Episcopalians; The Newman Club, for the Catholic students; The Wesley Foundation, sponsored by the Methodist Church; Westminster Fellowship of the Presbyterian Church; The Lutheran Student Association, which group carried things farther by the purchase of their own house near the campus on Birchmont Drive, The Kenfield Home, as it was known in town. (The Kenfield family went back to turn-of-the century Bemidji and was associated with lumbering and wood products, e.g., the Kenfield Box Factory. "The Kenfield Home" became one of the few grand old houses in town and a reminder of the lumbering era.)
    The Lutherans had this huge house for the L.S.A. activities, but then there were other, different Lutherans who had their own organization, Gamma Delta, "an organization of Lutheran Students of the Synodical Conference consisting of Missouri, Wisconsin, Norwegian, and Slovak synods and the Finnish National Lutheran Church." (Lutherans those days were less than united.) The last of the then new-on-campus religious groups was Bemidji Inter-Varsity Christian Fellowship, a local chapter of the international organization.
    It came as no surprise for school authorities to list "Church Attendance" as a category under "Clubs and Activities," the "explanation" there reading, "Students are encouraged to consider well the paramount importance of developing a sound religious philosophy."
    As to the other secular organizations, they of course changed with both additions and subtractions from ten years before that. By '59 there had been added

4) Information from Carlson gained in a series of conversations with him over the years. He had some wonderful tales to spin, many of which he asked me not to print. I asked him several times—yea, pleaded—for him to write up his own views and experiences as dean of students, but he declined to do so. His being brought in to implement this different policy meant his predecessors were out. No problem for Hobson, who continued on in other assignments with the same high quality he did everything. For Miss Kelly, however, it became a tragedy; indeed, it shall remain one of the saddest stories relative to faculty members. As the story is told, she could not/would not accept all the changes and new policies brought about by Martin, the dean of instruction. One night, in 1956, unbeknownst to anyone, a moving van came to her Bemidji home, loaded the contents and at dawn took them away, someplace. No one knew where she went exactly, let alone her address; no one in Bemidji ever heard from her again. It was not this writer's privilege to ever meet Miss Kelly (I came in 1959); all I ever heard—over and over again—was the above sad story. She is likely deceased at this writing, but no one seems to know that for sure either, despite those who tried over the years to keep close watch on Twin Cities obituary columns.

the following:

The American Humanities Club; the Bemidji State College Democratic and Republican Clubs; Future Business Leaders of America; Student National Education Association; German Club; Graduate Club; "Pep" Club; Photography Club; Physical Education Majors Club; Skating Club; Ski Club; Square Dance Club; and lastly, Women's Recreation Association. Taken all together, and given the existing cultural situation, these clubs and activities seemed entirely appropriate for that decade.

RISING COSTS

The tuition fees almost doubled in ten years, from $20 a quarter in '49 to $35 in '59, but non-residents still paid only an extra $5 a quarter. The student activity fee in that period inched up from $8 to $10 a quarter. All items considered, the estimated total expenses per school year to attend Bemidji State rose from $540 in '49 to $750 in '59. Northern Student editors, by then publishing biweekly, wondered in print if and how these escalating costs could keep on? When would it stop? (Those same questions may likely be repeated annually into the 21st century.)

1950s: TO BUILD AND EXPAND

The completion of the new Laboratory School in 1950 started major changes for Bemidji State. First of all its appearance was a showplace for the entire town. When visitors came to Bemidji, the locals drove them by to show off the new

Observers Watch Construction of First Post War Building
"The completion of the new Lab School in 1950 started major changes."

school just completed. An impressive sight to see. With towering, massive white pines on its north side, the handsome, three-story structure stood near the athletic field and overlooked Lake Bemidji.

Moreover, it was the first new, separate building on campus since Sanford Hall had been constructed back in 1920, and that fact alone added to its being an accomplishment to be proud of. Along with the educationally specific-sized classrooms, it contained both an auditorium and a small gymnasium. All in all, both kids and staff could hardly wait to get moved into this amazing structure following Labor Day, 1950.

Art Instruction Time in the College Laboratory School
"A kind of mystique identified with it . . . the waiting list to get in was long."

In its long history, the Lab School had gained the admiration of the citizens of the community. Indeed, it had a kind of mystique identified with it, best illustrated by the efforts of parents wanting to have their child enrolled there. The waiting list to get in was long. Some critics in town paid it a left-handed compliment by calling it a "brains factory" and a "snob school," a place for "faculty brats" to be indulged in someplace besides their homes. But the same critics wanted their kids there, too. (It is more than apocryphal the story of the father who went to the Lab School office to apply for his son's admittance on the same day the child was born.)

Professional people in Bemidji, who believed it desirable for their children to go out of town for college, nevertheless wanted their offspring to be prepared for further schooling by attending the local college Laboratory School.[5]

---

5)Many students who attended the Laboratory School grew to gain a loyalty for the school, even though they later had nothing to do with the College. Their fondness for the Lab School remained. This was recently demonstrated by the Alumni Office in planning reunions for the 75th Anniversary; it turned out the Lab School folks wanted their own reunion! And they got it.

It had a deserved prestige and a high standing in the community. The new Lab School, of course, opened up new space in the Main Building, almost enough to accommodate the ever-increasing numbers of college students arriving (575 in 1950).

Those added bodies had to have a place to stay; there had to be more dormitory space, but there appeared to be little land space left to build any more structures. Yet authorization had been given by the State College Board to build a new dorm! What to do? Solution: expand the campus; move north; annex city properties; take over that area called the "City Forest"; in effect, add 54 more acres to the existing 20-acre campus. And it was done. But not without testing tempers downtown and with school officials responding most carefully to common charges of "that damn College takin' everything."

Showing off a Birch Hall Room (1952); First Dorm Built Since 1920
"Across the street from Diamond Point Park . . . was the City Zoo."

But "everything" was not annexed, notably not the adjoining property directly north of the football/athletic field. That was Diamond Point Park, on Lake Bemidji, the municipal park and public boat landing; and no way was the city about to give that up. Just the mention of the possibility led to a verbal uprising in the local newspapers. *Vox populi.*

Yet the city did give up the land across the street from Diamond Point for the first of many residence halls to be built on its former property. Directly across from the park was the City Zoo, and thus the zoo would go, and never come back. Although a far cry from the Como Park Zoo in Minneapolis, it nevertheless had enough exotic animals, including camels, to make it a special place for the city to advertise. Understandably, most citizens were not pleased by the zoo's closing just to accommodate "the College,"—as it was usually called, and is called even to the present time, by most Bemidji townspeople.[6]

Behind the zoo area had been mainly woods, the City Forest, except for a small (950' by 450') portion next to Bemidji Avenue, owned and used as a practice football field by the high school, located just across the street. (The high school received $87,053 for this property from Bemidji State.) Tucked in the northwest corner of the Forest was, and still is, a state forestry station. With only this latter exception, the remaining acres—54 of them—became part of Bemidji State.

The school built the first of many buildings on their extended campus, Birch Hall, a residence hall, completed in 1952, at a cost of $700,000. Providing living quarters for 200 students, it was designed and constructed in two separate wings of student rooms (single-, double-, triple-occupancy available), one wing for men and one for women students. The wings were joined with a central office, reception lounges, and recreational facilities.

Beginning with Birch Hall, the growth of "the College" on its new property had begun and would continue with little letup for the next 20 years. "The City Forest" would gradually be denuded as trees were replaced by residence halls and a sprawling physical education complex.

The '50s building program continued, moving north from Birch Hall, one dorm after another erected along Birchmont Drive, before the building swung west along 23rd Street. All the dormitory buildings were named after trees: Birch, Pine, Oak, Maple, Tamarack, and Linden. The last, built in the '60s, briefly unnerved some local Republicans who, until they saw the spelling, believed it to be named for Lyndon Johnson. Giving tree names to the buildings made it easier than having to select, and inevitably not select, some person to be honored by having his/her name placed on a building.

To feed the expanding pack of "tunnel rats," a half-million-dollar food service building was attached to Birch Hall and opened in January of 1958. Its spacious dining room, with its room-length picture windows overlooking Diamond Point across the street, was a state of the art facility and would be another source of pride for all friends of the College.

With this new cafeteria, food service in the old one in the Sanford Hall basement, euphemistically called The Lower Level, was discontinued except for a snack bar, and the area became the next Student Union, "The Beaver Den," complete with a large picture of two busy Beavers painted on the wall. Three connecting rooms, each with tables and chairs, were available, the smallest room

---

6)Those citizens of a vintage to remember the City Zoo had those wags among them who said then and later that the zoo really did not cease operation. All that changed were the pens and the animals.

unofficially becoming the faculty room, including a long, long table where eminences could gather and smoke their pipes and cigars while sucking up the proverbial, medicinal union coffee, the substance never, ever known for its quality.

Students who wandered into the latter room were seen by other students as blatant "brown-nosers." The entire faculty came to the Beaver Den for coffee each day. President Sattgast made several trips a day to the union, seeing it as an opportunity to socialize and conduct important if unofficial business with both colleagues and students.

THE MONEY KEPT ROLLIN' IN

More state funds came for ongoing changes and expansion of the Heating Plant, first constructed in 1926 at a cost of $65,000. The plant was first remodeled and enlarged in '49 and received another $259,000 to be improved and expanded once more in '59, with latter changes more than doubling the heating capacity of the plant.

Primping in Pine Hall
"Those 1950s! Wow! Now that was really a weird decade. But weren't they all."

The big ending to a big decade of building and campus growth came with a million-dollar legislative appropriation for a new physical education complex to be located in the diminishing ex-"City Forest." The building's first unit was completed in late 1959, and consisted of a basketball gymnasium with seating for 3,100 people; a connecting Olympic-size swimming pool with six marked lanes, an electronic timing device, and bleachers on one side for 300 spectators; classrooms, offices, and a head office for the athletic director. Sadly, the athletic director who did most of the preplanning for the building, H.J. "Jolly" Erickson, did not live to see it completed. He died of a heart attack at age 53 on February 7, 1959. He had come to Bemidji State in 1938.

When finished, the new phy ed complex was a marvel to be seen. None other than Orville Freeman, the governor of the state, soon to be named secretary of agriculture under JFK, came to Bemidji to give the dedicatory speech at the grand opening. It was grand, both the building and all the positive changes for the school in the 1950s, and few enjoyed them more than President Sattgast. This was, after all, his first and only full decade as president. He could enjoy, yea revel in, what had happened to the once tiny college in the pines with 189 students that he came to in 1938.

A FACULTY MEMBER REMEMBERS PRESIDENT SATTGAST

"The past depends on who is looking at it," or so reads a common assumption of historians. Obviously any person who taught for any length of time under Sattgast would have his/her own views of the man. Of some special merit are the views of Richard Beitzel in that Beitzel himself served as vice president for academic affairs during most of the administration of President Robert Decker, 1968 to 1980. (Beitzel retired from the BSU chemistry department in 1992.) In his comments below, Beitzel concerns himself almost always with being a teaching faculty member under Sattgast. His wit and peculiar observations speak for themselves:

AS I REMEMBER CHARLES R. SATTGAST

I joined the Bemidji State College faculty as an instructor in chemistry in September of 1957. I first met Dr. Sattgast in the spring of 1957 when he came to Waterloo, Iowa, to interview me for a position in the chemistry department at Bemidji State College. I was instructed by phone to meet Dr. Sattgast at the airport. On the drive to my home from the airport Dr. Sattgast told me that this was his first-ever interviewing trip on which he was allowed by the state of Minnesota to fly. In the past he was required to travel by bus. He interviewed my wife and me in our livingroom. Dr. Sattgast was very, very enthusiastic about Bemidji State College. He told me how the legislature was considering, and he was certain that it would pass, a substantial increase in faculty salaries. He told how the faculty was a family. He asked me, after telling me that he wasn't supposed to ask, if I belonged to a church. When I answered to the affirmative, he described the wonderful Lutheran churches in Bemidji. He also told Josephine (wife) about the wonderful faculty wives' association and that she would certainly want to be a member. Once at the airport he called my principal because he wanted him to know that he, Sattgast, was in town and was interviewing one of his staff members. He offered me an annual salary of $5,700. Considering I was already making $6,000 with a guaranteed summer job in Waterloo and the knowledge that I would have to earn a Ph.D. if I were to accept this job, the Bemidji offer wasn't all that great. (Later when Dr. Sattgast offered our drama teacher $5,100 to come to Bemidji as Louis Marchand's replacement, my offer looked better. Our theater director was an excellent teacher and director.)

Later in the spring we visited the campus and were treated royally. BSC was indeed a family. John Glas, a Waterloo native, was most helpful. Drs. (William) Britton and (Harold) Peters had us over for dinner and it was very obvious that Bemidji State College was a friendly college that was concerned about its members. Bemidji appeared to be a city where Josie and I wanted to raise our family. As a result, we joined the Bemidji State College faculty in September of 1957 and we have always enjoyed the city of Bemidji and the University very much. I must confess I didn't mind nor do I mind now being asked about my church activities, and the suggestion that Josie join the faculty wives sounded like a good deal to us. I always felt that if I didn't care for my work place or my boss I would simply move to a better situation.

When I finished my doctorate at age 35, I requested a private interview with Dr. Sattgast to discuss my future at BSC. Dr. Sattgast told me that he considered me one of his top young faculty members. He also told me that I would be earning $10,000 per year when I was 40. At the time of this interview I was earning about $7,500. The year I turned 40 I was earning $10,000.

Dr. Britton, my office-mate and fellow chemistry professor, came into my laboratory one day and told me that Dr. Sattgast wanted to see me in his office _now_. I turned my laboratory over to Dr. Britton and I hurried down to find Dr. Sattgast doing paperwork on one corner of his desk. He looked up as I walked in, looking professional in my white coat. Dr. Sattgast said, pointing to his normal work station, "Doctor Beitzel, I was sitting right there and nitric acid began dripping on the top of my head. Dr. Britton told me that the problem is in your laboratory and I want you to tell me why nitric acid is running down into my office and hitting me on the head?" I told Dr. Sattgast that the drain lines in my laboratory leaked because they were old and needed to be replaced. Dr. Sattgast told me not to allow any more nitric acid to come into his office. I responded, "Yes, sir." I went back to the laboratory and turned off the water to two of our laboratory benches. To this day I have wondered how Dr. Sattgast knew he was under attack by nitric acid. Actually, it was more likely water, with maybe a few organic solvents. Besides, nitric acid would have left a yellow spot on his head.

In 1958 I wrote my first National Science Foundation grant proposal for a year-long inservice physical science institute for area elementary school teachers. Dr. (Jud) Martin served as my editor and Dr. Sattgast assigned his secretary, Mrs. Jake Outwin, to type the mimeograph stencil. We were eventually funded for two years. Dr. Sattgast was very excited about Bemidji State College's first N.S.F. grant. Dr. Sattgast's cup ran over when Dr. Britton obtained a series of N.S.F. summer institutes for BSC. The proposal writer's reward came in the form of extra pay for serving as institute director and faculty member. The all-expense-paid trips to Washington, D.C. for directors' meetings and evaluation sessions were also a form of reward. (It needs to be stated that Dr. Britton and I wrote and submitted a great many N.S.F. proposals that were never funded.) We earned our rewards several times over.

Dr. Martin introduced our new president, Dr. Harry Bangsberg, to the faculty as "Harry." After that meeting Dr. Britton and I both agreed that no one but no one, well maybe Dr. Brady, would ever call Dr. Sattgast "Charlie." Dr. Sattgast's first name was Doctor.

At our weekly faculty meeting Dr. Sattgast would occasionally address a faculty member by name. The faculty members with doctorates (25 percent doctorates in those days) were addressed as doctor—with a special emphasis on the doctor. When he called on non-doctorates the preceding Mr. and Miss was hissed. We young faculty all looked forward to the day that we would be recognized in a faculty meeting as doctor. I was so very proud the first time I was addressed as Doctor Beitzel in a faculty meeting.

When you were a young faculty member working on your doctorate, Dr. Sattgast would always ask you how your work was progressing. He always remembered your last report and expected continued progress. Dr. Sattgast made you feel that you were making a positive contribution to the College by working on your degree. You must remember that in those days the majority of the faculty were located in Deputy Hall where we saw Dr. Sattgast nearly every day, so he had plenty of opportunities to ask you about your degree.

Dr. Sattgast hated smoking. In 1958 Dr. Peters was president of the Minnesota Academy of Science, which meant that the state meeting was held in Bemidji. This was a big event for the BSC science division. At the close of the annual meeting and after the state science fair, Dr. Britton and I were showing a number of important people the chemistry laboratories. After the tour we were all standing in the hall smoking as Dr. Sattgast came down the hall. Just as Dr. Sattgast got close enough to be introduced to our visiting chemists, one of the chemists ground his cigarette on the floor. Dr. Sattgast turned purple and proceeded to give the chemist "whatever." Dr. Britton and I were very embarrassed; after all, the offended chemist was "Dr. Big Time." Finally things calmed down and after Dr. Sattgast left we apologized for Dr. Sattgast's behavior. Who knows what became of it all?

---

7)Manuscript from Beitzel on Sattgast dated December 18, 1992; in author's files. Interpreting Sattgast as president represents, of course, subjectiveness. As indicated, Beitzel's anecdotal commentary remains one of a hundred different views and experiences on and with Sattgast. Several attempts were made on my part to get some commonality of opinion on the Sattgast years by those who knew him reasonably well, but this seemed impossible. About all that could be agreed on was that the man was at all times 103 percent Bemidji State, a point dramatized by a common joke of the time that if one pierced the skin of President Sattgast, the blood came out in colors of green and white. Some alumni used words like "dynamic," "forceful," and a literal "eager Beaver"; other alumni thought him "eccentric" and "patronizing" and "out of the loop." A former resident director from Bemidji, serving a term during Sattgast's early years, labeled him "headstrong," adding, "When Charlie got up a full head of steam, he was hard to head off"; he concluded, "When shown the error of his ways, however, he'd come around. All in all he was a strong force for the school when it was most needed." Lastly, a faculty member who served under Sattgast for his entire presidency, concluded, "He was great in his early years, but as the years went on, he became a parody of his old self. The latter was sad to see. Like most of us, he didn't know when to get out. But he was definitely a man of the times and for that time. He was quite a Sattgast."

AN ADMINISTRATION IS GOOD—IF "THE HELP" IS GOOD
   All colleges and universities organize their schools differently. Bemidji
State's primary structure, from 1938 to 1992, was to operate administratively
through divisions, each division headed by a chairperson, appointed by the
president, who served in that capacity at the pleasure of the president.
   Although the number of divisions varied slightly each decade, there were
six such categories in the 1950s grouped together, if tangentially, by discipline.
The six were the divisions of education, fine and applied arts, health and physical
education, languages and literature, science and mathematics, and social studies.
   The umbrella-use of "division" made sense also in not requiring use of the
word "department," when in effect an academic department for many years might
be two people, or even just a single person. For example, Dr. Sam Chen, who came
in 1957, and whose fractured English became the bane of translators until his
retirement in 1978, was a "one-man econ department" in the social studies division.
Paul Grabarkewitz was alone in math until W. Richard Slinkman joined him in 1959
for a two-man show. (Grabarkewitz left in the mid-'60s to return to Nebraska;
Slinkman stayed on until he retired in 1992).

President Sattgast (hands on hips) Observes Camp Craft Class
"He took seriously the line . . . 'to develop a mature sense of responsibilities'."

There Are Division Heads; THEN THERE ARE DIVISION HEADS!

Teaching faculty can come close to the category of transients, with the BSTC exceptions already mentioned. Division chairmen (and they were all men) were to be leaders picked for their special abilities, as seen clearly by the president (but not necessarily by other faculty colleagues, who may not see as well). Yet chairmen, too, could, and sometimes did, drift on to Parts Unknown and different jobs as the muse moved them.

At Bemidji State, three special chairmen came early into their positions and stayed on to become veritable rocks of the school, holding their authority, and deserved honor and prestige, throughout the decade and the remaining Sattgast years, i.e., 'til 1964 and beyond. These outstanding figures were Carl Otmer Thompson, chairman of fine and applied arts, beginning in 1938; Philip von Rohr Sauer, chairman of languages and literature, beginning in '38; and Harold Truman Peters, science and math beginning in '47. The best triumvirate a college could have. They had both intelligence and wisdom.

The pipe-smoking (pipe always there, not always lit) Thompson had first come to Bemidji State in 1937 via St. Olaf College and grad work at the University of Iowa. Until he arrived on campus, wrote his friend and compatriot Sauer, Bemidji State was "tuneless." Thompson organized the A Capella Choir, and built it, and the department, into a first-class operation, to the later delight of the school's publicity directors. (More on music in a later section.) A pillar of and in the community, especially his church, he helped plan and design First Lutheran Church in town, making sure there were two choir lofts, and directed the main choir there for over 20 years.[8]

Dr. Sauer was a true scholar, holding advanced degrees from the University of Wisconsin and his doctorate from Freiburg University, Germany. He came to BSTC as an English professor in 1937. Teaching classes in English literature, and also German language, he was a man of many parts, with deep interests in a myriad of subjects, especially the arts (all of 'em) and theology, and he would be a mainstay in Trinity Lutheran Church in town.

Sauer was, and still is, as much known for his outdoorsiness as his renowned teaching and academic activities. Caught by the law that then required retirement at age 68, he was forced reluctantly to leave teaching at the end of the 1974-75 school year. However, with his home directly across the street from the school library, he has literally stayed close to the school ever since retiring. At the time of this publication (1994) Sauer is in his mid-80s but can be seen almost every day of the year—and winters don't stop him—taking brisk walks on/in/around/ through the campus, then stopping in to visit with his many friends. Hagg-Sauer Hall, of course, is named in his and Hagg's honor. (More on Sauer in a later section

---

8)"Carl O."—as he was often referred to behind his back—gave up directing the College choir in 1967, but not until he had handpicked his successor, Paul Brandvik. Thompson retired in 1971, spending much time afterwards working at his beloved 180-acre tree farm north of town on Whitefish Lake. Unfortunately, his retirement years were not many; he passed away in 1983 at age 77. The main recital hall in the music building was named in his honor; a large, colored picture of Thompson hangs on the wall at the entrance to the hall.

on languages, a section which he essentially wrote.)

Peters came to Bemidji in 1945, a combat veteran of World War II who was in on the Normandy Landing, D-Day, 1944, and lived to tell about it—but he did not much want to talk about it. With a Ph.D. from the University of Minnesota in biology, he had a special interest in, of all things, studying mosquitoes. He was forever collecting them while calling for help from others in collecting them, the latter less than enthusiastic about capturing live this "Minnesota State Bird," all too present and prevalent in the North Country. Like the other two, Peters participated actively in church work, his being at First Methodist Church.

On campus his science faculty came first; he watched them and watched over them and took care of them and supported them to the hilt. To what degree? Perhaps this answers it: He did not have to retire when he did in 1975, but chose to leave anyway that year because it allowed another person, who otherwise would have been "retrenched," the euphemism for being let go, to keep his job.

(Peters has turned into a "snowbird"; he winters in the south and returns to Bemidji in the summers. Prior to the trek south, he sits in on fall quarter non-science classes, taking and enjoying, he says, "all those things I wanted to know about before but never had time to do." The Harold T. Peters Aquatic Laboratory building along the lakeshore is named in his honor.)

HOW SCHOOLS SHOULD OPERATE; HOW SCHOOLS DO OPERATE

Certain assumptions exist about the operation of American schools, whether or not they are valid, and often they are not. The latter point doesn't become accepted until some time afterwards. Then new assumptions take over—until they too are replaced.

Bemidji State in the 1950s reflected these assumptions, starting with the role of the president, already mentioned. To the question (assumption?) as to who should be the primary classroom teachers, the answer appeared to be simple—men.

Omitting the Laboratory School teaching faculty (and another assumption was made for those teachers) and library personnel, there were only ten women out of a total of 75 instructors in college classes in the last year of the decade.

Their names and roles (and an update, if known) deserve mention:

Elsie K. Annis, associate professor of physical education, came in 1928 and by the late '50s was viewed by colleagues throughout the campus as one of the "grand-ol'-dames," a term of endearment then, of the school. Miss Annis retired in 1963.

Ruth Brune, who came in 1924, taught English; she also organized an American humanities curriculum that decade. She too gained a major reputation as a force to be reckoned with.[9]

9)Miss Brune and Miss Parker came to Bemidji State together in 1924, and they remained together throughout their teaching years, and beyond that in retirement. They lived together; they bought a lovely house together (on Lake Boulevard, overlooking Lake Bemidji). Each would contribute a lifetime of energy to their adopted school. Though they had their similarities, there were also obvious differences, with Parker more open and cordial than the more distant, cerebral Brune. When this then-young author joined the history department in 1963 and began research on College in the Pines, I was told by all means to interview Footnote 9 cont. on page 213.

Patricia Ellis, who began in 1957, taught the physical sciences and mathematics. Ruth Howe, who also started in 1957, taught physical education classes until she retired in 1986. (She then married; at this writing, 1994, she and her husband live in their Lake Bemidji home on Birchmont Drive).

Myrtie Hunt, who was teaching at Bemidji High School at the end of World War II, moved over to the College in 1945 as a professor of physical education, a role she continued until her retirement in 1976. Always interested in dance, she began the popular spring dance shows which by the 1970s replaced the prom as the biggest school event of the spring quarter. Myrtie—the name and almost-title associated with her—became well known for her outdoor activities, a passion that did not stop. (Although in her 80s, she still goes off on Canadian fishing trips, both summer and winter; and she continues to go antelope and elk hunting out west.)

Miss Ruth Lane, who came in 1945, remained a science teacher until her retirement in 1965. Miss Floraine Nielsen arrived in 1956 as an instructor in College music classes as well as a vocal instructor in the Lab School. She retired in 1987 and soon moved to Idaho.

Mabel E. Parker also came to the school in its earliest years (1924). Dr. Parker had the title of professor of sociology, but her various assignments included that of registrar; she retired in 1963 (she passed away in December, 1987). Miss Parker went ice skating, supported by a hockey player or two, on her 90th birthday.

Norma Lynn Wood came in 1957 as an instructor in art but left in the early '60s. Lastly, J. Ruth Stenerson joined the English department in 1956 and remained one of their shining lights for the next 30 years. Miss Stenerson became the quintessence of the kind, caring—but demanding—classroom teacher, as attested by legions of former students. She retired to her home on Birchmont Drive in 1986 but has remained academically active as well as being a community and church activist in the best sense.

WHERE FEMALES IN SCHOOLS "BELONG"

Just as "normal" an assumption at the time was the expectation that elementary school children should be taught by women, but the principal should be a man. Bemidji State's Lab School fulfilled this picture almost perfectly. (For the numbers of women on the faculties since 1945, see Appendix F.)

The kindergarten supervisor/teacher was Miss Marie Bishop, who started her position in 1950 and stayed in the same position until her retirement in 1976. She continues to live year-round in her home near the campus.

Arlene Fox became the first grade supervisor in 1956, but following the death of her husband, and her subsequent remarriage in 1959, she retired from

---

them as outstanding sources on early Bemidji State, which indeed they were. As a naive newcomer who then knew virtually nothing about either one, I went to their lovely home, hoping for full cooperation from both. It was not to be. Miss Parker was most gracious and cooperative in both answering questions and contributing information on her own; Miss Brune was neither. Given their togetherness of many years, it was more than eye-opening in 1959 for College faculty to hear the news of what happened to Brune/Parker on a recent vacation love-boat trip. Miss Brune not only met an elderly man; she married him! And she brought him back to Bemidji where the three of them lived together—apparently in harmony—in their lakeview home. This was, to put it mildly, "different."

teaching.

Second grade supervisor throughout the decade was Hazel Oas, who began in 1950, and stated that she loved every child who came through her door.

In the above line about the Lab School teachers being almost all female, the one exception was Donald Bye, the third grade supervisor, who came in 1954. Mr. Bye was way ahead of the game in seeing the real need for male role models on elementary school faculties. And he was certainly that, whether planning with his kids the next outdoor activity or arriving at the parking lot in the morning on his big motorcycle. When the Lab School closed, he taught College education classes, with social studies methods for elementary teachers his specialty. (He retired in 1984, indulged a little extra in his love of camping, and then became a snow bird, going to southern states in the winters and returning to his Bemidji home in the summers.)

Fourth grade supervisor of both tenure and merit was Hazel Hogenson, starting in 1943 and continuing until her retirement in 1974. (Miss Hogenson maintained active membership in the League of Women Voters, along with church and Sons of Norway activities. In 1992 she sold her home in town and moved into the new apartment complex located near the North Country Hospital.)

The fifth grade supervisor, starting in 1939, was Miss Alice Nesvold. This tiny lady could instruct a filled classroom by speaking almost in a whisper—and the kids responded in a whisper. A remarkable, soft-spoken person with great patience and great kindness for all. When she retired in 1972, it seemed more than natural that she went immediately to take care of a close family member who was in failing health, living in a southern Minnesota small town. (Alas, at this writing, it is sad to note that Miss Nesvold herself had to be committed to a nursing home, her mental faculties having failed her.)

The sixth grade supervisor was Bertha Christianson, one of the stalwart rocks of the Lab School since 1941. Miss Christianson retired in 1974 and since then has more than fulfilled the definition of "active retirement," less as a senior citizen but more as a seasoned-citizen. She has seldom missed a cultural activity on campus in the past 20 years. (And she is still lovely!)

Of the last three names listed—Hogenson, Nesvold, Christianson—School Principal Harry Bucklen said often and openly at the time that when it came to the combined competencies of his intermediate grade supervisors, he would not trade them for any three other Lab School teachers in the entire country!

The remark also says much about Principal Bucklen. He was beneficent. The son of a plumber in Bemidji, Earl Bucklen (whose physical dimensions were the ones used in planning, designing, and building the statue of Paul Bunyan in 1937; Earl was one big, strong man!) Harry Bucklen attended and graduated from Bemidji State Teachers College before going on for his master's degree at George Peabody College for Teachers in Tennessee. He was a supervising teacher at the Lab School before being moved up to principal in 1947.

In a nutshell, Harry Bucklen loved kids, and vice versa. In the mornings before school started, the kids would gather around him, and he would have a kind word and a pat on the back for every one before they left for their classes. Not that he could not be tough but he was essentially a man of reason; his logic worked wonders. His personal tragedy was a weak heart, a condition that kept him home on leaves of absence and that finally ended his life on May 21, 1961, at age 48. A little third grader was heard to say at this sad news, "Mr. Bucklen was an awful nice man." And he was.[10]

OOPS, THERE WAS A JUNIOR HIGH, TOO

Omitted thus far in the discussion of the Lab School faculty of the '50s is the junior high portion, but indeed they were there! And two out of three of the classroom supervisors were men. Teaching both social studies and mathematics, and of course supervising the omnipresent student teachers for these classes, was George W. Knox, who began in 1952 and remained in that particular position until 1959, when he changed assignments to become an off-campus supervisor of student teachers. A tall, fleshy, friendly man whose smile matched his girth, he had several irons in the fire at the same time, including a love for politics. Indeed, he wanted to run for public office, the legislature, until President Sattgast put the kibosh to it, reasoning/ruling this was not a proper role for a college professor. It would be another example of an assumption to be changed in the next decade.

Robert Baker, from nearby Blackduck, attended Bemidji State and returned to his alma mater in 1956 as supervising teacher of science and mathematics in the Lab School Junior High. He later replaced Bucklen as acting principal for the 1961-62 school year, at which time the junior high portion of the Lab School was shut down; there was much need for added classroom space for College classes, and moreover, a brand new public school junior high a block away enticed many Lab School students. Baker went off to more graduate school work at Oregon State, returning to campus as a member of the biology department. He remained there until he took early retirement in 1991. When he was an undergrad, he played a "mean trumpet" in the Bemidji State Swing Band. In the 1970s he started a radio show called "Baker's Bandstand," which featured, of course, the sounds of the Big Bands of the '30s and '40s. The show began on the College radio station and then in the '80s moved to the downtown studio of Minnesota Public Radio. In the fall of 1992 Baker and his wife Ruth left Bemidji—to the surprise of everyone—and

---

10) It is this author's pleasure to write that I came to Bemidji State in the fall of 1959 to work under Harry Bucklen as a junior high supervisor in social studies at the Laboratory School. For this position I was interviewed in Minneapolis by President Sattgast—but that's a separate story in itself. Just as no faculty member called Sattgast "Charlie," no faculty member called the principal of the Lab School anything but Harry. He was a wonderful man—fun, funny, smart, shrewd and perceptive to the point of being prescient—he was good to be around and have around. And a great school diplomat, as illustrated in this tale: I was in his office when a phone call came from any angry father protesting his daughter's having to read an "offensive, dirty book," To Kill a Mockingbird. On the phone Harry was peaches-and-cream and understanding and so sympathetic/empathetic that by the end of the conversation the father was apologizing to him for the phone call! Afterwards he just laughed and said, "Ahh, the joys of being a principal," then adding, "Censorship of either my teachers or of books is not my strong point." Following his death, there was an effort made by his staff to have the Lab School named in his honor. No way. The president simply sat on the request until both he and the request died. The building at this writing is called the Education-Art Building; it's accurate, but devoid of human substance.

moved to a home in St. Cloud, but he still returned to do his Sunday morning
Baker's Bandstand.

 The third important junior high supervisor was Dr. Frances McKee in
language arts and social studies, since 1932. Miss McKee had a big heart and a
delightful sense of humor. But she could be demanding when necessary and
certainly was not afraid to speak her mind to anyone when the issue of professionalism
was broached. Contemporaries indicated that President Sattgast was afraid of only
one person on the faculty, Dr. McKee, and whether this was true, the intimidation
factor of his being president did not squelch her. To many, she was a joy to have
at a faculty meeting. The mandatory retirement age of 65, made in 1975, required
her retirement in the spring of '76, and tragically she passed away that same
summer.

COUNTRY COUSINS "FARMED OUT"

 All Laboratory School supervising teachers were technically part of the
College faculty. Some Lab School status-conscious members didn't feel so sure
about that position, even when it said so in the school catalog. It was different when
the Lab School was in the heart of the Main Building; then they were right there
with all the others. But the new building some distance away made a few Lab
School folks feel like poor country cousins "far away on the farm." Moreover, it .
did not help with the staff's perception that Sattgast gave only half-hearted support
to the Lab School, compared to his predecessor, Deputy.

After 1957 the 'T' was Missing from Bemidji State Teachers College
"An era ended; another began. Looking good . . . but union coffee raised to a dime."

"HEAVEN IS A PLACE WHERE THERE ARE NO COMMITTEES"

All faculty—and that did indeed include the Lab School folks—were assigned to be on one or more faculty committees. This assignment went with the job, and was viewed as a necessary contribution to help make the entire school function reasonably well, and semi-democratically.

The number of committees seemed at the time to be too high, but this would be before the possibilities in that area were to be known. (By the 1990s, with the mind-boggling number of committees just with the faculty senate, the numbers of the '50s committees seem tiny.)

Faculty committees by decade's end included the following: Activities, Athletics, Classification, Conservation, Curriculum (everyone wanted that assignment; that's where the power lay!), Social, Financial Aids, Graduate Council, Health, Library, Public Relations, and lastly—and the one that made heads swim—the Committee on (more) Committees.

The above committees remained essentially unchanged between 1945 and 1975, the latter being the year when the faculty became unionized, with the legal right to strike, and committee memberships became "negotiated." (More on faculty governance in a later section.)

THE SHEPHERD EXHORTS THE FLOCK

Full faculty meetings were held once a month. In the early '50s they were held in the Little Theater "classroom" on the third floor of the Main Building, but as prof numbers kept growing, the Lab School auditorium became necessary to accommodate the group; and besides, the latter location had soft seats, while the former had only hard classroom chairs.

The president, of course, presided over these sessions, indeed dominated them. For the most part they were a combination of information and inspiration; yet Sattgast never forgot who were the "workhorses" on campus, and he regularly thanked and praised profusely all the faculty members for their ongoing work. Not that he couldn't inculcate the spirit of yet greater improvement for the throng—while suggesting even a possible perception that there might just be a few (unnamed) laggards.

At all meetings Sattgast for the most part was 1) positive, and 2) loud. Volume and sincerity went together. If there were ongoing themes/messages/dreams to drive home regularly, they were those of the absolute need for "faculty cohesiveness," the need "to serve the students and serve the region," the need for "a clean and neat-appearing campus and buildings" (he would personally walk the halls daily and pick up any debris off the floors and place it in wastebaskets), and never to be forgotten or omitted, Bemidji State must have the image of "the friendly College." The back-row cynics listening to his exhortations—and a few labeled them harangues—would snicker and scoff (behind his back), but Sattgast meant it; oh, how he meant it. One could question his decision-making but never his motives or sincerity.

TACKLING SACRED (NOT REALLY) "COWS"

One issue above any other at faculty meetings that roused even the semi-sleepers was for someone (fool?) to raise the question of the most sacred of cows, GENERAL EDUCATION REQUIREMENTS. Even a hint to tinker with existing required credits in gen. ed. could move some once-professionals into red-necked rantors. "WHAT!? Reduce the number of credits required in my department?! NEVER!" Sattgast, normally the pragmatist, was well aware of the danger of "gored sacred cows" and he tended to let sleeping dogs/cows lie. The issue of gen. ed.—retitled liberal education in the 1980s—has remained *ad infinitum* as a sore spot needing/not needing alleged improvements. And new presidents were forever wanting to tinker with the cow.

MORE IS BETTER

Some substantive issues came before the full faculty for decision making. For example, a major change in teacher preparation would be approved in 1959, but not easily and not until the topic was aired thoroughly. The change was the requirement that all students preparing to become teachers must complete one full quarter of student teaching. The supporters of the change cited both the desirability of extended practice teaching and meeting the growing need for student teaching off-campus, including public schools out of town.

When the entire school was in one building, including a school with grades K-through-9/the Laboratory School), there was no problem for College students to drop in on a Lab School class for a couple of hours a day before going off to College classes. Even the new Lab School building was reasonably convenient for one to be simultaneously a regular student and a student teacher.

Then the increasing numbers of students wanting student teaching at the same time could not be accommodated in the Lab School; soon they could not be accommodated in the Bemidji public schools, either, and there was a need for even more distant sites for these teachers-to-be.

So the change came with the new requirement of a full quarter (worth 16 credits) of student teaching. Some opposition came from the physical education division, their arguing the difficulty of fielding athletic squads when a player would be gone a whole quarter. They adopted and adapted, however, with athletes more carefully picking their quarter of teaching when their sport would be least affected. This policy of one full quarter of student teaching continued until the present; the only variation came in the 1980s to allow those few who want it a full school year of student teaching in an internship program.

MIRROR, MIRROR, ON THE WALL, WHO'S THE FAIREST ('50s PROF) OF THEM ALL?

Every school has one or two teachers who stand out above the remaining faculty. This determination is made over several years in a totally unscientific way. No votes are taken, no polling takes place, no one acts as cheerleaders for anyone else. But "the winner" is there! That person is known; it just happens that way. The word gets around. And everybody knows it. Emerging as not only the "Top Prof" but the "Intellectual of the School" at Bemidji State in the 1950s was Dr. Norman F. Christensen, professor of English.

To his students he was Dr. Christensen; to his colleagues he was "N.F."; to a select few friends he was "Norm." And none of the above would deny that he was a benign but somewhat awesome presence in his office and classroom.

Dr. Christensen, a native of Cass Lake, came to Bemidji in the fall of '46 when he, Phil Sauer, Ruth Brune and Margaret Kelly were the English faculty. He was born November 4, 1921, in Cass Lake; he took his B.A. at St. Olaf College (Northfield, MN) in 1943, his M.A. at the University of Minnesota in 1946, and his Ph.D. at the University of Wisconsin in 1960. His credentials were impeccable; the man himself fit the same category. Said a former student (Ivan Weir, '62) of him, "It is not enough to say I respected Dr. Christensen; I held him in awe." The ex-student Weir (now Dr. Weir in the BSU sociology department) added, "Dr. Christensen made you want to excel; more, he made you fearful of not excelling. He . . . had me so busy reading interesting books that I sometimes forgot to study for my tests, but I have no regrets. His presence in the classroom is as vivid today as yesterday; he gave me a lifelong appreciation of Hawthorne, Melville, and Aristotle's Poetics."

Of medium height, and a little on the stout side, Christensen spoke rather quietly, choosing his words carefully. He had little use for hyperbole and his well thought through ideas were always carefully hedged with qualifiers. Understatement and irony were his mode, in the classroom and on the street.

His thoughtfulness and scholarship carried through to curriculum matters. Division Chairman Sauer credited him in general as the person who made the English department both expand and flourish, and specifically for revising and strengthening the English major, changing it from 48 quarter hours required to 60. He also launched the communications course which was so popular in the 1940s, and he helped organize the American studies program in the 1950s.

Bemidji's loss would be Wisconsin's gain. He left Bemidji State in 1964 to head the department of English at the University of Wisconsin-Superior until 1977, after which he taught until he retired in 1987. Next to teaching he loved research, so much so that he continued to publish scholarly articles in retirement. He died August 13, 1991, at St. Luke's Hospital, Duluth.

His younger son, Mark, Ph.D., University of Minnesota, joined the BSU department of English in 1990, and thus N.F.'s influence remains on campus. Mark received a letter from John R. Bovee [B.S., 1954, and M.S., 1962] regarding his father. "Your father . . . was the best teacher I had in all my years in school. . . . I appreciated his magic ability to teach literature." So wrote Bovee, who in 1992 retired from the department of English, St. Cloud State University. He concluded, "I was glad to hear there is a Christensen still in the Bemidji State English department."[11]

HOW TO GRADUATE FROM BEMIDJI STATE
WITH A BACHELOR'S DEGREE

Though hardly that simple or easy, the figure of 192 credit hours has remained the same, whether in 1944 or 1994, whether for a B.A. or a B.S. degree. There was about a five-year period in the early '80s when the B.A. non-teaching degree was set at a lower 180 credits, but it was kicked up again to match the B.S. number.

One important name change came for BSTC graduates: Until 1939, four-year graduates received only a B.E. degree, bachelor of education, but requests/ pressures permitted the change to the more universal and elevated designation of bachelor of science.

THE (NON)SELECTION OF CLASSES

Regardless of when a student started, regardless of the major, regardless of the degree pursued, all students had to take classes in general education. The judgment of the faculty has always been GEN. ED. COURSES ARE GOOD FOR YOU!

And they were good, if one accepted the explanations in the school bulletins. The explanations/justifications read very much the same, regardless of decade, hence the representative catalog prose of 1958-59 (p. 38):

"The objectives of the interdivisional general education program include the general objectives of the College, together with the following:

1. "To give breadth to education in a day of overspecialization; to bring the student to a higher degree of self-realization, and to an increased awareness of the universe around him, and to induce mature use of leisure time.

2. "To give the student a core of information in each main division of knowledge and an acquaintance with the modes of thought applicable to each. This also helps the student select his major and minor fields of interest and lays the foundation for advanced work.

3. "To supply training in the skills necessary for further college work."

Certain classes and certain subjects were deemed so necessary as to be classified as "constants" in the bulletins of the 1940s, but the latter term would be dropped

---

11) My personal associations with Dr. Christensen were somewhat limited, but two things are remembered. I had his older son, Norman, Jr., as an 8th grader in the Lab School; the son won a reading contest one quarter, reading something like 75 books!— which very much pleased the father. He stopped by personally to thank me for something he much valued, but had little success with, he admitted. At the end of my first school year (1960), I was invited to attend a "stag poker party" at a cabin owned by industrial arts teacher John Warford. The road to the remote cabin was marked by homemade signs along the gravel road, reading "B.S. Seminar—Ahead," and soon some 20 men assembled, among them N.F. Christensen. What impressed me that evening as a mum newcomer was the obvious way in which all there deferred to N.F. Amid the male jocularity, with plenty of libation for all, with the usual and expected kidding, macho teasing, pointless verbal barbs flying around the smoke-filled cabin, no one, but no one, aimed any jibes at N.F. Even in social scenes with "hair down" and guards down and a casualness bordering on the sloppy and profane, N.F. was still viewed as "special."

by the next decade. Almost all basic disciplines would be included in general education, with some, like English, having the most requirements—a mandated three classes/twelve credits; in effect, a full school year of "Freshman English." This "constant" requirement did not change in 50 years.

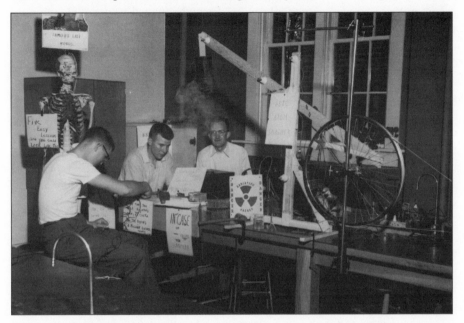

Could Rube Goldberg Build an Atom Smasher Like This?
" . . . occasional offensive odors emitting from their laboratories. "

Other areas of requirements saw some variations in the half century after the war. For example, the science area moved from six credits strictly in biology to nine credits that could be selected from a block of science areas. (By 1990 by far the most popular science requirement class for freshmen students had become the appropriately titled "Physical Science for Non Science Majors," usually called simply "PSNS.")

Social studies classes also once had a big slice of the gen. ed. pie, when for over 30 years all students had to take three quarters of Western Civilization. When these specific classes were dropped as a specific gen. ed. requirement in the 1970s, the number of sections of Western Civ. offered dropped from over 20 to less than five per quarter.

Other disciplines in gen. ed. seldom had more than one course requirements, e.g., art, psychology, speech, music, American government. The exception was physical education which had a five credit requirement to be obtained by taking only one-credit classes, the classes nevertheless meeting three hours a week! Understandably the latter area became a matter of full faculty concern—read fights—but would not be altered 'til the 1980s.

School bulletins advised students to complete their general education requirements by the end of their sophomore year, and with this in mind, laid out carefully in each year's catalog all the suggested classes to be taken by freshmen and sophomores. Although the vast majority of students followed the planned program, there seemed perennially to be discombobulated students planning to graduate who just happened to be a credit short in phy ed or missed the middle course in Freshman English, or forgot about the government class, and the like. *Sic Semper Studentes.*

Again, to make class selection easier and more understandable for students, the numbering system for courses began with 100 for freshman classes and ended with 400 for seniors (and eventually 500-numbering for graduate students). Hence the 300-numbering system indicated that those classes were upper division and for majors/minors in that area, and those higher numbers also gave warning to uncertain students to pick carefully when entering the high digit category, lest they get in over their heads. Again, without fail, every quarter found some first quarter freshman enrolling in some last quarter senior quantum physics class. Such are the exigencies of student life.

The secret in graduating—and it really was no secret—was to plan one's classes carefully, taking always the right courses and the right number of credits so that graduation came during the last quarter of the fourth year. This goal was admirable and feasible, and reasonably achievable at Bemidji State in those three decades following WWII. By the late 1980s, however, for a number of reasons—usually increased requirements in the major—many students had to go an extra quarter or more to fulfill graduation requirements; by 1990 it would be common to be "on the five-year plan."

TEACHER-ED: PRESCRIBED

Added help and guidance came for those students planning to become public school teachers, as indeed most students intended at Bemidji State until the 1970s when a major shift to non-teaching occurred. Regardless, school bulletins continued to lay out carefully, whether in 1944 or 1994, the specific outline of classes required for the elementary major and/or the secondary major. The former choice (grades 1-6 teacher licensure) allowed for few choices; classes were prescribed. The elementary major's schedule was filled with education courses, especially methods classes on "how to" teach . . . art, arithmetic, reading . . . and more. The secondary major (grades 7-12 teacher licensure) was of course tied to the student's academic major, e.g., science, English, etc., and required fewer courses in education classes, though still a sizable number (42 credits in 1950; 47 by 1990).

"The fly in the ointment" over the last half century in teacher ed planning has come from that downstate entity called, among words that can be repeated, "the State Department," the bug-a-boo and bane of teacher ed programs everywhere.

Always "they" have acted in the name of teacher education improvement, and with clear warning that unchanged programs would not be approved by them "unless." Thus forthcoming/ongoing/contradictive/mandated "suggestions" have continued to come forth to add to/subtract from (usually the former) existing teacher ed programs. These ukases got results, and raised always the question of who really does determine collegiate curriculums? At faculty meetings in which changes to the curriculum had to be approved, it became difficult, yea impossible, to counteract education-credit increases when criticisms/planned stoppages were met by the unanswerable line of power if not logic: The state now requires it or we'll lose our accreditation!

WHEN THE CRUNCH CAME FOR "SCHOOL MARMS"

Bemidji State began in 1919 as a normal school, a combination high school/college; its purpose was to train elementary school teachers, primarily for rural communities. A one-year normal school program, after high school, allowed the person who completed it to teach in any rural elementary school; the two-year, post-high school program permitted elementary school teaching in either city or country. Even after Bemidji Normal became Bemidji Teachers in 1921, with a curriculum leading to a four-year bachelor's degree, and licensing to teach in either elementary or secondary schools in the state, few students chose "the long route." Why go four years when you can get a license after one? Only gradually did the changes come over several decades, and they came because teaching requirements would be gradually raised. Behind upping the standards were both the law of supply-and-demand and the growing opinion that all teachers needed more schooling themselves before stepping into their own classrooms.

Bemidji State kept even pace with the shifting laws. Before the war BSTC offered the one-year program, but that ended after the war. There was still available in the late '40s a two-year program leading to what was called an "associate in education degree" (program outlined on pp. 44-45 of the '48-'49 catalog) which "provided for the education of elementary school teachers for kindergarten, primary and intermediate grades for both rural and urban schools." Not bad; still an "easy license" to achieve. Then came the '50s and a newly required three-year program before licensing, and along with it the terminology of a provisional elementary curriculum. Lastly, the boom fell with the state's decision that starting in the fall of 1961, all beginning teachers in Minnesota must hold a bachelor's degree. No more one or two or three-year Bemidji State options to get certification to teach. A very long era ended—for the better—in Minnesota public school history.

It should be pointed out if not emphasized that those teachers already teaching, who did not hold a bachelor's degree, were not stripped of their licenses. They could continue in their schools, and, in part only, were "grandmothered in." The crunch for them came in their eventually having to get a bachelor's degree in order to maintain their teaching licenses! In effect, they were told to go back to college or lose their jobs. And most came back in the summers to work on their degrees. "The retreads," as they were called, came back on campus, not happy about it perhaps, but nevertheless became aging undergraduates-in-the-pines.

(For Bemidji State this meant record summer session enrollments in the 1960s. Verily a body bonanza! Adding the numbers in both summer sessions of 1969 along with the extension courses that year, there were 6,878 students! The entire student body that fall was just over 5,000. Certainly a decade of multiple Beavers, young and old.)

ANOTHER TWO-YEAR SHOT . . . GONE

Bemidji State continued a single, two-year, non-teaching program long after the two-year teaching option was closed down. For its time, and what it was supposed to do, it served its few students well enough. Perhaps its appropriateness to certain times only is suggested by its being phased out on the 75th anniversary of the school in 1994. Bemidji State chose to get out of the two-year degree business. The associate in arts degree was discontinued. It had begun as an option for students, upon filing proper papers, to receive after completing all the general education requirements, 96 credits.

The usefulness of the "A.A." degree had been questionable, but among its uses was its desirability in transferring to other colleges or universities. To most schools, the "A.A." was the proof necessary that all general education requirements had been met and need not be repeated at the new school. In effect, the student with the A.A. began the junior year freed from more gen. ed. requirements. (This is still the ruling in the Minnesota State University System for transfer students coming in with A.A. degrees from junior/community colleges.)

Bemidji State had more A.A. offerings, however, than simply taking the basic core curriculum. The A.A. program was also for students seeking short term preparation for secretarial science and/or business management and accounting.

As indicated, the above programs had limited numbers-appeal, but the faithful few kept the A.A. offerings going for 50 years. If nothing else, they brought a form of almost comic relief to some stultifying spring graduation ceremonies. The A.A. grads were always last to be recognized. Thus, after the hours necessary to go through the ceremonies in bestowing degrees for the masters' folks, the honor grads, the B.A. grads, and finally the hordes of B.S. grads, and just when tired spectators believed commencement to be done, the A.A. graduates in the back row would be asked to stand—all five of them—and they too then got the full fulminations from the platform before coming on stage themselves to receive their A.A. specials. Now that era has ended. Just as well.[12]

---

12) It can be argued that Bemidji State has had a special two-year program since 1946, with no letup afterwards. The reasoning deals with the category of pre-professional planning and curricula designed specifically for students who enrolled at Bemidji State for two years only before transferring to some other school to enroll in a specific program that Bemidji State did not have. These pre-programs include recommended and/or required classes leading to a degree in forestry, engineering, medicine, mortuary science, pharmacy, optometry, agriculture, and the like.

THE FIFTIES HAD MORE THAN FAMILIAR FACES

A small Bemidji State offered more than the pleasant fact that everybody knew everybody else. There was the added dimension of human help from a faculty who then were more than names-on-a-door. The following personal story illustrates that added dimension:

"I [Jan Thompson] also want to pass along this little story about Dr. Ray Carlson [dean of students]. Might be useful for retirement party, etc. . . . tho I suppose there are many nice stories about him. Don and I were married when he was a senior at BSC. There was no student health insurance in those days, 1956-57, and I had no insurance where I worked. I cleared $88 twice a month, and our rent was $85 a month! It got a little interesting some months! Anyway, six weeks after we were married, Don had to have an appendectomy. It was more than routine . . . ruptured, etc., and Don was very ill. Even as he came out of the anesthetic, he was wondering how we were going to pay for this! The total bill, including both hospital and doctor, was $375. (Those were the days.) DR. RAY CARLSON, bless his heart, put out the word . . . and somehow came up with $300!!! We still do not know how he did it. Collections? Slush fund? Don's parents had died a couple years earlier, and we had NO ONE to turn to! We'll never forget his help! Hope we can do the same for someone sometime!"

Jan Thompson[13]

THE FALL OF '57 . . . IN THE STUDENT NEWSPAPERS. A TYPICAL YEAR?

Eagerness for the upcoming school year and happiness to be back on campus were both reflected in the early issues of the Northern Student that fall of '57. There seemed little to grouse about at the time. Students looked forward to yet another good school year, with a bigger enrollment and bigger plans for bigger buildings for a bigger school. And already a "new" school, too. That year the "T" for Teachers would be dropped in the title and the school became Bemidji State College. An era ended; another had begun. Looking good. The only unhappiness reflected in print in the first issue was a shocked student grumping about the cost of union coffee being raised from a nickel to a full dime!

At the convocation program held the last week of September, the cheerleaders took over and helped whip up some crowd enthusiasm prior to football coach Chet Anderson's introduction of each member on the squad. Despite the usual hedging, the coach still expected a good season, and he would be right. More in entertainment news came with the delightful shock that one of the country's biggest singing groups, the Crew Cuts, would be coming to Bemidji State, appearing at the same time with a major Big Band, Blue Barron and his Orchestra. Both groups were famous; almost every student knew only too well the Crew Cut's

---

13) Letter from Thompson sent to this author, letter dated April 19, 1984. Ms. Thompson at that time was the secretary to the student senate and I had written to her requesting the names of all the student body presidents at Bemidji State since the first election. After looking through the Northern Students, she was able to find almost all of the names and sent them to me (see Appendix G for the names), and in her reply she included the above wonderful anecdote. Letter in author's possession.

major song, "Sh-Boom." Their coming to Bemidji would be interpreted as a sure sign that the school was hardly a parochial place in Hicksville. Going national; going Big Time. Obviously a good year coming up. President Sattgast wrote his annual "Welcome to the Campus" letter in the first <u>Student</u>. He also announced that the tunnel being constructed between Memorial Hall and the Lab School would be ready for use by the fall of '58. More plans for the year came with Sattgast's happily telling about a scheduled tree planting day in the the College Forest, a 240-acre site acquired as tax-forfeit property 10 years earlier, thanks to super conservationist on the faculty, C.V. Hobson, who came up with the concept for school forests and worked for the passage of the School Forest Law, enacted in 1949.[14] A group effort would make tree planting day successful, said the president, who could rightly assume that students and faculty would be there together, grubbing in the dirt and planting those pine seedlings.

The student newspaper pointed out several news items to highlight that fall, all positive. Bright spots included an unprecedented 24 new teachers who came that fall of '57, bringing the faculty number up to 77, with the newcomers including Richard Beitzel, William Forseth, Samuel Chen, Roy Meyer, and Ruth Howe, all of whom stayed on until their retirements. Biology Professor Harold Peters served that year as president of the Minnesota Academy of Science, a mark of prestige for both the man and the school. In October the theater people produced the Arthur Miller play, <u>All My Sons</u>. By fall's end the Beaver football team shared the conference championship, which included wins over Moorhead, St. Cloud, and Mankato. Charlene Antos reigned as homecoming queen, along with princesses Barbara Droppo and Pris Fleener. Promoted by new Faculty Advisor Jim McMahon, the <u>Northern Student</u> would change from once a month to twice a month publication under Editor Ed Gutman, and the <u>Ah-Mic</u>, the student annual, would come out in May on schedule, 88 pages of the year's activities, thanks to co-editors Lois Moore and Roger Schmaus. (The word <u>Ah-Mic</u> is an Ojibway word meaning Beaver.)

The weekly convocations programs in January were typical in including varied presentations, with a professional baritone soloist named Edmund Karlsrud, the college wind ensemble, the Bemidji High School band, and a Paul Bunyan Week Special, each of these four programs taking up a scheduled convocation hour.

14) C.V. Hobson (1894-1966) deserves ink in any history of Bemidji State. The C.V. stood for Claude Vivian; he came to the school in 1931 as a science supervisor in the Laboratory School and moved to the college classroom in 1938 as a professor of geography and conservation. Eventually, for good reasons, he would gain the unofficial title of "Mr. Conservation." This role would include many areas, whether remonstrating with any individual who threw so much as a match on the ground, to his preaching the immorality of any hunter who shot a sitting partridge. Hobson was seen by his contemporaries as a major asset to Bemidji State. Best of all he loved students and strived to help them in every way. This part of him showed when he later headed the student personnel office. He had physical problems that never stopped him in his work. A small man of slight stature, he early developed a disease leading to bone deterioration and was eventually forced to use crutches. Moreover, he began losing his eyesight as well, but colleagues maintain he never complained; he instead showed a positive outlook at all times, despite his most difficult handicaps, and he never lost his sense of humor, the latter quiet and wry. He displayed publicly both courage and stubbornness each day he came to work in Deputy Hall because he had to walk up the stairs to his office (he wanted no help; he would not allow his office to be moved, just to accommodate him). This became more difficult year by year. As he approached retirement in 1962, his deteriorating health was obvious to all, but it did not change his pattern. He still chose to haul his body up those stairs, one painful step at a time, and onlookers could both see the sweat on his brow and hear the panting as he paused after each step. It sometimes took him better than 15 minutes to scale 23 steps, but he always made it. He was a walking lesson in determination and guts. The mark of the total man would be officially recognized in 1967 with the name of the C.V. Hobson Student Union.

Just as typical was a successful dance to end the 10th annual Paul Bunyan Week in February, with the coronation of Paul and Carrie, who that year were George Semchuk and Janice Hanson. The pattern in student entertainment continued with a student production of the musical Good News, and the Beaver basketball team played to cheering crowds, ending with a 10-11 record, not as good as the year before when they were co-champions in the conference.

At the end of the winter quarter, 15 students graduated; the Student Activities Committee announced that the request for funds for the next year would far exceed their income; the annual Religious Emphasis Week dates were announced; the editors twitted the student body for its poor turn out in voting for student elections; lettermen welcomed new members to the "B-Club," with a newspaper columnist questioning the wisdom of the initiation foolishness connected with membership acceptance; the College choir presented Brahms' German Requiem for the annual Easter oratorio; the English department announced plans for its 20th annual English Week while the science department made its own plans for hosting the fifth annual regional science fair, and the phy ed department did the same for the 14th annual Beaver Relays track and field competition. In this "typical" school year, the windup would come with the expected annual spring formal dance, final concerts by musical groups, a spring production of Shakespeare's Twelfth Night, student art displays, the baseball season ruined by snow, editors' goodbyes in the Northern Student, and lastly, of course, commencement ceremonies for 160 students, preceded by the then-typical baccalaureate exercises. The year 1958 was the 100th anniversary of the state of Minnesota, and graduation exercises included a Centennial Ballad, a kind of pageant with musical parts and spoken parts, all written by choir director Carl O. Thompson and presented by students from the music, speech and physical education departments. As seen in the pages of the Northern Student, it was a very special year.[15]

ONE PICTURE SAYS IT ALL: THE 1,000TH STUDENT!

In the first issue of the Northern Student in the fall of '58, there is a three-column picture of a scene at registration. With a smiling President Sattgast on one side, and other smiling faces around him, it shows a young man from Crookston, Alden LaRochelle, holding a large piece of paper on which is written the number 1,000. (He's the only one in the scene not smiling.) Another record enrollment had arrived, this one special because of the plus-1,000 tally. Turned out that it was barely that, the total making it to 1,003 students, but it was still a special number and a watershed year for Bemidji State. As to comparative numbers, even more

15) There was one news item of sadness, however. The November 15, 1957, issue reported the death of the president's wife, Bertha Sattgast. The paper noted that she had been deer hunting with their son and suddenly took ill; "she passed away shortly thereafter," read the brief statement under her picture. In an editorial in the same issue, both her role and how she played that role were noted, "Her gracious hospitality, dinners, senior teas, and open house, were enjoyed by both faculty and students who will long remember them. She worked diligently with the local Gray Ladies and organized the first troop of Girl Scouts in Bemidji."
All of the Northern Students have been bound and are kept in the History Center in the lower level of the A.C. Clark Library. They make engrossing reading today and they remain perhaps the best printed source for determining students' interests and attitudes in a given time period, along with presenting the school events of the times.

different from the wartime years, the men by Spring Quarter in '58 outnumbered the women on campus 653 to 385.[16]

The increased enrollment found the usual and expected problems, as noted in another headline, "Union Crowded as Enrollment Soars." The new buildings too posed the problem of what to name them, with Sattgast announcing that the existing

President Charles Sattgast Likes the Number (1958)
"By 1959 things just kept getting better and better, bigger and bigger."

as well as the newly planned residence halls would all be given names of trees indigenous to northern Minnesota, although when he used the linden tree as an example, he had to explain that the common name for such a tree was basswood, which name didn't have the nice ring to it compared to linden.[17]

ON A FORWARD ROLL . . .

As the end of the decade approached, Bemidji State College, no longer with the alleged stigma-designation of Teachers College, had a sense of solidity while at the same time it was on a forward roll. By 1959 things just kept getting better and better, bigger and bigger, and yet not so big that students became simply digits known only by their social security numbers. Little things suggested a one-

16) Northern Student, September 26, 1958, p. 1. The breakdown by class: 371 freshmen, 256 sophomores, 228 juniors, and 148 seniors. There were also categories of "special" students, including 10 graduate students, so the total could be raised to 1,026. If the totals do not seem to jibe, it's because of "how one counts" and "who one counts" as students. For example, is someone taking only one credit on campus still counted as a student?
17) Northern Student, September 26, 1958, p. 1.

big-family attitude. For example, the school newspaper made reference not to "the coach" but "our coach." Sattgast's Christmas greeting in the Student was addressed to "the College Family." Faculty members wrote chatty letters in the school paper telling about their vacation travels. The four classes met separately to hold elections for officers and plan class projects for the year. Freshmen wore their beanies and were properly humble before upperclassmen, and when the mild hazing ended in early October, the newcomers seemed genuinely pleased to be welcomed into full partnership with their hierarchical brethren. From the freshmen each fall came an elected Beanie King and Queen to participate in the big homecoming festivities. There was also the pre-homecoming pep fest, followed by the snake dance downtown through the stores and maybe the theaters, then back to the campus for a bonfire and cheers and singing, and finally the evening culminating with an all-school dance, the faculty included. Even as the faculty approached the 100 mark, they still pretty much knew each other, because almost all at some time each day slurped coffee together in the student union, then located in the basement of Sanford Hall. There they could match stories and wonder out loud which non-classroom duty the president would be assigning them to do next. Would it be to take tickets? Chaperone a dance? Serve as timers? Put up displays? Counsel at registration? Whatever, it was all part of the job.

For the wives of faculty members, the special social occasion in the fall was the Faculty Wives' Tea, hosted by the president's wife and the president of the Faculty Wives Organization.[18] Dances featuring national Big Bands continued to come to Bemidji and attract large crowds, as was the case with the Harry James band who played for the fall dance in '59. Likewise filling Memorial Hall each year in the late '50s was a musical group called the Tamburitzans, who played both a morning convocation program and a night dance. The Beaver athletic teams continued to have excellent seasons in the late '50s, with the football team again tying for the conference championship in 1959.

The record-breaking 1,233 student enrollment in the fall of '59 was by then ho-hum stuff, rating only a small blip as news in the Northern Student. The shock of 1,000-plus was behind them. Yet the fat numbers did not deter the ongoing student-made entertainment aimed at all and for all, whether at the weekly morning convocations, which included dates set aside for each class to present a variety talent show, or nighttime shows, such as the one the Korean War vets put on, calling it "College Life in the 1920s and the 1950s." Unsubtle comedy. Parodied lyrics. Soloists. Dancers. Quartets. Some blue lines, but more clever than raunchy. Fun and funny. And most important, all student-written and performed. Big crowds. Togetherness. The joy of college.

All of the above illustrated Bemidji State College in 1959; ten years later, virtually none of the above were still around. It would become a far different school by 1969.

---

18) President Sattgast remarried in 1959. His second wife, Mabel, was a widow whose late husband had been a college president in Illinois.

In the school year of 1959-60, there was still the mood and feeling of small-school unity, even if it were hardly a small school anymore. Solidity was there too in the form of an experienced, dedicated administration, there in their offices on "the hill." Solid "war horses" in the best sense sat in positions of authority, with names familiar because they had been there "forever" and were expected to be there forever: Sattgast, Clark, Glas, Martin, Hobson, Carlson, Thompson, Sauer, and Peters. The oligarchy.

At a level just below them there was arising by 1960 another slate of solid figures in the administrative staff: John Brady, placement and extension service director; Ed Aalberts, registrar; Don Stubbins, director of field services; Randy Nyquist, business manager; Robert Frazey, director of financial aids; Ida Mae Geittmann, director of housing; Don Dickinson, librarian; Harry Fritz, athletic director; Ruth Woods, school nurse; Roy Kendall, chief engineer; Marvin Ohman, chief custodian.

Bring on the Sixties.

The 1960s

T he early '60s were wonderful; the late '60s were terrible, a swirling turnabout summed up in the phrase, *THE DECADE OF HOPE AND DESPAIR.* Unfortunately, that phrase also applied to Bemidji State in that tumultuous decade.

No thinking citizen could by 1969 pretend that there were no national problems of the first magnitude. Emotional, divisive issues reached everywhere. Especially aware of national concerns are those communities where colleges are located because colleges remain a form of barometer, reflecting the nation's

Two Faculty History Profs Lead Protest March to Downtown (1969)
"Signing petitions . . . makes signers find out who their friends are--or were."

pressures and reacting to the many forces of deep social currents. Such was the situation for Bemidji State, a situation which had changed dramatically in that decade, in part because of a new president. Aside from any presidential shake ups, the national concerns by decade's end made the school no longer a quiet campus with a politically uninvolved, indifferent student body. Students were on the march, literally. Nowhere, not even in the timbered Minnesota north country, are people free from the ideas, attitudes, and powers of society at large.

By the end of the decade it seemed that every human act was heavy with symbolism. Americans could not eat a head of lettuce or lie on a redwood chaise lounge or open a door for a woman or wear a leather or fur coat or get a haircut— especially get a haircut—without their politics showing. Bemidji State students moved from a strict dress code in the early '60s to pure grunge by '69. Clothes are essentially a way to cover and decorate bodies, not expressions of political and social ideas; but in that decade clothes expressed culture and politics, imprecisely at times and directly at other times. For example, T-shirts became walking billboards to make brief editorials, "Bring the Boys Home!," "America: Love It or Leave It," "Turn On, Tune In, Drop Out," "Shoot the Boys at Berzerkley U," "George Wallace is Rosemary's Baby," "Save North Vietnam! Win Valuable Prizes."

Aerial View Showing the Denuded 'City Forest' Replaced by Dorms
"Overall, Bangsberg and Buildings were synonomous in the mushrooming growth."

Most Americans reacted negatively, as citizens did in Bemidji, to the outbreak of student protests. When Bemidji State students blocked all traffic on Beltrami Avenue by sitting down on the street in front of the Army-Navy Recruiting Office, demanding that the recruiters leave the building, public sympathy was hardly on the students' side. When two history faculty members led the march of students from the campus to the downtown City Hall, with a petition to the mayor seeking added support to end the war in Vietnam, local public reaction favored the end of faculty tenure right there on the spot. It seemed to many Americans in general and to Bemidji citizens in particular that students were acting nuts and that the whole country was coming apart. Not only were Americans in a war in Vietnam but they were also in a kind of civil war at home. Angry times, angry people: Doves vs. Hawks. Blacks vs. Whites. Reds vs. Radishes. Yippies vs. Y.A.F. Hippies vs. Straights. Parents vs. Children. Faculty vs. Students. Bemidji vs. Bemidji State.

Nationally, law enforcement agencies took a dim view of almost every extremist group and worked to infiltrate all of them. At some Ku Klux Klan meetings, federal agents in disguise outnumbered the regular members. Locally, the Beltrami County sheriff indicated he was more than ready to deal with student troublemakers. Bemidji citizens never did get used to the sight of machine guns on top of downtown buildings. Feds and narcs were everywhere, including secret agents planted on the Bemidji State campus. Troublesome times. Tea at the decade's start; turmoil at the decade's end. A 1959 graduate of nearby Hibbing High School, Robert Zimmerman, would by the summer of 1960 change his name to Bob Dylan, and his song said it all for the rest of that time period, "The Times They Are A'Changin' . . ."

The cultural tide shifted dramatically, shockingly. There was a common feeling among adults that somehow all the rules got changed in the middle of the game. The previous decade had seemed so pleasant, so simple. A rapidly expanding middle class moved to the suburbs; sex roles were decided at birth; parents raised in the insecurity of the Depression and World War II tried to give their children everything; Baby Boomers—many of whom would rebel in the Sixties—were fed society's rules: obey authority, control your emotions, fit in with the group, get a stable job with secure benefits—and don't even think about sex. SEX, DRUGS, & ROCK AND ROLL. Part of the culture of the 1960s. Jim Morrison. Janis Joplin. Jimi Hendrix. Live fast, die young. They did. In-a-gadda-da-vida, baby. The heady and idealistic years of 1960 and 1964 awakened activism and idealism in a new generation of college students, but by 1966 they felt betrayed having discovered that many Americans did not have the right to life, liberty and the pursuit of happiness and that fear of Communism could be used to silence dissent. Reform became equated with Reds; dissent towards this "holy war" against Communism in Asia became equated with treason. Many youth did not buy it. During the Vietnam era, 125,000 Americans sought political exile in Canada—the largest exodus of political refugees in American history. In fleeing their country, these war resisters repudiated the American Dream and turned upside down the idea of America as the land of the free and natural refuge for the world's oppressed. Were these resisters traitors or patriots? Did their defiance—and the general defiance of all youth in that decade—have a lasting impact on the nation, or were their actions an ephemeral movement of the times? How much was rebellion-for-the-hell-of-it?

The late Sixties' Youth Rebellion and Counterculture—inspired by music, drugs and the adolescent drive for independence—brushed aside every social rule learned and they substituted tenets of their own, dealing a strong blow to the repression and conformity of the era. Certain impressions and moods seemed real at the time: Everything was coming apart; a genuine revolution might occur; the country could become ungovernable; a civil war might break out. All Americans made fumbling attempts to adjust; some never found their feet again.

And to think that the decade started out so nice. . . .

◆ ◆ ◆

Buying the Books to Start a New Quarter and a New Life
"Who could assign the most books to read in a quarter? Bangsberg, with 13."

BEMIDJI STATE IN 1960

Little had changed for the school from 1959 to '60 that was not positive, except perhaps public transportation. Passenger trains to Bemidji had stopped running; students had to come by bus or car, and it was becoming increasingly more of the latter. The change, positive from the students' view, found more students owning their own cars. A sign of the times. The Prosperous Decade. The Affluent Society.

Charles R. Sattgast, president since 1938, could welcome the new decade in his usual blustering manner and take personal pride in learning that soon there would be a new million dollar science building that would bear his name. He could also boast of administering a college that had had seven straight years of enrollment increase. In the fall of 1960, 1,543 students registered for classes, but the enrollment came as no surprise as the increased numbers were expected. Bemidji State in 1960 was still primarily a teacher education institution. On campus the men outnumbered the women, but this would be reversed by decade's end. Ninety percent of the students in 1960 came from northern Minnesota; this percentage, too, decreased by 1969. As expected in the registration pattern, 88 percent of degrees that year were in teacher education. There were no bachelor of science degrees for non-teaching programs in 1960. Business administration, the major that would mushroom in growth in the next decade as a B.S. program, was in the '60s a B.A. degree. Off-campus classes were still important to the point that they made up 10.5 percent of the total 1960 registration. If the off-campus students were included as "regular students," the swelled enrollment number would have reached 1,724.[1] Things looked good at the decade's start and the demographics involving high school numbers made Bemidji State's future look even better. There were not only more high school students but more of them were planning to attend college. The "war babies" had come of age and these "baby boomers" began flocking to the colleges in record numbers. Bemidji State got its share; indeed, it got more than it could accommodate by the end of that extraordinary time period.

1960: STUDENTS BACK THE WRONG HORSE(?)
    A month before the November election day for president of the United States, the Bemidji State students held a mock election, and Republican candidate Richard Nixon carried the election with 56 percent of the vote compared to John F. Kennedy's 33 percent; the remaining 11 percent were undecided. By the actual election day on November 4, 1960, however, the students' voting in a second mock election reflected the exact voting pattern throughout the country. As close as close can be. In the tightest election this century, Kennedy squeaked out the narrowest of victories in American voting, and at Bemidji State Kennedy won by a vote of 336 to 333. Other offices were on that same Bemidji State ballot, including the office of congressman from the 7th District. The incumbent in 1960 was Coya Knutson, from Oklee, the only woman from Minnesota ever elected to a national office. Knutson lost that year, however, to Odin Langen. She lost the "real vote" and also the "mock vote" at Bemidji State. By decade's end, Knutson would designate Bemidji State as the official repository of her files, and anyone wanting to do research requiring her materials would have to come to Bemidji State to view the "Coya Knutson Papers," all carefully cataloged and preserved in the BSU library.

1) School information on the year 1960 taken from memo sent by Arlene Tangborn, director of institutional research, to Dr. Linda Baer, vice president for academic affairs; dated July 1, 1991. Memo entitled "Student Profile Comparisons - 1960 to 1990." In contrast to 1960, the 1990 enrollment had only 25 percent in teacher education programs, and only 68 percent came from northern Minnesota, with the number of metropolitan area students and international students more than 10 times the 1960 figure. The greatest difference, of course, was in the total on-campus enrollments: 1,543 in 1960 and 4,669 in 1990. The nine-page memo is composed mainly of statistical tables and pie charts, all together offering a wealth of comparative information on 30 years of changes at BSU. Memo in author's file.

"SAINT URHO'S DAY" BEGINS AT BEMIDJI STATE

There is a "national holiday" of sorts that falls on March 16, the day before St. Patrick's Day, called St. Urho's Day in honor of Finland's legendary patron saint who drove the grasshoppers out of Finland centuries ago and thus saved the Finnish vineyards and became the saint of the vineyard workers. Modern celebrants of St. Urho's Day tend to be located regionally at best, but some persons in the Finnish-American communities of northern Minnesota have adopted the "saint," with the small town of Menahga going further than most by also erecting a large wooden statue of St. Urho. The statue stands on Menahga's main street, which is also the major highway (#71 S.) running through the community. To those supporters caught up in this celebration, the proper colors of clothing to wear on March 16 are Royal Purple and Nile Green.

As to legends, Bemidji, of course, would claim fame primarily as being the proper home of the Northwoods' most famous legendary character, Paul Bunyan, and his faithful Blue Ox, Babe, both figures literally solidified as imposing cement statues standing along the Bemidji lakeshore in downtown Bemidji. The origins of Paul and Babe remain shrouded in mystery and controversy, but that is not the case with St. Urho. The latter resulted from the fertile mind and imagination of a Bemidji State psychology professor named Sulo Havumaki, appropriately a man of Finnish ethnic background, who moved to Bemidji in 1956. He alone can be credited with the beginning and growth, such as it is, of St. Urho's Day.

By 1960, the Northern Student would run a feature story regularly on Havumaki and St. Urho's Day, timing the article with an approaching March 16. Each article indicated that Havumaki had come up with yet more "evidence" of St. Urho, ongoing "solid documentation" that would answer all those scoffing critics who had denied the patron saint's ever existing. For example, the March 17, 1961, newspaper showed a picture of Havumaki holding a "mysterious package" that he said he had just received from Denmark. According to Havumaki, the contents were St. Urho's relics, including a portion of his jawbone. This latter object, he announced, he was bringing to the science laboratory to have tested by the carbon-14 procedure that would prove then and forever St. Urho's ancient embodiment. The science staff, however, he noted, did not yet have the proper testing equipment, but when they did get it, the "remains" of St. Urho would be presented for authenticity. Meanwhile, he'd hold on to the package. (He never let go.)

Havumaki, who had his Ph.D. from the University of Minnesota, told all St. Urho stories with a straight face, and after years of repetition, he could be convincing. At least he gained a small following on campus who dutifully wore their purple-and-green the day before St. Patrick's Day. He added a special wrinkle every year by announcing that there would be a St. Urho's Day parade through downtown Bemidji, and that national celebrities had been invited to be in the parade. Then just before the parade day came, he'd announce that the parade had been canceled for some particular reason. All this went well enough until the year he got a letter back from Vice President Spiro T. Agnew, who informed Havumaki that he would indeed accept his gracious invitation to be the grand marshal at the forthcoming St. Urho's Day parade in Bemidji, Minnesota. At that point Havumaki knew not what to do. But as luck would have it, a follow-up letter came the next week from the vice president's office telling Havumaki that something had just come up and that with deep regret Agnew could not be the grand marshal after all. Thus the parade was "saved" in that it could be canceled again.

After all the fun and tongue-in-cheek kidding over 10 years, personal tragedy came to Havumaki when he discovered that he had terminal cancer. He chose not to fight it with drugs or radiation; he chose instead to do as much as he could while he could still do it, and this included taking his family for a vacation trip to Finland. He died on April 14, 1970, at age 49. But St. Urho has lived on. He'd like that.

LEGISLATIVE PURSE-STRINGS

More students always require more financing from the state legislature, the rule-of-thumb once holding that students paid one-third of the costs and the state two-thirds. In the '60s it was even better for the students, in effect closer to a 30-70 split. (Alas, by 1994 it came closer to 40-60.)

Not that the state money came automatically. Each session found the Bemidji State president urging his staff to write/pressure legislators for full funding—and more, if possible. Legislators have historically responded the same way, regardless of decade or perhaps even century. To illustrate, Bemidji Representative Leonard R. Dickinson wrote on May 8, 1961:

"I am sure you understand that we are in very much of a deadlock, at the time of writing this letter, with respect to revenue, but I am hoping very much that this can be resolved without too much delay, and I am keeping in touch with the Committee. . . ."[2]

THE VIKINGS ARE COMING!

Added publicity came to Bemidji State in 1961 when the brand new Minnesota Vikings football team announced in April that they had picked Bemidji State as the site for their summer training camp. They stayed in Pine Hall and ate at the food services, but had a far better menu than what College students ate. A bigger boost in publicity could hardly have been imagined for both the school and the community. If every community needs its heroes, Bemidji gained an extra number of them, at least in the summertime. The players and coaches alike were

2)Letter from Dickinson, dated May 8, 1961, received by this author who had dutifully followed the president's urging to write legislators. Dickinson had an extensive career in the legislature in the 1940s, '50s and early '60s. He served in both the house and the senate, elected as a Conservative/Republican, although party labels were not used when he was in the legislature. The Republicans once picked Dickinson to run as lieutenant-governor, but the Democrats won that year, 1953. The Dickinson family goes back to earliest Bemidji and have always been connected with lumbering. At this writing (1994), Dickinson owns the only remaining lumber mill in the city, on Lake Irving, and at age 94, he still drives daily to the office and puts in a 9 a.m. to 4 p.m. workday.(Recent addendum: Dickinson died on March 13, 1994, at age 95.)

perceived as true celebrities and treated with a combination of awe and deference.[3]

As a new expansion National Football League club, the Vikings team began with a combination of both old and new players. Eventually 80 players came, vying for the 45 slots. Former star running back of the San Francisco Forty-Niners, Hugh McElhenny, was among the best known of the veterans, and kids followed him everywhere for his autograph. Head Coach Norm Van Brocklin, a once-famous quarterback, held the attentive stares of everyone. Then there was rookie quarterback Fran Tarkenton whose name meant nothing at the start, as witnessed by the same kids who initially never bothered him.

Public interest in the Vikings found crowds coming to the campus each day, rain or shine, to watch the Viking behemoths lumbering through their practices. Practices were held on the open field, beside Lake Bemidji, just south of the present football stadium. At that time there were no buildings even near the practice area; it was one, large, open field, with some viewers standing as close as allowed around the edges and others on the rising knoll of land to the west of the playing area.[4] By decade's end, one building, Hagg-Sauer Hall, would sit directly where the practice field had been, while on the surrounding sides came Bridgeman Hall, Sattgast Hall, the student union, and the A.C. Clark Library.

Each summer training camp culminated in a "practice game" between the Vikings and some other major league team. The game was played in the Beaver stadium, with crowds of spectators overflowing the bleachers and more fans filling both ends of the playing field. For some local sports lovers, it was THE event of the year! The game's ticket income went to the Bemidji State athletic fund, generating a substantial amount for its coffers, which made Bemidji State officials like the Vikings all the more.

Alas for Bemidji State, it all ended after the summer of 1965 when the Vikings moved their training camp to Mankato State to be closer to the Twin Cities, they said. It was great for Bemidji while it lasted, and almost everyone was sorry to see them leave.[5]

WHAT TO WEAR? WHAT CANNOT BE ALLOWED?

The issue of student dress arose in most public schools mainly because many young people wanted to imitate the looks and hairstyle of singer Elvis Presley. Campus administrators took it upon themselves to establish clothes conformity by instituting student dress codes. Bemidji State College drew up its

---

3)Who but Coach Van Brocklin could walk through the door of Bemidji's then biggest and best restaurant, Jack's Supper Club, and have the filled place shush to complete silence! The "celebrity status" terminology suggests honor for something worth celebrating, of course, but the Vikings nighttime notoriety at times superseded the daylight hours, with a different connotation to the term "celebration." Who but the Vikings could in one night drink a tavern completely out of beer?! The tavern was The Dutchman Bar, out of town, west on 5th Street, and faraway—and safe—from their coach, who ironically had the nickname of The Dutchman.

4)Among the viewers in the summer of 1963 was a newly-hired Bemidji State faculty member in music, Fulton Gallagher. He had just arrived from football-rich Pennsylvania, where interest in high school practices regularly found large crowds watching. Gallagher believed he was watching the local Bemidji High School squad practicing, not a professional team, and he could hardly believe what he saw! He went home and told his wife after seeing his first session, "That's the best high school football team I've ever seen!" Anecdote told this author by Gallagher, who swears it's a true story.

5)Least sorry to see them go were the mothers of star-struck teenage daughters, some of whom had reached the category of Groupies.

own set of rules for the start of the 1962-63 school year. At the time it all seemed reasonable.

A memo dated September 7, 1962, came from the office of the dean of students, and it was addressed to "All Students, Bemidji State College." The introductory line read, "At a summer meeting of campus student leaders and faculty advisers, it was agreed that a campus dress code should be established at Bemidji State College, commencing with the fall term of 1962." The next two short paragraphs recognized both the problem and the difficulty of dealing with the topic,

The Proper Look for a Proper (Alleged) Rebel in Protest Times
"The dress code seemed reasonable in '62 . . . by '69 the code seemed absurd."

and concluded with the line that "the common sense and good judgment expected of all students will render unnecessary a highly detailed listing of appropriate dress," after which came a listing of appropriate dress. Specifically for WOMEN, the Code of Dress "will exclude the wearing of slacks, shorts, Bermudas or Levis in the areas designated," that is, College classrooms, library, cafeteria, snack bar, and co-ed lounges. Moreover, "hair curlers will not be worn in any area unless properly covered and preferably not at all [sic]."

For College MEN: The foregoing principle "will exclude the wearing of T-shirts, athletic jerseys, shorts, Bermudas, and Levis in the areas designated." Next came the area of EXCEPTIONS, the first one (of five) reading, "Dress slacks will be approved for commuting women students when very cold weather would require such apparel." The final paragraph of the memo is headlined ENFORCEMENT, which went, "All students and faculty are expected to promote compliance with the foregoing dress code. It is hoped and anticipated that a positive climate of cooperation will make a program of enforcement unnecessary."

As indicated, the code seemed reasonable and acceptable to all in 1962.[6] By 1969, a dress code seemed absurd to almost all the students and half the faculty. For Dean of Students Ray Carlson, who initiated the original code, the reasoning

The Life and (Stilted) Times in the Early '60s Residence Halls
"In the '60s the buildings popped up on campus like proverbial mushrooms."

made good sense then and was viewed as a necessary part of his job. It all went together with the concept of *in loco parentis,* in place of a parent. For Carlson, certain moral duties were thrust upon him in his position as dean of students, be it dictating proper dress or proper behavior at school dances. In the latter area, for example, he felt duty bound to watch all couples dancing. If he perceived the dancers being too close to each other, he went up to the interlocked couple and

6)The topic of appropriate dress on campus had been discussed in the student newspapers, and these discussions included interesting letters. In the Northern Student of May 11, 1962, p. 2, a male student responded at length to an earlier article which stated that chivalry had died at Bemidji State. The young man responding blamed the alleged decline on women wearing slacks, "If girls wish to wear the pants like the men, they can be treated that way." After more discussion on his thesis, he ended his argument, "In conclusion, I would like to say that if the girls wore skirts rather than slacks, if the boys wore slacks rather than Levis, and if neither wore Bermudas to class, then we would recognize who is a lady and deserved such treatment, and who is a gentleman and likewise deserved such treatment. Possibly then chivalry would not die."

tapped each person on the shoulder, then giving his advice to allow sufficient space between their bodies, the situation summed up in the simple line, "Break it up." (Years later he would say with a laugh that he kept a ruler in his pocket so that he could measure the four inches of "proper distance" between dance partners.) Carlson saw his efforts to control dancing come to an end by decade's end, in part because at many dances no one danced; they sat on the floor. In the early '60s many faculty members came to student dances, sometimes as chaperones, but mainly because they wanted to come and in part because they were expected to come. By the late '60s, however, the faculty "stayed away in droves" and were no longer asked to serve as chaperones. Another form of "chaperone" had replaced them—policemen.

END OF AN AGE

Charles Richard Sattgast had become an institution by 1964. That January he began what would be his last months as president. Sixty-five years old at the time, and in failing health, he looked forward to the end of the school year and his planned retirement. Unfortunately he did not make it through the school year; he died of a heart attack on March 24, 1964.[7] In many ways the "old Bemidji State" died with him. Archie Clair Clark, an institution in his own right after 40 years on the faculty, took over again as interim president for the rest of the school year and through the summer; then Clark retired. The Old Guard was leaving, both literally and figuratively. (Clark died two years later on November 6, 1966, of heart failure.)[8]

More of the "old College" was slowly fading away. Before long, the school stalwarts—Chairmen Sauer, Thompson, and Peters—were no longer division chairmen. Sauer and Thompson had chaired their divisions since 1938, and Peters since 1945. They had been there so long and through such trying, stirring times that it seemed to many that they did not so much work at the College as that they were the College. But they were replaced. The old order changeth, making way for the new. A whole new era would start; a very different College would begin under Sattgast's successor, Bemidji State's third president, Harry Bangsberg. The remaining years of the '60s would be the Bangsberg Years, despite his tragic death

7) Because he served some 20 years as president, the documentation for the Sattgast years is voluminous. There are many boxes of "The Sattgast Papers" available in the history center of the library, and I tried to go through most of them, seeking certain letters and memos that he wrote which would answer questions on given topics and issues. However, one day in 1968 I learned that his papers had been expurgated on the orders of a vice president, and the same day I went to the administration building to confront the man who gave the order to his secretary to go through Sattgast's files and remove any "sensitive" materials. It turned out that we met just inside the doorway of Deputy Hall, and what followed immediately was a shouting contest at a distance of about six inches. The volume went to a high decibel count. Intemperate lines came from both red-faced parties, with phrases like "muckraker" being tossed about, along with a rejoinder about summoning the state's attorney general for the crime of destruction of state properties. Nothing came out of these verbal barbs other than bruised egos. However, certain documents of evidence are gone. Now unprovable, for example, are the pernicious rumors that Sattgast was trying to fire a certain science teacher, and that a certain resident director on the State Board was trying to fire Sattgast! Maybe it's just as well ... but historians will always view the destruction of documentation as a heinous crime. If you destroy the record, you destroy the truth.
8) Clark's primary roles had been as a professor of political science and chairman of the social studies division. It was in his latter position where "the old paternalistic College" was shown, illustrated by the planning of classes for the approaching quarters. Clark alone made the division decisions, seeking virtually no advice from anyone. For example, after 25 years of sharing an office with Clark, Harold Hagg had no idea of what classes he would be teaching nor what days nor what hours in the days until Clark laid the finished schedule on Hagg's desk.

in a plane crash in 1967. Many, but not all, of his policies would stretch through the rest of the decade and beyond. If ever there is an example needed of an institutional head who could turn a place around and upside down, be it for better or worse, it was Bangsberg at Bemidji State College in the 1960s.

THE SEARCH FOR A PRESIDENT

Following the death of Sattgast, the State College Board moved quickly to find a replacement. By April 24, 1964, the Board reported that 46 people had applied for the position and that that number had been narrowed down to six names by the Board. At that point the Board sought the opinions of the Bemidji State faculty. Acting President Clark called a special meeting of the faculty on April 29 to select an Advisory Board to the State Board, and after many names were submitted as candidates, an election was held and seven persons were chosen:

Don Dickinson, library; Louis (Jack) Downing, psychology; Harold Hagg, history; Robert Montebello, physical education; Harold Peters, science; Philip Sauer, English; and Carl Thompson, music. Sauer served as chairman and Downing as secretary. The Advisory Committee members were supplied with the credentials of the six candidates, and these were reviewed carefully.

The next step came on May 15, 1964, with the advisory faculty members driving to St. Paul to meet directly with the State College Board members for a final review and also meet the top candidates in person. The Bemidji group had narrowed their choices to two men, Bangsberg and Howard Bellows. It might be added that the State Board was at the same time seeking the first president for the yet-to-be-opened Southwest State College at Marshall.

In addressing the State Board, Downing told them that in the opinion of the Bemidji group, Bellows was better suited for Southwest's start-up while Bangsberg with his liberal arts background was the better choice for Bemidji. The State Board president then huffily reminded the Bemidji faculty that they (Bemidji) were not being asked for their recommendations, only their "evaluation," just in case the faculty forgot where the power lay.

Nevertheless, after the Board went into executive session, they selected Bangsberg. The motion to do so was made by the Bemidji resident director on the State Board, Herbert Olson, an attorney, and the motion passed unanimously. Effective September 1, 1964, at a salary of $17,000, Bangsberg was to begin his office. He was 36 years old at the time.[9]

A "NEW COLLEGE" ON THE ROAD TO BEMIDJI

In what became "typical Bangsberg," on the day he was chosen to be the new president, May 15, 1964, he rode back with some members of the Advisory

9) Much, but not all, of the public procedures in the selection of Bangsberg are laid out in the published Minutes of the State College Board for April and May, 1964; Minutes available in BSU archives. There is an excellent Bemidji State student paper, dated November, 1990, on "The Bangsberg Years" written for a Senior Honors requirement by Allen Kidd. He did his homework. His extensive bibliography reveals more primary than secondary sources, including lengthy interviews with at least a dozen faculty members who served under Bangsberg. Copy of paper in author's possession; also available at Honors Program office. Bellows, by the way, was selected in July, 1964 for Southwest State, which opened three years later.

Committee to see Bemidji State with his own eyes, before formally accepting the position. Halfway home, they stopped for dinner at a roadside restaurant. As the men were surveying their menus, the waitress asked if anyone cared for a cocktail. The Bemidji faculty members, conditioned by 45 years of two Methodist presidents— one president a total abstainer and absolutely death on booze, the other a temperance figure not far behind the former—looked sheepishly (longingly?) at each other but said nothing. Then Bangsberg piped up and ordered a drink, thus bringing Prohibition to a close after a half-century dry spell in Bemidji State social history.[10]

BIOGRAPHICAL SKETCH OF BANGSBERG

Harry Frederick Bangsberg, of Scandinavian descent, was born in Minneapolis, Minnesota, on April 7, 1928, the son of Marie and Roy Bangsberg. He grew up in LaCrosse, Wisconsin, and attended public schools there. He joined the Army in World War II and served as an infantryman in the Pacific Theater of Operation at war's end.

President Bangsberg and Family on Way to His Inauguration (1965)
"'I like books.' And he did. And he also liked others to read them."

After the war, Bangsberg attended three different colleges—LaCrosse State, Michigan State, and the University of Illinois—before taking his B.A.

10) For both confirmation and/or fuller details on above anecdote, consult two men who were there as witnesses, and who love to relate the tale, Montebello and Downing.

degree, *cum laude*, from Luther College, Decorah, Iowa, in 1950. He had majors in history and English.[11]

That fall of 1950 he began a master's program at the University of Iowa, completing his degree the next spring, and writing his thesis on the U. of Iowa during World War I. He then went to work full-time as a reporter for the LaCrosse Tribune newspaper, an employer he had worked for part-time as a high school and college student.

In 1952 he married Gertrude (Trudy) Moe of Eau Claire, a graduate of St. Olaf College. They had five children: Mark, born in 1953; Peter, 1955; Sara, 1957; Christopher, 1960; and Andrew, 1963.

Beginning in 1953, Bangsberg academically became a man on the make. He moved from position to position, always bettering himself; he seldom stayed over three years at any job. He taught one academic year (1953-54) at Western Illinois University before returning to Iowa to work on his doctorate in history. In 1956 he began in the history department at Eau Claire State, Wisconsin; in 1957 he completed his dissertation on the Columbo Plan and received his Ph.D.

In 1959 Bangsberg left the classroom for administration. He accepted the position as assistant director of the Wisconsin State University System in Madison, Wisconsin. In 1963 he moved to St. Louis as the first director of the Higher Education Coordinating Council of Metropolitan St. Louis, there to try to coordinate plans and programs of 20 colleges, universities, and public and private school systems. It was from this latter position that he moved to Bemidji the next year. Certainly a man on the move in a ten-year period.

Not incidentally, given Bangsberg's rising record, many at Bemidji State wondered just how long he would stay before moving on yet again. Was Bemidji State to be just another "springboard" for him?

BANGSBERG STARTS, LONG BEFORE HE HAD TO

Although officially to begin on September 1, 1964, Bangsberg began earlier. He came to Bemidji on June 14 and made his first public appearance at a Flag Day celebration in Library Park, downtown Bemidji. He spent the next days meeting people and getting oriented to both the school and community, and like all newcomers in town, trying to find a decent home to live in.[12] To acquaint himself more with the system in general, that summer he also attended the meetings of the State College Board. He intended to be fully oriented by Labor Day and ready to inaugurate his ambitious programs.

---

11) By pure coincidence, this author was a student at Luther College at the same time as Bangsberg. He, however, was a mighty senior when I was a lowly freshman. I remember him mainly because of his reporting work with the school news bureau. At Bemidji he said he remembered me at Luther, but he was being either kind or diplomatic; I don't think he knew me from Adam. What distinguished senior knows grungy freshmen?

12) Bangsberg was not a wealthy man, to say the least. Yet certain of the oligarchical faculty believed it was fitting and proper that he live in a "presidential house," not some ticky-tacky block house that just anybody (read history profs) might live in. "They" had his house picked out for him, a large, English-Tudor-style home at 2318 Birchmont Drive, and on Lake Bemidji, too. Very Lovely. Very Presidential. Very Expensive. "They" personally went to the local bank president for approval of a normally unsound mortgage arrangement. Bangsberg got his loan. Story told to this writer by Carl O. Thompson.

TO LOOK AT HIM . . .

Physically, Bangsberg was on the short side (5'6") and a bit chunky, with a full, round, boyish face, and sparkling—some said mischievous—dark eyes. Perhaps his most distinctive physical feature was his hairstyle: a short-cropped crew cut, a carry-over from his Army days, which style he never changed. On occasion his black hair was covered with another trademark of his, a black beret, which, in Bemidji, was certainly different.

BANGSBERG WAS READY FOR BEMIDJI STATE, AND VICE VERSA

Because Bangsberg had been on campus several times prior to Labor Day, 1964, and because many of his views were already publicly stated in the local newspapers, he did not arrive as a stranger when the school year began. Most of the faculty, staff and community had reacted favorably to his initial appointment and his later public positions so that they welcomed him as a breath of fresh air for all of Bemidji. Bangsberg did not let them down. He was a man-of-ideas-that-needed-doing, and the sooner the better, he indicated.

He got off to a fine start, establishing himself immediately as a friendly, personable man who seemed to remember everybody's name after one introduction.[13] At his first formal address to the faculty on September 14, he expressed his concerns forthrightly and declared the need for a new library, improved cultural opportunities, the establishment of a foundation to serve the school, and a greater emphasis on non-Western studies. In three years he would achieve all these goals.

Bangsberg also presented his agenda in the Northern Student, the newspaper carefully following his moves and his views. His positions also went out to the entire community as he became a frequently invited guest at meetings of the many civic organizations. On September 29, he expressed to the annual meeting of the Bemidji Chamber of Commerce his hope for warm town and gown relations— relations that needed careful monitoring during expansion of the campus and buildings and the losses of tax-properties. By the end of his first month in office, he had singled out what he perceived as the three major problems of the school: 1) the library building was too small and too limited in its holdings (it had 44,000 volumes but needed 150,000); 2) the curriculum needed revamping; 3) quality faculty needed to be rewarded and retained in those times of faculty-raiding.[14]

What followed point #3 gladdened the hearts of all teaching professors. To the surprise and joy of all, starting winter quarter he reduced the faculty teaching

13) Patrick Trihey, at this writing chairman of the biology department at BSU, was a graduate student in 1964. Along with other new faculty, he stood in a receiving line, along with his wife, Faye, when the president came through the line and introduced himself for the first time. Three days later Trihey happened to be at the post office when Bangsberg came in, and Bangsberg struck up a conversation, remembering both Trihey's and his wife's names. Later that year Trihey had his oral exam and who should come down from "the head shed" but Bangsberg, who sat in on the proceedings and asked Trihey insightful questions about his paper on the the College Forest, or C.V. Hobson Forest. Information provided by Trihey in an interview on October 15, 1990.
14) On Bangsberg's call for curriculum reform those in the audience could practically hear the groans all over the Lab School auditorium. "Reforms" always meant tinkering with general education, the sacred cow which always led to faculty concerns (read fights) whenever proposals came for changes. Every new president since Bangsberg has always wanted to "reform" gen. ed., and thereby stirred up a hornet's nest.

load from 16 to 12 credits! As retired English Professor Ruth Stenerson wrote in her "Memories," (p. 4) "When that requirement was lowered to 12, great was the jubilation—and great our puzzlement over why we still seemed to be as busy as ever."

Bangsberg wanted to know what the faculty thought about making the school a better school. To this end, that fall he called in every single faculty member individually to his office for the purpose of getting their views, and these he wrote down in longhand on long, legal pad paper. By Christmas, he had met privately with everyone, and everyone was duly impressed with Bangsberg. [15]

His newspaper background he put to immediate use, believing the major problem between faculties and administrators was lack of communication. He began a regular newsletter to facilitate this needed communication, setting the precedent that all presidents followed after him.

Bangsberg deliberately cultivated openness. He ran an open door policy well publicized and well known to students and faculty alike. All were impressed with this openness but more by his eagerness, his youthful exuberance, and his visibility everywhere on the campus, day and night. He seemed to show up everywhere.

He made it a point not only of coming to the student union both morning and afternoon, but also of dragging other administrators with him. The union then was in the basement of Sanford Hall and both its small size and the size of the student body allowed for a wonderful *esprit de corps*. Certainly the faculty then knew each other, something lost by decade's end when multiple growth meant separate lounges in separate buildings and separate faculties and even separate cliques within large departments. The curse of growth.

Bangsberg in the student union mixed with everyone. He exuded personality and genuine concern for all with whom he came in contact. And his sense of humor showed up there and everywhere else. For example, when land was being cleared for the building of a parking lot, Bangsberg was handed a napkin on which was scribbled, "Woodman, Spare That Tree!" The next day the president replied, handing the person his response which he had written on paper toweling from the lavatory in his office. (Bangsberg and his financial man John Glas also gained notoriety in the union for their squeezing two cups of tea out of one five cent tea bag.)

As new college presidents are expected to do, Bangsberg immediately became involved in the community. He joined the Rotary Club and became district chairman for the Boy Scouts. He not only joined First Lutheran Church in town but also did what most parishioners found unbelievable; he taught Sunday School. On weekends, he and his large family were regularly seen at the swimming pool or out

15) "The Bangsberg Papers," like the expurgated Sattgast Papers, somehow disappeared. There is virtually nothing available in primary documentation from Bangsberg's Office. What little there is from Bangsberg's time is in the form of brochures, clippings and scattered memorabilia, like some of his newsletters, all items kept in the Special Collections Room in the library. The really curious (read snoopy) wonder what happened to those legal pad notes he took so copiously, because he also solicited at the time information as to both what and who was wrong with Bemidji State, thus recording invective and diatribes.

skiing at Buena Vista Ski Area. At Buena Vista, he showed more courage than brains as a neophyte schussing down steep hills, legs wide apart and arms waving wildly in trying to prevent imminent physical chaos. Bangsberg also enjoyed fishing but lacked the patience required. According to Dr. Philip Sauer, the fish had to be jumping in the boat in order to please Bangsberg. One time, said Sauer, when the fishing was slow, Bangsberg threatened to strip Sauer's tenure unless they started catching fish faster.

SOMETHING NOT SEEN IN BEMIDJI: AN INAUGURATION
        Bangsberg chose to defer his formal inauguration until the next spring, on April 21, 1965. Because the previous president, Sattgast, had not been formally inaugurated way back in 1938, such an event was unfamiliar and there was much public interest in the planning for these festivities, even if there was uncertainty in what to do and who should do what. Nevertheless plans went ahead that would include plenty of pomp and parade, criteria expected by traditionalists and academicians, even if the ceremony had to take place in the College's cavernous basketball gymnasium. The court was selected because it held the most people, the expectation being that the place would be jammed with curious spectators, all wanting to be a part of a major academic rite never seen at Bemidji State. However, it was not jammed; most of the students stayed away, but least embarrassed by student absence afterward was Bangsberg himself, who indicated that if he were a student, he'd likely avoid this "pomp and foolishness," too. After all, it was a warm spring afternoon, he said, and why stay inside for a stuffy ceremony? Nevertheless, the ceremony went ahead, crowd or no crowd.
        The president of Eau Claire State College, Leonard Haas, a former colleague of Bangsberg, presented the formal charge, but the major address came from Bangsberg himself who entitled his remarks, "A Necessary Confluence." The address, delivered boldly with strong voice, stressed the two themes of more student involvement in decision making and more internationalization of the school. Said Bangsberg, "The merit of a true institution is whether it takes its students seriously." He ended his address by reciting an Edwin Markham poem that called for looking forward, not backward.[16]

TWO "EDUCATION PRESIDENTS"
        Bangsberg followed closely the national political scene and the goals and congressional acts of President Lyndon Baines Johnson, who declared himself to be, among many things, the "Education President." Following Johnson's election in 1964, and with it the election of an overwhelmingly Democratic Congress, this "Congress of Realized Dreams" passed a series of major bills for education in

---

16) The eight lines of the Markham poem are the last eight lines of College in the Pines (p. 215), the book ending with Bangsberg's charge to both himself and Bemidji State. For more information on the inauguration, see the printed inaugural program on file with the Bangsberg papers. For yet more information, see "Harry F. Bangsberg Fine Arts Complex Dedication Program," dated May 7, 1972, on file with his other memorabilia. Among students impressed with their president was Mary Lou Stark (now Mrs. Louis Marchand), a senior theater major in 1965 who directed a production that year. Bangsberg attended both performances and sought her out afterwards for his congratulations. Interview with Marchand on October 13, 1990.

general, including special acts to aid higher education. Thus federal monies by 1965 became available in large quantities to colleges, many of these new money-bills preceded by the word "Title." Bangsberg moved quickly and consistently to acquire Great Society funds for Bemidji State, resulting in a series of federal grants to the school ranging from smaller $50,000 grants to improve certain teaching areas to $464,967 to add a fourth floor to a planned new library. Overall, "Bangsberg" and "buildings" were synonymous in the mushrooming growth at Bemidji State in the 1960s. The days of penury were over.[17]

It is indicative of Bangsberg's views that the first major building to be constructed under his presidency should be a new library, and that the site of the library would be in the very center of the campus. That location became Bangsberg's testimony to the proper place of the library on any college campus. Not that anyone should have been surprised by this decision. After presenting a rather lengthy speech to the faculty, which he read from a manuscript, he looked up and added an impromptu line which summed up his philosophy, "I like books." And he did. He also liked others, like his students, to read them. He tried to teach at least one class each quarter, just to stay close to the classroom. Reportedly, Bangsberg was competing with Dr. Alexander Nadesan of the political science department as to who could assign the most books to read in a quarter, and Bangsberg "won" with 13.

The above-mentioned Nadesan reflected Bangsberg's agenda to move away from western civilization dominating the curriculum. Both Nadesan, a native of Indonesia, and Ray Jensen, a specialist in Asian history, were hired in 1965 to develop an Asian Studies program. Both hirings showed the direction of Bangsberg's shifting of the College towards the liberal arts, something he directly told the faculty he would be doing. He didn't hide it. Although his hiring philosophy pleased many, like those once small departments which suddenly ballooned in size (including history) there were others who were made nervous and felt threatened by "this pint-sized artzy-lover," as one disgruntled prof called him, adding, "Bemidji State was not meant to be a Carleton." Supporters of Bangsberg said he was going to "humanize the scientists," who shot back with their version, to "Simonize the humanists." Whichever side was "right," when Bangsberg was president, the humanists were winning.

HONOR THY FACULTY

In an attempt to give special recognition and promotion to classroom teaching, Bangsberg arranged for the selection of one professor to be singled out

17) Bangsberg was most effective also in getting state monies for buildings, resulting that decade in buildings popping up everywhere on campus like proverbial mushrooms. In addition to the library, credit goes to Bangsberg for either the construction or planned construction of both portions of the new union (C.V. Hobson Union), Maple Hall dormitory, and the high-rise (12-story) dorm, Tamarack Hall; a new food service building (Walnut Hall); a classroom building (Hagg-Sauer Hall); an aquatics laboratory building (Harold T. Peters); a field house/hockey arena (John Glas); remodeling of Sanford Hall, and a fine arts complex (Bangsberg Hall). The fourth floor to the new library (A.C. Clark Library), funded by the federal government, proved a bizarre challenge to Bangsberg in that it appeared that the original three floors would have to be completed and roofed (with state money)— and then the roof would be removed and the fourth floor (with federal money) added only then. Bangsberg restored sanity, and only one roof was built. See Appendix H, which indicates when each building on campus was built along with the square footage in each building.

annually and given the title "Lecturer of the Year," the determination to be made primarily by students. The first winner in this new development was history professor Eugene Mammenga, a young man of small stature but dynamic personality. (At this writing, 1994, Mammenga most recently served as Minnesota State Commissioner of Education, a not too shabby attainment for a former history prof.) The award and reward for this distinction seemed somewhat dubious, however, in that there was no monetary reward but only the "pleasure" of presenting a talk at a special convocation program open to the entire community.[18]

Andy Brown Talks in Large Lecture Hall in Sattgast Hall of Science
"From 95% in teacher-ed in '62 to 85% outside of teaching by 1990."

---

18) It was this writer's fortune to be selected the next year after Mammenga, receiving the same "reward." This practice of faculty selection was dropped after Bangsberg's death in 1967 and not resumed until 1981, when Dr. Charles Austad in education was chosen. By then the recipients received a check for $250. By 1990, the award figure went up to $1,000, thanks to an annual contribution from Burlington-Northern Railroad. By 1994, the figure hit $2,500.

While Bangsberg got along well with almost every faculty member, he also felt the need to "nudge" those who had not yet completed their doctorates. He made no secret that he wanted to increase dramatically the number and percentage of Ph.D.s on the faculty and he constantly irked the A.B.D.s with his constant innocuous line, "How's it going?" which question had nothing to do with their health. There existed at the time a form of monetary reward called "merit money"— raises that went only to those teachers with "merit," the latter often defined as an earned doctorate. In response to this less than welcomed "carrot," the faculty presented an original play written and directed by Louis Marchand and Jim Ertresvaag of the speech-theater department, the all-faculty musical, Once Upon a Merit Raise. 'Twas a not so gentle spoof, but Bangsberg and the whole large audience enjoyed it immensely. Once again, when the school was small, these "Faculty-Follies" were more common, but these ended when size disrupted the former community collegiality.

GOODBYE TO WEEKLY CONVOCATIONS

In his second year as president, 1965-66, Bangsberg eliminated the weekly convocation programs and replaced them with a few programs throughout the year featuring national figures and groups brought to campus. Aside from being a major shift in bringing cultural and popular arts to Bemidji, it eliminated any official time and place when the entire school community might come together.

As stated in an earlier chapter, convocations had begun when the College had begun with President Deputy back in 1919. President Sattgast changed the format to a weekly convocation in 1938, with student attendance voluntary, but President Bangsberg ended any regular programming. Bangsberg preferred to bring a few big names to Bemidji rather than have a weekly program of lesser lights. To some critics, the weekly convos smacked of high school assembly programs; they were seen as "parochial" and devoid of major cultural and intellectual value. However, not everyone was pleased with the new format; Bangsberg went ahead anyway, with mixed results. Initially the big names attracted big crowds, but by the second year, the big names sometimes attracted embarrassingly small numbers. Whatever the merits or demerits of Bemidji State's weekly convocation programs, they were never revived afterwards. Another era ended.[19]

IT WASN'T ALL PEACHES AND CREAM

Although Bangsberg's years were successful by most standards of

19) Lecturers brought in the first year included anthropologist Ashley Montagu on "The Superiority of Women"; Dr. Houston Smith of Massachusetts Institute of Technology on "Hope in World Civilization"; Thomas Ross on "The Central Intelligence Agency"; and poet John Ciardi, then weekly columnist in the now defunct Saturday Review. That spring the Norwegian National Symphony played in the basketball arena, and the crowd overfilled the arena. Second-year embarrassments came with Pulitzer Prize Winner Hanson Baldwin of the New York Times, with the tiny audience looking even tinier in the large high school auditorium. Afterwards, Bangsberg personally apologized to Baldwin. An unfavorite big name for a big crowd was Gore Vidal, who could hardly hide his disdain for his being in Bemidji. In a side note, after Vidal finished speaking that evening he was picked up and driven to Moorhead State, where he was scheduled to give a talk the next day. In the car, Moorhead English professors attempted to engage Vidal in conversation, but he refused to talk. His only complete sentence uttered between Bemidji and Moorhead was his crudely-phrased demand to stop the car so he could walk into the woods and urinate. So much for the line, "The bigger they are, the nicer they are."

measurement, there were many decisions of his that brought criticism both then and later. Ending the weekly convocations would be an example, along with his choosing an entire new slate of division chairmen while at the same time keeping all the former top administrators that he inherited. Many faulted him for his dramatic increases of certain departments, like foreign languages, and his obvious push for the liberal arts. A few departments were not only critical but had members near apoplectic in their belief that not only was Bangsberg not supportive, but he was leading the way to their demise. Some education division members fell into this latter category, and with good reason, because Bangsberg said often and publicly that there were too many education credit requirements for teachers-to-be when there should better be more subject matter credits instead. Also, Bangsberg came under fire for forcing division chairs to rate their faculty, in effect making them decide who in each department was the best and who was worst and who was in between. This was not a popular decision in this subjective area so sensitive to faculty egos.

Many believed that Bangsberg devoted both excess time and money to peripheral projects and purchases while neglecting core academic areas. For example, the 1966 equipment budget found a shortage of funds for basic supplies like paper and chalk and duplication needs while at the same time the school purchased its first sailboats. When Bangsberg first announced the sailboat purchases at a committee meeting, a professor immediately asked what type of duplicating machines they were. Bangsberg joined in the laughter that followed, but the sailboats stayed. Of course, there were a very few teetotalers who lamented the absence of one of their own in the president's office, and one element even believed that Bangsberg held impure thoughts and "leered" at pretty co-eds. Finally, for a substantive issue, there were those who opposed his taking a leave of absence for six months overseas when he had only been on the job for three years, the reasoning being that he should "stay home and tend the store." Bangsberg went anyway.

BANGSBERG JOINS VIETNAM ADVISORY TEAM

On November 18, 1966, Bangsberg asked the State College Board for a leave of absence without pay to join a team of seven other higher education administrators formed to help advise the government of South Vietnam on the development of public higher education in that country. Through the American Department of State, the Agency for International Development sponsored an advisory group of educators from the upper Midwest. The board approved Bangsberg's request, but not unanimously as one board member, Peter Popovich, voted no.

The Bemidji State campus reaction to Bangsberg's going to Vietnam was, like the State Board's vote, generally supportive, but not unanimous in that support. Most students and faculty believed his being asked to go was an honor for him personally and for the school in general. Those who backed Bangsberg's leave argued that he should be able to take a leave just as any other faculty member could, and besides he could make a needed contribution to this country allied to the United States. The opposition to his going included the argument that he belonged on campus; after all, that was what he was hired to do. He had initiated a number of programs that were just starting, e.g., the Honors Program, and his expertise in education was needed more on his own campus than in some far-off land. And coming up in the immediate future, when he planned to be gone, January through March, were the needed president's decisions concerning staffing, tenure, sabbaticals, promotions, and leaves of absence for others. Also there had been no precedent for a Bemidji State president to go anywhere far away for any length of time, other than Sattgast's going into the military in World War II, and that was entirely different. Aside from education consulting as an issue, or the question of on or off campus decision-making, many people perceived Bangsberg's mission as dangerous if not foolhardy, given the escalating war in that divided country. Many simply believed that he was taking a risky chance by going into a country enveloped in a war that was growing more dangerous every day.

Regardless of the opposition or the warnings of danger, Bangsberg left Bemidji on January 2, 1967. Prior to his departure from the Bemidji airport, he apparently expected only his immediate family to see him off, and thus he was at first surprised and eventually overwhelmed at seeing the airport terminal filled with wellwishers. It appeared that half of the faculty and their families were there to say goodbye and wish him well.[20]

Bangsberg joined the rest of the advisory team in Chicago, and on January 3, 1967, they flew to Saigon, Vietnam, with stops in Anchorage, Tokyo and Hong Kong. The team consisted of upper Midwest educators who were chosen because of their backgrounds in Asian international affairs and/or their connection with colleges still in the developmental stages. Especially perceived as useful advisors by the U.S. State Department were schoolmen with experience in campus building programs. Bangsberg filled the roles as both an expert in Asian history and campus building planner and builder. Collectively the group could make many useful suggestions that could aid Vietnam's institutions of higher learning. Dr. James H. Albertson, president of Stevens Point State University, Wisconsin, led the team as chairman. Albertson and Bangsberg, as vice chairman, were the two college presidents in the group.[21]

Throughout his stay in Vietnam, Bangsberg made regular reports back to

---

20) As one member of the big crowd who was there that day, this author can testify to the fact that Bangsberg was emotionally moved by this open display of community support and, in many cases, admiration approaching love. In typical Bangsberg style he moved through the entire crowd, personally thanking everyone there. Although hardly the proper setting, he did stand up on a chair and delivered an impromptu talk, one that trailed off because it became difficult for him to speak, with the tears welling up in his eyes—leading to tears on the faces of many in the crowd. It was truly an emotional time for all, especially when the moment came to leave and he turned and waved his final farewell just before boarding the airplane.

21) The other members of the advisory team were Dr. A. Donald Beattie, dean of the School of Business and Economics at Whitewater State University, Wisconsin; Dr. Vincent F. Conroy, director of field studies at Harvard's Center for Educational Research; Dr. Howard G. Johnshoy, dean of academic affairs at Gustavus Adolphus College, St. Peter, Minnesota; Dr. Robert R. LaFollette, staff member of the Federal Agency for International Development (and a member of the prominent Wisconsin LaFollette family); Dr. Arthur Pickett, professor of biological sciences at the University of Illinois, Champaign; and Dr. Melvin L. Wall, department head of plant and earth sciences at River Falls State University, Wisconsin.

Bemidji in his letters, and these were duplicated and sent throughout the College. His background in journalism came through in these missives as he wrote skillfully, giving both vivid descriptions and his interpretations of what he saw in his travels and visits to Vietnamese cities and schools. Like most American servicemen who spent some time in Vietnam, Bangsberg too revealed both his shock and dismay at the extreme inequalities of wealth that he saw all around him. The sheer number of hordes of poor and desperate people he saw made a major impression on Bangsberg, as revealed in his correspondence. In this context he noted the poorly equipped educational facilities in Vietnam, which found him making reference to understanding better the Arab proverb about the person complaining because he had no shoes until he met another who had no feet. The war around him could not be ignored, of course. When writing one letter from Saigon, he wrote about incidents of guns and loud shelling and running soldiers and the sky lit up with gunfire. He also wrote about rumors of a planned massive Viet-Cong attack coming at the time of Tet, the Asian New Year, an event that did indeed happen that next January of 1968. He also could report that the team's efforts were paying off and that they would be completing their reports and recommendations soon and then would be returning home to America.[22]

BANGSBERG, ENTIRE ADVISORY TEAM, DIE IN PLANE CRASH

On March 23, 1967, Bangsberg and the entire advisory team, along with the plane's crew members, were killed when their twin-engine Air America plane crashed into a mountain side north of Danang, South Vietnam. The crash occurred on the final leg of their planned flight from Saigon to Hue, the old imperial capital city. Rain and turbulence had forced the pilot to land first in Danang, but after a short wait on the ground, the pilot decided to complete the final 80 miles in spite of the inclement weather.[23]

The news of Bangsberg's death came to Bemidji on a Good Friday morning. Not only faculty, staff and students but the whole community went into emotional shock when the word came of the plane crash. Even by Monday and the start of another school week, many on campus found it difficult to resume normal activities, grief being so strong. An overflowing, somber crowd jammed the physical education arena for a memorial service on March 29 and they were met by powerful, emotional music from the College-community orchestra and the College choir. The service began with a prayer by the Reverend Ray Williams of First Lutheran Church, Bangsberg's church. Following were several brief tributes by persons representing different segments of the school and the state. These included remarks by John Ludwig, student senate president; Nick Welle, representing the community; J. Bevington Reed, chancellor of the State College System; Governor Harold Levander; and Eugene Mammenga, speaking for the faculty. History Professor Mammenga spoke for a large number of Bemidji people when he

22) Incomplete set of these letters by Bangsberg from Vietnam are available in the BSU Archives.
23) New York Times, March 25, 1967, p. 1, 3. The headline read, "Eight U.S. Educators on Vietnam Survey Killed in Air Crash."

compared the death of Bangsberg to that of John F. Kennedy, stating, "To many of us, March 23, 1967, will be not unlike that fateful November day of 1963, for we will always remember where we were when we heard, and things will never be quite the same with us again."[24]

WHAT IF . . .

Understandably there would be a great deal of speculation on what Bemidji State would have become, what it would have been like had Bangsberg— and Bemidji State—not suffered his untimely death. Despite those what-ifs being speculative if not pointless, the ponderings and probables continued as discussion topics for years afterwards but about all that could be agreed to was the fact that the school would have been "different" had Bangsberg been permitted to continue several more years as president. The passage of time since has allowed for more reflective judgment on the Bangsberg years, and among retired faculty members who have commented in print was the highly respected Ruth Stenerson of the English department. Teaching at BSC - BSU from 1956 to 1986, she came under the administrations of every president except the first one, Manfred Deputy. Her opinion thus has special meaning. In her "Memories of a Department," written in 1992, she stated, "I associate the greatest level of professional excitement on the faculty with the brief period of Dr. Harry Bangsberg's presidency."[25]

UNSETTLED TIMES

The period of time following Bangsberg's death was most unsettled on campus. In this sense it fit into the very mood of the nation which was equally unsettled. By the spring of 1967 the entire country was in the throes of deep divisions, with social and political anger escalating to meet the escalation of the civil rights disruptions, the growing war in Vietnam and the growing lies from the government. Unsettling also were the growing violence surrounding these emotional issues at home, and the concomitant growing disenchantment of the younger generation with the old for reasons connected with all of the above topics and more. Things were starting to unravel.

24) Tributes continued for weeks afterwards from both groups and individuals. Even at the June graduation, a representative of the U.S. State Department, Thomas Hughes, director of research and intelligence, came to Bemidji to pay honor to Bangsberg and his group for what they had done in serving their country. Five years later it still seemed more than appropriate to name the recently completed fine arts complex after Bangsberg because he had worked so hard to gain the initial appropriations. On May 7, 1972, in a special ceremony of dedication, the building became officially the "Harry F. Bangsberg Fine Arts Complex." For the occasion, a special memorial booklet was put together by faculty members Ruth Stenerson, English, and Keith Malmquist, art. The brochure contains a number of items about Bangsberg, including his inaugural address, graduation remarks, random quotes, memorial tributes and pictures. Booklet kept among the Bangsberg Papers, BSU library.
25) "Memories of a Department," p. 5. Copy of Stenerson's "Memories" in author's possession. While faculty historians are trained in grad schools not to get involved in "what-ifs," undergrads jump right in to the intriguing possibilities. Senior Allen Kidd wrote a paper in 1990 on the Bangsberg years and in interviewing faculty members who taught under Bangsberg (and there were still 36 faculty left in 1990 whom Bangsberg had hired), his last question to them was, "If Dr. Bangsberg were to visit BSU today, what would he say?" The general consensus, reported Kidd, was that Bangsberg would be pleased by the modern day school in general and particularly pleased with the faculty, administration, the internationalization of the campus, the Foundation, and the honors program. As for the students, however, Kidd concluded, "The student body is lazy and indifferent and has still not accepted the repeated invitations of Bangsberg and his successors to become more involved in the University community." Copy of Kidd's paper in author's file. Trudi Bangsberg and her five small children moved to Madison, Wisconsin, several months after her husband's death. She accepted a $330,000 cash settlement from the airline. At this writing, 1994, the children are grown and married, and Mrs. Bangsberg lives in Sarona, Wisconsin.

Disenchantment on the Bemidji campus was augmented by the strange if not bizarre actions of the State College Board, the designated overseer to supervise the State Colleges. The Board dithered, ducked, then dallied over Bangsberg's successor as president. No solidity came to that office for nearly two years, when Robert Decker finally took over on September 1, 1968. In between it was a mess for Bemidji State which somehow, in good British tradition, muddled through.

Demonstrators in '67 Demand a Permanent President for BSC
"A number of onlookers indulged in heckling the speakers . . . on a personal basis."

The old way of picking an immediate replacement for a president was altered by the State College Board who at first decided not to choose an acting president from the existing faculty but instead chose the chancellor of the System, J. Bevington Reed, to be the major "administrator" on the Bemidji campus, even if he would not be on the campus! The Board appointed Bangsberg's assistant John Glas as "campus executive officer." When the titles and job descriptions of both men were perceived as fuzzy, at best, the Board then named Reed the acting president, but he still stayed in St. Paul and governed via the phone lines. Reed's latter appointment came on April 1, which date had a connotation appropriate to the Board's curious decisions. After one month, this experiment in dual control was abandoned by the Board, and Glas was picked as acting president on May 1, 1967. At this same time Reed resigned as chancellor and returned to his native Texas. The bumbling machinations in all these changes and selections remain unclear, but certainly they included Bemidji faculty pressures, not too subtle, either in favor of or against certain administrators on campus about whom there were intense feelings as to their moving into the presidency. Tensions ran high. Exactly which side won/lost would depend on one's point of view afterwards. Either way, John

Glas moved into the president's office and stayed there for the next year and a half.

JOHN SAMUEL GLAS

Acting President Glas was born on October 1, 1910, in Waterloo, Iowa. He went through public schools there, graduating from West High School, after which he went to work for one year in the business office of John Deere Tractor Company, Waterloo. He then enrolled in the University of Minnesota and graduated with honors in 1933 with a bachelor's degree in business administration.

Mr. Glas married Elfrida Boysen of Pelican Rapids, Minnesota, a fellow student at the University of Minnesota, on March 25, 1933. Following his graduation, they returned to Waterloo where Mr. Glas was again employed by John Deere for six years. In 1939 they moved to Bemidji when Glas was hired by Dr. Sattgast to be the business manager of B.S.T.C. Although his duties remained similar, his title became assistant to the president in 1957; another title change came in 1968 when he became vice president for administrative affairs under Dr. Bangsberg. And, as noted, Mr. Glas became the acting president of BSC until Dr. Robert Decker was named president in September of 1968, after which Mr. Glas then returned to his position as vice president for administrative affairs. After 36 years of service to the school, he retired on September 30, 1975. Less than a year later, he died of heart failure on August 4, 1976.[26]

AGITATION MURMURS

Glas took office in unsettling times, and the subsequent year would be more unsettling than the previous one. This unnerving situation was true both on college campuses and the national level, the latter affecting the former. Washington, D.C., began to change more campuses than administration officials on all levels ever planned or wanted. By late '67 campus teach-ins had given way to pointed angry questioning, which in turn had given way to open protests. This evolving pattern was followed at Bemidji State, as seen in issues of the Northern Student in the months immediately following Bangsberg's death. To illustrate, two students had returned from participating in a peace march in New York City and wrote about their exciting experiences at some length, exhorting others to join the cause of stopping the war in Vietnam. One headline summarized a slowly changing BSC student attitude, "Voices from Underground: Students Demand Right to Think and Learn in Atmosphere of Freedom." (May 4, 1967; p. 3). The same page had two different student articles, both writers questioning the BSC dormitory policies in general and specifically mandatory hours for women but not for men, something found objectionable and cited as another case of double standards on campus. In

---

26) Information on John Glas supplied by his widow, Elfrida Glas, in a letter to the author dated January 23, 1993; letter in author's files. The Glases had three sons, John, Robert, and Richard, all of whom graduated from Bemidji State, and all were married as of this writing, 1994. Elfrida Glas had six grandchildren at the time she wrote her letter. Mrs. Glas worked part-time at the College and in 1960 she became the manager of the Beaver Bookstore. She retired in 1977 and lives in her home on Birch Lane, located directly across the street from the Education-Arts Building. Mrs. Glas continues being active in community and United Methodist Church work. Her husband had organized the Wesley Foundation Chapter at Bemidji State in 1947.

this time of questioning and cynicism, the Student editor wrote to defend the school newspaper, saying there was no need for an underground newspaper at Bemidji State; instead, the Student would be eager to take up the many causes coming forward. And issues did come forward in print and were viewed as positive. "Growing Student Dissent Can be Healthy Sign" preceded students' words to elaborate on that assertion, and when dismissal of student views was perceived, columnist Norm Hesseldahl fired back on May 11, 1967, p. 2, "The administration seems to doubt the seriousness of intent of the 'rebels' on campus." They certainly had definite changes in mind, both small and big. Although the cause and effect may be tangential, the faculty voted approval that spring of an ongoing student request to take classes on a pass or no-pass basis. But students had more substantive changes in mind than P/NP.

NEW SCHOOL YEAR, NEW "EVERYTHING"
In the fall start-up week of 1967, the first Northern Student showed Mr. Glas welcoming BSC's 4,000th student, Susan Bigelow, a transfer from Hibbing Junior College. That figure doubled the enrollment number of just five years before. This first issue included several warm welcoming letters, but the one from weekly student columnist James Conner laid out a different school year agenda, "This first column contains both a plea and a warning—a plea to all the campus 'rebels' to get organized; a warning that if they don't, this year's 'rebellion' will crumble from lack of solidarity like an elderly sand castle." His message for the need for organized and overt action on specific issues continued in his columns the rest of that school year. To add a journalistic contribution to issues and answers, the Student that fall began a column called "The Hot Seat," in which each week one faculty member was asked to reply in writing to a question posed by the editorial board. It allowed for far-ranging questions and answers, with the editor writing early on that "it appears as if the student power movement is in earnest." The newspaper editors were certainly in earnest about having a permanent BSC president named. This position was reflected in a variety of ways, including a picture of an office with just a paper-free desk and an empty chair; the caption, "The President's Chair . . . how much longer?" Incidents like student demonstrators meeting Governor Harold LeVander at the Bemidji airport, with signs asking the governor to speed the process of presidential selection, did no good other than to embarrass the other students there who welcomed LeVander as the major speaker at campus Political Emphasis Week. LeVander's near-dismissal of the sign-carriers did not deter the pro-president organizers who staged what became BSC's first "student protest demonstration." On November 9, 1967, "Some 50 students assembled outside Memorial Hall to hear Al Brusewitz, John Mattson, Norm Hesseldahl, and other speakers urge quicker action in hiring a new president for BSC" (Northern Student, November 16, 1967, p. 1). "A number of onlookers indulged in heckling the speakers, both from an ideological standpoint and on a

personal basis." The news article was written by student Hugh Bishop, who concluded, "The demonstration drew a number of faculty and administration onlookers, and there was somewhat more of an air of carnival than seriousness about the demonstration." Whatever it was or wasn't, it came to naught as far as imminent action on a new president.

YET "NORMALITY" CONTINUES

While it is things like drug use, student protests, angry letters and unnerving columnists which gained attention both at the time and later, all of the above are the minority news items in the student newspapers in the fall quarter of the '67-'68 school year. The school year began routinely: Freshmen came for orientation week, wore their green beanies and elected their Beanie King and

Native American Artifacts on Display in Sanford Hall
"Of all the Indians in Minnesota . . . to go to college, almost half have gone to BSU."

Queen (Carol Clarke and John Gill). Beaver athletics never faltered in inspiring student enthusiasm, and the homecoming queen contest was lively. (Sue Pooch won.) The on-campus building programs then in progress seemed carefully observed, whether it be the new student union or another dorm or the hockey arena or a new language laboratory going into Deputy Hall. Students appeared more upset by the perennial bugaboos of parking and bookstore prices and a disappointing football season than national concerns, let alone international issues like the Vietnam War, which was being protested in other colleges nationwide. At this stage not only did BSC students not protest the war but large numbers supported it. In the Northern Student there were several student-written pro-draft, and pro-Vietnam war letters, such as Al Nohner's comments, summarized in the headline, "U.S Must Challenge Commie Threat." As to student use of drugs, Leonora Dahle added a column on what this then-new drug LSD could do to any fool who tried it. Part of what kept the major issues simple was that most students did not spend a lot of time examining them. But by the quarter's end, an examination of national issues would be forced on anyone reading the student newspapers. Strong positions became clearly stated regularly from the front page to the back sports pages. Even sports became political.

"NORMALITY" NO LONGER "NORMAL"
        "Political Pot Starts to Boil" was a headline giving a good summary of the BSC campus as the year 1968 approached. Registrar Ed Aalberts provided in print the requested information on deferments from military service. Three BSU students (Smith Treuer, Walter Reed and Alan Goldknopf) opened a coffee house, a place less to drink coffee than to discuss issues, and they called it "The Back Door." A "Students' Rights Bill" was authored and sent before the student senate for ratification, and when that came through, the dorm girls were congratulated on "getting out of their cages." Alumni like Perry Patterson ('48) wrote to praise an editorial called "Thou Shalt Not Kill." In a "Hot-Seat" column, strong-willed, articulate history prof Jack Allen wrote, "I must confess at the outset to having crystallized my views on Vietnam almost to the point of dogmatism. I fully believe that we have blundered into a regional struggle beyond our national interests." He went on to call for a withdrawal of American troops from Vietnam. Despite the debates coming forward and heating up, Lucy Allebach saw insufficient student responses, her letter to the editor was headlined, "Two Wars Go On But They Do Not Upset the Calm BSC Ivory Tower." David Czarnecki, president of the campus GOP, agreed. He wrote to the state chairman, who had apparently asked for the results of a questionnaire on BSC student activism. Czarnecki sent a copy of his letter to the Northern Student, which reprinted it, including the last words of the opening sentence, "You must remember that the people who were exposed to it [the questionnaire] attend Bemidji State College, the apathetic college to the north."

BUT THE TIMES THEY WERE (really!) A'CHANGIN'
        In what was to be a neutral, non-Dove/Hawk response to Vietnam, the dorm council sponsored a "Vietnam Mail Drive" in December of '67, asking people simply to write letters or cards with only the address of "the men in Vietnam." But

neutrality was set aside by the Pine Hall prexy, Bob Montesano, "It's a good way for the people at home to play their part in this tragic war." Tiny articles like the following hardly stifled campus emotions: "Army Specialist 4, John P. Kurtz, a spring graduate of BSC, was listed as killed in action in Vietnam. Kurtz, who came from rural Argyle, had been previously listed as missing in action." (Dec. 7, 1967, p.1) Editor Hesseldahl called for the removal of Selective Service Director Lewis B. Hershey, who had issued a directive stating that draft-law protesters should be reclassified and drafted into the military. Student Elizabeth (Mrs. Ivan) Rogers wrote at great length on the virtues of civil disobedience as becoming "a proper tool of protest." And on and on as Bemidji State moved into the most tumultuous year of the decade, 1968.

1968 REMEMBERED

Rarely have there been headlines as big or as black as those of 1968. It was a wrenching, turning point year. Most people who lived through 1968 can remember it all too vividly, can still see the images of shock and mayhem and still feel the pervading sense that every societal nerve had been laid open to the icy chill of tragedy and the burning rage of denial and despair. In a year marked by political surprise, dissent and violence, Martin Luther King, Jr. and Robert Kennedy were assassinated; Russia invaded Czechoslovakia; President Lyndon Johnson was driven out of office as much as he elected to bow out. Richard Nixon won the presidential election by a narrow margin, campaigning on behalf of "the silent majority," the middle class whites who felt betrayed by liberals, threatened by blacks, and outraged by student protesters.

Around the world, students rebelled openly and protested violently. In Vietnam a partial bombing halt went into effect, clearing the way for the first slow steps to the negotiating table, but there was little mood for negotiating among sullen groups girding for battle on the home front. North Korea that year captured an American spy ship that got too close to land, the U.S.S. Pueblo, and months later the crew was returned, its captain disgraced. In Rome the pope decided to maintain the Catholic ban on birth control, triggering deep controversy within the church. But the revolution went on amid shocking decisions of Vatican I and II and III. The summer Olympics in Mexico City drew the largest gathering of athletes in history; the U.S. team returned home with nearly 100 gold medals, but the burning image remained of two black Americans giving the black-power salute as they received their medals while the band played The Star Spangled Banner. In Greece, to the dismay of many Americans, Jacqueline Kennedy married millionaire Aristotle Onassis.

The waves that were rising in 1967 crashed in 1968. The year seemed to lurch from one shock to the next, starting with the January Tet offensive in Vietnam which told the world that that inglorious war would not be ending anytime soon, and maybe not at all, considering the way it had been fought. What to do? Escalate?

Get out? The president said, "Stay," but then he got out of the presidency as the social fabric unraveled around him. Years later the late Abbie Hoffman, once "Mr. Hippie," was quoted as saying with characteristic sarcasm, "Yes, 1968 was a wonderful year. They don't make years like that any more." To which most Americans would add, "Thank God."

The year 1968 defies easy categorization. It was a culmination of the '60s rebellion—and yet the violence and cultural revolution persisted for years after. It was the end of eight years of Democratic presidents—yet their Republican successors continued some social and economic policies that seemed liberal 30 years later.

There were signal achievements in science. In medicine, surgeons in several countries successfully performed transplants of human hearts. And also came one of history's greatest adventures, the virtually flawless round trip to the moon by Apollo 8 astronauts. Upon their return, the men received a pile of letters, one particularly remembered for its message, "Many thanks. You saved 1968."[27]

A CIVILIZED RESPONSE

Somehow all campus members struggled through the rest of the '68 school year in a civilized manner, at least compared to some other campuses where disruption and violence became the fashion of the times. And yet there was an air of tension on the Bemidji campus as the debates—primarily on the Vietnam war— swirled throughout the school and made their impact, both visible and invisible, both loudly and quietly.[28] A few profs deliberately digressed daily from their course outlines to use the classroom as a forum to spout and sputter; a few other profs absolutely refused to permit the subject of Vietnam to be uttered in their privileged sanctuaries. However, lest anyone foolishly suggest this issue was far away and less than relevant, the Northern Student reported in January yet another former BSC war casualty: PFC William Larcher of Eveleth was killed in Vietnam.

Public forums on Vietnam occurred almost weekly, with scheduled talks finding large and interested and sometimes hostile audiences, depending on the listeners' Dove/Hawk penchants. Some faculty members jumped into the fray, with, for example, Fulton Gallagher stepping away from his music program to present a public talk he called "Pro Vietnam." And from the same platform the

---

27) For an added glimpse into the pop culture of that cataclysmic year, there are the top songs of 1968: "Hey Jude," Beatles; "I Heard It Through the Grapevine," Marvin Gay; "Love is Blue," Paul Mauriat; "Love Child," Diana Ross and the Supremes; "Honey," Bobby Goldsboro; "Sittin' on the Dock of the Bay," Otis Redding; "This Guy's in Love With You," Herb Albert; and "Woman, Woman," Gary Puckett and the Union Gap. The 10 highest-grossing movies of the year were: The Graduate, Funny Girl, 2001: A Space Odyssey, Guess Who's Coming to Dinner?, The Odd Couple, Bullitt, Romeo and Juliet, Oliver, Planet of the Apes, and Rosemary's Baby. There are also the top selling books: (fiction) Airport, Couples, The Salsburg Connection, A Small Town in Germany, Testimony of Two Men; (non fiction) Better Homes and Gardens New Cook Book, The Random House Dictionary, Listen to the Warm, Between Parent and Child, and Lonesome Cities. And lastly, the top TV hits of the 1967-68 season: The Andy Griffith Show, The Lucy Show, Gomer Pyle, Gunsmoke, Family Affair, Bonanza, The Red Skelton Hour, The Dean Martin Show, The Jackie Gleason Show, and Saturday Night at the Movies.

28) On a personal note, there was more than tension in the air when during one class period a male student said very loudly in my class, "I believe that any American soldier in Vietnam is nothing more than a berserk baby-killer," which line was met even more loudly by a girl from the back of the room who shouted, "My brother is in Vietnam right now defending his country for the likes of yellow-bellies like you!" From there the argument escalated both in volume and numbers, with students virtually erupting with vituperation. Only chairs, tables—and luck—kept the verbal fracas from turning physical at that point. By class time end, however, both sides returned to a position of quiet sullenness. Similar scenes were too common at BSC during that fragile time period when we were all on edge.

following week came philosophy prof Al Fenske on "Conscientious Objectors." Letters to the editor alternated between pro- and anti-war positions; these included some sarcastic letters from former BSC students who were then in military service. The Student editor at times tried to suggest impartiality by running a series of contrasting positions from figures like J. Edgar Hoover of the FBI and Minnesota

Student Protest Group 'Pledge Allegiance' Outside City Hall
"Public forums on Vietnam occurred almost weekly . . . and large audiences."

Senator Eugene McCarthy. Yet both the number and nature of articles in the Student made clear the editor's point of view: definitely anti-Vietnam War. Samples of the latter can be seen in just the headlines of selected articles and editorials: "Americans Should Be Getting Ready to Accept Vietnam Effort as Doomed"; "Morality Begins Where the Gun Ends, or See You in Toronto"; "Napalm is a Political Product"; "Reed College Grads Resist U.S. Draft"; "Bemidji Group Aids McCarthy in Wisconsin." There was also a cartoon of sorts portraying a military man bending over a little boy and asking him, "And what do you want to be if you grow up?" Thank goodness there were also diversions.

A SIGN OF THE TIMES . . . OR COMIC RELIEF?

Compared to the cramped and almost dingy union quarters in the basement of Sanford Hall, the new union was, in the slang of the day, "somethin' else again, y'know?" Plush carpets, soft lounge chairs, warm davenports, piped-in music, gentle lighting, two private dining rooms, two private meeting rooms, along with a U-shaped line of the expected dozens of chairs and tables going all the way around the building. And then that building was only half finished because by 1972 the completed union would contain two cafeterias, a dining facility to serve 500 guests, more lounges, a variety store, a large ballroom, game rooms—pool and ping-pong—and for those seeking either an escape from higher wisdom or finding transcendental messages from the rolling steel balls, a long row of pinball machines.

Although no reserved signs were placed on any tables or chairs, portions of the union became inhabited by certain like-minded or sometimes "geographic" groups. For example, there were "The Rangers," the students from the Minnesota Iron Range towns, whose seating area was appropriately known as "The Rangers' Cage." A distinctive group, these Rangers. In their speech pattern, some of them still had a tendency to substitute "d's" for the "th" sound, thus ending up with "Dat" rather than ("dan") "that." They could spoof themselves in this area, with a popular T-shirt reading "I'm From Da Raynch." As to appearance, the Rangers dressed conservatively, which middle-America would label "decent." Though they might wear jeans, both their pants and shirts—and hair—were neat and clean, as were

A Beaver Union Scene when Located in the Basement of Sanford
"Time was when everyone went to the union every day."

their politics: very mid-American.

There was another area where the recent Bemidji High School grads congregated. And naturally the recently formed fraternities and sororities had their niches picked out. Even the brown-baggers had a section to call "home." As suggested, no group was assigned any certain spot, but both herd instinct and conditioned response found each special group always going to its place. Then there were the hippies. In contrast to the decent-appearing Rangers and the semi-decent looking frats, there was that one section of the union known as "Hippie Heaven," where Bemidji State's alleged hippies hung out. What made them stand out was, of course, their appearance which was different, to say the least. Ragged clothes, dirty clothes, pure grunge. Both the men and the women wore earrings and necklaces and beads and flowers and floppy hats and big

work boots and open-toed sandals in warm weather when not barefoot. In their location they mingled and reveled happily in their maudlin unhappiness, and in just being there they put on a show for the rest of the school. Indeed, the Rangers would sometimes escort visitors from their own area over to the hippie section, just to show them, as one lad phrased it, "the asylum rejects," or as another observed, "It's like taking your company to the zoo."

Upstairs in the C.V. Hobson Union
"Since World War II, 'the union' has changed even more than 'the dorms'."

HIPPIE HEAVEN
BY THE LAKESHORE

The term "hippie" had first been used in 1965, when a newspaper man coined the term. The word was briefly used interchangeably with "beatnik" before the latter word became relegated to 1950s disaffected youth. The earliest hippie mecca was the Haight-Ashbury district of San Francisco, and apparently the first hippies there were the genuine flower people who honestly eschewed the old styles of middle-class culture and mores, asking only to be left alone to live as they wanted, free from the rat race of materialistically-minded, war-loving America; who really believed in "love power" and sharing; who rejected all violence and war, and who might be naive but at least were honest in living their convictions. Too soon the once-beloved "Haight" became infiltrated with all manner of undesirables, most of whom pushed the first massive use of drugs, and soon hippies became defined as "no more than beats plus dope," as certainly drugs influenced their culture. Dr. Timothy Leary, a fired former Harvard psychologist, declared himself the high priest of a drug religion and advised all to "turn on, tune in, and drop out." Acid, acid-rock, psychedelic posters, and festivals of hedonistic indulgence in music and drugs soon characterized a massive number of disaffiliated young people. The new culture, soon called "the counter-culture," commercialized itself rapidly and extensively and influenced young people throughout the nation, including some at Bemidji State College who scrounged around in their Hippie Heaven. The question asked then and later by outsiders was whether the Heaven students were indeed hippies, or were they only playing at it? Some observers believed they were playing a pathetic game of charades, which required only the surface acts of breaking the stereotypes of lifestyle, throwing off the pegged-pants, the blazer sports coats, the rep ties and button-down collars of Gant shirts, the penny loafers, all so popular just five years before. All had to conform in their non-conformity (a real non-conformist would have had a crew cut and not grown his hair down to his belly button). Not to dress sloppy, not to have unkempt long hair, not to wear beads and ragged jeans, not to love Joan Baez and Abbie Hoffman and Eldridge Cleaver would have put them out of their realm and thus not "groovy."

Moreover, as alleged white liberals, BSC hippies had convinced themselves that the way to relate and identify with all the blacks in America was to "talk black." Thus they went around "hey-manning" each other, all to the amusement and embarrassment of their intended brothers. At Bemidji State that meant all ten of them, mostly recruited athletes, all of whom avoided the bizarre-looking actors and actresses in Hippie Heaven. In an active political sense, however, the Bemidji hippie contingent did very little, if anything, unless some virtue can be noted in their abilities to shout obscenities, play guitars, broadcast the merits of Bugle wine, and occasionally scribble messages on lavatory walls. A few of these students were very bright, however (almost as bright as they thought they were), but they posed virtually no threat to school officials. In their chosen offbeat manners and mannerisms, they were more amusing than dangerous.[29]

THE RETURN OF THE ROUTINE

It was not all hippie-ville digression nor tensions of Vietnam talk, of course, in the winter and spring of 1968 on the BSC campus. A certain semblance of both order and normality came through loud and clear and was duly noted and appreciated. Amid the tough talk of letters to the editors and tougher editorial responses and tougher-yet columnists who ground out weekly polemics, the school newspaper revealed many more articles, features and pictures on what was essentially life-at-Bemidji-State. For example, all enjoyed the grand opening of the new student union; most enjoyed a little later the opening of the new field house and hockey arena; and many enjoyed the production on campus of The Mikado, directed by the aforementioned Gallagher. The school's brand new radio station, KBSC, finally got on the air, thanks especially to the two-year efforts of a dorm radio club headed by student technician-whizkid, Kris Geisen. Another successful Paul Bunyan Week came and went and was generally appreciated, especially the capstone concert by the then well-known New Christy Minstrels. Most concerts, naturally, were provided by individuals and groups from the College, whether a single senior recital by a scared music major or a massive College-community performance of Mozart's Requiem. However, an outside group of major prominence came to Bemidji that '68 spring, the Philadelphia Chamber Orchestra. Hence in an

---

29) One young man from Hippie Heaven did mimeograph on a half sheet of paper the formula for making pipebombs, and these were distributed all over campus, with copies lying on window sills and on classroom desks and union tables. It concerned this writer enough to find out the name of the person and go to the Records Office to check on his background. There I learned that he was from Blackduck, and there the matter was dropped, because I believed no true revolutionary bomber could come out of Blackduck.

Pres. Robert Decker Gives Talk and Awards at Homecoming
"His style was low-key . . . he kept his cool . . . he kept the lid on . . . unflappable."

ongoing broad cultural sense—athletics, music, art, literature, dance, speakers, indoor and outdoor fun (and keggers)—it was a proper, routine school year.

AN IMPROPER YEAR OF "ACTING ADMINISTRATORS"

Not routine was the shake-up in the school's administration. The administrative #2 position, the dean of instruction, Dr. Judson P. Martin announced his resignation after 22 years at Bemidji State. This action did not come as a big surprise. For reasons of his own—and all faculty had their reasons for his reasons—Martin chose to accept a dean's position in Missouri starting in April, 1968. It left the school with yet one more acting administrator, who joined the crowd: Acting president, acting academic dean, acting associate academic dean, acting chancellor of the State College System. Little wonder that Bemidji State partisans chafed at this school-on-hold and demanded action. Real action finally began with the State College Board's naming Dr. G. Theodore Mitau, chair of the political science department at Macalester College, as chancellor of the State College System. Mitau, at age 47, began his duties on July 15, 1968, and he moved into fast-forward to affect the entire System. In the next six years Mitau would make changes that would definitely alter the entire System, starting with his "putting the State Colleges on the map!" Mitau was a high profile figure who demanded attention and got attention and he did indeed awaken the entire state population to an awareness of the state's colleges. Noise and theatrics seemed to accompany the man everywhere. A small man physically, he talked dynamically even in small conversational settings, and on a speaker's platform—where it appeared he loved to be—his oratorical style was filled with gusto and rhetorical flourishes, whether bouncing up and down on his toes or waving his arms dramatically. People listened.

Legislators listened, too; better yet, they reacted and acted with imposing financial figures for a state schooling system that was leaving behind it the teachers college syndrome. The once-separate six State Colleges became under Mitau one large, ever-growing system to be noted and reckoned with—and funded as the fastest-growing institution in the state.[30]

A NEW PRESIDENT AGAIN

Bemidji State College received the news of the appointment of a new president one year, three weeks and two days after the death of Bangsberg. The Board announced on April 15, 1968, the appointment of Dr. Robert D. Decker, St. Paul, his position to begin at Bemidji State on September 1. Decker, age 45 at the time of his presidential appointment, had first come to Minnesota from Texas in 1966 to become assistant chancellor of the Minnesota State College System, working with his chancellor friend and fellow Texan, J. Bevington Reed. When Reed resigned and returned to Texas in May of 1967, Decker became the acting chancellor and held that position until the aforementioned Mitau began as chancellor July 15, 1968.[31]

ROBERT DAVID DECKER

Robert Decker was born in Hays County, Texas, November 12, 1922, the son of a county judge and rancher. In 1940 he graduated as valedictorian of his class from Kyle High School where he was also class president, president of the student council, president of the Future Farmers of America and captain of the football and track teams. Prior to entering military service during World War II, he attended Southwest Texas State College at San Marcos where he completed 87 semester hours while continuing his interest in both academic and athletic areas. He enlisted in the Army as a private and saw service in the Pacific theater of operations, including the Philippines and Japan. At war's end he was released as a first lieutenant. He continued his education after the war and received his B.S. degree in 1948 from Texas A&M. He returned to San Marcos where he was agriculture teacher for the Hays County Veterans' Vocational School for one year, and from

30) Mitau's flamboyant style, of course, did not appeal to all. The appellation of "Napoleonic" was often applied to the man and he would be seen as a chancellor as much interested in promoting Mitau as "his Colleges." He became well-known on all campuses for his frequent visits which he called "listen and learn" sessions, but to those who participated, Mitau listened little and learned nothing; he did all the talking. Although somewhat overstated, there was some truth to the assertion that Mitau reduced the role of all the campus presidents, aggrandizing power for himself in St. Paul. Yet if one seeks a special accomplishment of the man, it would be his success in the planning and eventual starting of a separate new State College in 1972, Metropolitan State College, headquartered in St. Paul, a totally different kind of school envisioned and fashioned by Mitau. He served as chancellor from 1968 to 1976; he died of cancer in 1979.
31) Unlike the usual Board pattern of selecting a president, that is only after a national search, the weeding down of candidates to a "workable number," and the interviews with some half dozen finalists before the final choice is made, the Board in this case believed they had the right choice right there in their office. Although BSC faculty eyebrows may have been raised at this different process, no hackles were raised and there was no public negative faculty response to the way in which Decker was chosen. Yet not all were happy with how it was done. By coincidence, at the same time Decker was made president of Bemidji State, the Board named Dr. Roland Dille as the president of Moorhead State, the latter continuing as president until his retirement in 1994. At the same time that Decker, Dille and Mitau began their offices, the College System had enrollments of some 33,000 students (BSC had 5,082 students that fall of '68), a total faculty of 1,100, and a total biennial budget of $100,000,000. Twenty-five years later the students and faculty numbers would almost double while the budget figure would be nearly tripled. The System allocation for 1993 was $282,874,558 but dropped to $277,721,578 for 1994.

1949 to 1955, he was a vo-ag instructor at San Marcos High School. He received his master of education in agricultural education from Texas A&M in 1954, and from 1955 until 1957 he worked as a research assistant for A&M at its Ag Experiment Station. From 1957 until 1959 he was assistant professor of agricultural economics at Sul Ross State College, Alpine, Texas.

In 1958 Decker received his doctor of philosophy degree in agricultural economics from Texas A&M. He remained at Sul Ross State until 1961 as associate professor of ag economics and economics before he became registrar. In 1961 he moved to Odessa State College, Odessa, Texas, where he was dean of admissions and registrar until he came to Minnesota in 1966, as assistant chancellor, then acting chancellor of the Minnesota State College System, the position held at the time of his selection as president of Bemidji State. At the time he moved to Bemidji, he and his wife Jacqueline had three children: David, a high school senior; Lynn, a high school junior; and Jack, a third grader.[32]

THE RIGHT PERSON FOR THE "WRONG TIMES"

Bemidji State from its beginnings has benefited from hiring the right president for that particular time period when a certain type of person was needed. Such was the case again with the arrival of President Decker in 1968 at a time period nationally on campuses that would have to be labeled, at best, convulsive. He became president during turbulent times, politically, socially, and economically. Student activism throughout the country had moved from questioning agitation to angry mob violence that literally found students taking over presidential offices by force, as witnessed at both Columbia and Cornell Universities. Although overthrow was hardly the situation at Bemidji State, nevertheless the ongoing student prodding and poking and general campus nervousness and frustration required a solid president, and Bemidji State had it in Robert Decker. He was unflappable. Mr. Calm. Mr. Rational. Mr. Fair. Whatever he may have been like on the inside was not visible; people saw only the outside, and hence publicly he portrayed without doubt that he at all times was totally in control, period. Or, in the slang-line of a student who watched him in the middle of a mild student demonstration, "That Texan is one cool dude." As to town-gown relationships, he felt strongly about this necessity and worked consistently to court townspeople and present himself as a president far removed from alleged "ivory tower irrelevance." He stroked, he schmoozed, he smoothed the ruffled feathers of an uptight community. The fact that he was still an active lieutenant colonel in the National Guard remained a notable fact for the greater community to observe. Yet his style was low-key; his

32) Information on Dr. Decker's background taken from the brochure at his inauguration, April 15, 1969. In his role as assistant chancellor, he was primarily responsible for curriculum studies, administrative organization of the six colleges, budgeting, and preparation of materials for the legislature, and thus he was very familiar with the operation of the State Colleges in general before taking the Bemidji job. Of immense contrast over 25 years has been the growth of the Chancellor's Office that Decker left. He and Reed, along with two secretaries, were then the entire Chancellor's Office. Twenty-five years later, there were 56 regular employees, so many as to have taken over an entire office building floor. There's a staff annual salary of over three million dollars. The chancellor, by 1993, made $103,000, and he had vice chancellors for various areas, and these in turn have administrative assistants and all of the above have secretaries. Certain BSU faculty members in the past few years (and this author is one of them), who have had to reach into their own pockets to pay for their own test duplication and student handouts in classes, have been less than thrilled by the bloated bureaucracy at the Chancellor's Office.

southern accent remained softly articulated in both conversations and speeches;[33] he appeared unemotional if not stolid; nobody but nobody intimidated him, neither mouthy students nor self-appointed faculty groups meeting clandestinely for the purpose of firing top administrators. Control he had plenty of. The times called for plenty of it. He kept his cool. He kept the lid on.

If disgruntled students were not enough trouble, and equally disgusted townspeople to match demonstrating students whom they at best tolerated, Decker came at a downhill time for federal and state monies. The money water well was emptying. The financial windfalls of the Great Society that had enabled Bangsberg to start new programs and institutes and build new buildings had declined drastically by decade's end. The golden money years of seemingly unlimited funds for

The Green-and-White Can Become the Black-and-(Blue) Gray & Wet
"Athletics participation. Was it worth all the work? Yes, yes, by all means, yes."

education had ended; the federal and state cash cows were drying up. Both internal and external forces seemed to prevent Decker from making major additions to the school either in new buildings or in programs. He would inherit scaled down budgets that required tough decisions, policy-planning that did not please everyone, and he battled a chancellor who wanted power over all campuses. Decker had to scramble just to hold on to what he inherited but could not (would not?) keep exactly what he took over to administer; he made decisions that again changed Bemidji State and moved it yet in another direction.

---

33) Of minor annoyance to some locals was Decker's initial pronunciation of Bemidji, which for his first half year came out "Bee-mee-gee." He finally got it right.

EASIER TO GROW THAN TO DECLINE

New President Decker arrived when student numbers were high and getting even higher. He was at the helm for the school's all-time peak on campus enrollment year of 1971 when there were 4,865 enrolled; he was also there three years later when the numbers dropped to 4,187. He first watched students scurrying to find housing everywhere, anywhere, from sleeping in dormitory hallways and lounges to being put up in the ancient, pre-World War I rooms at the downtown Markham Hotel. Later he also saw his dorm occupancy rates fall embarrassingly below capacity.[34] He hired the all-time BSU peak faculty of 233 in 1970; his low year came in 1976 with 188 on the teaching staff (in his last year, 1979-80, the number had risen to 197). He hired, he fired; in the latter category came for the first time the breaking of tenure, and it was called retrenchment. Whatever its terminology, tenured faculty were let go. Tough decisions. Unpopular decisions. Ultimately, the president must make them, and in his 12 years (1968 to 1980), the buck stopped often at the president's desk.[35]

AN AFFABLE FIGURE

Decker came to his office with a wide background of educational experiences, ranging from coaching a college rodeo team for three years to sponsoring a married students club. Naturally the first issue of the <u>Northern Student</u> (September 17, 1968, p. 1) presented a favorable feature on the new president, with the article allowing lengthy quotes from him to reflect his views on the school and on how it should be run. Of interest to many was his line in which he stressed "the chain of command," which phrase became interpreted differently, to mean either the determination of administrative responsibility (who's to blame?) or that one should not try to see the president until one has gone through "the chain of command" first. Soon his affable manner deflected the allegation of an unreachable figure distancing himself from the College-community. Just the opposite. His door was open. Soon he and his charming wife Jackie were seen everywhere; they made it to all the campus concerts, plays, and athletic events; to seemingly every community church dinner; both became active in the Methodist Church; both joined an array of community organizations and served as officers;

34) As suggested in a previous chapter, to arrive at "the exact enrollment figure" at Bemidji State for any year becomes a near impossibility in that there are so many variables, starting with the definition of a student. Is someone taking one credit to be counted as a student? Is someone taking a night course in Roseau a Bemidji State student? Are summer school workshop students "students"? Both how and whom one counts depends on the counter, and hence figures can be fudged or misleading and even misused. 'Tis not an exact science.

35) In the halcyon days of faculty growth—when some Septembers 40 new faces came on staff—the availability of top-notch, dedicated teachers became limited, which is to suggest that amid the flock of generally fine faculty members employed, there were included some "ringers" who are at this writing long gone, but not forgotten. Thankfully their days on the roster were limited, usually to one year, but some did not last even that long (one quit after seven days, another after a month, another went home to the West at Christmas in her husband's new car, and never returned—nor did his car), to which must be added for all of them, "Thank goodness." Among this unique group were a transvestite; one or more psychopaths; a female/male; several alcoholics; a peeping-tom; a druggie; a kleptomaniac; a wonderful con man who flaunted his "Ph.D." even though he had never graduated from high school (who planned to run off with a local housewife, even though he left her standing in a supermarket fresh vegetables section, still waiting); another deceitful science teacher who got a reputation as a wonderful instructor, despite no college degree; a philanderer of such devotion to his sideline that he died of a heart attack in a most compromising situation while out of town on Bemidji State business, his BSC school car parked outside the motel door. In retrospect they're found amusing; at the time they were disasters.

The Baby Boomers in Beanies
"The 'war babies' had come of age. BSC got more than it could accommodate."

they constantly hosted student and faculty groups in their home. In the old-fashioned collegial-community sense, they as a couple represented the College wonderfully well. Although he never in manner or appearance "dropped his guard" in his role as president, there was still the kind of "old shoe" about him; jus' plain Bob, aw shucks, one of the "good ol' boys" who was so easy to like because he worked at it to be likable.[36]

President Decker needed all these attributes and more when he took over in what were troubled times, but throughout his 12 years as president, he was always the best example of civility. During this period of conflict, civility served him well in the decade of the Seventies.[37]

36) Of immense importance in maintaining the proper image of a college president was Dr. Decker's wife, Jackie. She reflected genuine kindness and goodness, concern and responsibility, decency and honor. With her southern accent (still there after 25 years in the frigid North Country), she seemed the quintessence of charm. A wonderful person, and so much appreciated and admired that when the new faculty committee was picked to select Dr. Decker's successor, the advice that the committee heard most often was "try to get a president with a wife just like Jackie."
37) In a letter dated November 1, 1993, from Dr. Decker to this author, he explained how and why he came to Minnesota in February, 1966, "I first came to Minnesota to join Dr. Bevington Reed as an assistant to the chancellor in the central office of the Minnesota State College System. This was a good position for me because Dr. Reed and I had both previously been employed at Sul Ross State University in Texas. Reed took this Minnesota position providing he could have an assistant in addition to others already in the central office. As he and I had worked together real well in Texas, he invited me to join him in Minnesota. Later he decided to return to Texas and I was the acting chancellor of the System. My desire, however, was for a position on a college campus. When Bemidji State had an opening for a president, I applied for the position and was fortunate to be selected. Having visited the campus a number of times previously, as well as having gotten to know a number of the fine people working there, especially John Glas, I was anxious to be selected. When the board offered me the position, I was anxious for our family to hurry and move to Bemidji." Letter in author's files.

PROLOGUE

The 1970s

O n the third day of the 1970s, the results were published of a Gallup poll in which Americans had been asked whom they admired most in their country. The winners were Richard Nixon followed closely by his vice president, Spiro Agnew. It was not a good time for prophets.

Each decade is given a catchy, descriptive tag, a sort of tidy packaging that journalists and some historians find irresistible to use, like the Roaring Twenties and the Gay Nineties—when the word "gay" had a connotation decidedly different from its connotation a century later. But the decade of the '70s evades easy characterization. First, too much of historical significance happened; then, later in the decade, little happened. The years, in retrospect, tumbled after one another with sometimes stunning changes of events, of tone and of mood, much of it negative; at decade's end, the tumbling changed to slow motion, some of the change now positive. Eventually one historian would entitle his book on the '70s Nothing Much Really Happened, which sweeping title would hardly be accepted by those persons who survived those years. In the '70s, Americans became aware of not only a changing world but a changing planet.[1] Much happened!

The nasty, divisive bitterness over Vietnam in the early '70s ended in part with the war's end in early '73, but what followed was profound shock at the spectacle of Watergate in '74 and the revelation that a U.S. president conspired in his own downfall and disgrace. Shocking and disillusioning. Americans became

1) One measure of a decade is the kind of books that people were reading at the time. The best selling books in the 1970s were (in non fiction): The Late Great Planet Earth, by Hal Lindsey and C.C. Carlson; Chariots of the Gods, Erich Von Daniken; Your Erroneous Zones, Wayne W. Dyer; The Joy of Sex, Alex Comfort; Future Shock, Alvin Toffler; The Sensuous Man, "M"; Roots, Alex Haley; If Life Is A Bowl of Cherries—What Am I Doing in the Pits? Erma Bombeck; and The Total Woman, Marabel Morgan. In fiction: The Godfather, Mario Puzo; The Exorcist, William Blatty; Jonathan Livingston Seagull, Richard Bach; Love Story, Erich Segal; Jaws, Peter Benchley; The Thorn Birds, Colleen McCullough; Rich Man, Poor Man, Irwin Shaw; The Other Side of Midnight, Sidney Sheldon; Centennial, James Michener.

300

enveloped in a deepening crisis of trust about their government, but enough hope, optimism and pride returned by 1976 so that the Bicentennial could be enjoyed, even if the country then had something never before or since experienced, both an unelected president and unelected vice president. Unsettling times. In the early 70s, school busing controversies rocked the country both in the North and South, and Roe v. Wade in '73 touched off an abortion controversy which has not subsided since that court ruling. And throughout the entire decade the costs of everything went up, up, up, soaring prices tripped by an Arab oil embargo and the alleged shortage of gasoline. The long lines of American drivers waiting to buy a couple of gallons of gas had not been seen since World War II. Much had indeed happened in the 1970s.[2] (But the Vikings lost the Superbowl again and again and again.)

In 1976 the nation elected a new president from the South, one whose born-again directness, his promise not to lie, and his emphasized non-association with U.S. Capitol politicians, seemed to make him the right person for those troubled times. But double-digit inflation continued each of his four years, keeping him from having four more. The good news: By 1977 the U.S.A. was not involved in any war anywhere. The bad news: The good news never diminished the lasting troubles of the decade, from energy crises to out-of-control inflation to anti-Americanism culminating with hyper-chauvinists in Iran seizing Americans as hostages and holding them for 444 days! In that decade Middle East nations altered the power balance of the world.

Relentlessly, Vietnam shredded American omnipotence, and Watergate scandals befouled Americans' trust in politicians. Unfairly, all elected officials became tarred, as indicated by another poll in 1975 which placed politicians only one step above used-car salesmen as persons whom one could trust. Optimism, like sufficient oil supplies, became an endangered species. Depressing. A lost war. Body bags. A dishonored president. A suffering planet. Suffering pocketbooks. Inflation picked everybody's pockets without mercy, and both husbands and wives went to work, not because they wanted to but because they both had to work to try to keep up with the escalating costs of survival.[3]

The old verities of life faded. Once-shocking announcements became banal: "The air quality today will be unacceptable because of the smog"; "The fish from Lake _____ are unfit to eat because of pollution"; "Another child pornography ring has been discovered"; "Interest rates for home mortgages are

---

2) There are those who argue that a decade ends every year, every minute, even; that assigning the word "decade" to the period between years that end in zero is arbitrary at best and a childish affectation at worst. Though this argument on the surface has validity, it does not work out that well when normally applied to a ten-year block of time. For example, is it a reasonable time framework to consider when someone says, "Remember that wonderful decade of 1965 to 1975?" No, not reasonable; it's closer to absurd. Thus in the context of general public understanding, it makes more sense to lump time periods together that start and end with zeros, arbitrariness notwithstanding.

3) One newspaper columnist addressed the question of "What Worries Americans Most in 1979?" Answer: "Money. For the first time in the 23 years I have been doing the column, people are worried about money on the gut level. Husbands write in heartsick that their wives have to work to help them support the family. Wives who have no desire to seek work outside the home, say that they must and that leads to a lot of problems with children and home management. Senior citizens write me that they cannot pay their rent and buy food and medicine on retirement incomes." The Star, September 11, 1979, p. 17. In 1974, less than half of married men had wives who worked separate jobs outside the home; by 1994, the numbers increased to over two-thirds.

18 percent"; "Jobs scarce for college graduates." Familiar lines, to the numbing point.

By mid-decade the youth uproar had subsided, yea, ended. "Rarely in history has publicized activism been replaced so rapidly by apparent apathy, student dissent by silence."⁴ Both the draft and the Vietnam war had ended and the young people returned to mainstream culture, including seeking the goals of the American Dream, but the dream had become harder to fulfill. The times were against them. Jobs were harder to find; homes were too expensive to buy. The young were marrying later—if the partners married at all—and divorcing earlier. The most important thing in their world was not We but Me. The Me Decade. The old days, the old ways were harder to find, as hard to find as the Boston Braves, who were either in Milwaukee or Atlanta. Their baseball gloves came from Taiwan. Change, change. Nothing holds still. Yesterday's solutions become today's problems. Yesterday's radical hairstyles of the '60s became mainstream cuts, which meant on the long side, so that the Beatles' bangs looked middle-America on Main Street bankers ten years later. Ho hum. Just a slight trim, please.

Institutions like Bemidji State remained wards of the state and were subject to the rollercoaster economics of the '70s. Minnesotans joined their fellow Americans in accepting the stark realization that there were hard limits not only to the riches of the state, but also to the viability of the entire planet. Unsettling, yet solutions were expected. After all, if the government could put a man on the moon, it should also be able to clean up the garbage piling up on the streets—and fix the ozone layer a little later. And how 'bout jobs? And the shrinking U.S. dollar? Disturbing. In this atmosphere, in this uncertainty, Bemidji State moved into the new decade under constant pressure to be relevant. A challenge. Conflicts of values were sharp. Lively times for level heads.

◆ ◆ ◆

RESHUFFLE TIME: "MUSICAL (DEPARTMENT) CHAIRS"

Each new president at Bemidji State inherits both an existing administrative and curriculum structure, along with the persons within those structures. Robert Decker followed the pattern of Bangsberg in initially accepting both the job titles and the people in the top administrative positions. Again like Bangsberg, he soon changed some of the division alignments, along with some of the division leaders whom he renamed "heads" instead of "chairmen," thus inadvertently allowing wags to raise the possibility that "heads will roll" if they fall out of favor.

Bemidji State moved into the decade of the 1970s with the following top administrators: president, Robert D. Decker; vice president for academic affairs, Richard E. Beitzel; vice president for administration (and the next year, 1971, executive vice president), John S. Glas; vice president for student affairs, Cletus J.

---

4) James Patterson, <u>America in the 20th Century: A History</u> (New York: Harcourt Brace Jovanich, Inc.), 1983, p. 462. Evidence of all American apathy can be seen in the fact that in the off-year elections of 1974, barely 45 percent exercised the right to vote.

Kemper (Raymond P. Carlson, former dean of students since 1952, shifted into institutional research and two years later would have the title of vice president for external affairs, research, and development); registrar, Edwin J. Aalberts; dean of graduate studies, William A. Sellon.

The academic programs at Bemidji State under Decker continued to be administered under seven divisions, although the new president ended the division of social sciences and shifted those departments—along with a few other departments from other divisions—into different divisions. (Musical academic chairs, the rearranging pleasing some and irritating others who did not wish to be sent to such-and-such division.) While department chairpersons were elected for specific terms by department members, division heads were appointed by the president and served in that capacity at the pleasure of the president. Each division head was responsible to the vice president for academic affairs, and the following were the 1970 divisions and their heads: behavioral science, Lewis J. Downing; business and industry, John Warford; education, John Yourd; fine arts, Ronald Gearman; health, physical education and recreation, Victor Weber; humanities, Myron Swanson; and science and mathematics, Evan Hazard. In the next 10 years there were a few changes of heads, of course, along with minor realignments of division structures, but essentially Decker stayed with the above layout and basic "team" for his entire 12-year administration. Other top administrative staff leaders under Decker included: Lester Mattison, director of libraries; James McMahon, director of information services; Donald Dyrhaug, director of counseling; Robert Frazey, director of financial aids; John Brady, director of placement; Frank Borelli, director of college union; Donald Churchill, director of student teaching; Ernest Plath, director of elementary education; Gerald Nelson, Laboratory School principal; Donald Stubbins, director of field services; Alden Lorents, director of data processing; Rick Maynard, manager of residence halls; and Randolph Nyquist, business manager.[5]

THE GOAL: BUILDING A TRUE ACADEMIC COMMUNITY

All friends of Bemidji State have hoped at all times that all persons connected with the institution hold a true sense of academic community, that they collectively care for the goals and mission of the school. Friends hope for a genuinely-felt personal interaction of all faculty and staff members, with this sense of others in this shared role leading only to the greater good of the school. Collegiality in the best sense.

To achieve such a spirit of community is admirable; it may also be impossible. Certainly it cannot come via fiat or decree from the president or any of his top administrators. True community in the best sense is a gift; it is either there or it isn't there, and if it's there, it comes as a side effect of the entire operation.

5) Many long-term faculty members retired that decade. In alphabetical order: Ed Aalberts, 1978; Marie Bishop, 1976; John Brady, 1975; Arno Buntrock, 1978; Art Charvat, 1978; Bertha Christianson, 1973; Don Churchill, 1978; Harold Fleming, 1971; Ronald Gearman, 1977; Harold Hagg, 1976; Hazel Hogenson, 1974; Myrtie Hunt, 1976; Arloene James, 1979; Les Mattison, 1978; Robert Naegler, 1978; Alice Nesvold, 1972; Harold Peters, 1975; Phil Sauer, 1975; Carl Thompson, 1973. There were a number of tragic deaths: Sulo Havumaki died from cancer in 1970 at age 49. Deaths from heart conditions ended the lives of Russell Sawdey in 1978, James McMahon in 1975 at age 55, John Warford, 1977, at age 55, and Joe Free, in 1974, at age 63.

Community is built by many factors within the operation, the most important being a consensus on a fundamental sense of common values and an acknowledged common task or mission. (Sometimes community is built around a "common enemy," alas.)

Birdseye View of the Northern End of the Campus
"Returning students . . . never recognize the place."

Fundamental, common values are not easily agreed upon, however, making a sense of community at Bemidji State that much more difficult to attain. Add to the problem-formula the normally pleasant "problem" of large numerical growth in students, faculty and staff. The more there are, the harder it is to get acquainted and/or work closely with others. Insert to this equation new buildings and increased facilities. These shiny structures may be fine in themselves, but separate buildings make for more separation of personnel, with students and staff tending to spend most if not all of their time in one building where only a few specialized disciplines are located. By 1971, the BSU building boom had brought isolation and insulation to the long, narrow campus. 'Twas hard to mingle with others on spreadout acres when the coffee and the klatches are conveniently located in one building that is so easy not to leave during the day. Goodbye inclusion; hello exclusion. Make room for narrow compartmentalization, for department members who see only each other, for self-centered and self-serving agendas, for addressed frustrations vented to the same colleagues one deals with every day. So physically separated are some professors—for example, those in Bangsberg Hall contrasted with those "northerners in Blackduck," that is, the Physical Education Complex on the other end of the campus—that staff might not even meet, let alone get to know each other, even though they might have been there 10 or more years. It is hard to build community and collegiality under such conditions. (Not a few older faculty long for the proverbial "good old days.")

No college can be a utopian state, of course; indeed, some would argue that conflict and rivalry are good for a school. Departmental competition and a little tension produces smarter thinking and better products, leading overall to better quality and a better school, or so goes the reasoning. So fight, it's good for you. Darwin's thesis includes academic bloodletting, too, and the strong shall survive. 'Tis a cruel world out there . . . etc. However, college presidents seldom voice those arguments; they work to end arguments, to keep harmony, to build community and collegiality. Presidents have to look at the "Big Picture"; they'd rather not referee fighting faculty who have read too much Thomas Hobbes. Yet they must deal with, yea, ward off some vainglorious professors who get so caught up in orating their own self-importance and the importance of their particular department that it is a pity to compete with them by listening. The political world of academia very much exists at Bemidji State.[6]

GIVING CREDIT WHERE IT IS DUE

Some Bemidji State leaders have tried harder than others to promote this coveted sense of community. President Decker was one of them, along with his genial/crusty (depending on his mood at the moment) vice president, Richard Beitzel. An interesting pair. Although both men eventually suffered the slings and arrows of outrageous phone calls (plus snide letters, surreptitious faculty meetings; it goes with the territory), their severest critics must give both due credit for their ongoing efforts of 10-plus years to try to make the faculty and staff more of a community. For example, they sponsored and promoted annual faculty-and-spouse dinners held just prior to the fall start-up of classes, the dinners held at places like the Town and Country Club and Ruttgers Resort. Even if at times the gatherings appeared to be mob scenes (garrulous profs can raise noise levels akin to a riot in a parrot-house), even if name tags were secretly peeked at by many, the gatherings were still useful, fun, and they were always well attended. These dinners resulted in the desired goal of simple social mixing of diverse groups and individuals, if for a brief time period. In that short time all were reminded that they collectively were together at this school, and what they shared in common was the greater good for a greater school. Simplistic maybe, but it worked.

Mrs. Jackie Decker regularly hosted the Faculty Wives' social gatherings, including the annual tea. Again came the opportunity to meet new people and reinforce former friendships. Once again these were useful, fun and well attended, with the hostess being one with the rare gift of making all feel at ease and genuinely

---

6) When Woodrow Wilson—former history professor, former president of Princeton University—began his first run for a state office, he was met by the sneering admonition that he knew nothing about practical politics. To which attack Wilson replied that he knew all about politics, having learned and survived in the best of all political fire-storm training, faculty politics!

wanting to come back again. (This was in contrast to some previous administrators' wives, who reportedly used the name tag label less to meet the new people in attendance but more to "take roll" on who was/wasn't there for their stilted soirees.)

In the '70s, Decker and Beitzel (sometimes referred to behind their backs as the Tag Team Twins; each was always wrestling in the battle-of-the-bulge) began to sponsor a "stag night"—in the most benign definition of that loaded term—to which all the male members of the faculty were invited (usually at the Legion Club or the VFW meeting rooms), usually on a Friday night, for card games (bridge, whist, pinochle, a little poker), visiting, and lunching on cold-cuts. Interspersed all night long was free keg beer, compliments of the administration. The evening was neither genteel nor crude, and the party, such as it was, ended before midnight. This "night out" did allow once again profs from different disciplines to mix and mingle and swap yarns and tell lies and talk some shop, but always there was the "Big Picture" of the entire school, and everybody got to see everybody else in different togs (no ties allowed), in a different setting, and listen agreeably to pedants and bean-counters together laugh and kibitz and discuss something beyond their pinched and narrow subject matter specialties. It almost humanized everyone there. The "Head-Shed" administrators on "the hill" started the first one each year; then some other division members, feeling either guilt or thirst, picked it up and arranged for a second bash, and later third group, and on through the school year. And then *finis*. With the end of Decker's and Beitzel's administration in 1980, all of the above ended. Pity.[7]

1970
"AMERICA HAS NEVER BEEN DEFEATED IN THE PROUD 190 YEAR HISTORY OF THIS COUNTRY, AND WE SHALL NOT BE DEFEATED IN VIETNAM."
RICHARD NIXON,
April, 1970

"MY GOD! MY GOD! THEY'RE KILLING US!"
RON STEELE,
Kent State University freshman
May, 1970

No school year is easy for any college president, but the spring of 1970 will go down as perhaps the most difficult term for any college in the last half century. The above quotes display the emotions and polarization of the times. Nixon seemed

---

7) The obvious danger in lamenting the demise of these social functions is to idealize the past. Was it really that good a "community" in the 1970s? The broader question was raised in one of the lecture series sponsored by the Honors Council on April 29, 1993, when Dr. Charles Alberti, associate professor of education, delivered a paper on, "What Does It Mean to Build Community in the Academy?" Alberti was more sanguine about the present BSU community than were those listeners who had been at the school for many years, which brings back the original issue of idealizing the past. After Alberti's paper, discussion followed and the "old-timers" said it was a far better community atmosphere 25 years ago. The one area of agreement for the young and old faculty was to appreciate the ongoing civility on campus. Again, to contrast BSU with other campuses where faculty members hurl verbal barbs regularly and shout others down at times, Bemidji has represented the best in civil behavior.

intransigent on not getting American troops out of Vietnam; college students seemed equally unchanging in their opposition to the war, and the subsequent shooting deaths of four Kent State students by Ohio National Guardsmen blew the lid off campus restraints. Some campuses went nuts, like the University at Berkeley ("Berzerkley"). The immediate uproar found large numbers of colleges and universities stopping their schools' operations then and there; they immediately canceled the remaining spring term and canceled graduation exercises, too. Simply stop everything, shut the place down, and hope the great healer, time, would blow things over by the next fall.

A Small Portion of the 700 Students at the Kent State Service (1970)
"The Northern Student came out with a 16-page edition on 'The Kent State Massacre'."

Bemidji State canceled neither classes nor graduation. There was palpable campus tension and agitated, angry states of mind, primarily over the Vietnam War, but there were no negative student physical responses, no trashing of buildings nor rooms, no overturned cars set ablaze. The student senate requested that President Decker send a telegram to Nixon, condemning U.S. actions in Southeast Asia. He refused. His official administration response to the Kent State shootings—and American troops sent into Cambodia, which Nixon called an "incursion" and the students called an "invasion"—was to arrange for a memorial service for the victims of Kent State. Nothing else.[8]   (The Northern Student came out with a 16-

8) An estimated 700 students attended the outdoor service held on the steps and plaza in front of the union. There had been active agitation against the war all that school year, of course, the largest response being an earlier Moratorium March (to stop the war) of over 300 students and faculty, all wearing black armbands supplied by the student senate, to City Hall in downtown Bemidji, where they were met by City Manager Rudy Mikilich and former Mayor Fred Troppman. The latter, age 96, told the crowd that if he were younger, he would be marching with them himself. After a few brief statements, Mikilich thanked them for their non-violence and the crowd dispersed without incident. Mikilich had much earlier written an open letter to the people of Bemidji, pleading for calm; it was published in the Pioneer (October 15, 1969, p. 1), "On this day [of the Moratorium March] we have an opportunity to show our fellow Americans that Bemidji is an intelligent and concerned community. . . ."

page edition, much of it devoted to "the Kent State Massacre.")

DIVIDED FACULTY
Anti-war activism was not the sole domain of the students. The Bemidji State faculty divided themselves over the issue, but not proportionately. Although there may have been some/many/most(?) who opposed the war, only a very small number were willing to go public and sign their names under the following petition, "We, the undersigned members of the faculty at Bemidji State College, urge President Nixon to end our military action in Vietnam:
"Paul Pavich, Lorraine Cecil, Betty Rossi, Dolores Norman, Art Lee, Jack Allen, Michael Lamb, Martha Naegler, Betty Kvande, Al Fenske, Susan Erickson, Jean Leighton, Linda Grant, Ray Milowski, William Elliott, Ruth Stenerson, Arthur Charvat, Gerald Schnabel, P.S. Schievella, Wayne Mortenson, Harry B. Carrell Jr., Ken Henriques, Irvin Rotto, Charles Barnard, Kathryn Kruger, George Orton, Ronald Lycette, Piers Lewis, and William Lemly."[9]

A QUICK WASH JOB
Receiving the reputation for the most violent of student organizations against the Vietnam War was S.D.S., Students for a Democratic Society, which group had a sub-group calling themselves The Weathermen, made infamous by their "Days of Rage" in Chicago in 1969. Another sign of the times, literally, was anti-war graffiti, i.e., crude, homemade "signs" usually painted on walls, or any open spot with room to declare some brief statement. Graffiti can and often does stay there "forever," until it either wears away on its own or until some janitor finally gets around to removing it. One morning at Bemidji State in the spring of 1970, a new, spray-painted message appeared on the corridor wall outside the library; it read, "B.S.C. NEEDS S.D.S." By noon the message had been removed. The only semi-organized group B.S.C. did have that spring was SMAC, Students for a More Active Campus, with their leadership found also on the staff of the Northern Student (which had incorporated a peace dove to its logo). If nothing else, it contributed to interesting if didactic reading, the Student being the ongoing public forum for screaming debates.

RECOGNITION AND APPROVAL
That 1970 spring term was packed with turmoil and controversy on Bemidji's campus, but the overt reactions of the students to the fast-breaking world events was essentially modest and totally law abiding, in notable contrast to other communities and campuses across the state and nation where the social warp was ripped apart. This important fact regarding students' good sense was not lost upon

---

9) Signing petitions of such a controversial nature makes signers find out who their friends are—or were. The war brought out a depth of feeling that shook the foundations of higher learning at Bemidji State. Civility was sorely tested almost every day, with faculty deliberately avoiding each other, lest there be a flareup or worse. Of some interest, whatever it means, five of the above names were from the history department. On a personal level, I wrote a long novel in 1980 based on the events at Bemidji State during that gut-wrenching 1969-1970 school year and called it Jackpine Savage. It was "faction," that is facts wrapped in a fictional style. It somehow never made the New York Times best seller list; after three printings, it was discontinued.

the wider Bemidji community. As the school year came to an end, to a collective, almost audible sigh of relief by school and city officials, the board of directors of the Bemidji Area Chamber of Commerce published an open letter to the BSC students, thanking them and praising them for maintaining self-control and not using violence to achieve their goals. The letter read in part, "We have noted with pride the maturity you have displayed in the pursuance of your projects and concerns. You have shown by word and example that your goals can be accomplished by debate, reason and persuasion, rather than by disruption and violence." [10]

OTHER THINGS BESIDES "THE WAR"
        Bemidji State held events of interest far removed from the Vietnam War syndrome, of course, with sufficient people's time and energy readied for a variety of activities expected on a college campus. Two events started in the 1969-70 school year went on to become important traditions, specifically the first Christmas

The Twelve-Story Tamarack Residence Hall
"An impromptu panty raid, the Tamarack Tories surprising the Linden Loveleys."

10) The Bemidji Pioneer, May 18, 1970. In looking back on those years, one wonders when anyone on campus found time for school. Best remembered by a number of teachers were many male students who then made it very clear that they were enrolled only to avoid the war they detested so bitterly. A few also intimated none too subtly that if the profs gave them failing grades, they were essentially sending them off on the troop ships. Bitter blackmail.

season Madrigal Dinners, sponsored by the music department, and the first Eurospring program at Oxford. (Both topics are discussed in other sections of this tome.) The new Walnut Hall cafeteria opened for business and almost immediately achieved the moniker of "Wally's," a pernicious title that remained for subsequent entering class members to add to their vocabulary, implicit in its use being the absence of *haute cuisine*. But gourmands loved it! Completion also came on what would be Bemidji's tallest building, Tamarack Hall, the 12-story residence hall sticking high in the skyline and seen from considerable distance outside the city limits.[11] The college radio station, KBSB, then operating out of the basement in the lower Birch Hall, went FM, a change done with fanfare and a change well received by its listeners, even if the initial power was only 10 watts. Outside speakers of renown came on campus, among them Alex Haley, of Roots fame, who both lectured and fielded questions on the racial crisis as he viewed it. Former Prime Minister of Northern Ireland, Terrence O'Neal, gave a lecture on "The Troubles" of that troubled portion of Great Britain, reminding listeners that religious animosity would never be an anachronism and that the combination of religion and nationalism has been mankind's greatest curse in all its troubled history.

A RETURN TO NORMALCY, BY INCREMENTS

When President Nixon announced his "Vietnamization Program" of turning the war over to the South Vietnamese and bringing home American soldiers, this change and chance for peace brought some peace to college campuses.[12] When it was announced that the drafting of new soldiers would be based on the luck of the lottery drawing (New Years, 1970), a degree of fairness was perceived, with subsequent student acquiescence. (When the first drawing was held on national television late at night, male students in the dorms stayed up all night watching to see which number drawn would determine their military fate.) When the end of the draft came in early January of '73, near campus normality was restored. Finally, when the war finally ended for the U.S. on January 23, 1973, full normality returned. The end of the war was not celebrated, however, in the usual manner of parades and fireworks and happy snake-dancing; the news was received more with a grim sigh of relief and words, "Thank God that's over with." Never again. No more Vietnams.

The years between 1970 and 1973 may have been less turbulent on the Bemidji State campus but they had their moments. Sometimes these seemed minor. To illustrate, the student senate voted to drop its affiliation with the National

---

11) Travelers driving into Bemidji in the spring of 1970 could make out the town's four tallest structures peeking over the skyline: Tamarack Hall; the Federal Building, housing the Post Office along with other federal offices on the top floors; the dome of the aging County Courthouse with its statue of Mother Justice on top; and the high steeple and cross above St. Philip's Roman Catholic Church. What is also seen in these four buildings represents the major reasons for the small city's existence. It was the governmental center for the region, and in many ways the legal center as well as the church center; and the College of course added both a solid economic base as well as being the cultural center. Architecture tells a lot.
12) The maximum number of the numbers of American soldiers in Vietnam occurred in 1968 with 536,100; that same year found 14,592 Americans killed there. In this long conflict, 8.7 million Americans enlisted in the military while 2.2 million were drafted. Almost 16 million were deferred; some 150,000 became conscientious objectors while 570,000 were draft dodgers. Total American deaths in Vietnam: 57,660.

Student Association, believing that the N.S.A. was receiving funding from the C.I.A. As a sign of the times, all candidates for a B.S. degree were required to take a drug awareness course. (A <u>Northern Student</u> poll reported that over a quarter of the dorm students were smoking marijuana.)[13] Some anti-war events were major. For example, there were several student marches to the downtown area, marches that took shouters and chanters past both the high school and Central Elementary School. Most upset by these were the parents of the small children out for recess who had to hear shouted obscenities amid the ragged choral chanting of, "One, Two, Three, Four, We Don't Want Your F——— War!" One group of marchers in the downtown area all sat down in the middle of Beltrami Avenue, blocking all traffic, right in front of the Army-Navy Recruiting Headquarters (near the present Coachman Cafe) and demanded that the recruiters leave! They did leave, temporarily, but primarily to avoid potential conflict. Same way back on the campus where and when Army-Navy recruiters had set up tables in the lower union hallway and were soon confronted by nasty invectives that turned into a shouting scene. The recruiters did leave (via police escort) that area, permanently. One student "March on City Hall" found not only all the Police and Sheriff's Department personnel there to prepare for trouble but also brought were a half-dozen Northwest Minnesota Task Force, in full riot gear, waiting with their nightsticks outside City Hall. (See <u>Northern Student</u>, May 18, 1972, for six pages of pictures on "BSC Rallies For Peace.")

STUDENT ATTACKS AND SHATTERED GLASS AT BSC

The above headline might be interpreted in different ways. Given "the times," that is, the early '70s with the ongoing, raging campus protests against the Vietnam War, the headline seems to fit in with those national events. Not so. 'Twas an aberration. Though the above headline is accurate, the primary motivating force behind it all was a siege of warm weather in mid-February, 1971, in which it seemed the tensions and bizarre behavior on campus rose in direct proportion to the increase in temperature. Just before the evening meal, snowballs began to fly outside Pine Hall at students heading for Wally's, which missiles led to snowball fights of such intensity that windows were broken. Next came an impromptu panty raid, the Tamarack Tories surprising the Linden Lovelys. The men ran through Linden Hall, waving the loot of their pilfering over their heads. Casualties included much missing underwear, but also a couple of stolen stereos, and one man was sent to the hospital with a rupture, a victim of a swift kick by a 225-pound Linden Hall resident assistant. When the boys left to plot yet another raid on another dorm, the Linden Lovelys struck back with an equally surprising attack on Tamarack, called "Watchtower Hall," where the women got as far as the 8th floor before being turned back by water hoses, but not retreating before several pairs of B.V.D.s were

---

13)Drugs on campus have become a cliche' since the Sixties, but during the Vietnam War drugs were used more openly. On a personal note, I recall the pervasive odor of marijuana in the halls of Hagg-Sauer Hall; also remembered are the dilated pupils of my pupils in classes. All this semi-open drug use might be contrasted to earlier times; in the 1950s for example, the biggest drug problem in town was getting a prescription filled on a Sunday afternoon.

captured. During all this action, College radio station KBSB gave live reports from the 11th floor, with the station receiving constant phone calls ranging from, "I'll swap a pair of 38-D cups for a pair of shorts" to the rumor that "General Issimo Decker" was rounding up his troops for a massive counterattack, which outcome would find the student malefactors spending the rest of their term at "Graystone Tech," the prison at St. Cloud. However, the only forces from the outside that did come were two Bemidji police cars, the occupants of which restored order, but not until 1 a.m. The editor of the Northern Student, Dave Umhauer, reviewed these actions later (March 1, 1971) with a front page headline, "BSC is a Sane Asylum." He added that "a statement in the Atlantic Monthly, claiming that 10 percent of the American college population needs psychiatric care, is correct."[14]

TEAR GAS, ONE TIME ONLY

In the 75-year history of Bemidji State, only one time has tear gas been used on campus to "quell a disturbance." Once again the initial, primeval impetus was a warm March afternoon. Some students outside Birch Hall began throwing snowballs at nearby passing automobiles on Birchmont Drive, whose owners angrily reported as much to the police. Soon a squad car drove up, with two policemen in it; their car was also the target of flying snowballs. The snowballs came in such numbers and velocity that the officers at first did not choose to get out of their car. At last the cops eased out on the far side, and via a bullhorn, ordered the students to cease their snowballing forthwith. 'Twas not to be. More snowballs flew at the men in blue. At this point one cop, a veteran of many years on the local force and never one to be challenged by any College student, hauled out a tear gas canister and heaved it at some length, the device landing in the middle of the student crowd. Erupting gas fumes dispelled the group forthwith in all directions. All over? No. Although the "Birch Hall Massacre," as it was later flippantly called, could and should have ended there, it did not. The same bellicose policeman, with a billy club in one hand and his service revolver in the other, ran out from behind the police car and charged through the snowdrifts at some strays still hanging around the scene of the crime! The scared students made a beeline for the side door on the north end, with the angry cop right on their tails. At this point, thankfully, a dean made a quick appearance and persuaded the over-diligent policeman to not only put his gun back in his holster but also to return to his duties downtown. Agreed. All over at last, with a happy ending, sort of.

BOMB? NEVER. BOMB THREATS? ALWAYS.

Wherever and whenever campus bomb threats began remains unknown,

---

14) "Panty raids" on campuses went back to the 1950s, of course, to be reprised sporadically since then. (The Bemidji State "raid" of 1971 had the school newspaper quoting a local professor, "It really brought back memories.... It brought tears to my eyes.") The panty raid tradition as such virtually disappeared after the next year at Bemidji State with the advent of co-ed dormitories, that is, men and women living in the same dorm but on different floors. This early experimentation with college living arrangements brought national publicity to Bemidji State, not all of which was positive. Rumors had not only the two sexes sharing the same rooms but also sharing the same lavatories and shower rooms. The latter point produced the waggish slogan, "Save Water! Shower With A Friend." Wild, inaccurate rumors notwithstanding, Bemidji State has continued since then with the student options for co-ed dorms, a situation of 24-hour gender closeness that still raises a few eyebrows.

but their ongoing use remains an unfortunate example of copy-cat crime. The few actual bombings on various campuses throughout the Vietnam War were matched by bomb threats on most campuses. Such has been the case at Bemidji State since the Sixties, when threats have come almost annually. Because the potential for danger has been there in every scare (usually the bomb threats have been phoned in, but sometimes they're written), school authorities have always responded with alacrity and ordered immediate evacuation of the building threatened, then brought in the local authorities—along with ambulances and fire trucks—and searched the building. These threats have never been taken lightly, even though the large majority of them have come on warm spring days when presumably someone was looking for a good excuse to get out of classes. Always these disruptions have been perceived as a nuisance, and worse, discomforting, especially by those who have had to be awakened to leave their domiciles during the night—and in the wintertime. Two such threats came in March of 1971, the first caller telling the on-duty police officer at the desk, "You better get a lot of ambulances to Tamarack Hall. It's gonna blow up at seven." (Normally, one building would alone be specified as the alleged target, allowing the rest of the campus to go about with normal lives—and classes. But by the 1990s some callers expanded their targets to include "a bomb somewhere on campus," and thus shut down for hours the entire school.) Annoying as bomb threats have been, they beat the real thing.

THE VIETNAM YEARS ASSESSED BY A MODERN DAY STUDENT

In 1993, history major Tim Livingston wrote a brief history of this period in Bemidji State's history, and summarized his views:

"The school years of 1970-75 were exciting times. A full range of emotion is expressed in the pages of the Northern Student. There was a strong spirit of cooperation between the University and the town. Some campuses tore themselves apart with senseless violence, which created rifts in the community that have yet to heal. BSC students went about their protests lawfully and consequently retained the trust of the community that lasts to this day. City Manager Rudy Mikilich deserves a lot of the credit for the absence of violence when the students exercised their right to engage in public protest. The size of BSC grew at a tremendous rate during these years; it kept pace with the students' political awareness and intellectual aspirations. Growth distinguishes life from death, and in that sense, these were lively times. Peace."[15]

SEXUAL REVOLUTION SLOUCHES IN AT BEMIDJI STATE

High on the list of the social revolutions associated with the Vietnam-era protests was the sexual revolution, and with it the supposed end of hush-hush

15) Livingston, a senior from Minneapolis, wrote the paper as a student in this author's class spring quarter, 1993. He was a small child during the Vietnam War but his oldest brother had been a soldier in Vietnam, and Livingston wrote in an explanatory footnote in his paper, "I remember my mom glancing furtively at the television whenever combat footage was shown, my brother's latest letter jammed in the pocket of her bathrobe. She was scared, but never showed it openly. She wrote her son in Vietnam every day without fail. I cannot now imagine the terror she must have felt when he did not write back with the same regularity." The son/brother returned from Vietnam.

discussions on that topic that likely had kept more students staying up late in dorms talking about "it" than had any other subject. With the new openness there would be no more hiding of anything, no more pooling-of-ignorance on the mysteries of sex, no more limitations on the availability of contraceptives, no more unwanted pregnancies, or so went the assumptions. That was not the case at Bemidji State,

The Lure and Appeal of the Water on Lake Bemidji
"BSU is a small city of 'temporaries' populated by people just passing through."

as was seen when the school hired a full-time medical doctor for the Student Health Services at the start of the new school year of 1971. An American woman doctor, she was born in China to American missionaries who had been working there before World War II. At Bemidji State, she made clear from the start her views on premarital sexual relations and she did not bend in these strong views, despite concerted efforts on the part of some students and faculty to "bring her into the modern world." (The ongoing jokes and stories on campus, most of them blue, rose in proportion to her ongoing pronouncements.) A half year later the fact that she had not budged an inch was reflected in the school newspaper headline of February 7, 1972, "No Birth Control Devices for Single Students." A full year after that, February 8, 1973, still no change, and her position was quoted in the Student, "Not handing out contraceptives at the Health Center might be a deterrent to premarital sex. It was not God's will that we act this way." She gave no theological explanation for the concurrent rise in venereal diseases on campus during her years at the Health Center, even if the fraternities sarcastically saw the newest case of herpes as "the good doctor's revenge." The sexual revolution marched on someplace else. The Supreme Court had ruled that abortions were legal but not even referrals would come out of Bemidji State. Back to pooling collective ignorance.

ADJUSTING TO THE AFTERMATH OF VIETNAM: A "HAIRY" WORLD

Student physical appearance had taken on social and political meanings during the Vietnam War. The clothes and hairstyles supposedly said something, albeit imprecisely, about collegians' views on the war; they made "statements." Then the war ended and there was nothing more to say via threads and cuts. This led to a pleasant predicament; it was no more Hawks versus Doves, no more straights versus freaks. Freedom for all to dress individually. Students by the mid-'70s could and did dress any way they wanted to; there seemed to be no more required styles because no one was making any more alleged statements. So live and let live, and ignore the next guy. Wearing a vest (made from a rug) or a headband or a cowboy hat or a sash or a medallion or a fatigue jacket or a turtleneck (or a man's hair in braids) no longer got the wearer a second look. Ho hum. Big deal. Who cares? If there was a decided trend for men's appearance, it was in their hair being longer. Parental hassling of kids' hair lengths seemed to have ended in the early '70s. So, a hairy bunch on campus. (This was true of the faculty, too—in their new leisure suits. Long sideburns. Hair combed forward to hang over the forehead. Beards, goatees everywhere.) Some male students had hair far longer than that worn by most females, but this was no problem, other than confusing gender identification at times.[16] It was all so casual, so individualistic, so much a part of the "Me Generation." A cartoon of 1975 shows two men, the one dressed decidedly differently from the other, and explaining, "The trousers are the '30s, the tie is about the '40s, the jacket is into the '50s, the shirt is '60s, and that's what the '70s are all about."

Women students also went their individualistic ways. Skirt lengths—if they even wore a skirt or dress—varied widely to extremes, from tiny mini-skirts to long granny-dresses sweeping the floors. Their hair styles also tended to remain on the "longish" side, still a' la singers Joan Baez and Buffy Sainte-Marie. By 1975 the "new style" of clothing that did attract many—after T-shirts and black stockings—were bell-bottom slacks, with three-inch cuffs, the slacks textured polyester or

16) A woman English professor had always prided herself in addressing her students in class by the title of Mr., Mrs., Miss, or Ms. whomever, she had to give it up in the '70s, having embarrassed herself and her students too often by incorrectly calling someone Miss when that person was a Mister. The hair threw her off.

gabardine plaids, or houndstooth plaids, all to be worn with high, clunky platform shoes, a corduroy belt, and a bulky but plain blouse, all together producing the desired "layer look." (It all seemed so "Mod" at the time.)

The war had ended. So much for the problems of others. Time to find oneself in the wake of Vietnam, as the cliché went.[17] Time to get into personal growth, which in the '70s included everything from reading innocent self-help books to joining bizarre religious cults. And eat health foods. And shed the Beatles and replace them with the BeeGees; shed outdoor Woodstocks and go inside to disco. Goodbye pot, hello cocaine. And talk right; talk the proper slang of the day, man. Super, for sure, getting your head together, find yourself, coming to terms, getting it down, getting it on, rap sessions, coping, copping, commitment, prioritize, really sucks, mellow, meltdown, the pits; it goes with the territory.

POLITICS "MAKES STRANGE BEDFELLOWS" . . . AND TEACHER UNIONS

What happens to the state happens to higher education. What happens politically happens to higher education, too. For the first time in the history of Minnesota, the house, the senate and the governor were Democratic Farm Labor party, resulting in the 1971 passage of the historic state law, called the Public Employment Labor Relations Act (PELRA). This legislation enabled the faculty of the State University System TO BARGAIN COLLECTIVELY all contracts governing their terms and conditions of employment. Backed by a whole body of labor laws, PELRA authorized full unionization for the State College teachers, including the legal authorization to (gasp) strike.

Prior to PELRA, the teachers had been governed by a set of rules laid out in what was accurately if uninterestingly titled RULES AND REGULATIONS OF THE STATE COLLEGE BOARD, authorized by the legislature in general and specifically written by the State College Board, the official, designated manager of all the schools. PELRA superseded the managerial rights granted by the state's RULES AND REGULATIONS. It became a new ball game for all sides.

The faculty organization prior to PELRA had been just that, an organization only, with virtually no authority. It made changes in the heretofore hallowed "Rules and Regs" only by appeals of persuasion, pleas which were not always granted even a hearing, let alone the thoughtful consideration that could lead to favorable changes. To work on improvements, from each campus came two elected representatives to St. Paul several times a year, the combined group called the Inter Faculty Policies Committee. This small group, with a small budget, met regularly among themselves to plan strategies, and sometimes they met with the chancellor, who was the official representative of the State College Board. Although all parties involved had much in common, most important the good of the colleges, they had

---

17) For reasons not clear, most Americans in 1973 avoided the fact that the U.S. had lost the war in Vietnam. It appeared to fit into the rationalization of avoiding a problem by not thinking about it. Historian William Manchester suggests that Americans grabbed on to the successes of the space missions, notably landing Americans on the moon on July 20, 1969, as their way of dealing with their country's failure in Vietnam. It made "Peace with Honor" possible. Manchester, The Glory and The Dream: A Narrative History of America, 1932-72. (New York: Little, Brown and Company, 1974), p. 1157.

much that was not common in that they could not agree on many points of language (and the numbers/salaries) spelled out in the "Rules and Regs."

Following the passage of PELRA came first the faculties' voting on which bargaining unit they wanted to represent them; after considerable debate, some of it heated, the large majority voted to go with the Inter Faculty Organization (IFO), Minnesota Education Association related, as the exclusive bargaining agent. Thus the new IFO began a new era in Minnesota higher education, with the faculty NEGOTIATING future contracts, not simply accepting anything given to them. Moreover, starting in 1975, on each campus, the college president was required to MEET AND CONFER regularly with the representatives of the union/IFO, the latter also having the authority to initiate—and carry through to arbitration—official GRIEVANCES against administrative decisions if the IFO deemed this necessary.

The "good ol' days" for the college presidents were over. For the first time ever they now shared authority. Salaries were negotiated. It was different, to say the least, and not all presidents could at first handle it well. President Decker was one of those who found it difficult. Ever since he emerged from World War II as a U.S. officer (and he remained a lieutenant colonel in the National Guard while he was BSC president), he had usually been in positions of authority where he told people what to do; he didn't have to negotiate with anybody. Period. Prior to PELRA, his meetings with the faculty, if he wanted any meetings, had been to "meet and confirm" what he wanted, or at worst "meet and defer" that which he did not want. Hence those earliest, PELRA-mandated meet-and-confer sessions with Decker were not the most pleasant meetings; it was "them versus us," with a new adversarial relationship of Administration versus the Faculty. Goodbye to collegiality.

Some Bemidji faculty members refused to join the IFO, for a number of reasons. It was indeed a union, something some academics historically perceived as anathema and incompatible to both collegiality and the concept of intellectual free association; they were "beyond" unions, which existed only for the . . . uh . . . well, let's say it, blue-collar working men. Others would not join because they lost the election, when they voted for the American Association of University Professors and it lost to the IFO. A few who found the IFO too tame, too gutless, too company-unionish much preferred bellying up to a true union like the Teamsters. Then there were those who would not join because they were too tight to pay the dues. Yet all of the above who did not approve the IFO joined the category of "fair-share members"; that is, 85 percent of their dues (full dues almost $500 by 1994) was deducted from their salaries for the IFO whether they liked it or not. They did not like it.[18]

18) For an up-to-date IFO membership report, see Appendix I, listing all campuses with the 1992-93 membership and percentages. PELRA greatly affected the almost 40,000 state employees by 1992; the State University System employs 4,000 full-time persons, including faculties. 'Tis big business. The legislature in May of 1993 appropriated $355,020,000 for the seven State Universities for the next two years (out of $2,043,000,000 for all of state higher education). Bemidji State's share of the appropriation runs a little less than 10 percent, with $27,300,050 budgeted for Fiscal Year 1994 but $28,056,227 for FY '93.

. . . from tiny troop to BIG (NOT TOUGH) UNION

The IFO started out small, and like Topsy, just grew. It began with a small, almost all-volunteer staff and in 1974 an annual budget of $80,000; by 1994 the staff included three full-time professionals—directors of labor relations, governmental relations, and academic affairs—two full-time secretaries, and budget of $1,080,000. The president is a faculty member from one of the

Outdoor Science; Prof Bob Baker (seated by tree) Talks Conservation
"Baker . . . from Blackduck . . . knows Biology . . . and Big Bands."

Universities who, taking a leave of absence, serves a two-year term, and whose full salary is paid by the IFO. The IFO negotiates a two-year contract via their negotiating team, made up of faculty members representing each campus. The first collective bargaining agreement came in 1976. When subsequent new contracts have not always been reached by the time the new school year begins, the old contractual terms carry over. These carry overs have resulted in virtually continuous planning and/or negotiations; hardly is a contract approved when new contractual plans begin almost the next day. The terms and conditions of employment for faculty always have included the following categories: Academic freedom, grievance process, professional development and evaluation, salary, insurance, workload, retirement benefits, and faculty rights in cases of retrenchment, dismissal or non-renewal.

Whether PELRA was good for Minnesota higher education remains a moot point. It most decidedly has been good for the SUS faculties. IFO has been a force to be reckoned with; it has voting strength, some political clout (a full-time lobbyist) and money; its contracts have been the envy of other State University faculties who perceive Minnesota as one of the best states to be in during the 1990s. The most obvious sign of gains, of course, is financial. When PELRA was passed in 1971, the average base salary for the Bemidji State faculty without doctorates was $11,141; with doctorates, $14,995. By decade's end, 1979, non-doctorates averaged $17,185, and doctorates $21,867.[19] Given the escalating costs of living in the 1970s, the salary increases were not that great. The big jumps came in the next decade when the IFO negotiated a salary schedule, with a series of steps depending on rank, years of service, degrees held, and the like. The 1993-94 schedule shows those at Step 16—where most full professors rank (and a large majority at Bemidji State hold that top ranking)—making $55,626 as full-time, nine-month (168 duty days) teachers. Summer school pay is extra (1.5 percent of his/her nine-month base salary). In common parlance, these agreements are generally referred to as "the IFO contract" when in reality it is the IFO/SUS contract, or as the printed cover on each contract reads, "AGREEMENT between MINNESOTA STATE UNIVERSITY BOARD and INTER FACULTY ORGANIZATION." As noted, the PELRA law gave the faculty the right to strike, but no strike has occurred. There has never been an official vote taken to authorize a strike. "Straw votes," yes; real ones, no; threats, kind of. Yet that sword of Damocles hangs always in the air so that pernicious rumors of faculty striking manages to hit the campus to shock (sometimes please) students almost every year. Unlike other PELRA units on campus, the Bemidji faculty may writhe but do not rise.[20]

WATERGATE SPILLS OVER TO THE CAMPUSES

The Watergate scandal, with all its ramifications, led to the resignation of President Nixon in 1974. That same year it also led to both the federal and state governments passing legislation to protect individual rights. President Nixon said publicly that he was not a crook, but he and his ilk did crooked things, like pry into people's private lives and use/misuse pilfered information, then order federal agencies like the FBI and the IRS to hassle and punish his enemies. Congress responded with a law referred to as the Buckley Amendment but officially known as the Family Educational Rights and Privacy Act of 1974. The state of Minnesota added to it the state's Government Data Practices Act, a portion of which covers Student Rights and Data Privacy Policy. The thrust of both acts, of course, was to guard against the disclosure of private, personal information.

For colleges like Bemidji State, the laws were supposed to mean changes

19) Salary information taken from memo sent by Thomas L. Boates, professor of chemistry, and chairperson of the local IFO Salary Committee; memo sent to all the faculty and headed, "Why It's Hard to Pay for the Groceries." Though undated, the memo pertains to the forthcoming contract negotiations for the 1979-1980 school year. That same memo, with all the salary numbers for the 1970s, came back to be posted on faculty bulletin boards in 1994, with the new scribbled heading of, "Lest We Forget."
20) Council 6, the name given to the group made up primarily of the secretarial and janitorial staffs, went out on strike for two weeks in the summer of 1981. Of their over 200 members, only five would not strike. Many IFO members showed their support by walking in the picket lines with them along Birchmont Drive. Strikes also bring out bitterness; 13 years later, in 1994, there were still secretaries who would not speak to the five non-strikers. The Minnesota community colleges faculty went out on a two-week strike in March of 1978.

of policies—and attitudes—quick. Both were difficult to change, especially the latter. Nevertheless, from the Registrar's Office came a veritable stream of memos, first informing faculty members that they were all likely breaking the law and then reminding them they were still breaking the law. These memos/warnings/pleas/ threats have continued to come with no letup to the present date, which suggests how well the law was implemented. Some points of that law were clear enough: No posting of any grades beside any student names; nor even with their social security numbers for identification; no more leaving student book reports or term papers outside office doors for the students to pick up and unauthorized eyes to see; no more writing a letter of recommendation for a student that the student cannot see. Moreover, the school must permit students to inspect and review their education records, upon request; also, only information defined and publicized by the institution as "directory information" will be released without the express consent of the student.

Although the warnings seemed clear enough, all faculty did not abide by the rulings—or memos. Many said "piffle"—and worse—and went about their old ways, breaking the law established by the Buckley Amendment with reckless abandon. Some points of the law were vague, notably whether a student's grades could be sent home to the parents. The parents had a clear interpretation of this, especially since they were no longer raising their children but were financing them.

Each memo ended with the regular caveat, "Violations of the Data Practices Act can result in certain civil and criminal penalties." Between 1974 and 1994 there have been no civil nor criminal penalties adjudicated at BSU.

THE DOWNSIDE . . . AND THE STRUGGLE FOR WARM BODIES

As noted in an earlier section in the brief biography of President Decker, he was at Bemidji State's helm for the school's all-time enrollment peak of 4,865 students on campus in 1971. Three years later that figure had dropped to 4,187. In a system where funding depends almost entirely on the number of students (with the usual designation of measurement called FTEs, for Full-Time-Equivalents), dropping enrollments meant financial trouble. It meant cuts, reduced supply budgets, janitorial and secretarial staff lay-offs (they felt abandoned), deferred faculty hiring, and of course firing. Retrench. Cut back. Any way to save money, whether big or little amounts.[21]

That form of trouble trickled down fast to every department, with all of them scrambling to save jobs, and the only way to do that was to recruit warm bodies for classes. Standards went out the window; grade-escalation came in; after all, a passing student will return to occupy a chair—and pay tuition. Not much to be proud of as departments vied with each other to steal away students. While

---

21) The financial cutbacks came concurrently with the Arab oil embargo, the "shortage" that followed, and the plea of the federal government to save fuel. The entire Bemidji community then went on Daylight Savings Time, which in Bemidji in January and February made absolutely no sense. Although Bemidji State attempted to do its part in this patriotic appeal—and save money at the same time—this led to some bizarre actions on campus that winter of '74, with thermostats being turned down to the near-freezing point in classrooms, and only a portion of classroom lights allowed to be turned on. Decker personally went around to check campus buildings and snapped off many a switch in his rounds. Presidents do strange things.

official school admissions staff recruited students off-campus, many faculty did their own form of unofficial recruiting internally. Among ploys used were whipped-up new courses to appeal to student interests, and several of these took the form of mini-classes, that is a class for one or two credits at the most, with the class meeting perhaps only once a week or maybe half the quarter. While it is easier to single out other body-snatches, it should be admitted that the history department was as guilty as any. Among the history offerings came one-credit shots, for example, on the Big Band Swing Era, the Aztecs and the Incas, the Salem Witchcraft Trials, the Oregon Trail, and yes, the History of Bemidji State; also single-biography classes on names like Martin Luther, Eugene Debs, and Henry Ford. Course numbers were juggled, with ostensibly senior courses, previously numbered 400, reduced to "sophomore classes" at 200; same course, same everything, except that they would be more appealing to more students. Name changes brightened the appeal for some classes. For example, "Modern Germany" used to bring in all of five students, but simply changing the title to "Hitler's Germany" led to the classroom being filled up. None of the above, of course, could rescue the entire operation; faculty members were let go, even tenured professors.

THE DARKSIDE . . . AND THE NON-RENEWAL OF TEACHER CONTRACTS
        The aforementioned reduced enrollments led to reduced budgets which led to reducing staffing, and thus many teachers and non-teaching staff members were laid off. (Funding was based on the ratio of one faculty for every 19 students.) School officials found the legal problems in non-retention cases almost negligible if the person to be let go was not on tenure. All that was required was to follow a carefully laid out full due-process procedure, much of it involving proper dates of notification, proper letters, and the like. Almost all of the recipients of these non-renewal letters accepted their fates without challenge, but two professors in 1972 did not go quietly into that dark, academic night. One was a psychology professor and the other a political scientist, the latter somewhat special in that he was an Indian Sikh, complete with turban. Both men received their notices early in the school year and immediately began to do what they believed necessary to maintain their jobs, including holding private meetings with the president, conducting public meetings to air their positions, hiring attorneys, writing letters, seeking and receiving student backing to save them, and semi-storming a faculty senate session, demanding action. (Before the Sikh and his student followers could all get inside the senate meeting room, Senate President Fred Carr declared the meeting adjourned and walked out.) All this linen, more dirty than clean, appeared publicly in the student newspaper, which followed the ongoing struggles of both losing candidates throughout the school year. A final burst of protest was planned by them and their student followers to disrupt graduation ceremonies, but even this proved ineffectual and almost comedic. Graduation that year was held in the football stadium, with a large, indeed overflowing crowd there on a pleasant, sunny afternoon. The "protest disruption" called for the marchers to encircle the temporary speakers'

platform, where the president and all the invited dignitaries sat, at the point when graduates were to file forward and walk across the stage to receive their diplomas on the platform. However, this was the same time when many people came out of the crowd and went to the platform to greet personally the new graduates and take their pictures. The 50-some protesters thus marched around the stage but in so doing they mingled inadvertently with some of the crowd, and to the audience watching this milling about, it all seemed part of the general ceremonies. Hence the protest came to naught; same with the two men's jobs, and they soon left town.

THE DARKEST SIDE . . . AND THE BREAKING OF TENURE

Tenure: "The act, right, manner, or period of holding something, as a landed property or a position." So reads the dictionary definition. Regardless of its historic origins and *raison d'etre*—essentially the freedom to teach the truth as one perceived the truth, without fear of retribution—tenure eventually came to mean, for faculty members in the Minnesota State Colleges, a lifetime job. Tenure was viewed by profs as a continuing contract that assured them ongoing, steady employment. This notion ended in the 1970s.

Retrenchment: "A retrenchment is the layoff of tenured or probationary faculty members due to System or University budget reductions, budget deallocations, expenditure freezes, or unfunded increases in operating costs . . . ," or so reads Article 23 in the IFO/SUS contracts. This article would be the legal basis for ending tenure at Bemidji State in 1974 in what was inelegantly referred to by the faculty at the time as the "Great Wipeout." As was the case with the non-tenured positions not renewed, almost all who were retrenched accepted their fate—not happily—without challenge, but one person, again a political scientist, did challenge the ruling and fought it to the end. He lost. In between the first black letter in the fall and the final ruling of an unmoved state arbitrator in the spring, there was a messy, angry paper trail, so unpleasant, so upsetting, divisive and emotional, that by the time it was over, nobody "won." But tenure was the the loser.[22]

BEMIDJI STATE, 1975-1980, BACK TO (HO HUM) NORMAL

"Going to college during the Seventies was like going to town the day the circus left." So said Esquire. A University of Minnesota student added, "The Seventies were to history what the Edsel was to the automotive industry."

Bemidji State officials, and most of the faculty, were more than ready for a respite from the earlier conflicts and viewed comments like the above as the

---

22) Many departments were hit hard, history among them; four were let go in history in '74: James Hamilton, Arnold Lukkanen, Ashe Davis, and Dolores Norman. Norman would be retained, however, following the untimely death that spring of historian Joe Free. Hamilton returned to his native Iowa where he became a successful hospital administrator; Lukkanen at this writing is a Minnesota state assistant fire marshal; Davis, a Canadian, returned to Maple Leaf country but did not keep contact with BSU so there is no knowledge of his whereabouts or profession. In these non-retentions, where was the faculty union? Although IFO leaders wrung their own hands and held the hands of the non-retained, the only legal thing they could and did do was to make sure that full due process was provided everyone. In this effort they managed to secure an extra year or two for some people, simply because the administration had fouled up the process, usually missing time-line requirements. However, the IFO could only delay these executions, not stay them.

ramblings of those who suffered from terminal adolescence. 'Twas time to relax, ponder the past but plan for the future, a future with no more student marches. Good. No more sit-ins. Fine. No more screaming. Yeah! Back to normal school

Strolling the Long Lakeshore Campus
"If a single word describes student attire, the term 'casual' seems appropriate."

years, even though it meant cutbacks and bashed budgets. Tough economic times, but the school endured. (Many colleges did not endure; from 1960 to 1982, 119 four-year colleges closed, almost all of them private.) Despite shortages, Bemidji State was expected to perform "normally," too, which officially meant providing a complete undergraduate program in 70 areas, and a partial graduate program also. And, unofficially, the school had to circumnavigate the power-hungry chancellor's office and other state agencies always working to justify their existence.

By '75 it was time to enjoy a new status, too, a new designation of "University"![23] And maybe just get back to serious discussions again on—what else?—the weather, of course. Bemidji after all has so much of it.

Even the vice president for academic affairs commented on the changes in BSU students. Writing in his annual report (1975-1976, p. 2), Richard Beitzel observed, "In 1975-76, BSU experienced what is a national phenomenon; our students became serious. For example, they are requesting, as opposed to demanding, an increase in quality of not only instruction, but more importantly, an increase in quality of course content, i.e., Thermo Dynamics is once again a popular course."

WHAT THE SCHOOL WAS AND WAS NOT BY DECADE'S END

Bemidji State's history has been inseparable from the interplay of the needs and rights of students and faculty, of parents and communities, of the nation and of the world; of pressures within and without. The ongoing result—changes. One way to define an institution is not only to indicate what it was but also what it was not. In a spinoff to that kind of definition, institutional variations can be seen in what was once available along with what was later added and dropped. For example, certain traditions, givens that had been taken for granted, disappeared. To illustrate, the annual school yearbook, the AHMIC (Ojibway word for Beaver) was no more after 1972. It became a victim of an interplay of forces—after all, aren't yearbooks "high schoolish"? And wouldn't efforts be better given to social and political revolutions going on around us? So the AHMIC more faded away than died. Yes, officially budget problems were cited as the cause of death, but fully as important were interest problems, the latter shorter than the money. A Beaver yearbook could have been resurrected, but it wasn't; the rights have been there, but apparently not the needs.[24]

GOOD-BYE, PROMENADES

What had once been the biggest spring event on campus, the prom, became a suspended casualty before the decade even began. In a collegiate time period when any form of formal dress seemed anathema, the idea of putting on tuxedos and

---

23) The state legislature, recognizing the changing size and nature of the former State Colleges, had authorized the name change in the spring of 1975. No longer were any of them simple little colleges in the woods or on the prairies. Time to apply the appropriate titles. Bemidji could also change its name to reflect the new title, but was not allowed to place the word "Minnesota" in that title. In this ruling the University of Minnesota grads in the legislature protected their alma mater. That summer President Decker went public and sought input on a new name and several meetings were held on campus in which participants could present their views. Afterwards, Decker initially went with the name Northern State University-Bemidji, and he even went so far as to have a logo made and printed. See Appendix J. Just prior to the date when the announcement had to be made, however, he was persuaded that to call the school "Northern" would lead to the loss of identity for both the town and the school. Hence he acquiesced to the simple if accurate Bemidji State University, even though opponents pointed out the obvious interpretation that could be given when the name was reduced to just the three initials.

24) A half-hearted effort came for a senior yearbook in 1978 but it subsided before very long. The Society for Collegiate Journalists announced that they would provide the students with a book at no cost to the student and that fall they sent a photographer to Bemidji State to take senior pictures. The problem arose when the men students were expected to show up wearing suit coats and ties and the women in dresses or skirts; attire had to be "appropriate" or no picture would be taken. This ruling upset many, including the Northern Student Editor Karl Bremer who found the ruling insulting and absurd, and he concluded, "Thanks . . . but no thanks." He spoke directly about his fellow students (NS, January 11, 1978, p.6): "It appears to me that the suit coat (or is it leisure suit?) is not the most common sight around Bemidji State University. I believe the last time I donned one was over three years ago. . . . I certainly won't remember BSU for its nattily-dressed, double-knit students, but more likely for their flannel shirts and blue jeans."

long formal dresses for an evening of sedate dancing was perceived as a ritual belonging back with dinosaurs and Calvin Coolidge. What replaced the prom as the biggest social event of spring was the Dance Follies. It started small under phy ed teacher Myrtie Hunt, but by '79 the 13th annual dance show, under the direction of Marion Christianson, played four nights to overflowing audiences in Memorial Hall. So special has been this event to some students that it became the only reason for their enrolling in college. (The annual follies has continued in popularity since, the only change being its move to the new basketball court to hold the crowds; in 1994 Christianson still planned and coordinated the event. See section in Persons and Programs.)

Bemidji State bucked the tide in some social things, like abandoning homecomings in fall. Homecoming was not halted at Bemidji State. (Homecomings stalled by snowstorms don't count.) In that era of anti-establishment-anything, a number of universities dropped homecomings entirely, like the University of Minnesota, which only resumed holding them again in 1978. Bemidji State also went against the trend in fraternities and sororities. By 1970 most campuses were abandoning fraternities and sororities as irrelevant or worse; in Bemidji they just started getting off the ground at that time.

A combination of inside and outside pressures caused major changes in dormitory living over 10 years. The requirement that freshmen live in residence halls was challenged by the Minnesota Civil Liberties Union, whose views on the freedom to choose/not choose dorm living prevailed before the issue had to hit the courts. More changes came for dorm residents when they were permitted to choose the number of meals they wanted in a week, paying only accordingly. The co-ed dorms mentioned earlier became an option, as did the later option for graduate-only floors and "quiet floors." The dorm mother, she of ancient historical authority (and age), with powers almighty enough to lead to the suspension and/or expulsion of alleged culprits, was replaced by a student R.A., resident assistant, more counselor than cop. As to rigid, mandatory hours for women to be back in their vaults each night at a specific time, forget it; they went the way of the high buckle shoe and multi-layered petticoats. *In loco parentis* took a back seat; women students at last had their dorm rights, too. As to women historically standing and freezing outside on the dorm steps with their boyfriends in the wintertime, with howling winds and temps at minus 30, forget that scene, too. Invite the men inside. Lounges are available for many things.

NO MORE BEANIES

Although obviously in the category of historical trivia, another "given" dropped in 1972 was the requirement for new freshmen to wear beanies. Although these tiny caps did change in appearance over the decades—sometimes all green, sometimes green-and-white, with or without letters—they had been part of the expected and generally accepted college experience at the start of every school year. No more. The student governing board decision to abandon them came under the heading of ending hazing in general and in particular preventing specific students from being overly harassed by upper classmen. It worked. What hazing followed would be associated with the fraternities and sororities.[25]

'Button That Beanie' Went the Familiar Imperative for 50 Years
*"Another 'given' dropped in 1972 was the requirement
for freshmen to wear beanies."*

Some events of long tradition ceased because of outside pressures, indeed rulings, like the decision of the U.S. Supreme Court which ended, presumably forever, baccalaureate services on campus for members of the graduating classes. After separate religious services were dropped, there were a few years when prayers were offered at graduation exercises, but by decade's end, full separation of church and state would be applied at Bemidji State. The Court's ruling on abortions in '73 would be accepted eventually (when a new Health Center director

25)The issue of fraternity hazing continued throughout the decade, as noted by letters and columns in the student newspapers. A personal note, because this particular act made such an impression. I had a student in the late '70s who never skipped class, and then suddenly he didn't show up for two days. When he returned, I inquired about his absence and he told me that as part of his "orientation" into the fraternity he was joining, he and two other pledges had been awakened from a sound sleep in their dorm room, and while still in their pajamas, driven to Fargo, at which destination they were pushed out of the car and told to find their way back.

came by '75) so that by '79 interested students would be referred to the closest clinic at Fargo.

AND THE YOUNG SHALL . . . VOTE

U.S. Constitutional Amendment XXVI in 1971 permitted all citizens the right to vote at age 18. Again a sample of interplay of societal forces, the most familiar line of support going something like, "If a young man can get drafted and go fight for his country, he should certainly be allowed to vote!" Not all agreed, of course, with some opposition responding with their own familiar lines, "The young barbarians are at the gate!" or, "The inmates are being allowed to take over the asylum." Not to worry. Despite the potential for either power or mischief, voting enfranchisement authority among the young was used very little, with national polls soon showing that the age group least likely to cast ballots in America were those 18 to 22 years old. Not to worry in Bemidji, either, despite some townspeople's bogus charges of "hordes of College students coming over in swarms" to vote Yes on a school building referendum boondoggle "that us adults in town gotta pay for." A couple of profs (this author was one) did quick determinations from their large classes of students who actually did vote in the referendum and found the percentage at less than one percent; that message was sent to the Pioneer editor. That ended (for a while) charges of alleged suffrage misuse by 18-year-olds rocking the election boats.

In the early '70s, Bemidji State students continued to run for city offices, whether mayor or city council, and although they did not win, they kept trying. By decade's end they no longer tried. On campus the student elections around 1970 found many candidates who ran spirited campaigns, with relatively big student turnouts for elections. Alas, by 1979, candidates seemed few in numbers and apathetic in spirit, both figures and attitudes reflected in minuscule voting turnouts. Whereas campus editors once pleaded for reduced tensions and more common sense in the enthusiastic endeavors creating a charged political atmosphere, later editors pleaded for any sign of student life that might motivate dormant bodies to resuscitate sufficiently to enter the voting booths. (In 1971 there was one vacant seat for representative in the student governing council and there were 16 candidates; for the senate there were seven students running for one seat. By '79, finding two candidates to square off for each office was considered successful.)

Perhaps the extreme in BSU student candidates came in the early '70s when one student who was a card-carrying, genuine Anarchist—he lived alone in his van in Diamond Point Park—ran for senate president. In his campaign literature, he used a picture of himself holding a double-barrel shotgun across his chest, the scowling photo suggesting . . . well, a number of things, depending what the viewer saw in Michael Bakunin, revivified. He lost.

SHARE THE POWER, JOIN THE FACULTY COMMITTEES

Those students caught up in the general college activism of the early '70s found many wanting to be a part of the power structure on campus on those matters affecting curriculum, which meant their eagerness—yea, demands—to have membership on almost all committees of the faculty senate as well as serve at least as observers in all departmental meetings. President Decker was more than willing to accommodate students in their willingness to participate in these areas, and almost all the faculty agreed to have them join in their small group meetings. Participation was short lived. Perhaps the meetings themselves said more about the eventual outcome of these arrangements in that student participation began to fall off gradually as students joined faculty members who were falling off gradually into daydreaming and sleep at their boring meetings. Before too long almost all the committee-member students believed that perhaps their contributions to school governance could better be applied to some other arrangement.

AWAY WITH "THE OLD AMERIKA"

The above spelling is deliberate and the word was frequently written that way in those "Days of Trouble." It suggests, of course, a fascist nation, and according to the spellers, all the wrong things about the country that needed righting. For students to change these inherent wrongs, there came the cry to challenge all "the old ways"; to flaunt the new ways and styles; to flout the traditions and immoral laws: Away with establishment-set mores of society. Set civility aside for the greater good of calling public attention to the evils of Amerika and demand that they be expunged. Start with disrupting that one event that brings more people together on any university campus than at any other time in the year, graduation day!

The above prose included the thrust of most arguments of active college protesters. Almost none of the above could be applied to Bemidji State's protesters as to their actively acting on these positions and murky goals. Students may have talked the rhetoric, but they did not walk it. For example, there has not been one single student protest at any Bemidji State graduation in 75 years. (Yes, an earlier section mentioned a form of march at one graduation, but it was faculty planned and led in support of two fired faculty.) This declaration of "no protest," however, does not mean there were no individual idiosyncrasies seen primarily in dress, or maybe non-dress, at graduations, but they were not disruptive. For example, by 1970 it was common for some graduates not to wear academic gowns; presumably by this decision they made a statement against old traditions, but their attire—which included, for example, at different times one in Bermuda shorts and bunny-rabbit bedroom slippers; one in gown but wearing a Mickey Mouse cap, complete with spinning propeller on top; one with 1940s football helmet; one carrying homemade "board" on back of gown reading, "Eat At Joe's"—hardly constituted political or social protest, let alone disrupted any ceremonies. (Most faculty believed they added a needed sense of comic relief to otherwise boring ceremonies.)

Only one time was there a planned "student disruption" of sorts, and the motivation behind it remains mercifully unknown. It involved the fad of "streaking," a ubiquitous social phenomenon blithely presented, and blessedly brief in its faddish duration. At the start of the '78 graduation held in the field house, the last graduate had just entered through the open door on the west end of the building. The band was playing to an overflow audience so large that it would have forced a fire marshal to carry through on his oath to close it down for overcrowding. All the dignitaries were on the platform and President Decker was about ready to deliver his opening welcome. At that point two streakers ran up to the open door; they were wearing tennis shoes below and rubber-face ape masks above; nothing in between. Naked as jay birds. They stopped briefly to scan the scene and plan their running route through the field house and out the door on the other side. At that point, however, the commencement marshal ran up and blocked the doorway, arms outstretched, and bestowed upon them the message of NO WAY!—upon which they turned around and ran the other way. Hardly anyone in the vast audience even saw them; several wished they had. So much for planned graduation disruptions.

THE CALL TO CHALLENGE WENT MOSTLY UNCHALLENGED

The rhetoric of national collegiate protesters during the Vietnam War called for open student challenges to all the "old ways," whatever they might be or might mean: "UP AGAINST THE WALL!" "DON'T TRUST ANYONE OVER 30!" "CIVIL RIGHTS REQUIRE CIVIL RIOTS!" "WHEN IN DOUBT, BURN." The fiery clichés of the day built up one upon another, the whole anarchical pageant laid out in the 1971 book by infamous protester Abbie Hoffman, with its improbable title, Steal this Book.[26] At Bemidji State, however, except for those few areas already mentioned, the student challenges at Bemidji State were both few and almost always civil. A most extraordinary illustration of civility—indeed a virtual tradition at Bemidji State—happens at test time when the end of the class period comes and some students are still writing; at this point the next class members do not rush in but instead wait outside the door for the testers to finish. There have never been written rules to that effect nor any professorial dictum; it comes close to osmosis, something simply "picked up" by freshmen as to how things are done on this campus. A nice touch. A little thing, perhaps, but still telling. The Vietnam War syndrome did not alter this bit of civilization.

As to challenging statements made at lectures, this is something most teachers would welcome! Just to get ANY vocal response by a class member to a presentation is refreshing and certainly different. The normal pattern is so

26)Steal This Book (Grove Press, Inc., New York, 1971). Opening sentence: "It's perhaps fitting that I write this introduction in jail—that graduate school of survival. Here you learn . . . hatred of oppression." The first section is headed SURVIVE! after which come 12 chapters, each headed with the word Free, e.g., Free Housing, Free Money, Free Dope, etc. The last section is headed LIBERATE, followed by the F-word before the cities of New York, Chicago, Los Angeles and San Francisco. For whatever it means, this book was given to me by a student who stole it from the Hennepin County Library. (The Northern Student "progressed" from using the designation of "f—" in 1970 to spelling the entire word by 1979.) Because of a drug violation, Hoffman became a fugitive for seven years before resurfacing in 1980, at which time he lamented the youth of the new generation. In 1988 he was quoted as telling University of Alabama students, "The 1980s are the era of designer brains. You know, 'How can I cash in on a nuclear accident?' As I look around the movements, I don't see young people. They're not taught about that era [the '60s]. They know it as drugs, sex, rock 'n roll. They're not aware that it was a political struggle. I don't trust anyone under 30." Hoffman later committed suicide.

familiar—and so stultifying—as to be a classic scene caught forever in time: The prof finishes the lecture, and at the end of the hour turns to the class and asks, "Are there any questions?"—that line greeted by blank looks on student faces, and then stony silence. Nothing. (One history prof called his students "The Stones.") Perhaps osmosis infects the same freshmen who also learn the Beaver classroom culture that NO ONE asks questions at the end of the hour. (One student question, however, does get asked over and over again, "Is this going to be on the test?")

One national challenge was also taken up at Bemidji State in the early '70s, that of participating in "Who's Who in Colleges and Universities," first the selection of and then a later publication listing those students singled out for their contributions to their institution. To the nay-sayers, to those opposed to any Who's Who, this "old way" smacked of elitism; it was too openly snobbish, and if there's one thing that Bemidji State ain't, it's snobbish. So away with it, and it did go away, only to be revived again at the end of the following decade.

OUTSIDERS PROTEST OUTSIDERS

Outside speakers coming to Bemidji State could and did occasionally bring a form of community protests. A good example was University of Minnesota Professor Mulford Q. Sibley, noted political science teacher. Sibley was seen, by some, as notorious because of his outspokenness on a number of issues: never signing a loyalty oath, opposing the role of America in the Vietnam War, being an open Socialist—who wore a red tie each day. Prior to his speaking date on campus in 1971, the letters and phone calls of opposition began to appear; one strident caller had only one question for the school's president, "Who's gonna pay the bill for that Red S.O.B.?" When the day and hour came for Sibley's appearance, and someone was introducing him to the crowd in a filled Hagg-Sauer Hall auditorium, a student ran in shouting "There's a bomb planted in the building!" and everyone got excited except Sibley, who yawned. He was used to it. At that point everybody moved out of the auditorium and walked over to the Sattgast Hall auditorium, where Sibley gave his address. And no bomb. At decade's end, Sibley came back—still wearing his red tie—to an uninterested community, and he spoke in a classroom, there being no need for an auditorium.[27]

THE LAWS SPEAK

Women's sports revealed another change on campus, in part prompted by the 1972 law, Title IX, requiring gender equity on sports teams. Whereas the small number of women participating in sports were primarily competing in intramural contests at the start of the '70s, by '79 they had full, separate, intercollegiate competing teams in tennis, track, volleyball, basketball, field hockey, softball and

27) One outside figure who could still raise the hackles of the Bemidji American Legion in 1979 was one of the Berrigan brothers, ex-Catholic priests who had been excommunicated for their overt anti-war efforts. The town newspaper quoted several Legion officers who questioned allowing "Father" Philip Berrigan to speak at the Newman Center on campus. The Legion's position would in turn be challenged by responsive letters suggesting McCarthyism was alive and well in Bemidji. This author attended the Berrigan lecture, and remembers primarily the intoxicated man who stood up before Berrigan even began to talk and asked in slurred speech, "Are you still a priest?" When Berrigan said no, the man said very loudly, "Good," and then walked out.

swimming. Many in the latter program also took part in the women's synchronized swimming team, which put on a regular spring show for the public; but that was on its way out by decade's end. Women had also been a part of the Beaver's gymnastic

Gymnastics on 'the Bar' in Memorial Hall
"Additional programs lost were . . . gymnastics . . . Such are financial exigencies."

teams, before that sport was ended after 1972. Some things not possible to measure precisely had also dropped, with Beaver cheerleader advisor Marion Christianson telling the school newspaper in 1971, relative to declining school spirit, "It seems as though the crowd is merely entertained by the cheerleaders; crowds no longer participate in the yells." Students just sit on their hands and watch, was her observation and lament.

Some things were not new, they just seemed new—like teachers getting official, printed evaluations from their students, who also published them. The student senate hit a stone wall in the faculty senate, who blocked the students' ongoing call for a faculty-endorsed evaluation scheme. No way. Students returned to the hoary, hallowed criteria of word-of-mouth, rumor and testimonials, plus graffiti on the lavatory walls; nothing empirical, but it was all they had. Another not-new thing in the '70s was the students' abortive dream of allowing beer to be sold on campus. The trail of printed appeals, steadily increasing debates and testimony to this losing cause over five years would cause a lot of trees to fall for little or nothing. Even when the alleged last hold-out, the local city council, went on record with a 5-1 vote in favor of the suds to slosh on the union tables, the overweening state law of NO BOOZE on campus prevailed over everyone and everything. Another student setback, but only officially. Back to sneaking a handy-six or a clumsy twenty-four into the dorm rooms.[28]

LAB SCHOOL CLOSES

While certain changes of the decade would be minor, the closing of the Bemidji State Laboratory School after 1975 merits the designation of epoch-ending. The Lab School, as it was usually called, had always been an integral part of the Bemidji State. Indeed, under first President Deputy it was first among equals. But like so many phases of education in America, Minnesota lab schools had their moment in history—a long moment, as it turned out, roughly from the first one at Winona in 1860 until 1960—and then they gave way to the changing times. Their title told their purpose: To improve public school teaching through ongoing classroom experimentation. They were the educational laboratories on the campuses of all the teachers colleges. But by 1970 the schools were no longer primarily teachers colleges so that lab schools no longer fit the curriculum and majors, e.g., the vast growth in the areas relative to business administration. Bemidji State had dropped its lab school junior high in 1962, a decision caused as much by low enrollments (a brand new public school junior high building had recently been built, located only three blocks form the Lab School, and newness attracted that age group) as by the need for more classroom space for college classes.[29] The pattern of closing the kindergarten through grade six portions had already started throughout the state, and Bemidji State followed suit (St. Cloud State held out the longest, maintaining its lab school until 1978). Although there would be finger pointing in attempting to affix the blame for the BSU campus school's demise, it was neither simple nor fair to fault any single person. Again it was the mysterious "they" who decided to shut its doors. Yet few were that sorry to see it go; there was minimal

---

28) The power of advertising aimed at the age group of college youth can be confirmed in many ways, but none more so than in national commercials for beer. These have been too successful, this success sometimes bizarre and silly, as when cheering sections at Beaver athletic contests start shouting back and forth to each other the parrot-learned lines from TV, "Tastes Great" and "Less Filling," and too "successful" in making beer THE drug on college campuses. Alcohol is the social king; it remains the drug of destructive choice for most college students, including those at Bemidji State. The evidence is both anecdotal and statistical. Almost all damage in residence halls, violent and antisocial behavior, rapes and sexual abuse, and academic problems and dropouts are associated with alcohol consumption. It has been the most serious problem faced by all Bemidji State presidents, who do not lack awareness but do lack solutions. The seriousness of the problem makes any apparent glibness in the last paragraph inappropriate. In 1992 the legislature required all universities to implement programs addressing the issues of sexual harassment, sexual assault, and the larger issue of social justice. At BSU, this resulted in a program called "Responsible Men, Responsible Women." It became mandatory for every student to take this program.

29) This author was directly affected by the junior high closing; I was out of a job, being (along with Duane Daily in math and Gloria Witt in science) one of three non-tenured supervising teachers let go. So off to graduate school at the University of North Dakota, with no hope or plans of returning to Bemidji State. But an offer came the next spring, 1963, to join the history department in the fall, an offer accepted and appreciated; and it paid $7,200. It paid in other ways, too. The longer one stays, the more stories one knows.

opposition to its closing, and no public ceremony to mark its ending. It just "phased away," with few noting its disappearance. The folks most affected, of course, were those tenured faculty on the K-6 teaching staff, but all were accommodated by being shifted into teaching college education classes. More than coincidentally, several of those K-6 people were near retirement age and they did retire by decade's end. Whatever the causes of the closing might have been, it marked the end of a major epoch in the school's long history.

LIFE TEACHING LICENSES "CLOSE"

Rulings on teacher preparation and licensing have directly affected Bemidji State since it opened, and nothing has changed in that area since. The State Board of Education both giveth and taketh away; in 1971 it took away lifetime teaching licenses. After that year public school teachers were licensed to teach for a maximum of five years, after which the license had to be renewed, and renewal would be approved only if the applicant had improved himself/herself through "continuing education" programs. (Those who had their licenses before 1971, however, were grandfathered/grandmothered in; thus one teaching license granted back in '02 from East Armpit Junction Tech would be sufficient for a lifetime, or so the State Department ruled.) The new "continuing education" requirements had basic guidelines set by the State Department, but also allowed for individual school districts some discretion in defining "continuing education" and what it meant for relicensing. Definitions regularly included taking more credits at college, and thus Bemidji State continued to benefit from teachers—regularly if not kindly referred to as "retreads"—coming to the campus, mainly in the summers, for classes and workshops. From an educational point of view, the decision to do away with life licenses was one of the best decisions to come from that area often called "downstate" where "that Board" and "those people" have had a reputation for doing "dumb things."[30]

BUILDING MYTHS ABOUT BUILDINGS

The great economic swings in the 1970s made for uncertainties at Bemidji State; one of the major uncertainties concerned construction of new buildings. The previous decade had produced the biggest building spree the campus had experienced, with most of the credit going to President Bangsberg. Area legislators maintained throughout the '70s that the economy was so fragile that certainly there would be no money designated for new structures at Bemidji State. They were right; virtually no <u>new</u> buildings. And they were wrong; large grants came for what was called "remodeling" when the end result was essentially a new building anyway. The

---

30) The most common complaint and combined plea of public school teachers relative to the State Department of Education is a line so familiar as to be a kind of epigram: "Why don't they just leave us alone to teach!?" Brand new teachers coming out of Bemidji State receive only a two-year probationary certificate to teach, and only after that time can application be made for their first five-year license. Those ex-teachers who have let their licenses lapse must also get "continuing education" before their licenses will be renewed. While citizens of the state may wish that all licensing be based on scientifically tested, improved forms of teaching, alas it has been more based on supply-and-demand. Since 1971 that supply has been greater than the demand and thus all teaching candidates are told early "the facts of life," which mean that if they want to get a teaching job, they better be ready to leave the state.

remodeling of Hickory Hall (the former Birch Hall cafeteria) comes to mind, but two classic illustrations were the remodeling of Deputy Hall in 1978 and of Sanford Hall in 1979. Major, lengthy projects, both of them. Both buildings were stripped internally to the outer walls, and inside were built two basically new buildings at a total cost of $3,620,000. And yet the word game played throughout the time period was "no new buildings from the legislature; nope, nothing." Nothing succeeds like success.

Although smaller in both square feet and financing, literally new buildings also came in the '70s with an aquatics laboratory built along the lakeshore (4,000 square feet) and named for Harold T. Peters, and new maintenance-and-receiving buildings (15,000 square feet) on 23rd street, across from Maple Residence Hall. Although not a building, the skyway connecting Deputy Hall and Bangsberg Hall was completed in 1979.[31] Most financing had come earlier, but it was under Decker that Bangsberg Hall was finished in 1971 as well as the second phase of the new union in 1972. At decade's end one could legitimately ask who was the bigger builder, Bangsberg or Decker?[32]

R.O.T.C. COMES TO B.S.U.; FEW GET M.A.D.

The outside temperatures may have been cold but inside the temperatures rose over the decision to allow an Army Reserve Officers Training Corps program on campus. Amid controversy and some bitterness, the program—a military science minor—began in the fall of 1979. The proposal had been floated in an earlier trial balloon but the major votes and decisions came in the fall of '78, when the faculty senate voted to approve ROTC even though the student senate voted against it. When President Decker gave his final support that fall, and sent his recommendation down to the State Board, who also gave it their blessing, that was it; it seemed that ROTC would be a permanent part of Bemidji State's curriculum options.[33] From the administration's point of view, ROTC was a financial windfall for the school in general and for individual students in particular. Young men and women who chose ROTC—and it was strictly voluntary—had their tuition and fees paid, plus supplies and books, plus $100 a month for incidentals. Beginning students who were freshmen and sophomores and just starting the 27-credit program did not incur any military obligations later; however, third and fourth year

---

31) Townspeople, of course, followed the changes and usually gave their blessings to new structures and improvements. But not always to all. On a personal note, this writer was in a car with a city council member when we drove up and saw the then just-completed skyway. The councilman looked up, shook his head in wonderment and disgust, and said, "Lee, that's the biggest boondoggle this town has ever seen!" A rejection to that line could easily be found in the wintertime. The skyway, combined with the tunnels, completed the linkage that allowed students to venture virtually across the entire campus without having to go outside.
32) Sanford Hall had been built in 1920 as a girls' dormitory but it became mainly a place for faculty offices by 1965. Since its '79 remodeling, it has housed various agencies: Area Services, Vocational Education, Child Development, Alumni Office, Veterans Service Office, Upward Bound Project, Counseling and Placement Center, and Indian Studies and Student Services, Pier 9 (drug awareness program), and program offices of the Reserve Officers Training Corps. The one major change to the structure was the addition of an elevator on the north side in 1980. Deputy Hall continued as the main administration building after its remodeling (it was totally gutted, then rebuilt), but it also housed the school's radio and TV stations, plus the public TV station, KAWE; the mass communications program was also relocated there. Alumni may remember the large addition to Deputy Hall in 1948 for a library; in the fall of '93 the entire first floor of that addition became one large computer room.
33) "Permanent" lasted 12 years. The program was phased out by the spring of 1991, a victim of cutbacks in the military following the end of the Cold War.

students who continued through to finish the program did, upon graduation, go into military service as commissioned second lieutenants. The Bemidji State ROTC unit had a separate teaching staff headed by a lieutenant colonel; then came one major, two captains, and three sergeants, all salaries Army-paid, of course. Once the program got underway, there was no more hassle about it being on campus. The unit officers went out of their way to fit in with and adjust to the mores of the place, with uniforms worn sparingly by all involved. (Only at graduations, when uniformed young men and women provided the color-guard with their rifles were there open demurrals from those few who believed ROTC and ACADEME were inimical.) So low-key did they choose to be most of the school year that many students and a few faculty were not even aware of their presence. Yet reminders came almost daily to those who arrived by 7 a.m. because then they could see the ROTC groups in their regular morning exercises, notably jogging en masse and marching—in step—down Birchmont Drive to cadence calls. Commissioning exercises were done in the union ballroom, complete with a large concoction of all that might be identified with military showtime; then came the spiffy outfits, the spit-and-shined boots, the flags waving, the snappy salutes, all amid barked orders, grim visages, and ram rod stiff bodies at rapt attention. The variations in numbers to be commissioned each year ran between a low of 10 and a high of 20. The full numbers of those in the program each year also varied, with the figure of 100 a good ballpark, median number. The full pomp and ceremony came at the end of each school year with the ROTC Military Ball, usually held in the Bemidji VFW ballroom. For that event, the overused adjective gala has to be applied because then and there came full pomp and ceremony, with all the ROTC students and their superiors in their sharpest, neatest dress uniforms, their medals polished even shinier than the sheen of their shoes. Onlookers viewed the scene as right out of "An Officer and a Gentleman." To the ball came special, invited guests from out of town—usually top brass figures, some out of West Point, some with a general's star on the shoulder for the cadets to view with awe. A special time and place, and the capstone for a special unit. For many persons at Bemidji State in those years, the addition of ROTC put their school in the big-time league.

BIG-TIME GRADUATIONS

Bemidji State may not be Ivy League-old, but it does have ivy (covers the west wall of Deputy Hall) and one grand tradition, a splendid graduation ceremony. The colorful pageantry—banners and bugles, marching, and bands playing, displayed pomp and circumstance—usually associated with the Ivy-League schools has been adopted and augmented by Bemidji State at commencement time. Nowadays it's an impressive tradition to be proud of, but it has not always been that way.

Sometimes both individuals and institutions learn from the past, learn from their mistakes and make adjustments accordingly. Often one event will change the course of history, as it did for Bemidji's commencements. In the spurt of student growth in the early '70s, and the attending growth in number of graduates, the school experimented with commencement exercises at the end of both fall and winter quarters, there being a need based both on numbers and on requests from mid-year graduates who could not make it back for the spring graduations. These mid-year graduations were smaller, of course, and did not require the largest facilities; thus they were usually held in Memorial Hall or the ballroom of the Hobson Union. Given the different circumstances, and the scaled-down everything, these ceremonies seemed more quasi-events, with half-hearted numbers of students and faculty and interest and effort proportional to those numbers. Yet all in all they were muddled through somehow, until the fall of '78 when the general looseness in preparation turned the planned ceremony into an unplanned inconvenience and then a comedy of errors. Numbers fouled things up. Although the numbers of those planning to receive their sheepskins could be predicted with fair accuracy, the size of the crowd remained the unknown factor. This time the crowd was large, too large, unplanned-for large, not enough chairs to sit on. People standing around the sides of the room. People squished together, two kids sitting on the same chair. Mom and dad and gramma, too, with no place to sit. On the spot decisions were required, the big one not made until the faculty, who led the opening parade, began their march into the ballroom and down the middle aisle, heading for their several rows of chairs in the front. As the blackgowned profs lumbered forth, the commencement marshal sized up the situation quickly and, with good public relations sense, he instructed the faculty to keep on marching, and they kept marching right out the door, never to return that day. At least this decision provided more chairs for the family members to use, and besides, they did not come to see the faculty anyway. So ended mid-year commencements at Bemidji State.

Following the above snafu—an amusing blunder tucked away forever in the minds of those who were there—a small combination of interested faculty members and administrators began to meet and plan for a one-and-only spring graduation, but one so special as to mark it as THE school public relations event of the year. They succeeded; it became a ceremony marked by major ceremony. Any former image of colorless, parochial, woodsy Bemidji State was to be set aside, at least for one day. No more reverse snobbery and downplaying of honored academic traditions. Time for indulgence, time to dress to the nines; time for a little class! Begin by selecting the field house as the setting; no more trying to outguess and risk the weather in the football stadium. Plan. Plan big. Think big. Let those crowds of well-wishers see and hear something they'll remember. Make the many colorful banners and make them big! Start the proceedings with the grand march of all graduates and the full faculty walking two-by-two all the way from Memorial Hall to the field house, the marchers first ushered out with a blaring trumpet fanfare. And all participants in the long march dressed in flowing gowns and mortarboard caps, the graduates in their black gowns, representative alumni in their green and the top underclassmen in white; and the faculty with their regalia of multi-colored hoods flowing down their backs as they lead the procession, with the president and all the platform dignitaries at the very front. (The faculty line up by seniority, the oldest in front, with their white hair a symbol of their many years of service to their adopted school.[34]) Meanwhile, as the long line of marchers head down the middle of Birch Lane towards the field house, inside the field house the tuxedoed men and black-dressed women band members have been entertaining the throng with carefully selected, crowd-pleasing numbers. Then at the appointed time the big doors on the west side open up, the band swings into Elgar's "Pomp and Circumstance" and the advancing color guard, with flags waving, leads the lines into and through the building, passing by the crowded bleachers, to their assigned seats. Among the marchers are international students representing every foreign country attending Bemidji State, and these students wear the costumes and carry the flags of their countries, thus adding to the color. Pageantry has paved the way and set the scene before the actual graduation exercises themselves have even begun, and the latter of course has been carefully planned with the long-sitting crowd in mind. For the best example, there is no outside graduation speaker brought in for any major (read lengthy) address; moreover, the plan calls for every single graduate to march across the stage, have his/her name read for all to hear, shake the hand of the president and at the same time get their picture taken. Even if the individual name reading makes the afternoon last longer, few care because that is what it's all about. Bemidji State University graduations emphasize the graduates and their families (both the old and the young), who deserve a special time to appreciate higher education. If there is any doubt about hauling out ancient academic traditions, the ceremony concludes with the band playing and all rising to sing— in Latin!— "Gaudeamus Igitur" (Let Us Rejoice Always), a 1750 graduation song from England. Then it's over. The band plays and the marchers leave. An important event. A combination of panoply and panorama and tradition in one afternoon. It's memorable and leaves a positive memory for all in attendance. Bemidji State as a University never looks better than on Graduation Day.[35]

JUMBLED JOTTINGS AT DECADE'S END

If it's the "little things" that count, then certain "little things" about Bemidji State and the town should be noted as the year 1980 approached. Many

34) Bemidji State has precious few traditions, but faculty members marching in order of seniority is one of them. Newcomers at the end of the faculty line can look way to the front and in their relative youth they might wonder how all those old people in the front can still be teaching!? That statement was made by this author, who has been at both ends of the line between 1959-1994. At this writing in '94, the line will be headed by professor of biology, Evan Hazard, who came in 1958 with a new Ph.D. out of the University of Michigan.

35) Obviously, commencements take great planning and preparation, and credit belongs to several persons for their efforts. Among the most visible figures the day of the ceremonies is the University Marshal, an unclear title that does not delineate his role, but what the role means on graduation day is first to "Get the Show On the Road!" and make sure that everyone in the march is lined up in the right place and leaving at the right time in the right order and going to the right seat. The role requires an authoritarian figure who can keep order and bark orders and shape up the laggards—and prevent picture-takers from rushing up to the stage to muck up the ceremony—and all together have a sense of decorum and maintain that decorum under all circumstances. The role also requires someone with the voice of a hog caller and the lungs of an auctioneer. And all of the above have been found in the person of Gerald Michael Schnabel, professor of history, who has held the marshal role since 1979. A curious and unique tribute to Schnabel's knowledge of history come out in a student essay exam in a 1993 speech class. Wrote the befuddled student, "There is so much history that I would have to be God or Schnabel to fully grasp the exact situation during that time period."

pleased gourmands-in-a-hurry believed that Civilization had finally come to
Bemidji in 1976 when those Golden Arches could be seen on Highway 2 West, but
in three more years additional hamburger joints along the route would join
McDonalds to the point that that stretch of highway won the title of Gutbomb Row.
Students early in the decade could remember that empty section of jackpine forest
off Highway 2 West, but those who came at the end would spend time in the Paul
Bunyan Mall that emerged from the woods in the general malling-of-America that
decade.   In the spring of '79, dozens of students put away their ubiquitous
frisbees—and all the ambience implied by that curious form of boredom relief—
and volunteered their services to help sandbag the Red River banks, first for the
floods at Crookston and a little later the flooding in Grand Forks. Back on campus,
"mono" was still the "in" disease for diagnosis at the health service when nurses
didn't know what else was wrong. What was wrong with people's health from the
state's point of view was smoking, as identified in Minnesota's '79 Clean Air Act,
and the initial establishment of limited no-smoking areas on campus. However, the
smoke-free sections kept increasing in numbers and size till there were smoke-free
floors and then entire smoke-free buildings.   The whole clean-air, clean-lung
juggernaut culminated two decades later with a virtually smoke-free campus! (By
1990, huddled masses who yearned not to breathe free but rather to suck up a
precious cigarette could be found standing outside their buildings, heedless of
windchill factors or monsoons. Badly applied communist theory in this situation
found those from all walks of life—deans, janitors, vice presidents, freshmen—
huddling together without rank for their common cause, a cigarette.) The smoking
generations at early Bemidji State would find it most difficult to light up at their
school by its Diamond anniversary. Perhaps much happened in the '70s after all.[36]

WHAT'S BEEN DONE? ANNUAL REPORTS TELL (ALMOST) ALL

    At the end of every school year, all heads of units—chairpersons, deans,
coordinators, and the like—must write a comprehensive report which summarizes
the particular role of the unit and the individuals within the unit. All completed
reports go to the vice president for academic affairs who compiles them. The result
is a very fat "book," of sorts, a compendium of layered papers that can be measured
in pounds. Despite the intimidating size of each report, for any given school year

36) Assessments on any BSU time period from modern-day students make for interesting reading; obviously they view their
school's history differently. In the spring of 1993, a junior social studies major from Iowa named Karla Gransow wrote a 15-
page term paper reviewing BSU from 1975 to 1980, as part of an assignment for this author. For sources she used only the student
newspapers, and in her final paragraph she wrote her analysis, "As one can see, not much truly happened on campus in the five
years covered by this paper." Was she correct? Prior to her last comment, she chronicled some events she deemed at least semi-
important: the opening and naming of the Ila Mae Talley Art Gallery in 1975; the use by BSU of the former job-corps center
east of Cass Lake called Lydick Lake but renamed the Bald Eagle Center; the mixed feelings about placing sidewalks in the Hagg-
Sauer-library quadrangle; the snafu over first amendment rights about a "graffiti page" planned for the Northern Student which
the printer would not print because of vulgar language; a court trial over the non-hiring and non-renewal of contract of a husband
and wife who had both taught in the English department (BSU won); the flap over the removal of the original steps on Deputy
Hall; a Hall of Fame started in 1978 for former Beaver athletes; the BSU choir being selected to sing in Israel; students jamming
the Beaver Pond Bar on Thursday nights like sardines; the theft (and recovery) of the BSU sculpture called the Little
Fisherwoman; the Lamont Cranston band blowing the roof off M-100. All the above happened between '75 and '80, and so the
questions—what do they all mean? And how important are they? Present day readers, former students, and latter day historians
can judge for themselves.

it remains collectively the best single source of written but unpublished documentation available. (A complete set of annual reports are on file in the archives in the BSU library.)

These individually written summaries for the 1970s range widely each year, in number of pages or statistical evidence presented or the passions of the writers. The combined year's summaries are separated into categories: Graduate Studies, Teacher Education, Summer Sessions, Library, Registrar, Audio-Visual,

Sailing and Sailing Classes Just off from the Student Union
"Lake Bemidji ice freezes so solid and thick . . . the longest parking lot on campus."

Honors, Inter-Divisonal Programs; then Divisions: Behavioral Science, Education, Fine Arts, Humanities, Science and Mathematics, Health and Physical Education (and these division titles changed as realignments occurred), and within each division report are separate departmental reports written by the chairpersons. Everyone's report ends with specific recommendations for improvements, and even these requests can run several pages in length. All together the amount of information may be staggering but nevertheless this primary source documentation remains extremely important to the serious student of history attempting to learn more about Bemidji State in any given year.

For help in sorting out from the quantity, and maybe the quality, of the huge "book," each tome begins with a kind of cover letter, which is an overall summary of the year written by the vice president for academic affairs, after he or she has read and digested all of the submitted reports. The cover letter too ends with the V.P.'s recommendations to the president and the State College Board. The full summary takes up to 50 pages but in that relatively short space readers can get a profusion of summarized information on a variety of topics: the special successes of the year just ended listed numerically but in brief narrative form; numbers and names of new faculty, plus retirements and resignations; numbers on sabbatical leaves, leaves without pay, improvement grants, and research grants; promotions; number of doctorates and percentage by divisions and departments; faculty travels; new programs, both approved and waiting approval by the State Board; and all courses added and dropped; summer schools; enrollments (and graduates) broken down in quarters and by divisions and by departments; (even the number of official trips the V.P. took during the school year, plus where he went and why, are listed). And amid the V.P.'s assessments, along with the hundreds of pages that follow, are page after page of tables and charts and graphs and statistics. As indicated, the annual report is perhaps overwhelming in both numbers and verbiage but is nevertheless important material.

From the above reports came a list of the major accomplishments of the 1970s, as determined and stated by then vice president for academic affairs, Dr. Richard Beitzel:

- Bemidji State fully accredited in its undergraduate and graduate teaching programs by NCATE (National Council Association for Teacher Education); school to be reassessed in 10 years, 1981;
- Adult Education Evening Program (allowed persons to achieve a degree via night classes);
- New programs in Indian studies, environmental studies, outdoor education, social work and vocational education;
- B.A. and B.S. majors in humanities, 1973; geology, 1977; computer science, 1978;
- Appointment of an affirmative action officer;
- Expanded External Studies program; appointment of first full-time director;
- Career development program;
- ROTC program on campus;
- Annual department chairpersons preschool workshops;
- Computerized registration system, 1977; became model for rest of SUS;
- Full-time personnel director chosen; and,
- Summer writers' workshop conferences begin[37]

37) Cited by the division chair but not by Beitzel was the "accomplishment" of private telephones in each office in Hagg-Sauer Hall in 1974. Before the change, there was only one phone at the end of each hallway that was to serve all faculty personnel in the general area. In an interview with Beitzel at his Lake Movil cabin on July 10, 1993, Beitzel had almost all of the above mentioned points in mind when he was asked to come up with the Decker-Beitzel accomplishments that decade. In addition, he took credit for the naming of Hagg-Sauer Hall for the two men who had only recently retired at the time of the naming. He regretted not being able to achieve the naming of the education building after Bertha Christianson, who had been a Laboratory School supervising teacher from 1941 until her retirement in 1973. In a letter from Dr. Decker to this author, letter dated November 1, 1993, Mrs. Decker added two sheets entitled, "Things That Happened While Bob Was President." Most of the items she mentioned have been listed in the above text as stated by Beitzel and confirmed in the annual reports. However, she indicated some other things, "Increased number of cultural events on campus; encouraged town and area people to come on campus and encouraged faculty to become involved in civic affairs; built up community interest and awareness of the 'North Country' concept for area promotion; Fishing-for-Fun Contests, with proceeds going to scholarships." She added a wonderful anecdote on a planned student protest following the Kent State shootings in May of 1970. "The president's secretary, Martha Kaupp, would not let students have a 'sit-in' in President Decker's office because they did not have an appointment." Letter in author's files.

ROUTINE SCHOOL YEAR STARTS WITH A SHOCKER

The day before classes were to start in the fall of 1979, President Decker delivered his annual back-to-school address to the full gathering of all University employees. After 11 years, this procedure had become a routine for the audience who expected "the usual," starting with some bad Texas jokes and ending with his positive charge that all there would collectively work hard for another productive school year. In between the introductions and the conclusions, Decker would single out persons for praise, note major alterations in programs and staffing, comment on building changes and plans, and give useful information on budgets and allotments before sending everyone off to prepare for another school year. But this time his address was short, with all of "the usual" omitted; instead he announced his resignation as president: "I feel that it is time for a change after 11 years. Also I feel that it is in the best interest of Bemidji State University for me to resign now so that a new president can be selected in time to be personally involved in the process of selecting his or her own administrative team, with hopes that it will last for a long, long time."[38]   Following that last statement, Decker picked up the manuscript from which he was reading and strode out the door, leaving a shocked audience behind him.

Like Americans who were first shocked at the start of both world wars, and a little later were not that surprised, so too the employees at Bemidji State upon reflection could agree that Decker's resignation was not such a surprise after all. As was soon known, a number of factors had entered into his decision to leave, with the question both then and later being which was the most significant. These included his administration of 11 years, a rather long time period which made him subject to expected criticism. Understandably, he had made decisions that were not to everyone's liking. A few had bordered on the bizarre, like the decision of the previous spring (reversed by fall) to eliminate all chairpersons of all departments in order to save money. A $150,000 deficit in the Housing Office had been discovered back in May, and though there was never any suggestion of impropriety on his part, nevertheless the financial buck for sloppy management and bookkeeping stopped at the president's desk. About this time a new State University chancellor named Garry Hayes had taken over and he had definite ideas on what and whom he liked. Also, behind the scene was a tiny, rump group of disenchanted teaching faculty who met secretly and had their own agenda. Publicly, to clear the air, Decker had requested an outside review of the deficit, which Hayes granted, but Hayes then augmented the review to include the entire University operation and initiated a three-phase study of Bemidji State. Phase I consisted of an analysis by an external consultant; Phase II concerned the administrative structure, while Phase III involved revised structures and basic management functions. Vice Chancellor Emily Hannah coordinated the phase studies, reviewed proposals, and made her recommendations. All of these procedures were endorsed by the State

38) "BSU President R. D. Decker Resigns," The Pioneer, September 5, 1979, p. 1.

University Board (for the lengthy, detailed charges of the three-phase review, see Minutes of SUB, May 31, 1979).

Selected as the outside reviewer of BSU was Dr. Alan Guskin, chancellor of the University of Wisconsin-Parkside, who came on campus August 14 for two days of meetings, discussions and observations. He got an earful. In this brief time he met with a large number and variety of personnel, some who were the official representatives of their particular units and some who were not. After leaving Bemidji, he spent two days in St. Paul meeting with Hayes and the SUB. Guskin's findings and recommendations were later made public (the leaks came earlier), and collectively they would be referred to as "The Guskin Report." Perhaps most significant, Guskin recommended new administrative heads at Bemidji State who would not come from within the ranks. The SUB took these recommendations under advisement and did not officially act to implement them; unofficially is something else, with the public speculating on their behind-the-scene decisions. Considering all of the above, and more—along with the not-yet-stated notion that R.D. Decker was simply tired of the job and wanted out—his resignation that first week of school was less surprising. At the Board's request, he agreed to stay on as acting president until his replacement could take over.[39] The search then began for Decker's replacement.

THE BYZANTINE PROCESS OF PICKING A PRESIDENT

In Minnesota, the State University presidents are picked by the State University Board, and although that seems clear enough, the selection process has varied greatly since the first president was chosen at Winona back in 1860. These variations have been based on the degree to which the board is willing—or pressured—to share the selection-process with other interested parties. Sometimes the SUB has shared authority, sometimes not, and sometimes not enough, as was the case in the late '70s when the board set up a selection process for presidential vacancies at Mankato, Southwest, and Metropolitan State. Given the parameters announced by the chancellor, all three teaching faculties refused to participate, and so the Board went ahead without them. These same parameters were first announced as the procedures for the replacement of President Decker, to which the Bemidji faculty organization and the other bargaining groups all said no.[40] The Bemidji student senate also voted nine to two to protest the process. All groups called it "token participation" and wrote to Governor Al Quie and to some state legislators seeking their support for an alteration of the selection process.[41]

Even the Bemidji City Council jumped into the fray and contacted SUB Chairperson Arnold Anderson to request that the Board revise the process. Collectively, the protests/requests resulted in a hearing on October 23 of the Higher

39) Thanks to a policy established by former Chancellor Mitau, in office from 1968 to 1976, ex-presidents and chancellors, upon the recommendation of the SUB, could retire and be designated distinguished service professors with a salary commensurate with that high title. Decker received this honor upon leaving office; he also taught briefly in the BSU economics department before his election as a Republican to the Minnesota State Senate, where he served one term.
40) "Bemidji Groups Oppose BSU Presidential Selection Procedure," The Pioneer, October 3, 1979, p. 1.
41) "Senate Protests Presidential Selection Process," Northern Student, September 27, 1979, p. 1.

Education Division of the House Committee on Education, and afterwards politicians put the pressure on SUB to alter the process; the SUB agreed.[42]

Although still in an advisory position, the four Bemidji campus groups rejoined the selection process as the Advisory Search Committee and held their first joint meeting on November 27.[43] The ASC, chaired by Vice Chancellor Hannah, agreed to a preliminary screening by Hannah that would reduce the applicants (only 34 applied) to 25, at which point the full ASC would assess all applications and cut that number down to perhaps five finalists who would be invited to the campus for interviews.

Chairperson Hannah came regularly to Bemidji to meet with the full advisory group, who worked long and diligently to pare the numbers down. By early December the committee had reduced the slate to 12. After yet more deliberations and consultations, they selected five finalists who were invited to the campus for interviews the week of January 7 through 11, 1980. The finalists were Albert Anderson, president, Lenoir-Rhyne College, Hickory, North Carolina; David Barry, special assistant to the president of Antioch College, Yellow Springs, Ohio; James Schobel, president, Mayville State College, North Dakota; Charles Simmons, president, Lake Erie College, Painesville, Ohio; and Rebecca Stafford, dean, College of Arts and Sciences, University of Nevada at Reno. One by one— and one full day after another—they came on campus, for them to look at Bemidji State and vice versa. Although each candidate met groups and bargaining units separately, the day culminated when each candidate made a presentation to the full faculty and staff in the crowded auditorium in Hagg-Sauer Hall, and then answered often pointed questions. (The faculty buzzed steadily that week in making comparative judgments, and although no scientific poll was taken, the clear "winner" of the presentation hour was Stafford, whose intelligence, general poise and oratorical abilities simply overwhelmed her audience.) The following week Chancellor Hayes met with the full advisory committee and afterwards he exercised his authority and reduced the number further to three: Barry, Simmons and Stafford. That number became two when Simmons withdrew his name for the announced reason that "the match doesn't seem right between me and the University."[44] At last Hayes announced that the Board had voted unanimously on January 15, 1980, that Dr. Rebecca Stafford, age 43, would become the fifth president of Bemidji State and its first woman president.[45] Things were looking good as the 1980s began.

---

42) "Local Control Versus Centralization," The Pioneer, October 24, 1979, p. 1.
43) Committee members representing the faculty were Marjory Beck, Alan Brew, Richard Day, and Kenneth Lundberg; Carolyn Brule and Steven Schwanke served as BSU students on the committee, while Ida Mae Geitmann represented MSUAASF (Minnesota State University Association of Administrative and Service Faculty) and Shirley Bradley represented Council 6; Ed Nettestad represented employees not in a bargaining group; Lewis Downing, administration; James Sharp, alumni; and George Goodwin and Robert Welle, area representatives.
44) Quoted in The Pioneer, January 15, 1980, p. 1. Simmons had spent several years as a member of the history department at Moorhead State University, Minnesota, before starting an administrative climb that led later to a presidency for him.
45) "BSU's First Lady," Northern Student, January 17, 1980, p. 1.

The 1980s

T he '80s was not a user-friendly decade. Historians prefer to bundle years in blocks of time that try to make sense; world history writers prefer hundred-year packages—centuries—while American history scribes go for the shorter links to the past—the popular decades. Regardless, must not every decade bring about grand movements and momentous changes? No. Of course not. Major news events? Sure. However, while events can be precisely dated, news is little more than a first draft of history; newspaper headlines seldom endure as documents of import. In searching for meaning, elapsed time allows the luxury of retrospect. Until then. . . .

While not all became history, what made headlines in the '80s certainly caused a stir at the time. Among the people, places, and things making meaningful entrances: AIDS, Baby M., MCCL, fax machines, Margaret Thatcher, the Challenger disaster, Bernhard Goetz, Chernobyl, Garrison Keillor, Jarvik-7, AK-47, Pete Rose, crack, Lady Di, Lyme Disease, Bob Geldof, E.T., _Glasnost_, the greenhouse effect; homeless street people—and a "safety net"; leveraged buyouts, Boesky and Milken, Cabbage Patch dolls, Madonna, _Dynasty_, _Miami Vice_, "Who Shot J.R.?," Cuban Miami, Iran hostages, Vanessa Williams, Nicaraguan Contras, Noriega, microwaves, PC's, Rambo I, II, and III, Yin-Yin, the sleaze factor, Lech Walesa, Mount Saint Helen, Spuds MacKenzie, Bill Cosby, Vietnam Memorial, '80 Olympics; Geraldine Ferraro and Walter Mondale, Wayne Gretsky, Kabul, Oprah, _Cats_, Yuppies, Nancy, Donald Trump, Bear Bryant, Evan Mecham, Ethiopian Drought, Jimmy Swaggert, Oliver North, _Thirtysomething_, Gaddafi Bombing, Tiananmen Square, Bhagwan Rajneesh, _Back To The Future_, Rubic's Cube, Michael Jackson, the crumbling Berlin Wall. Headlines of the day, but not necessarily the stuff of long-range significance.

The major emblem of the '80s was not Wall Street with its message of "Greed is Good!" but the cheerful, reassuring President Ronald Reagan, who presided over the era. He cheered people up. Mr. Feelgood. At the height of his popularity in 1986, _Time_ magazine described him as a "Prospero of American memories, a magician who carries a bright, ideal America . . . and projects its image in the air." College students especially liked such talk of renewal from the nation's oldest serving president. On campuses where a few years before students had raged at their presidents, twenty-year-olds hollered "U.S.A. UP WITH AMERICA!" in response to Reagan's oratory. He captured the mood of the popular TV comedy series still running, _Happy Days_, even if realistically the '80s were not happy for too many Americans. His critics had labels for him like "amiable dunce," and journalists chronicled his many goofs, such as blaming redwood trees for air pollution. But the criticisms did not stick, and so he became the "Teflon President."

If there's one thing that Americans don't want from their leader, it's a sermon. Americans prefer pep talks, lines from their cheerleader reassuring them that they have to fear only "fear itself," being told that they're the best. When Jimmy Carter labeled the land as one of "malaise," Americans thumbed their noses at him in the voting booth. Reagan knew this instinctively; he also knew the country's basic political precept: No new taxes. And preferably no taxes at all. When Reagan campaigned in 1980, he promised to cut taxes, reduce deficits, reduce inflation, and rebuild the military to make America #1 again. One Republican called Reagan's ideas "voodoo economics"; this was George Bush, later to become Reagan's loyal vice president and ultimately president himself in '89.

Reagan's plan was called "supply side economics," the idea being that if taxes were cut, people would produce more and spend more to create even more jobs and greater prosperity, which all together would lead to higher government revenues. Everyone and everything would prosper. All men are equal, but some are more equal than others. Nothing new about that. Herbert Hoover had tried the same things during the Depression but it was then called "trickle down" economics. With strong popular support and congressional backing, Reagan's program sailed through Congress in 1981. But there was no immediate economic relief; on the contrary, the entire country was soon in the midst of a full-blown and devastating recession. Unemployment was high, inflation continued, bankruptcies and business failures skyrocketed, and family farms went on the auction block. When the crunch hit Minnesota, then-Governor Albert Quie gained the dubious distinction of having to call five special sessions of the legislature to muddle through expendable budget plans enough to squeeze by year by year. Of course Bemidji State in general again got caught in the economic crises of the early '80s, and specifically the burden of the school's maintenance, if not its very survival, fell on its brand new president, Rebecca Stafford.

Oil had been at the root of the nation's economic problems and it was only the eventual tumble in oil prices in '82 that relieved the pressures. The beneficiary of this reversal was Reagan; the slide in oil prices signaled the start of the recovery. With falling oil costs, the heart of the inflationary dragon was cut out, and Ronald Reagan looked like Saint George. Employment began to grow, and inflation, which had been running at better than 10 percent for 10 years, dropped to less than five percent the rest of the decade. The pro-business policies of the administration fueled the recovery, with the subsequent years leading to the sobriquet "The Business Decade." The rich got richer and the poor got kids. By the time the Good Times came back to Minnesota and Bemidji State, however, President Stafford was long gone. In a reversal of adjectives, "It was the worst of times, it was the best of times. . . ." Along came the right man at the right time for BSU, Ted Gillett.

The Southern Scene of the Extended Campus
"Faculty members on opposite ends of the campus never know each other."

REBECCA STAFFORD

Dr. Stafford served briefly as president of Bemidji State University from April 9, 1980, until her resignation on December 16, 1981. She was born in Topeka, Kansas, on July 9, 1936. She received all of her degrees in sociology: B.A.,

Radcliffe College, 1958; M.A., Harvard University, 1961; Ph.D., Harvard University, 1964. From 1964 until 1970, she served as lecturer in the department of social relations at Harvard. From 1970 to 1979 she was an associate professor of sociology at the University of Nevada-Reno, and served as chair there from 1974 to 1977 when she became dean, College of Arts and Sciences, at Reno. She did post-doctoral work at Harvard in 1978 at an Institute for Deans and Vice Presidents, and returned to Nevada as dean, the position she held when she accepted her appointment as BSU president on January 15, 1980, calling it "the most exciting thing that has happened in my entire life."[1]

Two days after the Board announced her selection, President-elect Stafford arrived in Bemidji on January 17, 1980, to be welcomed warmly on a cold day. The Chamber of Commerce sponsored a get-acquainted luncheon for her, while a similar reception, open to everyone, was held on campus. She also began the first in a series of meetings with administrative staff members and got acquainted with her office and her office staff. The overall mood of the time was not only upbeat but almost euphoric, with the banal phrase of "breath-of-fresh-air" used commonly in describing her selection. The greater college-community enjoyed the thrill of anticipation and looked forward with great optimism for Bemidji State with her as president. Following the receptions, she returned in late January to Nevada to complete her obligations there, commitments that lasted until April 1.

NOT EVEN A BRIEF HONEYMOON

President-elect Stafford had not yet arrived on campus when her first controversy emerged. In March it was revealed that moving expenses enabling her and her husband to leave their Reno home and relocate in Bemidji would be in the area of $18,000. After receiving several estimates, the State University Board agreed to pay the full moving expenses, and this news was trumpeted in the Minneapolis Star Tribune, which implied that the figure was bloated and that state taxpayers were being hit with yet another government-padded bill. None of this, of course, was the direct fault of Stafford, yet her arrival came under a faint cloud. Even finding a house to live in proved controversial in that it appeared that she reached agreements with a seller and then reneged, more rumors that small towns grab on to. She and her husband (they had no children) then rented a house near the University. Finally, on April 9, 1980, Stafford moved into her office on the third floor of Deputy Hall and thus assumed her full duties and responsibilities as

1)Stafford was quoted in a Northern Student article headlined, "Background of a President." This particular paper came out on October 30, 1980, just prior to her inauguration the next day as the school's fifth president. The four-day festivities surrounding the event included a luncheon for public school superintendents, counselors, and community college administrators. There was also a banquet for all BSU faculty and staff at the Holiday Inn the night before the inauguration ceremonies, while the night after the ceremonies there was a ball, also in the Holiday Inn, with music provided by the BSU Jazz Bands, complete with a grand march, led by Stafford and her husband, Willard Van Hazel, Jr. A busy week and weekend, with much finery trotted out for the several occasions. A silly issue was whether Stafford would wear the presidential medallion, made for Decker's inauguration by an artist-in-residence, Elmer Peterson (who would later make the huge bison figure standing on a hill near Jamestown, North Dakota, and also BSC's The Little Fisherman); in the middle of the medallion were welded an assortment of common screws, their featured appearance leading to many negative comments about it being/not being "art." She wore it.

president.[2]

Her first major public appearance came the next month when she presided over graduation ceremonies in the field house. Her appearance was impressive: She wore an all-red academic gown, reflecting her Harvard University background, attire which made her stand out amid the sea of black academic gowns all around her. She was at her best in addressing large groups and used the opportunity to say all the right things to the large assemblage of families and friends who came to Bemidji State to observe graduation exercises. The crowd had to be favorably impressed by this new, young, attractive, first woman president of the school. Much would be expected. Maybe too much.

GETTING ACQUAINTED: A TWO-WAY STREET

Stafford came just as the school year was ending, and her early efforts were spent in getting acquainted with the school, the programs and the people, and in getting people acquainted with her. Some things were new to both her and the school in 1980. A new public television station, KAWE, had set up operation on the second floor of Deputy Hall. Just across the hall was the University TV station, KBSU, which had been on the air since 1974. The school had begun to respond to both state and federal laws to make buildings accessible to the physically handicapped so that a ramp had been constructed into Memorial Hall and the restrooms had been remodeled in Hagg-Sauer Hall. By 1980 the term "janitor" seemed inappropriate, given the number of women employed, and the term "janitress" seemed both patronizing and dumb; finally came the appropriate designation of male/female custodians. (In 1980 the State University System had over 36,000 students enrolled—4,374 of them were at BSU.) The new ROTC unit held its first BSU commissioning ceremonies, making second lieutenants out of students Randy McGuire and Ray Born. By 1980, all outsiders had to be impressed by the large number of students working their way through college ("the scramblers"), with the majority in a financial aid program called work-study, which old timers saw as a form of WPA and cynics viewed as an academic pork barrel involving in its application little of each word in its title. Most Americans accepted WPA (Works Progress Administration) because it was necessary; same with the later work-study. Like its predecessor, it provided jobs and much useful work was done, even if there were aberrational abuses.

A TOTALLY NEW ADMINISTRATION IN A NEW DECADE

Stafford moved with deliberate speed to select her own team, her own administration, and in one year's time three new vice presidents began their terms:

2)While waiting for Stafford to take over, the school went into a kind of holding action, delaying major decision-making until her arrival. The annual report for the 1979-80 school year found the acting vice president using phrases like "put on hold" and "postponed until the new administration came on line." The famous, or infamous, Guskin Report of the previous summer had among its recommendations the need for outside persons in the top administrative positions. This stated need was implemented almost immediately with the resignation of Decker; five days before that, Vice President Beitzel had resigned to return to the chemistry department to teach. No administrators whose jobs continued only at the pleasure of the president would rest easy after the Guskin Report.

Thomas A. Faecke, administration; Roger B. Ludeman, student affairs; and Leslie C. Duly, academic affairs.[3] The new administration moved with suddenness that fall to rock and shock both the faculty and staff by requiring from every area a self-study called a "Program Planning and Review." Officially, as the opening sentence in the memo from the president's office read, "The need for comprehensive planning for financial resources and staff at Bemidji State University is acute." Unofficially, it required virtually all faculty and staff on the BSU payroll to justify their existence or be terminated. "A bombshell," said most faculty; "More wasted time, effort, and paper-shuffling, all of which will never get read and end up gathering dust on administrators' shelves," said many; "Time for creative justification," said others, and a very few said, "This is exactly what this school needs." Outsiders said, "It's about time."

The order went out not only to each academic department but also to all non-teaching areas. Thus the directors of counseling and financial aid and area services were forced to file their reports alongside German and geology and geography. The format for all to follow was the same, starting with Staff/Faculty Data, followed by the big one, Roman Numeral II, PROGRAM, under which came subtitles: "Importance to the University, Evidence of Programs/Service Quality, Evidence of Academic Quality—" which included the question, "Why are they better or we better?"; "Additional Resources to Improve Programs and How They are to be Used"; "Impact of 25 Percent Reduction"; "Designation Sought." The latter phrase had all responders specify the category under which they wished to be designated: 1) Center for Emphasis 2) Major Program 3) Minor Program 4) Service Area.

Before any self-study efforts had even started, the administration made it very clear that they intended to aid, promote and continue primarily Centers for Emphasis so that virtually all self-study units went for that designation; choosing any other category appeared to be some kind of academic death wish. This desire for Center for Emphasis came out in every report, with one reviewer specifying on his title page: "A Justification for the Designation of Center for Excellence."[4]

SURVIVAL TACTICS, A' LA ACADEMIA

The scramble for survival began with alacrity. With it came an equal number of grumbles and roars, even if the warning from the administration was clearly stated in their memo on what the completed documents would mean for each unit: "This document will govern our staffing plan for the next six years . . . and

---

3)Duly was selected in June of 1980 and Ludeman in July, '80; Faecke in November of '81. According to one administrator, still in office in '94, still not wanting his name mentioned, "When Becky [Dr. Stafford] first arrived on campus, all the 'wannabes' buzzed around The Queen Bee like shameful, sycophantic drones." Duly replaced Acting Vice President Willard F. Bornschlegl, who returned to the education division; Ludeman's title as vice president came as a result of the Guskin Report. Prior to his coming, Jon Blessing had served that role as coordinator of student affairs (Blessing stayed on as assistant to Ludeman); Faecke replaced Carl Long, who left the University, as did Ludeman leave in 1988 and whose V.P. position was not replaced.
4)Only one unit, ROTC, chose the designation of minor. Being essentially outside the school with their own staff paid by Army, they did not have anything to worry about. Programs like German chose major program, only because they were part of the general foreign languages which went for Center for Emphasis. Rare was the academic area that did not go for the brass ring; just one, political science, asked for "major program" designation—and ended up defending its very existence.

every biennium thereafter. Reallocation of resources will utilize existing vacancies and retirement where appropriate...." In other words, get busy or you may be gone in a short while. Thus the personnel in all departments and various programs began to organize, to form committees and sub-committees and make individual assignments, collectively to gather and sift documentation and write it up and rewrite and add more numbers when and if they looked good, with all to be completed and submitted (in duplicate) in final form by D-Day, December 18, 1980. It was a major scramble all fall, involving much overtime work, and not a few side/snide comments made along the way. In size, some self-studies were longer and thicker and heavier than the regular annual report compendium, and when all reports were piled one on another, they measured three and a half feet high.

Several stages of evaluation followed the submission of the reports, culminating on March 2, 1981, with President Stafford announcing which department or program or unit made which category; in the faculty vernacular this translated as "who'll live and who'll die." Twenty-five units were judged, nine in non-teaching service areas. The 16 teaching areas which received the initial hallowed designation of Center for Emphasis ranged from elementary education, which had the most annual graduates at 122, to economics, which had the least, two. In between, and in order of the most graduates per year were: business education, physical education, social work, English, mass communication, criminal justice, community service, accounting, biology, industrial technology, music, history, sociology, and geography. Though the adjective was not formally used, these 16 were perceived as the "best"; those not in the ethereal circle were . . . lesser on the scale.[5] Those lesser on the scale made enough noise to be heard in St. Paul; the endangered species put up a fight, as illustrated by a three-page, single-spaced letter addressed to President Stafford, which began, "We believe that the proposed destruction of the political science department is both unwise and unjustified," and went on to explain and plead the department's cause.[6] Taking the biggest hit of all was counselor education; that program was phased out entirely. Stafford also indicated her intention to add 13 new staff positions, presumably to the Centers for Emphasis, while deleting 23 positions in other areas. Obviously there was a very upset faculty as a result of all these machinations, so much so that by May the president began to waffle over definitions, or, as the student newspaper headlined it: "Centers for Emphasis Redefined," explaining that Stafford had recently accepted a new definition, which included three sub-categories: "Centers for Emphasis of recognized quality, necessary Centers for Emphasis, and unique

5)Stafford's recommended list was announced on March 13; the Northern Student of April 2, 1981, listed the departments under the headline: "Staff Cuts May Hurt Sports, P.E." Despite phy ed making top designation, Vice President Duly was quoted as recommending to the president that one major sport be eliminated (he did not say which one) and that only one of five current staff vacancies be filled in phy ed, reducing the complement from 20 to 16. Whether it is coincidental or cause and effect, the same issue reported the retirement of Chet Anderson as head wrestling coach after 25 years.
6)Letter from chair of political science, dated March 20, 1981. Letter found in miscellaneous file of some Stafford papers that are part of the program planning and review reports, the massive documents kept in a storeroom on third floor of Deputy Hall. Political science had been recommended for elimination as a major, along with speech and Russian. All would survive, however, and Stafford learned about applied Minnesota political science when some top state DFL figures stepped in and put the pressure on her. For a sampling of both student and faculty disgust, see Northern Student, April 2, 1981, p.1, under headline "Inconsistencies Cause Anger."

Centers for Emphasis." Amid the word games, still perceived as coming out best were those of "recognized quality," which were music, psychology, biology, history, industrial technology, education, geography, sociology, environmental studies, business administration, financial aids, counseling, career development, and placement bureau. The fact that some areas on the new preferred list had not made the first cut stirred up even more turmoil among the disgruntled. Stafford would not have won any popularity contest at this time, something she acknowledged forthrightly: "To be president, you have to give up being liked. You have to hope that you're respected."[7]

THE VIEW FROM THE TOP

The general consternation among faculty, staff and students lasted the entire 1980-81 school year. Given the ongoing amazed dismay and general confusion that went with program reviews, almost all were extra happy to have the school year end, just for a respite from the turmoil. Stafford served only one full school year as president, and at the end of that year, the student newspaper co-editor, Rob Hotakainen devoted two pages to interview questions and answers with Stafford. Both the questions and her replies give added insight about her short period as president:

Question: You've been president of BSU for over a year now. What's been your greatest accomplishment?

Stafford: *"What I think will be my greatest accomplishment has not been accomplished yet, which is the whole program planning and review. That's what I've been spending most of my time on. . . ."*

Question: In your estimation, what is BSU's image and how do you want to change that image?

Stafford: *"Well, the image comes from outside. It comes from [presidents, the SUS board, teachers, community] a composite of data collected from all of those fairly informal sources. I think our image is that we're a bit soft on rigor, that we don't know where we're going, that we have set our priorities, that we're really going off in many directions. . . . Hockey and teachers were what we're known for, and so I would like to change the image by balancing liberal arts and vocational education. . . ."*

Question: You've named Centers for Emphasis. In an era of declining resources, to what extent are you willing to push this quality?

Stafford: *"That's hard to say. What I am already willing to do is redirect resources. We'll take resources from one area and put them in another. Certainly all new resources that we come upon will go to the Centers for Emphasis."*

Question: " A lot of faculty members are complaining that you're inaccessible."

Stafford: *"I bet every president has had that charge leveled at them. The difficulty is that there are many, many constituents on campus, and each of them thinks that they are the only constituents that need to have some of my time."*

7)Stafford quoted in the Northern Student's last issue of the school year, May 14, 1981, p. 3B.

Question: Mark Morphew, our former student senate president, criticized you rather severely, saying you ignore student needs and student auxiliary services and that you're too far removed from the students.

Stafford: *"Well, again, Mark is making the same argument. I'm only one person. I would simply not be able . . . to run every piece of the University. So I have administrators running each section of the University and they have a lot of authority to make decisions. I know constantly what is going on. I know what the student senate is doing every week, even though I don't sit there for two hours and listen."*

Question: "You're criticized for traveling a lot. You went to England at a very crucial time for the University. . . People say, 'Well, Becky's on another one of her trips and Vice President Duly is running the store again.'"

Stafford: *A lot of people don't have a perception of what a president does. A president is a boundary maintenance person. A president is expected to be the person between the inside and the outside, so there is a great deal of traveling required for the job. I spend a lot of time in St. Paul. I can't get away from that as long as we're a part of the System. I visit many schools in northern Minnesota. I made the England trip to take a look at the Eurospring program. We've got to make some big changes in that program."*

Question: What other criticisms have you heard about your performance as president?

Stafford: *"Well, I had a man criticize me the other day. He called me up and said, 'What is this bit about excellent education?' And I said we are working on a real thrust for excellence in the '80s. And he said, 'Well, I don't think people in northern Minnesota want excellent education.' I have also been criticized for being too much in favor of the liberal arts. I have also been criticized for not paying enough attention to the liberal arts."*

Question: How's it feel after one year in "power"?

Stafford: *"Oh gosh, I don't think it's being in power. I try to be the one person that balances the needs of the faculty, staff, and the various constituencies. Somebody once said when they were very angry that I have to do what the faculty wants me to do, that I'm employed by the faculty. And I said, 'Oh no, I'm not. I'm more employed by the students.' But that doesn't mean that I'm going to do everything the current crop of students wants me to do. I have to look at the current, the past, and the future. It's always a very, very lonely job because you're nobody's friend. If you're somebody's friend, you're not doing your job because then you're pandering to one particular constituency. To be president, you have to give up being liked. You have to hope that you're respected."*[8]

8)Northern Student, May 14, 1981, pp. 2B, 3B. Even that category came hard for her. Although she did have her admirers, there were more critics, even when both sides acknowledged the difficult financial times. English Professor Ruth Stenerson, on the faculty from 1956 to 1986, wrote in her Memories of a Department (1992), "The tension over financial matters and policy was evident during Dr. Decker's administration and disagreements between him and some of the faculty were hard to resolve, but I came to appreciate him as a fine human being—which I still do. I was not enthusiastic about his successor, Dr. Rebecca Stafford. Most of the English faculty, I believe, mistrusted her interest in our discipline and were glad when she (and Dr. Emily Hannah of the Chancellor's Office) left. A part of the dislike toward them was no doubt the result of their being the first women we worked under at that level of administration, but most of it was a result of their ineptness in handling interpersonal relationships." pp. 5-6.

Dining at 'Wallys': Walnut Hall, the Primary Campus Cafeteria
"Gourmets may have their doubts . . . gourmands love the place."

BRIGHT SPOTS AMID THE TURBULENCE

The 1980-81 school year had its bright spots, of course. For the 4,000-plus undergraduates on campus, there was always something bright to discover and enjoy, even if an extra dollar per credit surcharge was slapped on them for winter and spring quarters. The new figure ($13.20 a credit) was grudgingly accepted as a necessary evil, a way to survive the economic crunch of the times. Some building improvements were perceived as bright, although all people in remodeled Deputy Hall that fall were still dodging carpenters and ladders, boxes and dollies, painters and electricians; it eventually came out all right when all the work was completed by Christmas. Because it was a U.S. presidential election year, the school got caught up in the spirit of the lively campaigns. The Northern Student served as a kind of political billboard before the editors made their choices just before election time, and afterwards they found that most of their endorsed candidates did not win, starting with the incumbent Jimmy Carter. The controversial issue of the legality of beer on campus seemed to go through the ballot boxes O.K.; the city voters approved the referendum, but even then brew-in-the-union did not quite make it. (So back to the popular night spots of the time: The Bare Bear, T-Bone's, Gene's Place, Corner Bar, Turtle Club, and the old Vogue North which had been renamed The Viking.) In early January, the local fire marshal closed Memorial Hall for public use, citing violations of codes. He did permit the then-annual Ol' Tyme Fiddlers' Contest to take place, with a large crowd coming out on a night so frigid that folks were hoping the temp might get up to 25 below zero. The Michael

Johnson concert the next week, however, had to be moved to the high school auditorium. The PAM (Peaceful Alternatives to Militarism) group on campus kept making the news with protests, like picketing and protesting draft registration. (Two Bemidji State students, John LaForge and Barb Katt, remained so committed to PAM goals that they continued their protests throughout the country that entire decade, protesting to the degree that they spent time in and out of federal prison.) Father Carl Kabat, one of seven people then awaiting sentencing for destroying the nose cones of two nuclear warheads in Pennsylvania, spoke on campus and unsettled his audience. A student senate motion to eliminate the armed ROTC military color guard at commencement exercises was declared "out of order" by the student senate president. Consumer advocate Ralph Nader spoke at BSU as part of the MPIRG (Minnesota Public Interest Research Group) Energy Fair. In sports, the Beaver hockey team ended the season with a 27-4 record; the basketball and football squads won only one game each, while baseball ended with a 15-18 record. The theater and music people provided an abundance of music and theatrical events, with plays like Rimers of Eldritch, See How They Run, and The Boyfriend.

SOMETHING NEW (AND GOOD) FROM STAFFORD

The school year came to an end with a new bright spot inaugurated by the new president, an Honors Convocation. This has been held annually ever since. All classes were canceled between the hours of 9 a.m. and noon for the program held in the Beaux Arts Ballroom on Monday, April 27, 1981. The time was set aside to give public honor primarily to students for their academic achievements, with each program or department selecting their top student or students for that year. All the winners were called to the stage to receive their certificate of award and get a public handshake and congratulations from the president, too. Five special awards had monetary stipends, then $200 each, in five categories: The Distinguished Teacher of the Year, the Distinguished Faculty Researcher, the Outstanding BSU Employee, the Outstanding Student, and the Outstanding Student Paper/Work of Creativity. Prior to the announcement of awards, an address was given by Dr. Oscar Anderson, former president of Augsburg College, entitled, "Toward a Higher Pragmatism." All in all, a special event, a proper event. A reminder of what a school is to emphasize—and honor.[9]

DEFINITELY NON-ADMINISTRATIVE DUTIES

Summers at Bemidji State have normally been more relaxed times for everyone. Most of the students, staff and faculty are not around in summertime, and the pace slows down for those who are on campus. Administrators usually find

9)Receiving the Teaching Award was Dr. Charles Austad, education; Research Award to Dr. Charles Fuchsman, director of the Center for Environmental Studies; Outstanding Employee, Nickie Petrowske, supervisor of the secretarial pool in Hagg-Sauer; Outstanding Student, Robert Hotakainen, from Sebeka, who was the co-editor of the Northern Student; Outstanding Student Paper went to Paul Hedtke, from Baudette, for his paper, "Software Development for the Fast Neutron Hodoscope's New High Density System." In the interview with Stafford in NS, May 14, 1981, p.2B, she was quoted as saying, "The second greatest accomplishment [after program planning and review goals] that I feel very strongly about is the Honors Convocation. Third would be all the speaking I do on the quality of education and the way in which my school visits have, I would like to think, had some effect on enrollment."

fewer problems to deal with and live less hectic lives for these few months, when the daylight in the north country hangs on until 10 p.m. Quiet times, usually. Not so for administrators in the summer of 1981, when almost all of the secretarial, janitorial, and maintenance staff went on strike in late July.[10]   While striking picketers and their supporters marched with their signs up and down the sidewalk along Birchmont Drive in front of the school, school functions went on essentially as usual, whether classes or workshops or clinics or band camps. All of the usual functions of each day required the usual secretarial and janitorial functions: Letters still had to be written, office shelves dusted and floors swept, wastebaskets emptied, and yes, lavatories cleaned also and toilet paper replaced. For the next two and a half weeks, Stafford and her top administrators—including some unhappy division heads pressed into service—performed duties never mentioned in their job descriptions. Top administrators were assigned responsibility for specific building cleaning and maintenance, the amount of work requiring weekends, too.   One senior personnel aide moved about the campus each day to do as much as possible of the basics in each assigned area before rushing off to do something somewhere else, and this included placement bureau typing for a while, picking up debris from the grounds, working on intra-campus mail deliveries, and the like. Each employee signed in and signed out when coming to or leaving a building; those names and numbers were reported daily to St. Paul. There were a few open acts of vandalism during the strike, along with regular nuisance phone calls. For example, the state fire marshal was called to come to Bemidji to examine—and close down— Memorial Hall facilities in the middle of a music camp, when some one thousand high school students were using the building. A junk car was hauled in at night and placed in the middle of the main loading ramp to try to prevent garbage pickup. The tires on the car of one non-striker were slashed. The tensions on campus continued and were exacerbated by individuals not in the striking units but still wanting, sometimes demanding, to flaunt their views. Thus some persons made a show of deliberately walking through the picket lines on their way to their jobs, with something less than social chitchat exchanged; others refused to cross the picket lines and honored the strikers by, for example, refusing to deliver ordered supplies. Each day the vice president for administration drove a school truck to the mall to pick up supplies there from state truckers who would not cross the lines on campus. To the relief of everyone, the strike ended on August 11, and gradually the place returned to normal and the summer atmosphere came back to the more casual ambience associated with it, but by then the summer was nearly over. Some invisible scars would remain from that strike, however, the wounds taking a long time to heal.

FISCAL WOES CONSTRAIN AND CONSTRICT
The financial crunch in the early 1980s affected the operation of Bemidji State in ways that not only threatened the regular operation but even gave rise to

10) The union that struck on campus was AFSCME, American Federation of State, County, and Municipal Employees.

rumors of its discontinuation. Bad rumors may be easy to start but they are hard to beat back. For reasons never clear, other than fiscal difficulties, by January of 1981, words to the effect that Bemidji State would be closed reached the outer public so that phone calls came to the president's office offering both solace and surprise: "We're so sorry to hear that Bemidji State will be closing. . . " "Is it TRUE what we heard? . . ." However, like Mark Twain's reply to the newspaper story that he had died, reports of BSU's demise were "greatly exaggerated." Hard times had hit so severely by 1981 that legislators traveled throughout the state taking testimony on how to save money, and eventually Governor Al Quie called another special session of the legislature to attempt to manage the crisis. For all state agencies, of course, the crunch meant cutbacks at best and closings at worst. Once again survival required dogged, ongoing exertions on the part of friends of Bemidji State. The entire Bemidji community got behind a variety of lobbying endeavors, efforts that included the Chamber of Commerce sponsoring chartered bus trips in January to St. Paul. It was a struggle, indeed, but eventually the combined lobbying efforts paid off in the major sense that BSU remained as viable as before, its budget essentially the same as the previous year.[11]

One obvious result of these financial woes that fall of 1981 was the scuttling of the previous year's agonizing Program Planning and Review plans/predictions/threats. Whether departments or units had ratings of "Centers for Emphasis of Recognized Quality" or not made no difference at that point because there was no extra money anyway to fill all the planned new positions that were supposed to go to the centers. So virtually nothing changed. Much ado about nothing. Faculty reaction to the abandonment of PPR was mixed; some cheered, others jeered, but all sides agreed that it had been a lot of work, a lot of turmoil, a lot of bitterness—for nothing! Not all were forgiving of Stafford and all the commotion she had caused over plans and programs and changes that never occurred.[12]

STORMS AT HOME, MAN-MADE AND OTHERWISE

Not all the problems which hit Bemidji State that fall of '81 were man-made. Ten years earlier the school had leased the former Job Corps Center east of Cass Lake as an outdoor recreation center and a kind of extended campus. It became a wonderful spot for retreats, seminars, environmental study programs, workshops, and faculty social and professional gatherings. The facilities included small dormitories, a kitchen and eating area, and even a small gymnasium. It was

11) The old saw runs, "A friend in need is a friend indeed." For Bemidji State in the early 1980s, that line would be changed to, "A friend indeed is . . . the chairman of the Senate Finance Committee." Gerald Willet, DFL, Park Rapids, served as the chair of this powerful committee and he was indeed a friend of Bemidji State in these difficult times.

12) In talking recently with faculty members who were employed during the Stafford years, the one issue most remembered by them were those planning proposals that got them worked up then and still got them agitated when they thought about them later. Said one man, "We were so busy with meetings and planning and writing that whole year that I wonder how we ever got around to teaching classes. And what came out of them? Nuthin'." It would be too easy then and later to be critical of Stafford on this issue, but even if her plans were not implemented, they did force all faculty and staff to come to grips with some important issues that needed to be confronted, and in that sense the University benefited by taking careful measure of itself. Perhaps all the acerbic critics of Stafford should first contemplate the Writer's Prayer: "O Lord, help my words to be gracious and tender today, for tomorrow I may have to eat them."

a little village/campus way out in the middle of the woods. Located some 30 miles from Bemidji on Lydick Lake, it was renamed the Bald Eagle Center and it got good use and a good reputation as a desirable forest retreat run by and for people connected with the University. Then came a summer storm of such severity that it ripped through the camp, destroying enough of the buildings as to make the place unusable. The damage came just when BSU's lease was up for renewal in '81, and rather than repair the buildings, the U.S. Forest Service decided to return the land to its natural state. Like the many logging towns that once surrounded Bemidji, the Bald Eagle Center campus slowly disappeared back to nature.

OTHERWISE

The real storm in the fall of '81 was man-made, or in this case, woman-made: President Stafford resigned in the middle of the school year. On December 16 she resigned and announced that she had accepted the appointment as the executive vice president of Colorado State University in Fort Collins, the position to start on February 1, 1982. She added, "The offer from Colorado State was a rare opportunity in my career and one which I did not feel I could turn down." The Northern Student's banner headline the next day ran, "Stafford Quits."

Once again came the initial reaction of shock which was soon followed by the absence of any real surprise. After all, her interest in another position had become well known on campus so that the debates over her leaving had been under discussion for some time. Although there was no campus consensus about any ethical duty to remain as president, at least through the school year, almost all persons connected with Bemidji State felt used and let down. Perhaps the Northern Student editorial (December 17, 1981, p. 6) spoke for most; it was headlined, "It's Time to Move On, Dr. Stafford." Wrote the editor:

"Many predicted Stafford's resignation; some expected it. But it was still a shock. Stafford's bold planning in academia and budget areas have helped Bemidji State. She won our loyalty two years ago. We placed our trust in her. We were a University tired of a do-nothing president. We begged for leadership, and she gave it to us. She let us down. Even by interviewing for the job, she let us down. It's probably best she's leaving. Actively pursuing another job when she promised to dedicate herself to this one was a slap in the face. Her credibility was irrevocably shaken. She invalidated anything she ever said. . . ."[13]

The announcement of her leaving came just before the Christmas break. The students' reactions reflected the expected diversity of opinion, evidenced in union coffee comments and a little prose in the school paper. Two students, however, carried it further by burning Stafford in effigy. Wearing ski masks, they carried a crudely-constructed dummy, clad in a blonde wig, and placed it in a snowdrift just outside the union's big windows. Just in case the figure was not

---

13) Among the surprised was Tom Faecke, vice president for administration, who had been interviewed the month before by Stafford. After he came from Washington State University to be interviewed, he too heard the rumor about her possible departure and before their session ended, he asked her pointblank if she intended to leave and she said no. Comment made by Faecke to this author on July 18, 1993. Faecke is a Bemidji State graduate, class of 1969.

recognized, the pair had hung a sign reading "Becky" around the dummy's neck. They then set it on fire and ran away. Inside the union, students witnessing the scene displayed reactions equally mixed. Some laughed, some cheered, some revealed shocked disgust. The <u>Northern Student</u> editorial response later was headlined, "Effigy Burning Regrettable."[14]

A PARTY OR A WAKE? THE LAST GOODBYE

Dr. Stafford came in under a cloud, created a storm cloud over the campus that lasted most of her 20 months at the helm, and she left under a cloud of controversy, albeit a snowy one.[14] Just before the Christmas vacation began and just before Stafford left office, there was a final social gathering for her, with all faculty and staff invited to stop by for coffee and cake on the third floor of Deputy Hall, just outside her office. But what "the party" was all about was not clear. Some saw it as an "Honor Coffee," a form of congratulations on her new, presumably elevated position; some saw it as some kind of wake, with a last sip of Folgers denoting the dear departed heading west; a few observed it as "Good Riddance Time" which would bring out for this short-termer only the true hypocrites to sup among the other brown-nosers while uttering falsities of such quantity and quality sufficient to shame the entire school; others viewed it as simply a proper going away gathering which required swallowing any prejudice towards her and instead bringing forth all alleged Minnesota nice, or at least enough to allow a decent display of congeniality for a civilized goodbye. After all, she had done some good things for the school.[15]

And besides, it was again time to look ahead and think about a new president; meanwhile, it was also time to adjust to an acting president. That would be Richard Haugo, BSU Placement Bureau director, who would serve the next eight months, until July 30, 1982.

RICHARD ROLAND HAUGO

Dr. Haugo was born July 11, 1925, in Ellendale, Minnesota, the first child of Aslak and Irene Randall Haugo. The next year the family moved to a farm near Sheyenne, North Dakota, where eventually four sisters and two brothers were born. The Haugo family was the only one attending the one room country school near their farm. While Haugo's father was a first generation Norwegian-American, his mother was predominantly English, Scotch and Irish in her ethnic background.

---

14) Continuing this cloud metaphor, in the summer of 1993 this author was in a discussion with a female colleague who had been at BSU over 20 years. In commenting about Stafford's leaving, she said, "On the day she resigned, the black cloud hanging over this campus just disappeared. Poof! The sun shone again! It was wonderful! And if you put that in your book and use my name, I'll shoot you."
15) Not yet cited among her contributions was her inauguration of an event held during graduations, that is BSU selecting and honoring each year a Distinguished Minnesotan. The first one picked in 1981 was nature writer Sigurd Olson, and each year since then some person has been honored; after Olson, Karl Kassulke, Janet Dearholt Esty, Frederick Manfred, Dr. John Najarian, Dr. Harlan Cleveland, Muriel Buck Humphrey Brown, Elmer L. Andersen, Curtis L. Carlson, William S. Marvin, Meridel LeSuer, Veda Ponikvar, and Nellie Stone Johnson. Stafford stayed only briefly in Colorado before accepting the presidency of Chatham, a small women's college in Pennsylvania. In March, 1993, she was chosen as president of Monmouth College, West Long Branch, New Jersey, a position she holds at this writing. This author wrote two letters to her, asking her for her own interpretations of her year and a half as president of Bemidji State. She did not reply.

Because of the Dakota drought in the 1930s, the Haugo family moved to a farm near Erskine, Minnesota, in 1937, and Dr. Haugo graduated from high school there in 1943. After a two-year term in the Navy, serving in the Pacific theater of operation during World War II, he spent time working on a road construction crew until he enrolled at Pacific Lutheran College, Tacoma, Washington, in 1946, for one semester and two summer sessions. He did not return to college for the next 11 years.[16] In between he worked in a variety of manual labor jobs for companies

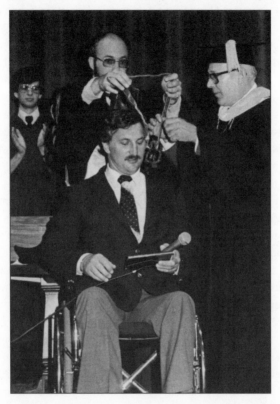

Ex-Viking Kassulke Receives 'Distinguished Minnesotan' Award ('82)
"An event held during graduations . . . BSU selects and honors a Minnesotan."

up and down the West Coast, including a lumber company, a smelting and ore-processing plant, a furniture company, a paper-bag company, and Kaiser Aluminum.

16) Biographical information received from Haugo, upon request of the author. His terse cover letter read, "Art, I believe this is bland enough to be accepted and uninteresting." But he was wrong in his terminology. For example, he told why he left college in 1947. He had attended a convocation session in which the speaker gave a fiery address which condemned American unions "as led by agents of the Soviet Union," and the man went on in his "blatant request of the student body to write their congressmen asking support of the Taft-Hartley Bill." Haugo continued, "By accident, I walked out beside him through a corridor and told him I wished we could have had a representative of the unions opposing the bill on stage with him as I wondered if we received an unbiased view, etc. He asked my name and less than one hour later I was called out of my next class and seated in the dean's office . . . and told that if I ever insulted a major contributor again [the speaker represented Weyerhauser Timber], I would be asked to leave. After some discussion [Haugo told the dean he had just fought in a war in behalf of freedom of thought and speech], with my becoming quite angry at the regimentation, I told him it would not be necessary to ask me to leave because I was leaving—today. And that day I withdrew. I am still trying to decide if I should regret that hasty decision or not." Letter in author's files.

In the meantime, the Haugo family had relocated to the Bemidji area, and in visiting his family, he became impressed with Bemidji State and the community. He decided to move there and enrolled in 1958, majoring in industrial education. While in College, he worked nights as a maintenance mechanic and welder at the newly built Nu-Ply plant. Following graduation in 1961, Haugo accepted a teaching position with the Grand Rapids, Michigan, schools. He also enrolled in the evening courses at Michigan State University but returned to Bemidji State in the summers and completed his master's degree in 1963. He began teaching in the Bemidji State in 1965 as an instructor in industrial technology. While attending BSC during the summers, he met Dorothy Warner, a Bemidji native, who worked in the Records Office, and they were married in 1966. (They raised three children, Linda, Gail, and Ann.) Like most faculty members, Haugo assumed other duties and functions in addition to his teaching, such as serving in the faculty senate and later as the president of the faculty association; chairing the first Affirmative Action Committee; and working towards a doctorate, which he received in 1969 from the University of North Dakota. In 1975 he was selected as the director of placement, the position he was in at the time he was picked as acting president. Let Haugo describe those times and events in his own words:

"By fall of 1981, BSU was facing rather serious problems. A revenue shortfall impacted all state institutions and agencies. In addition, a wage increase which had been granted was not covered by that year's allocation to the University. The shortfall, compounded by the perception that Bemidji State was not enrolling its share of the System's students, indicated the possibility of staff reduction. Discussion of possibly closing one or more of the State Universities and some community colleges included Bemidji among those mentioned. . . .

"In December of 1981, President Stafford was granted a release from her contract. Since there would be a time lapse between her starting date and the appointment of a new president, it was necessary to select an interim president. Dr. Garry Hays, then chancellor, had been in Bemidji December 22 to talk with members of the community . . . about the selection process. Many names were mentioned around campus as possible appointees, but the two who seemed obvious contenders [Haugo did not name them] had withdrawn from consideration. It came as a surprise to me that my name surfaced as one being considered. . . . Hays called asking for my resume and asking that I plan to interview with the Board as one of two candidates being considered. The interviews were held in St. Paul on December 30, and immediately after the vote, we were notified that I had been selected . . . the actual starting date to be January 16, 1982. Dr. Stafford . . . took time to provide valuable assistance which enabled me to make a smooth transition. . . . The entire president's cabinet was most cooperative . . . [and] operated as a collective, and I felt true strength in each member's contribution. I saw part of my role to be that of an outreach representative. . . . No group or organization asking that I speak to them was refused. During those seven months I spoke to 27 clubs, to classes, and to prospective student groups. I continued to represent the President's Office on the Intergovernmental Council, a group of community leaders dedicated to advancing the interests of the greater Bemidji area, and I served as chair of the Chamber's Economic Development Committee. . . .

"The projected $825,000 budget shortfall for the 1982-83 academic year presented the greatest difficulty during my interim presidency. . . . [Haugo went on to talk about the stress caused to the school over this expected shortfall.] However, it later came as a tremendous relief to me and to everyone concerned . . . to learn that . . . the budget projections were becoming more positive. Consequently, we did enter into a period of relatively improved budget conditions, lasting through the 1980s.

"The situation within the State University System in 1982 was unique. In January there were acting presidents at Bemidji, Winona, and St. Cloud [in the latter place and position was Ted Gillett, who would become the new BSU president that summer, starting August 1]. During the second week of each month the presidents of each campus met with the Board Office staff. At the February 9-10 meeting, Chancellor Hays informed the System presidents that the president of the SUS Board had asked him to resign, and that he would . . . on February 11. The announcement was a shock to the presidents. . . . Meeting with the other presidents . . . and having an opportunity to visit with them was tremendously valuable. I came to know and respect Ted Gillett at these meetings. . . .

"Perhaps most reassuring during the entire seven months was the relative calm and the cooperative spirit that existed on campus, constantly reminding me of the warm, friendly institution that had meant so much to me as an older-than-average student 25 years earlier. In fact, it paralleled the camaraderie experienced working nights at the Bemidji Nu-Ply plant while attending Bemidji State. I was happy that I could return a measure of gratitude in this short assignment."[17]

PICKING A PERMANENT PRESIDENT FOR THE '80s
The above heading had special meaning, following the short-term presidency of Stafford. The school looked not only for a figure to restore a sense of calm and order, but also for one who would stay around a while—at least five years—and who would not be using the school as a springboard to leap away at the first opportunity. Following Stafford's resignation, the faculty moved quickly to select an executive committee of 13 who met with the State Universities' vice chancellor of academic affairs, Sheila Kaplan, on January 7, 1982, in Bemidji to work out a procedure in picking a new president. As usual, there was disagreement on both the process and the size of the search committee. Kaplan had met with the

---

17) Excerpts from a seven-page manuscript Haugo wrote, at this author's request. Everything about the manuscript is "pure Dick Haugo," from the timeline (he got it in early) to the true humility of the man. His selection at the time was appropriate in that he was a kind, conscientious, well-meaning and sincere caregiver of and for Bemidji State. He served briefly, but honorably and well. When his successor Gillett became president, Haugo went back to his position as director of Placement, Counseling and Educational Services; he retired from the University in 1988 to become a hobby farmer, running a small beef operation on his farm in Guthrie, some 15 miles from Bemidji. On a personal note, I asked Haugo on his last day as acting president what it felt like to be president, and he replied, "Ah, shucks, it really wasn't that big a deal."

various campus units and learned that the faculty preferred a smaller group while other units wanted a larger committee. A compromise on both the numbers and representatives was reached, one in which all applicants' papers would go directly to the campus search committee to begin the narrowing down process that would reduce the final number to four or five finalists.[18]

Other agreements included: A timeline for the process, culminating with the Board's official selection on May 11, 1982; the preparation of a standard rating sheet for each candidate, and the understanding that a candidate must receive a "yes" vote from two-thirds of the search committee members in order to remain as a viable candidate; the final search committee's top four or five choices to be brought to Bemidji for interviews (with the Board maintaining the right to add up to four of their choices to that final group, though it turned out that they did not add anyone); each committee member to write his/her evaluation of the finalists but not rank them in order of choice; findings to be given to the Board members for their perusal before they voted their selection.

The search committee at Bemidji State consisted of 18 members representing nine different groups; non-voting member Kaplan chaired the committee.[19] The committee had much work to do in that there were 55 applications and thus 55 lengthy sets of papers to read diligently before making a determination on who would or would not make a good BSU president. Eventually, after many lengthy sessions of the search committee, by April 2 the number was reduced to five finalists. In alphabetical order they were: 1) Leslie Duly, then vice president for academic affairs at BSU 2) Lowell (Ted) Gillett, acting president at St. Cloud State University 3) Terrance Hogan, dean of faculty for graduate studies at the University of Manitoba, Winnipeg, Canada 4) Peter Ristuben, dean of the State University of New York—Empire State College at Buffalo 5) Carson Veach, director of the Altoona campus of Pennsylvania State University. More meetings later, the number was narrowed down to three men: Duly, Gillett, and Ristuben, who were invited to campus for interviews and meetings that lasted all day, the final act of each being an oral presentation, with a question and answer period, to the entire faculty and staff in the auditorium in Hagg-Sauer Hall. The listeners/watchers were also asked to fill out forms on each candidate and give the completed forms to search committee members, who then wrote their final appraisals to be sent to the State Board. The board would interview the three and vote on their selection

---

18) Heretofore the State University Board Office had done most of the early winnowing process, presenting only their choices to campus search committees. For more details on official faculty actions in the selection process, see unpublished faculty association minutes for the months of January through May, 1982, minutes on file in the Bemidji State library. For published information, see Minnesota State University Board Minutes for the same months, their Minutes also on reserve in the school library.
19) Representing the teaching faculty were six members: Marjory Beck, Ray Jensen, Gerald Smith, Peter Smith, Richard Slinkman, and Art Lee. Student senate representatives were Jim Elwell, Brad McDonald, and Kirby Johnson. MSUAASF had Mark Paulson and Lorraine Cecil, and Council 6 had Alice Toninato; Judy McDonald represented the deans; the MAPE rep was Dave Waldon, and Joe Vene represented the alumni. Community representatives were Donna Kunz and John Baer, while George Goodwin represented the Native American community. In a personal note, as a member of the committee, it might be revealed that we fought mightily at some meetings, with the volume high enough to match the temperatures of several highly agitated souls (I was one of them, too). It should also be noted that Chairperson Kaplan ruled fairly and impartially, never pushing her own choice over others, although obviously she had her favorites, too.

May 11.[20]

The scene shifted to St. Paul and the Board Office where each of the three candidates was interviewed by the chancellor, the vice chancellor for academic affairs, and selected members of the chancellor's staff. Then came more interviews before the full Board, in alphabetical order, with the Board taking a break between interviews. Campus interest back in Bemidji was so high that the school's radio station, KBSU, broadcast live from the Board Office to inform listeners what was happening. Finally, at the end of the afternoon on May 11, 1982, the State University Board voted unanimously in favor of Lowell R. (Ted) Gillett to become Bemidji State's sixth president. On August 1, 1982, Gillett began what would become an eight-year term. From the point of view of the search committee, the process worked about as well as could be expected.[21]

LOWELL RENO GILLETT

Dr. Gillett was born on February 23, 1925, in Minneapolis, the son of Ethel and Reno Gillett. He went through the Minneapolis public schools, graduating from Roosevelt High School in 1943. He attended Gustavus Adolphus College, St. Peter, Minnesota, graduating from there in 1947 with a major in English. He began his teaching career that year as a high school teacher and coach in Amboy, then moved to Sherburn, then to Austin (1951 to 1962), where he was also assistant principal. In 1954 he received his M.A. degree in educational psychology from the University of Minnesota. In 1962 he began his doctoral work at the University of North Dakota, completing his degree there in 1965 in educational psychology. He began his career in the State College System at St. Cloud in 1962 and remained there until he left for Bemidji State 20 years later. He had a wide range of roles at St. Cloud as a member of the education-psychology department, as acting dean of the school of education, as acting vice president for academic affairs, as dean of the graduate school, and as acting president of the University.[22]   When he came to Bemidji that summer of 1982, Dr. Gillett, who preferred to be called "Ted," and his wife Ardis had two grown daughters, Judy Dittberner and Amy, both Minnesota public school teachers.

---

20) April 15 and 22 issues of the Northern Student, 1982, give lengthy quotes from each of the candidates. The search committee never took an actual vote on the candidates, but it would be no secret nor surprise that the committee members reached no total consensus on any one person. In the last written appraisals to be written by each committee member, there was to be no ranking of first, second, third, or so ordered the chairperson, but "ranking" occurred anyway simply by the way each candidate was written up.

21) A social studies major named Maria Stumpf wrote a brief term paper in 1984 on the selection of Gillett as president. After the appointment, she asked some members of the search committee about their views. Student Senate President Brad McDonald thought the committee was too large, that the three students "were forced to stick together, and that the faculty members were very strong." Gillett was chosen, said McDonald, because "the other candidates were not impressive enough and that Dr. Gillett was known." Faculty member Richard Slinkman, wrote Stumpf, "stated that there was over-representation by groups except the faculty; [the committee suffered from the inability] to check up on applicants because of state privacy laws, and that the committee was too large." Slinkman believed Gillett was chosen because "he was well qualified, the least controversial, and Board members wanted him." The Ristuben supporters passionately believed he was the best BSU president we never had. Overall, Slinkman felt that the process was a "vast improvement" in comparison to the past selection. Stumpf's paper in author's file. Ms. Stumpf was chosen in 1985 as the Outstanding Student of the Year.

22) As St. Cloud's acting president for one year, he was not permitted to be a candidate for that position. The month before Gillett was picked by the Board for Bemidji State, the Board had named an economist and vice president at a Minneapolis bank as St. Cloud's new full-time president, but he resigned less than a week after he was selected. His name was Dr. Sung Won Son, and the St. Cloud newspaper had a bit of fun with that resignation, running the headline, "Son Rises, Son Sets."

MR. RIGHT

If ever the cliché about the right-man-right-place had meaning and application, it was the coming of Ted Gillett as president of Bemidji State in the summer of 1982. If his predecessor Stafford did not fit in—"like ketchup on lutefisk"—Gillett did—"like ketchup on french fries." He, and his equally socially adept wife, Ardis, quickly absorbed and were absorbed by the College community. A good fit, an easy fit. Gillett brought stability and solidity to a campus low on morale and high on cynicism. Stafford's abrupt abdication still smarted. When Gillett arrived, he immediately addressed the issue of his plans to stay, making it crystal clear by what he said; at age 57 he was not on any academic make, and he had no plans to jump anywhere else. Indeed, he said that he intended to remain as Bemidji's president until he retired (and he did).[23] Such early assurance was reassurance to a campus still feeling burned. Gillett's statements as well as his manner and mannerism were reassuring.

Physically, Gillett was a tallish, robust, athletic figure, with big, strong arms and hands. He walked with a limp, however, a carry-over from an earlier tragic bout with polio.[24] The most appealing aspect of the new president was his style. He avoided posturing and pretensions at all costs. He was devoid of pomp; he eschewed any trappings of his office; he talked in the vernacular, and he could talk hunting and fishing, sports, and Bemidji weather with the best of them. An English major in college, he clung to the notion that language should be clearly written and spoken in everyday terminology. Nothing fancy about him. No educational gibberish spouted; no pie-in-the-sky foolishness; no high-falutin' dreaminess. Mr. Realism; the ultimate pragmatist; the quintessence of common sense, and yet despite the one-of-the-boys settings and the relaxed atmosphere he chose to cultivate at meetings, there was never a doubt that he was the president, that he was in charge, and that nobody better try to push him too far. He would listen intently to others' pleas; he might laugh and joke; he told stories (badly)—but he would make his own decisions and stick to them. He came to Bemidji under no illusions; he knew the situation well and knew what had to be done and how he would proceed. He later wrote:

"When I arrived, my broad goals were to bring stability to the University, broaden its impact, and to develop greater depth, strengths, and diversity across all facets of the campus. I did not have a plan tailor-made to fit my philosophy and values but preferred instead to assess the existing strengths (and areas in need of

23) Comments in the first student newspaper of the new school year, September 22, 1982, pp. 1-2. In an extensive question and answer interview with editor Terry Gunderson, the article headlined, "Gillett Brings Experience, Stability to BSU." There are also several pictures of a smiling, genial-appearing Gillett. His later "official photo," however, the one he chose to use in most publications, showed him not smiling, indeed more glowering, and gave him almost an intimidating appearance to those who did not know him. In the words of an undergraduate who looked at Gillett's scowling countenance, "Geez, he looks like a Mafia hit-man."

24) Gillett was one of those hundreds of victims in the 1950s who were struck down, literally, by polio. When it hit him he was a high school teacher in Austin, married, and the father of two little girls. Initially he was paralyzed from the neck down and was taken immediately to the Sister Kenny Institute in Minneapolis where he underwent lengthy and extensive treatment. It would be the lowest point in his life and career. Eventually he recovered the use of all limb muscles except for those in his one leg, and thus he walked with a decided limp, and often used a cane. Said one surprised faculty members who first saw him going across the campus, "He walks with a limp!" Replied a second, more perceptive prof, "Ah, yes, but most importantly, he walks."

improvement) and adapt specific plans to the needs and strengths, after I better understood these factors. Over the first year to year and a half, I tried to tailor our efforts to deal with specific issues. Many of these were highly interrelated. . . . Frankly, BSU was not in good shape in many important ways—image, morale, enrollment, finances, admission standards, etc., yet there were many outstanding qualities on which to build—generally high quality of faculty and staff and a strong reputation for commitment to the individual student. But all of the key component groups recognized the difficulties we faced and worked together to build a strong University. While we didn't always agree, we jointly developed a culture of working together for the common good."[25]

Les Duly Makes a Point to Ardis and Ted Gillett
"Initial doubts on how well they would work together. Not to worry. A good team."

NEW MAN, SAME STAFF

To the surprise of many, Gillett chose to keep the same top staff members, most notably the same three vice presidents whom Stafford had hired: Duly, academic affairs; Faecke, administrative affairs; Ludeman, student affairs. Duly, of course, had been Gillett's competitor for the presidency and some people initially had their doubts on how well they would work together. Not to worry. They made a good team, a good pair, with Duly viewed as the "idea man"—filled with great plans dreamed of, and sometimes dreamy—and Gillett the "common sense man"—who weighed all plans carefully and thoughtfully before making a

25) Comments written in his two-page cover letter, dated August 9, 1993, sent to this author, who had requested from each president his/her interpretations on the issues and accomplishments of their administrations. Selections from his responses will appear later in the text. Letter and commentary in author's file; to be placed in the BSU archives. Former President Robert Decker had initially agreed to write his interpretations of his years in office and he began these efforts, but he had to give them up in 1993 because of a lingering illness.

decision. But let Gillett describe his own style: "I would describe my administrative style as setting goals, conferring openly as possible with those key component groups, and working in a systematic fashion to achieve them. Often I delayed action, particularly with controversial issues, waiting for the propitious moment, and then tried to act firmly and decisively. . . . There were many things that I knew needed to be done, but I tried to time the decision to have the most positive (sometimes the least negative) impact."[26]

THE PUBLIC MAN

As the new kid on the block, community people looked forward to seeing him in person, something available most publicly when Gillett and his wife were scheduled to ride through town in an open convertible as part of the '82 homecoming parade. Then everybody could finally get a look at him. Alas, the rain came that morning in such volume as to cancel plans. There was no parade of any kind; no floats, no marching bands, no open convertibles, no king and queen ceremony— and no Beaver loss, either. In a game played in a drenching rain to a diehard crowd of only the faithful few, Bemidji State ended a 20-game losing streak in football, with a 14-10 victory over U-M Morris. (To show it was no fluke, the team won the next week's contest, too.) In the stands sat a soaked but not sullen Gillett; he hardly ever missed any Beaver home athletic contests.[27]

If the townsfolk missed the Gilletts that first homecoming, they had ample opportunities to see and meet them later in many places and on many occasions. He realized that good community relations were of obvious importance to the success of the University. He made a conscious effort to attend functions of all kinds that were primarily focused on the school, but he also made it a point to attend community functions whenever possible. Thus he and Ardis showed up at high school events, the Paul Bunyan Theatre, the Arts Center, fund drives (cancer, heart, Hospice dances), Friends of the Library, Santa Lucia breakfasts, and the like, which included the multitude of year 'round church-basement dinners. He even went to the area lutefisk suppers—and loved lutefisk!? He joined the Rotary Club (Duly was also a member), and became a board member for the Chamber of Commerce. He played a major role in the formation of the Joint Economic Development Commission and felt so strongly about it that he assigned a faculty member (Art Gullette) two-thirds time as its initial executive director for the first 14 months of its operation. If Ted and Ardis Gillett were not "everywhere," they weren't too far away. The Gilletts became—and remain—very active in the community.

26) Source: Gillett's cover letter. See footnote 26. Gillett added, "I've often used the Bill Mauldin cartoon (from Up Front) to illustrate how I tried to balance the need to take action with the need (particularly in the early days of my BSU tenure) to maintain campus morale and stability. You may recall Willie and Joe as artillery spotters. They occupied a foxhole directly under a huge German tank. Using the field telephone, the message was, 'Able Fox. This is Able Fox Five. I've got a target but you've got to be patient.' As to his partnership with Duly, Gillett throughout his eight years as president constantly acknowledged, yea venerated, the help and support of his vice president.

27) Gillett's obvious ongoing interest in all BSU athletics was not always perceived as positive by some personnel who believed his interest was too much, too slanted in that area as contrasted with other areas, both extra-curricular and curricular. Such is the lot for all presidents who must perform a balancing act in the impossible goal of keeping all sides happy. How much he aided/overaided any athletic squad remains a moot issue, but on a personal note, I did overhear him mumble one time, "I'm not going to allow any BSU team to be any conference doormat as long as I'm president." And he didn't.

FIRST THROUGH THE EYES . . .

The new president felt strongly about the physical appearance of the campus and acted to make it more attractive. He argued that first impressions for any visitor coming to the campus were tremendously important, so much so that both prospective students and faculty could be swayed one way or another as to whether to come to Bemidji State. Nature had already bestowed on the school the lovely lakeside setting that was the best in the entire state, and that natural beauty was enhanced by campus tree plantings, notably more pine trees to maintain the image of the college in the pines. Then came more and more flower beds and shrub-plantings, along with watered, well-groomed lawns, and a campus devoid of trash, the latter picked up each morning by custodians assigned to the job. Gillett believed that how people felt about themselves was directly impacted by the physical environment surrounding them; it also affected what others thought of the school. The result was a clean and neat-appearing campus. Every day was Arbor Day to the new president.[28]

PROBLEMS: WHERE TO START!?

When Gillett arrived in 1982, the state of Minnesota was in an economic recession that threatened to cause major funding cuts which would necessitate large personnel reductions. The problem of projected cuts was compounded by declining enrollments. Fall enrollment in '82 was 4,311 students, down 118 from the year before. The perceived threats to the institution seemed real enough, augmented by certain legislators who engaged in repeated political posturing which included threats to close one or more State Universities. Bemidji State was mentioned prominently as a candidate for closure, and the combined negative combination at the time had led to high anxiety and low morale on campus. Admission standards had also been compromised during this period as one approach to address the enrollment problem, but this also affected the image of the school ("the College of Last Resort?") and caused faculty to work with some students who were not well suited to collegiate instruction.

The new administration developed a number of strategies both to resolve and counter the above issues. Among the strategies were deliberate public and private statements expressing the president's absolute confidence in the long-term vitality of the school and its importance to the region. He marshaled power and hard evidence to argue both logically and politically that it made no sense whatsoever to even consider closing the only four-year university in northern Minnesota. Don't even think about it! Moreover, maintained Gillett, there was absolutely no chance that this would occur. The quality of the faculty, the staff, the academic programs, the education provided, the cultural opportunities, and the individual attention focused on student needs became concepts widely publicized and widely understood. His was a first-rate sales job.

---

28) Although it might appear trivial, a second physical change to the campus came in a simple but useful way when each building had added to it some large lettering to indicate clearly, and at a distance, the name of that particular building.

To stem the enrollment decline, innovative and expanded recruitment practices were implemented. They paid off. Gradually enrollment stabilized, then came the slow process of growth, the increases coming alongside increased admission standards. The official standards had required all applying students to be in the top 50 percent of their high school graduating class or have an ACT score of 21 in order to be admitted, but through the lean years there had been large numbers of exceptions granted. Throughout the rest of the '80s, implemented standards moved upward (from 25 percent to 33 percent to 40 percent) so that the 50 percent target would be achieved as the new decade began. (No more snide image of "The Ol' Miss of the Muskeg for Morons.")[29]

SAVING STAFF, LIVES AND MORALE

There are few things worse for morale on a college campus than letting faculty members go. (Technically they are not "fired"; they are "retrenched," or "terminated" or "non-renewed" or simply "let go." Whatever the euphemism, they do not have a job anymore at the college.) Nobody is happy about this, except perhaps the accountants who have to balance the financial books. As indicated in an earlier section, allowing non-tenured faculty to be "non-renewed" is bad enough but retrenching tenured staff is an academic abomination. Yet such were the economic times in the early 1980s that faculty cutbacks were occurring regularly throughout the state and nation. But they did NOT occur at Bemidji State because of a deliberate policy adopted by Gillett. It was a gutsy, personal gamble for him, as he explains:

"At a time when significant personnel reductions were thought to be required, I made the commitment that whatever personnel reductions became necessary would, if at all possible [Gillett's underlining], be accomplished through attrition, and that probationary and tenured personnel would be protected. In my view, this optimistic commitment required actions to give it validity. Two examples will illustrate. First, several terminations were rescinded. Second, renewal contracts were offered to both first and second year probationary personnel at a time (actually December and February) when funding necessary to implement these decisions was not available or assured. These were gambles that should they backfire, would undoubtedly have resulted in an extremely short tenure for my presidency. Nevertheless, it was my conviction that for quality education to occur, the morale of the faculty and staff were of utmost importance and was worth the risk."[30]

He won. The faculty won. The students won. It was a gamble won, in which there had been many potential losers.

FROM THE STUDENT PERSPECTIVE

Administrators in higher education look upon autumn from a different

---

29) In Gillett's commentary, he wrote, "It was (and is) my belief that lowering admission standards to achieve greater enrollment was an approach that might bring short-term results, but would, over a longer period, prove damaging to the image of the University, and thus to enrollment." p. 1.
30) Source: Gillett's commentary, pp. 2-3.

Perusing the Stacks in the A.C. Clark Library
"By 1990 there was no more card catalog . . . by 1997 a new library."

perspective than students attending those schools. The former tend to view the times in somber tones, seeing at best diminished budgets and cutbacks here and there, and at worst the end of western civilization as they once knew it. Students, however, see any new school year with a vibrant and positive view: Buildings filled with fun and excitement, seeing old friends and meeting new ones. They're close to elation to be returning. Time to live!—and live it up! Most faculty also look forward to the fall start-up after a couple of months pursuing other endeavors and conjure up another good school year with their colleagues and students. So let those fossils "on the hill" worry about the down-state machinations of the legislature; the rest want to enjoy another school year in 1982 and 1983. And there was plenty to enjoy, even if it might seem routine to the jaded. The aforementioned football squad had a couple of victories under peripatetic new coach John Peterson, and the womens' field hockey team—in their gold uniforms with the plaid skirts—kept their ongoing, winning ways under coach Betsy McDowell. They achieved a 20-

7 record that year, including wins over Division I and II schools. The student senate announced their exploration of adopting the semester system, reinventing that wheel of fortune on a topic that never stopped moving from being studied to death. Flamboyant art critic, Robert Hughes, whose Time articles were used in some English classes as an example of overwriting, came on campus to make pronouncements. The much-heralded Luther College Choir, under Weston Noble, representing the finest in the Lutheran church colleges' vocal tradition, sang a concert to a packed auditorium, with impressed listeners leaving with the opinion that the Bemidji State Choir under Paul Brandvik was equally as good. The Northern Student had a gadfly that year who consistently wrote well-written articles which unnerved most readers; he was a bright young man named Tim Graham, a kind of William Buckley clone, and he produced sprightly columns like "Social Security Should be Phased Out," and "Why I Like Secretary James Watt (A Lot)."[31]

Students appreciated the fact that their new president ate noon meals at the union, and mingled with students and that he picked students at random each month to come to his office to visit, just to find out their views on subjects. Despite head hockey coach Bob Peters being gone on sabbatical for the year, interim coach Mike Gibbons did a fine job, guiding the Beavers to a 30-7 win-loss record, one that led to the national NCAA Division II tournament in Boston, where the team took second place. The theater folks produced three special plays that year, Juno and the Paycock, A Funny Thing Happened on the Way to the Forum, and Close Ties. A December thaw found the school's biggest parking lot, Lake Bemidji, swallowing autos and fish houses, to the amusement of all except their owners. February found residents fighting the expected disease called Cabin Fever, the prescription for cure including a trip to the Eelpout Festival in Walker, and the local sled dog races on Lake Bemidji. And what can take away more from the constricted mind than the culinary delights at Wally's, whomped up by Max Morphew? The asbestos scare/ plague, like some sci-fi amoeba juggernaut lumbering over Planet Earth, struck the Bemidji campus, too, with Bangsberg Hall singled out for a cleanout forthwith. The courtyard between the two unions was finished and became a testimonial to Portland Cement. Some half-dozen students planning to graduate at the end of the year with an environmental education major found out to their unhappy amazement that no such major existed, and learned that they were really mass communication majors after all, the closest thing their credits could fit into in time for commencement. Not happy campers. The "father of Bemidji State Music," Carl Thompson, died that spring. Jon Wefald, new State Uuniversity chancellor, via the route of state commissioner of agriculture and then president of Southwest State University in Marshall, came to town to review the troops.[32] Biology Professor Evan Hazard,

---

31) Young Mr. Graham, a social studies major, was an activist in his political beliefs. In the fall of 1984, he began an entirely new campus newspaper to rival the Northern Student, even if the entire theme of the paper was political. Once Ronald Reagan was re-elected, however, the newspaper ceased operation.

32) If there seem to be too many BSU presidents in a short time, Southwest State University at Marshall has been a revolving door for presidents over its entire 25-year history. This was pointed out in Joe Amato's brief history of the school, A New College on the Prairie: Southwest State University's First Twenty-Five Years, 1967-1992 (Crossings Press, Longmont, Colorado and Marshall, Minnesota), 1992.

after eight years of researching the subject, published a scholarly book, <u>Mammals of Minnesota</u>. The school newspaper published a delightful April Fool's edition and tweaked many a nose amid the foolishness. The fourth annual edition of student writings, <u>Loonfeather</u>, came out, timed with the respected English Week. Native Americans held their sixth annual pow-wow on campus. All in all, another year, semi-normal, semi-typical, except, of course, there was the official inauguration of Bemidji State's sixth president, Lowell R. Gillett, on February 12, 1983.[33]

BACK TO REALITY, BACK TO LIVING ON LESS

Gillett put people first and supplies second in his policy decision not to lay off faculty in those hard economic times of the early 1980s. The draconian nightmare of school closing did not occur, of course, but significant cuts, $314,000 for the 1982-83 school year, had to be made somewhere ($825,000 had been the earlier prediction). Because salaries made up 80 percent of the budget, the paring came in other areas, specifically library resources, equipment, supplies, duplication, and maintenance, all areas slashed to the bone. The school made do with what it had, and what it had was running out and wearing out too fast. It was a serious problem, with one instructor keeping a private supply of toilet paper in his office drawer, just in case. Cuts in the early '80s continued to be made wherever a few dollars could be saved, and thus library subscriptions to some academic journals were canceled, little-used telephones were removed from some offices, and mailings were restricted to those absolutely necessary. Still, the University plugged ahead successfully, and by decade's end, with a degree of relative prosperity restored, the staffs had received the good word that they could once again start ordering books and supplies.

AMID THE SHORTAGES, A BUILDING BOOM!

The reductions, the paring, the cutting back had been in the school's instructional budgets, but entirely separate was another category, the capital budget, which means new and repaired buildings. Bemidji State capitalized very well in this second kind of budget (no pun intended), making major improvements to the campus in the 1980s. The former Laboratory School building was totally renovated, the old (1950) structure knocked to the ground, with only a few steel girders left poking high in the sky, and then rebuilt in 1986 as an attractive, modern facility well-suited to meet the needs of the education programs and the art department (the latter FINALLY got some decent facilities). That building, like all of the other buildings by decade's end, became handicapped-accessible. It was

---

33) It was somewhat unfortunate that Bemidji State was used to inaugurations by the time it came for Gillett's turn. Nevertheless, the proper procedures were produced and the academic regalia hauled out once again, but festivities were reduced to one night and one morning, at Gillett's request. There was a well-attended banquet at the Holiday Inn on the evening of February 11, 1983, with the president of the University of North Dakota, Thomas Clifford, as the featured speaker. The next morning—a Saturday morning—found the official ceremonies, with the aforementioned Chancellor Wefald delivering the Charge to the President. For more complete information, copies of both the four-page inaugural and banquet brochures and the 14-page inauguration ceremonies brochure are on file in the Bemidji State library. For news coverage and pictures of the events, see the <u>Northern Student</u>, February 16, 1983. The <u>Students</u> since 1980 are in bound volumes and shelved in the library.

renamed the EDUCATION-ART BUILDING. The discovery of asbestos in two important buildings ended up being a proverbial blessing-in-disguise for Bangsberg Hall and Hagg-Sauer Hall in that both ended up looking far better than before, especially Hagg-Sauer Hall, which had been a drab, unattractive, virtually an ersatz "rabbit hutch" that illustrated the aesthetic problem of letting state building construction contracts go to the lowest bidder. The "new" Hagg-Sauer became attractive, for the first time.[34]

Sattgast Hall, the science building first constructed in 1962, was also totally renovated and rebuilt in 1989. The new building's design and construction illustrated how the school in general and the science programs in particular had changed in those years in between. The original building housed four majors, largely teacher-education programs, and there was only modest need for laboratories. The new Sattgast building housed 11 majors, the expanded programs focusing more extensively on business and research applications of science and heavily oriented toward laboratories. The shift in emphasis had basically reversed at Bemidji State since the original building was constructed, from 95 percent of the science students preparing to be teachers in 1962, to 85 percent preparing for scientific careers outside of teaching by 1990.

The last large building constructed on campus was built in 1989, the large/huge (85,000 square feet) Recreation Fitness Center already mentioned. Achieving funding for the center was a major accomplishment, and yet this is Gillett's brief written comment on that matter: "Perhaps the single most significant physical improvement in making the campus more attractive to students has been the construction of the recreation building. BSU was clearly the campus in the State University System most in need of indoor recreational opportunities based on location, weather, and lack of existing facilities. We had by far the poorest facilities in the System. [In that same legislative bill,] we were also able to incorporate major renovations of the P.E. Building into the plan, and a new football field and all-weather track were also included." A modest appraisal, certainly, by Gillett, and thus inadequate language for something that so dramatically changed the face of the campus. It's an amazing structure! And primary credit for it must go to Gillett.[35]

A BEMIDJI STATE BUILDING GETS NATIONAL ATTENTION

Something radically new on a college campus, and yet a proper sign of the

34) The asbestos removal itself, followed by the rebuilding process, took an entire school year for completion for each building. Hence the faculty members in Bangsberg and Hagg-Sauer (in alternate years) had to find temporary quarters on the first floor and lower level in Pine Hall, built in 1959 as a residence hall. Thus all faculty involved found themselves once again living in a college dormitory room. (Another good thing that came out of the move was the forced cleaning-out of faculty offices. Unofficially, the tally vote for the worst, messiest, most discombobulated office of all was a tie vote between Wagner Collins and Art Lee, with each malefactor trying to give the dubious honor to the other.)
35) Gillett's prose appeared in his written commentary, pp. 4-5. His bland wording omits any reference to the long struggle to get that particular building. Nor do his words even hint at the emotion he felt the day the measure passed in the legislature. Following the vote, Gillett called his wife to tell her the good news, but he was so emotionally choked up at the time that he could hardly speak. Gillett's overall successful building programs—in those times of fiscal restraint—obviously said much about his connections downstate, or as one of his friends phrased it, accurately but fuzzily, "That guy sure knew his way around St. Paul." He did. Among his legislative connections perhaps the most important was Senator Gerald Willett, Park Rapids, the chairperson of the Senate Finance Committee. In the House was Bob Johnson, Bemidji, a BSU grad, and an indefatigable supporter of his alma mater.

times (1990), was the renovation of Pine Hall into apartments for single parents. This former residence hall, built in 1959, was getting run-down and shabby-looking inside, and something had to be done. It was rebuilt into a series of 28 apartments, with one, two, or three bedrooms, for students who were single parents. This unique arrangement was not only the first one in the state but was the first one in the whole country. The program, Housing and Urban Development certified, brought national attention, with inquiries and later imitations, from all over the nation. Certainly the need was there at Bemidji State, where over 300 single parents

Family Returning to their Home in the Former Pine Hall
"Something radically new on campus . . . apartments for single parents."

were enrolled, many if not most needing affordable housing close to the campus. Prior to the construction of the apartments, a daycare center was operating in the former Pine Hall lounge. The daycare facilities were subsequently extended outside where playground equipment for children was installed, something not usually found on university campuses. The whole scene was certainly different, with the other College students at first a bit surprised at hearing crying babies and sometimes meeting little toddlers in the tunnels. Despite some initial problems the first year, authorities soon deemed it a wonderful venture, one that directly met the educational needs of many Bemidji State SOTA students, allowing them true fulfillment of their educational dreams. In keeping with the theme of giving residence halls names of trees indigenous to the area, the new housing project became officially the Cedar Apartments.

As Gillett made plans for his retirement after June 30, 1990, the State

University Board made good on his late request for a special kind of structure, one that would really set the campus off. Like many others, Gillett believed that over the years too many people unfamiliar with Bemidji came on the campus and really had no idea where it "started." There was no discernible entrance to the school, just a series of buildings and grounds and sidewalks laid out in a long string beside this big lake. This was a problem, minor perhaps, which could be solved simply enough, the Board willing. Gillett got, in effect, a kind of "going away present" from the Board in the form of the construction of an imposing two-column brick archway on the corner of 14th Street and Birchmont Drive, just down the sidewalk from the main entrance into Deputy Hall. And written on the arch—the official "entrance"—in big gold letters is BEMIDJI STATE UNIVERSITY. The new structure, called the Alumni Arch, added a nice touch of class to the institution. It also provided a proper spot to place the two little statues of the "monk scholars" who once stood on tiny ledges at the entrance to Deputy Hall, but had to be removed when the entrance was changed. (Between that time and their new placement, the statues sat for 20 years on the floor of the lavatory in the president's office.)

Not all the building and renovations done in Gillett's eight years were accomplished by him alone, of course, something he freely acknowledged then and later. Nor did he get all he hoped for, notably a new library. The existing A.C. Clark Library he described in his commentary as "an under-sized, poorly designed facility." The best that came out of his effort to replace it was "planning funds" for the renovation and expansion of the A.C. Clark Library, following extensive studies; but "studies" can take forever, or the whole project may be abandoned by new legislatures. Nor did he get the needed renovation funds for the industrial technology programs in Bridgeman Hall. (This area too reflected the changing times. When built in 1964, it was for one, and only one, program—industrial arts— with four staff members. Thirty years later, there were 15 staff in four programs: Technical illustration/graphic design, industrial technology, technology education, and vocational education.) Nor did he get sufficient funding for the planned new Indian Center, one that will be located on the present-day Bangsberg Hall parking lot, and it was supposed to rival Bangsberg Hall in size and importance. At the time Gillett retired in 1990, about $75,000 had been raised for the Indian Center ($2 million was needed). Though a substantial figure, Bangsberg Hall need not fear immediate architectural rivalry. Nor did he get a science center on campus when he could have had one essentially "for the asking," or so maintained some science profs who found Gillett's objections in this matter untenable, and later unforgivable. Nor did he get enough parking places, but then nobody before him or after him did either. (Last minute addendum: the '94 legislature voted $8.1 million for a new BSU library, to be completed in 1997.)

THE BUGABOO OF PARKING STALLS

Few endeavors lend themselves more readily to self-delusion than the presumed availability of a place to park. At BSU there are never enough stalls for automobiles, which seem to multiply each year like fruit flies. On the surface, this whole subject seems both trivial and unnecessary to mention, yet there are few issues that can stir people up more than the difficulty or impossibility of finding a place to park. Constantly there are frustrated drivers unable to find a stall, who then for reasons of their own park illegally, believing it to be a temporary malfeasance that will be corrected as soon as they get out of class. Alas, by then they've likely been ticketed at best, or at worst have found their machines towed away and impounded. An expensive proposition either way, both in money and stress. When driveways of homeowners near the campus get blocked, the driveway owners get angry, which leads to the police being called, which leads to ticketing—and likely towing—which leads to more frustration and anger. Nobody's happy. Poor BSU presidents, as though they did not have enough problems, have actually gotten phone calls from housewives living near the campus who were planning to have a church circle meeting and expected the president to make sure there were enough places for the circle members to park that day.

Adding more designated parking lots, although helpful, has proved an inadequate solution for every president, with the unhappiness starting when parkers are allegedly overcharged for their parking stickers, and continuing when they come late to campus and find their lot already full. A mess. In the 1980s, and since, commuters to Bemidji State not there by 8 a.m. might just as well forget it and plan to park on faraway Bemidji Avenue, if they're lucky. For a while, nearby Diamond Point Park became the place for overflow traffic, but city tree lovers persuaded the city council to kill that option. Back to the streets. Back to Lake

The Perennial Problem of Parking--and Getting Ticketed
"Few endeavors lend themselves more readily to self-delusion than . . . parking."

Boulevard where the denizens besieged City Hall to close the entire street to daylight traffic, by which they meant NO PARKING! That request failed, so a petition went to the president to DO SOMETHING!

(There is some good news about Bemidji winters as they relate to parking. The Lake Bemidji ice freezes so solid and thick that it makes for a very large parking lot; indeed, the longest and biggest parking area "on campus." Its use continues into Spring, permitting viewers to witness malingerers or late-to-class-students whose cars sink through the ice in part or in toto. Thus March drivers have always the thrill of anticipation as they venture forth on Lake Bemidji ice.) Administrators who may want to ponder expanded curricula, and promote higher order thinking skills, instead have at times been reduced to ameliorating ('tis impossible to solve) the crushing traffic problem, and Gillett was no exception. He acknowledged the situation with complete honesty when he wrote, "One of the main sources of tension with the community is the issue of on-street parking. We developed a minimum of 400 additional parking stalls, which reduced but did not eliminate the problems. One hundred twenty-five of those stalls were created at the Recreation Building when we worked a cooperative deal with the city to purchase three homes and construct the parking lot which we then purchased from the city through a series of annual payments."[36] Certainly the new lot helped, but it was not enough. Back to the streets.

THE ONGOING GOAL OF IMPROVED INSTRUCTION

Following World War II, vast numbers of veterans returned to college under the G.I. Bill. For a variety of reasons, both valid and invalid, academic prestige gradually became associated with universities highly involved with research, both pure and applied. In 1945 that meant primarily one Minnesota school, the University in Minneapolis, but 30 years later the educational situation had changed substantially so that the once tiny Minnesota teachers colleges had themselves become large schools and universities. Some sought to emulate the U of M, with a correspondingly diminished emphasis on the importance of undergraduate instruction. This siren song of research and graduate work had appeal to some new universities, but Bemidji State never succumbed to that temptation in any significant way detrimental to its undergraduate teaching programs. While no Bemidji State president has denigrated the importance of research, all have set the tone and direction of the school by placing the strongest emphasis on classroom instruction, something Gillett acknowledged clearly: "It was my belief that the instructional role of faculty should be emphasized even more strongly.... With the development of the Honors Convocation, we gave a strong public focus to student achievement. The same was true with the faculty awards which, both in terms of teaching performance and in specialized research, recognized excellence but granted the

36) Gillett's commentary, p. 12. So desperate was the need for more parking that the lines in the Bangsberg lot were repainted closer together so as to get more cars in. Getting in and out of the cars was the driver's problem.

highest award to the Teacher of the Year."[37]

It is one thing to emphasize good teaching as the seminal aspect of a university's operation, but it is another thing to hire and retain excellent teachers. Recruiting and holding skilled and stimulating professors genuinely committed to teaching students has been the key to the quality of the instructional process at Bemidji State. Presidents take pride in that fact. There are many variables in hiring, factors that both positively and negatively influence the ability to attract and keep high quality classroom personnel. Northern Minnesota may be attractive to some but not to others; BSU can be perceived as either too big or too small, and the like. Then too there has always been the issue of faculty holding a doctorate, or terminal degree—a factor so significant in many colleges that tenure should not be granted to anyone unless that coveted doctorate was in hand. This kind of restrictive reasoning either drove away or resulted in the non-retention of some outstanding classroom teachers, and Bemidji State lost its share over the years. In the 1980s, however, that rule was not applied in many instances where the school employed persons who did not hold a terminal degree but who exhibited excellent potential— and got tenure. Moreover, the school invested in these same people through the use of sabbaticals, faculty improvement grants, and other leaves which permitted most of them to complete their degrees eventually. This bending policy all in all paid off handsomely. In 1982, only 47 percent of the faculty held the terminal degree, the lowest percentage in the State University System; by 1990 the percentage had increased to 71 percent, the highest in the System. This fact has not been overlooked, and the esteem of BSU has been raised significantly in the eyes of the faculties and administrations of her sister institutions.[38]

THE WORLD BEYOND, FAR BEYOND BEMIDJI, & Fosston, & Roseau, & Gonvick . . .

Bemidji State historically has drawn at least two-thirds of its enrollment from northern Minnesota, resulting in a student body which has had limited opportunities for personal contact with people of international cultures. No more. The school has undertaken a comprehensive program to create expanded opportunities for interpersonal contacts with international students on campus along with opportunities to travel to and study in other countries.

37) Gillett's commentary, p. 6. While this choice each year was well accepted and well received by the faculty, less acceptable in the 1980s under Gillett and Company were the annual "merit money awards." Each spring the administration singled out 10 faculty who, in the administration's judgment, deserved an extra financial award of $1,000 each for meritorious service. Despite the administration's good intentions, the process tended to be viewed by most faculty as "demerit non-awards," for those who were not selected—and many were hurt and angry because of it. When only 10 out of 210 faculty seemed meritorious, the remaining 200 "unmeritorious" felt overlooked and slighted. The issue became an annual sore spot, and at first the only thing the faculty organization could do about it was to convince the administration not to publish the "merit winners" until the final test week of the spring quarter, at which point the boiling point of the losers would be least affected. Finally, at the decade's end, when the administration was convinced of the deleterious effects of these "merit raises," the money instead went into the scholarship fund.
38) By 1993, the percentage of doctorates had gone up to 76 percent, still the highest in the System. The fact that the SUS chancellor chose to send his own son to Bemidji State at decade's end spoke eloquently of the school having the best undergraduate program in the state. Gillett, in his commentary (p. 6), paid tribute to faculty members Mike Field, Chuck Austad and Russ Lee, who in 1986 inaugurated the Center for Professional Development to assist in the improvement of teaching. The center is still going strong at this writing, 1994. The project was totally faculty designed and operated—and externally funded (Title III, Bush Grants)—with participation entirely voluntary. Any faculty member can request and get both analyses of his/ her classroom teaching skills and help in improving them.

In 1982, there were only 15 international students, including Canadians, on campus; by 1990 there were approximately 250 students, representing over 30 countries. (By 1994 there were some 300 students from 35 countries.) In 1982, foreign study opportunities were limited essentially to the Eurospring program in England and the continent. By 1990 the expanded opportunities for students and faculty to study abroad included an annual Sino-summer travel program; a faculty-exchange at Laioning University, China; participation in the two-year Akita (Japanese) program, or at the University at Kasai Gaida, Japan; study at Vaxjo University, Sweden; Year Abroad at Oxford, England; and a year-long program at Petaling Jaya Community College, Malaysia. All in all, programs a long way from Beltrami County and the days of the Normal School.

Among the important on-campus initiatives were the internationalization of the curriculum, including a requirement in general education for all students to take a minimum of 12 credits approved as global, multicultural and/or gender study. As to a major, there became available an international studies field of emphasis designed to complement other majors that may have an international or cross-cultural orientation. Outside the classroom, each academic year a particular all-school academic topic or theme or focus is selected, around which is infused programming, lectures, films, mini-courses, seminars, and the like, all to promote the topic (country) and tie the theme together over an extended time—and in all this heighten an all-school awareness of a world really not that far away from Beltrami County. (The 1993-94 theme was "Focus on the Middle East.")

Graduating Senior and Family Friends from Malaysia
"In 1982 there were 15 international students . . . in 1994, 300 from 35 countries."

The initial area for recruiting foreign students was in Southeast Asia, especially seeking high-ability, highly motivated students who would be academically successful and contribute to a campus academic atmosphere that would further challenge all students to perform at a high level.[39]   The screening process for international students became more rigid in the 1980s, with all required to have a demonstrated English language competency along with sufficient financial backing. No more surprise arrivals at the Bemidji Greyhound Bus Depot of non-English speaking "wannabe" BSU students with five bucks in their pockets and knowing only words to the effect of "Now you take care of me." Not that all the '80s contingents had their English down pat; most of them carried their dictionaries with them their first year on campus, which helped them get by. Yet the befuddled international students could never look up definitions that might help them pierce the code of American school slang, lines like: "Deece, man, like the max. I've got some kick tunes and I'll bring my box, but can you come up with some barley? Y'know?" There's English, and then there's "American."[40]

This recruitment of overseas students was not totally educational nor altruistic nor philosophical; it was practical, too, because the infusion of significant numbers of well-qualified international students also assisted in reversing the enrollment decline projected for the '80s. It might also be noted that for many of these international students, the costs of attending Bemidji State were relatively low, indeed, a university-education bargain, compared to educational costs in their own countries. Their coming became a good deal for all parties concerned, a true win-win situation, not that there were not problems or concerns. There would be culture shock for each international student, of course, starting with the weather. Most of the Asian students—and the Ethiopians—had never seen snow, let alone experienced a winter like Bemidji's. Nevertheless, almost all of them stayed on for four years, adapting to the clime and adopting long underwear and goose-down parkas. Overall the large numbers of foreign students made the University a true university, a school more attractive to thoughtful American students, and a factor in advancing the basic plan to enhance the academic image of Bemidji State. Bemidji State was no longer isolated nor insulated; it had become a part of the "Global Village."

FOUNDATIONS, FUNDING AND FATTER FIGURES

The goals of a school foundation are more than simple fund raising. There's a broader goal closely allied with other initiatives leading to increased prestige for the University. This is particularly important with public school figures—counselors, faculty, administrators—who remain influential in assisting high school seniors in selecting the school of higher education they will attend.

39) On a personal note, and with mixed feelings, I can report that in my two American history survey classes taught in spring quarter, 1993, with over 200 students enrolled, the highest test scores went to a young woman from Hong Kong.
40) Translation, of sorts, "Fine, man, it's the best. I've got some great songs, and I'll bring my tape player, but can you bring the beer?" Every generation of young people adopts its own slang. Those who were in college during the Vietnam era said "groovy, far out," and "right on" a lot, and they did not have conversations, they had "rap sessions." Some of the terms were so widespread and remained current for so long that they made it into the next round of dictionaries. Money, for example, is now listed as one of the meanings of "bread," and "rap" has come to mean talk. But, however "groovy" it might be at one time period—as when "wheels" meant "car"—the next generation would scoff at such terminology. The one word appraisal that seems to have hung on for two generations is the term which bestows the highest accolade on anything, namely "neat."

The initial push for a Bemidji State Foundation began with President Bangsberg but the idea did not really get going until 1969 under President Decker. As a non-profit, tax exempt corporation, the Foundation was empowered to solicit, receive, and administer gifts, bequests and trusts for the University, its departments and programs. The Foundation Board of Directors has consisted of area business and professional persons, alumni and faculty, and has been responsible for establishing policies. The earliest years found some success, with gifts to the school ranging widely from the expected cash or checks to real estate to gifts in kind (art, books, collections, boats, building supplies); in 10 years' time the funds went from $1 to about $150,000 which figure, though hardly monumental, said one board member, "was better than a kick in the shins."

The need for more funding was obvious because there was a greater need for scholarships; and as state appropriations cannot be used for that category, BSU Foundation monies were almost totally designated for scholarships, with a small portion for recruitment. Initially, all fund raising was aimed locally, and only gradually did the range of effort go out of town, at first targeting alumni via telephone in what were called "phonathons." The rewards came with increased contributions so that by the mid 1980s, the assets approached three-quarters of a million dollars, a notable achievement, accomplished by a variety of persons who did fund raising part-time only. Therein lay the problem and thereby came the decision in 1986 to restructure the administration and employ a single development specialist, a vice president for development (Dr. Dave Tiffany became the first V.P.D.). With one person devoted almost totally to development, the Foundation work moved literally far and wide, expanding the range as well as targeting different potential donors, notably large corporations. Success with the latter can be noted, yea celebrated, in the 1990 bequest of $750,000 by 3-M Corporation of St. Paul to Bemidji State in a specified endowment fund to be used for the employment of a Native American to teach classes in accounting. The Foundation's ongoing changes and improvements have included an expanded phonathon appeal, and creation of a special Business Administration Alumni Chapter. Each fall, starting in 1989, the school has sponsored a Twin Cities Alumni and Friends Dinner, with a featured speaker coming from the campus faculty to address former students and ongoing friends of Bemidji State. In total, the growth of the Foundation funds from these changes has been dramatic; as of June 30, 1993, the Foundation assets totaled $2,807,513.64. Given these numbers, the Foundation Board authorized scholarships totaling $152,025 for the 1993-94 school year, and combined with the other University scholarships (e.g., the Bookstore alone gave $112,560), the grand total came to $342,257. (For a breakdown of scholarship sources for the latter figure and school year, see Appendix L.) These dollars translated into over 100 scholarships presented, and over the past 20 years, more than 2,200 students have been helped by the Foundation. Besides that internal source, over 250 students each year are helped by awards and scholarships from outside sources, including Blandin Corporation, Lakehead Pipeline Company, wood processing plants, education associations, PTAs, churches, and the like. Those awards average just over $900 for the 1993-94 year. All of the out-of-town help to the Foundation has been greatly appreciated, certainly, but the primary supporters over the years have been in the Bemidji community, thanks in part to the perennial promotion by the editors of the Bemidji <u>Pioneer</u> who reemphasize over and over the powerful economic impact of the University on the community.[41]

The Study of Ojibwe by and for Native Americans
"Geographically, Bemidji State sits in the middle of four reservations."

OTHER NEW AREAS OF EMPHASES

By decade's end, which coincided with the end of Gillett's tenure as president (June 30, 1990), certain school decisions stood out because of the

41) A <u>Pioneer</u> editorial of August 27, 1993, illustrated their supportive position: "Because of the groundswell of community support garnered in the recent past in response to BSU as it struggled through tough state budget times, one shouldn't have to conduct a 'hard sell' to ensure the BSU Foundation a successful community drive today and Friday. Those tough state budget times haven't gone away." The editor went on to point out the multiplier-effect and the school's amazing economic impact: "BSU'S payroll last year totaled $18.9 million. Add to that some $17.6 million in direct student expenditures and $1.9 million in BSU expenditures in the local community and BSU's total expenditures amount to $38.5 million. Using the accepted multiplier effect for the number of times money exchanges hands locally before leaving the community, BSU's economic impact on the community approaches $92.3 million annually."

particular emphasis placed upon them. Such decisions were made for a variety of
reasons, including sign-of-the-times responses as well as pressures on the
administration for changes. For example, the importance of women had been
promoted, as reflected in several areas. More classes and more new courses are now
offered to show the historical importance of women. A women's studies program
and minor have been added, along with a new Women's Resource Center. Gender,
along with race, became a significant factor in hiring, resulting in the employment
of a full-time affirmative action officer (Lorena Cook is the first such officer in her
official role as assistant to the president). The school also emphasized its special
responsibility and opportunity to advance the education of Indian students. Thus
an Indian Advisory Council was formed; an Indian counselor was employed to
develop Indian Student Services; Native Americans into Medicine, a cooperative
program with the University of Minnesota-Duluth was started, and the drive began
to build a new Native American Center on campus. (For more on the BSU Indian
programs, see section on Programs and People.)

The administration made deliberate moves to improve both visibility and
communication with constituent groups as well as promote the school's successes.[42]
Thus began a regularly published President's Newsletter and an alumni newspaper
called Horizons. For community and area citizens, the administration began a
series of popular "Campus Community Breakfasts" on campus, each featuring a
speaker and a topic of general interest. The breakfast—coffee, orange juice and
sweet rolls—starts at 7:30 a.m., the main speaker begins by 8:00 a.m. and
everything concludes within the next hour. The president also starts each school
year with an "Opening Day Breakfast" for all University employees held in the
ballroom of the Hobson Union. The session allows time for all present to get an
update on school news, to get to see if not meet new staff members introduced at
the time, and lastly to hear the major address of the president, who lays out the "state
of the state university" as he sees it for the coming year. (These opening-school-
year sessions also allowed for certain high jinks between President Gillett and Vice
President for Academic Affairs Les Duly, as the two played ongoing tricks on each
other, all to the enjoyment of the suddenly-attentive audiences. Indeed, soon these
fall openers were awaited by all, just to see what special goofiness the president and
vice president would come up with each time. They were most creative, especially
in returning and re-returning to each other two ugly statues of pink plastic
flamingos. Each opener was judged afterwards by audiences deciding which of the
two got the upper hand over the other one that particular year.) More promotion and
inter-staff socializing in the eating category included the president's annual free
spring bratwurst—and sauerkraut and baked beans and potato salad—luncheon
held outside (in good weather) and viewed as a nice gesture for all to end the school

42) Considerable "high visibility" came because of Beaver sports teams, especially the hockey squads who regularly played in
national tournaments throughout the decade. When the hockey squad went 31-0 in 1984 and won the NCAA Division II title,
the print was big. Nor did it hurt BSU when hockey star Joel Otto signed a professional contract in '84 with the Calgary Flames
of the NHL. Also the Beaver basketball team played Stanford University in Palo Alto, California in 1983, permitting some good
picture-taking for publicity purposes later. Same with the swimming team that year ('83) competing against the University of
Minnesota, and barely losing 69-64.

year with good feelings and a full stomach.

While the campus community breakfasts brought in some speakers of at least state, if not national, recognition, the Distinguished Lecture Series at night brought in "the biggies" from all over the world. Viewing the role of the University as in part providing major cultural and academic opportunities for all people in the area, BSU fulfilled this role by bringing to the campus persons of major renown, international leaders like the former prime minister of Great Britain, Lord Harold Wilson, as well as well-known, sometimes controversial personages like William Buckley, Jack Anderson, Arthur Meier Schlesinger, Jr., and Bettina Gregory, all of whom appeared in Bemidji in the late 1980s. Given the high costs for each speaker's address, only about one big name per year could be afforded.

A SCHOOL FOR ALL AGES—BY LAW

The major trend in the '80s as to new students coming to BSU was increasing numbers of older students, the aforementioned SOTA (Students Older Than Average), this group so important as to make BSU the campus with the highest percentage of SOTA students within the State University System by 1990. (BSU also had the highest percentage of ethnic minority students in the SUS.) Though not as large in numbers, there was also the other end of the age scale, high school students ages 15-16-17 taking classes at BSU. This latter group came as the result of a 1985 law, the Post Secondary Options Act, the intent of which was to allow juniors and seniors in high school to take college classes not available in their high school—and the state would pay the tuition-credit costs (the local school district having its state funding reduced accordingly). Like all programs with good intentions behind them, the act brought some abuses when initiated. With Bemidji Senior High School being only two blocks away from the BSU campus, high school students came in large numbers (100-plus to start with) to take college classes, and some took all their classes at BSU, which allowed them to use their credits both at the high school and get college credits, too. Indeed, a few students on their graduation day from high school already had two years of college credits to their credit. While the vast majority of high school students since '85 have come on campus only briefly to take a class or two (about 75 students each quarter by 1990), some out-of-town high school students (about 25 a year) have become full-time students, living in the dorms for the entire school year. All this illustrates again that neither high school nor college is what it used to be. . . .

WHAT IS NOT THERE BY 1990

The obvious changes to the University can be determined in part by noting what was "not there" by decade's end. Like beauty being in the eye of the beholder, BSU's changes—and what they meant—depend on the person chronicling and interpreting them. To illustrate, by 1990 a trip to the A.C. Clark Library could/did confound the uninitiated in electronics; there was no more card catalog. Attempts to determine the availability or location of any document required basic computer skills, the PALS on-line computer eliminating forever the card catalog. This change led to many older profs going to the library and quietly asking some freshman there to please help them find a certain book on that funny machine. (Moreover, the "library of the future" may be one with no books or magazines; all that information will be on computers.)

Students starting the decade could take a B.A. degree with 180 credits; by 1985 that number had been upped to 192, the figure required for all bachelor's degrees. The heavy hand of the Chancellor's Office in St. Paul led to the demise of certain graduate programs. Some departments, like history, had both an M.A. and an M.S. graduate program in 1980 and had neither by 1990. (By 1994, although there were 10 M.S. programs available, the only M.A. options left were in English and biology.) The falling enrollments of the early '80s, however, had been reversed so that by 1990, again depending on how/who one counted as a student, the round figure of 5,000 could be claimed. By then none of the 5,000 students could buy on campus a cup of coffee that came in a styrofoam cup; ARA Food Services had replaced styrofoam with paper cups, in keeping with the wish of the environmentalists. Nor could one smoke in any building on campus, with the exception of one room of the Hobson Union set aside for the puffers. Nearly each year of the decade, the campus newspaper had helped promote that one special day called D-Day, then meaning Don't-Smoke-Day—nor the day after, nor. . . .

Some campus faculty figures were gone by 1990, venerable "old-timers" like Ray Carlson, who retired in 1984 after 32 years—but who managed off and on to teach a class or two and who helped struggling grad students complete their theses. Head football coach John Peterson left to join the pros as a scout, and he was replaced by Kris Diaz, a former Moorhead State assistant coach. Women's field hockey teams were no more by decade's end, a lamentable loss felt strongly by loyal if small-in-number supporters. No more were SUS students limited to Minnesota campuses, because in 1990 the "eighth campus" became available for all in Akita, Japan. Only a few Minnesotans chose to go to Akita, but the special few who did go came back as converted Nipponophiles.

Another sign of the times. It was not that the Peace Corps representatives did not come to the BSU campus to recruit volunteers in the '80s, it was only that they came infrequently, there being a more limited campus interest in volunteerism than 25 years earlier. Campus idealism had shifted more to environmental goals, and there was no lack of push and promotion by the student newspapers for awareness that would lead to action. Think Globally, but Act Locally. Recycle, re-use, no plastic, recycle, re-use . . . reinforcement. Nor was there any chance to ignore the DANGERS OF ALCOHOL on campus. It was hoped that the concepts pushed in Alcohol Awareness Week would become understandings and attitudes held by every student every year, but alcohol abuse remained a major problem that would not be close to being solved by 1990.

Half amusing, half annoying in 1990—and for many it was either all one way or the other—was the potential "absence" of Bemidji's most famous citizens, the Paul Bunyan and Babe statues. The two tall figures, standing mute and immobile on the lakeshore, are symbols of northern Minnesota in general and Bemidji in particular. A local writer—who said later it was all tongue-in-cheek good American fun—suggested in print that the statues of Paul and Babe were so much schlock; they were "artistic embarrassments" and they "should be hauled off

Bemidji North Country, Very Much Canoe Country as Well
"Before all the ice goes out . . . the boats go in."

to the prairie backwashes." All such talk would have stayed locally emotional—and nasty—had not the alleged story about "Bemidji Paul Bunyan's Statue Being Torn Down" reached the Minnesota Associated Press Bureau, which in turn soon made the news on CNN, CBS and WGN. By this point the "fun" was no fun at all, but Paul and Babe stayed put and emotions died down, sort of. (In 1987 the town had given their two top citizens a 50th birthday party, a bash that lasted off and on all summer long, and it made a fine excuse for an all-Bemidji High School reunion.)

Also not amused in 1990 were students resisting a pressure group from downstate who wanted to change the name of the State Universities so that Bemidji would become "Minnesota State University-Bemidji," a' la Wisconsin's way of designating its universities. No way. No change. No change either that decade for BSU students who took their lives in their hands each time they tried to walk across Bemidji Avenue. Some things haven't changed since World War II.

Someone else would not be on campus by the end of 1990. President Ted Gillett retired June 30, after eight years at the helm. In keeping with his style, he made his decision clear the year before so that there would be plenty of time to select his replacement. Gillett officially made the announcement of his retirement at the start of the 1989-90 school year at the all-school Opening Day Breakfast. When he got to this part of his talk, the words did not come easily, and he spoke with choking hesitation as he relayed the mixed feelings he had about leaving Bemidji State. The new school year began along with the extended process of selecting a new president for the 1990s. So ended another decade and another presidential term at Bemidji State, but it was time to look forward, not backward, to new leadership for those years as the 20th century wound down to the year 2000.

"DEJA VU ALL OVER AGAIN"

The search for a new president began in earnest in early September, 1989, starting with the formation of an official campus search committee. After the usual wrangling among the group members who would send representatives—and the votes taken—23 persons were chosen who represented the several constituencies. Individually, the search committee members started the long process by reading the application materials, some almost book-length in quantity, of some 60 candidates, and the committee met regularly on Fridays to discuss applications and afterwards cull out those deemed least desirable. Their efforts led to the candidate numbers being reduced to eight by December 15, at which point a sub-committee of seven members conducted what were called "airport interviews," meaning the eight semifinalists were brought to Minneapolis, with the majority arriving by plane, for personal interviews. By February, 1990, only three finalists remained in the running: 1) Dr. John Agria, vice president for academic services at Thiel College, a private liberal arts college in Greenville, Pennsylvania; 2) Dr. Leslie Duly, vice president for academic affairs at Bemidji State University; 3) Dr. Catherine Tisinger, president of North Adams State College, Massachusetts. On three separate days, the three of them came before Bemidji State committees for viewing and interviewing, the day culminating with their oral presentations made to an all-school assembly. Questions and answers followed each talk.[43] The candidates then went to St. Paul and essentially went through the same process with members of the

State University Board. On March 7, 1990, the SUS Board voted unanimously in choosing Dr. Duly to replace Gillett as Bemidji State University's seventh president, Duly's position to begin July 1, 1990.

The process of picking a new president had commanded more than six months of ongoing, intensive efforts that were both strenuous and costly to carry out. Applications came from every region in the country and probing letters and phone calls had been made to these regions. The sifting and winnowing process was stressful for the search committee members who dutifully carried out their mandate to judge each candidate carefully and honestly. SUS representatives also traveled to the home colleges of the finalists, the trips preceded and followed by hours and hours of reading and discussions. Yet when the choice was at last made to pick Gillett's successor, he was located only 45 steps away from Gillett's office.

Understandably, back on the Bemidji campus, there was little surprise and no shock at Duly's selection. Most faculty members expected it, and all constituent groups easily acquiesced to the choice. He was the "known" candidate; "better to bear the ills we have than to fly to others we know not of," or words to that effect bespoke the basic campus attitude. Many (but not all) were pleased, and a few were ecstatic at the selection, most notably Gillett. Obviously in Duly's selection there were distinct advantages for both Duly and the entire University. After 10 years as vice president, Duly knew the school and its operation as well as anyone, and vice versa. There was no one-year time lapse for the usual orientation of a new president. (There was also no honeymoon time accorded him.) Duly could simply pick up where he had left off and hit the ground running, as it were; the obvious difference was that he was the #1 man instead of #2, and the presidential move to his new office was simple, too; it was only 45 feet away.

---

43) The Northern Student conducted their own questions-and-answers to the top three candidates, all printed in the February 21, 1990 issue, p. 2.

The 1990s

I NTO THE 21ST CENTURY. *The trends that characterize a decade are not always neatly confined to a ten-year period; they can come and go, resulting in their being almost faddish. Some of the images associated with The Second Gilded Age, the 1980s, began to wane as 1990 came closer. For example, the slipping popularity of TV shows about the rich and fashionable, such as* Dallas *and* Dynasty, *suggested a shift in American values toward more concern for a struggling middle class, and the two worlds of black America. Other trends, however, notably in electronics use, expanded in quantum jumps. The public witnessed an explosion in communications technology so that by 1994 a personal computer could be found in a third of American homes. Computers' abilities to store massive amounts of data increased every year; the electronic office and the electronic home had arrived, and the workplace of the '90s would belong to those who came prepared with current skills, and were ready to retrain as often as necessary during a career lifetime certain to see ever more technological change and challenge. By century's end a child may go into a museum and ask about a funny-looking machine on display, only to be told, "Oh, that's a typewriter."[1]*

BEYOND THE COLD WAR. Even as the Soviet Union receded in power and then crumbled by 1991, the first Afro-American to be America's top military man, Colin Powell, Joint Chiefs of Staff commander, reportedly told a NATO commander who was still preoccupied with the Communist threat, "Smile, Jack. We won." The end of the Cold War removed the Soviet Union as America's main

---

1) The years 1982-1990 of BSU President Ted Gillett illustrate the changes in historical documentation. As with his predecessors, I had asked Gillett to save for historical purposes all the letters and memos that went out from his office in his term, to have them boxed and put away in reserve. At this request he looked at me quizzically before replying, "Everything's on the D.G. [Data General]." His entire administration is essentially recorded on computer.

ideological enemy, but new post-Cold War challenges quickly appeared, notably in the Middle East and in an Eastern Europe vulnerable to regional and ethnic conflicts. George Herbert Walker Bush, the first sitting vice president since Martin Van Buren to be elected to the presidency, was no clone of Ronald Reagan. He lacked the former's abiding conservatism and promised "a kinder, gentler administration" for the '90s. If that line didn't trouble too many, his later, "Read My Lips: No New Taxes" did—after he went back on his word and approved a new '91 tax bill. Yet the deficit he inherited from the Reagan years, along with Bush's own preference for foreign affairs, kept him from articulating a clear domestic agenda. The "hero president" of the Persian Gulf War (90 percent approval rating) became in one year a victim of the collapsing economy around him. If America could apply itself so purposefully to war, why couldn't it do the same for the problems of its inner cities, unemployment, the recession, the disintegrating family, the environment, the threat of AIDS? Where's the leadership on domestic issues? The results of those questions: In 1992 Bush was able to accomplish what few incumbent presidents had done before, lose the next election. He lost to a baby-boomer, a boyish-looking Southerner named Bill Clinton. The United States had had eight recessions since World War II, and in each case the economy had rebounded within six to 16 months. Not so in the first half of the 1990s, with recovery slowed by a massive federal debt, overburdened state and local governments, and decreasing consumer confidence. Main Street became Bleak Street. Unemployment moved beyond seven percent nationwide; industrial and white-collar layoffs spread; and in many families someone had either already lost a job or feared it might happen soon. Unsettling times in the early '90s were, as usual, reflected in the operation of America's colleges. Back to the British motto of "muddling through," somehow.

Once again, in that period the sound bites made indentations in American minds. Names and news that pulsated through the airwaves between 1990 and 1994 included S&L Crisis, "Quayle" hunting, the Threepeat Chicago Bulls, Roseanne, Karaoke, Dr. Kevorkian, ozone holes, Reginald Denny and Rodney King, Prozac, the obscene "L" word for the Democrats, third-wave feminism, Moonwalk, Iraqi aggression or Kuwaiti oil?, Guns 'n Roses, The Bridges of Madison County, North Stars do Dallas, National Health Plan/s/s/s, the Kurds, Murder in Miami, Mississippi floods, Tailhook, Larry King Live, Elvis sightings, Somalia in/out?, Achy-Breaky Heart, Soviet Union: 1917-1991, H. Norman Schwarzkopf, CD-ROM, Phonegate, "Wilding," Israeli-PLO Peace Accord, Lotto Largesse, Jurassic Park, car phones, sexual harassment, family violence, "designated drivers," Joe Camel, Shevardnadze in Georgia, Iacocca, drive-by shootings, Hillary Rodham Clinton, Los Angeles riots, Cuba after Castro? Late night talk shows after Carson? The Judds after Naomi? Tipper and Al, Beavis and Butthead, Deconstruction in lit and fashion, gays in the military, 20/20, Desert Storm, the Mall of America, Aidid, the Peace Dividend?, the Twins and Toronto and Toronto again. And always the many controversies: Planned Parenthood v. Casey, Clarence Thomas v. Anita Hill, Murphy Brown v. Dan Quayle, Gorbachev v. Yeltzin v. Hard-liners, H. Ross Perot v. Democrats and Republicans, Crips v. Vice Lords, Cable v. Networks; Grunseth v. Perpich v. Carlson v. Boschwitz; Tonya Harding v. Nancy Kerrigan; To Live and Die in L.A.? O.D.'d on O.J. Simson.

In sexual matters, Americans in the early '90s seemed to be saying "no" to the casual experimentation of the preceding years. Here AIDS was central. Campaigns promoting safe sex may have made many angry but the overall education managed to make the activists more cautious. It appeared that hedonism was out, monogamy—and even celibacy—was in. Sexual activism on college campuses was hardly out, of course, nor were venereal diseases. At Bemidji State, the Student Health Service continued to have ongoing business, notably in chlamydia infections. The times had indeed changed: By 1994, condoms were readily available in several places on campus, in the variety stores and from the vending machines in the student union lavatories. Free condoms for students were also available for the asking at the Health Service.

TOWARD A PLURALISTIC SOCIETY. The 1990 census counted 246.9 million Americans. By far the most dramatic shift since the 1980 census was the changing racial composition of the land. In 1990 one in four Americans had African, Asian, Hispanic, or American Indian ancestry, up from one in five just 10 years earlier. The country had emerged as a fully pluralistic society. In 1941, Henry Luce, the publisher of TIME and LIFE magazines, confidently predicted the beginning of an "American Century" when World War II ended. As the nation approaches the year 2000, it seems likely that the 21st century will be known not as an "American Century" but as a "Global Century." Economically, power will be shared among multiple players, in sharp contrast to the immediate postwar period when the U.S. dominated the world economy. The new world order will be characterized by interdependent capitalist market economies organized around major world trading blocks. The new century will likely be more favorable to the Pacific Rim and European Community countries, by 1990 already emerging as strong contenders in global markets. It would be great irony if the U.S. "won" the Cold War, only to have jeopardized its status as a world economic leader in the resulting peace. That the U.S. no longer dominates the world does not mean that the country is on any inevitable decline toward obscurity and powerlessness. This emerging new multiculturalism and the new world order will shape the future of the U.S. and the globe in the next century. These important concepts were not only recognized in 1990 by the new president of Bemidji State University but were ideas that seemed an integral part of his attitude and policies. Once again the school seemed to choose the right man for the changing times as the University moved towards the 21st century.

◆ ◆ ◆

Leslie C. Duly (president 1990-1993)
"So engaging a scholar . . . He was both a gentle man and a gentleman."

LESLIE CLEMENT DULY

Bemidji State's seventh president was born September 26, 1935, at Kenmore, New York, the son of Leslie H. and Lucille Duly. He was raised and educated in the Kenmore area. He graduated with a bachelor's degree, *cum laude*, from the University of South Dakota in 1957, with a major in history. He married Diane Hewes on April 20, 1957, at Crete, Illinois; they would have three daughters and one son. Duly received a Fulbright Scholarship and studied at the University of Melbourne, Australia, receiving his master's degree in history in 1959, with an emphasis on land policy of Australia. With a National Defense Educational Fellowship and a Ford Foundation Research Award, he completed a doctorate in history in 1965 at Duke University's Commonwealth Studies Institute with an emphasis on British and Commonwealth land policy of South Africa. He also lived and studied at the University of London and the University of Cape Town, South Africa. After teaching history at Memphis State University in 1963-64 and at Mount Holyoke College in South Kaley, Massachusetts, from 1964 to 1968, he began a 12-year career teaching history at the University of Nebraska, Lincoln. At Lincoln he also served as fellow and director of university studies, a program for highly-motivated students. In 1976 he received a special award for teaching excellence in the humanities. He was a member of Phi Beta Kappa, and he wrote extensively, contributing to a number of scholarly journals, writing primarily about various aspects of the British Empire. He served as editorial consultant for several publications, especially those focusing on international studies. Although he had limited administrative experience at Nebraska-Lincoln, Duly came to Bemidji in 1980 as vice president for academic affairs. As chief academic officer, he was responsible for academic programs, cultural diversity programs, faculty development, and for creating and promoting international studies.

"JUS' PLAIN LES"

The preceding summarizes the formal, official life and educational background of President Duly, but it was the human side that the students and faculty knew and saw every day. He was both a gentle man and a gentleman. He virtually glowed with kindness and civility. He appeared devoid of anger, and if he had a bad temper, no one on campus saw it; the most that might be revealed was fluster. What the campus saw was his steady temperament: Easy going, smiling, joking, happy and friendly, characteristics which could be observed from first thing in the morning when he got out of his car in the parking lot and people could literally listen to him whistle indecipherable melodies as he walked briskly to his office/s in Deputy Hall. A smallish man, slightly built, with bright eyes that could twinkle mischievously, the bespectacled president was a natty dresser who always wore a tie, which was never loosened despite the heat of the day or the heat of the argument. And no matter how heated the argument, he always, but always, kept his cool, even when on rare occasions a few malcontents virtually badgered him and pushed him (too) far. (Observers to some of these scenes believed Duly would have had every right to pop a few of these boorish persons in the nose. Such a notion was absurd, of course; he didn't even raise his voice in arguments. His was always the voice of reason and calm.) His devotion to Bemidji State was so strong as to make him a workaholic, a trait that at first seemed admirable but later appeared excessive; he seemed always to be somewhere on campus. Always working, always planning, always promoting the University, and always serving, literally. Certainly he'd be there on campus. When there was some kind of social gathering with food and refreshments, Duly would be the one going around the room the entire time with a coffee pot, filling people's cups and making conversation. The president was the one who personally dished out the ice cream at every social, the one who fried the hamburgers and passed out more bratwursts, the one who brought and then cut the cake at the monthly Meet and Confer sessions with the IFO Union Executive Board.

Duly's commitment to students and their wants and needs never stopped. Illustration: The day after he became president, he revealed offhandedly his plans to live in Tamarack Hall dormitory for a week, to be with students day and night, eat with them at Wally's and listen to their concerns. And he did. And he enjoyed it!? Dr. Duly loved fun, loved puns, and promoted the same shamelessly, to wit: "Do More With Les" and "Let It Be Duly Noted." Then his eyes twinkled. Humor was part of his leadership style and regarded by nearly all as an admirable quality about him because his humor was never unkind, never destructive. This president who seemed to know everybody's name was so unassuming but so engaging, a "scholar in president's clothing."

Many believed Duly to be at his absolute best in front of crowds, notably when he served as a master of ceremonies. An articulate spokesman, he not only spoke fluently—and always with a touch of wit—but he managed somehow at every occasion to say all the right things.[2] People looked forward to social gatherings which the president would attend, whether as the main speaker or simply as a fellow guest, because he talked so well and so nicely and was so courteous to everyone, whether in a one-on-one situation or part of a small group. He genuinely liked people, and he loved Bemidji State University. The entire school became a kind of extended family for him. He loved what he was doing and he was doing what he loved.

The down-side of this warm, genial, verbal president was the difficulty of some students, faculty, chairpersons and deans to get any response from him, let alone a clear, explicit yes-or-no answer. Some people left his office believing they had a yes when they really had a no, and when he sometimes said semi-facetiously that the best he could do was to offer "a definite maybe," not all listeners were amused at the line, or at the waffling. It became a left-handed compliment when faculty members frequently said that President Duly was a very nice man, too nice. (There were disputes and open disagreements with the president's priorities, of course, but these were issues of judgment outside of his personality. His one central quality was integrity to do what he believed was right.) More criticisms came during his first two years when he was faulted for either unwillingness or inability to "let go" of certain decision-making powers. His personal, hands-on desire to be in on everything appeared to hamstring administrators under him. Those 10 years of his as vice president handling the nuts-and-bolts of the operation appeared hard for him to give up. Again he meant so well, but his constant involvement in so many areas sometimes delayed quick responses to important questions and issues. Thus many things moved slowly, such as some hiring, some firing, some program additions/elections, exasperating many of those persons involved.[3] However, by the start of his third year, he showed far more willingness to turn the daily running of the store over to others while he concerned himself more with larger policy-making and the needed state politicking. He was very good at the latter, with Minnesota State Senate Majority Leader Roger Moe later observing, "President Duly was not your typical university president. He was always pleasant, always

2) Understandably, not all persons connected with Bemidji State would agree, especially some of those in athletics, because at a few social situations in which athletics was the basis for the gatherings, some of his comments seemed inappropriate, if not gaffes. For example, at one Holiday Inn athletic fundraiser, Duly spoke about the elimination of swimming as a varsity sport. It would be charitable to state that he did not appreciate, let alone understand, athletics.
3) A few faculty members most happy at his foot-dragging were those who were scheduled to have their contracts run out, but who, because of administrative delays and missed deadlines, got to hang on an extra year, and sometimes longer. As indicated in the previous section, Duly was an excellent vice president. By his tenth year in this capacity, he was the senior academic vice president in the System and so knowledgeable about the entire State University operation that he became the major source of information and help for other administrators. It became a cliché among state officials that if anyone had any difficult question about the SUS, "Call Les Duly up in Bemidji."

smiling. He had success with the formula that 'sugar works better than salt'."[4]

INAUGURATION WITH A TWIST

Each Bemidji State president has come to the position with certain goals, certain biases, certain predispositions for future emphases, which in Duly's case became publicly clear at his inauguration ceremony on November 2, 1990, in Memorial Hall.[5] In his choosing what and who should be on the program, it became obvious to all that the new president had cultivated a global perspective that he would be promoting through his office. He was an internationalist, a promoter of cultural diversity, points observed throughout the colorful and upbeat ceremony, from the University Band's playing of "O Canada," to a message delivered in the Ojibwe language, to a greeting by the consul general from Australia, to international students—most wearing the costumes/clothes of their homeland—as special delegates to the inauguration. Duly's address was entitled ". . . or 21," and in it he gave the clear reminder that the institution existed to serve students, students, and more students, and after them, all citizens in the region. The ceremony ended with the audience singing the venerable Gaudeamus Igitur, and the participants marched out while the band played "Waltzing Matilda" (the "unofficial" national anthem of Australia) adding a final and appropriate touch to this president so immersed in global perspectives and multiculturalism.

MAKE NO MISTAKE ON WHERE HE STOOD

President Duly had an extraordinary vision of the potential of the University, and indeed of education itself, in coping with a difficult and often mean-spirited world. If was the very breadth of his concept of education which puzzled and annoyed some of his colleagues as much as it encouraged them to do more than they thought they could do. His firmness of commitment to intercultural understanding and the world beyond Bemidji came out in many ways, but none more straightforwardly than the opening lines of the BSU undergraduate catalog for 1992-94. Under "Educational Philosophy: President Leslie C. Duly," he wrote:

"Bemidji State University is a comprehensive regional University committed to the education of students so that they may live as responsible, productive, and free citizens in a global society. While the University offers a wide variety of undergraduate and graduate educational programs, all are designed to build upon and extend the foundation of a sound liberal education. Such an education fosters the wisdom of historical perspective, the understanding which

4) Statement made by Moe on May 12, 1993, at the Service of Remembrance for Duly held that day in Bemidji.
5) Copy of the inaugural program in the BSU archives. Following the pattern set by his predecessor, the festivities were low-key and limited to a few basic events held within two days. The night before the formal inauguration there was a banquet in his honor held at the Holiday Inn, at which time and place the mirth of the man spilled over to a happy evening for the large audience in attendance. The major address was given by Duly's friend of many years, Dr. Robin Winks, professor of history, Yale University. Immediately after the inaugural convocation the next day, there was an open public reception in the ballroom of the student union. That evening there was an inaugural celebration and dance at the Holiday Inn, featuring the music of the BSU Jazz Bands. Planning for the all events was performed by the Inauguration Committee: Bea Knodel, chair; Jerry Abbott, Linda Baer, Kristine Cannon, Cindy Dahl, Jerry Havel, Judy McDonald, Al Nohner, Gerald Schnabel, Linda Sutherland, Arlene Tangborn, and David Tiffany.

Diamond Point City Park Surrounded by the University
"Building anything there . . . raised the hackles of the townspeople."

comes from an appreciation of the intellectual and cultural achievements of different societies, a willingness to explore diverse views, and a desire to contribute to those creative processes by which human cultures are ultimately formed and sustained."

Dr. Duly took office when the economic terminology of the time was filled with phrases like "down-sizing" and "staff reductions" and "leaner and meaner." The latter was not in his vocabulary. Yet he met the tough economic exigencies head-on and at all times he was the optimist. His optimism was infectious, particularly for his immediate staff, who joined him in his enthusiasm on behalf of the University as the keeper of the flame of internationalization and multicultural understandings. He kept the two top vice presidents he inherited (Tom Faecke in finance and Dave Tiffany in development), and by September 1, 1990, brought in a new vice president for academic affairs, Dr. Linda Baer, a sociologist by training. She had been professor of rural sociology at South Dakota State University, and later held the position of administrative associate in strategic planning, working with the South Dakota State president prior to her joining the Duly administration.

ENTER THE OPPOSITION

The financial pie to be divided up at Bemidji State each year can be and has been divided many different ways, and it is the president who holds the carving knife; he or she determines who gets the biggest pieces and who gets the crumbs. In the pie-slicing-and-distribution to the waiting hands, there are always the less than happy crumb-getters, or those who believe they've gotten but a few morsels.

To the woebegone crumb-catchers, Duly's financial commitment to the seemingly wispy goals of multiculturalism was just so much pie in the sky (and a few added the word "nonsense"). There were those for whom short term needs were more compelling and who had little sympathy for this visionary in the president's chair who could wax eloquent about the strain of altruism running through all cultures and nations, while back on his campus there was a desperate need for more sections of English or biology or criminal justice, with more instructors, more equipment, and more supplies for the weary profs teaching classes with too many students. Expecting the president to take better care of all the monetary aches and pains of departments operating on tight budgets, and to mediate all disputes among faculty groups competing for larger shares of the economic pie, many profs did not share in the president's inspiration to make the University an institution of global significance. The malcontents were there in goodly numbers and suffered from that common academic disease called "turf mentality." Duly fought 'em, and won. It did not always make him popular, but he said he was not in that position to win popularity contests. To the end he remained the keeper of the pie, harassed on many sides; the losers could fault his judgment but never his integrity. Amid the ongoing turmoil over "sliced pie," he remained the unquenchable optimist, this despite political, institutional, and personal burdens which might have crushed a less visionary and resourceful person. He may have been small physically, but he had great strength of character. In the Duly years (1990-93), BSU could be compared to one big family which, like all families, is not always happy, not always in agreement, but still together for a common cause as stated in the president's philosophy: "A teaching-oriented school committed to the education of students."

MAKING THE UNIVERSITY FIT THE DEFINITION
        The word "University" is thrown around loosely, as "loose" describes some definitions of what a university is and isn't. The state legislature in 1975 had authorized all the "State Colleges" to change their names to "State Universities," which they did. To match the dictionary definition, however, a few schools also changed their organizational makeup. Bemidji State's did not change immediately; for example, BSU continued to operate its academic programs under divisions, not colleges. A change came about under President Duly in 1992, and the definition of University was fully met: "An institution of learning of the highest level, comprising a college of liberal arts, a program of graduate studies, and several professional schools, and authorized to confer both undergraduate and graduate degrees" (Random House College Dictionary, 1980, p. 1437). In January, 1991, Duly announced his intention to move the school from divisions to colleges, but the actual changes came only after many meetings and actions and reactions to a variety of structural variations presented by the administration to the faculty. Thus a year went by before the official new titles were announced and implemented. There would be three colleges: the College of Arts and Letters, the College of Social and

Natural Sciences, and the College of Professional Studies. Each college was headed by a dean, appointed by the president; each department, headed by an elected chairperson, would be in one of the three colleges.[6]   The intent of the restructuring included the effort to make all colleges about equal in the number of faculty as well as to have like-minded departments combined appropriately under one heading—one college—but these intentions were not easy to carry out.[7] Connected with all three colleges is a Graduate Studies and Special University Programs unit, and from the latter is another grouping called the School of Integrative Studies (Honors, Indian Studies, International Studies, Peace and Justice Studies and Women's Studies).[8]

THAT DIFFERENT BUILDING . . . ACROSS THE STREET
        Since the mid 1930s, all Bemidji State students have observed a unique, white house standing on the corner of 15th Street and Birchmont Drive, just across the street from the A.C. Clark Library. One did not have to be a student of architecture to recognize the distinct characteristics of its art deco design. This different, oddly-shaped house was strange in style and looks, especially for Bemidji. With its smooth surfaces, flowing lines, and repetitive, geometrical detailing, the house was a classic example of the "Streamline Moderne" variant of the art deco style popularized nationally in the 1920s and 1930s in homes of wealthy people who tended to live in Florida or California, not Bemidji. Incoming freshmen had reason to believe that the impressive-looking building, with its rounded corners and rounded window frames, was part of the campus and was, in all likelihood, the president's house. After all, it looked as if it should be the home of the president. Wrong. It was the home of businessman David Park, whose contractor completed the house in 1936. The house was purchased by the Bemidji State Foundation and the Alumni Association from Park's widow, Wanda Park, in December of 1991, for $92,000.
        David Park was a prominent businessman in Bemidji, and the owner of the largest creamery in the region. In the mid 1920s, at age 23, he had moved to Bemidji and bought a bankrupt creamery. Soon, Park built it up and expanded its operations to where he was considered by his contemporaries as one of the major entrepreneurs in northern Minnesota. Park owned both a fleet of trucks and his own railroad boxcars for shipping dairy products to the east coast. Park also owned smaller creameries in area towns as well as the David Park Company Creamery in Bemidji;

6) Departments in the College of Arts and Letters include English, history, mass communication, modern and classical languages, music, philosophy, theatre and speech communication, and visual arts. The College of Social and Natural Sciences includes biology, chemistry, criminal justice, economics, geography, math and computer science, nursing, physics, political science, psychology, and social relations and services. In the College of Professional Studies are accounting, business, industrial technology; health, physical education and recreation, and professional education.
7) Understandably, some departments would have preferred being assigned to a different college, and a few departments wanted a separate college of their own. All faculty were involved in the official naming of each college, producing some interesting if glib suggestions like the College of the Natural and Unnatural Sciences. Full consensus on names was difficult to achieve. For example, in the CAL there was a strong element preferring to adopt the more common designation of College of Arts and Sciences, but they lost out to the CAL proponents.
8) If all the changes of who's under whom, et cetera, seems confusing, that's because it is confusing. Some sense of the new order can be gained by observing the 1992 flowchart of the responsibilities of the vice president for academic affairs; see Appendix K.

The David Park House and the New Home for Foundation and Alumni
"Incoming freshmen had reason to believe . . . it was the president's house."

the creamery's public specialty in sales was Luxury Ice Cream. With an ice cream sales outlet right on the street, Park was in some ways a forerunner of Dairy Queens. Many people coming to town to shop on a summer Saturday night did not believe the shopping was complete without a stop to buy a nickel ice cream cone at the Park Creamery.

Built in an area that was then almost devoid of other houses, the 5,326 square-foot Park house was designed by architect Edward K. Mahlum (who was also one of the architects who designed both the Bemidji High School auditorium building and the Clearwater County Courthouse in Bagley). Mahlum grew up in Norway, but his formal training was in the Midwest. The walls and floors of the Park House were made mostly of poured concrete, which gave the smooth shape to this striking building shaped like a grand piano. Its uniqueness was later verified by its being the only house in Bemidji that is noted in the National Registry of Historic Residences.

By early 1992, both work on the house and fundraising for its full restoration began, and both were successful. A year later, donations had exceeded $125,000. This total included contributions of materials and services as well as cash donations and pledges. The first major project was the replacement of the roof, followed by a complete reworking of the electrical system. All of the windows and frames were also replaced (a courtesy gift of Marvin Windows of Warroad); window drapes were given by Anderson Fabrics in Blackduck; damaged plaster was removed and replaced; and all exterior paint was removed by using compressed air and corn cob grit instead of sand. Moreover, the former garage was converted into offices, and a handicap accessible restroom was added. Much work was done and most of it done by legions of volunteer labor. The new paint job on the outside made the place gleam with all the class that the striking building symbolizes. The official dedication came on October 2, 1992, as part of homecoming. The ceremony was complete with bands playing and ribbons cut and finger-food served for a supportive crowd of 150 who squeezed inside. A letter of congratulations from Governor Arne Carlson was read, and the Alumni Association presented a framed photograph of Eleanor Roosevelt being greeted by David Park in front of the living room fireplace. (Mrs. Roosevelt had spoken at a Minnesota Education Association teachers convention in Bemidji in 1955; the Parks were her hosts for her brief stay in town.)

Called officially the David Park House, the building currently (1994) houses the BSU Foundation, Alumni and Special Events offices. Students and student organizations are encouraged to utilize the conference (the former master bedroom) and meeting rooms upstairs, free of charge during business hours. The recreation area downstairs holds up to 40 people and can be used for social gatherings, banquets and small dances. The facilities are also available to community groups for a small fee.

What had seemed to newcomers to be part of Bemidji State since 1936— and was deemed ever afterwards as something really desirable for the school to obtain sometime, some day—finally did become part of the University 55 years later. A real touch of class because it is a building of class.[9]

FOUNDERS WALK: THE START OF FORMAL
RECOGNITION OF BEMIDJI STATE'S BENEFACTORS

Since the school's opening 75 years ago, there have been those who believed that recognition needed to be given to the many persons who gave special assistance to the school's operation, especially in those earliest, formative years. While everyone seemed to agree that this was a good idea, virtually nothing was done that in any way formalized publicly those needed honors to individuals so deserving of public recognition. Finally, by 1990 a campus committee was formed to meet and determine who and how many should be recognized, the criteria for recognition, and how that formal recognition might be accomplished. Despite this "early" start, a combination of inertia and funding problems delayed action until the spring of 1993, when at last the decision was announced that a Founders Walk would be established on campus. Commemorative plaques of honor would be attached to the brick columns that support the archway-entrance leading to Deputy Hall, this location being one of the most prominent on campus and regarded as the official entrance to Bemidji State. It was further announced that Absie P. Ritchie

9) In a Northern Student article on the Park House (September 22, 1993, p. 3), Wanda Park, David Park's second wife, and the widow who sold the home to Bemidji State, was quoted as saying, "That house was the only house in the area at that time [1936] and there were only two college buildings in existence. We could see the lake from our house. I wanted the College to have it. I didn't want to sell it to just another individual." At the time of the purchase, an individual had indicated his interest in buying it and turning it into a bed and breakfast. The original cost of the Park House in 1936 remains unknown, with the best guesstimate put at $40,000, a princely sum in those Depression days when two-story homes could be purchased for less than $1,000.

would be the first person so recognized by Bemidji State.[10]

The timing for this commemoration event was not coincidentally the day chosen as the kick-off event for the school's 75th anniversary celebration. It came on July 15, 1993, 80 years to the date that the announcement came via a telegram from St. Paul that Bemidji had been chosen as the site for the new state school. To note that special day and date, and honor A.P. Ritchie at the time, a full program for a sizable crowd was held in the Beaux Arts Ballroom of the union, with talks both short and long by various figures ranging from Bemidji's mayor (who read a proclamation) to a spokesman for the Ritchie family (five of the six surviving children of A. P. Ritchie were there, along with their extended families) to a BSU history prof who dwelled at length on that one special day, July 15, 1913, while giving tribute to the importance of Ritchie making it so special. After the inside ceremony ended, the crowd moved outside to the archway on the corner of Birchmont Drive and 14th Street for a second ceremony which had some very brief talks before the official unveiling of the plaque by members of the Ritchie family. (Among the crowd and participants in the latter ceremony were ex-BSU Presidents Robert Decker and Lowell "Ted" Gillett, and former Acting President Richard Haugo.)

The 6" by 12" brass plaque read:

A. P. RITCHIE
1869-1950

School Superintendent, Postmaster, County Commissioner, School Board Member; Chairman, committee to bring state normal school to Bemidji. Instrumental in founding current Chamber of Commerce, securing Carnegie Library, establishing Diamond Point as a City Park, and building public school system.

The precedent and pattern for formal recognition have been set; more persons can now be chosen in the future.

WHO WILL TELL THE WORLD? THE PRESIDENT

President Duly was the school's best ambassador and publicity agent. He did not stint on proclaiming the good news whenever there was good news to trumpet, even though he was humble with his own personal accomplishments. For Bemidji State, however, he heralded highlights both personally and in print. A one-man ad agency. A missionary determined to tell the world about the school he loved. And as he neared the end of his third year as president in the spring of 1993,

---

10) Ritchie was singled out as the man most responsible for getting the 1913 decision to locate the state's newest normal school in Bemidji. For a more complete discussion of his activities in this matter, see College in the Pines and the chapter "The Normal School Fight: 1907-1913." For a description of the impromptu, wild celebration in Bemidji the day the decision was announced—and Ritchie's reactions—see pp. 33-34. For the school's formal recognition of outstanding alumni, see Appendix P. The 1994 recipient was Lloyd G. Pendergast, the legislator most responsible for getting state money to build the first building.

there was much to crow about. His well-written newsletters (BSU News) called regular attention to school successes, like the striking item below:

"Each year, U.S. News & World Report identifies colleges and universities that meet a specific level of excellence. Highlights of their research appear in the magazine while the rankings of all schools are published in the book America's Best Colleges. In the listing of the midwestern colleges and universities, Bemidji State is the highest-ranked Minnesota State University. . . . Although any university needs to be careful in using the information contained in the publication, it is noteworthy because it shows that people beyond the campus look favorably on BSU."[11]

In the same publication, Duly called attention to the public attention given the school, emphasizing an article in the Minneapolis Star-Tribune which had mentioned the important research in vitamins by BSU chemist Dr. Gary Evans. Duly went on to list more accomplishments of the 1992-93 school year and with obvious great pride, he wrote, "Periodically, we should pause and consider those bright moments that bring pride to the University community. By no means all-inclusive, the following is just a sampling of some good things that have happened:
• The first choir ever selected from a Minnesota public college or university to sing at the American Choral Directors Association National Convention [in Texas] was the Bemidji choir.
• Funding was received from NASA to continue a five-year study on the effect of radiation on eye tissue.
• A faculty member [CarolAnn Russell] was elected to membership in the American Center of PEN, the only world-wide organization of literary writers.[12]
• BSU received a $315,000 grant from the McKnight Foundation to fund summer programs for gifted Native American students."

LITERALLY "HANDS ON" SUPPORT FOR CULTURAL DIVERSITY

President Duly's enthusiasm for promoting global awareness and cultural diversity never waned. The entire month of April, 1993, was designated Cultural Diversity Month, with the theme "Undo Discrimination and Prejudice." This ongoing awareness culminated with something called Hands Across Campus in which students and faculty came together on the lakefront by the union on the morning of April 22. At the noon hour all in attendance literally joined hands in one big circle. Prior to the joined circle there were cultural performances of dances and songs presented by students representing various nations, races and cultures. Over a dozen booths representing different cultures had been set up on the lawn and spectators could go from one to the other and look over the artifacts ranging from clothes to paintings to brochures. Duly, of course, was in the middle of all of this.

11) BSU News, Bemidji State University, Vol. 11, No. 12; April 2, 1993, p.1.
12) In other articles and speeches, Duly often sang the praises of English Professor Will Weaver, a nationally published author, who had major success with a novel, Red Earth, White Earth. CBS later did a two-hour television show based on this book about Indian/white relationships. Weaver's next book, A Gravestone Made of Wheat & Other Stories, won the Minnesota Book Award for fiction in 1989. A Bush Foundation Fellow, Weaver published his most recent book in November of 1993. This work, Striking Out, is a baseball novel for young adults (Harper/Collins). Weaver's literary agent is the Lazear Agency in Minneapolis.

Behind the show time and the free lunch provided that day there had to be financing, and this too Duly had worked on, seeking grants for support. The Ford Foundation would award Bemidji State a two-year $236,000 grant to pursue the project named "New Directions in Developing and Implementing a Multicultural Curriculum: Models of Change and Transformation." Duly was on a roll, and then suddenly it ended for him.

PERSONAL AND INSTITUTIONAL TRAGEDY STRIKES AGAIN

On May 8, 1993, just two weeks before commencement, President Leslie C. Duly, age 57, died suddenly from a massive heart attack at his Bemidji home. The Northern Student's headline of May 12 summed up accurately the school's response: "President Duly's Death Stuns BSU." The attack had come suddenly on a Saturday afternoon, apparently without warning. That morning Duly and his wife had gone shopping, then stopped for noon lunch before returning to their house in Lavinia, on the east side of Lake Bemidji. Soon after arriving home, the couple were in the middle of plans for some needed window curtain installation when Dr. Duly had his attack.

The University held a "Service of Remembrance" for Dr. Duly the next Thursday, May 13, in the Physical Education Complex gymnasium. The Duly family requested that the remembrance be a celebration of his life rather than a morbid memorial service; they also specified that the service be non-religious in nature. As a result, the one-hour-and-ten-minute service was entirely upbeat; indeed, an element of levity was part of the comments of many of the 11 persons who spoke. The speakers represented a spectrum of Minnesota and the State University System, and they included the SUS chancellor, the head of the state senate, several faculty members, the alumni and student senate presidents, and a town representative. Speaking for the Duly family was daughter Abigail Duly, whose manner and comments represented just what the family wanted for the occasion. Her words were upbeat and positive, and at times she was humorous as she illustrated her father's character with amusing anecdotes. Among several quotable lines near the end of her talk were, "He knew everyone's name.... At BSU were the best years of his life. . . . He loved this place."

One speaker presented a unique oratorical style. Dr. Annie Henry, professor of professional education, the only African-American on the faculty, spoke with strong feelings of her warm association with President Duly. Her style was reminiscent of the famous "I Have a Dream" speech of Dr. Martin Luther King when he began each segment with the line, "I have a dream." Dr. Henry's line repeated over and over again was, "I knew a man," followed by her recollections of what President Duly had done for her personally as well as his steady efforts for commitment to all persons of color. Her conclusion: "You have fought the good fight. . . . You deserve a rest." In the large audience attending, it seemed appropriate that in one section of the bleachers sat almost all the international students enrolled at BSU; they knew they had had a friend in President Duly.

Equally appropriate in the ceremony was a Native American Honor Song played and sung by the Bemidjigamaag Drum Group. Other music selected for the occasion by the family was a string quartet playing Pachelbel and a soloist who sang "On the Road to Mandalay." A reception followed the service in the Beaux Arts Ballroom in the union.[13]

As indicated, Duly's death came at the end of the school year, which is also the time when there are so many all-school "teas" held in behalf of persons retiring from the faculty and staff. In the past it was a given fact that President Duly would not only be in attendance at every one of these retirement gatherings but would be literally serving coffee and cake and visiting with everyone. Thus, even after Duly's passing, people by habit still felt almost compelled to look around and expect to find the president. For some, this feeling was unnerving; for others it was a form of quiet testimonial and recognition to this man who remains an integral part of the institution.

The obituary in the Bemidji Pioneer made reference to his body being cremated but there was no indication as to the final disposition. Only months later did it become semi-public knowledge that early in the morning on graduation day, May 28, 1993, three members of the faculty selected by the Duly family distributed his ashes across the campus grounds.

HOLDING-ACTION TIME, AGAIN

The death of President Duly resulted once more in Bemidji State's administration going into a partial holding action until a replacement could be selected. By necessity, some of the school's remaining top leaders soon had a series of new titles with the word "acting" in front of them. The appropriate temporary presidential replacement was Dr. Linda Baer, BSU's senior vice president for academic and student affairs, a position she had held since 1990. The SUS Board acted almost immediately after Duly's death to name Dr. Baer as acting president, and two weeks later (May 25, 1993) interim president for one year only, until June 30, 1994, or until a president was named following a national presidential search.[14]

13) Service of remembrance program available in A.C. Clark Library archives. The basic themes emphasized by all the speakers were Duly's dedication to the school, his infectious smile and his gentle humor, and his efforts to raise consciousness over issues of cultural diversity on campus and beyond the campus. The Pioneer editorial on Duly on May 12, 1993, was headlined accurately, "Duly Tireless Worker for Community, BSU." Duly was survived by his wife, Diane; three daughters, Susannah (Daniel Bogucki) Duly of Duluth, Melissa (Martin) Semerau of Hammond, Indiana, Abigail Duly of Grand Forks, N.D.; a son, William (Susan Knisely) Duly of Minneapolis; his mother, Lucille Duly of West Amherst, N.Y.; two sisters, Priscilla (Ray) Kuntz of Clarence, N.Y., Lucille (Wilfred) Schoepf of Chester, S.D. He was preceded in death by his father.
14) Once again a Presidential Search Committee was formed over the summer of 1993 to make recommendations for Duly's replacement. Initially there was an air of urgency in getting the search committee members chosen so that they could begin the process by Labor Day, but not until late October did the full 26-member committee meet for the first time. Chairing the committee was Mike Lopez, vice chancellor for student affairs of the State University System; secretary to the committee was Lorena Cook, BSU's affirmative action officer. The two SUS Board members were Corey Elmer of Moorhead and William Ulland of Duluth; Dr. Robert Bess, interim president at St. Cloud State, represented the System presidents. Ms. Nellie Stone Johnson represented the Minnesota Higher Education Board. There were six BSU faculty members: Richard Gendreau, Ray Nelson, Gerald Schnabel, Louise Mengelkoch, Thomas Boates, and Donald Bradel. Dale Ladig and Allen Nohner were there for MSUAASF; Jaclyn Ryder represented AFSCME and Council 6 while Evonne McKinzie had several constituencies: MAPE, Middle Management, Nurses, and Confidential Unit Employees. There were one graduate student, Melissa Baker, and two undergrads, Marina Nadarajah and Torrey Westrom. Gerald Norris represented the BSU administration; Jim Ghostley, BSU Foundation; Caroline Adrican and Will Antell, Alumni Association; Judy Roy, Native American/minority community; finally, there were two representatives of the area business community, Emily Lahti and Tim O'Keefe. As of January 1, 1994, there were over 100 candidates or nominees for the position of president of Bemidji State University.

Baer agreed to the Board policy of her not being permitted to be a candidate for the permanent presidency. "In accepting this appointment, I intend to further build on the vision and planning developed by Dr. Duly and the administration," she said at the time. After openly seeking the advice of the faculty, Baer named Dr. Jon Quistgaard, dean of Graduate Studies and director of Undergraduate Admissions, as acting vice president for academic affairs. The latter's new position of course required yet another appointment; Dr. Gerald Norris, dean of the College of Professional Studies, became acting dean of Graduate Studies. All the rest of the administrative staff remained in their same positions.

Dr. Baer, 43, took hold immediately and acted with a combination of good common sense and assuredness to finish one academic year and start another, the school year that would mark BSU's 75th anniversary. She caught on fast. In her thoughtful, deliberate and low-key style, she impressed all with her decision-making skills, so much so that the operation of the school slipped nary a cog. It was a good year. (Indeed, as the 1993-94 year went forward under her guidance, not a few on the faculty and staff wished that she were a candidate for the job she was performing so well.)

Linda L. Baer
(interim president 1993-1994)
"Small wonder there was little trepidation . . . she took hold immediately."

LINDA LOUISE BAER

Interim President Baer was born September, 7, 1949, in Spokane, Washington, the daughter of Lyle Larson and Mary Buckland Larson. (At this writing, 1994, her father is still living; her mother is deceased. Linda Baer also has three sisters.) She was raised and educated in Washington, attending grades K through 12 at West Valley School District, Millwood, Washington, a suburb of Spokane. She began her post-secondary studies at Washington State University, following her bachelor's degree in sociology with a master's degree in the same discipline from Colorado State and a doctorate in sociology from South Dakota State University. In 1969 she married Norman W. Baer; they have one son, Scott Benjamin, and one daughter, Elizabeth Jean.

Before coming to Bemidji in 1990, Dr. Baer held several positions at South Dakota State University, including director of the Center for Innovation Technology and Entrepreneurship, administrative associate in charge of data collection and strategic planning, and associate professor in the rural sociology department. She was also project director for an initiative to develop partnerships between the university and South Dakota tribal colleges. She published extensively in the areas of rural sociology and educational quality and received numerous honors, including the Great Plains Sociological Distinguished Service Award, and being listed in Outstanding Young Women of America.

BAER LEADS OFF ANNIVERSARY CELEBRATION

The official start of the 75th anniversary school year began with opening remarks by Interim President Baer at a college-community luncheon held in the student union on July 15, 1993, exactly 80 years after the date that Bemidji was selected as the site for the state's newest school. She also announced the theme of the 75th anniversary year, "Making A Difference", and she spoke directly to this theme, stating clearly and boldly what Bemidji State had stood for in the past and what it would stand for in the future. In her conclusion, she stated: "WE ARE COMMITTED . . .
• to preparing students who will make a difference;
• to faculty and staff who make a difference;
• to diversity which encourages a variety of people; the multicultural, traditional, nontraditional student and faculty and staff who make a difference in whom we serve and how we serve them;
• to developing and maintaining a committed alumni who make a difference;
• to the citizens of Bemidji, who through their involvement and support make a difference;
• to a future which includes expanding regional coverage and boundaries that will make a difference, and;
• to a successful Foundation, that through the gifts and scholarships make a difference."[15]

Her thoughtful words were not empty rhetoric. Not only did she mean it, she could prove it. The combined efforts of the alumni and community people, for example, affirmed work already done. The Park House across the street was a tangible reminder of the commitment to help the University. A network of 200 alumni was in place to contact legislators statewide; they had already been called on for action in the early months of 1993 and would be prepared for duties each succeeding year. Fund raising activities had set new records so that in 1993 nearly 4,000 alumni, contacted via the phonathon (sometimes called "friend-a-thon" or

15) Dr. Baer's manuscript for her July 15, 1993, talk was requested by this author and the papers are now in his files. Her title, "Making a Difference", was subtitled "Quality Education, Research and Service." Her remarks began the program that day, and after she finished her formal talk, she continued as mistress of ceremonies for the full program that followed in which the late A.P. Ritchie was honored as the first nominee for the new FOUNDERS WALK. (See earlier section.) As a personal note, but one that led to the revelation of an extraordinary commentary on BSU, I was visiting with former President Gillett before the festivities began. We talked about how the school had changed for the better and almost offhandedly he quoted a recent member of the SUS Board who had told him simply, "Bemidji State is the flagship of the System."

"friend-raising") had pledged more than $117,000 to the school. The B-1000 Club grew to 600 members as it moved toward its goal of 1,000 members who pledged to contribute at least $100 each year. Alumni constituents continued to play an active role. For example, said Dr. Baer, the Indian Alumni Chapter provided invaluable counsel on issues relating to the building of the Indian Center. The number of contacts with alumni grew, whether at the annual Twin Cities Alumni Dinner, which featured an address by a favorite BSU prof brought in for the occasion, or chapter meetings in Hong Kong and Malaysia! Bemidji State had truly spread out to become global, as President Duly had wanted, and Dr. Baer made it clear that she intended to carry on his work. Small wonder there was little trepidation for staff, faculty and students under Interim President Baer when September of '93 came up quickly and the school began its 75th anniversary school year.

START-UP TIME: MORE MINORITIES BUT FEWER STUDENTS OVERALL

Minority enrollment at Minnesota's seven State Universities rose by more than five percent in the fall of 1993, while overall enrollment fell by nearly as much, according to the figures released by the State University Board. The Board indicated that 2,320 minority students were enrolled at the seven state schools, up 5.3 percent from the same time the previous fall. Overall enrollment fell 4.7 percent in the System, from 60,499 to 57,617. The decline was expected because of fewer high school graduates statewide, poor economic conditions aggravated by the summer's floods, and tighter admission standards. Moreover, the SUS Board also had asked most schools to reduce or contain their enrollments to ensure workable class sizes and quality instruction.[16]

Of major importance in the changing numbers at BSU in '93 was the increase in the number of transfer students (519, up 41 percent) while the size of the freshman class went down (553, down 6.5 percent). Essentially, maintaining Bemidji State's enrollment in the 1990s meant that the number of transfer students was becoming equally important as the size of the incoming freshman classes. The times and the school had indeed changed.

The make-up of the teaching faculty had also changed. In the general category of Employment of Underrepresented Groups, terminology used by the BSU Personnel Office, there were 73 females, or 31 percent, employed out of a faculty of 239 persons, as of September 9, 1993. (By contrast, 30 years earlier there were 27 women out of 115, or 23 percent.) Under the designation of Minority, 22 (or nine percent of the total faculty) included seven American Indians, one black,

---

16) The State University Board released the numbers to the media and an AP story to that effect ran in the Bemidji Pioneer on October 15, 1993, p. 3. The same news story listed BSU's enrollment at 5,009, a considerable difference from the BSU Registrar's Office memo of September 22, 1993, giving the on-campus head count at 4,693. Again, it's both how one counts and who one counts. Overall, BSU's enrollment was down 4.8 percent from the fall of 1992. The biggest drop was felt at Moorhead State; their '92 enrollment of 8,455 dropped 10.7 percent in '93. As usual, in the fall of '93 St. Cloud had the largest enrollment with over 14,000 while Southwest State at Marshall had the smallest at just over 2,500. For a complete listing of BSU's enrollments from 1919 to 1994, see Appendix D.

nine Orientals, three Asian/Pacific Islanders, two Hispanics.[17]

JUST PASSING THROUGH . . . AND GIVING CREDIT WHERE IT IS DUE

Bemidji State is a small city of "temporaries," populated by people just passing through. And all of them need and want help. A changing community such as Bemidji State consists of many parts, some large and others small. Separately, each operates to serve students in the best possible manner, and collectively they contribute to the overall strength and direction of the University. It's always been a team effort for 75 years.

Only the naive believe that all teaching and learning are done in the classroom. By 1994 one of the largest components within the school, the Department of Residential Life, worked hard to integrate student services with academic life. This is no small undertaking. With 1,500 students living on campus, the residence halls provide students an environment which supports and complements the classroom experience. The staff is concerned with each student's adjustment to the school and with ensuring the maximum growth possible throughout their time in the residence halls, their home away from home. To facilitate this process, "the dorms" employ both professional and paraprofessional live-in staff. The professional staff members have backgrounds in counseling and student development theory. These individuals supervise paraprofessional staff whose training covers such diverse topics as peer counseling, confrontation and mediation, crisis management, domestic violence, cultural diversity, and gender issues. The residence halls have become much more than just a place to sleep and eat. Just living there is a special "classroom experience" of its own.

Over the years, dormitory residents have become more and more involved in community projects. These have included working at the soup kitchens in the town churches, collecting food for food shelves, becoming Big Brothers and Big Sisters, working with the mentally retarded, helping in the nursing homes, providing labor for Habitat for Humanity, and making other community contributions. The overall positive effects of residence hall life have been shown in demographic data which indicated by 1992 that on the whole, "dorm" students achieved better grade point averages than students residing off-campus. Bemidji State's residence halls have been much more than board-and-room places, or "a crash-pad to camp out"; the residential life program has become a planned experience. The old Sanford Hall of 1924 was considerably different from the dorm complex and its programs of 1994.[18]

17) Information on faculty makeup from John Arneson, director of Personnel Services, in a memo from his office dated September 28, 1993. Memo in author's file. Arneson's figures included non-teaching faculty personnel, e.g., counselors, librarians; the teaching faculty numbered 219, 64 of whom were women. For both the changing size of the faculty and the number of women employed since 1945, see Appendix F. As to the limited number of faculty representing minority races, perhaps an anecdotal incident best reflects what BSU is like/is not like in 1994. In the spring of 1993, a young woman from Texas came to Bemidji to be interviewed for a position in the music department. When she looked around the room at the people there, her first remark was, "I have never seen so many blue-eyed and blond-haired people together in my entire life!"
18) For most students attending Bemidji State since the 1950s, there's been a pattern of different domicile living, usually starting out with freshmen and maybe sophomores residing in a dormitory. Then comes "advanced age" and the desire to "go on one's own," finding like-minded friends and renting rooms off campus. Freedom. Now. By the time they're mighty seniors, the goal is a rented and furnished apartment. Go out with class—and total independence. And a fat student loan. It's worth it. (By 1994, the average student debt exceeded $7,000).

If "the dorms" had changed considerably by the 75th, even more changes had come to and with the student union. The '94 Hobson Memorial Union cannot be contrasted to '24 because there was no union then; but even by '54 or '64 or even '74, the union was primarily just a place to go and sit and visit between classes, maybe play cards, and have a cup of coffee. Although those things are still done, there's so much more available. In the summer of '93, the lakeside section of the union was renovated, giving it a whole new, snazzy look, with new, snitzy services, too, for the 1993-94 students. Some of the new things included a Pizza Hut,

The Modern Residence Hall Living Quarters
"The Department of Residential Life. . . employs professional live-in staff."

Gretel's Bake Shop, Deli Corner, Grille Works, Tortillas Mexican Bar, and a section just to buy Leghorn Chicken. The new things joined the old things: A Lakeside Food Court, a large smoking room (the ONLY room on campus where one can legally light up a cigarette), variety stores (one in the union, the other at Walnut Hall), pinball machines, pool and ping-pong tables, and a TV area with chairs in a semi-circle for sitting and watching. The west end of the union is also the headquarters of the union-sponsored Outdoor Recreation Center, which plans, promotes and carries out a variety of outdoor trips both instate and out of state (lots of ski and hiking trips). And of course there are free film nights and it's the union which is the primary agent on campus for booking and bringing in outside bands for dances and concerts in either the Beaux Arts Union Ballroom upstairs or in M-100 next door. The dining service of the union (ARA) also operates Walnut Dining

Hall, the main cafeteria for residence hall students during the daylight hours, but the new "Wally's" includes an After Hours pizza parlor where students can purchase pizza and sub sandwiches, buy pop and snacks, rent videos, and make photocopies. By 1993-94, the main Walnut Hall dining area was opened to the public at all times, with prices at $3.10 for breakfast, $4.35 for lunch, and $5.10 for dinner. All of the meals are "as much as you can eat." Wally's added a Mexican Bar, Egg Line, Potato Bar, Rice Bar, Hamburger Line, Pasta Bar, and soft- serve ice cream and yogurt machines. They also offered catering service to the community, from fancy top of the line banquets and buffets to refreshment deliveries. In conjunction with all of the above, the union has sponsored what is called the Free University. During the entire school year, at virtually no cost, students and staff can attend a multitude of short-short "classes" (no credits)—at least two each week— which range from tie-dying to wine tasting to twisted-paper-basket-making to Buddhist contemplation to resume writing to "How to Catch More Walleyes." Since World War II, "the union" has changed even more than "the dorms."

SO WHAT DO WE HAVE BY THE 75TH?

In moving both into the 21st century and towards the next special celebration, a BSU centennial, friends of Bemidji State might ponder where the school is in 1994. To begin with, the enrollment has held rather steady for 10 years at about 5,000 students, that number including both on-and off-campus students. Almost 70 percent are from northern Minnesota and more than 50 percent are female; 35 percent of the student body is over the age of 25. An overwhelming number—75 percent—of Bemidji State's 33,000 graduates live in Minnesota, with 7,000 of them living in the Twin Cities area. In the most recent years, the transfer students from the region's community and technical colleges have almost equaled the number of entering freshmen. More and more, BSU has become a senior-level University for northern Minnesotans who have no easy alternative, public or private, for completing their baccalaureate degrees.

Bemidji State has taken seriously its commitment to ensure that its academic programs and services reflect national standards. For example, although it causes nearly all faculty in the professional education area a lot of work, and for a special few a tremendous lot of work (and pain and frustration), the school has jumped through every suggested hoop in order to maintain its accreditation with NCATE, the National Collegiate Association for Teaching Education. The nursing program, offered in cooperation with 12 area community and technical colleges, has required careful and ongoing coordination—and schmoozing—with its sister schools while also meeting the high standards of accreditation by the National League for Nursing. And the highly specialized industrial technology model-building program has been the only one in the country and cannot turn out enough graduates for corporations in Minnesota and elsewhere. All of the above reflect the requirements of being quality-driven, performance-based, and result-oriented.

Slipshodiness is not tolerated.[19]

The geographic location of Bemidji has meant both opportunity and responsibility to serve the Native American population that surrounds the community. Thus BSU has 200-plus American Indian students enrolled each year, and has produced more American Indian graduates than any school in Minnesota. That area of leadership has been supported by such sources as the Ford Foundation in cultural diversity; the Northwest Area Foundation in general education; the U.S. Department of Education, and a host of public and private supporters for BSU's work in human, environmental, and global studies. Over the past 10 years, almost a million dollars a year has come to the school in support of multiculturalism in general and Native Americans in particular. In October of 1993, the school held ground-breaking ceremonies for the construction of a new Native American Center, with completion expected by the end of '94. That plan changed dramatically. At the time of the ground breaking, the plans called for a small, modest structure, but then the 1994 legislature, just before a literally wee hour, 3 a.m. adjournment on May 6, included in its bonding bill $1.1 million for an American Indian History and Policy Center on the BSU campus. So it is happily back to the drawing boards for a large, immodest structure to correspond to the fat new numbers assigned to its construction. In this case the delay to its completion is a welcomed one.

The institution as a whole has learned to live with decreasing budgets in the 1990s, as have all the individual departments which have been most affected by the cuts. No department has been immune from cutbacks, and if "it's the little things in life that count," then there's extra concerns for those dozens of instructors who've gritted their teeth when being informed that they cannot get duplication work done in the amounts needed, let alone get computers for their offices. Although the budget figures themselves are massive ($26,710,000 for 1993-94), compared to the penury days when Manfred Deputy was president, some still resent what they see as penny-pinching, like the elimination of five sports for men and women (swimming, cross country running, cross country skiing, men's tennis, women's golf), like the canceling of the job of a counselor in drug and alcohol-education, like the elimination of the whole department of office management and business education. Cutbacks also have meant scrapping plans to add needed faculty in places like criminal justice—with 175 majors—where there were only three faculty when five were needed. Other departments made similar cases for needed help—which never came. "The budget says No," has been the irrefutable answer to the question of "Why?" Yet trying to understand the multifarious ledgers of the annual budget has been an arcane art form, a veritable enigma wrapped in a puzzle, with one SUS president complaining publicly that the SUS budgets have been purposely obscured so that no one really understands them except for the vice

19) In what will go down as "memorable moments" for everyone who was there, Tom Swanson, professor of music and director of bands, spoke to the entire faculty of the College of Arts and Letters at a start-up session on September 7, 1993. His topic dealt with the general need, yea passion, for excellence demanded at Bemidji State. In his powerful presentation, Swanson wore his heart on his sleeve as he drove home the driving need for required quality, with statements like, "In no way is this a second-rate school," and, "We are not one notch lower than the University of Minnesota." Fully remembered as much as his words were his infectious enthusiasm and style. It was wonderful; he was wonderful.

chancellor of finance, and he isn't talking.

Each time period in BSU's history has had its own jargon which may or may not have long-lasting effects. By 1994 this vocabulary has meant buzz words like "political correctness," "gender free," and "T Q M"—Total Quality Management–"legislative audit" (or "paralysis by analysis") "outcome-based education," "restructure," and "redefine." In this new vocabulary of word shifts, former nouns have become verbs, e.g., access and input. People don't "communicate" anymore, they "interface" and "network." Equally part of any changing times in public education are panaceas, or what are perceived as such by many, if only briefly, as the welcomed cure-all. For Minnesota's public schools in the early '90s, it has been "outcome-based education," whatever that exactly means. (Former BSU History Prof Gene Mammenga, state commissioner of education, was "let go" in the summer of '93 by Governor Arne Carlson because of some alleged failure to act on outcome-based education, though neither of them was sure what OBE precisely meant, let alone how/when/where it was to be implemented in Minnesota.) In the SUS, the hottest buzz word (a panacea?) since 1990 has been something with the eye-and-ear-catching title of "Q-7," with the meaning "Quality - Indicators" in seven areas to be mastered by all students: Higher Order Thinking, Scientific and Quantitative Literacy, Global Awareness, Multicultural Understanding, Readiness for Work and Career, Responsible Citizenship, and Community Development. Presumably, with Q-7 in the required curriculum, each graduate from henceforth shall go forth only after all seven indicators have been met satisfactorily. The problems for Q-7 implementation have been multiple, ranging from definitions to departmental applications to exit exams. By '94, Q-7 had become semi-stalled because of the familiar obstacles: proposal approvals, evaluations, strategies, and many more, including financing.[20]

The information-future is now. What BSU certainly had by the 75th was a vast network of computer networking that has never stopped growing or changing. (Stacked to the ceiling in a storeroom in Hagg-Sauer Hall at this writing are boxes and more boxes of old computers; they're out-of-date; they're obsolete; they're three years old.) In the spring of '93 the University decided to install a campus computer network with the goal of providing fiber-optic network access for every office and classroom. When completed by 1995, the network will provide access to the VAX academic computer (access to Internet and academic E-mail), the PALS library system, the Data General administrative computer system (access to administrative E-mail and course registration information), the file servers in the SuperLab, and other computing resources that are not only national but international. The component will bring building networks on line to access the full complement of services. Exponential technology growth. Among illustrative services will be students doing all their class registration by telephone. The Brave New World is

---

20) Q-7 may turn out to be exactly what BSU has needed; Q-7 could indeed lead to a vast improvement in the education of its students. Then again none of the above could happen, and Q-7 could go down in history as yet another educational fad that had its moment and then faded away. Stay tuned.

here. Luddites not welcomed.

While it's the gee-whiz electronics that amaze the many, area residents have still appreciated the old-time basics that BSU supplies to the community. For instance, the science department has been doing a public service in water testing since 1969 by analyzing well water, at the request of well owners, for safe drinking.[21] Though easy to dismiss as minor, this kind of public service has helped promote the image of the school as being something more than steeped in ivory-covered irrelevance. Others in the community look forward to coming on campus

The Annual 'Science Fair' in Memorial Hall
"Different academic departments continue to serve the public in different ways."

at least every other week just to see the latest art exhibits (and to attend the receptions and gallery talks that are sometimes part of them) arranged throughout the entire school year by a Talley Gallery director. Since 1983, the director has been Sandra Kaul. And almost always the outside speakers who come on campus have a time set aside to address the general public. Once a month, as mentioned already, speakers are brought in, with the presentation given in the union ballroom at Campus Community Breakfasts. With the working public in mind, these breakfasts start at 7:30 a.m. and end by 8:30. It's good P.R., but still an applied illustration of the dictum that the University is there to serve the public.

Different academic departments continue to serve the public in different ways, such as sponsoring annual programs to bring guests to the campus. For example, the political science people, under Dr. Alexander Nadesan, have sponsored a mock United Nations forum for the past 11 years, a colorful event that has brought in hundreds of high school students over that time period. The mathematics department has held its annual spring math contest since 1974 and has had as many as 800 contestants in a single year. There are other departments performing public services—and P.R.—but the granddaddy of departmental public programming is that of the English department, which has sponsored an annual English Week for over 50 years! Service remains the name of the game.

EARLY RETIREMENT OPTIONS IN THE '90s

The fiscal uncertainties in the state and nation, along with shaky college enrollment projections based on the declining number of Minnesota high school graduates, led the legislature to try to find ways to cut back spending and ultimately to save money in ways that were least harmful to both the personnel at state institutions and agencies and the agencies and institutions themselves. Different incentive proposals for early retirement were floated about before a rather generous bill passed the legislature in 1993. To qualify, an employee had to be age 55 or over with 25 or more years of service, or age 65 with one or more years of service. Eligible employees who contributed to the general employee retirement plans (for BSU faculty, this meant the Teachers' Retirement Association) could choose one, but not both, of two options: 1) paid hospital, medical and dental insurance from retirement until age 65, or until eligible for coverage through a spouse or some other employment; or 2) a retirement incentive of an additional one quarter of one percent for each year of service, up to a maximum of 30 years.

Retirement benefit calculations were to be computed using a person's high-five average salary. Even prior to this '93 bill, the faculty union (IFO) had worked out an early retirement program so that at age 55 one could retire and receive a full salary and paid health benefits for the next year. If the retiree was somewhere between 55 and 64, his or her next year's salary-figure-settlement declined on a sliding scale. Both the old and the new early retirement options—the latter extended to January 30, 1994—made many BSU personnel get out their calculators to determine the fiscal feasibility of early, voluntary retirement. The bottom line numbers apparently convinced over a dozen teaching and non-teaching personnel that the 75th anniversary year was a good time to separate officially from the University in the Pines. Among them are faculty Evan Hazard, Robert Melchior, Charles Holt, James Elwell, Irv Strom, Gerald Smith, and William Kelly. Staff members who will retire are June Bender, Esther Dexter, Darrell Little, Dave

Waldon, Arleigh Chandler, Nickie Petrowske, and Evelyn Gladhill.

On the "elder" end of the age scale, by 1994 a federal ruling had gone into effect which declared forced retirement laws for college teachers at any age to be a form of age discrimination and thus illegal. Thus in effect a professor at BSU can teach "forever," a prospect conjuring up images of 95-year-old, drooling, senile pedants tottering off to classrooms to deliver shaky lectures in wispy voices to audiences less than thrilled by the ancient orators. Once again came the cliche' that colleges are not now what they once were. (In reality, however, the oldest BSU classroom teacher in the 1993-94 school year was age 68, and that person retired at the end of the school year.)

THE STUDENTS AFTER 75 YEARS

All of the aforementioned items—budgets, acting presidents, phonathons, E-mail, retiring faculty, residence halls, NCATE, fiber optics, Q-7—become totally irrelevant without adding to them the ingredient on which all are based and all are dependent, the students. In ringing the changes of administrations and staffs and buildings and programs, it is too easy to overlook the justification for Bemidji State's existence, the students. Without students there would be no *raison d'etre* for those 87 acres of state-owned campus, all those buildings, all those employees, all that spending. . . .

And to the reasonable question, "What are students in '94 like?" comes the reasonable answer, "Compared to what?" All the years since World War II have been alike in that Americans wanted to get things back to normal, but this dreamed-of normality was difficult to determine because normal has always been a weasel-word defined differently at different times and, of course, by different people. In commenting about what BSU students are like by the 75th anniversary, there is the obvious need to generalize—and justify generalization by adding that generalizations are generally true.[22] To proceed. What is easiest to describe about the '94 students is their appearance in classes. The dress code at Bemidji State is to have no dress code. The trend driving fashion trade is a fickle one in which the outfit that was so recently to-die-for is soon not-to-be-caught-dead-in. If one were to use a single word to describe attire, the term "casual" seems appropriate, and for many students the adjective "carefully" should precede the description. Also the word "eclectic" applies to student dress, and although there's a little bit of everything, it's primarily "jeans/slacks and . . . something else," the latter something in the form of some kind of top which might be a sweater, T-shirt, sweatshirt, flannel shirt, or sport shirt. What stands out as different is a woman wearing a dress or skirt to class or a man

22) There happen to be some solid statistics on what the 91-92 students were like; they came out in a memo from the Financial Aid Office, "A.C.T. Profile of Financial Aids Applicants' Report" (code 2084). Based on 4,419 BSU applicants, the office memo reported, "The typical dependent applicant came from a family with an average parental income of $35,819 and total average assets of $42,248. The average family contained 4.1 members; the average age of the older parent was 48 years, and 63 percent of the families had two incomes. Approximately 18 percent indicated they came from one-parent homes. The typical family had $2,948 in cash, savings and checking, and 90 percent owned their homes, with the average home equity at $25,454. Also 28 percent of the families owned a farm or business with an average net worth of $39,343. The average parental contribution for applicants was $2,931. The typical dependent applicant had savings and net assets of $435, and average total income of $3,318." The three-page memo in author's files.

wearing a shirt and tie, not that this doesn't happen; it's just . . . er . . . different.

Perhaps in the category of "fad" are the large numbers of '94 students who wear baseball caps every day, regardless of season. Presumably these caps are "cool," and added sophistication apparently is gained by the wearer when the cap is worn backwards. For some, this headgear is so omnipresent as to seem a part of their bodies; they've got them on morning, afternoon and night, with some doubts about their even being removed at bedtime. Like some large-billed tumor growth, the caps—with logo designs calling attention to the likes of the "Twins" and "John Deere" and "Beltrami Co-op"—parade forth daily in the halls of academe, with no sound and no fury and signifying . . . nothing.[23]

As to basic attitudes and manners and general deportment of Bemidji State students in the classrooms, the fitting one-word description would be "civility," the appellation being most positive as well as accurate, at least in this author's opinion. The relationship between students and teachers is almost always one of mutual consideration and respect. Refreshing egalitarianism. Students are considerate of their teachers, at least within their hearing, displaying manners and mannerisms that are in no way obsequious on one end nor smart-alecky on the other. Almost always profs are addressed by title; rare is there any first name chumminess solicited by teachers, something that most students seem to prefer—and respect. Overall, the relationship between students and faculty has made Bemidji State a wonderful place to teach—and to learn. And over 75 years faculty have held a mantra-mission known but seldom stated, let alone put in print: "Take them (the students) from what they are when they come to what they can and should be when they leave."

Bemidji State students have always been "scramblers" in the best sense; and yet, as college students, they have reflected the times surrounding them. In the early '90s, the economic times have not been that great so there is little surprise that the Bemidji students have been more job-oriented and less socially concerned than those in some previous decades.[24] There's a common campus culture marked by no-nonsense emphasis on materialism, promoting self-success measured by good jobs and dollars. But not that many dollars, not that foolish notion of super-big-bucks dreams. That's for unattainable C.E.O. positions and winners of lotteries. Unrealistic. For many students, success means simply future survival, and a

---

23) For men to wear hats/caps in the BSU classrooms has become apparently acceptable to most professors. To my knowledge, there are only two of us left who require students to remove their caps before the class period begins. Almost all students affected willingly acquiesce to this quaint, Victorian notion of decorum when requested, but a few shed those caps with obvious reluctance and a clear body language denoting dismay (read Ticked Off); nevertheless the caps are removed. As to changing styles, one observes with more wonderment than shock the variations in men's hairstyles that even 25 years ago would have seemed impossible. Some '94 styles, of course, draw more attention than others (a drooping earring on the man does contribute to the cause), notably the "layered look," which style old-timers hadn't seen on boys since the Depression times when poor kids getting haircuts had soup bowls placed on heads, with all the hair hanging below it lopped off. Same comparison with jeans—then called overalls in the Depression—being more in style in '94 if they are ripped and torn and have unpatched holes in them. "Oh fashion, what shins are uncovered in thy name." Then again, it's "cool."

24) In a conversation with this writer on October 20, 1993, a Beltrami County social worker, Lloyd Johnson, hearkened back to the late 1960s and early '70s when he said BSU students "came by the carloads" to do volunteer work in and around the community. "It was great! They were great! Nowadays we hardly get a one." As to shifting attitudes towards the U.S. military, a Marine recruiting officer told this writer (conversation in the union on October 26, 1993) that the "Minnesota campuses vary widely. At Concordia in Moorhead they go out of their way to avoid us; across the river in Moorhead State they welcome us. At Bemidji State, well, they're sort of in between. Mostly they just leave us alone."

college degree makes that simple goal more available. Verily, life's a struggle; school's a struggle, but it's worth it because there is a better life out there with a degree. When the pragmatic mind gets wrapped up in the personal survival code, some other things by default—not a calculated decision—take a back seat. Planned careers produce value conflicts. Thus despite the University's ongoing push and

Touring the Labyrinthine Sidewalks
"Gradually . . . every building made handicapped-accessible."

promotion of multiculturalism on and off campus, it has been a constant problem to combat dulling sensitivities to the plight of the less fortunate in general and racial minorities in particular. Apathy towards society's ills has been tough competition for an age group on campus more inclined to look out only for good ol' #1, themselves.

First things first. As to BSU students any time or year, always, regardless of decade, young people possess the same characteristics of exuberance, game playing, and peer group identification. What does differ from era to era is the specific actions in game playing and the shifting mini-codes that distinguish the in-group from the rest. There's a school that exists on the surface for all to see; there's also a "school" that exists below the surface that only those in it know about. Between the two schools have emerged thousands of successful scramblers who have graduated. For most Bemidji State students, life is too serious to be taken too seriously. So they have fun, and they can laugh at themselves as well as at others. They certainly have made their professors laugh, too. It was refreshing for the philosophy professor to write on the board in big letters, THE UNEXAMINED LIFE IS NOT WORTH LIVING, and return the next day to find the student rejoinder, THE UNPREPARED LECTURE IS NOT WORTH HEARING. Discerning faculty have acknowledged how they were enriched by their students, the students' tolerance of instructional atrocities, and the mutual encouragement when profs connected with them. Learning and teaching can be such fun. And nothing has ever beaten the one-on-one faculty-student relationships so available at Bemidji State. It is not an impersonal place. Students have names—and personalities—as well as numbers; as do the faculty. Together they find insight and share time after classes and agree to talk again soon. Mutual motivation, mutual affection. Indelible imprints have been made on both sides, something often not realized until reunions years later.

The make-up of the student body has changed dramatically by 1994. Not even close is the homogeneous class of 1964: Dominantly white, age range 18-22, traditional majors (mostly professional education), and traditional ethnic/cultural influences. It's different; they (the students) are different, as illustrated by Dr. Kay Robinson, BSU professor of speech, who wrote a profile of her '93 class: "The age range was 17-70. It was not bright white; there were four international students—three from Asia, and one from Africa; English was their second language. There were at least two dyslexics in the class, two students with multiple-personality disorders, three battered wives, two recovering alcoholics, and one student with substantial hearing loss. These were the ones I knew about—there may have been others."[25]   Dr. Robinson continued, "To say that I can no longer approach this course in the same way as I have in the past is a substantial understatement," and she went on to declare the obvious if difficult need for flexible responses to student needs "that were not even known to my professor." In her description and analysis of the students as she anticipates they will be, she lays out the challenge for all instructors for this new Bemidji State—that in many ways is already here.

TOWARDS THE CENTENNIAL: A NEW MERGER AND A NEW PRESIDENT

One era ends, another soon begins. A new president takes over also. What will happen to Bemidji State in the next quarter-century is unknown—and a subject

---

25) Kay Robinson's written remarks appeared in a four-page pamphlet published by the Bemidji State Center for Professional Development (Metamorphosis, vol. 8, no. 1, November, 1993, p. 4) under the headline, "The Changing Profile of the Classroom Community."

historians generally attempt to avoid. It is always difficult to determine the significance of what happened in the past, let alone to try to speculate on what the future will hold. For Bemidji State the crystal ball for the approaching years becomes even cloudier because of a monumental decision made by the 1991 legislature to unite under ONE higher education board ALL of Minnesota's seven State Universities, 18 community colleges, and 33 technical colleges, the merger to go into effect July 1, 1995. That date marks a new era, a new beginning for Bemidji State University. It will be "a new ballgame." Small wonder that there was initial opposition to the merger, and later, at this writing, 1994, there are still many uncertainties about what will happen and what and when the merger's effects will shake out to signify. (For state appropriations to these three units before the merger, see Appendix N.)

As of April 1, 1994, the list of candidates for the BSU presidency had been reduced to five men, one of whom would be chosen president by the SUS Board on May 5, 1994. The five finalists were: Lee Vickers, president of Lewis-Clark College, Idaho; M. James Bensen, president of Dunwoody Institute, Minneapolis; Phillip J. Farren Jr., vice president for administration at Emporia State University, Kansas; Phillip L. Beukema, vice president for academic affairs at Northern Michigan University; Lee A. Halgren, provost and vice chancellor for academic affairs, University of Wisconsin--Platteville.

Despite all the ongoing speculation and prognostications, what all this merging will mean for Minnesota, higher education, the new system—and Bemidji State—will not be revealed until it happens, and even after that it will be years before any valid conclusions can be drawn as to the wisdom of the legislature's action.

While almost all people connected with Bemidji State had, by 1994, discussed—and cussed—the new merger off and on for four years, not many had put their thoughts in print. One important person who did so was Interim President Linda Baer, whose published comments on the complicated topic were thoughtful and enlightening, as well as challenging.[26] She began her essay, dated October 15, 1993, by telling about a gathering of the heads of various state higher education institutions involved in the merger who had met to discuss obvious issues, challenges, concerns, and opportunities that needed to be addressed before the actual implementation of the merger took place. She admitted frankly that none of them at that time knew, or could know, the full implications of the merger; but they speculated anyway, and they conjured up some interesting metaphors. Wrote Baer, "One proposed that the new system would be like a train, driven by an engine that pulled the cars, which were designed to serve varying functions, after they got on the track. The question of who was the caboose never came up.

---

26) Her remarks were first published in the Bemidji State University NEWS (vol. 12, no. 5, October 15, 1993, p. 1), a monthly newsletter from the president's office. Those same remarks appeared in the Bemidji Pioneer, October 27, 1993, p. 2. There had, of course, been fierce opposition to the merger since the day it was announced, but because ultimately the opposition to the merger would be ineffective, it seemed pointless to discuss at length their multitudinous concerns, despite the shrillness in the partisan debates over those concerns. It happened, period. It's over, so get on with it.

"Another group likened the system to a quilt, where regional patchworks were stitched to a single, larger piece blanketing the state. Others thought the analogy of a garden was best, especially when carrying forward the imagery of planting the seeds of inquiry, cultivating the crop of learning, and harvesting the fruits of education." Dr. Baer added the obvious about both the opposition and its outcome: "There have been many attempts to sidetrack the train, unravel the quilt, or plow up the garden since the 1991 legislature mandated the merging. . . . Only reality remains. A 12-person board is in place to guide the process and Dr. Jay Noren has been on board as chancellor for seven months to shepherd the union."[27]

Dr. Baer called special attention to the fact that "on October 11 [1993], a large and important segment of those affected by the merger made history in Duluth. Faculty from BSU, the Arrowhead Community College System, and regional technical colleges met for the first time ever to discuss the theme of collaboration among the institutions in northeast Minnesota. . . ." She made clear that they—the faculties, administrations, staffs and students—are all in this new structure together so they should make the best of it. In her conclusion, Dr. Baer essentially summarized the new Bemidji State and its charge for the future: "The structure of higher education must join other institutions to become more adaptive and responsive to the needs of students. The vision is to be the best and most integrated system, one that is relevant and responsive to the demands of the 21st century. Many challenges remain: change itself, structure and function, efficient use of facilities and staff, and control of administrative costs by eliminating duplication, to name a few. While there are still enough roadblocks to slow the process, one that we cannot allow into the process is fear—both of an old system of delivery that won't die, and of a new system unable to be born." Her message was succinct and clear, something that needed to be said, heard, and applied as D-day came closer.

Historians have their own line applying to the changing scene and the start of another era—in this case the new Bemidji State on the horizon: "For each age is a dream dying for another to be born anew." Yet, whatever is anew, whatever the exact future may be, history suggests that as long as Bemidji State continues to operate as it has operated in the past, certain givens—educational, cultural, social, aesthetic opportunities—can be routinely expected and available for the citizens of Bemidji and the wider community of northern Minnesota. Thus there can and should be optimism in the Minnesota North Country. Social historian Lewis Mumford studied American communities in general and concluded, "A community not irrigated by art and science, by religion and philosophy, by the love of learning, and the opportunity to learn, day-upon-day, is a community that exists only half alive." Considering Mumford's criteria, the greater northern Minnesota community

---

27) Noren, a native of Willmar, Minnesota, came at age 48 to the new position from the University of Wisconsin-Madison, where he was vice chancellor for health sciences. A new board to implement the merger meant that the other three governing boards would be soon eliminated. Those board members—and the three chancellors' offices with their large numbers of employees—became lame-ducks after 1991.

shall remain fully alive because of the school in their region known as the University in the Pines.

The End[28]

---

28) This marks the end of the chronological sections on Bemidji State's history. However, there are two more sections following which take a different approach. The first one is called "Persons and Programs," the title revealing the contents, and the second is labeled "The Eye (and Ear) Catchers," which discusses Bemidji State's most public programs, music and sports.

Commencement Marchers Commence Long Walk to Ceremonies
"The archway-entrance . . . regarded as the official entrance to Bemidji State."

Note: Just prior to publication of this book, the State University Board on May 5, 1994, picked the new president for Bemidji State; he is M. James Bensen, a 1959 graduate of Bemidji State. For a brief biography, see next page.

BENSEN NAMED BSU PRESIDENT

A Bemidji State graduate, class of 1959, M. (for Maltin) JAMES BENSEN, was selected as the next President of Bemidji State University in a unanimous vote by the Minnesota State University Board on May 5, 1994. He was one of four finalists interviewed by the Board that day. Bensen, age 57, will begin his presidency on July 1, 1994, as BSU's eighth permanent president.

The day after his selection, Bensen come to the Bemidji State campus to meet with media members and to attend an extended-noon-hour public reception in his honor held in the Crying Wolf room of the Hobson Memorial Student Union.

Bensen, a native of Erskine, Minnesota, graduated from Bemidji State with a degree in industrial education and physical education. He received his master's degree in 1962 from the University of Wisconsin-Stout, specializing in industrial education, administration, supervision, and curriculum. He holds a doctorate degree (Ed. D.) from Pennsylvania State University (in 1967), with specialties in curriculum, administration, and educational development.

At the time of his selection as Bemidji State's president, Bensen had been the president for six years of Dunwoody Institute, a private, non-profit, and endowed institute of science and technology in Minneapolis, a school that enrolled approximately 3000 students. Prior to Dunwoody, Bensen was the dean of the School of Industry and Technology at the University of Wisconsin-Stout, Menominee, Wisconsin. When he left Bemidji State in 1959, he began his professional career as a teacher and coach in the Erskine public schools until 1962 when became a high school teacher in Minneapolis. He left there to become an instructor at Stout and--with time off to earn a doctorate--stayed on, moving up and through the ranks to become a dean in 1980.

Dr. Bensen has over 60 publication in journals, chapters in books and periodicals. He also made on the average of 100 presentations a year at conferences, seminars, and conventions held on the local, state, national and international levels. Moreover, he has had to turn down some 500 speaking engagements each year. Among his many awards was his receiving the "Distinguished Alumni Award" from Bemidji State in 1984.

In selecting Bensen for president, State University Board President Elizabeth Pegues was quoted as saying, "The Board believes that Dr. Bensen's strong background in applied education will complement Bemidji State's efforts to serve as an institution on lifelong learning for residents in northern Minnesota. He also will bring to the presidency the knowledge and experience he has gained as a highly effective administrator."

When all five candidates for the position came on the campus in early April, 1994, to see and be seen, to hear and to be heard, certainly it was Bensen above all the rest who showed the most enthusiasm and vigor--and layed out ambitious plans and exciting ideas--at the public meetings. Words like "dynamic" and "fire-ball" and more positive phrases like "putting Bemidji State on the map" followed his lively presentations and the question-and-answer sessions. Of all the candidates, Bensen generated the most audience emotions as listeners responded to his style and manner. Understandably the responses to Bensen varied widely, with almost no neutral listeners afterwards. He stirred people up!

It is that manner and style, that same enthusiasm, his optimism, those ambitious ideas of Dr. James Bensen that collectively make Bemidji State supporters believe that once again the right person has come along at the right time for the University in the Pines. As the school moves quickly towards the year 2000, the institution pins major hopes, dreams and desires on its new president. It looks good, he looks good. All Bemidji State's loyal backers and supporters should always be historical optimists; that's someone who believes the future is still uncertain.

M. James Bensen
"Strong background will bring a highly effective administrator."

Persons and Programs

W HAT'S NEW?
Bemidji State University offers undergraduate and graduate programs in approximately 60 subject areas. Many of these areas are those familiar and expected at all colleges; however, some programs are less than standard curricula, and it is the latter which will be emphasized in this section.

Caveats and Rationale

Singling out some programs as "special" and leaving out others becomes often a judgment call, of course, and can be interpreted as implicitly suggesting less significance for the unmentioned areas and/or departments. Not so. Not true. Or at least not meant to be slighting to programs and people not mentioned. Few could argue the "unimportance" of such basic studies as, say, mathematics and the sciences, art, the humanities, and, yes, history. The fact that all of these mentioned are required for all students in their general or liberal education requirements gives testimony to their inherent value. In this section, however, they shall be passed over, alas, because of their "basicness," even though extensive histories could/ should(?) be included on all of them. Indeed, a few above-mentioned departmental histories have been written.[1] In the following sections, the selected programs have been placed in alphabetical order so as to avoid any suggestion of which is best and/ or least good.

---

1) The English department, for example, has several documents relative to its role at Bemidji State, the most important being a 12-page, unpublished manuscript by long-time department chair (1938-69), Philip R. Sauer, entitled, "Highlights in the History of the Bemidji State English Department from 1921 to 1969," written in 1992. There is also an 11-page unpublished paper by former faculty member Ruth Stenerson (1956-86) called "Memories of a Department," which she wrote in 1992. Both documents available; they're kept on file in the current English chair's office.

423

ARROWHEAD UNIVERSITY
        Where is it? What is it? To uninformed Minnesotans, the name and
location hold an element of surprise and curiosity, with most people wondering
what it's all about. Does Arrowhead University have a campus? How do you get
there? Who runs it? Is it one of those branches of the main University in
Minneapolis? Different sounding school; never heard of it. . . .

        Bemidji State essentially runs what is officially named the Arrowhead
University Center, whose central headquarters are in Hibbing, with a small staff
headed by a director appointed by Bemidji State. The center began in June of 1989
with an appropriation from the legislature to the State University System to provide
upper division and masters degree programs for place-bound people in northeastern
Minnesota, the Arrowhead region of the state. Although Bemidji State had since
the 1960s been providing educational services to this area usually called "The
Range," the services were limited and sporadic. However, with the Arrowhead
University Center founded and funded, the programs for the region became
formalized, with a full-time BSU director in Hibbing, who also plans and cooperates
with other higher education institutions in the region. Officially, the AUC is
governed by a Board of Providers made up of the heads of all the higher education
institutions in northeastern Minnesota: Bemidji State, College of St. Scholastica,
University of Minnesota-Duluth, Arrowhead Community Colleges, and Range
Technical Colleges.
        With programs and classes coordinated by the director, the AUC currently
offers baccalaureate degree programs in accounting, applied psychology, human
services, business administration, and elementary education from Bemidji State; a
management degree from St. Scholastica; and a criminology degree from U of M-
Duluth. Bemidji State offers a master's degree in education, and St. Scholastica
offers a master's degree in management. The center serves about 300 students per
quarter, and has had over 250 people earn degrees since the center began five years
ago.
        Classes are held on the campuses of Itasca Community College in Grand
Rapids, Hibbing Community College, and Mesabi Community College in Virginia.

Interactive television is being used whenever feasible, and there is extensive academic support from Bemidji State's External Studies program (see following section). The director's office is on the Hibbing Community College campus and at this writing, 1994, the director is Loren Hoyum, a BSU graduate, with Dorothy Ojala as his assistant and Kay Lahti, secretary.

This outreach activity, this semi-satellite campus, this "university in the mines," has gone a long way towards positioning Bemidji State as a leader in higher education in northern Minnesota and has done much to fulfill BSU's stated mission "to contribute to the intellectual, social, cultural, and economic development of society of northern Minnesota."[2]

THE CENTER FOR EXTENDED LEARNING
The Center for Extended Learning, as the name suggests, coordinates and promotes classes and programs primarily away from the main campus. Its origins in general go way back to 1925 when the school offered its first off-campus extension classes in the summertime. These outside offerings were expanded in the mid 1950s, with classes available during the school year as well, mainly graduate classes for in-service public school teachers.

As word of the success of these extension classes spread, more requests came for more graduate classes and even more requests for undergraduate offerings. By dint of administrators spending many hours on the road as well as on the telephone, the network of extension classes spread far and wide across northern Minnesota. Newly hired faculty by the early 1960s often had a clause in their contracts specifying that part of their teaching load during the school year would be off-campus teaching, either at night or on weekends. Geographical expansion included an off-campus center in White Bear Lake, north of St. Paul, established in the late 1970s, to offer primarily graduate courses. The delivery of whole majors to the Iron Range area started in 1974, and the popularity of these offerings led to the creation of the Arrowhead University Center in Hibbing in the late 1980s. (See previous section.)

The overall coordinator for all of the above programs has the title of director of area services, and Edward G. Gersich has served as director since 1971. Gersich, a 1965 graduate of BSU, has served his school in many capacities: assistant registrar, assistant to the academic vice president, and director of Common Market; along with his off-campus duties, he was also made director of summer sessions, an assignment which includes both planning and coordinating the two regular five-week sessions along with all workshops, short courses and special projects offered either session. A busy man.

---

2) Politics naturally played a role in its origin. Iron Range legislators had worked without success to achieve a separate State University on the Range, but when this did not occur, legislators went for the next best thing to provide the needed higher education programs for people living there. Bemidji State Presidents Ted Gillett and Les Duly both worked hard with legislators, first to get the funding and then to set up the programs. Other Bemidji State leaders who were early and strong supporters of these efforts for AUC were Ed Gersich, director of the Center for Extended Learning, and Lorraine Cecil, coordinator of the External Studies program. Collectively, theirs was no small achievement.

A busy woman. Under the direction of Ida Mae Geittmann, associate director of area services, an extensive array of non-credit classes was also developed and offered in the early 1970s. The main thrust of such courses was to make Bemidji State the hub of local educational activities. Classes included such diverse subjects as photography, cake decorating, and pet care. Assistance in community projects was also assigned to this area, with special help from Ms. Geittmann in establishing a senior citizens center in Bemidji. As an outgrowth of such interest, a very successful Elderhostel was established on campus (see separate section), with Geittmann as the first director. The outgrowth continued with a strictly Bemidji State name and BSU-sponsored overseas study program called Seniorhostel, a program mainly the work of English Professor Kenneth Henriques (see his name connected with Eurospring, too), who set up educational programs—they were more than basic tours—in countries all over the world. With the retirement of Geittmann in 1982 and the growth of the Community Education Program offered through the Bemidji school district, the non-credit classes declined and gradually disappeared. Elderhostel remains as vigorous as ever, as does Seniorhostel, although both programs have been reassigned to another office. (Ms. Geittmann, who began at Bemidji State in 1957, may be remembered more for her 15 years as director of housing. Until she came, there had been five directors in six years. A strong, tough administrator, she brought stability—and no nonsense—to the residence halls.)

EXPANDED OPPORTUNITY: A DEGREE "IN THE NIGHT"

Evening class offerings on campus also came to be promoted and coordinated by the Area Services Office, allowing the administrators to work out programs for students to earn an A.A. or a bachelor's degree in administration, industrial technology, accounting, or the humanities by attending night classes only. This fulfilled the dream of many potential students who had wanted degree work but were unable to attend school during the day because of holding down full-time jobs. These "nighttime majors" provided the necessary outlet for dozens of frustrated, daytime workers; the opportunity to achieve a degree was received wonderfully well.

The term "Area Services" was so broad that a change in name became necessary. Although the change had been discussed before, in 1981 a small incident moved the staff into action. A plaintive, telephone query came to the Area Services Office in Deputy Hall as to when "someone" would be out to fix the roads. This obvious miscommunication caused the staff to reconsider the name of their office, and by noon that day the office was re-christened the Center for Extended Learning. The center remains a vigorous component of the campus in terms of academic offerings. For the 1991-92 academic year alone, more than 200 extension courses were offered in over 20 communities. There were over 1,300 undergraduate students who produced close to 6,000 credits and nearly 700 graduate students who produced nearly 2,000 graduate credits. That's "area services."

ELDERHOSTEL

Although now discredited, one of the ancient "givens" held in higher education was that colleges were for those young Americans between the ages of 18 and 22. That quaint notion went sailing out the door after World War II, and it never came back. The G.I.s returning to their schools proved that not only could these "older students" hold their own, but they were better students overall than the younger set, that block in the 18-22 allegedly magic age group.

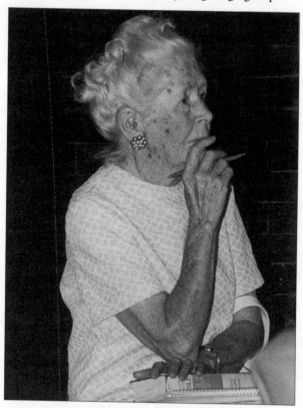

The Elderhostel Program
"The real action in life is inside the head."

The trend of SOTA—Students Older Than Average—arrivals on campus continued after the G.I.s were gone with their degrees, so much so that by 1990 the average age for Bemidji State students was 29.

Yet there were out there in America a vast number of potential college students who viewed even those persons age 29 as "kids." Collectively called senior citizens, they may have experienced a slowing of body motor skills but not of their minds. They wanted to take college classes also, but not for degrees (Many of them already had degrees, some more than one.) Nor did they want the added stress of tests and homework and grades. They just wanted to learn more!

It was for the above seniors that Bemidji State added the program called Elderhostel in 1978, and by 1990 it had grown to become the largest Elderhostel program in any college or university in Minnesota.

Age 60 is the minimum age for acceptance in Elderhostel, but it is common for some students to be in their 80s, and a few students have been 90 or more. All of the preregistration is done via the mails—with sometimes a few phone calls. The enrollment for each week is capped at 50. The students arrive on campus on Sunday and receive their dormitory room assignments. (Some folks have not been back to a dormitory room for 50 years.) The semi-Spartan quarters, including the sharing of lavatories, goes with the territory of Elderhosteling. Meals are taken at the school cafeteria, the students getting in line with all the rest of the undergraduates for their chow.

Classes begin Monday morning and continue through Friday. Usually there are three academic classes offered daily, and students may go to all or one. They're supposed to go to at least one class, but no roll is taken so absences mean nothing. What is most different from regular college classes is the absence of assignments and testing. They may be curious and want to learn, but they don't want to be required to put any of that learning down in blue books. Enough already.

Afternoons are mainly activity-oriented, such as walking, swimming, dancing, aerobics, and sometimes sightseeing around the region. Always there's a trip to Itasca State Park to see the start of the Mississippi River, and often they take a trip to an Indian reservation - and recently to the Indian-owned and run Bingo Palace in Cass Lake.

The week ends with a special banquet, with "diplomas" bestowed on all. The group then departs on Saturday, and a new group comes the next day. The once summer-only Elderhostels have more recently been augmented by both fall and spring programs, but for some reason there has been little interest in attending winter Elderhostels in Bemidji. (?)

Students come from every state in the union. It is common for some participants to work their way across the country, going state to state, one Elderhostel week at a time. They maintain, correctly, that it's a great way to see America.

As for the Bemidji State faculty chosen to work with them, let English Professor Ruth Stenerson give her summation, which views are representative of those of all the instructors:

"Teaching in an Elderhostel program from the inception of the program on for a few years was a great experience. Those people were captivating! What a joy to teach poetry, fiction, whatever, to people who had enough life experience to really understand what an author was dealing with! When I saw some of those Iowa farmers nodding their heads and taking notes in response to Edna St. Vincent

Millay's 'Renascence,' I was hooked on Elderhostel. One summer my course had to do with characters from Hebrew Scriptures. Probably because of that, about a third of the ones attending that week were Jewish. I really felt accepted when a rabbi in the group indignantly corrected my pronunciation of the name Abraham. 'That is Avraham!' he almost shouted. If he hadn't become involved, he wouldn't have cared. I have always enjoyed older students. . . ."[3]

EUROSPRING

Time was for Bemidji State students when a "trip East" meant traveling all the way to Duluth. No more. Time was when the accepted culmination of a college experience, if one were enrolled in an Ivy League school, meant an extended tour of Europe. No more just for Ivy Leaguers.

Bemidji State started a successful program in 1975 for overseas study and overseas travel and called it Eurospring. The program includes five weeks of study at Oxford, England, followed by three weeks of travel throughout Europe before returning homeward to Minnesota in time for spring graduation.

At Oxford, the Bemidji State students sleep, eat, and go to classes in one large, red brick building, Wycliffe Hall, located about 15 minutes' walk from the center of the "City of Spires." The part-old, part-new extended building, simply called "Wycliffe," is actually a theological college and seminary for the training of Anglican priests. Wycliffe students and faculty are on an extended spring break for the five weeks that the Bemidji State students are living there. These "regular students" return to their dorm rooms and classes two days after the Bemidji State students have left for the Continent. It's a way for their seminary to make some extra money in this "down time" period, but the regular year-'round staff at Wycliffe Hall find it "different" to have a building full of young, eager, sometimes bumptious, active Americans. Overall the culture shock is good for both groups.

In charge of the academic program at Oxford, and himself chief lecturer, is Dr. Allan Chapman of Wadham College, Oxford University. Since the program was initiated, Chapman, a veritable walking encyclopedia, has come each fall to the Bemidji campus to help explain the details of the program to students interested in going. While at Bemidji, Chapman also delivers an annual lecture to the general public, and over the years it has become the most highly-attended lecture of the school year.

Bemidji students enroll for Eurospring for 16 credits, the usual number taken whether on campus or not, before the group flies to England the first week of spring quarter. The class offerings have been determined by joint agreement with

---

3) Miss Stenerson was a member of the English department from 1956 to 1986. Her comments above appear in a small, 11-page paper entitled "Memories of a Department" (p. 9) written in 1991. Copy in author's possession; more available from BSU English office. On a personal note, it was Miss Stenerson who convinced me to teach in the Elderhostel programs, and with reluctance and hesitation at first, I tried it. Turned out that without a doubt, they have been the best students I've ever had in my 35 years at Bemidji State. I've also received my most wonderful put-down from an Elderhosteler, about age 85, and it came following my hour-and-a-half lecture on Bemidji and Bemidji State! She came up afterwards and said, "Young man, [I liked that line] years ago, after too much effort, I finally finished reading Moby Dick. When I could at last stop and put the book away, I said to myself, 'That's more about whaling than I ever cared to know.'" She then walked away.

Chapman and Bemidji State. When students are not in classes they are free to go wherever they choose, and many choose to spend as much time as possible in London.

AH, LONDON-TOWN

Oxford lies about an hour's journey west of London. A bus—or in England, a coach—leaves and returns to the medieval city every half hour, allowing easy and regular transportation to and from this massive and cosmopolitan metropolis. All students have taken advantage of this proximity, especially in the opportunities to attend London theaters and museums.

Every Saturday, as part of the program, the students—with an English guide—take a motor-coach day long field trip to see some place and/or something special. These sites have included Stonehenge, Salisbury Cathedral, Bath, Greenwich Naval Observatory, Bristol, Windsor Castle, and more (there seem no end of castles to visit); every year the group goes to Stratford-on-Avon for a tour of Shakespeare's home city and while there, sees a Shakespearean play at the Royal Theater.

In proper European style, the classes and term end with the one and only exam, consisting of extensive essay questions. The next morning the group travels by coach to the coast, catches a ferryboat to the Netherlands, and the following day begins a whirlwind, three-week tour of the major European capitals on the Continent. Then it's back to Frankfurt, Germany, and the flight homeward. At that point, after two months overseas, students are truly ready to go home. A tired but happy (and broke) group back from a school term never to be forgotten.

Virtually every student who has been on Eurospring has afterwards concluded, "That was the best quarter of my entire time at Bemidji State!"[4]

EXTERNAL STUDIES

The External Studies Program at Bemidji State University is part of the Center for Extended Learning. In order to appreciate and understand more fully the impact of the program on the University community, consider that since its inception in 1974, nearly 9,000 students have been aided; over 2,000 (2,267 by June, 1993) students have graduated, and almost all of the graduates would never have been able to do so without the availability of this program. Interested persons need to consider its historical development along with the procedures and policies which govern its existence. It's different; it was controversial when it started and has remained in that category ever since.

---

4) Inaugurating this program involved several faculty, with much credit going to Professor Kenneth Henriques, then of the English department (1965-88), who himself received an M.A. degree from Oxford University. Henriques had maintained personal connections with Oxford University professors and he made the arrangements for the annual planning and programming. Henriques personally directed the three week bus tour portion of the program for 10 years until his retirement. On a personal note, it was this author's good fortune for my wife Judy and myself to be part of Eurospring in both 1985 and 1990, and thus give validity, I hope, to the excellence of the program and the degree to which students have found it so wonderful. Although Eurospring is the oldest and largest of overseas study programs, Bemidji State has also initiated a growing program (since 1986) with the Peoples Republic of China, with annual tours there called "Sino-Summers." There is also a small program with the University of Vaxhos in Sweden. At this writing (1994), Jan Weiskopf-Smith is coordinator of all international studies programs.

BACKGROUND

Bemidji's External Studies Program can be traced back to June 6, 1972, when then-Chancellor G. Theodore Mitau issued a press release in Alexandria, Minnesota, which suggested the possibility of an external degree in the State University System. To the uninitiated, it seemed too good to be true: Achieve a bachelor's degree and never have to leave your home. Nothing, of course, is quite that simple. Mitau's trial balloon was followed by a series of meetings. Each campus designated a number of interested faculty to attend a workshop on the subject in St. Paul in December, 1972. Members of the Bemidji campus committee included Lorraine Cecil, Marjorie Beck, Edward Gersich, Paul Parthun, Duane Sea, Lowell Vaughn, and Richard Haugo, who served as chair. The workshop dealt with the concepts involved, procedures to be used, and the benefits of an external degree. Afterwards, the campus committee was charged with studying existing external degree programs on other campuses in other states before eventually making suitable recommendations for a Bemidji program.

Several meetings and months later, the committee planned a curriculum and procedure to fit an adult, off-campus population. This had to include both a concept and a means of delivery. Furthermore, the program provided a way of evaluating what students already knew—and a way to receive "academic credit" for that knowledge in their programs. This would be a true external degree with separate requirements and matriculation procedures, and yet it was not to be a self-designed curriculum. Students must adhere completely to the major/minor requirements specified by departments whether they are on campus or in Camp Swampy (and not a few students have been incarcerated in prisons).

A TOUGH PRODUCT TO SELL

Perhaps understandably, not all departments would participate. Not only were some faculty indifferent to the program, but a few were openly hostile. These detractors saw external studies in terms of the old "correspondence school" syndrome which bordered often on being questionable, if not a complete sham. If the local opposition was not enough, about the time the program was to be formally presented for approval, the State Higher Education Coordinating Board decided that the HECB would not approve any new programs until their members had personally conducted their own studies, something HECB seemed to be doing *ad infinitum* and *ad nauseum* in their ongoing effort to simultaneously justify their existence and build an empire.[5]

5) The acronym HECB does to most teaching faculty what the legendary bullfighter's cape does to the bull. Although grudging consideration may be given to the concept of having some agency working to coordinate the functions and duties of all the state's colleges and universities, the classroom folk tend to view the HECB as a combination of mischief-makers, program-throttlers, power-grabbers, and money-gobbling paper-shufflers biased against the state-sponsored schools. And those are the kinder pejoratives, considering the easy availability of descriptions to those with short fuses and short descriptions. If HECB has been consistent in anything, it has been in their forecasts for projected enrollments: They have not been correct in 25 years. Lest this appear to be a one-person acerbic response, historian Joseph Amato, in his history of Southwest State University (A New College on the Prairie, Crossings Press, Marshall, Minnesota, 1991), observes with horror the growth of HECB from a staff of 25 and a budget of one million dollars in 1969 to its staff of 82 and a 70 million dollar budget in 1992 (pp. 10-11). Meanwhile, the teaching faculty wonder why they can't get chalk to use in their classrooms.

Despite built-in abhorrence for almost anything new on campus, the BSU senate easily approved the External Studies program on May 7, 1973, and the school administrators assigned Dr. James Hamilton of the history department as the first coordinator. He served half-time in External Studies and the rest as a classroom teacher, with British history his specialty. The first students were admitted in November, 1973, and they numbered only 44 when Hamilton left Bemidji State in June of 1974. Lorraine Cecil of the English department replaced Hamilton as full-time coordinator and she remained in that role until her retirement in June of 1993. In effect, External Studies and Lorraine Cecil have been one and the same since its start; the marriage has been a good one. It was most certainly productive. (She promoted, she protected, she shepherded the flock. On the telephone she could talk almost anyone into almost anything, whether encouraging some timid soul from East Armpit Junction who might be half contemplating taking a class, or imploring some warden from some prison to let such-and-such convict complete his BSU degree from his jail cell.) She always got results.

The program limped along at the start, however, receiving a small grant from the State University Board Office for its first two years only. But in 1975 it was made a part of the Area Studies Office, and soon the numbers grew as the program became better known. Among the popular earlier majors available was community service, the kind of thing for those students who just "had to have a college degree in something, anything!" But that degree is no longer available; it was the same with industrial technology, which was also phased out. At this writing (1994) students may complete an A.A. and/or a B.A. or B.S. in criminal justice, social studies, and history, but all of them are non-teaching degrees. Portions of other majors such as Indian studies, political science, psychology, and social work are also available, and when extension classes are added to the formula, a quasi External Studies degree can be attained. The Arrowhead University Center at Hibbing adds yet an extra incentive for External Studies students because through Arrowhead students can, via a combination of classes, achieve several different degrees, namely in accounting, applied psychology, business administration, and elementary education. The juggling and transfer of credits became an art-form.

External Studies. Something new/old has been added to BSU's missions, an extra benefit demonstrating that there's another form of the University far from the main campus which truly serves the needs of its citizens located in the North Country or in Parts Unknown, from Bena to Guam. Observers might say this was less than an idea whose time had come than one which never went away.

FOREIGN LANGUAGES
WHAT A DIFFERENCE A . . . PRESIDENT MAKES

For the first 40 years at Bemidji State, foreign languages teaching on campus remained just that, "foreign." Languages were not promoted; teaching staffs did not exceed two faculty members, and students often avoided the few offerings that were available.

For example, in 1957, with 847 students enrolled, at then BSC, only 65 people took any foreign language. (It was worse that year in Moorhead State, where 61 students took a foreign language, while at Winona State the number was a paltry 37.)

Languages under both Presidents Deputy and Sattgast were not stressed. The exact reasons why remain unclear, but among them was the American time period when the immigrant experience was still so strong that schools like Bemidji State worked diligently and deliberately to remove any hint of "foreign-ness" that the students brought with them. (Getting rid of the s's from "dose Scandinavian accents vussn't eassy, den; yeah-sure, yew-betcha.") Not that languages were totally excluded, for Deputy did hire one teacher—and one only—of foreign languages in his 19 years as president. He employed Clara Schuster in 1921 to teach both German and French, and he offered both beginning and second year studies in both languages.

Schuster retired in 1937. Arriving that year (he had recently returned from a year's study in Germany) was Philip R. Sauer who agreed to teach, temporarily, quarter-time German in addition to his classes in English. "Temporary" for Sauer lasted the next 25 years. But he loved his German! In 1938 Sauer and his students also publicly produced a German play, <u>Panne vor Alt-Heidelberg</u>. Help in foreign language teaching remained small in numbers, and provided short-lived careers for the few who did come. For example, Dr. Donald Schier came in 1939, planning a career (teaching French) in Bemidji, but he got drafted into the war in 1941 and never returned to Bemidji afterwards. The war years were lean in every way. Sauer received only short-term help from Charlene Dieterich in 1942-43 to teach Spanish, but with BSTC's total enrollment that year at 141, there were not enough students left over for Spanish classes, so they were dropped.

The postwar years found little improvement in staff numbers, despite near annual requests of Division Chair Sauer to add one full-time instructor for German, one for French, and one for Spanish. In 1957 Sattgast agreed to add one teacher only, in Spanish. Indeed, a native Spaniard, Dr. Anthony de Soto, was engaged to teach his native language. He did not work out well; worse, it backfired. Although de Soto obviously knew his mother tongue, he did not teach it well and was fired. (His credentials were spurious, too.) But he did not go quietly into that dark Spanish night. As Sattgast told Sauer, "You and I can share a jail cell. Vicious de Soto is suing us." Nothing came of the suit.[6]

ACH DER LIEBER!—and RUSKIES!

A native Ukrainian who fled a Mennonite community just ahead of the Soviets, but an American by then via Canada, came to Bemidji State in 1957 to teach English. His name was Henry Dyck, and given his background—made

---

6) Anecdote quoted in memo to this author from Sauer dated December 12, 1992. Memo in author's file. A request was made to Dr. Sauer for information, and his response came in a five-page memorandum he entitled, "Highlights in the History of Foreign Languages at BSU, 1921-69."

obvious by his heavy foreign accent—Dyck agreed to teach the Russian language too. He remained until 1967 and by then had firmly established a Russian program. Its uniqueness was seen in it being the only Russian program in the state outside of the University of Minnesota. Dyck not only taught Russian and talked Russian, he "looked Russian." A tall man and on the robust side too, he wore a high beaver hat in the winters, making his appearance that much more stereotypically Russian.[7]

Real relief came for Sauer in 1962 with the hiring of Dr. Clive Cardinal to teach German, relieving Sauer, after 25 years, of any more German classes. Cardinal's expertise allowed his teaching of advanced third and fourth year German and he strengthened the tiny program. Still, when new President Harry Bangsberg arrived on campus in the fall of 1964, the foreign language staff had only a fourth-time Russian teacher, a half-time Spanish teacher (Aileen Canfield), and only one full-time member, Cardinal, in German. That would change fast under Bangsberg, who provided a renewed vision of the intellectual (and boom-time) academic challenges of languages.

Though short (1964-67), Bangsberg's term nevertheless found him building up the department with the hiring of five full-time professors: (1) Richard Day came to teach French and remains at the present writing (1994). French alone became a two-person department when Jean Leighton joined the staff in 1969; she retired in 1991. (2) Irvin Rotto was brought in primarily to head up the Russian studies program after Dyck left. With his added linguistic skills, however, he also taught both Latin and Norwegian. Rotto also taught Russian literature in translation, plus courses in Russian history. (Rotto retired in July of 1993.) (3) Ernest Ashley taught Spanish, driving home that there was no way to learn the language except through hard, hard work, drill, drill, and more drill. (The hard-driving Ashley continued in the position until his retirement in 1983; soon after retirement, however, he died suddenly from a heart attack.) (4) Richard Krummel was employed primarily as a German teacher, but he also taught beginning Greek. (Krummel stayed until he retired in 1990; he and his German-born wife still live in Bemidji.) (5) Mary Ann Hunter was hired with the above group to teach Spanish (she left in 1968 and was replaced by John O'Boyle, who retired in 1989).

Along with these several full-time language teachers, Bangsberg also added part-timers such as James Zeller, Stephanie Fechner, and Enid Swanson. (Mrs. Swanson was the wife of Myron Swanson, who replaced Sauer as division head in 1969. She continued her part-time teaching and was an effective classroom teacher, whether with little Lab School children or college students. She also promoted and strengthened the German Club. At this writing Mrs. Swanson is retired and living in Florida; her husband died in 1992.)

---

7) Henry Dyck, a fine storyteller about his days in Europe, may be remembered as the man who could roll his r's like no one else. His great love—of which he spoke openly—was literature, a term he could pronounce with such mellifluous tones that it could send the listener running immediately to Shakespeare. He represented the "Old World" in the best sense, demonstrating his overall passion for all things Classical. His wife Kathryn, who also taught in the English department, was an accomplished violinist, and they wanted their two daughters and son to grow up in a milieu of Kulture. They moved to Mansfield State College, Pennsylvania in 1967. During a trip to London a few years later, Henry dropped dead on a London street. Kathryn still lives in Mansfield and is now retired.

Thanks to President Bangsberg, the foreign languages program became no longer "foreign"; he built it up and it never let up, remaining a reasonably large (seven full-time; four part-time instructors by 1994) and viable unit ever since. With increased size came a change in status. In 1970, foreign languages moved out of being only an "area" within a division to the proper designation of department. Again, in a deliberate attempt to reflect changes and update terminology, the department members in 1983 voted to drop the word "foreign" and substitute instead the word "modern." With the additions of both Greek and Latin—and a little later Chinese and Japanese—their new and present title became "Department of Modern and Classical Languages."

Japanese Teacher Reaches to Japanese-Language Charts
"Foreign languages are no longer 'foreign'."

The best may be yet to come. At this writing, the State Board of Education is phasing in a requirement for two years of a foreign language to be taken in high school, prior to the student's coming to college, which decision when/if fully implemented will have a positive effect on all college language departments. Although several members of the BSU department have come and gone in the past 25 years, one stable—and tenured, finally—position has gone to Dr. Nancy Erickson, German teacher, who began in 1981 as a part-time adjunct teacher and gradually moved forward to become the new department chair in 1993. She's lively, full of ideas, a hard worker, and a promoter and protector of her department. Modern and Classical languages at BSU look good; Bangsberg would like that.

THE FUNTASTIC DANCE FOLLIES

MODERN DANCE 1945-1976: Both the modern dance beginning and advanced classes began in 1945 at Bemidji State Teachers College. The classes and a program for the public were mandated by the administration when Dr. Myrtie

Hunt was hired for the women's physical education department.

The first program, or "modern dance show," was held in 1946 at the Bemidji High School auditorium, since there were no facilities adequate for the performance at the College. There were a total of eight students involved in this program, and the audience was small but encouraging. No budget had been allotted, so for costumes the dancers turned to Norma Fenson-Olson, who, with the help of her mother Ella, graciously designed and made all of the costumes. In that first dance show was a young soloist named Marion Fenson who would eventually inherit control of the show from Dr. Hunt and bring it to its current level as the Funtastic Dance Follies. Today she is known to everybody as Mrs. C - Marion Christianson.[8]

There were one or two more programs held at the auditorium, but due to inconveniences it was moved to Memorial Hall (M-100), on the BSTC campus.

An Early 'Funtastic Follies' Dance Group (on stage in Deputy Hall) c. 1955
"It started small . . . and then played four nights to overflowing audiences."

Each year Memorial Hall was prepared with makeshift stage equipment, practice hours, housekeeping necessities and access to music, like phonographs or pianos, all to make ready for the dance show. Memorial Hall also provided the most important resource—space.

Soon came Orchesis, a club for dancers. This was formed to generate ideas for the program. With the use of films and visits to other schools with dance programs, along with the students' own creativity, ideas grew, and helped shape individual or group numbers for the show. Students were happy to discover that by using basic principles of movement and reaching into their own resources for individual expressions, the results were delightful. Gradually the dance show

8) Obviously, the annual spring dance shows are not "programs" in the academic and curricular sense, but they have been so important that not mentioning them is a disservice to the hundreds of students who have been a part of them since 1945. Information supplied by Jon Langhout, Jr., who not incidentally is Marion Christianson's son-in-law.

gained the participation of the men on campus. This took some gentle nudging on the part of girlfriends and a very important curriculum class, social dancing, resulted ultimately in several athletes joining in as dancers. This meant a further gain in interest in the dance show when the fellows were seen to take part. As a result more numbers were added to the program and soon the troupe included a hundred dancers! Of course the audience also expanded, and the Student Activity Committee, seeing the need for financial help, allotted funds for this purpose.

All the accompaniment that required music was taped on a master reel from various record albums, 33s, 45s, and 78s. When the sound system was put in place on stage, audio helpers and stage hands took charge. The tape had everything on it and was the single most important prop the program used. One year the master tape was stolen! There was no time to make another tape so a mad scramble ensued. Everyone in the show was alerted and told to bring their records! After many anxious moments, the music came in, from rooming houses, dorm rooms, homes and wherever. One very helpful student gathered them all together and when the performance was about to start, she would hand the sound man a record and tell him which song on the record to play for that number. The show went on.

At first, leotards were the standard costumes for dance classes, and with either a short skirt or a long flowing skirt, this basic costume was retained for some performances. At one of the programs a dancer wearing a skirt was leaping across the stage and her skirt came loose and floated behind her, but she just sailed on and finished the dance. As numbers, variety and participants in the show increased, costume design became more individualized.

Also the popularity of the dance show, in the eyes of the public, necessitated the addition of another night's performance. In 1975 the show expanded from one to two nights.

The last modern dance program under Dr. Myrtie Hunt was presented in 1976. As the dancers gathered together backstage just prior to the start of the performance, there was nervousness and anticipation - but reminding them of their hours of practice as she did each year, Dr. Hunt sent them off with the statement, "This is your hour of truth." In 1977 the dance show was directed by Pat Schneider, who was assisted by Marlene Techau. It was the next year, 1978, when Marion Christianson took over and brought the dance show into the contemporary age. Her first action was to rename the show the "Funtastic Dance Follies."

THE FUNTASTIC DANCE FOLLIES, 1978-PRESENT: In renaming the dance show, Mrs. C also sought to increase the emphasis on variety to gain even more students. She also added third and fourth nights to accommodate the growing crowds, which were reaching numbers of over 500 each night. Crowds were lining up around the block from Memorial, down past Deputy Hall on Birchmont Drive. At one performance the crowd was so overflowing that President Decker and his wife Jackie had to sit on the floor of M-100 to view the show! Then, in 1981, the Funtastic Dance Follies made the big leap of moving to the basketball gymnasium in the Physical Education Complex. This has provided more space for dancers and the public. The curtain was moved from M-100 and decorations and a false floor were added to make it more like a stage. In the gymnasium the show could play to a larger audience and now routinely draws 600-800 spectators per night, with Friday and Saturday shows often exceeding 1,000!

Technical problems have added to the challenge of putting together such a performance. Twenty minutes prior to one of the sold out shows, the stage crew was setting up the light board and BANG, it blew! The hall filled with smoke and many people had to go outside to get some fresh air. Coming to the rescue was long-time technical advisor Vance Balstad, who has been Mrs. C's right hand man in putting together the dance show year after year. He wasn't able to dim the lights, but he was able to turn specific lights on and off with a last minute plug arrangement. Another time a dancer forgot his pants for one of his performances and had to run back to his dorm during the show to get them. He made it just in time, nearly out of breath. The show went on.

Mrs. C soon moved the Sunday evening performance to the afternoon, allowing families to bring their children and have them home early. She also incorporated the use of assistant directors and student directors to help with the additional chores that came along with the expansion. Over the years these directors have been instrumental in achieving the success that the dance show has enjoyed. Starting in 1978, 32 people have held this position, including Marie Hasty, Jo Pfeffer, Terri Beck, Tami Blanchard, Anita Beckeris, Becky Gunderson, Cindy Evanson, Dave Nelson, Melodie VanKampen, Mary Lynn Humbeutel, Donna Smahel, Dennis Schuemann, Kiersten Heide, Sharon Neppel, Cindy Stalock, Teresa Theis, Jeff Stern, Barb Ruzynski, Kim Mavetz, Chuck Veilleux, Brent Jeffers, Kris Winge, Julie Renaud, Rita Meyer, Suzy Christianson, Greg Gargano, Brett Harrison, Darren Yerama, Jon Langhout Jr., Chris Mahoney and Sue Kylmala. A multitude of other students, too numerous to name, have held many responsible and important jobs in this production.

As far as numbers of people, the show has expanded to having over 200 dancers plus support personnel directly involved in this production. Another important addition was the inclusion of an official emcee. This all-important position has added spice and a level of professionalism that makes that show all the better, and has been held by 11 people, including Rick Robbins, Robin Melcher with Pat Peterson, Jeff Stern, Jeff Olson, Dennis Weimann, Jeff Kennedy, Brian Bissonette, David Terry, Jon Eisele and Howie Leathers. Other people at Bemidji State University that have played a part in many of the dance shows include Becky O'Keefe, Dr. Muriel Gilman, Andy Wells, Bill Crews, sound man Dr. Lee Hawk, and former emcee Jeff Olson, recently the alumni director at Bemidji State University.

Making variety a priority, Mrs. C's philosophy has been to have something in the program that appeals to everyone in the audience, and this has resulted in a montage of numbers. The numbers have ranged from Broadway's "New York, New York" to "Disco Duck," children's numbers to spiritual numbers, and international numbers to country-western. Some of the most notable numbers have been "Shall We Dance," "The Cowboys," "Colors," "The Curly Shuffle," "Native American Sneak Up Dance," "Blues Brothers," "Barney," "Beep Beep," "The Cossacks," "Greased Lightning," "Heard It Through the Grapevine," "Summer Nights," "Gary, Indiana," "Mountain Music," "You Dropped a Bomb on Me," "Boogie Woogie Bugle Boy," "Chorus Line," "Standing on the Corner," "Last Dance," "Surfing USA," and "Mame!" Some of the classics have included tap and soft shoe, waltz, and Latin numbers, a kids' number ("Barney's Back Yard"), BSU cheerleaders, BSU dance line, humorous-surprise skits and "all guy" numbers. And an international flavor is evidenced as the show routinely displays dances from all over the world, including numbers from the Ukraine, Malaysia, Germany, Tahiti, Sweden, Japan, Scotland, Africa, India, Austria, and Hawaii.

THE HONORS PROGRAM

"The first duty of a college is the creation of an authentic intellectual community within each classroom . . . in which the things that are taken for granted are the things that count. AND THE THINGS THAT COUNT ARE IDEAS."

—Max Lerner

Like most colleges and universities during the tumultuous 1960s, Bemidji State sought to redefine and broaden its basic character through curricular change and redirection. In 1964 the innovative presidency of Harry F. Bangsberg began. Although brief and tragically ended in 1967, the Bangsberg years witnessed a renewed stress upon the liberal arts as the foundation of the intellectual enterprise and the creation of exciting, alternative forms of learning. Included in the latter category was the laying of the groundwork for an Honors program for intellectually superior students.

What had been a traditional aspect of education for some other schools was then new to Bemidji State; yet making the change was not easy. All of the usual faculty fears were manifested, from those who saw little but intellectual anarchy, to those who feared erosion of their territorial turf, to those who saw it as snooty elitism and antithetical to the role and mission of "plain ol'" Bemidji State. The road was bumpy to start with and smoothed out only gradually.

Since its inception, however, the Honors program has provided a sense of intellectual excitement and academic challenge to those who have participated in it, students and faculty alike. As one observer put it simply, if inelegantly, "That whole thing is tailor-made for a different breed of cats." As to its acceptance at Bemidji State, even 10 years after its start, cerebral professor Charles Fuchsman, environmental scientist, who was in the program from its initial phases, would challenge doubting colleagues in his address to them entitled, "The Bemidji Honors Program - Doubts and Affirmations." Said Fuchsman, "If in fact the Honors program connotes aspiration to superior education, perhaps it is our professorial colleagues and our University administration who need the Honors program more than our Honors students do."

The Honors program was a long-time-a-bornin'—and had a host of parents, mainly in the forms of committees, one after another, starting with an *ad hoc* group in 1964, and only semi-concluding after the first class of 43 students entered the program in the fall of 1969. Its implementation, however, was only the start of ongoing changes and refinements to the program, and some of those later changes were radical indeed.

Although not that simple to summarize, a few basic points emerged in this program: (1) Honors students were to be exempted from the usual general education requirements, these being replaced by an individualized program of study; (2) all Honors classes would be fully interdisciplinary, each course to be broad in scope with viewpoints presented by professors from each area. The courses would not be oriented towards the memorization of facts and the development of mechanical skills, but rather towards an overall conceptual appreciation for the field of endeavor; (3) the faculty who would participate would themselves have an interdisciplinary perspective and commitment, and they would function in a team-teaching, not turn-teaching situation; (4) lastly, the Honors scholar would be required to complete a departmental Honors activity, normally a senior research paper, in his or her major field, upon which effort the student would be examined orally.

FINALLY, SUCCESS AND STABILITY

An important milestone in the Honors program came with its first graduates in 1972; the Honors students at the graduation ceremony wore distinctive gold bachelor's hoods, an item of apparel that has marked them as special students ever since. Stability came to the program by the late 1970s, with 150 to 175 enrolled in the program each year since then. It's here to stay. (The program has also provided a side benefit to the entire campus community. Starting in 1975, it has annually sponsored the Honors Council Seminar and Lecture Series. Approximately eight lectures are presented each school year on a variety of topics.)

"THE THINGS THAT COUNT ARE IDEAS"

The true college is that small enclave in the midst of a busy world where the life of the mind and the advancement of knowledge and understanding are guarded and treasured with a sense of both their fragility and essentiality. Bemidji State has met that definition in its Honors program.[9]

9) Information taken from an excellent brief history of the Honors program written by Professor Gerald Schnabel of the history department, dated April 24, 1984. Its title, "And Gladly Would He Learn and Gladly Teach," with the subtitle, "An Essay and Remembrance in Celebration of the Fifteenth Anniversary of the Bemidji State University Honors Program, 1969-84." Copy in author's file; copies available at Honors Program Office in Hagg-Sauer Hall. Of much use in the 27-page essay are the dozens of names of faculty members who shepherded the program through the Byzantine path of committees and sub-committees, and finally implementation. Schnabel also added the several changes since 1969. There were four different chairmen of the Honors program before Dr. Michael Field was named chair #5 in 1974. The fact that Field is still there at this writing (1994) speaks well of both the program and Field himself.

INDIAN STUDIES PROGRAM

Geographically Bemidji State sits in the middle of four Native American reservations: Red Lake, Leech Lake, White Earth and Nett Lake. Little wonder that the school should be the location of educational services for the large Native American population both in and around Bemidji.

Scene from Annual Spring Pow Wow held during Indian Week
"Mind-boggling gifts like 3-M's . . . demonstrate the importance of Native Americans."

Organizing a program for Native Americans and hiring its staff took seven years from the time of the first formal discussions in 1962. In the 1960s, two motivating factors moved Bemidji State forward on behalf of Native Americans, the 1964 Civil Rights Act and the 1968 U.S. Senate report: "Indian Education: A National Tragedy—A National Challenge." The response by two institutions of higher education in Minnesota was almost immediate. Both the University of Minnesota and Bemidji State implemented Indian studies programs in their schools in 1969, and Bemidji went one step further with the establishment of an Indian Studies Center the next year. A director of the Bemidji center was hired; an Indian studies minor was proposed and accepted; and an Ojibwe language instructor soon would be employed, with the language classes leading to an Ojibwe minor in 1973.

Enrollments of Native Americans increased dramatically. From an estimated 50 students in 1970 to almost 400 by 1990, Bemidji State gained (and still has) the largest Native American enrollment of any Minnesota college or university. Of all the Indians in Minnesota who have chosen to go to college, almost half have gone to Bemidji State.

The Indian studies major was accepted by the faculty senate in 1978, and by that time a Council of Indian Students had been formed and an annual Indian Week initiated (in 1973). The latter has consistently included a pow-wow and an Indian meal, with the general public invited for both. Moreover, since 1973, there's been an annual banquet at which the speaker has been a nationally prominent Indian. At the banquets awards are given to outstanding Native American college students. Many area high school Indian students are invited to attend for the dual purpose of gaining increased appreciation for their heritage and at the same time being encouraged to consider attending college themselves.

Significant improvements came in the 1980s with the establishment of (1) an Indian Students Services program; (2) an American Indian Advisory Council; (3) a Native Americans into Medicine program, in conjunction with the medical college at the University of Minnesota-Duluth; (4) a BSU Indian Alumni Chapter; and (5) an American Indian Science and Engineering Society Chapter. Obviously, the programs for Indians at Bemidji State have changed dramatically, and overall they have achieved considerable success since their inceptions.

Native Americans in colleges have been organized on all levels, from campus to state to nation.[10] The year 1994 marked the 10th anniversary—and annual convention—of the Minnesota Indian Education Association. There is also a national IEA, and there is regularly a BSU delegation in attendance at the IEA national meetings.

Clearly, according to the BSU administrations and directors, much has been done, but there is much more to do. A major goal has been the construction of a new Indian Studies Center on campus to replace the current small center, an old house on Birchmont Drive located across the street from the Lutheran Student Center. (The Indian studies offices are located in Sanford Hall.) Fulfillment of that goal got underway in April, 1993 when President Les Duly announced publicly that fundraising had yielded over $85,000, enough to hold groundbreaking ceremonies in October of 1993 for a two-story, octagonal building with offices for faculty and staff as well as a computer room, a kitchen area, a conference room, and a multi-purpose space where classes, pow-wows, and workshops could be held. Duly indicated that the construction would be completed by the end of 1994.[11]

10) A historic agreement between BSU and the Leech Lake Tribal College, Cass Lake, was signed on December 1, 1992, when the presidents of both schools (Les Duly and Larry Aitken) met to sign the agreement. The plan allowed tribal college students to transfer up to 24 quarter hours upon admission to BSU. Northern Student, December 16, 1992, p. 1

11) As with the location of all new buildings on campus, there were widely varying opinions on where the construction should/ should not take place. No one opposed the Indian Center itself, only its location. Initially the building location was planned for that small woods located south of Birch Hall, between Birch Lane and Birchmont Drive. Petitions against this proposal came almost immediately, the opposition finding the choice inappropriate both because of the crowding in this limited land area, and the threatened loss of the only woods left on campus. The new center will not only replace the old, but also will be in that same location. Addenda; last minute change: the '94 legislature voted $1.1 million for and Indian Studies Center, and thus all the plans had to be altered, including the new location. Stay tuned.

The biggest financial boon to Indian education specifically and education in general for Bemidji State came in 1991 with a million dollar endowment gift from the 3-M Corporation in St. Paul, the annual interest on which must be used to employ a Native American instructor to teach classes in accounting. To date this stipulation—and goal—has been fulfilled. Mind-boggling gifts like 3-M's have demonstrated the impact on a changing Bemidji State and the importance of Native Americans.

The topic should not be abandoned before acknowledging the problems with Native American education at Bemidji. Indian leaders have been the first to recognize the perennial problem of retention of Native American students once they come on campus. The students come all right, but not enough of them stay. For this problem alone, an American Indian counselor has been employed since 1991, with the appropriate title of Native American retention counselor. Already this influence has been positive, and the entire Native American program has been judged a needed success. Bemidji State has met the challenge and has met many (but not all) of the needs of northern Minnesota's indigenous people.[12]

KAWE, PUBLIC TELEVISION, CHANNEL 9

Including a public TV station in the special category of Programs and People at Bemidji State University may seem to be stretching it, but given the background of the station, it makes sense. KAWE is, sort of, a part of BSU.

Citizens of Minnesota North Country today flip on their TV sets, and if they are searching for something educational, they seek channel 9 which brings in public TV from a station headquartered in Deputy Hall on the campus of Bemidji State University. This routine action too easily suggests that public TV has been around "forever" and that Bemidji State was the originator and the natural location for the station. Not so. And certainly not so simple and easy. Because public TV is currently viewed as a virtual extension of the University's charge to serve the region, the history of KAWE—and a lengthy history it would be, if all were told—deserves at least cursory telling.[13]

The idea for a public television broadcast facility to be located in northern Minnesota goes back to the 1950s, with much of the initial credit going to Ray Witt, then principal of Bemidji High School. Witt met Harold Fleming, chair of the education department at BSC, who was just as interested as Witt, and both of the

12) Credit for successful American Indian programs at Bemidji State belongs to many people, starting with the directors chosen, all but the first one a Native American: Alan Brew, Gerald Vizenor, Don Bibeau, and the current head, Kent Smith. Closely associated with the program (since he came in 1984) is Donald Day, whose position has had several title changes so that by 1993 he became the director of Minority Student Services, his role to include all persons of color. (Not incidentally, in the entire State University System, which in 1994 is over 50,000 students, only 3.3 percent are students of color.) Don Day joined the Bemidji Lions Club after he came in 1984, and he is the only person of color out of 119 members. Not to be forgotten in BSU's Indian studies is the delightfully droll Ojibwe Language Professor Earl Nyholm, who came in 1972 and replaced the first Ojibwe language teacher, Selam Ross. Nyholm has another major skill which he practices almost every summer; he builds birchbark canoes, an art he has demonstrated at the Smithsonian Institution.
13) Special thanks to this section on KAWE must go to Lee Hawk, chair of mass communication at BSU, who first convinced this author that public TV is indeed a special "part" of BSU and needs to be in the school's published history. Hawk also personally had most of the documentation connected with the station's founding, data surpassing 100 pages, which he pared down to less than a dozen pages that he presented to me on November 5, 1993 and I cut that drastically to three lonely pages; document in author's file. The interpretations as to who deserves the most credit for KAWE are Hawk's—and his documentation backs his conclusions.

schools they represented agreed with them that the concept of educational television was good but neither school could afford it. Nevertheless, the men continued their plans and discussions and brought in a third interested party, Lowell Vaughn, also from BSC.

Witt and Vaughn decided in the early 1960s to promote their TV goals by visiting with area superintendents in towns primarily west of Bemidji, and eventually a number of convinced school leaders met together in Crookston, which seemed to be the logical center for a major television station when and if it was approved. That meeting, and others that followed, led to the formation of the Northwest Regional Development Commission, the first of several organized groupings formed to acquire a TV station in northern Minnesota.

In the meantime, the Federal Communications Commission assigned an educational channel to Bemidji, UHF channel 32. Since most area sets then received only VHF, Principal Witt, acting on behalf of his school board, in 1966 requested from the FCC a change in the kind of channel, along with a different number. Simultaneous with Witt's request, the Bemidji Pioneer filed a dissenting response to the FCC as the newspaper then wanted a VHF low power station of its own. The FCC, however, decided to grant Witt's channel request change and assigned the Bemidji school district a VHF channel, 9. But victory was yet far down the road. The Bemidji school board next received a small federal grant of $7,419 to hire a consultant to do a feasibility study, and afterwards the New Jersey consultant's report made it clear that a significant educational TV station was far beyond the capabilities of a single school district.

After that rejection, Witt and Vaughn (Fleming had retired) decided to try to improve their chances by expanding the size of the constituency. They went back to the multi-school NWRDC group who then tried in 1967 to receive a substantial federal grant, but they were told their numbers were still too small even to be considered. The same response had been given to a group of school leaders from the far western school districts, and so the two groups joined together (that took a year to work out) and formed a larger Northwest Minnesota Educational Research and Development Council. But they did not join together in their opinion on where any new TV station should be located, one group favoring University of North Dakota and the other Bemidji State College. More disagreement came from some superintendents who did not want any college involvement anywhere, arguing loss of control for the originators of the project. Witt apparently convinced the doubters that a college would have to be involved as the only workable solution and it would either have to be at Bemidji State or it wouldn't be anywhere. (The Minnesota legislature would not offer any assistance to UND.) Enter John Yourd, chair of the BSC department of education, into the equation (and conundrum). It was his task to solicit support from Robert Decker, the BSC president, for the concept of a TV station and the assurance that the College would provide the needed space. Decker agreed to both ideas and appointed a committee—of College and community and area school board representatives—with Vaughn as chairman to plan the next step in the process, soliciting financial support. However, the Vaughn committee was hampered in fundraising for the College because the proposed station was not—and is not today—a College television station. The school districts also could not supply money because it was beyond the realm of their responsibility. Solution-in-part: A non-profit organization named Bunyanland Educational Television was established in 1970 with Vaughn as chair, and at the same time the earlier committees were terminated. Little happened in the next five years, however, to bring channel 9 into anybody's home, with one important exception: permission for its location at Bemidji State. Since the TV facilities would not belong to the school, permission had to be secured in the form of a legislative bill. State Senator Gerald Willet, who represented northern Minnesota, was sold on the idea of having the station on the BSC campus and he guided the needed legislation through the legislative intricacies necessary. President Decker did the majority of the testifying before the legislature, justifying BSC's interest and support in the project.

One more and final name change came in 1976 when a board member from Bagley, the Reverend Milan Davig, convinced the TV planning group to drop the word "educational" from its name and replace it with "public" so that the whole new title would become: Northern Minnesota Public Television. Agreed. Agreed also was the hiring of a professional fundraiser for regional private donations while at the same time going to the state legislature AND the federal government (Department of Health, Education and Welfare; HEW) for the big sums necessary for construction to begin forthwith. It worked. A touch of drama was added when a deadline for the HEW application was reached only when Yourd flew to Washington, D.C. and hand-delivered the needed documents, with only a few hours to spare. HEW granted $600,000; the legislature came up eventually with $615,000, plus another $30,000 from the Governor's Rural Development Council. Other grants applied for and received were $100,000 from the Blandin Foundation, $100,000 from the Upper Great Lakes Regional Commission, $76,000 from Dayton-Hudson Foundation, $85,000 from the McKnight Foundation, $85,000 from the Bush Foundation, and $5,000 from Burlington Northern Foundation.

The successful funding goals dovetailed with the planning and subsequent remodeling of Deputy Hall in 1979-80, which incorporated appropriate space for the new TV station. Moreover, the University's own small TV station capitalized on this in-house remodeling project by revamping its own facilities which were located just across the hall from the planned public TV station. During this period the governing board took up the issue of call letters, and a variety of letters were presented for approval—KJLY, KNCP, KKNC, KBJI, KBMJ, and KAWE, the latter recommended by language professor Earl Nyholm who said that KAWE is an Ojibwe Indian word meaning "top priority" or "first in a sequence." The FCC assigned the new channel 9 station to be KAWE. On June 1, 1980, at 8:05:54 a.m., station KAWE-TV signed on the air and began regular programming for the first time. It was a long time a'comin'.

Over the decades since World War II, when the magic of television gradually transformed itself from "magic" into the category of "one vast wasteland," when by 1994 one of the highest rated network TV shows actually advertised that it is a silly sitcom based on nothing, when kids growing up have by age 12 witnessed something like 5,000 TV murders, stations like channel 9 are a welcome and necessary oasis in that wasteland, and Bemidji State is proud to be a part of it.

DEPARTMENT OF MASS COMMUNICATION

The department of mass communication has evolved over many years from a series of individual efforts in the various media to the eventual merging of those efforts into a single department in 1988. The University's newspaper, the Northern Student, the oldest form of "mass comm" at BSU, existed long before the department was even considered, let alone established. James McMahon (came in 1957), while serving as public relations director for BSU, also served as advisor to the Northern Student. As a result of his close relationship with the print media, he developed a series of journalism courses that were offered through the division of language and literature. This was the start of what would be a separate department

Jim McMahon

"The start of Mass Comm . . . a wonderful, fun, funny, cigar-chomping DFL Irishman."

30 years later. (Author's addendum: Jim McMahon was a wonderful man. The words genial, outgoing, warm, fun and funny may be hackneyed terms, but nevertheless describe this remarkable, cigar-chomping, politically active [DFL, of course] Irishman who it was impossible not to like. A native of Maine, his east coast accent accentuated only a part of his specialness. Aside from his being just a lovable character, he brought fine journalistic skills which carried over to Northern Student editors and publications as well as all-school publicity, as he was a one-man news service. Not incidentally, McMahon began the first fall journalism conference in 1959, which has continued since and which has brought hundreds of high school students to the campus.)

RADIO WAVES; TV FLICKERS

BSU's radio station began in the mid 1960s through the efforts of students who desired an alternative to the only radio station in the area, KBUN-AM. The students constructed an AM carrier-current radio station in a dorm room and began broadcasting news and music throughout the campus in 1965. The station, KDRS-Dorm Radio Station, was funded by the Student Activities Committee and was strictly a student facility. One of these students, Kris Geisen, was hired in 1967 as BSU's director of audiovisual services. He carried the idea of a campus radio station a step further by applying for the first FM-licensed station north of Brainerd. His idea was to extend BSU radio services to the entire Bemidji community and provide educational, entertainment, and cultural programming to an unserved area of Minnesota. The Federal Communications Commission granted the license in 1969, and in January of 1970 the 10-watt station went on the air from studios in the basement of Birch Hall. Once on the air, the new station needed a manager and director. Geisen was reassigned from audiovisual services to the new position of director of broadcasting under University President Robert Decker. It was in the early 1970s that the development of BSU television also began through audiovisual services. Geisen, as part of his master's degree project, used a $20,000 state grant to design and build a portable, closed-circuit television production center on campus. Early use of the television system was to support educational and instructional efforts on campus only.

As the student-operated KBSB-FM and KDRS-AM cable radio operations developed, an agreement with Elmer Langhout, owner of Bemidji's Midwest Cable, was reached. The FM station and the first locally-originated TV services began broadcasting 24 hours a day over the Bemidji cable system in 1971. The TV portion of the service, although it received much attention at the time, was very rudimentary compared to 1990s standards. It comprised a black-and-white TV camera pointed at printed announcements on 4 x 6 inch file cards that rotated on a pair of bicycle rims driven by a small electric motor. The hand-printed or typed cards included various announcements of BSU and community non-profit events.

The instructional television system expanded into a small TV studio during the same period, from 1969 to 1971, under the direction of Vern Thomas, audiovisual center director; Bruce Hough, television coordinator; Tom Miller, graphics coordinator; Bob Smith, photo coordinator; and Andy Wells, equipment facilitator. As student and faculty interest grew, short news and public affairs programs were produced and inserted into the FM radio and closed-circuit TV broadcasts.

As interest in the potential of broadcasting grew on the part of both students and faculty, Decker and others in the administration became increasingly interested in the development of an academic program in the area. In 1969, John DeSanto was hired by Ronald Gearman, dean of the fine arts division, to begin a communication media department. DeSanto, along with photography instructors Ron Gezelka and Mike Barnett, began teaching added journalism and photography classes. McMahon also taught several journalism courses. Things then moved fast. When DeSanto first arrived on campus and was looking for his office, he met Geisen in Deputy Hall. After a brief discussion, Geisen agreed to begin teaching broadcast courses in audiovisual services. These courses expanded rapidly due to strong interest resulting from student involvement in the existing radio and TV facilities.

STRUCTURAL EXPERIMENTATION: FEELING THE WAY TO INDEPENDENCE

As audiovisual services expanded, mass communication instructors began offering courses in photography, television, and media through the education department. The loosely-organized mass media courses were consolidated into a communication media department in 1974, under the chairmanship of Bob Smith. In 1975, audiovisual services and the communication media department combined their teaching efforts into a communication major. The radio station director position and funds were channeled through the communication media department instead of the president's office. Later, the departments were merged under the division of humanities and fine arts to provide both communication courses and audiovisual services through one department. (If this seems confusing, it's because it was confusing.)

In 1978 Peter Nordgren was hired to operate the radio facilities and Geisen moved back to the audiovisual area. Dave DeVries and Dan Younger were hired to operate the TV facilities. The rapidly-growing program offered emphasis areas in photography, public relations, journalism, and broadcast. When funding was provided to remodel Deputy Hall in 1979, provisions were made to house the TV facilities, the radio station and the Northern Student in that building.

AN "UNNATURAL MARRIAGE"

In late 1979 Nordgren resigned as radio director and Lee Hawk was hired in his place. He and Paskvan began transferring the broadcast facilities to Deputy

Hall. Peggy DeVries, the newspaper advisor at the time, moved that operation from the first floor of Deputy Hall to the room beside the radio station. By 1981 the new radio, television and newspaper facilities were completed and in use. In 1982 DeVries resigned and Roy Blackwood was hired to teach journalism and advise the Northern Student. The department that year merged with the speech/theatre department to form the department of speech/theatre and mass communication. The merger was part of a requalification of academic programs mandated by the State University Board. As part of this reorganization, the photo program, with instructors DeVries and Younger, was moved to the visual arts department. The department merger brought together faculty and students of widely divergent interests, and created a strained working atmosphere for the following six years. Geisen served as chair during the first three years of the newly established department, after which that responsibility switched to theatre faculty.

In spite of administrative difficulties, the communication program continued to flourish. The radio station increased its power to 130 watts and converted to stereo. The television station adopted three-quarter-inch, all-color format. The stations provided broadcast laboratory experience to hundreds of students, with a secondary mission of providing information to students both on and off campus. By 1987 it had become apparent that the speech/theatre and mass communication merger was not working. Judy McDonald, dean of the division of humanities and fine arts, after consultation with department members, decided the departments were too diverse to remain together and a separation was effected. The new department of mass communication was established in 1988, with Hawk as chair. Under his guidance the department has reestablished its own identity, and has developed a curriculum that provided a balance between the theoretical and applied courses appropriate for a major within a liberal arts context.

Louise Mengelkoch was added to the staff in 1989 to teach journalism and take over advising the Northern Student. In 1991 the faculty recommended that operation of the Northern Student should become a University, rather than a departmental, function. They recommended that the paper assume its broader identity beginning with the 1992-93 school year. The paper has relocated in the student union and operates under the direction of a media board. The board consists of members of the community-at-large as well as faculty and students. Mass communication students still provide the majority of the staff of the paper, but the new configuration is conducive to involvement by others as well.

The television and radio facilities have continually upgraded their equipment and facilities since the move to Deputy Hall. The radio station has acquired a digital editing system for audio production and is considering a total, computer-assisted programming format. The television station has made a transition from three-quarter-inch to half-inch format and has acquired new digital video-editing equipment.

The department offers three $500 scholarships each year. Two are awarded to outstanding students in broadcast and print. The third goes to a Native American student who declares mass communication as his/her major.

The mass communication faculty in 1994 consists of:
Dr. Lee Hawk, broadcast (department chair)[14]
Dr. Roy Blackwood, journalism
Mr. Kris Geisen, broadcast
Ms. Louise Mengelkoch, journalism
Mr. Roger Paskvan, broadcast (TV director)
Mr. Robert Smith, broadcast (radio director)

DEPARTMENT OF NURSING

Northern Minnesota needs nurses. Bemidji State serves the educational needs of northern Minnesota. So start up a baccalaureate nursing program. The logic seems simple enough, but it took many years to move from the talking stage to the actual nursing degree program.

Informal talks started in the 1960s and formal talks in 1973 for the purpose of both increasing and improving the pool of nursing personnel in northern

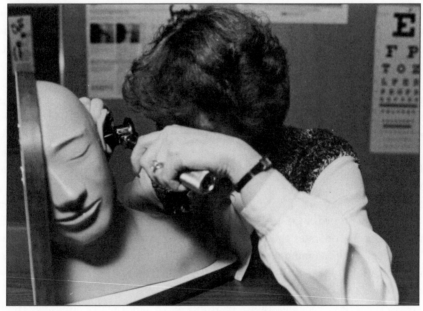

"Other than not hearing well, how do you feel?"
"Nursing . . .The uniqueness of the program is matched by the delivery."

14) Information on mass communication department came from Chairman Hawk; indeed, Hawk wrote essentially the entire section. His manuscript had a brief cover letter, the entire letter reading, "Well, here it is in all its fame and glory. As you might imagine, there are a lot of man-hours involved in this document and I'm not sure if it tells the entire story. Good luck with editing, and let me know if there is any information I can provide." His information seemed more than adequate, and as to editing, well, who is one to edit the script of those who are in the business?

Minnesota. In 1977 the Minnesota Higher Education Coordinating Board, an agency of the state legislature, issued a special report recommending facilitating an improved program in general for nursing preparation and specifically recommended that Bemidji State establish a nursing major to better serve its geographical region. The HECB noted that 21 percent of those in nursing in Minnesota were prepared at the baccalaureate level, but only 12 percent of the nurses in Bemidji's service region were baccalaureate nursing graduates.

Despite the immediacy of the need for change, virtually nothing happened until the fortuitous—and coincidental—arrival of Joelyn Scriba in Bemidji in 1979. Her husband, Robert, accepted a position at BSU in the theatre department, coming from Jamestown College, North Dakota, where Mrs. Scriba had chaired a nursing program there; she brought a background of experience immediately recognized by BSU officials. Still, not until 1982 was Joelyn Scriba appointed on a full-time basis to develop the requested and needed program at Bemidji State. At this point, more meetings and coordination were begun with area nursing personnel in an attempt to work out a final curriculum that involved collaboration among 12 post-secondary institutions (almost all technical and community colleges) in northern Minnesota. The numbers involved were enough to make the final outcome difficult to attain, but perseverance paid off. When a curriculum was finally agreed on by year's end, it received overwhelming support from area nurses, nursing agencies, two area health systems, and two health consortia groups. On to the legislature for financial support.

Following the necessary formal approvals from all official agencies involved, a line-item-funding approval for a nursing program was granted Bemidji State in May of 1983. Next came the hiring of two more nursing instructors, Diane Rose and Riki Scheela, who joined Ms. Scriba, and the first classes were offered in winter quarter of 1983. At last the program was off and running, and the first graduates completed the major in the summer of 1985. (An additional staff member, Jane Carlstrom, joined the teaching staff in 1984; in 1989, Elizabeth Bridston replaced Carlstrom and was herself succeeded by Ranae Womack in 1991.) The program has run effectively since '84, resulting in job placements of 100 percent. Would that all programs could do so well.

The Bemidji State program is unique in that it offers only upper division work. It builds on nursing preparation already completed. Each student who enrolls must already (1) have completed a program for registered nurse graduates of diploma and/or associate degree levels; (2) be licensed to practice as a registered nurse in Minnesota or be a graduate with license pending; (3) show evidence of completion of a minimum of 30 quarter hours in non-nursing courses, including 10 quarter hours in science and mathematics, and 10 quarter hours representing social and behavioral science; (4) show evidence of completion of lower division credits in nursing; and (5) show evidence of a cumulative grade-point average of at least 2.50 (on a 4.0 system).

As indicated, the Bemidji State nursing program builds upon preparation already completed in previous training. Those students who are accepted into the program enroll in a variety of courses that include mandated nursing classes as well as a few selected non-nursing classes. Of the 66 credits for the major, 13 represent elective courses in many disciplines. All of the above are meant to carry through their stated goal:

"The . . . program aims to provide the diploma and associate degree graduates with a broadened educational base for the improvement of nursing practice, preparation for meeting future health care needs, preparation for graduate study in nursing, and an opportunity for continued professional development."

How times have changed. Prior to 1983, the only Bemidji State "program" for nursing was a kind of pre-nursing suggested curriculum of two years, after which the student would transfer to some other college. Now that's reversed; students come back to Bemidji State after some training somewhere else. The whole thing falls under the rubric of regional service and the supposition that that is what Bemidji State is all about. Approximately 20 students complete the nursing curriculum each year. The anticipated enrollment for 1994-95 is 60 majors.

The uniqueness of the program is matched by how the program is delivered. In noting the requirements to get in, it is obvious that the interested applicants are not 18-year-olds just out of high school. Almost all of the participants maintain employment in nursing while pursuing the degree. On the average, nursing students have had to commute about 100 miles one way to get to the classes on the BSU campus. Result: classes on campus are scheduled in "block times," taking up a half day and sometimes a full day, but only one day a week. Again in response to location and need, some classes are offered off-campus at sites most convenient for attendance, and two classes have been delivered via interactive audioteleconference to seven sites simultaneously, representing over 50,000 square miles. That's adopting and adapting to North Country territory.

SOCIOLOGY
WHAT A DIFFERENCE A . . . DECADE MAKES

Among the more appealing programs at Bemidji State the past quarter century have been those in sociology and the related area of social services. Perhaps these growing areas reflected the shifting societal needs in that same time period. Whatever the explanation, these diverse BSU programs, revolving around that rubric of social services, showed increasing student appeal, especially for those who would be given the acronym of SOTA, Students Older Than Average. The core of the programs was sociology. That discipline has come a long way in 50 years, evolving from virtually nothing to become a major program. For its first half century, sociology was attached to some other program, usually in the division of social studies, and it remained a one-person department, of sorts, with Dr. Mabel Parker (1924-63). Even when it moved to two persons (Ed Stokes, Ken Skogen) in the mid-1960s, it still made the less than positive category of "service area," filling the needs of general education or other departments' requirements for majors and minors, but having nothing of its own. It was an orphan waiting to be picked up by someone else. Then the changes began. A third sociologist (Leland Blazer) was added in 1968 and an anthropologist (Alan Brew) in 1969 to be a part of the new Indian studies program launched that year—and to offer an anthropology minor. Several part-time persons from the Beltrami County Welfare Department also began to teach classes, this in response to a request from the administration, via demands from the region, for development of a social work major. Students flocked in. This major was among the first in Minnesota to be accredited (1974) by the Council on Social Work Education. Again in response to the administration's request, as well as a regional demand, a criminal justice major and minor were developed and approved in 1973. Even more students came forward to fill this interest and need. In the same year faculty from sociology worked with faculty from psychology to develop an interdisciplinary community service major. Once more it became a program of considerable student interest and has evolved into the present (1994) applied psychology major.

In 1980, anthropology merged again with sociology, and that year the title was changed to the current designation: Department of Social Relations and Services. The membership consists of 12 full-time faculty, including four in sociology, four in social work, three in criminal justice, and one in anthropology. The ex-orphan, sociology, has indeed come a long way.[15]

SPACE STUDIES

The subject is old, very old; the program at Bemidji State is new, brand new. Modern day space exploration and the question of its continuation is moot only in the sense that scientists ask not "Should we go?" but instead ask "When?" The only constraint upon space exploration activities is budget, not desire, according to those many dedicated scientists steeped in a passionate interest in space studies.

The subject still reaches out in the nightly television news to all Americans who can still get interested in space exploration, although there is less of the fanatical enthrallment with outer space probing in the 1990s than was seen in the 1960s. But space studies is wide-reaching in personnel involved, and it is so much more than moon shots and astronauts because so many varieties of persons and positions are involved in the general program. The word about its multiplicity needs to get out now. Also, by 1980 it was apparent to the National Aeronautics Space Agency that more than just narrowly-trained space scientists or engineers were needed for the future. NASA employs people in business, law, psychology,

15) Information supplied by Dr. David Nordlie, who came to Bemidji State in 1970 as chair of the sociology department. There is no coincidence between his coming and the subsequent departmental growth and changes for the better. Hired the following year as the first full-time social work faculty member was Lyle Lauber, a former social worker himself, who worked and planned together with Nordlie. Movers and shakers, both of them. Progressive reforms have also included the M.A. in applied behavioral science. There have been some recent changes in the department, of course; e.g., criminal justice is now (1994) a separate department. Also a Center for Social Research began in 1989, and currently a sociologist is serving on a small committee to develop a new peace studies program.

medicine, sociology, history, and many other professions. On the BSU campus, some science professors believed strongly that as a premier undergraduate state institution, the school should produce knowledgeable graduates capable of working in almost any space related industry. Target groups for inclusion within this career work force were women, minorities and the disabled.

In response to the general need for more and more broadly trained persons in space exploration, BSU, through the College of Social and Natural Sciences, joined with the University of Minnesota and Augsburg College to form the Minnesota Space Grant Consortium in 1991; the three schools received a substantial four-year grant from NASA to inaugurate space studies programs on their respective campuses. Each school that was selected as a NASA grantee was free to develop programs that fit its individual needs and character. Bemidji State developed a unique academic program known as the space studies minor, an interdisciplinary program which provides an undergraduate emphasis that fits with almost any major field of study, whether that major be psychology or physics. Another goal of the BSU program is to prepare future public school teachers to be more knowledgeable about space exploration.

Bemidji's space minor is unique among those in the University as well as the college scene nationally. Most schools participating in NASA-sponsored programs (one consortium in each state is recognized and funded by NASA) focus on outreach to the area K-12 schools, have only a one- or two-course introductory offering in their general curriculum, or have an established graduate education program in space science or aerospace. Bemidji's plan seeks to provide a broader based, pragmatic educational experience that will result in increased employment opportunities for students and/or to make public school teachers more intelligent, understanding, and supportive of one of mankind's most intriguing, ongoing mysteries, outer space.[16]   It's new, it's different, and it works.

THEATRE—ALL YEAR 'ROUND

The last years of World War II and the immediate postwar years saw extraordinary changes in Bemidji State's theatre programs. The exploding college population brought a flood of new talent for ambitious shows, and an attractive new speech-drama minor stabilized interest for many students. The minor was an excellent fit with other humanities students who planned to teach in secondary schools.

BSTC then had a one-person theatre "staff," and even that single professor could not devote full-time to drama and speech; he or she also had to teach classes in Freshman English. The turnover in staff between 1944 and 1948—(in order)

16) Information on space studies minor at BSU supplied primarily by Dr. John O. Annexstad, the BSU space studies director and associate director of the Minnesota consortium. As a former employee of NASA who worked directly in the Johnson Space Center, Houston, Texas, before coming to Minnesota, Annexstad knew his way around scientists and space shots and consortia and grants very well. He is a promoter, a go-getter, and a devotee of the program and BSU was fortunate to land him on campus (where he is officially an associate professor of geology). The basic core of the space studies minor consists of a two-quarter sequence of four credits called Introduction to Planetology I and II. The third required course is a mini-thesis or capstone course that covers a space-related theme within the student's area of interest. To round out the preparation, each student then selects 16 credits from a long list of interdisciplinary courses.

Elizabeth Anderson, Marie Robinson, Betty Jane Wenzel, and Earle Winters (he stayed until 1955)—made for artistic variety but also some uncertainties.

The major problem for theatre, however, was the lack of a suitable performance space. For major shows with large casts, the College used the Bemidji High School auditorium, but its cavernous size and inadequate acoustics were problems. Casts had to learn to project excessively to be understood, but in the auditorium's "dead section," even loud projection was inaudible. The only performing space at the College was the assembly room located on the main floor of Deputy Hall. Although an intimate space for theatre, it did not have adequate staging; the room could not even be made totally dark.

Notwithstanding the performing space problem, the number, quality and variety of productions in the late '40s was impressive. Marie Robinson initiated plays for children; high interest in the shows necessitated the busing of area students to see the productions in the high school auditorium. Wenzel continued the tradition with plays such as Pinocchio, and Winters followed with similar shows with and for children. These productions had strong audience appeal; many of the performers were either in or had graduated from the local high school's excellent theatre program.

A major change in BSTC's theatre came in 1950 with the construction of the school's first post-war building, the Laboratory School. Kindergarten through ninth grade students moved out of Deputy Hall, vacating significant space. The top floor classroom which had been used by the junior high classes was converted into a small theatre with a proscenium opening of 25 feet. The theatre space was intimate all right, with seating for only about 100 spectators on metal chairs. (Because this was one of the larger rooms on campus, it was also used as a classroom and the meeting place for the many faculty meetings President Sattgast called.) Director Winters was eventually able to "own" the stage-space entirely, allowing great savings in time, effort and materials involved in the moves into and out of the high school auditorium. Still, it took 10 more years for the space to be fully equipped with adequate lighting and sound.

The enrollment stability of students interested in drama—and most stayed for four years—produced an increasingly skillful acting pool. The staff person, however, had to have considerable endurance as well as theatre skill. There was no assistance from trained staff, and the director was responsible for every aspect of a production from staging and acting through setting design, carpentry and painting, makeup, sound and lighting.

The periodic presentation of a play by Shakespeare always represented a high point in the seasons for several years. Director Betty Wenzel staged A Midsummer Night's Dream and toured to area high schools. Director Winters produced Othello, starring Wes Balk, one of the outstanding arts graduates of the University for several decades. Director Marchand presented Macbeth, again casting Balk in the lead role. While Marchand was on leave in 1958, his replacement for the year, Robert Copeland, directed the Shakespearean comedy, Twelfth Night. Such productions—well before any area TV—were well attended by the community and students from area high schools, something which spoke well for the literary sophistication of the region's schools.[17]

ENTER PAUL BUNYAN PLAYHOUSE
The start of the summer Paul Bunyan Playhouse in 1951 in a recreation hall at Ruttger's Birchmont Resort, located five miles north of town on Lake Bemidji, was a major impetus for change in theatre student training and in the College's support and attitude towards its own program. The financial assistance from the College to the playhouse in its first decade was the single most significant factor in its stability and growth. Director Winters had in 1949 envisioned a summer stock theater made up of BSTC personnel and operated by the College, but ultimately it was an outside director and a board of local supporters who founded the operation and who have governed it, from 1951 until the present (1994). It is the state's longest running summer theatre, something of considerable pride to the community which has supported it steadily. In 1992, the board, with private donations, purchased the Chief movie theatre in downtown Bemidji and moved its operation there.[18]

The summer theatre gave wide opportunities for many Bemidji State players to work with professionals. Another pattern of summer productions found the first show of the long season directed by a Bemidji State theatre staff person, with an all-local cast, many of whom were college students. The evolving summer playhouse attracted growing and loyal audiences, and the school's summer course offerings included credits for work—and even internships—at the theatre. This became an attractive choice for non-theatre students as well as "drama kids." The entire community has continued to benefit from this special form of summer-and-winter live entertainment; a real "plum" among the pines.

NEW DIRECTOR, LIKES JOB, STAYS 37 YEARS
A 1948 graduate of Bemidji State, Louis Marchand, took Winter's place in 1955, and he liked it well enough to stay until his retirement in 1992. Soon after his arrival, a speech-drama major was approved (in 1957), and the next year Marchand got approval and funds to renovate the performing space in Deputy Hall as well as purchase up-to-date lighting. Despite these improvements, a major handicap for shows on campus continued to be the small stage along with the

---

17) In the past 10 years, BSU's theatre directors have less frequently chosen Shakespeare, primarily because of concerns about sufficient acting rosters. Dr. Kay Robinson produced Much Ado About Nothing in 1987, and in the spring of 1993, Robert Scriba staged a powerful production of King Lear. Afterward he expressed his great pleasure with the cast and the performances, but was concerned about the audiences' limited understanding of the play; a total audience of over 1,000 attended King Lear. The department planned for 1994 a production of The Tempest to incorporate Chinese theatre elements.
18) The decision to leave Ruttger's Resort, a summer symbol of vacation, after 40 some years was not an easy one to make. However, after that agonizing decision, the board effectively conducted a major fund-raiser and secured the needed funds. With almost all volunteer labor—and contributed supplies—the old movie theater was revamped with total facilities which won over the initial doubters. Furthermore, whereas the Ruttger's facilities were used only in the summers, the new theater downtown gets used year 'round for a variety of cultural events.

location of the theatre-shop-storage facility in the Deputy Hall basement, three flights below the performing space. Lots of tired leg muscles resulted from this arrangement.

Theatre Director (for 37 years) Louie Marchand and Friend
"Theatre on 3rd floor . . . shop-storage in the basement . . . tired leg muscles."

As the number of students increased in the Sixties, additional staff came to the program: James Ertresvaag became half-time English and half-time speech and drama in 1961; Joan Reynolds was hired in 1963 with responsibility for the speech communication portion of the program, and Louis Marchand was relieved of the Freshman English courses he had been teaching. Added help to the department came in 1965 with the hiring of a full-time technical theatre person; by 1970 the speech-theatre staff had increased to four full-time and two part-time teachers, including a speech therapist, Mildred Pedersen.

The "Great Day" for theatre came with the opening of the fine arts building, Bangsberg Fine Arts Complex, in the fall of 1971. The students and staff who moved from the out-of-date, out-of-space alleged theatre on third floor Deputy marveled at what they found in Bangsberg: A Main Theatre (seating 290), a Downstairs Theatre (seating 100), make-up rooms, costuming storage and work places, a scenery shop with wood and metal working equipment, sound and lighting booths, light-hanging areas, a fly gallery and overhead counterweight systems—in short, all that a theatre-training facility should have to prepare students for theatre work. Even if it took several years before all the glitches were worked out of the various systems, students and staff loved and appreciated all of it. Marchand directed the dedicatory production of <u>I Never Sang for My Father</u> in May, 1972.

The production had challenging difficulties presented by last-minute lighting installations. During the opening night performance, all the lights mysteriously went out—but the cast members continued their roles and dialogue, as though nothing had happened. The audience determined that the lights-out bit was all part of the play and was not aware that anything had gone wrong. Few in the theatre were happier to have the lights suddenly come back on again, however, than director Marchand.

The new facilities at Bangsberg found the two principal programs located there—theatre and music—collaborating regularly on large-cast musical productions, from fun musicals such as L'il Abner to classical fun musicals such as The Marriage of Figaro. The '70s saw a wide variety of presentations, from serious shows for adults to spectacular fully-staged plays for children such as Treasure Island.

The close relationship between the College and the summer stock playhouse began to change in the late '70s as changing enrollment patterns eroded the summer workshop population. Reductions in funding meant reductions for school support to the playhouse, and by 1980 the summer theater kept only a modest connection by using the College's technical theatre person as its administrative officer. But the good news was the growing financial success of the summer theater which thus became less dependent on financial transfusions from the College. The summer theatre, too, had grown up and gone out on its own.

The 1970s saw a greatly varied theatre production schedule as well as regular curricular adjustments as the demand for secondary teachers in Minnesota schools declined. The B.A. in speech and drama was more attractive to students who planned to continue in graduate school for advanced degrees. Many students sought more extensive technical theatre training and upon graduation moved directly into full-time theatre jobs. Other graduates of the theatre program found the training an excellent foundation for a variety of jobs in the arts, student services, creative advertising, media communications, and publishing.

The opportunity to present plays for children on a well-equipped stage found an annual series of longer plays such as Pinnochio, and area school children were bused to the theatre mornings and afternoons for an entire week. A small touring company also visited some of the region's schools with plays that could be staged in elementary gyms.

The end of the 1970s and the early 1980s saw a cluster of retirements: the University speech therapist, Mildred Pedersen, who had also taught public speaking and English as a Second Language to international students, left in 1979—she was not replaced. James Ertresvaag retired in 1981, and the department found an able replacement in Kay Robinson. Joan Reynolds retired in 1983 after 20 years, but she was not replaced. The various financial crises that confronted the University and the entire System in the early 1980s resulted in significant staff reductions both in full-time and in part-time personnel.

In 1974, University theatre had seen the departure of George Terhune, the technical director and designer who had been responsible for the concept and planning of the new theatre facilities. He was followed by David Weiss who stayed for several years; Robert Scriba became technical director and scenographer in 1979, taking on responsibility for the production facilities and equipment. It had been obvious to all the staff and the University that the lighting and sound equipment in both of the performance theaters were failing, and efforts began to purchase replacements. Eventually, the theatre's sound systems were replaced and the lighting control systems were brought up to contemporary national standards in 1990. Repeated reductions in financial support continue to handicap the theatre program in the 1990s, and with fewer full-time staff than the department has had since the early 1960s, the outlook for the future is uncertain.

The wall outside the main theatre in Bangsberg Hall is covered with pictures portraying scenes and cast members from previous Bemidji State theatre productions. Whether viewers see them as history or nostalgia, artifacts or art forms, they serve as reminders that there is no special university unless it has special theatre productions. Theatre holds up the looking glass for the world to see. The world is, after all—as the Bard said—"a stage."

The Eye (and Ear) Catchers

No college anywhere operates in seclusion. Although certain individuals and entire departments within a school may feel secluded at times, even the most remote and esoteric field does peep out semi-publicly, if just a tiny bit. However, many, if not most, programs at a college get little publicity because the public interest is just not there for basic, if not ho-hum programs.

Some academic departments seem to prefer anonymity. Not only are they disinterested but also uninterested in receiving public exposure via newspapers and/or television as to what they have been doing. They, like the late Greta Garbo, "vant to be alone." Conversely, other academic areas desire public exposure but do not get it, which may be unfair, but their feelings are not ameliorated by the philosophical line of President John F. Kennedy, who admitted that "life is unfair."

At Bemidji State, "life is unfair" to a variety of persons and programs who have received little if any public attention, let alone acclamation, over the years, despite their obvious successes. One which comes to mind is a small physics-engineering program developed primarily by Dr. Ron Anderson; this department appeals to a talented few students (a half-dozen grads a year) who end up getting into the best graduate schools and employed by super science industries like Argonne Laboratories and McDonnell Douglas Corporation. Yet that is not the stuff of headlines.

Industrial technology (the phrase "industrial arts" is moving into dustbin terminology, soon to join "manual training") has had, among several successful options, a model building program so special and rare as to be partially duplicated perhaps by only two other colleges in the nation. But that too fits no segment in television news features.

The accounting faculty has had so many successful students "breezing through" the national C.P.A. examinations (some 60 between 1984 and 1992) that the accomplishment could not be publicly ignored, especially when one young man (Todd Sladky) in 1984 ranked second among all 70,000 national exam takers in the country. Indeed, this acclaim led to Bemidji State taking out a full page advertisement in Time magazine to extol the virtues of the school in general and the accounting program in particular. Nevertheless, neither the local nor regional media leaped forth to herald the event, and the happy C.P.A.s would have been ignored except for submitted articles on said subject sent out by the school's news bureau. Life is unfair for the numbers-crunchers, too.

What catches the general public's attention needs to be feature material, something show biz-like, maybe competitive, perhaps splashy, certainly of human interest and appealing to the eye and ear; "newsy" or entertaining things that the college offers which the public likes to read about, and maybe go personally to see—and hear. Enter the two Bemidji State programs that most fill and fulfill the public's desires for entertainment: music and sports. Those two areas most catch the eyes and ears of John and Jane Public.

MUSIC

In all American institutions of higher learning, music deserves its rightful place in the curriculum and in the social and cultural life on the campus and in the community. Performing in a music group gives students socially and esthetically satisfying outlets for their personalities. Furthermore, music reaches into the community and beyond when the college bands, orchestras and choruses perform.

History is people; the history of a college music department is the story of people working together to develop one of the fine arts essential to a well-rounded curriculum. The study of music is a strict academic discipline, but in a college community it reaches beyond the classroom. A community with a college or university is the most fortunate of towns or cities.

THE START . . .

Bemidji State first opened its doors to students in 1919. Shortly thereafter, in 1922, the first president, Manfred Deputy, hired the school's first music teacher. Only one person would be in a music education position for the next 15 years. During this period, this lone teacher had three major responsibilities: 1) teaching music to the children in the Laboratory School, 2) supervising the student teachers who were practice teaching the music segment of their program, and 3) providing an opportunity for the college students who wanted to participate in performing groups. As to the last point, by the end of the 1920s, the school had a glee club made up women, but a few men joined them on occasion as soloists.[1]

1) Dorothy McMillan, who was the first music teacher, was hired in 1922. She served the school two years and then Harriet Johnson replaced her, staying from 1924 to 1930. Inez Donaldson was the third teacher, in the years 1931-36. Source of information: an unpublished, 17-page mimeographed personal history of the music department (1919-72) written by Carl O. Thompson in 1972, soon after his retirement. The first 14 pages are in narrative form. The remaining pages update the departmental changes and list the personnel by category, e.g., choral, piano, etc. and the year each person was hired (from 1919-92). Copy available by contacting the music department office, Bangsberg Hall. All quotes of Thompson in the text are taken from his personal history. Thompson was gallant to omit the known fact that his predessor, Ms. Donaldson, was given to fainting at the end of each of her concerts.

Going 'Forties Style' at the Annual 'Remember When' Concerts
"Jazz studies program . . . it's pure nostalgia for many gray-haired in the audience."

Music became a part of every all-student convocation program under Deputy, and thus all students had some music in their lives. The song book used included hymns and folk songs. This all-school singing came both at the beginning and at the end of the twice-a-week convocation programs. Student creativity in music began early. In the school's second year of operation, as part of a song-writing contest, the song "Hail to Thee, Bemidji College" was composed, with music by Raymond Nelson and words by Marie Krogseng. This college song would be sung frequently at a variety of school functions for 25 years and remains one of the official school songs, albeit little known to students and staff after 1950.[2]

Despite the school changing in 1921 from a normal school to a teachers college, not until 1937 did Deputy make any changes in the music offerings so that the secondary field of educational training could get equal emphasis with the elementary. In 1937 he hired not one but two people to teach music, the aforementioned Carl Thompson (see footnote 1) for vocal work and Milton Dieterich for band and orchestra. Because of them, that fall brought three Bemidji State musical firsts: an *a capella* choir, a full college concert band, and a College-community orchestra. Moreover, uniforms were purchased for the band and for the first time there was band music at athletic events.[3]

2) See next page for copy of words and music to "Hail to Thee, Bemidji College." In a nostalgic reminder of the postwar days, a '48 graduate, Dr. Perry Patterson, sang "Hail to Thee, Bemidji College" at the alumni reunion homecoming luncheon in 1991. He later put the song on cassette tape for the school archives. Dr. Patterson, a Bemidji native, retired in 1992 from the drama department of Sioux Falls College. He had earlier written a tribute to Carl Thompson which appeared in a 1983 Bulletin of the Alumni Association: "We knew him as an energetic and dedicated teacher and choir director. In his teaching he was a kind, soft spoken, almost shy man; a true gentleman, highly sensitive to every nuance in the classroom. He had the nicest way of telling one that the placement was wrong on the high note.... Yes, Carl O. Thompson was a beloved director. He cared about students, the fine arts, the College, the community and the role of things that are really important in the universe. His influence was profound in the lives of so many over the decades." "Hail to Thee..." was also sung at the 1994 BSU graduation as part of the 75th Anniversary celebration.

3) Thompson mentioned in his brief, informal history that Dieterich was a fine cello player and his wife a good violinist. With a student pianist named Katherine Gennes, they formed a trio which performed widely in the area. Thompson went along as bass soloist and Professor A.C. Clark narrated, as well as presented separate talks as part of a general program "in a great number of area high schools." Thompson concluded that these programs "had much to do with the sudden rise in enrollment at the College." Thompson had previously sung in the St. Olaf choir under famous director F. Melius Christiansen.

Hail to Thee, Bemidji College

Words by Marie Krogsang

Music by Raymond Nelson

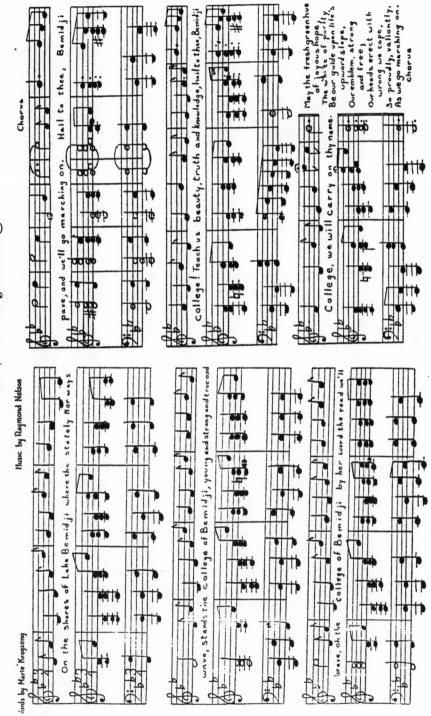

As to the choir's start, Thompson observed that "talent was somewhat limited and the tenor section had to be made up largely of baritones," but nevertheless the College choir presented the first Christmas concert, and that concert has continued annually since 1937.

During the spring of the same 1937-38 school year, the Bemidji Civic Oratorio Society was formed to sing the Messiah. The College-community orchestra joined with the College choir and choirs from Bemidji and the surrounding areas in singing this popular oratorio. Again the pattern began of an oratorio being presented on campus every year, with variations of selections; most frequently performed besides the Messiah were Mendelssohn's Elijah and the Creation by Haydn.

In that first year this two-man department also established the first music major of 38 credits. That year the department was even allowed a part-time person to teach piano, and one piano-teaching part-timer continued until the war years.

The war years? Let Carl Thompson's line summarize them: "The war years were lonesome years on campus." From his department, his sole compatriot Dieterich left to join the USO, the United States Service Organization, leaving the reduced band and tiny orchestra to be led by part-time directors from the local high school teaching staff, Earl Kerns and Elmer Christianson. The a capella choir went back to being a girls' glee club.[4] When World War II ended, there came some understated words from Thompson, "There was general rejoicing on campus when the war was declared over."

A "RENAISSANCE MAN" ARRIVES

With the war ending, wrote Thompson, "Men were turning to the campus, much to the delight of the girls. The returning veterans were serious about their academic work."

And Thompson was serious about building his music department. Of two new men hired for the 1946-47 school year, one—Ronald Gearman—remained until his retirement in 1977. Gearman had recently been discharged from the U.S. Navy and at the time he accepted an appointment to Bemidji State the position was not full-time. As an inducement to come, he was given a free apartment in one of the barracks buildings in exchange for managing this ersatz dormitory. As a further enticement, he would be permitted to keep the fees received for teaching piano lessons. By the time he arrived on campus, however, the financial situation had improved so that he was hired on a full-time basis to teach piano and music theory (but he did live in the barracks one year, all he could stand).

Gearman possessed several special skills. Not only did he play classical piano to public performance level, he also tuned pianos and built harpsichords; he

---

4) Of his glee club experiences, Thompson wrote, "One spring day the glee club went to Grand Rapids, Minnesota, to give a concert. While they were there, a snowstorm developed. I was fortunate to have Dr. Clark along as a manager and public relations director. It took the two of us until five o'clock the next morning to get the girls back home as we spent most of the night shoveling the cars out of snow drifts." Not incidentally, Clark and Thompson built homes next to each other on Lake Bemidji, north of the College along Birchmont Drive, when that area was empty, if not wilderness. At the time of their building, both men took a ribbing for locating homes "way out there in the sticks."

Beaver Fight Song

"Go Bemidji Beavers..."

would later be responsible for developing a minor in piano technology and he wrote a book on the subject.

In his teaching of music theory, Gearman stressed creativity and demonstrated as much. In 1947 he and his class collectively wrote the words and music to the <u>Go, Bemidji Beavers</u> fight song in one class period in an advanced harmony class (the vets could not abide the old school song). The catchy pep tune became an immediate hit and has remained as <u>the</u> school song until the very present, even if Beavers in all decades since never did learn all the right words (see previous page).[5]

(The other music man hired in 1946 along with Gearman was also a victim of the housing shortage in town. To induce his coming to Bemidji State, he was given a small, makeshift apartment in the Power House on campus. Maybe that's why he only stayed one year.)

The creativity of Bemidji State music students showed not only in remote classrooms but also publicly. Each spring, from 1948 through 1966, an annual Creative Music Convocation was held in Memorial Hall. Compositions presented were composed, arranged, rehearsed and conducted or performed by students as part of their regular work in music theory classes. (With Thompson in charge of all convocations, scheduling the above was no problem.)

BEMIDJI MUSIC GOES NATIONAL

The year 1948 goes down as an important year in the history of the music department. Prior to that time, discussions had been held regarding the start of a summer music camp for junior and senior high school students. Then came action. Selected to organize and promote such a camp was the new (he had come the year before) band and orchestra conductor, Maurice Callahan, who also discussed the future camp with townspeople, like Bill Bender.

The music camp idea proved to be productive, and more. It took off! The first Summer Music Clinic attracted 100 students; 25 years later it attracted 1,300 students. It evolved from a one-week camp to two; from just band to all facets of music (band, orchestra, choir, piano). In the next 25 years the clinic served over 12,000 students and directors and became a positive force in the development of music education in the state. Each clinic session ended with the grand public performance, and these concerts attracted standing-room-only crowds in Memorial Hall. Some big national names in band music came to Bemidji in those halcyon summers: Paul Yoder, Vaclav Nelhybel, Glenn Cliffe Bainum, Lt. Col. Arnold Gabriel, Lt. Col. William Santelmann, Charles Minelli, Clifton Williams, John

5) Gearman represented a true Renaissance Man. Besides the aesthetic, refined, advanced musical theory he knew and loved so well, he was equally good as a car motor mechanic. How many men with doctorates in music (Columbia University, 1953) could also serve as an auto mechanic in a General Motors garage? (Gearman did repair work on the side for his friend Buster Spaulding. Then again, they had much in common in that Buster had—and played—a grand piano in his auto showroom.) Gearman also built houses, many of them. He developed property on Lake Beltrami, built a road in, and sold lots of lots. At this writing, German and his wife Millie spend their summers in Bemidji and their winters in Gainesville, Florida; he likes the cultural things that go with a university town. After retiring he finished and published his book, <u>Piano Tuning, Regulating and Repairing</u>. In 1993 he donated one of his handmade harpsichords to the music department.

Paynter, and Alfred Reed, to name only a few of a veritable Who's Who in American Band Music.

But the real work horses and the unsung heroes of all the successful musical extravaganzas have been the Bemidji State band directors who were also the camp directors: Callahan (1948-52); Edgar Gangware (1953-66); Theodore Thorson (1967-83); and several directors since 1984.[6]

FIFTIES FIGURE IN BEMIDJI STATE MUSIC

In the fall of 1952, Edgar B. Gangware became director of bands, replacing Callahan. His specialty was percussion, and his percussion ensembles became well known through their performances in many public schools. It was emblematic of success that Gangware's percussion groups were honored by invitations to play at Minnesota Music Educators conventions in Minneapolis. This was clear evidence of their success, and his.

Gangware's wife Euana, called "Debbie," was a fine musician also. What made her reputation were her solo performances on the harp. She also taught part-time in the department as a piano instructor.[7]

In 1956 Floraine Nielsen became supervisor of music in the Laboratory School and teacher of elementary music methods for College students. Aware of the need for new music methods, she spent a year studying music in Europe (1963-64) and returned with new information on and great enthusiasm for what would be called "The Orff and Kodaly Methods" of teaching music to children. Her enthusiasm over these creative forms of music teaching led her to co-author a book on these methods with a University of Wisconsin musician.

In 1957, President Sattgast agreed to add an orchestra string specialist to the music faculty, and Howard Mickens, a former member of the Chicago Symphony, was selected. Mickens, who had a delightful sense of humor, was a lively teacher and director and the orchestra made steady progress under his direction.

The department moved beyond "the basics" in 1959 when Noel Stevens was hired as the first woodwind specialist. He paved the way for the hiring of a

---

6) Information on summer band clinics taken primarily from two unpublished documents written by Betty Masoner, who has been a part of every summer clinic since 1948 as a percussion teacher. Her first "book" is a 41-pager entitled, "A History of the Bemidji State College Music Clinic, 1948-72." The second is 23 pages long and appropriately called "A Continuing History of the Bemidji State University Music Camp; From the 25th to the 35th Year, 1973-82." Both documents are filled with voluminous information on all of the camps, their directors, outside artists, applied faculties and music areas taught, concert pieces performed, and much more. These documents are available from the BSU music office. Her two histories should answer almost anyone's questions about this once-successful summer program. Unfortunately, that last sentence suggests the need for an update, and that takes some of the shine away. Obviously there were these wonderful, golden years for the music camps, but they did not (could not?) last forever. Even in 1982, Masoner wrote in her last page of narration (p. 13), "On the national scene the country is suffering from serious economic problems referred to by some as a recession. . . . On the state scene the economic problems are even greater than the national average. All of this might have an effect on the camp. . . ." And it did, along with side factors of a changing teenage culture, and a few BSU music men and women simply wearying after years and years of extra efforts. The 1992 summer camp brought less than 200 students to the clinic, and only 130 came in 1993.

7) Physically, Ed Gangware was a hulking bear-of-a-man who was wont to say that he better represented the stereotypical wrestling coach than a band director. Although an assertive person, he could also laugh at the thought of audiences wanting/ not wanting to go to a night of "drum solos"—but many did want to go because his percussion groups were that good. Unlike the hundreds of faculty who came to Bemidji and later left (Gangware left in 1966), he kept a home in town, a large cottage on Lake Bemidji, directly across from Pine Hall residence hall. Edgar and Euana planned to return after his retirement from a college he taught at near Chicago. He retired in (1992) but tragically, Debbie Gangware died in a car accident soon afterwards. At this writing, his Bemidji home still stands empty. (A sad last minute addition. Ed Gangware died in late February, 1994, at age 70, from a heart attack.)

brass specialist, Thomas Swanson. All in all, the 1950s were good for Bemidji State Music, and the 1960s would be even better![8]

SURGING SIXTIES

With the rapidly expanding numbers of students in the 1960s came the commensurate expansion of the music department, along with changes in personnel.

Felix Spooner, who had spent most of his life in the South, came to Bemidji in 1963 as orchestra director. He made ongoing contributions as a string bass teacher and as a performer. He commuted regularly to Duluth to be the principal string bass player in the Duluth Symphony Orchestra as well as playing in small combos in and around Bemidji. With his unique experiences in New Orleans playing with jazz groups, he made popular—like 150 in a single class—the music department's general education course called "Folk, Jazz, and Rock"; he knew them well.[9]

Another top musician arriving in 1963 was Fulton Gallagher, an opera specialist. He had been a district winner of the Metropolitan Opera auditions and a soloist with the Indiana University Opera Theatre before coming to Bemidji. Yearly productions of operas on campus followed his arrival, with productions including Mozart's Marriage of Figaro, Bizet's Carmen, and Gilbert and Sullivan's Mikado. Eventually (1975) he developed the almost too-popular (tickets impossible to procure) "Opera Night," an evening starting with a gourmet supper and featuring a wide variety of selections from operas, sung by his students. It is opera for people who don't like opera.[10]

By 1965 the department determined the need for a specialist in brass instruments. The aforementioned Tom Swanson was added to the staff, and oh, how he loved to play the trombone! Under his guidance, the brass sections of the band and orchestra showed great improvement, or so wrote Carl Thompson, who added, "He is known as a 'taskmaster' by his students, but they respect him and willingly work under his teaching to become outstanding brass performers."[11]

Theodore Thorson became the band director in 1966. Wrote Thompson about Thorson, "Dr. Thorson is a very friendly and personable man who makes friends easily, and is a great asset as the administrator for the summer music clinics.

8) In this section, names of those who came and left after a year or two are not included.

9) Spooner had eclectic tastes in music, including a love for barbershop-style singing. He both directed the barbershop chorus in town and sang baritone for some 20 years in a local quartet called The Timbertones. His wife Lois played the viola and she also gave piano lessons. They loved to travel in their camper, and Spooner chose in the late 1980s to go two-thirds time, taking winter quarters off for time down South. He took full retirement in 1991.

10) Gallagher experienced a number of different jobs, if not careers. He was elected department chairman in 1971, following Carl Thompson's retirement, and in 1980 he became the dean of the division of fine arts and humanities. In the early '80s he took a leave of absence from Bemidji State to become a vice president for development at a private women's college in Pennsylvania, Chatham College, but he returned two years later to Bemidji, choosing to become a classroom teacher once again, something in which he excelled. (His enthusiasm for music has been infectious; he may be a rare figure who plays wonderful piano while standing up.)

11) Comments written on p. 7 of Thompson's unpublished history of the music department. Swanson continued in the department filling many roles, from department chairman to orchestra conductor to band director. At this writing, 1994, he is the revered taskmaster-band director (since 1977), with the interesting and useful style at concert-time of turning to his audience and "explaining" certain selections to the uninitiated. His whole family is musical: His wife Bonnie teaches elementary school music; she also plays horn in the orchestra. His son is a high school band director; his daughter is studying opera in Boston.

The quality of band music has improved under his direction. . . ."[12]

At first they started as "faculty wives" who participated voluntarily in this or that College musical group. Then they became part-timers, teaching just a class or two or giving a lesson or two in their specialties. And finally they became regular staff members in the music department. Such was the case for two "faculty wives"—Roberta Sellon, a violinist; and Sylvia Dyrhaug, a pianist—both of whom became part-timers in 1967. Their qualifications were obvious: Roberta Sellon was picked as first-chair violinist in the orchestra and remained in that #1 position until her full retirement in 1989. (Her husband William retired in 1985 from the industrial arts department.) Dyrhaug's prowess on the piano was demonstrated publicly over the years, with some orchestra concerts including one section in which she performed a major piano concerto. (Both Sylvia and her husband Donald—a member of the psychology department—retired in 1993.)

CHOIR TURNED OVER TO BRANDVIK

As to a highly significant event for music at Bemidji State, let Thompson's interpretation speak for itself:

"One of the biggest changes in the college music department took place in 1967 when I retired from all choral activities and Dr. Paul Brandvik was added to the staff as choral specialist. [Brandvik was a graduate of Concordia College, Moorhead; he sang in choir there under Paul Christiansen. Prior to his arrival at Bemidji, he had been the music director at Pelican Rapids, Minnesota, high school. When hired, he was in graduate school at the University of Illinois.] Choral activities have expanded greatly since he became the director. The Bemidji Choir has gained international reputation for excellence. [They have represented the United States four times at the international choral festival, the Europa Cantat in France, Austria, Belgium, and Switzerland.] They have also been a featured choir at the Music Educator's National Conference in Atlanta, Georgia and at the Northwest and North Central Regional Conventions of the American Choral Directors Association. Every three years the choir undertakes a foreign concert tour. . . . [In 1988 the Bemidji Choir performed two concerts in Carnegie Hall in New York, flew to Yugoslavia to sing in the Dubrovnik Festival, then continued with concerts in Hungary, Austria, Czechoslovakia. In 1991 they represented the United States at the Europa Cantat in Victoria-Gasteiz, Spain. In 1993 they sang for the National ACDA Convention in San Antonio, Texas.] He has continued the tradition of the Christmas concert and the annual oratorio production each

12) The peripatetic Thorson had an equally varied career at Bemidji. The short, bouncy man brought equal liveliness to the concert band (1966-76), including a penchant for extra promotion. For example, he arranged to have famous trumpeter Doc Severinson, of the Tonight TV show band, brought on campus to play with his Bemidji band. Thorson also served a stint as department chairman as well as the aforementioned band clinic director. A life-long collector of antiques in the music field, he eventually gave his extensive library of old sheet music to the University. Following retirement in 1984, he served one year in the state legislature. Like many of his colleagues, he became a snowbird, wintering with his wife Margaret in Tucson, Arizona, with summers back in Bemidji near Lake Irving.

spring. His greatest innovation has been the development of Madrigal Dinners for the public [started in 1968], before the Christmas season. The music is performed by a small vocal ensemble, called the Chamber Singers. He also began a high school invitational choral festival called Chorfest. Dr. Brandvik continues to be in demand as a clinician and conductor in this country and Europe." (from Thompson's manuscript, p. 7)

Choral Director Paul Brandvik in Front of Madrigal Dinner Singers
"Dividends . . . Irrelevant if presidents knew 'The 5th' to be Beethoven's or Seagram's."

FINALLY A MUSIC BUILDING (Almost)

The need for a fine arts building had been known for many years. Whenever the Legislative Building Commission came to the Bemidji campus, their members were always shown the intolerable conditions under which music, art, speech and drama faculties had to operate to try to develop their programs. The needs were apparent to all, the afflicted and non-afflicted alike actually feeling sorry, and sometime embarrassed, for some of the alleged facilities that fine arts was forced to use. For example, the assignment to have band instructors' offices in the barracks—"the shacks"—was insulting.

Yet no substantive change came until a new president came. Dr. Harry Bangsberg took office in the fall of '64 and almost immediately began discussions with Chairman Thompson, Dr. Russell Sawdey, chairman of the art department, and Louis Marchand, chairman of the speech and theatre department. Afterwards,

Bangsberg presented a plan to the Legislative Building Commission for a large complex to house the three departments, as well as a 2,000-seat auditorium. They bought it, in part. From the legislature in 1965, Bangsberg succeeded in getting what was called "planning money" for Phase I, that is, the planning of the future construction of a building housing music, speech and theatre. (Alas, nothing then for art.) From the 1967 solons came approximately $3,000,000 for building this first phase. (There would be no more "phases" financed; to date, no large auditorium has been built--but "hope springs eternal...")

The regrettable and untimely death of Bangsberg in March of 1967 did not slow down the building plans. Acting President John Glas appointed Ron Gearman as chairman of the Faculty Building Committee, which worked closely with the teaching faculties involved in planning the layout and the rooms.

At last, in 1969, actual construction began, but not until the fall of 1971 did the music department and the department of speech and theatre move into their new facilities (86,878 total square feet). Essentially, the speech and theatre folks are "downstairs" while music is "upstairs," although building-sharing is done—not always with smiles—by the two groups involved. On Sunday, May 7, 1972, the building was officially dedicated and named in honor of the late Bangsberg.

Rather than saying the technically correct "First phase of the Bangsberg Fine Arts Complex," it was immediately labeled Bangsberg Hall. It was simpler, and besides there was no second phase forthcoming.

Bangsberg Hall contains a 300-seat main theater with a fully equipped stage, a sceneshop, a downstairs experimental theater, a "green room" which can be used as a classroom, nine regular classrooms, a recital hall (Thompson Hall), piano technician's room, individual practice rooms for speech and 50 practice rooms for music (in the building were 26 Steinway grand pianos), an audio visual recording room, rooms for percussion, instrumental practice rooms, instrument repair room, a music library/listening room, 35 faculty offices, and, lastly, storage rooms. And though not planned that way, it's easy for visitors to get lost in Bangsberg Hall.

Of the many new buildings that grace the beautiful campus, Bangsberg Hall is viewed less as a plain classroom building than as a "class building," i.e., one where quality was not spared, even if the construction contract went to the lowest bidder. (Still, at the time it was the most expensive building per square foot—$35—in the SUS System.) 'Tis a lovely structure, its beauty seen more on the inside than the outside, the latter's dark-bricked, windowless west side giving some observers the image of an American Bastille. But the theater inside and the across-the-hall Thompson Recital Hall are marvelous, especially compared to the truly lugubrious facilities that preceded them.

Now the bad news. Bangsberg Hall, the southern-most building on the long-extended campus along the lakeshore, was built on a residential block. All the homes were purchased by the state; all the homeowners had to find new homes

somewhere else. Understandably, not all townspeople were happy about the new
Bangsberg Hall. Once again "the College," then portrayed as a devouring serpent,
had consumed yet more of "our land." Nor did the city council members cheer
loudly to have lost all that tax-paying property.[13] (Yet it was either there or
Diamond Point City Park, which very suggestion raised the hackles of the
townspeople.)

LEVELING OFF IN THE '70s IN ALL EXCEPT QUALITY

Bemidji State music had made dramatic changes. It moved from being a
one-person department in 1945 to having a dozen full-time staff 25 years later, and
then stayed at that size. By the '70s, Bemidji State moved from "regionalism" to
become recognized for its high quality throughout the entire state and beyond.
Augmenting its quality was music history and theory teacher, plus cello instructor,
Patrick Riley, who came in 1973.

From the public's point of view, a school's name-in-the-paper is usually
associated with its athletic squads. That has not been the rule for Bemidji State
because its music fame was established and then maintained—and kept regularly
in the public eyes and ears. This recognition has been a major achievement for the
entire school.

For all of the recent school presidents, music has been a wonderful asset
in their ongoing work with state legislators. To have the school praised publicly for
something besides athletics has warmed the hearts of every Beaver prexy, and
along with the intangible praises have come very tangible rewards, like green
money to maintain the operation. Presidents have come to know on which side
some financial bread is buttered, the musical side. It has paid dividends in support
for the department, and it remains totally irrelevant whether presidents personally
knew "The Fifth" to be Beethoven's or Seagram's.[14]

Legions of Bemidji area citizens have equally appreciated the quality
offerings coming from the local University music department over the decades.
Indeed, many area retirees have made it very clear that they chose to come to live
in Bemidji because of the school's cultural offerings in general and musical
offerings in particular.

---

13) The majority of the houses on the block were bought by one man who had them moved north of town where they sat on a
small hill, side-by-side and looking like some used house lot. Actually, he had created an instant slum. The slum owner soon
went insane and was committed. His houses eventually were either sold or deteriorated and collapsed on the spot. The hillside
is again bare. Of all the houses on the Bangsberg Hall block, two were not immediately torn down nor moved off. They had
been owned by faculty members Phil Sauer, English, and Sulo Havumaki, education. The Sauer home was temporarily used as
a "Journalism House," responding to the overcrowding in Deputy Hall, but it too caught the wrecker's ball by decade's end. The
Havumaki house still stands, at this writing (1994), and though a variety of college groups have been assigned to use that location,
the last dozen years it has served as the center for Native Americans and has a sign on it reading "Anishinabe House," translated
very roughly as the First/Original Settlers. All the remaining area in that empty block was converted to automobile parking.
14) Two special music programs in particular went off campus and permitted Bemidji State presidents to use them for good will
and good advertising in general and political hay in particular. They are the Madrigal Dinner, and Opera Night. Following the
week of Madrigal Dinners in Bemidji at Christmas-time, the group goes to Minneapolis for two nights of performances; in the
audiences are selected figures who are guests of the president. Not only has the Bemidji president used these dinners for school
promotion but the chancellor of the State University System has joined in and added his list of special guests, too. The same
applies to Opera Night, held annually first in Bemidji and then in the Twin Cities in late March or early April. In 1993, the Opera
Night group also, by invitation, sang in Florida.

AUGMENTED STAFFS FROM CREATIVE JUGGLING

The number of faculty since 1970 is deceptive because there have regularly been a near-equal number of part-timers to match the full-time dozen in the department.

After 1970, financing for music positions, or the lack thereof, led to a variety of means of augmenting faculty numbers. Part-timers came on line with different designations: graduate assistants, artists-in-residence, visiting Fellows in music, grant recipients, special services program, visiting instructors, applied fee instructors, Indian artists-in-residence, and adjuncts. Such creativity—or juggling— or finagling—has kept the music programs going wonderfully well since the official full-time staff leveled off.

The above categories have been noted in part because within them over the past 25 years have been some superb musicians who brought great pleasure to large, fascinated audiences. Although lack of space prevents their receiving the praise they deserve, at least their names deserve mention: Karen Bradley, Mark Gruett, Mary Ann Witmer, Roy Berg, Phil Jorgenson, Linda Wagner, Kathy Terhune, Dennis Murphy, Lynda Peterson, Arvid Knutsen, Lyn Wedlund, David Murphy, Lyle Jewell, Joe Vene, Abigail Riley, Margaret Maxwell, Ann Lamb, Betty Masoner, Cathie Hatch, Terry Hemsworth, Julie Konecne, Ken Wold, and Dan Risness. And likely more who were missed. (Sorry.)

Too many of the above were/are "members" of the department for many years, but are kept in a virtual state of "peasantry" via some non-tenure-track designation. Not that the department would not like to have hired most of them full-time; there just has not been the financing. And thus came this twilight zone status that never could mean steady employment for these part-timers. Grateful audiences can only say collectively, "Thanks for the musical memories!"[15]

BEAVERS GO JAZZY

Of the more recent personnel "specialists" who came to the music department (and stayed, and "conquered") was Steven Konecne, primarily a tenor-saxophone player, who was brought in to teach woodwinds, and to head the jazz studies program—something far different from anything the first two college presidents would have had in mind, and which they likely never would have allowed. Before long (he came in 1979) he had not one but two Jazz Bands on campus, named for logical if not euphonious reasons: "Jazz Band I" and "Jazz Band II." Their popularity has never diminished, and it soon carried over to the general

15) Missing from the list of names above is John Keston, missing because he, virtually alone, escaped the category of artist-in-residence, a temporary position when he started, and shifted it into a full-time, tenured job. Keston was British-born. He and his wife Ann came to Bemidji in 1975 when John became a voice instructor. John was a popular singer (a tenor) and actor, and with his cultivated accent and manner he could charm the snoose box away from a deranged lumberjack at Gene's Place. Over the years Keston starred in many campus musical productions along with summer productions at the Paul Bunyan Playhouse at Ruttger's Resort. Keston became well known for his jester role in the Madrigal Dinners, also. He was good enough to perform a one-man show called (and about) "Aging," which he presented around the North Country. He also teamed up with soprano Karen Bradley and they portrayed—and sang the famous songs of—Nelson Eddy and Jeanette McDonald. "Jolly good show." Keston retired in 1989. For the department musically, as the non-grammatical but still meaningful line goes, "He would do them proud." This single, tiny segment on Keston is representative of the musical success stories that could be told on all of the above "peasantry," because all of them "done 'em proud."

public with their annual "Remember When" sessions, two nights of Big Band music played for dancers and listeners. It's pure nostalgia for many gray-haired in the audience. (Both jazz bands play, changing sets over the evening. They even add singers/canaries and enthusiastic trios doing Andrews Sisters numbers.) And not to be forgotten is their annual Jazzfest, held in February, a month which requires special warming up.

WHERE TO FROM HERE?

As the department moves past the diamond jubilee year and towards the end of the century, the chair's position has gone into the hands of the fine orchestra director, Dr. Brian Runnels, who came in 1987 to both direct and teach percussion. He represents the "new age" chairperson on campus, starting with his mastery of the computer. He is a solid, sensible, young (age 37) man—who nevertheless dreams of unlimited, skillful string players coming forth from the North Country— whose talents and personality augur well in planning for the musical future, while meeting the existing problems that surround the department today. He's a pragmatic optimist.

A CONDITION SHORT OF PERFECTION

Despite an overall success ratio that would be the envy of other, competing departments, the faculty members in music would be the first to admit that all has been less than perfect over the years.

For too many music positions since '45, their Bemidji stay has been a near-revolving door, despite the carefulness of preparation. Standard scenario: the department spends months reviewing applications, then painstakingly weeding them down to a half dozen finalists, reducing carefully that figure to three or four and bringing them (and paying their expenses) to campus for interviews, followed by more discussions and haggling among the selection committee. Finally a decision's made to offer the contract to so-and-so, with the reasonable expectation that their newest colleague will come on board and remain at Bemidji State forever and ever, amen. Then that person leaves/flees after a year or two. Not good.

Probably the music department set a dubious record in brevity of tenure for a college band director. One James Johnston was hired to direct the band in 1977. He came, he saw, he packed his bags and left town seven days later, never to return.

THE MISSING CONCERT HALL

Another concern. Facilities for concerts remain a perennial problem for directors, especially facilities for large audiences. The dream of a new, acoustically fine, large auditorium has remained a dream for half a century. Among the several performing groups affected has been the choir, with Director Brandvik trying and giving performances all over Bemidji. It appeared he had finally found every acoustical advantage he desired for concerts in the St. Philip's Catholic Church, but that ended when the church was torn down in 1990. Back to campus—with side-trips to Trinity Lutheran Church—to the ballroom in the student union for most choir concerts, but when it comes to full oratorios, it's back to Memorial Hall/M-100/the Old Gym, a place no one really likes for memorable music.[16] Something has always been lost in that building, whether it's the no-back bleachers on both sides or the metal-back folding chairs on the floor. And the entranced concertgoer glancing away from the soloists because the eye was caught by an extended basketball hoop or a gymnast's ring hanging from the ceiling has been sadly reminded of the absence of concert hall ambience. (A few Bemidjians have refused to go to any production if it's to be in—gasp—Memorial Hall.)

WHAT IS THE FUTURE OF BEMIDJI STATE MUSIC?

The above reference to the lack of an adequate large auditorium should in no way detract from the overall excellence of the music department. So what can be expected? There's a familiar line of reasoning that goes: if it's so good now, then given more time, it will be even better. Not necessarily. The late Martin Luther King, Jr. had an insight on the notion of "time" improving anything. King declared time to be "neutral" as far as change is concerned. He was referring, of course, to civil rights for all citizens and the common assumption that things just automatically get better over time. Not so, said King; there will be no improvements unless people work for them. That simple. It is in that framework that the music department gets inserted into the equation. Hence music will get no better, and perhaps will not even stay the same, unless people work at it. Realistically, this concept of a continued fine music program must also be "worked at" by those figures who determine the degree of funding and support for music, namely the president, vice president and the dean. Where their values lie relative to the importance of music affects directly the program's future.

The man who essentially started the whole thing, Carl O. Thompson, "Mr. Music," had something positive to say about this topic in 1972. Today his brief statement stands out as a challenge to the current and future music personnel moving Bemidji State towards centennial times and beyond: "The future of the music department is in the hands of people today who will guide the department, I am sure, to greater and greater heights of excellence." He was right in '72; may he be right again in 2002.

SPORTS

Near the end of the classic tale of King Arthur and the knights of the Round Table, the aging king looks back on his life and wonders if all his earlier efforts were

---

16) The availability of the fine North Country arts has always required proper adaptation to the elements. On a personal note, I recall during a particularly frigid afternoon viewing a large man rushing in somewhat late to a major musical production of Brahms' Requiem being performed in Memorial Hall. On the surface, the man appeared to be a true "Jackpine Savage." He wore a thick stocking cap, was heavy-bearded, and wore big boots which he had trouble removing. He began to pull off a heavy, duck-down coat and was struggling to get it over his head. Finally he succeeded, and what emerged was a handsome man wearing elegant black formal wear, complete with tails. It was Paul Brandvik. The formal concert could begin.

worthwhile, and would they be remembered? For an answer he approaches a young lad with his questions and concerns and is rewarded with the response: Yes, yes, by all means, it was worthwhile, and yes, it would be remembered.

Shot-Put About to be Launched
"Title IX was a hot topic . . . it brought the women's athletic program in the limelight."

To the thousands of young people who at some point participated in Bemidji State athletics over 75 years, two basic questions might be asked of them: Was it worth all the work? Will it be remembered? And the answer will be the same: Yes, yes, by all means, most certainly, yes.

Students participated in Beaver sports because they wanted to be a part of something they deemed to be valuable. If they might claim a fleeting glimpse of glory along the way, that would be an extra bonus, but most important was to be a part of something they believed important in their lives, and sports was important.

Whatever the sport, whatever the team, it was never easy to be on it. One had to work hard to make the squad and the initial lessons were hard work and the survival-of-the-fittest. The competition was both against others and oneself, but from it all came a better person.

Those who were part of some sports program—any program—left Bemidji State with an added pride in themselves, a sense of personal accomplishment just a little bit beyond the normal, and a camaraderie with fellow team members that would last a lifetime. A life-long lesson would be learned from sports, namely to believe in oneself and what can be accomplished by dedication and hard work. At the same time, enjoy it. Have fun. Yet good things in sports do not happen by themselves. These require guidance, someone in control, someone to show the way and guide the way. They're called coaches. The vast number of Beaver players came straight from high schools where they may or may not have been heroes; either way, when they arrived on campus they were young in age and young in experience. The process of change over four years is called maturation. The coaches led them to that last stage. Most athletes left Bemidji State with not only their degrees but also a pride in themselves at what could be accomplished through hard work and dedication to a purpose.

Over the decades since leaving Bemidji State, the physical skills would diminish, but there would be no diminishing of those favorite colors, the green-and-white of Beaver players' uniforms. And always but always there would remain the memories. Yes, yes, it was most worthwhile indeed.

WHEN IT ALL BEGAN

Intercollegiate athletics began at Bemidji State in 1921, with basketball. Track was added in 1924 and football in 1926. Baseball came along in 1933 and hockey in 1946, to round out the so-called major sports. Following, and sometimes in between, came a number of so-called minor sports, an unfair terminology in that they were anything but minor for the participants. Perhaps, like beauty, the importance of any given sport is in the eye of the beholder.

Like academic programs over the years, the coming and going of specific Beaver sports activities realistically depended on available financing. Alas, when the funds got cut back—and they were—something had to go, leaving always a most unhappy group of young people who saw their favorite activity dropped, for example wrestling in 1983 and men's swimming in 1991. Additional programs lost were women's swimming, women's field hockey, gymnastics (men and women), cross country running (men and women), cross country skiing (men and women), women's golf, and men's tennis. Such are the financial exigencies of collegiate athletics everywhere.

A few sports activities emerged briefly, got dropped, emerged again—and got dropped again, for good. Among them were weight lifting, last seen in 1950, and boxing, gone forever after 1947. A sport once viewed as minor, like hockey, came and went a couple of times until it finally, like Lazarus, came back to life in 1959 and went forward with such vigor as to dominate Bemidji State sports life since the late 1960s.

WHAT'S IN A NAME?

Change alone has been the ingredient in sports history that can be counted on. Among the obvious changes have been the names and the makeup of the conference in which Bemidji has been member. In the 1920s Bemidji belonged to the Little Ten Conference, consisting mainly of junior colleges. In the 1930s and 1940s, only the teachers colleges in the state were members and appropriately it would be labeled the Minnesota State Teachers Colleges Conference. Change came again in the mid 1950s when Michigan Technical College at Houghton was added. Along with this addition came the name change reflecting it: Northern State Teachers Colleges Conference. When the legislature permitted the word Teachers to be dropped in 1957 from the Minnesota public colleges, so too did the drop come to the conference name. To some viewers, however, the new Northern States Conference sounded too much like Northern States Power, the utility company with which sports did not wish to be confused. Thus by 1960 came an unmistakable name change that served the participating schools—and some colleges came in while others left—well for the next 30 years: Northern Intercollegiate Conference, and usually referred to simply by the three letters "NIC."

Lastly, one more title change went into effect in the spring of 1993 when the Northern Sun Conference (women) and the NIC (men) merged to form for both the men and the women the Northern Sun Intercollegiate Conference. Along with BSU were (and the year they joined): Moorhead State (1932), Northern State (Aberdeen, South Dakota; 1978), Southwest State (Marshall, Minnesota; 1969), University of Minnesota, Duluth (1932; withdrew in 1949, readmitted in 1976), University of Minnesota, Morris (1966), and Winona State (1932).

FACILITIES: WHAT ATHLETES HAD TO USE

For sports participants and spectators alike, even more significant than the changes in things like conference names were the playing facilities used by the different sports teams over the past 75 years. The most accurate assessment in any description of overall changes is the hackneyed but oh-so-honest phrase, "From the ridiculous to the sublime." The former can be seen in the school's first "gymnasium" for the first basketball team of 1921. It was located in the Main Building (Deputy Hall), with a playing court of 20 by 40 feet. The latter (sublime!) can be witnessed by anyone stepping inside the newest addition (1989) to the sports complex. The view of the vast Recreation Sports Center expanse can take the breath away! It's huge (85,765 square feet)!

That first basketball court became more of a place for player conditioning. Most games were played in the town Armory building, but after Bemidji High School built its "new" school in 1922, "The Peds" (as the sportswriters frequently called the college teams) played some games in the high school gym, too. Those two locations provided the only options for basketball at Bemidji State for almost the next two decades. Not until the gymnasium (Memorial Hall) was completed in 1939 did the big change come. (More later on that oddest of all buildings on campus, Memorial Hall).

The first football field was built along the lakeshore, down the hill and north and east of the Main Building, Deputy Hall; it ran lengthwise, paralleling Lake Bemidji, that is, north and south. Started in 1924, it was completed the next year. Football officially began at Bemidji State in 1926, when there were exactly 26 men enrolled in the entire school that fall quarter.

Football spectators stood along the sidelines, with some fans running up and down the sidelines the entire game, depending on where the line of scrimmage was located. Improvement for viewers came in 1931 when the industrial arts classes built wooden bleachers. Aside from clearing more brush around the edges and bringing in needed fill, the football field served the school until the present one, running east and west, was built in 1940-41. (Again, more on that later.)

The sport of track began in 1924. Work on the track took place simultaneously with the work on the football field and the track was completed in 1925, completion being a relative term.

Impressive changes came for track and football in 1935 when lights were installed for night games. The lighting system then had high ratings for illumination, with a total of 60,000 watts shining forth. The lights were mounted on eight posts, 60 feet high. True community support came through for this lighting enterprise, with donations from individuals, groups and organizations totaling full payment of $2,400.

Bemidji State began baseball in 1933, but the team had to share the playing field with Bemidji High School, which had received the land in 1927 as a gift from five town sports supporters (C.W. Vandersluis, C.L. Peglow, John West, W.L. Brooks, and H.A. Krebs), who stipulated that the land had to be used for athletics or else it would revert back to them. At this writing (1994), the land is used for four softball fields and is owned by the University. Its purchase from the high school for $87,053 in 1960 came at the same time the school began its expansion program north of the original campus, adding 54 acres to the existing 20. (See section on the 1950s.)

Hockey started semi-officially at Bemidji State in 1946, although there had been informal pick-up games played before then. Practice facilities were the local lakes, with Lake Bemidji the primary ice spot; games were played in the town's city arena, an enclosed area downtown (where Northland Apartments are currently located). But there was no heat inside, and only a single bench around the rink for spectators. The games there ended when the roof literally fell in on the arena on January 4, 1949. The collapse was caused by a combination of too much snow and high winds. Some half dozen young children were skating at the time of the collapse, but they were not hurt and managed to escape through windows. At the same time about 20 more skaters were in the warming house section but the roof held up over them. The remaining games that season were played on Lake Bemidji until the caterpillar used to scrape snow off the ice fell through the ice.[17]

WHEN GOOD THINGS HAPPEN IN BAD TIMES

The Great American Depression hit Minnesota like a pile-driver, and public institutions like Bemidji State Teachers College joined the victims of hard times. That the school survived at all approaches amazement; that it actually grew and practically boomed in the late '30s is more amazing.

The school had fumbled along without a single new structure since 1921,

---

17) For more information on Bemidji State and what the times were like on campus when the earliest sports began, see College in the Pines, pp. 72-105. Certain sports have been omitted in the main text above because they began later; wrestling, for example started in 1954. Cross-country track began in 1957, gymnastics in 1960, and swimming in 1964. The sport of men's tennis was first listed in 1928 when there was a match with Hibbing Junior College; then it was apparently dropped to return for one year, 1933, then was dropped again 'til '39; dropped once more in the war years and restarted in '46; and finally was dropped again in 1980—but women's tennis continues! (It started in 1970.) The great boost and boom for all college athletics nationwide came in those post-World War II years. Because both the ages and experiences of the returning veterans were so much more advanced (many had played in military service), the quality of the play of the teams was extraordinary! For many aficionados, the postwar years in the colleges were the "Golden Years of Athletics."

and thus there was no hyperbole in the '37 school newspaper headline reading, "Hope of Decade Realized." The realized dream was a new physical education building; construction began on the same in 1938, with its use starting in 1939. For its day, the Gymnasium (Memorial Hall) was a marvel! People drove for miles just to see it. High school boys in the region played their district basketball tournaments there, and witnesses described the dropped jaws of young lads who had just walked in—they had never seen a building so big in their lives!

For architectural buffs, it reflected wonderfully well the art deco style still popular at the time. The rounded corners, the rounded curlicues in the expansive lobby, even the aluminum hand railings rolled into twisted, curved round balls at the ends, made it less a building than an art form to treasure.

The playing floor dimensions ran 50 by 90 feet. According to the plans, the two bleachers on either side held 1,200 people, but on the night of the dedication, February 9, 1940, an estimated 1,800 had squeezed inside to enjoy watching the Beavers defeat the Mankato Indians, 38-27. "Mr. Minnesota Football" himself, University of Minnesota coach Bernie Bierman, just coming off the golden age of Gopher football, was the main speaker that night.

If the coaches and fans were pleased with the playing facilities—and of course there were also elaborate shower rooms and lavatories for the teams—other faculty members found similar pleasure in the levels below and above because of the added and badly needed classroom space. (Over the years the lower level contained/housed the entire industrial arts department, the student union, the school post office, and the bookstore. At this writing, 1994, the lower level is taken up entirely by the bookstore and the printing services facilities.) All so grand!

Considering the grandness with which most folks at the time viewed Memorial Hall, it seems almost churlish to suggest any flaws. But there were flaws on a scale that almost landed a half dozen men in jail (they went before grand juries but were not indicted); flaws that make that particular building the oddest structure on campus. It simply is an unfinished building. How many freshmen over the years have explored the upstairs area, following steps up and up and discovering that they lead to nowhere?! Spooky. There are doors on the east wall which open into space. The original plans show a second gym, a large swimming pool; and several more classrooms, but they were never built because the school ran out of money building what is there, an unfinished building. Corruption? Bill padding? Favoritism? The charges came forth, but were never proven in the courts. Meanwhile, to hide the aesthetic mess on the east side, long, wooden two-by-sixes have been added, ostensibly to make it look "arty" but really there to cover up a botched building.[18]

NEW PHYSICAL EDUCATION BUILDING, NEW FOOTBALL FIELD TOO

Putting men to work was the goal of President Franklin Roosevelt's New

---

18) A student who had explored the curious halls and doors in the remotest parts of Memorial Hall became intrigued enough to write her senior honors paper on the subject. Written by Pamela Docken in 1987, copies are available in the Honors program office; this author also has a copy. For a very brief background on the events leading up to the funding for M-100, see College in the Pines, pp. 131-132.

Deal programs in the Depression decade of the 1930s and the earliest '40s. Within that larger program were an array of planning agencies, collectively derided by detractors as "alphabet soup," the negative term referring to the letters by which these multi-agencies were known.

The specific "soup program" that most benefited Bemidji State athletics was the W.P.A., the Works Project Administration. Federal funds had been designated by W.P.A. officials for both the new gymnasium and a total athletics facilities building program for Bemidji State, the new football field being part of the latter.

The greater goal for W.P.A. was to meet the need for employment as well as to produce necessary construction projects, benefits thus coming for both individuals and communities. Combining funds from the state of Minnesota relief program with larger W.P.A. funds, the work on the Bemidji State athletic fields began in 1940 and was completed the next year at a total cost of $60,000.

It should be emphasized that the completion time for this relatively small federal project was longer than normal, but those were not normal times. For the men lucky enough to be employed, their hope was for the project to last as long as possible. Who knows when or if there would be another job? Consider, for example, the height of the football field compared to the land level in adjacent Diamond Point Park. The higher level of the football field occurred because it was filled in by W.P.A. workers, bringing one wheelbarrow load of dirt at a time. And it took a long time because the "workers" took a long time. Bulldozers and dump trucks could have done that job much faster, but efficiency was not the goal.

Little wonder that critics of the W.P.A. programs everywhere, including many in Bemidji who came to watch the construction work on the local college campus, redefined W.P.A. to stand for "We Poke Along," or "Workers Playing Around," and worse—and saw all those projects as a foolish government boondoggle.

When it was completed in 1941, Bemidji athletics had a new football field and bleachers; they also had a new football practice field, a softball diamond, a soccer field, a new 440-yard track, a concrete court for handball and basketball, and four concrete tennis courts. A major improvement! In all this construction, school officials protected and preserved as many of the big white pines as possible on the construction sites. A "College in the Pines" required pine trees, and Bemidji State had (and has) some big beauties.

Open at both ends of the field, the cement bleachers on each side of the football field are 180 feet in length and 40 feet in width. There are 15 rows of redwood seating in each section and the wood sits on steel frames, also 180 feet long. The permanent grandstand seats can hold approximately 4,000 people. In securing W.P.A. funding, BSTC President Sattgast had to ensure government officials that the cement bleachers would be more than just seats for spectators to watch athletic contests. Thus the north bleacher section is also—if one can picture it—a potential "Grecian Theater," with arts-loving spectators sitting in the south bleachers watching the grand production across from them. To date, this potential theater has remained just a concept. (Ahhh, the ruses required to get federal funding. . . .)

There are heated press boxes on both sides, each originally capable of holding a dozen people. (The press box on the south side was enlarged and improved in 1958. Soundproofed, the box was divided into two nine-by-twenty seven foot units, holding some 30 people.)

In 1957 new (and still there) lights were installed for the football field which included a total of 96 1,500-watt Westinghouse lamps. The lights are mounted on six Tulito Towers, two on each end of the field and two center towers, the latter towers being 90 feet high and each holding 24 lights. The end towers are 70 feet high and contain 12 lights each.[19] (New lights were installed in 1992, a cooperative venture by BSU and Bemidji High School.)

Although the Depression produced more victims than beneficiaries, Bemidji State athletics made the latter category in those years right before World War II.

THE SPORT OF HOCKEY STARTS/RESTARTS YET AGAIN
After a 10-year layoff, the sport of hockey began once more in 1959, thanks to a new instructor (and coach) who came that year, Vic Weber. The absence of any playing area and the need to build such a rink was initially met not by some

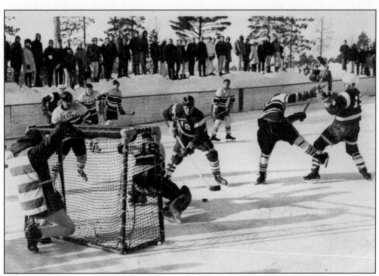

Outdoor Beaver Hockey (c. 1960)
"Crowd fickleness . . . depended on the weather conditions on game days."

19) Those football light poles have produced an ongoing problem since installed, namely finding someone willing to crawl up to the top of those high towers and replace the burned out bulbs. As to the seating capacity in the stadium—in these last years flippantly referred to as "the Beaverdome"—the true test in seating capacity came when the Minnesota Vikings trained at Bemidji State (1961 to 1965) and played practice games in the stadium against other National Football League teams. Crowds then were estimated at over 5,000. Both the Vikings and the Beaver teams could agree that when it came to lovely locations for a football field, Bemidji State won that contest easily.

million dollar appropriation from the legislature but by a couple hundred bucks from the Student Activities Committee. (The players wore old football jerseys.)

No big-time, indoor palace to start with; just the opposite: a small-time, outside rink located 200 feet east of Bemidji Avenue, 200 feet west of the current ice hockey area. The outdoor rink had the barest of necessities, starting with the most important: ice dimensions of 200 feet by 85 feet, the figure that met the official collegiate hockey specifications.

Crowd fickleness—and attendance at these home games—depended less on the won-lost records of the teams than on the weather conditions on the days of the games. Beaver hockey then was for the brave-at-heart who had the good sense to dress warmly. Games were played in the afternoons, but even that meant little sustenance in that dreaded month of January. What limited crowds there were at the time stood mainly on the top of the snowbanks surrounding the rink, and on severely frigid days spectators spent as much time running to and from buildings or cars to warm up as watching the games.

Temporary wooden bleachers from the football field were hauled over to the rink and were placed on the west side (sun at their backs); they held about 300 spectators. There were also some lights for night use. Twelve light poles surrounded the rink, each with 1,500 watts, collectively providing sufficient illumination for team practices and for general student recreational skating nights.

The return of hockey to Bemidji State began with limited (read primitive) facilities, but that did not deter the growth of the sport. Indeed, maintenance of the program was built on the premise that someday, maybe someday soon, Bemidji State would have an indoor arena. (The "someday soon" took another eight years.) So meanwhile, they enjoyed the games in the fresh air. "Fair-weather-fans" can be defined differently in hockey country.

NO MORE "GYM"; NOW IT'S A "COMPLEX"

The expanding BSTC campus moved out and away from the lake in the 1950s. Adding 54 acres from that mostly uninhabited expanse called the City Forest, the school's growth into the new acreage began with Birch Hall dormitory (1952) and continued with more residence halls built up the line, directly north of Birch Hall, during that decade. Then came the major leap westward from the roadside dorms to the empty, forested center area and the construction there of a new gymnasium and a swimming pool in 1959, thanks to an earlier million-dollar appropriation from the legislature.

This physical education complex—eventually a labyrinthian expansion of three separate, major buildings—began with Unit "A," which included essentially a basketball court and swimming pool. At the time just "A" unit was completed, it appeared massive! The added fact that it stood on a location where there had been only a woods before made it that much more impressive to see.

The previous marvel of the Memorial Hall facilities was dwarfed in comparison, and once again the high school basketball tournament boys went pop-eyed at the biggest court they'd ever seen, proving that size is always relative. The playing floor on the new basketball court was made of hardwood maple; it was 126 feet wide and 121 feet long. Seating capacity for games and other activities was approximately 3,100. This capacity was (is) tested each March when high schools play tournament games there.

Spectators did not walk on the floor but entered at either end of the main lobby, going up one-half level to a balcony nine feet in width, then proceeding down into the telescopic bleachers. Exiting spectator traffic moved out via this balcony and down to the main lobby. (The dimensions of the main <u>lobby</u> are larger than Bemidji State's first basketball court in 1921.)

Players and officials alone moved from dressing rooms to the gym floor through the lower corridor, thus having no direct contact with the spectators. For its time it was state-of-the-art all the way, with built-in protection from "foreigners" scuffing their feet on the precious playing surface.

NOT TO FORGET THE SWIMMING POOL

The swimming pool, built concurrently with the gym, was located on the southern side of the building (with a long hallway in between the pool area and the bucketball court); this was the second part of Unit "A."

The pool was 42 feet wide and 75 feet long, with six marked lanes seven feet in width. A balcony on one side provided seating for 300 spectators. On the deep end of the pool were two one-meter diving boards and one three-meter board. For special effect, there were underwater sound and lighting equipment; there were also underwater observation windows.

Although the pool was overshadowed simply by the size of all the accouterments connected with the new basketball facilities on the other side, it nevertheless had an immediate impact and appeal to the community in 1959 because it was the first school in the area to have an indoor pool. That made it something special, and both students and non-students plotted ways they might be able to use it somehow, sometime. For faculty there was a special perk in that Sunday afternoon was set aside for pool use by family members for a nominal fee. That offering was snatched up and enjoyed, becoming a weekend ritual for pleased parents and ecstatic kids. (When anything is new, it's always so special. Ten years later, Sunday "pooling" was canceled, due to lack of interest and participation.)

What really made the pool a place of noise and excitement for over 20 years (1968-91) were Coach Lee Ahlbrecht and the Beaver swim teams. (See later section for men's teams records.)

BOOM TIME FOR HOCKEY! THE BOYS COME IN FROM THE COLD

The most natural sport for northern Minnesota is hockey. The most natural place to play it is outside, there being no dearth of natural ice in the North Country.

Nor will it melt away 'til March. Something else is natural: creature comfort. If the exciting sport of hockey can be good outside, then it has to be great inside, or so ran the rationale.

Did Minnesota legislators like hockey that well? Not! To simply build an indoor rink proved insufficient justification for funding to wary legislators. They wanted evidence of need demonstrated by building-use far beyond blue lines painted on ice, with circles here and there, and mesh cages on either end. Other uses? No problem. The most obvious need coincided with the changes on campus in the 1960s: More students, measured no longer by the hundreds but by the thousands. And about 40 percent would graduate, the resultant ceremony bringing on campus more people in one day than ever showed up in Bemidji the rest of the year. It can be the day of the school's greatest public relations effects. More first impressions are made by campus visitors at commencement than any other day. Vast crowds are either impressed positively or negatively. That is more than enough reason to hold commencement in an impressive indoor setting—that just happened to be a hockey arena, too.[20]

More pitches for a large arena were made in behalf of an argument for an "auditorium" of sorts that would attract traveling entertainers of national prominence for people of the region to enjoy. Big names, big crowds, big money, big profits.[21]

Other sports teams joined in to move the terminology away from a simple, selfish hockey rink to a major field house with multiple athletic uses. Baseball backers especially argued with total, irrefutable reasoning that spring comes so late in the North Country that there just had to be an indoor place of wide dimension for preseason workouts. This way when the snows melted off the ball diamond (in April? May? June?), the Beavers would be ready—ready to start the season. Similar pleas came from tennis squads. A field house would allow room for some half dozen indoor courts.

Whichever above pitches swayed the legislature may never be publicly known, but publicly seen soon was the addition being built to the existing Phy Ed Complex, and it too was big! On the blueprints it was Unit "B" of the Physical Education Complex; officially it would become the John S. Glas Field House, a fitting memorial to a Bemidji State business administrator (and acting president,

20) Historically, college commencements are expected to be held in the school football stadiums in June. That month is more than significant for Bemidji State; it's crucial. Weather is the extenuating circumstance, but June commencements worked out reasonably well in the football stadium. However, in the 1960s student pressures came for a school year ending early, certainly before June 1 (pragmatic Beavers are eager to get at those summer jobs before the rest of the schools let out). Hence came May commencements that found crowds sometimes facing/enduring inclement weather in the Beaverdome, and somehow a wet, snow-covered sheepskin lost some of its intrigue. It was a welcome relief to get the arena; it has been used for graduations ever since and has worked out wonderfully well. All importantly, the presidents have worked assiduously to make commencement day the kind of day that shows Bemidji State at its best. Lots of pomp with no bad circumstances.

21) The hockey arena has been used almost annually to bring on campus at least one nationally-known musical person or group, this despite acoustical problems in the cavernous location. The most regular promoter—and booker—of performers has been KAWE, the public television station whose facilities are on campus (second floor of Deputy Hall). They have brought in mainly country-western singers who have played to full houses, and thus been a moneymaker for the TV station. Bemidji State sometimes books a special entertainer for homecomings, e.g., Lee Greenwood, John Denver, Rick Nelson, Jim Croce, Muddy Waters, Tim Weisberg. Sometimes it's special rock bands, e.g., Gary Puckett and the Union Gap. (Rock groups have continued to come regularly to the campus since the '60s but usually put on their performances in Memorial Hall and sometimes the union ballroom.) The Bemidji Chamber of Commerce holds an annual sports show at the end of the hockey season, soon after the ice is removed. Some church group conventions get held there in the summers, so the arenas do get multi-use, as first planned and promised.

and an ongoing athletic supporter during his many important years on the faculty, 1939-75). However, in the daily vernacular, the new place was just called "the hockey arena."

The new arena adjoined Unit "A," the west side thus becoming the campus building closest to Bemidji Avenue. Between the avenue and the building was built one big, long parking area, seen initially as too big and unnecessary, and proven afterwards to be insufficient in size to accommodate the mushrooming automobile numbers.

A small but literally "telling" item would be added soon after the arena's completion, namely a large school "billboard/marquee," located at the west end of the parking lot, next to Bemidji Avenue. Initially workmen came weekly with a ladder, crawled up to the sign area, and inserted large, black letters to announce the coming school events. Useful, helpful, promotional. (A new age computer in 1990 replaced both the original billboard and the hand labor needed for informational changes. Today there's a somewhat smaller "billboard," but all the daily information provided 24 hours a day—starting with the time and temperature—is typed in from the office of the news services director, whose office is in Deputy Hall.)

When Units A and B were measured together in square feet, they totaled 121,586. Considering that Memorial Hall had only 53,893 square feet, small wonder that the latter was seen as "small"—and old, and quaint, and unworthy of any major sports; let it be for . . . ah, . . . er, . . . intramurals.[22]

The first hockey game played in the John Glas Field House, November 17, 1967, attracted a standing-room-only crowd estimated at over 3,000 people. The added fact that the hockey team won the N.A.I.A. national championship in Saint Paul that year kept the crowds at near capacity. No surprise. This initial newness of the building might have kept the crowds coming, regardless, just to see the largest hockey arena in northern Minnesota. More than likely the crowd sizes would have soon faded along with the newness of the structure, but this did not happen because the Beaver hockey teams just kept winning and winning, essentially for the next 25 years. The combination of winning teams and big crowds is a standard formula, of course. Curiously, it has become somewhat peculiar in the last quarter century when Beaver hockey has <u>not</u> ended up in first or second place and has <u>not</u> gone to the national tournament finals. So consistent have they been in winning that the local wits said they hoped the University would become a school worthy of its hockey teams. The new building, the new coach (Bob Peters came in 1966), the new era in Beaver athletics all went together nicely. It was, to say the least, a most pleasant, fortuitous happening for the University. (More on Beaver hockey in a later section.)

---

22) For the year of construction and the square footage of every building on campus, see Appendix H. Several buildings have multiple dates, indicating they were either remodeled or added on to, e.g., Deputy Hall, Sanford Hall, Sattgast Hall, Education-Art Building, Hickory Hall, and several residence halls. As noted several times, the building boom construction essentially decimated this rather large woods located within the city limits, i.e., the City Forest. For pre-boom students, this forested area had the name of Tipperary and became a gathering spot for semi-secret social activities, which in the vernacular comes out as a lovers' meeting place and/or site of great beer keggers in the middle of the woods. The forest would end; the lovers and the keggers would not. There are still lots of empty woods around Bemidji.

Post Game Pure Locker-Room Joy
"And always but always there would remain the memories."

BEMIDJI STATE ATHLETICS
Section I: The First 40 Years—Men's Teams, Coaches, Records, Summaries—1921-1961

OVERVIEW. In the following section on Beaver athletics, an attempt is made to survey men's sports very briefly from their starting point (basketball begins in 1921) through 1961. The coverage comes in different ways, however, with football and basketball season summations (next pages) in statistical form, listing the years, won-lost-tied records, and the coaches by name. Remaining sports are wrapped up with the briefest of narratives. There are a number of problems in this first section of reporting, the most significant being the omission of the names of any of the athletes participating. Despite their absence, the fact remains that Bemidji State athletics have existed for one reason only, the same reason why the entire University exists, for the students themselves.

Section II: Beaver Sports Since 1961—Men's Teams, Years, Coaches, Records

The same format of basic statistical information is used for recording football, basketball, baseball, swimming, and golf since 1961. This abbreviated reporting style can be justified only in the space saved, but with it comes the assumption that truly interested readers can draw their own conclusions and interpretations simply by perusing the numbers; moreover, information is provided on where to find more information on each sport. The one Beaver sport which receives emphasis in this section is the program that has most dominated the school the past quarter of a century, hockey.

MEN'S BASKETBALL
INDIVIDUAL COACHING RECORDS: 1921-1961

Coaches	Year	Total Years	Won	Lost
Fremont Wirth	1921-24	2	2	9
E. A. McPhearson	1922-23	1		

Although an 18-game-season, BSTC teams played high schools and those scores were not recorded.

E. Wayne Beck	1924-26	2	1	14
Raymond Mendenhall	1926-28	2	4	15
Eldon Mason	1928-31	3	15	17
Jack Sterrett	1931-35	4	16	32
Reuben Frost	1935-37	8	76	57
James Witham	1942-44	2	12	7
Hjalmer (Jolly) Erickson	1944-46	2	24	6
Stanley Hall	1947-54	7	105	48
Harry Fritz	1954-58	4	42	48
Jack Vinje	1958-62	4	48	43

FOOTBALL
INDIVIDUAL COACHING RECORDS: 1926-61

Coaches	Year	Total Years	Won	Lost	Tied
Raymond Mendenhall	1926-28	2	6	5	1
Eldon Mason	1928-31	3	8	9	2
Jack Sterrett	1931-35	4	11	15	2
Reuben Frost	1935-38	3	7	14	1
Hjalmer (Jolly) Erickson	1938-55	17	51	53	5
Chester Anderson	1955-61	6	25	19	4
John Kulbitski	1961-62	1	3	6	0

"Mr. Athletics"—Jolly Erickson

A total of 32 different coaches served on the Bemidji State staffs over the school's first 40 years, and six of the 32 were students at the time. H. J. (Jolly) Erickson had the longest tenure of the 32 coaches and deserved the title of "Mr. Athletics" for that time period. Erickson began coaching in 1938 and stopped in 1954. In addition to this primary coaching position in football, he also by necessity coached basketball, track, tennis, and golf at different times during his 20 years at Bemidji State, 17 as a coach.

Erickson's hometown was Moorhead, Minnesota, where he attended public schools and college, graduating from Moorhead State in 1930. He began his teaching and coaching at Bemidji High School and started part-time coaching at the College in 1938. The next year he moved to a full-time position at Bemidji State during the school years, and he spent the next three summers as a graduate student at the University of Minnesota where he received his master's degree in 1941. His coaching interests were wide and strong at Bemidji State. He originated the Beaver Relays track event; he also began coaching clinics, bringing to the Beaver campus such widely known sports figures as Terry Brennan, Adolph Rupp, Forest Evashevski, and Henry Iba. He also served as head coach of the North team in 1952 in the annual all-star high school football game in Minneapolis. For reasons of health, he gave up coaching in 1954 but remained a classroom teacher. Tragically, Erickson died of a heart attack on February 7, 1959, at the age of 53.

TRACK

The first recorded information on track and field competition at Bemidji State dates back to 1924 when a Bemidji team participated in the Hamline Relays, but no results were listed. Therein lay a regular problem that decade and beyond in determining track meet outcomes because the reports after the meets would be phrased as "no results" whenever high school teams participated in the competition. Adding to the complications of the usual won-lost-tied recordings of most competitive sports is the nature of track scoring when it involves relay teams vs. individual sports, first-second-third places, and the like. The above problems can be seen throughout the 1920s when there were indeed BSTC track teams, but virtually no records were kept of their track meets as all contests had included high school teams, hence "no results." One of the few facts to record is that the first track coach was E. Wayne Beck in 1924.

In the 1930s there were presumably more track activities, with seasons including dual, triangular, and quadrangular meets, such as the latter event in Virginia in 1932 when Bemidji State took third place. Unfortunately, this decade also found most track meets going down in the records as "no results." The pattern of unrecorded outcomes continued into the 1940s, and even when Bemidji State inaugurated its Beaver Relays in 1943, there is no recorded report of the competing teams and individuals. Like most things at Bemidji State, the big boost in numbers and interest came after World War II, and thus all-college track meets were held and results finally recorded. For example, Bemidji won first place at its own '47 Beaver Relays, and the next year took first (of nine teams) at the Hibbing Invitational. By the 1950s there were established annual all-conference meets; the highest the Beavers came out that decade was second place in 1956. Things changed in 1959 with the hiring of a new track coach, Vic Weber. A competent, diligent, highly organized person, as well as an assertive spokesman for physical education in general, Weber cajoled, pushed, and promoted the sport of track and field into a new stage of importance and success for the next 20 years.

BASEBALL

Geography has hurt baseball at Bemidji State more than any other sport. Late-arriving warm weather in spring has often hampered the program over its checkered history, and at times cold weather has ruined it by ending the season forthwith, as in 1954 when on May 3 a foot of snow fell on the diamond—and stayed there most of the month. Given the nature of Bemidji's geographic latitude, every baseball season has become touch-and-go, weather the determiner of how many games get played at home. (Weather at all times has given Beaver sports fans in general the thrill of anticipation.)

Baseball made its debut in 1933 under coach Joseph Hahn, with only three games played, two with high schools (scores not recorded) and one with St. Cloud State; the Beavers lost 3-2. That may not have been an auspicious beginning, but what followed was worse because 13 years went by before another Beaver baseball team was assembled. Again, it came after the war when in 1946 Arthur Caskey coached this one team that played one game against Moorhead State and lost it, 11 to 2. The "season" was repeated exactly in '47, except for the losing score which was 18 to 3. Improvement in '47 was seen in that the team wore uniforms provided by the school. At least they looked better.

These truncated seasons of playing no more than three games lasted until 1952 when eight games were played (Beavers won 3, lost 5), and the approximate latter number of games played became regular the rest of the decade. They had two winning seasons in the 1950s: a 4-3 record in 1953, and a 7-3 season in 1956. Paul Meadows coached for four years, 1952-55; Harry Fritz coached in 1956 and again in 1958. Keith Mooney coached in 1957.

As in track, a new coach took over baseball at decade's end. Robert Montebello, who had played shortstop for Ohio State University, brought both physical and psychological skills to the Beaver diamond in 1959, and he launched a significantly improved program into the next decade and beyond. Both the number of games played and the number of wins increased. He even began a form of "spring training" in the sense that the baseball squad went south for the one week between winter and spring quarters, and there they played southern teams, averaging a game a day. In his first year Montebello's team went 6 and 10, which in itself may not seem that great, but compared to the 0-16 record of the year before, it was a monumental improvement. The arrivals of both Montebello and Weber were only two of the many good things that happened to Bemidji State athletics as the decade of the '60s began. (Weber retired in 1984 and Montebello in 1987.)

GOLF

Intercollegiate golf had a slow development at Bemidji State. There is no record of golf team competition before 1946, and very limited competition reported after that in the next four years. Like the sport of track, men's golf got on a regular schedule in the 1950s with several dual meets each spring and the season-ending conference meet in the fall.

The school, of course, never owned its own golf course. Home meets were scheduled at the Bemidji Town and Country Club, located six miles north of town, overlooking Lake Bemidji. The 18-hole course has maintained an enviable reputation as being among the finest courses in the upper Midwest. It was the headquarters for the 1967 National Association Intercollegiate Athletics Golf Championship.

Bemidji State's golf teams' best showing in the '50s conference meets were two second places, one in 1951 and again in 1955. (Yet again a new coach, Dave Lehmann, took over the sport and 11 team championships were won between 1968 and 1990. At this writing, 1994, Lehmann is still the golf coach.)

WRESTLING

Wrestling began in 1954 with a student coach, Jack Willhite, himself an outstanding wrestler. From that year forward, however, wrestling at Bemidji State meant essentially one man, coach Chester Anderson. When Chet took over in 1955, he took a group of inexperienced young men and within a year had them competing on equal terms with the rest of the teams in the conference, and he never let up. An intense, devoted, charged-up coach, Anderson came in a winner and went out the same way. He did not like to lose, nor did his wrestlers. Their won-loss record over a quarter of a century bespoke this attitude. (BSU later had conference championships in 1972, '73, and '76. Anderson retired from the faculty in 1981; wrestling was dropped in 1983.)

CHECKING "THE OLD NUMBERS"

For statistics on the wrestling program year by year, and all of the Bemidji State sports from 1921 to 1961, there is a source available from the BSU physical education department office, a vast compendium of sports information all in one "book." It is an unpublished masters paper of about 200 mimeographed pages (not numbered) entitled "A Brief History of Intercollegiate Athletics at Bemidji State College" by Lawrence Evans Erie, dated November, 1962. Only a small part of Erie's paper is narration; the major body consists of page after page of statistical data. Despite a few inaccuracies, any reader desiring to know the particular scores and opponents for any season in any sport up to 1962 should be able to find the answer in this tome. In that sense it is a very useful document for basic information.

CHECKING "THE NEW NUMBERS"

For year-by-year information on competitive sports since 1962, interested readers can find the answers by checking the annual Recordbook published by the Northern Intercollegiate conference (before 1991-92) and since then published by the newly-named Northern Sun Intercollegiate Conference, the latter organization separating the publication into books, one for women's and another for men's sports. These sources are rife with statistics, mainly numbers about sports in one given school year, although some sections list "the leaders" in dozens of categories, going back to the early 1950s. The near endless stream of numbers upon numbers becomes numbing after a while, and for most readers, even the truest of fans, there is probably more information in these Recordbooks than one would ever care to know. (Complete set on file in Phy Ed Complex.)

For true numbers-crunchers, however, along with the curious wondering which Beaver holds which record for which sport and in which year, the Bemidji State News Service has published since 1971 an annual Media Guide for each sport, with separate Guides for men's and women's teams. This brochure-style publication gets down to the nitty-gritty, presenting virtually "everything." For example, in football under the section on "Passing," there come the categories of "Most Attempts," "Completions," "Percentage," "Touchdowns," "Interceptions," (and) "Yards," after which are listed the year, the player, the opponent, et al. For more illustrations, in the women's Guide for basketball, one page is devoted to individual records, under which come 13 categories ranging from "Most Field Goals Made" to "Most Free Throws Made" to "Most Blocked Shots." Certainly "the numbers" are there for all Beaver athletics since '62 for those who seek them. (For access to the BSU Media Guides, contact the sports information director, whose office is in the Phy Ed Complex.)

Section II: Women's Athletics–History of Women's Athletics 1969-1992

THE PHILOSOPHICAL PERIOD

Women in competitive sports at Bemidji State University have a history that details not only the growth of women's athletics from nothing to a sophisticated program of intercollegiate athletics but also a 180-degree change in the thinking and philosophy about the place of athletics for women in the University's extracurricular program.

Although the thrust of this section is to trace the development of an athletic program for women from the late 1960s through 1980, it would be incomplete if some recognition of the part played by students and faculty in the pre-1965 years were not included. Prior to 1965, college women in sport had been largely overlooked in college and university extracurricular programs throughout the country. The situation at Bemidji State University was no different. However, in spite of this campus environment, a program of sports for women at Bemidji State University did exist. It was funded and managed by students themselves, with generous support and guidance by faculty in the women's physical education department. The faculty believed that participation by Bemidji State University women undergraduates in sport with undergraduate women from neighboring institutions was both beneficial and fruitful to the student in her undergraduate professional development. The student organization which managed this program with the aid of a faculty advisor was known as the Women's Athletic Association (WAA) and later the Women's Recreational Association (WRA). The majority of student members were physical education majors.

Their program consisted of weekly meetings for sports of an intramural nature and recreational outings. Trips were few but they highlighted the quarter's activities. Students traveled in faculty cars and enjoyed a special faculty treat. They left early in the morning and returned to Bemidji late in the evening of the same day. The outings were known as "sports days" or "play days" and once at the host school, students usually played several games with each of the other institutions which had also been invited. Uniforms were generally a clean rendition of the PE class outfit, usually white. Teams in the same outfit, which frequently occurred, wore different colored pinnies. These trips were eagerly anticipated by the students. Perhaps they traveled twice a quarter, or traveled once and hosted a sports day at home.

For years WAA and later WRA applied to the Student Activity Committee for modest funding but were denied because the Student Activity Committee claimed their club was a private affair supported by membership fees when in reality the club was open to all women students. The modest membership fee they

Women's Field Hockey
"No more 'sports days' . . . by the '70s the athletic program was thoroughly established."

did charge supported their program. WRA was the seed for the athletic program to follow. It became the student sounding board for their wishes for a more sophisticated sports program than the students and their advisor were capable of providing. As these desires became more open and the dialogue louder, WRA began to shift its focus to a more competitive sports program and the assistance of faculty as teacher/coach was sought while that of the faculty advisor concept faded. This emphasis-shift was also taking place in the other neighboring institutions, and women physical educators began to question and to explore the possibility of establishing a more formal program of athletics for women. This program, they stated, meant university funding, assigned coaches, game schedules, team travel, won/loss records, etc. No more "sports days" but rather a coalition of neighboring schools with mutual interests and loyalties to the group to which they all belonged. Concordia College of Moorhead, Moorhead State University, University of Minnesota-Morris, University of North Dakota, North Dakota State University, and Bemidji State University came together and formed the Minn-Kota Conference, which was fully functioning by 1969. The conference and its athletic programs were a direct outgrowth of the "play days" of the WRA's earlier years. It is believed that the Minn-Kota Conference was one of the first athletic conferences for women in the country.

The strength of the Minn-Kota Conference rested on the geographical proximity of the six institutions, the strong faculty friendships of an earlier era, and the fact that the women were excluded from any athletic considerations by their respective institutions as well as the men's conference and by the NCAA and NAIA. This meant they were quite free to grow in the early years of Minn-Kota as their conscience dictated, and the Minn-Kota members did essentially that.

The early years were difficult for the group but the effort was of a philosophic nature as the faculty women schooled in an earlier "non-competitive program for women" philosophy struggled to adjust to new ideas and to reconcile these with their early professional trainings. Meanwhile, the sports program grew. It is important to point out that the women faculty had to go through this period of discussion in order to provide students with a solid, well grounded athletic program. Students, on the other hand, focused on the athletic program. The whys and wherefores that captured the women faculty were lost on the students. Conference sports were identified as field hockey, basketball and track, but it was not long before gymnastics, swimming, volleyball and softball were added. Bemidji State University participated in all but softball.

The early 1970s were busy years. They saw an intercollegiate program emerge from the 1960s extramural sports program. Funding for travel, equipment, uniforms and supplies grew and/or was allocated for the first time. Athletic schedules and meetings were commonplace and other institutions in Minnesota were beginning to look for alliances similar to that of Minn-Kota. As the national organization, the Association of Intercollegiate Athletics for Women (AIAW), began to form in 1971, the Minnesota institutions moved toward establishing their own state group (MAIAW) to facilitate schedules and to provide a network within the state for the dissemination and discussion of all matters relating to athletics for women. Bemidji State University continued to affiliate with Minn-Kota but rounded out its game schedules with other Minnesota schools. The MAIAW system appeared to work rather well. The women physical educators responsible for the programs learned much about women's athletics in a short period of time.

Bemidji State University assumed a leadership role in the formation of Minn-Kota, MAIAW, and later the Northern Sun Conference. Dr. Marjory Beck of the women's physical education department at Bemidji State University served as a member of the organizing committee for the three groups. She later became the first chairperson for each organization. Bemidji State University was a charter member of Minn-Kota, MAIAW, AIAW and the Northern Sun Conference.

By the mid-1970s, the women's athletic program was thoroughly established. Dr. Beck was serving as the women's athletic coordinator. Coaches were receiving a modest amount of released time for coaching duties and the facilities were scheduled for both the men's and women's practices.

Title IX was a hot topic. Its passage in the 1972-73 academic year brought the women's athletic program into the limelight as never before, both at Bemidji State University and elsewhere. Support for the women's athletic program by the Bemidji State University community, the town, and by parents of athletes leapt ahead. Several events in addition to the passage of Title IX accounted for the program's new-found popularity.

The addition of the field house to the Physical Education Complex brought the offices of men and women physical education faculty and coaches together for the first time. The Phy. Ed. Complex became the primary location for both departments. This facilitated much athletic articulation between the groups.

The complex addition plans called for a switching of men's and women's locker rooms. The women moved into a space considerably larger than they had before while the men inherited the original women's locker room to which had been added more space. This switch gave the women two rooms off the main locker rooms, spaces which the men had used as team rooms. In the late 1970s the women turned one of these rooms into a much needed training room, and the other into a weight room to support their athletic program. (By 1994, seperate no longer exist. They now have coed rooms for training and weights.)

The women's teams were consistently turning in winning performances, especially in field hockey, volleyball, swimming and gymnastics. Some teams went to national championships. In particular field hockey was a national qualifier seven times and the highest finish was seventh nationally.

The Bemidji State University community began to be interested in what the women were doing. Attendance at home games (although never very big) did grow. Faculty from other disciplines showed interest in the program, perhaps because some of their majors were athletes. The Northern Student began to carry stories about the women's games.

Men and women athletes began to form professional friendships because of a mutual interest in a sport. This was unheard of in the 1960s. Men began to work at women's games and vice versa. Even though it might have been a class assignment for phy. ed. majors, the students were free to choose which game they wished to work.

For the 1975-76 academic year, the state mandated maintenance and equipment funds for women's athletics. The women in charge of the athletic program were to be fully and solely responsible for the fund dispersal of $19,846. These monies enabled women's athletics to procure uniforms and warm-ups for each sport (gone were the tired yellow shorts and shirts). Equipment that was needed, but never before owned, and replacement equipment and supplies were obtained. It was wonderful to have for the program many of the items that had been needed for so long.

By 1975 one new position was allocated to the women's physical education department and two replacement positions were made available. In 1975 the women's athletic program earmarked the new position as women's athletic trainer. This individual came to Bemidji State University to serve as athletic trainer and in addition to plan and organize the women's athletic training room and the women's weight room.

And finally, the students themselves began to ask for athletic scholarships and by 1975 a modest amount of scholarship money became available. The monies for women student athletes grew over the years and the method of dispersal changed as the women's athletic program at Bemidji State University matured.

It is unclear just when the first meeting for the formation of the Northern Sun Conference began, but the Universities in the Minnesota State University System plus the University of Minnesota-Duluth and the University of Minnesota-Morris began to think seriously about such an arrangement in 1976-77. This step was taken by women faculty in the member institutions because they realized that inequities in funding and staffing caliber of athlete and coaching expertise were creating problems, with the haves and have nots competing against each other. Dr. Beck represented Bemidji State University at these organizational meetings and served as the group's first chairperson in 1977-78.

In the spring of 1978, Dr. Beck asked to be relieved of the athletic coordinator's position. Ann Lowdermilk assumed the responsibility. She inherited a well-established and solidly funded program. She was appointed women's athletic director and served Bemidji State University as the first titled women's athletic director.

It was with reluctance, but by mutual agreement, that the Minn-Kota Conference disbanded in 1979. For Bemidji State University it was replaced by the Northern Sun Conference which more closely resembled the men's Northern Intercollegiate Conference. Minn-Kota had served BSU well during the 1970s decade of growth and acceptance of women's athletics. As a viable extracurricular

A Game of Concentration, Skill, and Endurance
"Those who were part of some sports program. . . left with an added pride."

program at Bemidji State University, Minn-Kota had influenced the establishment of MAIAW and Northern Sun and may perhaps have extended influence in other women's athletic programs as well.

The Women's Athletic Programs Come of Age

The 1980s brought change again. The women's program began to resemble the men's program. Moreover, personnel and staff responsibilities were changing, new ideas were introduced, athletes represented many different majors and they played only one sport whereas their predecessors of the '70s played a sport each season.

Title IX was being interpreted somewhat differently at this time. There was a national movement towards integrated programs and Bemidji State University followed the trend. A change of BSU presidents and campus reorganization resulted in one combined department of physical education providing for different faculty responsibilities. Released time for coaches improved and the women's athletic program retained its identity. But change was in the wind. The 1980s might be considered a period of securing and pinning down that part of the 1970s program which was solid and discarding that portion which failed in some way to fit into the 1980s model.

The 1990s Era

In the early 1990s, the women's Northern Sun Conference and the men's Northern Intercollegiate Conference merged to form one conference - the Northern Sun Intercollegiate Conference (NSIC).

WOMEN'S BASKETBALL
INDIVIDUAL COACHING RECORDS: 1969-92

Coaches	Year	Total Years	Won	Lost
Ruth Howe	1969-76	8	90	42
Ann Lowdermilk	1977-80	4	42	50
Jo Carpenter	1981	1	2	21
Joan Campbell	1982-85	4	70	43
Sherri Mattson	1986	1	25	3
Mary McDonald	1987-89	3	43	38
Doreen Zierer	1990-1992	3	42	41

Championships/Post Season Play
Minn-Kota Conference Champs (2 times)
1974 - Coach: Ruth Howe
1976 - Coach: Ann Lowdermilk

Northern Sun Conference Champs (1 time)
1986 - Coach: Sherri Mattson

NAIA DISTRICT 13 CHAMPS (1 time)
1986 - Coach: Sherri Mattson

NAIA National Tournament Participant (1 time)
1986 - Coach: Sherri Mattson

NAIA District 13 Runner-up (1 time)
1990 - Coach: Doreen Zierer

WOMEN'S FIELD HOCKEY
INDIVIDUAL COACHING RECORDS: 1969-85

Coach	Years	Total Years	Won	Lost	Tied
Betsy McDowell	1969-85	17	338	80	18

Championships/Post Season Play
Minn-Kota Conference Champs (8 times)
1971, 1972, 1973, 1974, 1975, 1976, 1977, 1978

MAIAW Minnesota State Champs (6 times)
1975, 1976, 1977, 1978, 1979, 1980

AIAW Region Champs (4 times)
1975, 1976, 1977, 1979
2nd place finish 1978

AIAW National Champion Qualification and Participation (7 times)
AIAW - 1975, 1976, 1977, 1978
NCAA III - 1982, 1983, 1984

WIM Conference Champs (4 times)
1982, 1983, 1984, 1985

WIM Conference was formed in 1982 specifically for field hockey, as the Northern Sun Conference schools did not compete in field hockey.

The Bemidji State field hockey program was dropped as an intercollegiate sport in 1986. This was due to lack of colleges in the Midwest offering field hockey programs.

WOMEN'S VOLLEYBALL
INDIVIDUAL COACHING RECORDS: 1969-1993

Coaches	Years	Total Years	Won	Lost	Tied
Thelma Ahrens	1969-71	3	20	12	0
Stephanie Schleuder	1971	1	11	3	0
Sharon Purdy	1973-74	2	26	7	0
Pat Rosenbrock	1975-1976 1978-82 1985-89	12	293	219	4
Jan Gudknecht	1977	1	32	12	1
Linda Anderson	1983-84	2	38	60	0
Jean Musgjerd	1990	1	13	20	0
George Stowe	1991-93	3	31	72	0

Championships/Post Season Play
Minn-Kota Conference Champs
1971 - Coach: Thelma Ahrens
1972 - Coach: Stephanie Schleuder
1973 - Coach: Sharon Purdy
1974 - Coach: Sharon Purdy

1977 - Coach: Jan Gudnecht
1978 - Coach: Pat Rosenbrock

<u>Northern Sun Conference Champ</u>
1988 - Coach: Pat Rosenbrock

<u>NAIA District 13 Champs</u>
1987 - Coach: Pat Rosenbrock
1988 - Coach: Pat Rosenbrock
6 time Minn-Kota Conference Champs
4 time 2nd place in MAIAW Tourney
1 time 2nd place in AIAW Region 6 Tourney
1 time Northern Sun Conference Champs
2 time 2nd place in Northern Sun Conference

INDIVIDUAL SPORTS

Although complete statistical data is not available for the individual sports during the 1970s and 1980s, it is a well known fact that gymnastics, tennis, skiing, swimming and track and field programs were very competitive, winning cross country runs and cross country skiing conference championships during this time frame.

CROSS COUNTRY SKI TEAM: A BRIEF HISTORY

The BSU Cross Country Ski Club was formed in the late 1970s as a part of the Outdoor Program Center in the Hobson Union. During its status as a club, the women participated in AIAW National Championships and the men participated in the National Collegiate Ski Association Championships. In 1986, it became a varsity sport for both men and women, with Dr. Muriel Gilman the coach. During this time both the men and the women participated in the National Collegiate Ski Association (NSCA) events. Both the men's and women's teams successfully qualified for the national meets most years. The highlight for the men's team was in 1991, when they were third at the national meet in Bend, Oregon. The women's team highlight came the next year, in 1992, when they placed third at the national meet in Lake Placid, New York.

Fifteen athletes were named to the NCSA All-American teams of NCSA Academic All-American teams during the six years the varsity team was in existence. Of these athletes, the most outstanding scholar-athlete was Margaret (Borchers) Adelsman, who was named three times as the outstanding Academic All-American and second team All-American.

Women's Athletic History
1969-1993
1. ERAS:
  - Pre-1965 - WRA era (synch. swim/dance show)

- 1965-69 - Pre-athletic era/extramural sports era (also planning for MKC)
- 1969-70 - First year of women's athletics at BSU
- 1971-81 - AIAW era/Title IX era (Note: most women athletes PE majors)
- 1982-91 - Dual membership: NAIA/NCAA II/"Grove City"
- 1991-   NCAA era (Division II)/gender equity "push"
- 1994-95 - 25th anniversary of BSU women's athletics

2. AFFILIATIONS

Minn-Kota Conference (MKC)
1969-70 to 1978-79 Charter Member

Northern Sun Conference (NSC)
1979-80 to 1991-92 Charter Member

Northern Sun Intercollegiate Conference (NSIC)
1992-93 to Present Charter Member

WIM (Wisconsin, Iowa, Minnesota)
1982-83 to 1986-87 Charter Member

AIAW (Region 6; MAIAW)
1971-72 to 1981-82 Charter Member

NAIA (District 13)
1981-82 to 1990-91

NCAA, Division II
1982-83 to Present

3. MILESTONES:

1969-70 Minn-Kota Conference established. M. Beck first president.
First year SAFAC funding ($3,400).
Three sports added (for a total of seven).
M. Beck named women's athletics coordinator.
Status change from extramural to intercollegiate sports.

1971-72 AIAW established (also MAIAW); BSU becomes charter member.
First president of MAIAW: M. Beck.

1972-73 First year released time for coaches of women's sports (5%/sport).
SAFAC funding up to $10,000.
Title IX passed.

1973-74 First year M&E funds for women's athletics ($2,087).

1975-76 Title IX implementation target.
First year athletic grants for women ($600); divided equally among all sports.
State mandated M&E funds earmarked for women's athletics ($19,846).

1976-77 (T.9 influence).
Hired a women's athletic trainer (M. Gilman) w/ M&E funds.
Established a women's training room.

1977-78 Built a weight room in the women's locker room.

1978-79 Funding from all sources greatly increased:

M&E	=	$32,867
SAFAC	=	$30,754
Athletic Grants	=	$12,150

First Women's A.D. named: A. Lowdermilk (separate men's/women's programs).
First year for indoor track (sports increased from 7 to 8).
Final year of Minn-Kota Conference.

1979-80 First year women's coaches receive released time for recruiting.
First year of Northern Sun Conference (all Minnesota State Universities).

1980-81 Men's and women's physical education departments merged.
State-mandated M&E "bulge $$" ends. (reduction from $21,428 to $9,669).

1981-82 Add softball, cc running, golf; drop swimming (move from 10 to 8 sports).
Final year of AIAW, nationwide mergers.
P. Rosenbrock named acting women's athletic director.
First women named to the BSU Athletic Hall of Fame.

1982-83 National affiliation shifts to NAIA (Dist. 13) and NCAA II/III.

1983-84 IFO/MEA contract mandates released time for coaching (3 tiers).
Drop gymnastics (women's sports reduced from 10 to 9).

1984-85 NSC changes: St. Cloud and Mankato move to North Central Conference.
First Lady Beaver Golf Tournament (fundraising for women's athletics).

1985-86 Drop field hockey; add cross country skiing.

1986-87 <u>Women's and men's athletics merged; B. Peters named athletic director.</u>
M. Christianson named associate athletic director.

1988-89 Drop women's golf (women's sports reduced to eight).

1989-90 <u>Women's and men's athletics unmerged; M. Christianson named women's</u>
<u>athletic director.</u>

1990-91 NAIA membership dropped. Both programs NCAA II.

1991-92 NSC/NIC merger: Northern Sun Intercollegiate Conference (NSIC).
cross country running and cross country skiing dropped; women's sports
reduced to six.

1992-93 Women's and men's athletics reporting structure changed: from dean PAS
to president (through vice president for administrative affairs).

*Section III: Beaver Sports Since 1961–**Men's Teams, Years, Coaches, Records***

STUDENT BODY AGITATION: HOW HAVE STUDENTS
REACTED TO (ALLEGED) BAD COACHING?

If Bemidji State students have gained a reputation for anything over many years, and that reputation was required to be reduced to one hyphenated word, it would likely be non-demonstrative.

Bemidji State has never been a seedbed of radicalism. With rare exception— the student protests and marches of the late 1960s—Bemidji State has drawn "a different breed of cats" than that element who show up at the University of Minnesota. Bemidji State students may writhe but seldom rise.

This generalization has held true for sports at Bemidji, also. Most students who are dissatisfied with a coach or program show their dissent with their legs; they stop going to the contests. (Yes, on a few occasions there have been grumping letters in the <u>Northern Student</u> calling attention to a certain coach's "limitations," but that's about the limit of opposition.)

Only twice in 75 years have there actually been actual "student marches/protests" on behalf of some coach. Both involved basketball coaches in the 1960s. The first protest was a march, of sorts, to the president's home, seeking not the firing but the retention of the coach. (They were a happy and courteous group of perhaps 35 "protesters," many participating because they were out for a walk on a warm spring night and joined in just to see what was happening.) The president opened his door, walked out on the porch, and received pleasant applause from the students standing in his yard. He listened, then accepted a petition, then said he'd take it under advisement, and went back in, after which the crowd dispersed.

Upshot: The coach was "let go" anyway.

The second "protest" did gain some media attention in that newspaper reporters came and took pictures of "the coach" being hanged in effigy from an oak tree just outside the front door of the phy ed building. (It was near Halloween and stuffed dummies were readily available.) Less than a half-dozen students were behind the "hanging," but they were sincere, yea obsessively driven, in their message to fire this particular coach because of the man's egregious "mistakes" in general, and dumbest-of-dumb decisions the night before when he "gave away" the

Beaver Baseball

"Given the nature of Bemidji's latitude, every season has become touch-and-go."

game. (Their "joke": "Next year let _____ go to work for Target; there he can sell games instead of giving them away.") Upshot: The coach stayed. Poetic justice (?): The next year BSC won the conference (12-0) and he took the Beavers to the NAIA district playoffs.

Not that unhappy students do not grouse about certain coaches. The student union finds tables of grumbling, disgusted students who almost daily have "roast coach" for lunch, but there the protest stops.[23]

FOOTBALL
INDIVIDUAL COACHING RECORDS: 1962-1993

Coaches	Years	Total Years	Won	Lost	Tied
Chester Anderson	1962-66	4	18	15	1
Don Palm	1966-69	3	9	16	1
Jim Malmquist	1969-74	5	15	27	2
Larry Mortier	1974-75	1	2	7	0
Don Turner	1975-78	3	14	15	0
Richard (Sparky) Adams	1978-82	4	3	35	1
John Peterson	1982-89	7	30	40	3
Kris Diaz	1989-	5	9	40	0

YEARLY BSU BASEBALL RECORDS

Coach	Year	Total Years	Won	Lost	Tied
Bob Montebello	1962-1987	26	275	457	2
Doug Smith	1988-1994	7	131	145	3

MEN'S SWIMMING
Men's Swimming Coaching Highlights

Coach	Years	Highlights
Don Palm	1964-67	Conference champions 1966, 1967 NAIA second-Place finish, 1967
Bob Leahy	1968	Conference champion
Lee Ahlbrecht	1969-1991	Conference champions 1969, 1970, 1971 1972, 1978, 1979, 1980, 1981 NAIA Top 10 finishes 12 times, highest were fourth-place finishes in 1979, 1980, 1984 and 1985

GOLF CHAMPIONS
Men's Golfing Conference Championships:
1968, 1969, 1975, 1976, 1978, 1981, 1983, 1986, 1987, 1988, 1989

---

23) Pity the poor presidents when it comes to campus athletics. Theirs is a difficult job whether teams win or lose. Even the least supportive have not allowed any team to become a patsy and thus gave some support to athletics and in so doing immediately received criticism for too much backing!? Any university president can list the three basic requirements for overall success: 1) athletics for the alumni, 2) sex for the students, and 3) parking for the faculty.

BASKETBALL
INDIVIDUAL COACHING RECORDS: 1962-1993

Coaches	Year	Total Years	Won	Lost
Wesley (Zeke) Hogeland	1962-67	5	65	46
Dave Hutchins	1968-81	14	142	201
Karl Salscheider	1981-85	4	42	71
Will Baird	1985-86	1	12	15
Karl Salscheider	1986-94	8	98	118

HOCKEY
INDIVIDUAL COACHING RECORDS 1947-50, 1959-1994

Coach	Years	Total Seasons	Won	Lost	Tied
Jack Aldrich	1948	1	1	9	0
Eric Hughes	1949-50	2	17	13	0
Vic Weber	1960-1964 1966	6	42	19	2
Wayne Peterson	1965	1	10	1	1
R. H. Bob Peters	1967-82 1984-94	27	582	200	34
Mike Gibbons	1983	1	30	6	1

The first intercollegiate hockey game played in the United States of America was in 1888 when Brown University defeated the Harvard squad, 6-0. Hockey as a competitive sport at Bemidji State began in 1946, sort of, even if there was no faculty member as school coach, no rink, no uniforms, few interested players, and an equal uninterest in College financial support for yet another sport viewed then as not much needed. Who would have believed that 20 years later the hockey program would have grown in size, interest and support to the degree that it rivaled basketball and football as the school's most popular form of athletic competition. In less than 10 years after that, by 1970, hockey had surpassed both of its rivals. Hockey became the biggest in student and town popularity for one simple reason, the teams won most of the time. Indeed, the Beaver squads first became—and then remained—essentially nationally-ranked powerhouses. (For confirmation/information, see won-loss charts previous pages; for dramatic visual impact, see the dozens of banners hanging along the southern wall in the BSU hockey arena.)

Considering Beaver hockey's humble beginnings after World War II, its fragile existence for the next three years, and then a 10-year period of no games at all (1949-59), its later mushrooming growth and subsequent fame make its dominance even more remarkable. And yet a hockey season is as natural to northern Minnesota and Bemidji State as . . . well, . . . winter. They have gone very well together. The game is rooted in northern Minnesota tradition in part because of Bemidji's close proximity to Canada.

From International Falls to Brainerd, hockey has been a way of life for hundreds of young lads and Bemidji State became an extension of that way of life for dozens of talented young players raised in the northland. High school hockey in the state goes back some 75 years, although there was no state tournament held until 1945 when Eveleth won it. Northern teams continued to dominate the state meets until the 1960s, when Twin Cities' programs began catching up with their northern rivals—and soon these southern teams snared more than their share of high school state tournament titles.

Beaver hockey has a relatively brief history but yet one that can be considered as rich and successful as any small college in the country. The school has produced some of the top players in the nation, with many making All-American status, some playing on U.S.A. Olympic teams, and a few making it to the professional National Hockey League. Also, more hockey coaches have been produced from the BSU program than any other institution in the Midwest, a factor that has helped in recruiting even more and better players.

When Robert H. "Bob" Peters was hired to take over the hockey reins in 1966, a dynasty had begun, although few knew it at the time. Peters came to Bemidji State from the University of North Dakota, where as head coach he had led the 1965 Sioux to the Western Collegiate Hockey Association (WCHA) championship and third place in the National Collegiate Hockey Association (NCAA) Division I tournament. Peters had an admirable 42-20-1 record at UND and was named the 1965 WCHA "Coach of the Year." As the assistant coach in 1963, Peters helped the Sioux win the NCAA title.

The first championship for the Bemidji State squad came in Peters' rookie year (1966-67) when the Beavers won the Minnesota Collegiate Championship with 13-5-1 record, and the home games were played on the outdoor rink. The dynasty had started. The first national title followed in the next season as the 16-8 Beavers won the National Association of Intercollegiate Athletics (NAIA) crown. That season also found the first games played on the Beavers' own indoor ice. Their November 17, 1967, field house debut was spoiled, however, when the Minnesota National team scored a goal with 50 seconds remaining in the contest to win 6-5. Over 3,000 fans that night made up the standing-room-only crowd.

Subsequently, neither the large crowds nor the general success of the hockey squads have ever let up. In 1968 the Minneapolis Tribune declared Bemidji State as having "possibly the best small college hockey team in the world," and they lived up to that kind of billing by winning four consecutive NAIA championships. At one point they set the collegiate record for the longest winning streak of 42 games. The Beavers became such a dominating force as to win nine of the last ten conference championships awarded before the International Collegiate Hockey

Association suspended operations after the 1978 season. A few knowledgeable aficionados of the sport believed those early Golden Years and those "dream teams" (Bryan Grand, Blaine Comstock, Terry Bergstrom, Jim McElmury, Terry Burns, Barry Dillon, Charlie Brown, Bruce Falk, Jude Boulianne), could never be equaled, but they soon were, and soon there were new stars, such skilled players as Mark Eagles, Mike Alexander, Drey Bradley, Gary Ross, Scott Johnson, Rod Heisler, Jim Scanlan, Jamie Erb, and Gary Sergeant, the latter leaving after one year to play for the U.S. National Team, then the Minnesota North Stars and the Los Angeles Kings. Joel Otto played four years as a Beaver before signing with the NHL Calgary Flames in 1984. Dale Smedsmoe joined the Toronto Maple Leafs and McElmury the Colorado Rockies. This was big time hockey.

And on and on Bemidji State hockey went forward . . . the big crowds . . . the winning seasons . . . the tournament playoffs. . . . Yet another national championship in 1986 gave Coach Peters the unique honor of his Beaver teams winning a title in each of four national affiliation championship games. And recently one more NCAA Division II national championship title came in March of 1993 in a 24-7 season. Little wonder that in 1993 Peters would join a tiny group of hockey coaches with 600 wins—and Peters had the highest win-loss percentage among all active collegiate hockey coaches.

Bemidji State made it back-to-back NCAA Division II national titles in 1994 with tournament wins over the University of Alabama in Huntsville, the games played in Huntsville. The Beaver come-from-behind victory in this, their eleventh national crown, occurred with a 2-1 sudden death overtime win. Bemidji State fans attending the contests in Huntsville were outnumbered 6,400 to 51 but these numbers did not deter their enthusiasm. Led by the all-student-run band, the Red Line Swingers, the 51 Beaver backers endured a 25 hour bus trip from Bemidji to Huntsville, but the rides became more than tolerable because of the outcome. The disappointed reporter for the Huntsville Times summed up the tournament with the unique line: "It was a hellish end to a heavenly hockey weekend." (March 13, 1994, p. 9D).

Beaver hockey fans, unlike those for the other sports, have not ridden the emotional roller coaster of seasonal ups and downs because, with the exception of one year, hockey squads have been steady winners since 1960. It has been exciting and it has been remarkable. Bemidji State University as an institution has benefited mightily over the years from the publicity—yea, national recognition—that has come because of its hockey program. It has put the whole town on the American map for something besides Paul Bunyan and cold winters. Nothing succeeds like success, and thus Coach Peters' simple, succinct, superb understatement: "The players are well-informed of the program's success when they enter it. Tradition is a lasting victory."

The End

APPENDICES

Appendix A

All State University System Programs

MSUS ACADEMIC AREAS WITHIN THE STATE SYSTEM:

BEHAVIORAL SCIENCES
    Counseling
    Psychology
BIOLOGICAL SCIENCES
    Aquatic Biology
    Biochemistry
    Biology
    Biomedical Science
BUSINESS ADMINISTRATION
    Agribusiness
    Accounting
    Business Administration/Management
    Economics
    Finance
    Institutional Management
    Insurance
    International Business
    Marketing
    Quantitative Methods & Information Systems
    Real Estate
BUSINESS EDUCATION
    Business Education
    Office Administration
COMMUNICATIONS
    Mass Communications
    Radio, TV & Film
    Journalism
    Speech/Speech Communications

COMPUTERS AND COMPUTER SCIENCE
  Computer Information Systems
  Computer Science
EDUCATION
  Curriculum & Instruction
  Early Childhood & Family Studies
  Educational Administration
  Elementary Education
  Secondary Education
  Reading
ENGINEERING
  Computer Engineering
  Electrical Engineering
  Industrial Engineering
  Materials Engineering
  Mechanical Engineering
ENGINEERING TECHNOLOGY
  Electrical Engineering Technology
  Engineering Technology
  Industrial & Technical Studies
  Industrial Technology
  Manufacturing Engineering
  Mechanical Engineering Technology
  Photographic Engineering Technology
  Photographic Science & Instrumentation
ENGLISH
  Creative Writing
  English
  Linguistics
  Literature
ENVIRONMENTAL STUDIES
ETHNIC/MINORITY STUDIES
  Indian Studies
  Latin American Studies
  East Asian Studies
  Minority and Ethnic Studies
  Scandinavian Studies
FOREIGN LANGUAGES - WESTERN ALPHABET
  French
  German
  Spanish
  Other

FOREIGN LANGUAGES - NONWESTERN ALPHABET
>	Russian
>	Arabic
>	Chinese
>	Other

GEOGRAPHY
>	Geography
>	Local & Urban Affairs
>	Urban & Regional Studies

HEALTH SCIENCES/EDUCATION
>	School & Community Health
>	Nursing
>	Physical Therapy
>	Vocational Rehabilitation Therapy

HEALTH TECHNOLOGY
>	Medical Technology
>	Nuclear Medical Technology
>	Physical Therapy
>	Biotechnology

HOME ECONOMICS
INDUSTRIAL ARTS
INTERDISCIPLINARY STUDIES
>	American Studies
>	Human Relations
>	Multidisciplinary Studies
>	Women's Studies

LAW/CRIMINAL JUSTICE
>	Legal Assistance/Paralegal
>	Corrections
>	Criminal Justice
>	Law Enforcement

LEARNING RESOURCES
>	Educational Technology
>	Information Media
>	Library Media

MATHEMATICS
PERFORMING ARTS
>	Music
>	Music Management
>	Theatre Arts

PHILOSOPHY

PHYSICAL EDUCATION AND RECREATION
    Athletic Training
    Physical Education
    Recreation, Park & Leisure Services
PHYSICAL SCIENCES
    Astronomy
    Chemistry
    Earth Sciences
    General Science
    Geology
    Physics
POLITICAL SCIENCES
    History
    International Relations
    Political Science
PUBLIC AFFAIRS
    Community Education
    Community Service
    Human Services Planning & Administration
    Public Administration
SOCIAL SCIENCES
    Anthropology
    Social Science
    Social Work
    Sociology
SPECIAL EDUCATION
    Special Education/Special Education Administration
    Experiential Education
    Early/Exceptional Education
SPEECH SCIENCE
    Communications Disorders
    Speech/Language Pathology
VISUAL ARTS
    Art
    Art Administration
    Art History
    Art Studio
    Commercial Design
    Graphic Design
    Industrial/Technical Illustration

Appendix B

Greetings From the Board of Directors
BEMIDJI STATE UNIVERSITY COMMENCEMENT

Presented by Elizabeth A. Pegues
President, Minnesota State University Board
May 22, 1991

President Duly, Platform Guests, Faculty and Staff, Students, Friends . . . and the CLASS OF 1992: Good Afternoon. I am pleased to bring you greetings on behalf of the Minnesota State University Board of Directors. Participating in a commencement ceremony is as exciting for me as it is for the graduating student. It presents me with the opportunity to share in your accomplishment and to also reflect on my Board responsibilities. Only at Commencement do the two things converge: RESPONSIBILITY and ACCOMPLISHMENT. The mission of the State University System is to provide affordable, accessible education of high quality, which will enrich individual lives . . . increase economic opportunity . . . and to promote a caring and just community. The seven State Universities within our System are committed to the exploration and dissemination of knowledge . . . development of cultural, intellectual, and humane sensitivities . . . improvement of professional, scientific, and technological competence . . . and enhancement of personal values and purpose. Bemidji State University reflects that mission. I extend our Board's thanks to the University and congratulations to these graduates.

While most of my work deals with academic policy and governance, I am cognizant that the real work takes place on the campus . . . and in the classroom. I wish to thank the faculty for their outstanding work in academic planning, and enthusiastic teaching. I also thank the administrators and staff for their efforts in supporting these students with advice and counsel . . . and for helping to maintain a vibrant and stimulating learning environment. I am confident that this graduating class has been well prepared for the future. Finally, I wish to extend the Board's thanks to these graduates' strongest supporters. Thank you - wives, husbands, and significant others. Thank you - mothers, fathers, children, brothers and sisters, and other extended family members. Thank you - babysitters, employers, neighbors, co-workers, and friends of these graduates. Thank you for your encouragement . . . your sacrifice . . . and many times, your patience. Without your help, many of these people would not be here now.

Last month, we all watched this nation take an embarrassing step backward, [Los Angeles Riots]. We discovered that our country is, after all, less perfect than you and I had hoped and believed. For you graduates, this ceremony, as serious, and exciting, and memorable as it may be, is not the end. It is the beginning. . . . The beginning of new challenges . . . new horizons . . . new opportunities . . . and new dreams. We look to you to make a difference. On behalf of the Board of the Minnesota State University System, I wish you every success.

Thank you.

Appendix C   **Beltrami County**
1990 Census
Total Population: 34,384
Figure written in each square is the
population per township

Unorganized No. 1
42

| Benville 98 | Spruce Grove 81 | Minnie 9 |
| Lee 50 | Hamre 27 | Steenerson 44 |

Unorganized No. 2
4

Waskish
111

Upper Red Lake - Unorg.
23

Ponemah 790

Shotley
57

Shotley Brook (Eland) Unorg #2 23

Battle 53

Woodrow
97

Kelliher
100

Kelliher
344

75

Cormant
199

Shooks
217

Red Lake Reservation

Little Rock 714

Red lake 1068

Redby 787

Lower Red Lake Unorg. 200

Lower Red lake Unorg. 62

Quiring

O'Brien
80

Langor
186

Hornet
225

Funkley
15

Alaska 256

Nebish
301

Roosevelt
180

Maple Ridge
95

Durand 135

Hagali
255

Hines
556

Tenstrike 184

Summit
237

Blackduck
718

Buzzle
277

Liberty
473

Turtle Lake
838

Port Hope
505

Turtle River 62

Taylor
133

Birch
85

Lammers
390

Eckles
805

Northern
3638

Turtle River
799

Sugar Bush
113

Moose Lake
166

Solway 74

Jones
230

Wilton 171

Grant Valley
1040

Bemidji 245

Bemidji 2660

Frohn
1151

Ten Lake
651

Brook Lake Unorg. 3
176

Bemidji: Population

Ward 1	2217
Ward 2	2219
Ward 3	2235
Ward 4	2250
Ward 5	2324
Blackduck	718
Kelliher	348
Funkley	15
Tenstrike	184
Turtle River	62
Solway	74
Wilton	171

Appendix D

Fall Quarter Headcount Enrollment at Bemidji State University 1919-1993

Year	On Campus Classes			Other Classes*			Total Enrollment all Classes		
	Undergr/Unclass	Graduate	Total	Undergr/Unclass	Graduate	Total	Undergr/Unclass	Graduate	Total
1919	38		38			0	38	0	38
1920	138		138			0	138	0	138
1921	211		211			0	211	0	211
1922	270		270			0	270	0	270
1923	331		331			0	331	0	331
1924	322		322			0	322	0	322
1925	294		294	20		20	314	0	314
1926	293		293	12		12	305	0	305
1927	252		252	11		11	263	0	263
1928	233		233	21		21	254	0	254
1929	242		242	29		29	271	0	271
1930	241		241	27		27	268	0	268
1931	322		322	16		16	338	0	338
1932	395		395			0	395	0	395
1933	329		329			0	329	0	329
1934	283		283			0	283	0	283
1935	267		267			0	267	0	267
1936	257		257			0	257	0	257
1937	229		229			0	229	0	229
1938	361		361			0	361	0	361
1939	410		410	15		15	425	0	425
1940	501		501			0	501	0	501
1941	383		383	14		14	397	0	397
1942	283		283			0	283	0	283
1943	141		141			0	141	0	141
1944	146		146	9		9	155	0	155

Year	On Campus Classes			Other Classes*			Total Enrollment Classes		
	Undergr/Unclass	Graduate	Total	Undergr/Unclass	Graduate	Total	Undergr/Unclass	Graduate	Total
1945	184		184			0	184	0	184
1946	575		575			0	575	0	575
1947	598		598			0	598	0	598
1948	573		573			0	573	0	573
1949	604		604			0	604	0	604
1950	575		575			0	575	0	575
1951	462		462			0	462	0	462
1952	471		471			0	471	0	471
1953	511		511	33		33	544	0	544
1954	601		601	30		30	631	0	631
1955	706		706	9		9	715	0	715
1956	846		846	108		108	954	0	954
1957	840	7	847	208		208	1048	7	1055
1958	1024	13	1037	194		194	1218	13	1231
1959	1297	21	1318	238		238	1535	21	1556
1960	1511	32	1543	181		181	1692	32	1724
1961	1645	61	1706	211		211	1856	61	1917
1962	1833	121	1954	251	17	268	2084	138	2222
1963	2094	110	2204	288	62	350	2382	172	2554
1964	2499	148	2647	229	44	273	2728	192	2920
1965	3036	163	3199	173	18	191	3209	181	3390
1966	3425	130	3555	129	182	311	3554	312	3866
1967	3959	134	4093	153	308	461	4112	442	4554
1968	4275	217	4492	271	319	590	4546	536	5082
1969	4457	277	4734	192	190	382	4649	467	5116
1970	4535	288	4823	153	727	880	4688	1015	5703
1971	4640	225	4865	307	440	747	4947	665	5612
1972	4348	277	4625	236	473	709	4584	750	5334
1973	4085	238	4323	340	874	1214	4425	1112	5537

Year	On Campus Classes			Other Classes*			Total Enrollment all Classes		
	Undergr/Unclass	Graduate	Total	Undergr/Unclass	Graduate	Total	Undergr/Unclass	Graduate	Total
1974	3870	257	4127	258	640	898	4128	897	5025
1975	3963	245	4208	664	583	1247	4627	828	5455
1976	4134	250	4384	456	796	1252	4590	1046	5636
1977	4147	252	4399	574	325	899	4721	577	5298
1978	4032	218	4250	538	492	1030	4570	710	5280
1979	4014	270	4284	739	511	1250	4753	781	5534
1980	4148	226	4374	703	710	1413	4851	936	5787
1981	4257	172	4429	473	236	709	4730	408	5138
1982	4105	198	4303	308	282	590	4413	480	4893
1983	3938	159	4097	316	110	426	4254	269	4523
1984	3817	167	3984	326	188	514	4143	355	4498
1985	3756	187	3943	369	223	592	4125	410	4535
1986	3697	215	3912	381	231	612	4078	446	4524
1987	3776	202	3978	375	407	782	4151	609	4760
1988	4138	217	4355	428	252	680	4566	469	5035
1989	4360	247	4607	378	207	585	4738	454	5192
1990	4400	258	4658	496	269	765	4896	527	5423
1991	4448	262	4710	503	180	683	4951	442	5393
1992	4445	228	4673	391	196	587	4836	424	5260
1993	4263	207	4470	357	164	521	4620	371	4991

*Includes extension, senior citizens, external studies and workshops.

Appendix E
Sample of Historical Trivia

The 50s were a strange trip. One of the biggest stars of the time played an accordion; a picket was a kind of fence; people called Arthur Godfrey's gentle kidding of commercials freedom; a starlet named Joan Weldon was renamed in a contest sponsored by a luggage company; people found communists under every bed; pants were so narrow around the cuff that you couldn't get them on if you were wearing socks; it was the Eisenhower years. And people say that the 1950s may be in for a revival. This section will treat some of the phenomena of the era. In the meantime, take a look at these names—they were all big numbers during the 1950s, beginning with:

Sherman Adams
Holden Caulfield
George Nader
Julie Adams
Denise Lor
Marian Marlowe
Haleloke
Snooky Lanson
Maggi McNellis
Yolanda Betbeze
Colored people
Greenwich Village
North Beach
Julie London
Cisco Kid
Coonskin Caps
Bernard Goldfine
Alger Hiss
Rosenbergs
H-bombs
SAC
Vikki Dugan
Tony Curtis & Janet Leigh
Piper Laurie
The Thing
Cinemascope
3-D movies

New York Giants
Brooklyn Dodgers
Dick Contino
Florian Zabach
Rocky Marciano
Which Twin Has The Toni?
Margarine With A Red Button
Nickel cokes
1/2 inch belts
The Chemise/The Sack
red lipstick
white lipstick
Elaine Stewart
The New York Yankees
"Bobby Thompson's Home Run"
Sortilege
The Stork Club
Studio One

Milton Berle   Red Buttons

Playhouse 90
Existentialism
Juliette Greco
John Agar
Audie Murphy
Brainwashing
Igor Gouzenko
Bulganin
Malenkov
Mary Hartline
Roxanne
Faith Domergue
Cecile Aubry
Pink dress shirts
Charcoal suits
Henry J
Captain Video
Steve Allen
Yalu River
Pusan
William Holden
marty
madras
"Knock, knock"
"Have you heard about his brother Enos?"
Strike It Rich
Sputnik
Stu Erwin

I Remember Mama
Tab, Rock, etc.
Wrestling-Georgeous George
Abstract Expressionism
Mickey Spillane
By Love Possessed
Roller Derby
Buckle-back trousers
Beat Generation
Silent Generation
Desert boots/fruit boots
white bucks
pegged pants
D.A. haircuts
circle pins
crew cuts/flat tops
peroxide streaks
M.G.'s
Raymond Loewy
waist cinchers/merry widows
45s
fraternities
drag races—"chicken"
Dave Brubeck
clip-on bow ties

Stalin

Faye Emerson

Appendix F
BSU Faculty Since 1945

(Memo to author from Arlene Tangborn,
Office of Institutional Research, Oct. 15, 1992)
Your request for the number of faculty by gender and/or race since 1945 is a
difficult one to fulfill. Part of the problem involves the time of the year the numbers
are taken, part-time/full-time, teaching/non-teaching, FTE versus headcount, etc.
I searched some of our files for reports that have been produced over the years and
zeroed in on on-campus "teaching" full-time faculty. Full-time faculty are those
who, in the most part, teach at least 50% of their loads. Laboratory school, library,
and counseling non-instructional positions are excluded.

I used fall quarter of each year as the base reporting period. While I did not get data
for each year, I hope the following is of some assistance. You will note that the
number of women versus men was not accessible until 1961.

Fall Quarter   The Number of Full Time Teaching Faculty

1945-48 and 1955 numbers were extracted from load studies found in my files:

Fall Quarter	Number
1945	23
1946	32
1947	38
1948	39
1955	35

1961-67 numbers were extracted from faculty rosters found in my files:

Fall Quarter	Number
1961	90 (25 women)
1962	99 (28 women)
1963	115 (27 women)
1964	131 (30 women)
1966	184 (40 women)
1967	212 (45 women)

1968-1991 numbers were extracted from the U.S. Department of Education reports:

Fall Quarter	Number
1968	198 (# women not known)
1969	213 (# women not known)
1970	233 (# women not known)
1971	207 (38 women)
1972	195 (35 women)
1974	191 (32 women)
1976	188 (29 women)
1977	191 (33 women)

1978	200 (37 women)
1979	197 (34 women)
1980	176 (27 women)
1981	171 (25 women)
1983	184 (34 women)
1984	180 (39 women)
1985	202 (47 women)
1987	225 (59 women)
1990	226 (62 women)
1991	208 (54 women)
1992	218 (63 women)
1993	213 (62 women)

Appendix G
Bemidi State Student Body Presidents

1929-30 Erma Atwood	1969-70 John Borg
1930-31 Roscoe Stilwell	1970-71 John Borg
1931-32 John T. Schuiling	1971-72 Dave Sorenson
1932-33 Harold Hoganson	1972-73 Michael Conway
1933-34 Stan Oksness	1973-74 Dennis Erickson
1934-35 William McNelly	1974-75 Chris Wegner
1935-36 Glenn Holty	1975-76 Pat Pelstring
1936-37 Robert Doty	1976-77 Gary Gunderson
1937-38 Walter Schuiling	1977-78 Tom Gray
1938-39 Milton Bentley	1978-79 Mark Morphew and
1939-40 Lewis Doty	Alan Bates
1940-41 George Taylor	1979-80 Al Bates and
1941-42 John Schock	Ross Millar
1942-43 Winston Benson	1980-81 Mark Morphew and
1943-44 Priscilla Hepokoski	Brad McDonald
1944-45 Eva Mae Cann	1981-82 Brad McDonald
1945-46 Faith Fleener	1982-83 Tom Anderson
1946-47 Joseph Logsdon	1983-84 Dave Ghostley
1947-48 Louis Marchand	1984-85 Dan Olson and
1948-49 Earl Gregoire	Mark Holmquist
1949-50 Bruce Atwater	1985-86 Jill Sannes
1950-51 Harry Welinski	1986-87 Roxanne DeVries
1951-52 Wes Balk	1987-88 Erich Campbell
1952-53 Wes Balk	1988-89 Scott Anderson
1953-54 William Marchand	1989-90 Valerie Field
1954-55 Paul Welter	1990-91 Jeremy C. Havel
1955-56 James Baril	1991-92 Gina Fink
1956-57 James Baril	1992-93 Katie Kelly
1957-58 Dave Trompeter	1993-94 Marina Nadarajah
1958-59 Dave Trompeter	
1959-60 Dennis Nord	
1960-61 George Welte	
1961-62 Jerry O'Neil	
1962-63 Larry Jorgenson	
1963-64 Lynn Smith	
1964-65 Ed McDunn	
1965-66 Jim Lindberg	
1966-67 John Ludwig	
1967-68 Al Brusewitz	
1968-69 Jack Hamre	

Appendix H
Bemidji State University
Summary of Existing Academic and Support Space

Buildings:	Year Completed Additions, & Remodeling	Total Square Feet in the Building
Bangsberg Fine Arts Complex	1971	86,878
Deputy Hall	1919, 1928, 1949, 1979, 1981	78,656
Heating Plant and Garage	1926, 1949, 1964, 1965, 1978, 1984, 1991	20,317
Harold T. Peters Hall	1972	3,999
Boat House	1969	1,200
Sattgast Hall	1962, 1989	84,248
Memorial Hall	1940	53,893
Sanford Hall	1920, 1979, 1980	17,012
Hagg-Sauer Hall	1970	82,478
Bridgeman Hall	1964	33,772
A.C. Clark Library	1966	68,073
Education-Art Building	1950, 1986	53,342
Stadium	1938	19,911
Hickory Hall	1957, 1964, 1979	29,423
Physical Education Complex	1959, 1967	121,586
Maintenance Building	1978	8,080
Receiving	1979	6,240
Electrical Sub-Station	1960	220
Pump House	1953	80
Recreation-Fitness Center	1989	85,765
Skyway	1979	2,428
Tunnels		25,520
Total Academic and Support Space		883,121

Other Buildings:

Hobson Memorial Union	1967, 1972	76,756
Birch Hall	1952	62,184
Linden Hall	1959, 1964	67,565
Tamarack Hall	1969	88,410
Pine Hall	1959, 1961	89,397

Walnut Hall Food Service	1969	57,167
Oak Hall	1965, 1966	128,550
Maple Hall	1967, 1968	94,635
Boat House	1988	1,800
Total Other Buildings Space		666,464
Total Space of all Buildings		1,549,585

Appendix I
IFO (Inter Faculty Organization; the faculty union)
Official Membership Figures as of 1 December, 1992

Campus	Total Faculty	Members	Non-Members	Percent Total
Akita	44.8	31	7	81.6%
Last Year		28	9	75.7%
Bemidji	253.3	195	36	84.4%
Last Year		195	34	85.2%
Mankato	701.8	479	136	77.9%
Last Year		464	140	76.8%
Metropolitan	124.5	68	5	93.2%
Last Year		67	5	93.1%
Moorhead	399.3	323	47	87.3%
Last Year		336	35	90.6%
Southwest	139.9	127	5	96.2%
Last Year		127	7	94.8%
St. Cloud	702.8	539	93	85.3%
Last Year		537	100	84.3%
Winona	390.6	305	35	89.7%
Last Year		287	28	91.1%
Totals:	2757	2067	364	85.0%
Last Year:		2041	358	85.1%
Percent Change:	1.27%	1.68%	1.33%	

Appendix J

What Might Have Been:

FIRST NAME-CHOICE,
later changed, when the school became
designated a University in 1975.

(President Robert Decker changed his mind just prior to
the deadline decision in the Spring of 1975 and instead specified
Bemidji State University as the official title.)

Appendix K

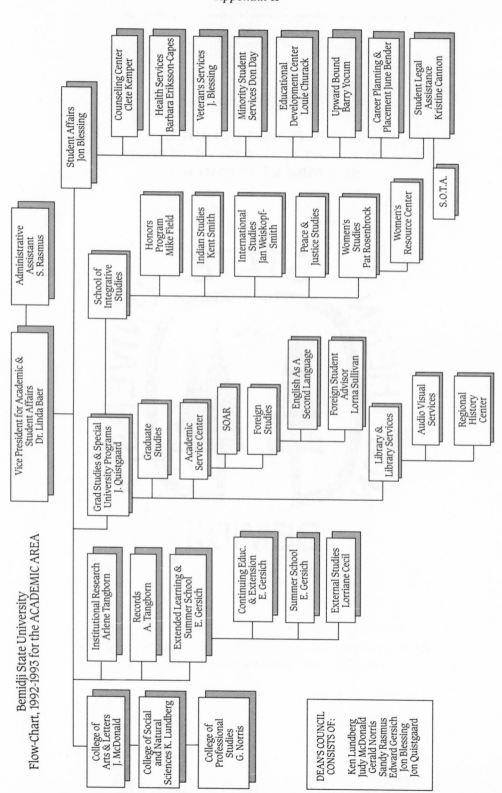

Bemidji State University
Flow-Chart, 1992-1993 for the ACADEMIC AREA

Vice President for Academic & Student Affairs
Dr. Linda Baer

Administrative Assistant
S. Rasmus

Student Affairs
Jon Blessing

Counseling Center
Clete Kemper

Health Services
Barbara Eriksson-Capes

Veteran's Services
J. Blessing

Minority Student Services Don Day

Educational Development Center
Louie Churack

Upward Bound
Barry Yocum

Career Planning & Placement June Bender

Student Legal Assistance
Kristine Cannon

S.O.T.A.

School of Integrative Studies

Honors Program
Mike Field

Indian Studies
Kent Smith

International Studies
Jan Weiskopf-Smith

Peace & Justice Studies

Women's Studies
Pat Rosenbrock

Women's Resource Center

Grad Studies & Special University Programs
J. Quistgaard

Graduate Studies

Academic Service Center

SOAR

Foreign Studies

English As A Second Language

Foreign Student Advisor
Lorna Sullivan

Library & Library Services

Audio Visual Services

Regional History Center

Institutional Research
Arlene Tangborn

Records
A. Tangborn

Extended Learning & Summer School
E. Gersich

Continuing Educ. & Extension
E. Gersich

Summer School
E. Gersich

External Studies
Lorriane Cecil

College of Arts & Letters
J. McDonald

College of Social and Natural Sciences K. Lundberg

College of Professional Studies
G. Norris

DEAN'S COUNCIL CONSISTS OF:

Ken Lundberg
Judy McDonald
Gerald Norris
Sandy Rasmus
Edward Gersich
Jon Blessing
Jon Quistgaard

Appendix L

BSU Scholarship Sources - (1994)

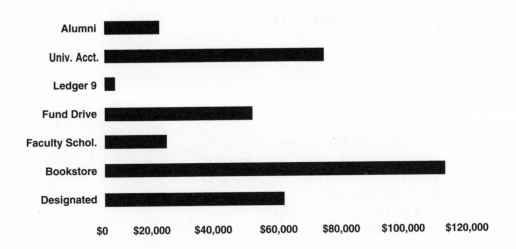

RECIPIENTS
BSU Scholarship Breakdown

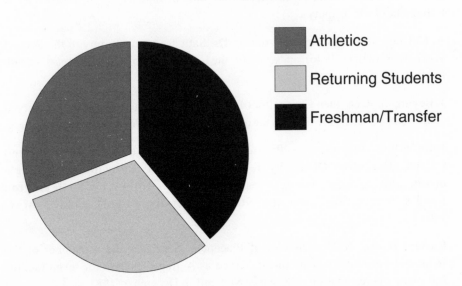

Appendix M

THE PRESIDENTS OF
BEMIDJI STATE NORMAL SCHOOL (1919 - 1921)
BEMIDJI STATE TEACHERS COLLEGE (1921 - 1957)
BEMIDJI STATE COLLEGE (1957 - 1975)
BEMIDJI STATE UNIVERSITY (1975 -   )

1. MANFRED W. DEPUTY 1919 - 1938
        E. Wayne Beck, Acting President 1938
2. CHARLES R. SATTGAST 1938 - 1964
        Archie C. Clark, Acting President 1942 - 1946
                    1964
3. HARRY F. BANGSBERG 1964 - 1967
        J. Bevington Reed, Acting President 1967
        John S. Glas, Acting President 1967 - 1968
4. ROBERT D. DECKER 1968 - 1980
5. REBECCA STAFFORD 1980 - 1981
        Richard R. Haugo, Acting President 1982 - 1982
6. LOWELL R. GILLETT 1982 - 1990
7. LESLIE C. DULY 1990 - 1993
        Linda L. Baer, Acting President 1993-1994
8. M. JAMES BENSEN 1994 -

NOTES:
E. W. Beck was Acting President for one month, January, 1938, following the retirement of Mr. Deputy.

A. C. Clark served as President during Dr. Sattgast's tour of duty in the Second World War II (1942-1946), and again for the five months following Sattgast's death in 1964.

J. Bevington Reed, then Chancellor of the Minnesota State College Board, served technically as Acting President in the month following the death of Harry Bangsberg.

John Glas, Assistant to President Harry Bangsberg, was appointed Campus Executive Office by J. Bevington Reed following Bangsberg's death, and became Acting President of BSC following J. Bevington Reed's resignation from the State University Board, circa 1 May, 1967.

Richard Haugo, BSU's Director of Placement Services, and a member of the Industrial Technology Department, served as Acting President for seven months following the resignation of Rebecca Stafford in December, 1981.

Linda Baer, vice President for Academic Affairs, served as Acting President for a year following the death of Duly.

* * * * * *

MANFRED W. DEPUTY
President of BSNS/BSTC: 1 May, 1919 - 1 January, 1938
    b. Vernon, Indiana, 27 October, 1867
    d. Lake City, Iowa, 13 March, 1947
    EDUCATION:
Southern Indiana Normal School, Indiana
B.A., University of Indiana, Bloomington, Indiana, 1904 (Education)
M.A., University of Indiana, Bloomington, Indiana, 1905 (Education)
Ph.D., University of Indiana, Bloomington, Indiana, 1947 (Education)
    PREVIOUS ACADEMIC POSITIONS HELD:
Rural Elementary Teacher, Indiana
Principal, High School, Hayden, Indiana
Principal, High School, Paris, Indiana
County Superintendent of Schools, Jennings County, Indiana
Superintendent of Schools, Columbia City, Indiana
Supervisor of Teacher Training, Eastern Illinois State Normal School, 1909 - 1911
Director of Elementary School, Mankato Normal School, 1911 - 1916
Principal, City Normal School, Kansas City, Missouri, 1916 - 1919
    PRESIDENTIAL INAUGURATION: None
    RETIRED AS PRESIDENT: 1 January, 1938
    NOTE: Mr. Deputy was elected president at an annual State College Board meeting (reported in the Bemidji Daily Pioneer, 20 June, 1919), his position to begin for the summer term starting Monday, 23 June, 1919. He did not have a formal inauguration ceremony.

* * * * * *

ELTON WAYNE BECK
Acting President of BSTC: January, 1938
    EDUCATION:
B.A., Coe College, Cedar Rapids, Iowa, 1913 (Education)
M.A., University of Iowa, Iowa City, Iowa, 1916 (Education)
Ph.D., University of Iowa, Iowa City, Iowa, 1937 (Education)
    POSITIONS HELD AT BEMIDJI STATE:
Instructor-Professor, Education, 1923-1948 [rank(s) unknown]
Instructor, Psychology [or Educational Psychology]
Advisor of Men, 1923-
Director of Placement, 1923-
Physical Education coach, 1924-26
    RETIRED FROM BSTC FACULTY: 1949

* * * * * *

CHARLES R. SATTGAST
President of BSTC/BSC: 1 February, 1938 - 24 March, 1964
     b. Mount Vernon, Illinois, 26 January, 1899
     d. Rochester, Minnesota, 24 March, 1964
     EDUCATION:
Extension, University of Illinois, Champaign-Urbana, circa 1918
Certificate., Southern Illinois Normal School, 1922 (Education)
B.S., University of Illinois, Champaign-Urbana, 1923 (Education)
M.S., Leland Stanford University, 1926 (Education)
Ph.D., Columbia University, 1938 (Education)
     PREVIOUS ACADEMIC POSITIONS HELD:
Elementary School Teacher, Marlow, Illinois, 1918-1919
Dairy Extension Agent, University of Illinois, Urbana, Illinois, 1919-1920
Superintendent of Schools, Richfield, Kansas, 1923-24
Assistant Professor, Extra-Mural Education, Colorado State College, Greeley, Colorado, 1926-29
Associate Professor, Extra-Mural Education, Colorado State Teachers College, Greeley, Colorado, 1929-1930
Associate Director, Extension Department, Colorado State Teachers College, Greeley, Colorado, circa 1929-30
President, Sioux Falls College, Sioux Falls, South Dakota, 1930-37
     PRESIDENTIAL INAUGURATION: None
     DIED IN OFFICE: 24 March, 1964
     NOTE: Dr. Sattgast's arrival in Bemidji during the winter of 1938 made any formal inauguration ceremony difficult. Instead, he and his family were given a faculty reception on 30 January, 1938, a community reception on 4 February, 1938, and a student reception (a dinner) on 11 February, 1938.

* * * * * *

A. C. CLARK
Acting President of BSTC: 1942-1946 (for President Sattgast)
Acting President of BSC: 1 April - 1 September, 1964
     b. Iowa Falls, Iowa, 27 May, 1896
     d. Bemidji, Minnesota, 5 November, 1966
     EDUCATION:
B.A., Ellsworth College, Iowa Falls, Iowa, 1916-17 (Social Studies)
M.A., Teacher's College, Columbia University, New York, 1923 (Social Studies)
Ed.D., University of Southern California, Los Angeles, 1941 (Social Science)
     PREVIOUS ACADEMIC POSITIONS HELD:

Instructor, Social Science, Mankato High School, Mankato, Minnesota
Principal, New Ulm High School, New Ulm, Minnesota
Instructor, Social Science, Ely Junior College, Ely, Minnesota (Social Science)
POSITIONS HELD AT BEMIDJI STATE:
Instructor, Social Science, 1924-38
Chairman, Division of Social Science, 1938-42; 1946-64
Vice President, 1946-
Director of Publicity, various dates
Director of Placement, various dates
Director of Public Relations, various dates
PRESIDENTIAL INAUGURATION: None
RETIRED FROM BSC FACULTY: 1 September, 1964

* * * * * *

HARRY F. BANGSBERG
President of BSC: 1 September, 1964 - 23 March, 1967
b. Minneapolis, Minnesota, 7 April, 1928
d. Near Da Nang, Vietnam, 23 March, 1967 (plane crash)
EDUCATION:
B.A., Luther College, Decorah, Iowa, 1950 (History and English)
M.A., University of Iowa, Iowa City, Iowa, 1951 (History)
Ph.D., University of Iowa, Iowa City, Iowa, 1957 (History)
OTHER ACADEMIC POSITIONS:
Instructor, Social Studies, Western Illinois University, 1953-55
Associate Professor, History, Wisconsin State University, Eau Claire, 1957-59
Assistant Director, Wisconsin State University System at Madison, 1959-63
Executive Director, Higher Education Coordinating Council, Metropolitan St.
    Louis, Missouri, 1963-64
PRESIDENTIAL INAUGURATION: Bemidji, Minnesota, 21 April, 1965
DIED IN OFFICE: 23 March, 1967
NOTE: In January, 1967, Bangsberg undertook a tour of Vietnam with
seven other American educators. Sponsored by the State Department's Agency for
International Development, the group was charged to assist the government of
Vietnam in developing a public higher education system. Bangsberg embarked on
the two-month trip to Saigon on 2 January, 1967. On 23 March, 1967, just three
weeks before the group's scheduled return to the United States, their twin-engine
Air America plane crashed in the mountains north of Da Nang. The entire
delegation of eight was killed.

* * * * * *

J. BEVINGTON REED
Acting President of BSC: 1 April, 1967 - circa 1 May, 1967
OTHER ACADEMIC POSITIONS:

Chancellor, State College System, Minnesota, 1 July, 1966 - circa 1 May, 1967
> PRESIDENTIAL INAUGURATION: None

RESIGNED FROM THE MINNESOTA STATE COLLEGE SYSTEM: circa 1 May, 1967

> NOTE: Reed did not hold a permanent position at Bemidji State College; he served only as its brief interim president after the sudden accidental death of Harry Bangsberg. He was appointed Acting President by the State College Board on 1 April, 1967, though he preferred to think of this only as a temporary administrative role. He appointed Bangsberg's assistant, John Glas, as his Campus Executive Office to deal with campus matters in his absence. Glas assumed the post of Acting President when Reed suddenly resigned his post about 1 May, 1967, to assume a position in Texas.

* * * * * *

JOHN S. GLAS
Campus Executive Officer, 3 April, 1967 - circa 1 May, 1967
Acting President of BSC: circa 1 May, 1967 - 1 September, 1968
> b. Waterloo, Iowa, 1 October, 1910
> d. Bemidji, Minnesota, 5 August, 1976
> EDUCATION:

B.B.A., University of Minnesota, 1933 (Business)
> POSITIONS HELD AT BEMIDJI STATE:

Business Manager, 1939-58
Assistant to the President, 1957-68
Campus Executive Officer, 3 April, 1967 - circa 1 May, 1967
Vice-President for Administration, 1968 - 1 October, 1975
> PRESIDENTIAL INAUGURATION: None
> RETIRED FROM BSC ADMINISTRATION: 1 October, 1975

* * * * * *

ROBERT D. DECKER
President of BSC/BSU: 1 September, 1968 - 5 September, 1979
Acting President of BSU: 5 September, 1979 - 9 April, 1980
> b. Hayes County, Texas, 12 November, 1922
> d.
> EDUCATION:

Southwest Texas State College, San Marcos, 1940-41
B.S., Texas A&M, 1948 (Agriculture)
M.A., Texas A&M, 1954 (Agricultural Education)
Ph.D., Texas A&M, 1958 (Agricultural Economics)
> PREVIOUS ACADEMIC POSITIONS HELD:

Instructor, Agriculture, Hayes County Veterans Vocational School, San Marcos, Texas, 1948-49

Instructor, Agriculture, San Marcos High School, Texas, 1949-55

Research Assistant, Agriculture, Texas A&M, July, 1955-September, 1957

Associate Professor, Agricultural Economics and Economics, Sul Ross State College, Alpine, Texas, 19570-61

Registrar, Sul Ross State College, Alpine, Texas, 1959-61

Dean of Administration and Registrar, Odessa College, Odessa, Texas, 1961 - February, 1966

Assistant to the Chancellor, Minnesota State College System, February, 1966 - 1 July, 1967

Acting Chancellor, Minnesota State College System, 1 July, 1967 - April, 1968

> PRESIDENTIAL INAUGURATION: Bemidji, Minnesota, 15 April, 1969
>
> RESIGNED AS PRESIDENT: 5 September, 1979
>
> ACTING PRESIDENT OF BSU: 5 September, 1979 - 9 April, 1980
>
> SUBSEQUENT ACTIVITIES: Minnesota State Senator, 1988-1990
>
> Minnesota Higher Education Coordinating Board, 1990 -

* * * * * *

REBECCA STAFFORD

President of BSU: 9 April, 1980 - 16 December, 1981

> b. Topeka, Kansas, 9 July, 1936
>
> d.
>
> EDUCATION:

B.A., Radcliffe College, 1958 (Sociology)

M.A., Harvard University, 1961 (Sociology)

Ph.D., Harvard University, 1964 (Sociology)

> PREVIOUS ACADEMIC POSITIONS HELD:

Research Sociologist, Harvard University, 1964-1969

Lecturer, Sociology, Harvard University, 1969-70

Associate Professor, Sociology, University of Nevada, Reno, 1970-74

Professor, Sociology, University of Nevada, Reno, 1974-77

Dean, College of Arts and Sciences, University of Nevada, Reno, 1977-80

> PRESIDENTIAL INAUGURATION: Bemidji, Minnesota, 31 October, 1980
>
> RESIGNED: 16 December, 1981
>
> NOTE: Dr. Stafford resigned on 16 December, 1981, announcing that she

had accepted the position of Executive Vice President of Colorado State University, Fort Collins, with duties to begin on 1 February, 1982.

* * * * * *

RICHARD R. HAUGO

Acting President of BSU: 16 January, 1982 - 30 July, 1982

> b. July 11, 1925
>
> d.

EDUCATION:

B.S., Bemidji State College, 1961 (Industrial Technology)

M.S., Bemidji State College, 1963 (Industrial Technology)

Ed.D., University of North Dakota, 1969 (Industrial Technology)

PREVIOUS ACADEMIC POSITIONS HELD:

Instructor, Industrial Technology, 1965-68

Assistant Professor, Industrial Technology, 1968-70

Associate Professor, Industrial Technology, 1970-75

Professor, Industrial Technology, 1975-88

Professor Emeritus, Industrial Technology, 1988

Director of Placement, 1976-83

Director of Counseling and Placement, Bemidji State University, Bemidji, Minnesota, 1983-88

PRESIDENTIAL INAUGURATION: None

RETIRED FROM BSU FACULTY: 28 January, 1988

* * * * * *

LOWELL R. GILLETT

President of BSU: 1 August, 1982 - 30 June, 1990

b. Minneapolis, Minnesota, 23 February, 1925

d.

EDUCATION:

B.A., Gustavus Adolphus College, Minnesota, 1947 (English)

M.A., University of Minnesota, 1954 (Educational Psychology)

Ed.D., University of North Dakota, 1965 (Educational Psychology)

PREVIOUS ACADEMIC POSITIONS HELD:

Teacher and Coach, Amboy Public Schools, Minnesota, 1947-48

Teacher, Sherburn Public Schools, Minnesota, 1949-51

Teacher and Assistant Principal, Austin Public Schools, Minnesota, 1951-62

Graduate Assistant in Education, University of North Dakota, 1962-63

Professor, Educational Psychology, St. Cloud State University, St. Cloud, Minnesota, 1963-82

Acting Dean, School of Education, St. Cloud State University, St. Cloud, Minnesota, 1965-67

Acting Vice President for Academic Affairs, St. Cloud State University, St. Cloud, Minnesota, 1975-76

Special Associate Vice Chancellor for Academic Affairs, Minnesota State University System, 1977-78

Dean of the Graduate School, St. Cloud St. University, St. Cloud, Minnesota, 1967-75; 1976-77; 1978-81

Acting President, St. Cloud State University, 1981-82

President Emeritus, Bemidji State University, Bemidji, Minnesota, 1990 -

PRESIDENTIAL INAUGURATION: Bemidji, Minnesota, 12 February, 1983
RETIRED AS PRESIDENT: 30 June, 1990

* * * * * *

LESLIE C. DULY

President of BSU: 1 July, 1990 - 8 May, 1993

b. Kenmore, New York, 26 September, 1935
d. Bemidji, Minnesota, 8 May, 1993
EDUCATION:

B.A., University of South Dakota, 1957 (History)
M.A., University of Melbourne, Australia, 1959 (History)
Ph.D., Duke University, 1965 (History)

PREVIOUS ACADEMIC POSITIONS HELD:

Assistant Professor, History, Memphis State University, 1963-64
Assistant Professor, History, Mt. Holyoke College, 1964-68
Associate Professor, History, University of Nebraska, Lincoln, 1968-70
Professor, History, University of Nebraska, Lincoln, 1970-80

POSITIONS HELD AT BEMIDJI STATE:

Vice President for Academic Affairs, 1980-90

PRESIDENTIAL INAUGURATION: Bemidji, Minnesota, 2 November, 1990
DIED IN OFFICE: 8 May, 1993

* * * * * *

LINDA L. BAER

Acting President: 8 May, 1993 - 24 May, 1993
Interim President: 25 May, 1993 - 30 June, 1994

b. Spokane, Washington, 7 September, 1949
d.
EDUCATION:

B.A., Washington State University, 1970 (Sociology)
M.A,, Colorado State University, Fort Collins, 1975 (Sociology)
Ph.D., South Dakota State University, Brookings, 1983 (Sociology)

PREVIOUS ACADEMIC POSITIONS HELD:

Assistant Professor, Rural Sociology,
    South Dakota State, University, Brookings, 1983-87
Associate Professor, Rural Sociology,
    South Dakota State University, Brookings, 1987-90
Director, Center for Innovation Technology and Entrepreneurship,
    South Dakota State University, Brookings, 1989-90
Administrative Associate, Data Collection and Strategic Planning,
    South Dakota State University, Brookings, 1987-90
Director, Partnership Program, Native American Tribal Colleges and South
    Dakota State University, South Dakota State University,
    Brookings, 1986-88

POSITIONS HELD AT BEMIDJI STATE:
Vice President for Academic Affairs, 27August, 1990 - January, 1992
Senior Vice President for Academic and Student Affairs, February, 1992 - 8 May, 1993
Acting President 8 May, 1993 - 24 May, 1993
Interim President, 25 May, 1993 - 30 June, 1994 (Appointed by the State University Board, Tuesday, 25 May, 1993)
          PRESIDENTIAL INAUGURATION: None

* * * * * *

M. JAMES BENSEN
President of BSU: 1 July, 1994 -
          b. April 8, 1937
          d.
          EDUCATION:
B.S., Bemidji State College, 1959 (Industrial Education)
M.S., University of Wisconsin--Stout, 1962 (Industrial Education)
Ed. D., Pennsylvania State University, 1967 (Educational Development)
          PREVIOUS ACADEMIC POSITIONS HELD:
Teacher and Coach, Erskine Public Schools, Minnesota, 1959 - 62
Teacher, Department Chair, Independent School District #279,
          Minneapolis, Minnesota, 1962 - 64
Research Associate, Pennsylvania State University, 1964 - 66
Professor of Communications, Education and Training,
          University of Wisconsin--Stout, 1966-1989
Director, Technology Education, University of Wisconsin--Stout, 1970 - 76
Associate Dean, School of Industry and Technology,
          Wisconsin State University--Stout, 1976 - 80
Dean, School of Industry and Technology,
          University of Wisconsin--Stout, 1980-89
President, Dunwoody Institute, Minneapolis, Minnesota, 1989 - 94

(Selected by the State University Board as BSU President on 5 May, 1994; to take office July 1, 1994)

Appendix N

1993-'94
State Appropriations by Category

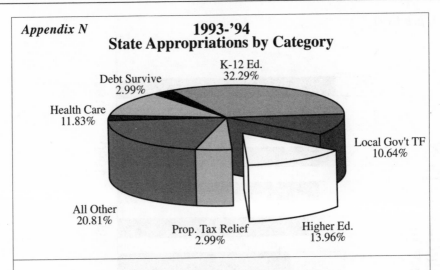

K-12 Ed.
32.29%

Debt Survive
2.99%

Health Care
11.83%

Local Gov't TF
10.64%

All Other
20.81%

Prop. Tax Relief
2.99%

Higher Ed.
13.96%

Higher Education Appropriations

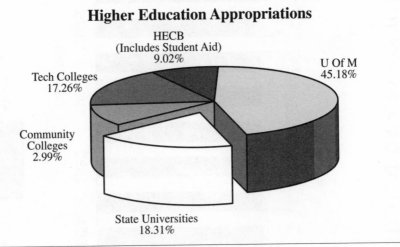

HECB
(Includes Student Aid)
9.02%

U Of M
45.18%

Tech Colleges
17.26%

Community
Colleges
2.99%

State Universities
18.31%

State University Budget Allocations

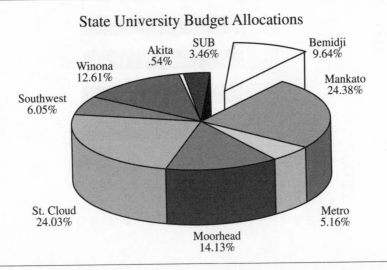

SUB
3.46%

Akita
.54%

Bemidji
9.64%

Winona
12.61%

Mankato
24.38%

Southwest
6.05%

St. Cloud
24.03%

Metro
5.16%

Moorhead
14.13%

Appendix O

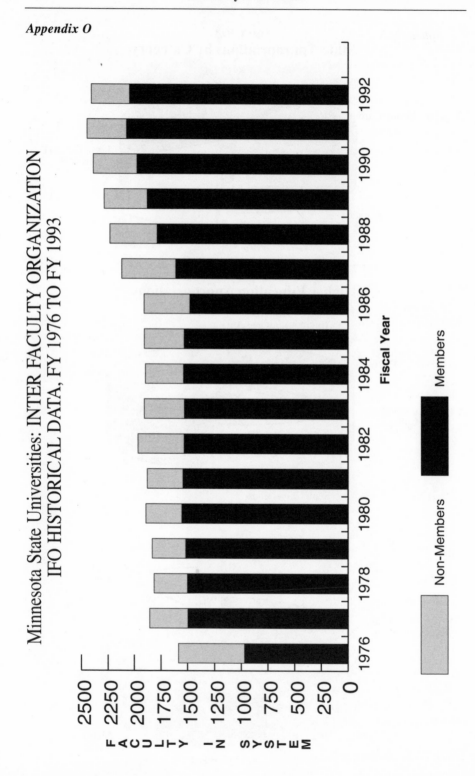

Minnesota State Universities: INTER FACULTY ORGANIZATION
IFO HISTORICAL DATA, FY 1976 TO FY 1993

Appendix P
Bemidji State University's Outstanding Alumni
Year selected in bold faced type

1972 George Welte '61 & '77
1973 Dr. James Ghostley '55
1974 Raymond Miller '59
1975 Bertha Christianson '39
1976 William R. Howe '51
Guy Vena '60
1977 Farley Bright '36 (deceased)
George Goodwin '64 (deceased)
Dr. Irvin Keeler '29 (deceased)
Eleanor Kipp '30
Dr. James Witham '38 (deceased)
1978 H. Wesley Balk '54
John Schuiling '32
1979 Margaret Galloway '37
Margaret Harlow '36
Grace Nugent '23
Eleanor Traut '39
Robert Vleck '65
1980 Dr. Carl Knutson '47 (deceased)
1981 Margaret Berg '60
John Borg '71
Susan Chianelli Jacobson '71
Lillie Kleven '37
Dr. Elwood Largis '65
Dr. Robert Olson '62
1982 Gail Gantz-Bergsven '65
Dr. Richard Haugo '61
Dr. Dwaine Marten '58
Edwin Nordheim '41
Virgil Prestby '63
1983 Lillian Ailie '34 & '63
Paula Bruss Bauck '42
Robert Drake '71 & '80
Lt. Col. Clark Gilbertson '72
Richard Hegre '57 & '59
Dr. Royal Netzer '27 (deceased)
1984 Runae Anderson '70
Dr. Will Antell '59
Dr. James Bensen '59

Merle Bryant '46
Gary Olson '50
1985 Jay Griggs '70
Harvey Westrom '57
1986 Bill Clark '53
Joseph Graba '61
Dr. Bill Kirtland '53
Dr. Malvin Skarsten '22
1987 Dr. Caroline Czarnecki '50
Dr. Herbert Fougner '43
Dr. Ronald Ostman '65
Dr. Sheldon Ramnarine '71 & '72
1988 Fred Schmit '78
John Schmit '58 (deceased)
Paul Schmit '60
Erna Meyer Schuling '40
1989 Dr. Jack W. Miller '56
Roxanne Nawara '73
Dr. Perry W. Patterson '48
Jack Wilhite '55 & '63
James Williamson '86
1990 Helen Gill '76
Colonel Gerald Green '60
Ethel Roesch '36
Willis Stittsworth '53
1991 Jerry Abbott '60
Donald E. Hoganson '38 (deceased)
Robert D. Johnson '52
Everal Vermilyea '38
1992 Marion Christianson '50 & '71
1993 David G. Odegaard '66